Respond in Writing

Respond in Writing

Ricki Heller

Seneca College

THOMSON

NELSON

Australia   Canada   Mexico   Singapore   Spain   United Kingdom   United States

THOMSON

NELSON

Respond in Writing

by Ricki Heller

This book is dedicated to M., with love

Editorial Director and Publisher:
Evelyn Veitch

Acquisitions Editors:
Chris Carson and Anne Williams

Marketing Manager:
Cara Yarzab

Developmental Editor:
Rebecca Rea

Production Editor:
Bob Kohlmeier

Production Coordinator:
Helen Jager Locsin

Copy Editor:
Sarah Weber

Creative Director:
Angela Cluer

Proofreader:
Cy Strom

Interior Design:
Tammy Gay

Cover Design:
Ken Phipps

Cover Image:
Detail from *Untitled,* 1/1, stitched monotype, by Tara Cooper

Compositor:
Tammy Gay

Printer:
Transcontinental

National Library of Canada Cataloguing in Publication Data

Heller, Ricki, 1958–
Respond in writing

Includes index.
ISBN 0-17-616855-9

1. English language—Rhetoric.
2. Essay. I. Title.

PE1471.H44 2002   808'.042
C2001-902353-7

Contents

Part 1: Thinking, Reading, and Writing Critically

Chapter 1   Reading Texts

Chapter 2   Writing Essays: Responding to Texts in Writing

Part 2: Readings

Chapter 3   Description

Chapter 4   Narration

Chapter 5   Example

Chapter 6   Process

Chapter 7   Classification

Chapter 8   Comparison and Contrast

THEMATIC Contents

Business/Economics

Canada

Education/Learning

Family

Feminisim/Gender

Health/Well-being

History

Humour

Language

Modern Culture/Trends

Morals and Ethics

Multiculturalism

Nature

Personal Narrative

Politics

Popular Culture

Psychology/Sociology

Relationships

Science

Sports/Leisure

Suicide

Technology

Traditions/Rituals

Travel

Writing

Preface

The general approach of *Respond in Writing* is to stress writing as a skill, one that can be learned and applied like any other. Based on the premise that students must first be able to analyze a text and assess their own reactions to it in order to respond intelligently to a piece of writing, *Respond in Writing* tackles the skills of critical thinking, critical reading, and writing essays in a logical sequence that allows students to practise these skills after reading about them. Throughout the book, the intent is to treat the topics in a direct, practical manner that involves and engages students and encourages them to recognize the links between skills attained in the classroom and the kinds of writing they will continue to do in their nonacademic lives. Central to the approach of *Respond in Writing*, as well, is the concept that real-world writing, while it may differ in its ostensible objective, content, or formal structure, shares all the important underlying principles of essay writing: it must be clear, coherent, structured, and comprehensible to a reader. As they begin to understand these parallels, students will come to appreciate the links between what they are doing in their English classes and the communications skills they employ in the rest of their lives.

How the Book Is Organized

Chapter 1 begins with an introduction to critical thinking and analysis, including distinctions among emotional reactions, opinions, inferences, and facts. Next is an overview of the reading process in three general stages (pre-reading, reading, and post-reading). A sample text, complete with model student responses to the reading, is provided. Chapter 2 examines the writing process in three major stages (pre-writing, writing, and post-writing) that parallel those in the reading process. Unlike many other texts, *Respond in Writing* treats three types of essays: those that draw on students' personal experiences, those that require a student to respond directly to a reading (and draw evidence from that reading), and those that analyze fiction.

Chapters 3 through 11 examine the traditional rhetorical modes (description, narration, exposition, and argument) in order of increasing difficulty. For each mode, an introductory section describes and defines the mode and instructs students on how to write an essay in that mode (following the general steps already laid out in Chapter 2). The sections on each rhetorical mode conclude with a selection of readings that illustrate the mode (though many texts can be used to illustrate more than one mode).

Following each reading is a set of questions structured in three incremental steps, each representing a more sophisticated level of cognition. The first section, "Understanding the message: Comprehension," tests the student's basic understanding of the meaning of the text (both its vocabulary and content). Next, "Examining the structure and details: Analysis" asks the student to analyze the text by breaking it into component parts. Analysis questions focus on the defining characteristics of the text (the thesis, major points, style, and so on)—that is, how the message is presented. Finally, "Formulating a response: Inference and interpretation" elicits the more sophisticated responses involving personal reactions, evaluation, interpretation, and critical assessment; at this point, students consider "why?" Finally, each selection ends with three essay questions, at least one of which asks the student to employ the same rhetorical mode just illustrated. The others allow the student either to respond directly to the text (for example, in an essay that requires references to the text) or to use the text as a springboard for an essay about a more general topic (for example, to support an argument with examples drawn from the student's own life and experience).

With the exception of some classic fiction, all readings were published after 1990. Most are Canadian and feature a broad range of interests, viewpoints, and authors. Though many of the topics cover timeless subjects such as friendship, family, or fishing, others relating to current events, technology, or the sciences are as up-to-date as possible. The range of authors (from well-known voices such as David Suzuki, Margaret Laurence, and Tomson Highway to others who are not yet household names) is extensive. Texts from a variety of sources each illustrate common principles of clear thought, organization, structure, and presentation of ideas. At the same time, readings are short enough to read in one sitting and are stimulating in subject matter, sparking the student's interest and thereby encouraging enthusiasm both for studying the readings and for responding to them.

Chapter 12 offers fiction selections from a variety of authors, arranged chronologically. Classics such as Kate Chopin's "The Story of an Hour" and Margaret Laurence's "The Loons" are presented alongside works by other established Canadian writers such as Timothy Findley and Alistair MacLeod, as well as those by newer writers such as Anita Rau Badami and Camilla Gibb.

Chapter 13 provides a comprehensive guide to the Modern Language Association (MLA) and American Psychological Association (APA) documentation formats, including in-text citations and references. For each potential reference source, students are shown both the advantages and disadvantages of using the source and are encouraged to assess its credibility and validity. In addition, a section on the summary (with a sample selection and a summary) is included. As well, an extensive section on electronic research is included, providing the most up-to-date formats for both MLA and APA documentation.

Finally, a note about the editorial treatment of the essays and stories reprinted here: each reading in the book preserves the editorial style it had in its original form. In keeping with standard editorial philosophy, neither the author nor the publisher edited the readings to make them conform to a single editorial style. Consequently, the attentive reader will notice differences from reading to reading in punctuation, capitalization, and spelling styles, and in the treatment of numbers.

Other Useful Features of the Text

Respond in Writing also provides a series of aids to understanding, including the following:

- DEFINITION: Definition boxes flag short definitions of key terms (set in bold type) that are discussed at greater length in the chapter. These definitions provide a handy review for students once they've worked through a particular chapter. In addition, each of these terms (along with others) is defined in the glossary at the end of the book.

- TIP: Tip boxes indicate short, practical tips to simplify or demystify techniques discussed in the chapter and make the process easier for students (for instance, how to develop a thesis sentence or choose appropriate details to support a comparison and contrast essay).

- SNAG: Snag boxes highlight common writing difficulties or pitfalls encountered by many students. Snags inform the student about the problem and suggest simple, direct ways to avoid or correct it.

The text also provides an abundance of concrete examples both to illustrate concepts and to provide practice exercises for students. Examples are chosen from a wide range of subject areas and interests to appeal to as large a student population as possible.

A Note on Language in the Text

Every effort has been made to use gender neutral language whenever possible in *Respond in Writing*. If appropriate, the plural pronoun "they" is used; otherwise, I've elected to use the inclusive "s/he" rather than the more cumbersome "he or she." In addition, to reflect current changes in professional writing throughout Canada and other countries, I have used contractions (both of Canada's national newspapers regularly employ contractions). The book's informal, relaxed style helps to reinforce the notion that writing is part of our day-to-day lives. At the same time, *Respond in Writing* also makes it clear to students that a professional style must employ Standard English and adopt an appropriate tone.

Acknowledgments

In creating any from-the-ground-up textbook such as *Respond in Writing*, many people contribute to the shape and evolution of the project. Heartfelt thanks go to all those at Nelson Thomson Learning who contributed to the text from its inception through to its final format: Joanna Cotton, Anne Williams, Chris Carson, Tammy Gay, Evelyn Veitch, Vicki Gould, Nicole Gnutzman, and, most especially, Rebecca Rea and Bob Kohlmeier for their support, advice, and encouragement. Thanks go as well to the many reviewers who read the manuscript in its myriad incarnations and provided thoughtful, detailed, insightful, and highly useful suggestions: Tim Acton, Capilano College; Angela Carlyle, Red Deer College; Arlene Davies-Fuhr, Grant MacEwan Community College; Moira de Silva, Kwantlen University College; Ingrid Hutchinson, Fanshawe College; Declan Neary, Humber College; Linda Reiche, Algonquin College; Ilona Ryder, Grant MacEwan Community College; Linda Smithies, Humber College; Valerie Spink, Grant MacEwan Community College; Thom Sunega, George Brown College; Deborah Torkko, Malaspina University-College; Lucy Valentino, Centennial College; and Judith Wintonyk, Sheridan College. Thanks also go to my friends and colleagues whose valuable input and feedback moulded and improved the book: Angie Azouz, Laurie Bell, Mara Bordignon, Ela Borenstein, Judith Carson, Burke Cullen, Brian Flack, Robin Flamer, Carla Flamer, Enid Gossin, Diane Hallquist, Grant Heckman, Irene Kanurkas, Bev Kravitz, Eva McCarney, Kathy Pearl, Linda Siomra, and, in particular, Alexandra MacLennan. Finally, I'd like to express my appreciation to the many talented writers whose work appears in the readings, and to my students—future, present, and past—who both inspired this text and for whom it is intended.

Part 1

Thinking, Reading, and Writing Critically

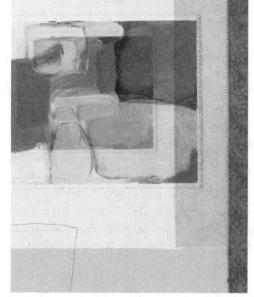

CHAPTER 1

Reading Texts

If someone asked whether you enjoy reading, how would you respond? For many of us, the answer depends on our motivation for reading. If you read material of your own choosing, the task is almost always enjoyable, even easy. Magazine or newspaper articles, text on Web sites, the latest work-related journal—all may be absorbed effortlessly and can be read perfectly well at a desk, on a bus, even in a noisy cafeteria. But when you're asked to read something you wouldn't normally select, or when you're *required* to read, the task may feel frustrating or even onerous.

An effective way to compensate for this slightly reduced enthusiasm when reading materials that don't naturally hold your interest is to employ critical reading, a method we'll examine closely in this chapter. By contributing the necessary effort, concentration, and motivation to the task of assigned reading, you can make the process as effective—even as enjoyable—as reading for pure pleasure.

Learning to read critically becomes much easier if you understand how reading fits into the larger context of communication in general. Like any acquired skill, reading ability improves with study and practice. Once you know the steps in the process and can apply them, you'll notice the many benefits that critical reading can bestow: your reading speed, comprehension, and retention will all improve.

COMMUNICATIONS LOOP: READING AND WRITING AS A FORM OF COMMUNICATION

Think of reading any text as participating in the larger process of communication. What factors are necessary for "communication" to occur? Initially, every attempt to communicate involves someone with something to say, someone s/he says it to, and the actual message being conveyed. No matter which method of communication you imagine—handwritten letter, e-mail, sign language, heated debate—these three components (often labelled **sender, receiver,** and **message**) of the basic **communications paradigm** or **feedback loop** are always present. The entire operation can be illustrated as follows:

FIGURE 1.1 The Communications Paradigm

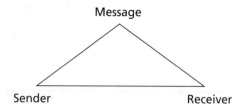

A fourth component, feedback, is also required for the sender to confirm that the communication was successful. **Feedback** allows the receiver to acknowledge both receipt *and* understanding of the message. In other words, you may send a message to someone else, but if s/he either doesn't receive it at all (for instance, if your e-mail server is down) or doesn't understand it when it *is* received (as when a taxi driver who speaks only French hears a message spoken in Cantonese), no true communication can take place.

CRITICAL THINKING: AN ESSENTIAL TOOL FOR READING AND WRITING

What Is Critical Thinking?

Critical thinking will help you both to construct effective messages as sender and to understand more fully those you receive. The idea of thinking as a skill we can develop may sound paradoxical at first; after all, don't we already know how to

> **Critical thinking:** the process by which you closely examine and consider a message and, using analysis and logic, formulate your own assessment of its validity

think, and don't we do so all the time? Critical thinking, however, is a more formal, deliberate operation, one that involves the ability to focus on, and carefully analyze, what we read and hear. While critical thinking may include a range of mental operations (from using logical analysis or principles of creativity to adjusting one's attitude or enthusiasm level while tackling a problem), the common basis of all critical thinking is *using thought to reach a rational, logical conclusion about or assessment of any particular message.* It is an active process in which you use your intelligence to review and assess what's being presented to you.

How to Think Critically

A key skill in critical thinking is the ability to draw **inferences**—logical conclusions based on **facts.** Maintaining objectivity as you reach conclusions is essential to drawing useful and valid inferences. For instance, most of us would hesitate to believe a neighbour who confidently asserted, "Well, I know that cigarettes don't cause health problems—my cousin's been smoking a pack a day for five years and he's as healthy as a horse." We'd immediately question the accuracy of this assertion. Can a single person provide enough evidence to prove that smoking isn't bad for us? What contradictory evidence exists in the rest of the world? Does it *make sense* to believe our neighbour? What proof does the speaker have? In the end, we would have to come up with our own conclusions by carefully examining, in an objective manner, all the evidence. Similarly, critical thinkers decide for themselves, based on facts and objective data; they are not swayed purely by emotional messages, their own biases or prejudices, or preconceived notions—all of which are subjective measures.

In addition, critical thinkers are aware of their own emotional reactions to a reading and how these might influence their conclusions. In their academic lives, students want teachers who mark fairly and base their assessments on the work submitted rather than how the teacher feels about a particular student. In the same way, critical thinkers develop their responses based on the objective merits of a reading rather than emotional reactions to it. Even if the subject matter is controversial, is something in which they're not particularly interested, or is based on a topic of which they disapprove, critical thinkers are able to recognize that the quality of the writing and the writer's argument, its structure, and its presentation can still be good. It's possible to concede that rapper Eminem has talent, for instance, even if you disapprove of his lyrics or public persona.

To think critically, you must analyze and evaluate what you read, ultimately deciding whether you believe its message has value. A central skill in critical thinking is being able to distinguish between objective statements or responses (those that can be supported by evidence) and subjective ones (those that are based more on emotions than facts). A good critical thinker uses inferences rather than **opinions** or **emotional reactions.** This means using observation and logic to determine whether a text makes its point effectively or not.

DEFINITION

Facts: irrefutable units of information that can be objectively measured and confirmed

Inferences: your own logical conclusions based on, and supported by, the facts

Opinions or **emotional reactions**: responses based on strong feelings or personal experiences (such responses may not always be logical)

TIP

Testing the logic of conclusions

How can you tell if your conclusions about the messages you've read are logical? The most obvious question to ask in this case is, "Do the facts support my ideas?" Then ask, "What information, if any, contradicts my conclusion?" Assess the source of the information. Is it a reputable source? Is it current? Finally, even when the facts don't contradict your ideas, you must still ask, "What is the likelihood that this is true?" In other words, just because a particular conclusion is *possible* doesn't necessarily mean it's *probable;* often, several different conclusions are equally valid, given the same set of facts.

EXERCISE
Drawing conclusions through inference

To help you distinguish among facts, logical inferences, and subjective responses, try this exercise. First, read the following passage. Next, look at the list of statements below it and try to determine how *likely* each conclusion is, based on the information (facts) in the **paragraph;** assign each statement a score from 10 *(definitely true)* to 1 *(definitely not true)*.

As you decide on your answers, think about how you derived each conclusion. On what are you basing your ideas? Is there a specific statement in the passage that backs up your inferences, or are they only implied? Your ability to support your inferences when a conclusion is not irrefutably true will help you choose evidence for your ideas more judiciously, thereby producing stronger essays.

> My parents were married for a total of 39 years. In all that time, I never once heard my father say "I love you" to my mother. On Mother's Day or her birthday, a new plant or bunch of flowers would magically appear on the kitchen table, a card propped against it with the signature "from Your Husband." Dad didn't even write his name! As my mother read the card, she would start to cry. On their anniversary, they always went out to dinner, just the two of them, and returned long after we children were asleep. The next day, life would resume as usual, and it would take another year before the flowers appeared on the table.

Which statements are absolutely true? Which are likely? Which are based entirely on the reader's own assumptions or emotions?

1. The father never bought any presents for his wife other than flowers.
2. The mother was unhappy with the arrangement.
3. The couple were married almost four decades.
4. Despite the lack of verbalization, the husband loved his wife.
5. The couple enjoyed each other's company.
6. The gifts from the father were enough for the mother.
7. The father was thoughtless and unimaginative.
8. The couple were never affectionate toward each other.
9. The couple never said "I love you" to each other.
10. The couple were shy and reserved even after 39 years of marriage.
11. Something special existed to keep the couple together.

As you develop critical thinking skills, you will find they help you immeasurably no matter what kind of reading you undertake. You'll find more information about critical thinking as you work through the reading process.

The Characteristics of Critical Thinkers

Here is a list of the most prominent qualities of critical thinkers. Continue to work on developing these skills as you approach each of the readings in this text.

- *Critical thinkers rely on objective evidence.* For any inference they draw, critical thinkers use specific details, facts, and examples (either from life or the readings to which they respond) as a way to support their assertions.

- *Critical thinkers are willing to set aside personal and emotional reactions.* If a writer discusses the benefits of a 50-hour work week, for instance, the reader is willing to put aside her or his aversion to the concept to examine instead how the writer presents an argument.

- *Critical thinkers use logic and probability to assess the relative value of assertions or ideas.* Critical thinkers arrive at conclusions not only because they "feel right" but, primarily, because they can be backed up by evidence and fact.

- *Critical thinkers don't automatically accept everything they read or hear.* Critical thinkers tend to ask a lot of questions; they challenge the information they receive, asking themselves whether the sources are valid, the arguments hold water, or the ideas make logical sense. A cure for AIDS would be a wonderful scientific discovery—but if it were reported in a daily gossip tabloid, we'd most likely question the sources and wonder whether the "cure" were also substantiated in other, scientifically reputable, papers.

CRITICAL READING: UNDERSTANDING WHAT YOU READ, ANALYZING THE TEXT, EVALUATING THE MESSAGE

When you read what someone else has written, you receive the writer's message as part of an intended communications loop. Ideally, you would understand fully what the writer has put on the page, and then have the option of responding to it in person. Since most of us read outside this ideal scenario, it helps to consider as closely as possible both the sender (the author) and the message itself (the words on the page) in order to gain a clear understanding of the writer's message—in other words, reading in a more structured fashion than when you read for pleasure only. This activity is known as **critical reading.**

Reading critically allows you to understand and evaluate a text as effectively as possible. By the time you assess your own reaction and formulate a written response, you have become a new sender creating a new message that can be received by others. But how do you decide *what* you think about a particular reading, or the manner in

DEFINITION

Critical reading: the process through which you draw inferences and develop logical interpretations of a text by considering the writer, the content (what the writer actually says), and the structure (how it's put together) in order to understand and respond to it

which you wish to respond? Using the steps that follow will help you navigate through a reading and generate a thoughtful, reasoned response.

Like any organized activity, critical reading can be divided into subactivities. While these steps may not be separated this clearly in reality, they will help direct your actions while you read. Remember, though, that in reality these steps will often overlap, and the process is not perfectly linear.

The **reading process** can be divided into three basic stages: pre-reading, reading, and post-reading. In pre-reading—everything you do *before* actually reading the selection carefully—you get the gist of the message and prepare yourself to delve into it more deeply. During reading, you carefully and systematically work your way through the entire text, while speculating about its meaning. Finally, in post-reading, you review and collect your thoughts, evaluate what you've read, and begin to formulate a response to it. The steps described below focus primarily on reading nonfiction texts, but you can apply this method, with minor modifications, to fiction as well.

PRE-READING: Getting Ready to Read

How do you prepare yourself to tackle a reading assignment? Below is a full list of the different activities in the process. Again, you should feel free to adapt these to your own specific preferences or situation to make the most of your reading. It's possible to condense or even eliminate some of these steps and still read effectively; ideally, however, you'd have time to work your way through the entire list.

1. *Prepare yourself mentally for the task of reading critically.* As best you can, eliminate any psychological barriers to reading. This step has two parts: eliminating negative *attitudes* and letting go of *thoughts that interfere with concentration.* To begin with, you will need to decide for yourself that you are *willing* and *prepared* to concentrate on your reading. In fact, simply affirming this decision in your own mind focuses your attention on the task at hand and encourages you to take your reading more seriously. At the same time, it may be difficult to concentrate if a multitude of other concerns repeatedly intrude on your consciousness. A concerted effort to put other worries aside and

focus (for the time being) exclusively on the reading can help you retain what you read, thereby making the process more effective.

2. *Prepare your physical environment.* In this step, take whatever measures are necessary to ensure that your environment is as conducive as possible to thoughtful reading. This might include removing external distractions (such as the noise of a nearby television or radio) or finding a comfortable working environment with adequate space and lighting.

3. *Skim through the text for general information and cues.* This type of preview provides a general sense of the subject, the writer's approach, and any other relevant information that can focus your reading. A preview prepares you for the more intensive and directed reading to follow by providing some familiarity with, and other links to, the information as you read. Admittedly, you'll have fewer such cues to examine in a short story as opposed to a nonfiction text, but don't skip this step nonetheless. Even short stories sometimes have individual sections, headings, or, at the least, an introductory and concluding passage.

Consider these points:

- *The length of the piece.* Try to allot enough time to allow a complete reading of your text, from start to finish, in one sitting. If you can't read the entire piece, aim for at least a major section up to a natural break (if a story is divided into parts, stop after one section, for instance). Reading in units or "chunks" allows you to comprehend the writing more completely and to remember what you read more effectively.

- *The title of the piece.* Titles frequently reflect the content and purpose of a piece of writing. At the same time, titles can also be used to establish certain expectations in readers' minds that will enhance the ultimate impact of a selection. For instance, the title "Ecologically Friendly Cars" implies a discussion of vehicles that produce minimal air pollution. A short story entitled "The Lottery," on the other hand, might create expectations of someone winning something, of a monetary prize, or perhaps simply of the notion of good luck. Imagine a reader's surprise, then, to discover that Shirley Jackson's short story "The Lottery" describes a small-town ritual in which an annual lottery takes place, but the "winner" is then stoned to death by the rest of the agitated mob! The title prepares the reader to expect something good, thereby emphasizing the horrific and ironic ending even more.

- *The author(s).* If you recognize an author's name, your knowledge about that person can also help to prepare you for what you're about to read. Is the writer an expert in the field, a reputable professional? Are you familiar with the author's **style?** (Knowing that a particular writer uses complex, dense language could help you determine the time required to read the selection, for instance). Knowing the geographical location or historical period in which an author lived can also be useful, since it places her or him in a general context that may reflect on the subject matter. A serious article on brain surgery, for example, written by a reputable surgeon who lived in 1919, would nevertheless offer little in the way of groundbreaking techniques for today's readership.

- *Visual cues to meaning.* Some texts provide boldface headings, italicized words or titles, footnotes, sidebars, diagrams, illustrations, or other elements that help to organize the material and clarify the meaning. If these do not occur in the text you're reading, it's still a good idea to read *just* the introductory paragraph(s) and the concluding paragraph(s)—especially in a short story—as a means to understand the general framework of the text.

- *The genre.* Whether a selection is prose fiction, nonfiction, poetry, or drama will also shape your approach to it. The differences between nonfiction essays and short stories (fiction) are considerable and are addressed in Appendix 1. For now, knowing whether something is factual or has been created by someone's imagination can also influence how you respond to it.

4. *Create a personal road map for your reading.* Finally, one of the best ways to increase understanding is to generate some questions you'd like answered as you read. These may be based on information you've gathered while previewing the text and should be designed to clarify any vague points, concepts, or terms. You might wonder about the title: to what does it refer? How serious is the writer about the subject matter? What did the writer mean by "the most important element in any retirement plan"? By creating questions *before* you begin to read, you focus and direct your activity, so you can be more actively engaged as you proceed through the selection; the questions provide a *reason* to read more attentively, because you'll be searching for answers. You'll also learn almost immediately which areas of the text prove most difficult or puzzling, so you can return to these later.

Don't be intimidated by the number of steps in pre-reading. *In fact, all of these activities should take no more than 5 to 10 minutes.* Remember that this stage is designed to prepare you to read carefully and to provide a *general* sense of the topic and content of the reading. You can always return to the unanswered questions later on.

READING: First Time through the Full Text

Once you've completed the pre-reading activities, you've already begun to think about the selection to some degree and probably have a general idea about its content. At this point, you're ready to attack the text as a unit. Armed with your questions and your general impressions, you can actively read through the work, looking for answers and trying to understand more completely the author's message and the structure of the writing.

Here are some of the ways to enhance your read-through:

1. *Read with a pen or pencil in your hand.* Again, active reading means reading with your mind—and in this case, hand—primed and participating. Having a pen in hand allows you to jot down any reactions, comments, or questions that come to mind immediately, before they slip away. This physical participation in the process also further increases the chance that you'll pay close attention to, and ultimately remember, the material.

2. *Ensure that you understand the literal meaning of the writing.* As you work through the text, it's important to understand what the author says on a literal level *before* you can really begin to analyze and assess your reactions to it. Lack of comprehension may lead to subsequent chaos if you forge ahead with an initial interpretation of a reading even when you don't fully understand some part of it. Since your interpretation of an early passage may affect your understanding of the remainder of the selection, the best way to avoid such mishaps and save time in the long run is to ensure understanding *as you go*. To check your comprehension, try to **paraphrase** as you read. (For more on paraphrasing, see Appendix 2.) If you are able to relate, in your own words, what the writer has said well enough to explain it to someone who *hasn't* read the selection, you've probably achieved an adequate level of comprehension. (Comprehension questions following each selection will also help to test your understanding.) The sample reading that follows provides some examples of paraphrasing to help you improve your own paraphrasing technique.

   In addition, look up words you don't know. To maintain the momentum as you read through a selection, consider circling, highlighting, or jotting down *all* words you don't understand as you encounter them. Then, immediately look up only those that are *essential* for you to understand the basic sense of the paragraph while reading through; save the others for when you've completed reading the entire essay or story. This way, you'll still achieve a valid *general* impression of the writing the first time through, but won't ignore the new vocabulary that is so important to build as you develop your own writing proficiency.

3. *Try to determine the author's purpose, intended audience, and tone:*

   Purpose. The author's purpose in a piece of writing is the same as the objective; that is, what s/he hopes will happen as a result of people reading the selection. In other words, what reaction or change in the reader was the author trying to evoke? Purpose usually falls into one of three types: (1) to entertain, (2) to educate or inform, or (3) to persuade. If a writer simply wishes to amuse you for a time, but is not concerned about your personal opinions or beliefs on a topic (as in a syndicated humour column in a newspaper, for example), then the purpose is to entertain. If, on the other hand, a writer tries to educate you by providing information not previously known to you (as in a biology textbook), then the purpose is to inform. Finally, if a writer attempts to change your mind with her or his words, the purpose is to persuade. In other words, the writer tries to convince the audience that her or his viewpoint is valid and worthy of adoption. While persuasive writing may include *both* informative *and* entertaining material, its primary purpose is to convince the reader of something. A letter to the editor explaining why Canadian taxes are too high has a persuasive purpose, even if the message is presented in an entertaining way: the writer hopes to convince the readers that taxes should be lowered and hopes that readers will protest against current tax laws. Depending on the writer's purpose, your own assessment of the reading may change. You will most likely have more stringent requirements for an author's supporting points if it's clear that s/he is trying to persuade you than you would if s/he were merely trying to entertain you.

Audience. The audience is the intended readership for a particular piece of writing. Writers alter their language according to the audience they address. If a physicist writes for an audience of other scientists (say, in a professional journal), the writer assumes a certain base level of knowledge that might not exist in the general population and uses language appropriate to that group.

Tone. Like tone of voice, the tone of a piece of writing lets us know the writer's true feelings about it—her or his attitude about the subject matter. Is the writer being sarcastic? Is s/he conveying a sense of sadness? Anger? Whatever the emotion you sense from the writing, that is the tone of the piece. Tone is also expressed through **diction,** or word choice. When a writer describes a rainy scene as "sodden, grey and dull," the feeling evoked is quite different from that in the description of "a light and refreshing mist of rain." The first elicits sullen, sad emotions, while the second is actually upbeat and positive. Tone is a crucial aspect of writing, since a satiric tone (one in which the writer is poking fun at the subject matter), for instance, can trigger an inaccurate interpretation of a text if taken seriously. Be careful when reading to detect any nuances that indicate tone.

4. *Try to uncover the text's structure and underlying meaning.* Attempting to answer your pre-reading questions will give you a head start toward understanding the author's underlying meanings. But the way a work is structured also conveys its message. Look for patterns or devices that connect ideas; notice any sentences or phrases you think are imbued with particular meaning

and search for repeated phrases or words. You should also try to determine the essay's thesis (main idea in a nonfiction article) or story's **themes** (central ideas or abstract concepts in fiction) while you read. (Chapter 2 covers these concepts in more detail.) Finally, look for links among ideas; for example, consider how the last paragraph (the conclusion) connects to the previous one, to the introduction, and so on.

POST-READING: Reviewing What You Have Read

In this part of the process, you formulate a solid interpretation of the author's message, your reaction to it, and your assessment of it. Here are the steps in post-reading:

1. *Write a quick summary of the essay or story.* You need not write a formal summary at this stage; rather, jot down, in your own words, your initial impressions of the main message and major points of the text. (For more on summaries, see Chapter 13.) This way, you'll establish a good synopsis of what the article or story says. In addition, this brief version of the selection will most likely capture its key ideas.

2. *Try to determine the thesis of the text.* The thesis in a nonfiction text is the writer's main idea or the message that is conveyed through the piece. In other words, if you had to sum up the writer's point in a single sentence, what would it be? The thesis is the core of the argument, the idea around which the essay is built. Finding the thesis is a good exercise because it tells you in a condensed form what the author is saying. (Chapter 2 provides more detail about thesis statements.)

3. *State the main points that support the thesis.* What are the main points of support that the writer uses to back up the thesis? Each paragraph normally contains one major point. You can find these by locating the **topic sentence** in each paragraph (often the first sentence). You'll also probably notice the introductory and concluding paragraphs at this stage and how they fit into the whole.

4. *Answer any unanswered questions.* Once you've read through the selection and have pondered it somewhat, go over it to answer any as yet unanswered questions. You may need to read the selection again or conduct some research to understand some of the references more fully. At this point, you may find an Internet or library search on the topic or author useful to broaden your understanding.

   In addition, make use of any questions provided with the selection; these are designed to help you delve more deeply into the material. Still, don't worry if you don't have all the answers at this point; you can always go over the selection again. Then, if you're still uncertain about aspects of the text, bring your questions to your class discussion or talk to other students who are studying the same reading.

5. *Clarify your responses to the reading.* Once you are satisfied that you understand *what* the writer is saying, begin to think about your reactions and responses to it. Do you think the writer's points are valid? Are the arguments presented logically? Is the writer biased? Do you agree or disagree with what the writer says? Do you think the text is well written? Remember that any inferences you draw should be based on solid evidence. Reaching a particular conclusion about a reading simply because you "have a gut feeling" or "feel that way" is tantamount to convicting a criminal for murder because you don't like the look of his moustache or nose ring: the reaction is based on an emotional response, without being grounded in fact.

CRITICAL READING: SAMPLE TEXT AND RESPONSES

To help you become familiar with the process of reading critically and try it out yourself, a sample reading selection and a student's responses to it follow. While we can't include every thought that may drift through the reader's mind, the comments recorded here represent initial *thoughts, questions,* or *ideas* that surfaced as the student read the article. As you read the selection, decide whether you agree or disagree with the writer and with the student's assessment of the article. The text is presented in a format consistent with that of all other readings in this book, including essay questions and a vocabulary section.

How did your responses compare with the student reader's? Remember, there is no one "correct" way to delve into the text; the pre-reading stage is designed to help you simply *begin* the process of thinking about the writing.

Now, armed with pen in hand, you're ready to start reading. Here's how our student reader tackled this part of the task. Her commentary is written on the page itself. Once again, pay attention to the ways in which the student's thought processes and commentary match or differ from your own.

The Canadian Way

by Charles Gordon (b. 1940)

Charles Gordon is a columnist for the Ottawa Citizen *and* Maclean's *magazine. He is the author of four nonfiction books, including* At the Cottage *and* The Canada Trip *(both published by McClelland & Stewart) and a novel,* The Grim Pig *(also published by McClelland & Stewart). Gordon is married with two grown children and lives in Ottawa.*

PRE-READING

What are your own opinions about Canadian culture? In this article, originally from *Maclean's* magazine (1999), Charles Gordon explains why he thinks Canadian culture is foundering. What does Canadian culture need to flourish? Do you believe that Canadians are unduly influenced by our neighbours to the south? How would you define what is distinct about our culture in Canada? What kinds of activities do you consider worthy of your spare time?

STUDENT'S PRE-READING RESPONSES

1. The length of the piece

   This doesn't look excessively long, and I have set aside an hour to work on it. I could probably read this entire thing through from start to finish in one sitting.

2. The title

   It looks like he's going to be writing about something Canadian-- the Canadian "way" of doing something. The title makes it sound as if it applies to the majority of all Canadians, as if there is one "way" we all share, some history or tradition.

3. The author

   The bio says that Charles Gordon writes for the <u>Ottawa Citizen</u>. Does this make him an authority on what is "Canadian"? Since he writes in Canada's capital, he might have a better view from "the inside" than the rest of us. As a regular newspaper columnist for a reputable paper, he's been trained to do proper research. He should be a fairly reliable source.

4. The source of the article

<u>Maclean's</u> is a Canada-wide weekly newsmagazine known to be reputable. It's also been around a long time and has a huge circulation. I'd expect them to print material that is factually accurate and fairly trustworthy. It's also fairly recent, 1999.

5. Visual cues to meaning

In the opening paragraph, Gordon seems to be indicating that shopping is the most important activity for Canadians. There must be some significance to "shopping" here—maybe that we do it too much? Or that we shop for unnecessary items ("exotic birds," or "something you've never heard of, but everybody is getting one"). How does shopping connect to "the Canadian way"? At the end, he suggests that we have "created" a culture. So it looks like he's going to be talking about Canadian culture.

6. Create a road map for your reading

Questions to be answered while reading:

a. What does Gordon mean by "the Canadian way"? Is there one way of "being" that he thinks applies to all Canadians?

b. Why is shopping so significant? Why does he mention it in the first paragraph?

c. What is the culture at the end that he thinks we have chosen?

d. What are the factors that determine a Canadian culture? What parts of culture is he dealing with?

e. Do Canadians shop too much? What kinds of things do they shop for?

f. Who are the sources of Canadian culture?

g. Who is the intended audience of the piece? What is its tone? What is its purpose?

h. What is the thesis or main idea of the piece?

This sounds like Seaway Mall to me.

There is one of those wide, crowded avenues of shopping centres and strip malls in Ottawa, as there is in every city, and when you drive laboriously along it on an early Saturday afternoon, you get a sense of where all your neighbours are. This is confirmed when you hit the stretch, at the former outskirts, where all the big-box stores are.

Like Home Depot? Look this up.

Image of chaos and confusion

Sounds like a midway fair.

The parking lots are jammed, people driving distractedly around, fighting one another for parking spaces, the hotdog carts outside the store doing a flourishing business feeding dedicated shoppers who pause briefly to catch a bite before venturing inside again to face the merchandise.

There is a giant hardware store, a giant home furnishings store, a giant auto dealership, a giant lumber store, a giant pet store (Aisle 2: exotic birds; Aisle 4: snakes and lizards), a giant electronics store (Aisle 3: something you've never heard of, but everybody is getting one), and other giant places. Aside from the fact that many of these stores are foreign-owned, this street seems to have little to do with Canada's cultural identity debate. But there may be a link. It is that our true culture is shopping and everything else takes a back seat.

Ha, ha! Humour!

The idea that Canadians have no distinct "identity"

In what way can shopping be a culture?

It's an idea worth thinking about as we begin another round of discussions, in the wake of the magazine policy settlement and more closings of Canadian bookstores, about Canadian culture— what it is, whether it is worth saving, and, if so, how to go about doing it. In the broadest sense of culture—the range of activity from hockey to opera— Canada is doing very well in one way and rather badly in another.

Look this up

Two points being made, good and bad.

The good news is that the workers in the cultural sector—the musicians, writers, actors, composers and painters—are doing good work. In terms of sheer volume, the output of those who toil in the cultural fields far surpasses that of their predecessors. There are more Canadian books, movies and plays. In terms of quality, our stuff has been recognized around the world and its reputation grows.

That's the good news. The bad news is that this great work is being done largely by volunteers. Not that they are volunteers voluntarily. But they are being paid like volunteers. Actors and musicians frequently perform for nothing, or next to it, in the hope of catching a break. Authors do the same. Rare is the Canadian novelist who does not have to supplement his or her income with other work. For every Canadian who is now a star in the United States, there are many equally talented ones slogging away in this country for little recognition and less money.

Canadian culture does not generate enough money in Canada to support those who produce it. That's the problem. The reason there is not enough money is that there is not enough of an audience. This is where the neo-conservatives leap gleefully off the bandwagon shouting: "If people don't want it, then we shouldn't support it, and would you pass me that copy of *Sports Illustrated* when you're finished?" Certainly that's the easy way out. Give up on supporting our culture, throw open the doors to the Americans (even wider than they are already), relax and enjoy *Gilligan's Island VI: The Wrath of Ginger.*

But those who respect what Canadian artists and performers do, and don't want it to be swallowed up in a tidal wave of American blandness are not prepared to give up the fight. The question is: what sort of fight should it be?

We have tried various forms of protectionism. Although some of them have worked reasonably well (such as Canadian music quotas on pop radio), they are falling out of favour with the high priests of international trade and will not last. Because of the recent cutbacks in grants to artists and arts groups, a lot of discussion is focused on the role of government, but no amount of government support can make our culture self-supporting. The answer is not to restrict the foreign competition or subsidize the domestic product, but to make the market bigger.

In other words, the answer is us, the audience. We have to support the stuff, vote with our feet and our wallets, buy the books, attend the theatres and the galleries, and, yes, the ball parks and arenas, because you may notice that sport has been going south as well.

Why don't we do it? It is not lack of money. The recession is over. Canadians are spending money again, and not all of it on the necessities of life. North Americans are spending $6 billion a year on their pets. Casinos are thriving.

What keeps us away—or what we think keeps us away—is lack of time. We are terribly busy, we always say, what with working harder than ever before (because of all the labour-saving devices we have been given at work) and there is no time to do anything, and even if there was, we are tired. Yet there we are, on Saturday, bumper to bumper, heeding the siren call of the merchandise piled floor to ceiling, the bunny rabbits in Aisle 6, the DVDs in Aisle 9, narrowly averting incidents of shopping-cart rage. There is no question that this is hard work, physically and emotionally exhausting. No wonder we are too tired to go out. No wonder we flop in front of the TV set. There is Sunday shopping now, and we have to rest up.

In all this, we have unwittingly created a culture. The question we have to ask is whether it is the one we want.

QUESTIONS

Understanding the message: Comprehension

1. What is the "magazine policy settlement"? How is it related to the issue of Canadian culture?
2. Explain how, according to Gordon, Canadian culture "is doing very well in one way and rather badly in another."
3. What does Gordon mean when he writes in paragraph 6, "Not that they are volunteers voluntarily"?
4. What is meant by the term "shopping-cart rage"? What similar term(s) does it imitate?

Examining the structure and details: Analysis

1. How many different rhetorical modes does Gordon use in order to prove his thesis?
2. Reread paragraph 3. What examples of merchandise does Gordon supply? What do these items have in common with each other? Why do you think Gordon chose them?
3. How long is Gordon's introduction in this essay? How long is his conclusion? How are the introduction and conclusion related? Why do you think he makes the conclusion as short as he does?

Formulating a response: Inference and interpretation

1. What is the irony in Gordon's title?
2. What is the tone of this essay? Provide examples to support your answer. Why do you think Gordon chose this tone?
3. In paragraph 7, Gordon writes that it's wrong to "Give up on supporting our culture, throw open the doors to the Americans (even wider than they are already) . . ." Do you agree that we are excessively influenced by our neighbours to the south? Why or why not?
4. What do you think Gordon's purpose is in this essay? Is he successful in achieving it? Why or why not?

Essay questions

1. What is your view of the kinds of shopping that Gordon criticizes in "big-box stores"? Discuss your own approach to this aspect of Canadian culture.
2. What do you think defines "Canadian" culture as opposed to any other? Write an essay in which you discuss the characteristics that make our culture truly "Canadian."

3. In "The Canadian Way," Gordon suggests that Canadians' behaviour fails to promote or support Canadian culture. What does Gordon imply we can do to save our unique culture? Support your answer with examples from the article.

VOCABULARY

magazine policy settlement: legal settlement in which American-based magazines are required to print separate Canadian-content editions

neo-conservatives: political and economic conservatives whose beliefs arose in opposition to the perceived liberalism of the 1960s

averting: avoiding; preventing

Notice that while the student reader remained respectful of Gordon's argument, she also felt free to question his assumptions and even disagree with him. Did you come up with any of the same questions? Don't worry if your questions are different or if you think you haven't got enough. You'll develop more as you continue to read, as the topic starts to become clearer, and as you begin to recognize your own reactions to what you read.

Notice, too, that the reader used paraphrasing to help her master the more complex phrases or ideas, and she looked up any words that would hinder her as she moved from start to finish (she also reminded herself to look up other words and ideas later on).

Here's how our reader responded to questions about the author's purpose, audience, and tone:

STUDENT'S READING RESPONSES

Purpose:

> Even though the writing is entertaining in places, I don't think this is the writer's main purpose in writing. It's also educational; he mentions certain facts about Canadian culture and leisure. Most of all, though, the author seems to be trying to persuade us that we need to create and preserve a unique "Canadian" culture that is valuable to us. I think his major purpose is to persuade.

Audience:

> He's obviously addressing this information to Canadian readers, since he's asking us to support our own cultural activities. He's also probably interested in more educated or middle-class readers, since those are the ones who would be familiar with "big-box" shopping and the kinds of cultural activities he mentions: books, theatres and galleries, sports events.

Tone:

> There seems to be a mixture of a serious tone (he uses factual data to support some points) and a sarcastic tone (making fun of Gilligan's Island or "shopping-cart rage"). At the same time, he's also a bit angry, saying that we as Canadians are spending too much time and money on "bland" American culture rather than our own. Overall, I'd say this is a somewhat angry, even negative, tone.

As you can see from this student's response, it's possible that several aspects of a reading may still remain vague after a first encounter; the student didn't yet have a fully developed sense of Gordon's argument at this stage. As she reread the selection and answered the questions accompanying the reading, these points became clearer. Nevertheless, her initial reading certainly allowed the student to identify the major topic (Canadian culture) and some of the main points in the article. Finally, she began to react to what the author says, either agreeing or disagreeing at times, or commenting further.

POST-READING

As she continued to ponder the selection, the student attempted to clarify all confusing terms and conducted a search on the Internet using search terms such as "big-box store" or "Canadian culture" in order to answer some of the text's post-reading questions (for more information on all types of research, see Chapter 13). Notice, too, that she continued to generate more questions even at this late stage (she added her own questions and ideas in parentheses). Depending on time constraints, she might have followed up on these new questions as well; in any case, they helped her examine the argument in greater depth and served as part of her brainstorming material as she began to respond to the reading. As you read, think about how you would treat some of these same issues.

Now, here are the post-reading activities and sample responses to them:

STUDENT'S POST-READING RESPONSES

1. Write a quick summary of the piece.

   In "The Canadian Way," Charles Gordon seems to be suggesting that we spend our time shopping rather than taking advantage of Canada's unique culture. We don't realize that we are allowing our native culture to suffer as a result, because we don't support it.

2. Determine the thesis of the selection.

   If we are not careful, the only kind of culture that Canadians will support and share will be a pervasive "shopping" culture.

3. State the main points of support for the thesis.

   a. The cultural debate in Canada is linked to the notion of excessive and unnecessary shopping at places like the huge and impersonal big-box stores.

   b. We need to ask ourselves what Canadian culture is, if it is worth saving, and how to save it.

   c. The quality and quantity of Canadian culture these days is improving, but it is not making a profit because so many of the "workers in the cultural sector" are neither paid well nor recognized for their contributions. (But if the quality is so good, why aren't more people taking advantage of Canadian culture? In fact, it seems to me that it is growing. I know people who buy Canadian books and magazines, or watch Canadian TV shows. Still, there aren't a lot of really great Canadian productions; you hardly ever see Canadian films in the movie theatres.)

   d. The reason the workers are not paid enough is because there is not enough of an audience for the culture being produced in Canada. (I think there would be an audience if we knew about it and if it were of high quality. I've always enjoyed the Canadian novels I've read. But he's right about the American influence; we all watch American TV, have cable TV with hundreds of American channels and swoon over American movies and movie stars. When's the last time a Canadian movie had the kind of hype that the Jurassic Park movies have?)

e. Canada has tried various ways to protect Canadian culture; some have been successful while others have not. (Radio quotas are a good idea. Now that we're all listening to more Canadian musicians, we realize how good the music is. What would happen if they tried the same thing with television or movies?)

f. We're not patronizing Canadian culture very much because we say we lack time; yet we have time to shop at mega malls and big-box stores. (I'm not so sure it's merely a matter of time. It's obvious that people have time to watch American TV or movies, or to line up for hours to get tickets to American rock bands. Have we really been socialized to believe that "American is better"? Maybe that's part of the problem, too.)

g. The culture we are creating may end up to be one we don't want. (Does he mean a "shopping culture" or a culture that prefers U.S. products to Canadian ones?)

4. Answer your unanswered questions and solidify your impressions.

By this point in the process, our reader realized that some of her earlier questions had already been answered (such as why shopping is mentioned at the beginning of the article, or which sources of Canadian culture are cited). She also discovered that some of her initial questions were not as relevant as she'd originally assumed (for example, learning about the actual products that Canadians are buying became less important as she continued to read). After reviewing her still unanswered questions, the student realized she'd need to do some further research to clarify.

Once she discovered that many of her guesses had been correct (for example, "big-box stores" does, in fact, refer to enormous theme stores such as Home Depot or Chapters), the student began to formulate her own reactions to and opinions about what Gordon is saying. By working through the selection carefully and responding to all the questions generated, she developed a clear grasp of Gordon's points and what he says about our culture. She also recognized that she disagreed with some of Gordon's ideas (for example, she questioned whether lack of time is the only reason Canadians spend so much money on American culture).

In your own post-reading process, you'll probably find that you, too, will need to delve a little more deeply into the writing and its context before you'll completely understand the author's message or purpose. It's important to note, however, that not everyone works best by jotting down *all* ideas on paper, as our student has done. For some of you, working through the pre-reading, reading, and post-reading activities may remain primarily a mental activity. Still, it's important to run through these steps in order to read purposefully and solidify your own response and reactions to what you read.

By the time she had finished rereading "The Canadian Way," the student had not only established her sense of Gordon's thesis and approach but also developed her *own* opinion on the topic—a perfect starting point to begin building an essay in response to the reading.

CHAPTER 2

Writing Essays: Responding to Texts in Writing

Why Write? The Benefits of Writing Essays

A common lament that's familiar to most college and university English instructors is, "Why do we have to write *essays*? Essays don't exist in the real world. We may never have to write another essay again as long as we live." While there may be some truth to these charges (essays are rarely part of one's work life—except, perhaps, in the case of English professors!), the skills you acquire through writing essays will continue to serve you long after you graduate, in almost every instance in which written communication is required.

An essay, unlike most other types of writing, demands that you exercise a constellation of skills not regularly coinciding in any other type of writing. Essays oblige you to think critically, present a logical argument, organize ideas in an outline, provide specific details and support, express your ideas clearly, convince a reader—all while responding to something that you have already read. How many other kinds of writing demand all these skills? In other words, once you've mastered this form, the rigorous, challenging nature of essay writing will prepare you well for any other writing assignments or day-to-day writing you may undertake. In a way, an essay is a kind of crash course in many different kinds of writing skills.

This chapter takes a closer look at the qualities of good writing and helps you develop the skills required to construct effective, well-written prose.

What Is Good Writing?

Good writing begins with an awareness of the writing process and what distinguishes it from other forms of communication. The key points about writing in general are discussed below.

Writing Is Different from Speaking

If you had the choice between telling a person something or writing it, which method of communication would you choose? For many people, oral communication is almost always preferable. When asked to write, these people think, "I sometimes have great ideas, but I just can't transform them into words . . . when I try, the language sounds too simple, and I don't get my message across," or "I just can't think of anything to write."

Why do so many people struggle with writing? Simply put, they lack practice. Even with the prevalence of e-mail and the proliferation of written communication today, most of us spend most of our time communicating orally with others; it makes sense that we're more comfortable speaking. In addition, talking allows us to add visible cues (such as gestures) or other aids to understanding (such as asking questions, providing immediate feedback, and so on) to our messages. Furthermore, we usually don't need to worry as much about grammar (and not at all about spelling) when speaking. Expressions perfectly acceptable in speech ("There's so many people in that gym!") are unacceptable if we write Standard (grammatically correct, relatively formal) English.

The easiest way to become more comfortable writing is simply to *do it*. Write, write often, and write in as many different contexts as you can. Think of writing as any other skill that you can improve with practice. After all, you're aiming to become a *competent* writer, not this millennium's Shakespeare. Just as you would never expect to ski like an expert if you hadn't practised your technique beforehand or expect your future spouse to cook a gourmet meal if s/he'd never before set foot in a kitchen, good writing, too, requires practice—ideally, on a daily basis.

Good Writing Uses Critical Thinking Skills

By the time you've read and re-read a text and formed your own interpretation and beliefs, you're ready to start formulating a response in writing—an essay. Like reading, writing essays requires you to think critically and use logic, in this case to present your ideas to an audience. If you review the communications paradigm from Chapter 1, you'll notice that as a writer, you're in the position of sender. Accordingly, it's useful to consider both your readers (the receivers) and the specific details of the essay (your message) as you write.

Good Writing Exhibits Common Characteristics

Whichever type of writing you examine, you'll find that the best samples share a set of traits that distinguish them from more mediocre efforts. In particular, good writing shares the following common characteristics:

- *It has a purpose.* Whether it aims to entertain, inform, or persuade, or aims at a combination of all three, good writing has a purpose that directs the writer.

- *It has an appropriate structure.* Even highly informal writing, such as an e-mail to a friend or a note stuck on the refrigerator door, is structured according to particular rules or conventions appropriate for that kind of writing. Structure also contributes to the unity of the writing (it is focused on one topic at a time) and its coherence, or connectedness (ideas flow smoothly from one to the next). If you're aware of structure, your effectiveness as a writer increases.

- *It uses language effectively.* Good writing uses language appropriate to its context: a quick note informing your wife that you've gone out to the corner store uses one kind of language; a note to your daughter's teacher uses another. Knowing when you can "relax the rules" and when you must adhere to Standard English is important to writing effectively. Using language well also means you'll get your message across clearly and succinctly.

- *It makes sense.* Good writing is easy to follow; its logic is clear. Even if the writer rearranges chronological details or presents ideas unconventionally, the meaning should still be evident. The reader should never have to search for meaning unduly hidden behind the words. Good writing makes sense.

- *It is complete.* Key ideas are never omitted in good writing; the writer ensures that the reader has everything needed to understand the message.

- *It has a unique voice, or personal style.* The best writing samples convey a sense of the writer's unique personality. Personal style may be less obvious in purely expository or informative writing (such as in a textbook), but it should be recognizable nonetheless. Style is what makes the difference between a dry, boring text and one that continually engages the reader, prompting curiosity and interest.

- *It sometimes breaks the rules.* Like experts in any field, experienced writers know the rules well enough to be able to break them on occasion. As communicators today, we face a set of language rules in transition; what's considered effective or well written is currently being redefined. (For example, the use of the first-person "I" in essays, previously shunned, is now quite common; and the popularity of Web sites, with their clipped, fast-paced style, also affects our definition of good writing.) Good writers know when they can modify, bend, or alter the rules for a desired effect. Take note, however: good writers also make it perfectly clear that any unusual or atypical structures are *deliberate* and not caused by ignorance or laziness. Unless you feel extremely confident in your abilities, it's best to stick with the rules at first before venturing out into more experimental kinds of writing.

THREE KINDS OF ESSAYS

This text looks in depth at three conventional types of essays dealing both with fiction and nonfiction readings. (While other kinds of essays exist, these three are the most common styles used in college classrooms.) With one basic set of principles to guide all three types, you'll be set to tackle any kind of essay question.

Essays Based on Personal Experience

In this type of essay, you develop a general topic suggested by something in a reading. For example, Amy Tan's article, "Mother Tongue," touches on topics such as English as a second language, second-generation Americans, and mother–daughter relationships. A typical personal-experience question about this reading is, "After reading Amy Tan's article, 'Mother Tongue,' describe a special relationship you have had with an older relative."

A personal-experience essay such as this is built on your own experience with, and knowledge of, the topic. A good personal-experience essay presents its thesis (main point) with support from your own life and learning.

Essays That Analyze a Nonfiction Reading

In this type of essay, you focus on the contents of the reading itself and closely examine, analyze, and respond to the contents and/or structure of the selection. Your responses are based on what the author has written, and any support you provide is drawn from the selection itself. In "Depression Can Strike Anyone," Diane Francis discusses the debilitating disease of clinical depression. A question that asks you to analyze this reading is, "Does Francis succeed in convincing the reader that depression 'is a hideous disease'? Write an essay in which you argue one way or the other, citing examples from the article to support your argument." Any answer to this question must use information from the reading itself, and any support will be gathered directly from it as well.

Essays That Analyze a Short Story (Fiction)

In essays based on fiction, you also focus directly on a text by examining its structure and contents; you read a short story closely and support any inferences you make with specific details or quotes from that story. Here's a sample question: "Discuss the image of the tattoo in Camilla Gibb's 'ID Me.' How does having a tattoo influence each character's life?" Your task as writer is to determine your own interpretation of this image in the story and then develop a thesis and outline around which to construct your essay.

A Common Approach for All Essay Types: Three Stages of Writing an Essay

As with reading, you can maximize your chances of writing well by following some straightforward guidelines. The **writing process** can also be divided into three stages: pre-writing, writing, and post-writing.

As you'd expect, pre-writing refers to all those activities occurring before you actually start to write the essay draft. Pre-writing includes thinking about the topic, planning, and other preparation (gathering background information or details, for instance). In the writing stage, you compose your first draft of the essay. In post-writing, you refine what you have written; at this stage, you focus on correcting errors, polishing the prose, and making any other changes necessary to improve the work overall. Ideally, you'll have the opportunity to write more than one draft before you engage in the final stages of post-writing.

Pre-Writing: Preparing to Write

What are your tasks during pre-writing? As the term suggests, pre-writing involves all activities *before* you actually start to write the essay. In fact, a common error students make is to spend too little time on this stage. A major portion of the work on the essay *must* begin before you actually start to write; plan to reserve a substantial portion of the time allotted (even up to one-third) for pre-writing activities.

Use this stage simply to think about the topic, getting your ideas and approach straight in your own mind. Because pre-writing primarily involves thinking, you'll once again need to call on critical thinking skills at this stage. Once you spend sufficient time thinking about a topic, you may be pleasantly surprised to find how much you have to say. (In fact, a dearth of ideas is more often due to lack of pre-writing than lack of knowledge.) Then, transforming the pre-writing ideas into sentences and paragraphs may be less of a hardship than you expect.

TIP

Preserve the pre-writing

If you want to ensure your essay treats its topic thoroughly and is well constructed, be sure to work through pre-writing. Pre-writing is the best guarantee that the argument of your essay will be clear and well thought out, and won't omit any essential points that slipped by as you rushed to write your draft.

The various steps in pre-writing are listed below. While most people follow this order of steps, there is, as with all creative work, overlap and movement back and forth between the steps.

1. Choose a general topic

Writers are often furnished with only a general subject area and must narrow this down to a single topic even before they can *start* to think of a thesis, or statement about the topic. In order to approach your essay assignment efficiently, you should understand the distinction among subject, topic, and thesis.

A **subject** is a very general area of interest, one that can usually be summed up in a word or category heading. For instance, pollution, education, freedom, pets, or leisure are subject areas. Often, your instructor will assign a very general subject, and it's up to you to narrow it down to a topic.

A **topic** is a single aspect of the subject, one subcategory or part of it. The topic can often be stated in a phrase or clause. For instance, effects of pollution on farming in Alberta, phonics as a method to teach reading, freedom in Kate Chopin's "The Story of an Hour," Seeing Eye dogs, or working out at the gym are all topics. Because subjects are simply too broad to serve as the basis of an essay, you'll need to select a topic before you can move to the next step.

A **thesis** is your own statement *about* the topic, phrased in a single sentence. The thesis states your viewpoint on the topic and represents the main point or message of your essay. "In Kate Chopin's 'The Story of an Hour,' the only way Mrs. Mallard can achieve freedom from her marriage is through death" is a thesis.

DEFINITION

Subject: a very general area of interest, usually expressed in a word or two
Topic: one specific part or subcategory of a subject, usually expressed in a phrase or clause
Thesis: the main argument or point of an essay

TIP

Choosing an audience

After you've been assigned an essay, double-check with your professor to see whether s/he has an intended audience in mind. Most often, class assignments assume an audience of your peers—that is, other college-educated readers who have knowledge similar to yours.

TIP

Choose a topic that interests you

The best way to generate ideas for creating a successful essay is to ensure that you are *interested* in your topic. Begin with something you know about or something that intrigued you in the reading selection. Even if the topic is assigned by your professor (and is not one you'd normally consider), you can generate ideas that interest you. Focus on something that appears incongruous (if you think the writer is contradicting herself or himself, for instance), something puzzling, or something that elicits a strong reaction (particularly if the topic isn't naturally appealing to you). With this base, you'll be more likely to write something that has meaning for you and that will, therefore, be more interesting for your readers to read.

2. Consider your audience and purpose

Before you begin to plan *what* to write, it's important to consider your audience (for whom you are writing) and your purpose (what you wish to accomplish with the essay). (For a review of audience and purpose, see Chapter 1.) Sometimes the assignment itself establishes these details. If not, first take some time to imagine the major characteristics of your chosen audience: How old are they? What is their educational level? What kind of language do they use? Which terms do they already know? As you write, your sense of the audience will help to determine writing style and content (such as vocabulary, types of supporting details, depth of explanations, and so on). If you're aware of the needs and expectations of your intended audience, you can cater to those needs and expectations, and your audience will be more likely to understand and accept your message.

Next, consider your purpose. The purpose of an assignment may be left open or may grow out of the specific topic and thesis you choose. If you write about shopping as a substitute for power (a means of expressing financial clout), you may decide to approach the topic in a serious vein, perhaps even conducting research to support your ideas. In this situation, an informative or persuasive purpose would be most appropriate. If, however, you choose to poke fun at the ways people shop to exert control over their lives, an entertaining purpose would be a better choice. It's important to consider purpose early in the process because your purpose helps to shape the form, structure, and details of the essay.

3. Generate ideas about the topic

During this step, decide what you think *about* the topic. This viewpoint will form the basis of your thesis sentence and the foundation of your essay.

You probably already know more than you realize about any given topic. In this stage, examine your existing knowledge, feelings, reactions, opinions, or other ideas about a topic to determine your position on the issue. If the essay assignment asks you to address the contents of a selection directly (for example, whether you agree or disagree, whether you think the author made her/his point effectively, and so on) you might have all the information you need right there in the reading itself. Similarly, if you are asked to write about a short story, outside research is not *required* to produce an effective argument, although it can certainly serve to support your ideas.

Let your thoughts wander over the topic at hand: does anything immediately come to mind? Generating ideas—sometimes called **brainstorming**—about the topic allows you to determine how you respond to it, how you feel about the issue, or what your own opinions are. The purpose here is to generate as many ideas as possible associated with your topic so that you can begin to determine where you stand, which areas you already know well, and which others you must consider further (or research), if necessary. Do this without worrying about whether the ideas seem logical or not; don't censor or judge at this point. Brainstorming means allowing all your ideas about a topic to surface and recording these without discounting any at first. Later, you'll discard the redundant or unimportant ideas. You hope ultimately to generate enough ideas about the topic to extract a thesis (your main point for the essay) and support for it.

DEFINITION

Brainstorming: a collection of techniques used in pre-writing to generate ideas freely about a given topic

There are several methods for generating ideas (brainstorming). All of these techniques encourage you to create associations with the topic or develop ideas that emanate from it. The goal at this early stage is to allow as many thoughts as possible to occur, without censoring or limiting them. Just as some of the zaniest ideas have formed the basis for the world's most brilliant inventions, an unlikely association or afterthought on a brainstorming sheet may ultimately lead to an original, insightful essay.

Here are some common brainstorming methods:

CLUSTER TECHNIQUE. To use the cluster technique, begin with a general topic in the centre of the page and draw branches with associated ideas emanating from it. Include similar points, opposing points, connected concepts—virtually anything that comes to mind and is related to the topic. See what associations grow from the central idea and indicate each of these on individual branches. Each of the resulting thoughts may then lead to something else. The

FIGURE 2.1 The Cluster Technique on Keeping a Diary

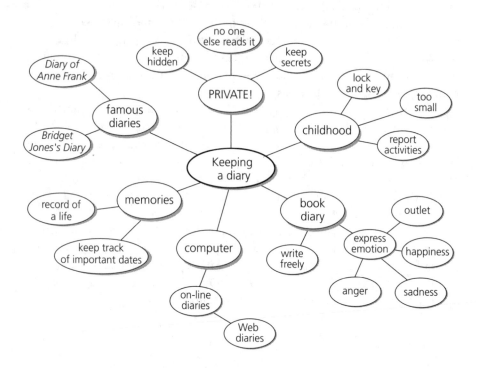

final diagram (see Figure 2.1) will provide a host of ideas about your topic, and these can be used to structure your essay.

As you go, pay attention to any particularly dense portions (with lots of smaller branches) or repeated concepts. These highlight areas of particular interest or usefulness.

Figure 2.1 shows an example of the cluster technique. The writer's topic is "keeping a diary." Notice how each idea naturally leads to another, as sub-branches sprout from larger ideas.

Eventually, our student generated a number of ideas about this pastime. From here, she can decide which specific aspect of diary writing she wishes to consider for her essay.

FREEWRITING. This method of brainstorming allows you to work with full sentences rather than a diagram if this is more comfortable for you. Nevertheless, freewriting, as the term implies, also encourages spontaneous associations and unstructured writing. When you freewrite, simply let your mind wander over the topic, allowing ideas to lead where they may. If one sentence prompts a new idea in a new direction, simply follow its path until you think of something else. The only imperative is that you continue to write about the topic for a designated time period, say 5 to 10 minutes. Freewriting is a written form of "free association," allowing ideas to float through your consciousness without interruption. Because this method liberates your mind from the kind of structure that will be required later on in the writing process, you may find that some of the ideas that surface surprise you.

Here's an example of freewriting on the same topic, "keeping a diary." Notice how the writer lets one idea lead naturally to another, yet never veers far from the topic at hand.

STUDENT'S FREEWRITING

It seems as if I've always had a diary. I've kept a diary since I was a little girl . . . I remember the first one I got for my tenth birthday, with a lock and key! I really believed nobody could get into it. But of course, my little brother Ethan broke into it and then I started hiding it, well it really is a private activity. I can be so open in my diary, no need to worry that anybody's going to judge me. Unless they find it, I guess, and then I'd be in trouble. What would happen if somebody discovered my diary? I bet it's horrible for famous people, they don't want all those secrets revealed, the face lifts and breast implants. That could certainly cause problems! For me it's just a way to get out my thoughts and dreams, never just a list of what I did that day. I've put in some pretty personal stuff and boy I'd hate it if anyone else read it. But I enjoy rereading it once in a while, like after we moved. I sat in my bedroom and went through my old diaries. I was amazed at how much I've changed, and how my ideas are so different now, like my attitude towards friends and school. I got a big laugh out of it too when I read how I was so heartbroken after Danny broke up with me in eighth grade, what a BABY. Him, not me, that is! He didn't even tell me in person, he did it over

(continued)

the telephone. Coward! Well, the diary helped me at the time because I was in a new school and I didn't have new friends yet and the diary was kind of my best friend... it's sort of like a friend I guess. I find that when I'm really happy about something or really sad, that's when I feel like writing in it. Now I write it on the computer because it's faster, but I sort of miss the old books.

Embedded in her freewriting are the writer's ideas about her topic, those that she can later enlist for use in an essay.

CATEGORIES OR LISTS. Ideas seem to organize themselves almost of their own volition when we start with subject headings and list things under them. For some people, writing category headings and recording all related ideas under each one works well to generate ideas about a topic. Divide your topic into separate parts or categories, then jot down anything that comes to mind in relation to each heading.

Here is one student's list of categories and corresponding ideas about the topic "favourite leisure activities."

STUDENT'S CATEGORIES AND NOTES

GOING OUT

   MOVIES:
fun to watch, escapism, cool heroes

   PARTIES:
- at home
   fun with friends, see my girlfriend
- at clubs, dances
   big zoo, lots of fun, loud noise, can yell and sing, dance with the crowd

SPORTS:
- on teams: soccer, basketball, etc.
   physical development, learn skills, fun with the guys

(continued)

- as audience: hockey games, football, basketball
  going with the gang, cheering, audience experience

- working out
  get in shape, feel good about myself, see my friends

STAYING HOME

VIDEO GAMES:
- playing with the guys, learn new techniques, improve my game, win!

TV:
- favourite shows, laughing at <u>The Simpsons</u>, after school relaxing before homework, relaxing in the evening, good for boredom

MUSIC:
- listen to CDs, watch videos, trade music with friends

HANGING OUT:
- have pizza, go over to Jeff's house, surf the Net, work on my Web page, e-mail the guys

This list of categories will later help the student pinpoint what he will say in an essay about the topic.

JOURNALIST'S METHOD. Since journalists must provide key facts and details up front in their newspaper articles, they're routinely taught to answer each of the questions "Who?" "What?" "When?" "Where?" "How?" and "Why?" in their opening paragraphs. You can use these same questions to focus your ideas about a topic. Generate questions—as many as you can—that begin with each of these words and jot down the answers. Try to make the questions as interesting as possible rather than use those most obvious. Instead of asking, "What is my favourite leisure activity?" play with variations on the question: "What do I do when I'm bored?" "What do I do when I want to relax?" "What do I do when I want to be alone?" "What do I do most frequently?" "What do I enjoy most when I'm with friends?"—and so on. The more varied the questions, the broader will be the range of answers and the more material you'll have to start your essay.

Here are some questions generated about the same topic, "favourite leisure activities."

STUDENT'S ANSWERS TO JOURNALISTS' QUESTIONS

WHO do I do my leisure activities with?
Jeff, Amol, Patrick, Marco, my family, no one

WHO decides what I'll do?
sometimes depends on the guys, or if my girlfriend is busy; sometimes my dad if it's family time

WHAT do I do for fun?
Sports, videos, Web page, music, parties, hanging out, watch television, dancing

WHAT is missing from my leisure?
need a car, would make it much easier, and more cash

WHAT am I not doing that I'd like to do?
try snowboarding, maybe go travelling with my girlfriend

WHAT do I do when I'm bored?
call a friend, call my girlfriend

WHAT do I do most frequently?
sports, hang out with the guys, Web page

WHEN can I have leisure time?
after homework, after part-time job, Saturday nights

WHEN do I enjoy leisure activities the most?
birthday party at Jeff's, laughed till we were sick

WHERE do I spend my leisure time?
at home sometimes, (TV, Web page, music, etc.) and at the gym, dances, friends' houses

WHY is it enjoyable?
doing things I choose, relaxing, learning stuff, fun, with friends

HOW can I have better leisure time?
avoid boredom, try new things, call up my friends, get together

When he reviews his notes later on, the student will pick out those ideas that best contribute to his essay.

4. Narrow to a thesis

By this point, you should have at least one full page of notes, points, ideas, or sentences that grew out of the assigned topic. Within the contents of this page you hope to find the leading idea for an essay—the thesis.

To help pinpoint a thesis, take a closer look at the ideas you've generated. Look for key points or for repeated words or patterns in your notes. By reviewing the notes and questioning what you think *about* the topic, you can determine your own viewpoint—your thesis. For instance, the student who brainstormed using categories and the journalist's questions, above, reexamined his notes and noticed that almost all the activities he mentioned focused on interaction with others. By asking himself questions such as "What does this say about leisure activities?" and "How does this help characterize my approach to leisure?" he eventually formed a thesis: "No matter how I spend my spare time, my first choice is to spend it with my friends." This thesis reflected his own viewpoint about the function of leisure in his life.

Your thesis is the core of the entire essay and serves as its guiding principle; everything else in the essay should serve to support, explain, or prove the thesis.

CHARACTERISTICS OF AN EFFECTIVE THESIS. How can you tell if your thesis accomplishes the task set out for it—effectively stating the main idea of the essay? Here is a list of the major characteristics of a good thesis sentence. Whenever you write a thesis, cross-check it against this list:

- *An effective thesis can be stated in a single sentence.* While some professional writers may present a thesis in more than one sentence and others never write one in the essay at all, a good thesis *can* always be expressed in a single sentence, and a one-sentence thesis should be your initial goal as a writer. The thesis should state both your topic and viewpoint (the idea about the topic) as clearly and directly as possible.

- *An effective thesis presents a clear viewpoint.* The thesis should indicate your viewpoint about something, a viewpoint that may not necessarily be shared by others; it is your own "take" on the topic. What is it that the essay will tell us *about* this topic? The thesis answers this question. To determine if the thesis is effective, ask these questions: "Is it possible to disagree with this statement? Are there some people who might hold alternative views that are also valid?" Even descriptive or narrative essays, which are highly personal, should indicate the writer's viewpoint, and if the essay's purpose is to persuade your readers, then your thesis *must* be argumentative.

- *An effective thesis is stated near the beginning of the paper.* Because the thesis lets your reader know your main point and actually directs the contents of the essay, you should state your thesis early on in the paper. Most often, the thesis is positioned as the last sentence in the introductory paragraph.

- *An effective thesis is never a question.* Since the point of the thesis is to present your viewpoint on the issue, a question suggests you haven't yet decided what it is. While it's okay to include questions in the essay itself (and even in the introductory paragraph), using a question as the thesis is never acceptable.

- *An effective thesis is neither so broad that it allows only a generalized treatment of the topic nor so narrow that it eliminates any possibility for further development.* Narrowing down to a thesis that works but also proves interesting enough to carry an entire essay is one of the most challenging tasks in essay writing. If a thesis is too general, to support it fully may require more writing than you are willing or able to do. For example, the sentence "Sports enable us to keep in shape" may be true, and it also expresses the writer's viewpoint. However, in order to prove *all* the ways that *all* sports contribute to good health would take far longer than most students have to write their papers. On the other hand, the sentence "My basketball team has five players" proves itself in its words; since this statement is already true, it leaves no room for development.

- *An effective thesis is supportable.* You may have a great idea that presents an original, interesting viewpoint, but if there is not enough support (evidence— either from the text or from other sources) to back it up, then it's not a viable thesis. Ask yourself if you could think of at least three strong, convincing points of support (reasons why your thesis is valid). If you can't, then you need to discard this thesis—no matter how dear it is to you—and try again.

Remember that in developing a thesis you are really deciding *what you think about a topic.* In order to determine a clear viewpoint, you must carefully examine the topic and your brainstorming ideas. If you need to, conduct some research as well at this point.

Once again, let's examine the essay topic "keeping a diary." By reviewing her notes and contemplating the topic further, our student eventually decided on the tentative thesis "Keeping a diary has been a beneficial experience for me." Look again at the list of criteria for a strong thesis and ask yourself if it qualifies as an effective thesis sentence. Why or why not?

When the student checked the list of criteria, she decided that her thesis was too broad, since "beneficial" is a rather vague descriptor. She determined what, exactly, had made the activity beneficial, and revised the thesis as follows: "Keeping a diary has helped me to grow as an individual." At this point, she felt, the thesis was both specific enough and argumentative in its approach. Even though it could be further refined as the writing process continued, it provided a good starting point to begin writing the essay.

TIP

Developing an interesting thesis

The best thesis statements are those that tell the readers something *new* or *different*, something they had not previously considered. While the statement "Moving to a new city by myself taught me a lot about independence" is a viable thesis, it's not one that holds many surprises for readers. Something a bit less obvious, such as "Moving to a new city highlighted all my personality flaws," holds more appeal and may also provide your readers with something they had not anticipated reading.

5. *Organize your ideas in an outline*

Once you have a thesis in mind, decide how, specifically, you'll support it in the **body** of your essay. How can you state your case so that a reader will naturally agree with you by the time s/he finishes reading your essay? How can you write in such a way that the essay naturally substantiates the thesis sentence? Choosing main points of support and organizing them in an **outline** will help to accomplish this task.

DEFINITION

Outline: a basic plan, or blueprint, of an essay, containing the thesis and main points of support

Some students shudder merely *reading* the word "outline." To them, an outline feels too restrictive, like a bad contract they've already signed that forces them to comply with its terms and conditions whether they like it or not. In reality, an outline, like any plan, serves only to *direct* you as you build the essay, but is not, like a signed contract, legally binding. An essay's outline ensures that you've previewed the essay's structure from beginning to end and allows you to catch any glaring omissions or errors *before* you write an entire draft. At the same time, a flexible outline still allows you to introduce new ideas, make deletions, or implement changes as you write. If you have a clear sense of where your essay is going, your reader is more likely to be able to follow along as well.

To establish supporting points for the thesis, ask yourself, "How do I know this is true?" or "Why do I believe this?" Jot down all the answers you come up with. (In fact, you may find that many of the supporting points for your thesis are already present on your brainstorming sheet.) Aim for a list of 5 to10 supports for your thesis. Then, review the list and decide which 3 to 5 are most suitable for the essay. You may realize that several points can be regrouped under a larger heading, or that some can be eliminated because they contain repeated or unnecessary information. The idea is to end up with 3 to 5 points that you feel provide all the *essential* support (not necessarily all support of any kind) for the thesis.

ORDERING POINTS IN AN OUTLINE. There are three methods of ordering points. Depending on your topic and your approach, decide which works best for you:

1. **Spatial organization.** This method orders points according to their location. Used mostly in descriptive essays, spatial organization begins at one point in space and proceeds logically through to a final point. For instance, in describing your favourite beach, you might begin at the hill near the hotel, where chairs dot the lawn. Next, you'd move to the beach itself and the beachgoers' activities there. Finally, you'd proceed to the shoreline and ocean and describe the bathers frolicking in the water. However you order your points, the movement must seem sensible and logical.

2. **Chronological organization.** In this method, you organize points as they would naturally occur in time. For instance, to write about the process of adjusting to college life in a new city, you might begin with the period just before leaving home; next, you'd discuss the first few days or weeks adapting to your new lifestyle; finally, you'd write about your day-to-day activities after adjusting to the new location. Chronological order makes the most sense whenever confusion could result by rearranging the points. Narrative and process essays are most often ordered this way.

3. **Emphatic organization** (order of importance). Emphatic order is most useful when writing argument essays or if your points don't demand a chronological sequence. In this method, you order ideas from the least forceful to the most forceful; in other words, you end with your most convincing point. Emphatic order works to enhance the psychological effect of the essay, working incrementally as it steadily convinces its readers. This method also avoids anticlimactic endings caused by revealing the best idea too early. Emphatic order builds points in order of importance, so you end with a flourish.

The student who wrote about leisure activities, above, used the thesis "No matter how I spend my spare time, my first choice is to spend it with my friends." His three points of support are as follows: (1) I feel accepted as part of a group; (2) I share skills and information; (3) I have fun. Since each of these benefits occurs in varying degrees every time he's with friends, chronological order isn't relevant.

To order the points emphatically, the student must decide which benefit is the most important to him, which next important, and which least important. After some thought, he organized the points as follows: (1) I share skills and information; (2) I have fun; (3) I feel accepted and part of a group. To this student, feeling accepted was the most important benefit of spending time with his friends. Another student may have ordered the points differently. With emphatic order, the specific sequence of points depends on what *you* perceive as the most important point; it may not be the same for two different writers.

6. Decide on specific support for the main points

Once you've determined your major points, you must find sufficient detailed support to back these up in the essay. Finding support involves choosing specific examples, illustrations, details, or explanations to substantiate your ideas. These may come from research on the topic or, if you are responding directly to the content of a reading selection, from passages or quotes you cull directly from the original article or story. Every major point you make should be supported with something specific, whether from the text to which you are responding, from research, or from your own knowledge.

Writing: Composing a Working Draft

With a plan in place, the next stage is to compose a full draft of the essay. If you write simply to get your ideas down on paper (or on-screen), this goal is actually less formidable than it may sound. At this stage, don't worry too much about spelling, punctuation, or whether you've found the perfect word—you can attend to these issues later. Aim simply to create something concrete that you can craft into a successful essay. If you don't assume that your first draft is the only draft, you'll alleviate some of the pressure to perfect the entire essay at this stage.

Keep the following points in mind as you work through the first draft.

1. Keep the writing and revising functions separate

Studies have shown that we use different parts of our brains for creative thought (such as when we generate new ideas or imagine new concepts) as compared with analytical thought (such as when we examine our writing to search for grammar errors or to improve the structure). Many students, however, attempt to do both simultaneously: they generate ideas as they write, at the same time trying to correct and refine the expression of these. As a result, they succeed in shortchanging *both* parts. It's better for you—and for your essay—if you approach the task in two stages. Get the content down first, without agonizing over grammar, spelling, or sentence structure. Then, work with the draft to polish and improve both the technical aspects and the writing style. It may help to approach the revision stage as you would an in-class grammar exercise, in which you correct the work sentence by sentence.

2. Write to get the ideas on paper, not to create a "perfect" draft

As you write, keep in mind your main points and ideas and how they relate to the thesis. If you've established a strong thesis and good supporting details, the bulk of the essay's content is already on paper; your task at this point is to transform those ideas into sentences and paragraphs. At this stage, you likely won't come up with many new ideas, so simply expand the ideas you've already organized.

Keep in mind that even professional writers often work when they're not in the mood, and their first drafts, too, are far from perfect. Don't judge yourself too harshly at this stage. Since everyone needs to start somewhere, once you write a

TIP

Tackle the middle first

If you're having trouble starting your draft, you may find it easier to compose the body of the essay (the middle paragraphs that cover points and supports for the thesis) first, and save the introduction and conclusion for later. This way, you'll have a better idea of how the argument takes shape, as well as how the tone and purpose are conveyed, and you can tailor your introduction and conclusion to fit the body. Since your thesis and points already direct the content of the essay, you won't *need* the introduction to get started.

TIP

draft (even if the use of language falls short of your expectations), you've got a good beginning. Remember, it's easier to improve an existing essay than to write something excellent from scratch.

3. Make use of any shortcuts or abbreviations that will help you move smoothly through your draft

If you regularly use abbreviations or symbols while taking notes, continue to employ these while writing your draft. For instance, if you assign a number to each quoted passage while taking notes, you can insert the numbers, rather than copy the entire passage, in the appropriate places in your draft (obviously, you'll need to copy out the entire quote for a final draft).

4. Take a break

If at all possible, try to put your draft aside for a period of time—ideally, a day or more—before you launch into post-writing. A break allows your mind to rest and recharge, allows your ideas to crystallize, and often allows you to recognize errors or gaps in logic that you wouldn't otherwise notice.

Post-Writing: Revising, Editing, and Proofreading

At this point, you're almost there—you've written a first draft that expresses your viewpoint about your topic and supports the thesis with several points. Your attention to detail in this stage, post-writing, can make the difference between a mediocre essay and an exceptional one. In general, *revising* refers to those changes that improve the overall content or expression of ideas, while *editing* refers to changes that correct errors in mechanics; that is, failure to adhere to the rules of English. A third function, *proofreading,* refers to those changes that correct formatting or typographical errors in the essay.

As the word "revise" (which literally means "to see again") suggests, now is your opportunity to examine the essay with fresh eyes. You shouldn't expect to alter any of the fundamentals at this point, but careful revision may uncover gaps, flaws in logic, omissions, or unnecessary details that should be corrected. Infrequently, the entire argument may be found wanting, and you may decide to begin anew (with a brand new thesis), though such drastic alterations are rare if you have carefully followed the processes of pre-writing and writing.

You'll do two types of revision when writing essays. The first examines the *structure and contents* of the essay (the thesis, outline, supporting points, details, paragraphs); the second involves *style* (the expression of ideas, the diction, and so on). During revision, you review the entire essay analytically: you reexamine your basic premises and ensure, first, that you still believe in them and, second, that you express them in the best way possible.

The steps involved in post-writing are described below.

1. Review the underpinnings of your argument

While it would be highly unusual for you to lose faith in your thesis at this late point, it does occasionally happen. Perhaps you need to reword the thesis to bring it in line with what your points actually say. Perhaps a small change to the thesis will transform your argument from a competent to an exceptional one. Whatever the case, if you find that your thesis just doesn't "cut it" at this point, you must either repair or replace it.

2. Check the outline, major points, and supporting details

Do you still feel that your major points are the best ones to prove the thesis? Sometimes, the act of writing a draft uncovers further proof or evidence that can be incorporated into the outline. Don't be afraid to add, delete, or rearrange points at this stage, if necessary. If you use a word processor to compose the essay, rearranging paragraphs is easy with the cut and paste functions.

3. Ensure that you're satisfied with individual paragraphs' structure, length, and support

Does each paragraph have a topic sentence? Is the logic within the paragraph clear? Do you provide enough support, and is the support explained clearly? Do you use sufficient **transitions** to link ideas? Are quotes integrated correctly and smoothly into the text? (For more about integrating quotes, see Appendix 2.) Each of these points will contribute to the overall effectiveness of the contents.

4. Include a title

Every essay should be given a title. A good title, as you saw in Chapter 1, both informs the reader about the contents of the essay and enhances the reader's enjoyment and appreciation of the essay. Don't short-change your essay by omitting this important detail. (If you find yourself at a complete loss, you can always state the major topic or article about which you are writing as a title.)

5. Revise for style

At this point, try to imagine yourself in the position of your readers. Would the argument make sense to them? Does it appeal to the knowledge or perspective of the readers? Does it use language that is both clear and in harmony with your purpose?

Style encompasses word choice (**diction**), sentence variety, and wording in general. Just as personal style is reflected through choice of attire or home décor, writing style reflects the uniqueness of each writer and reveals the writer's personality.

Style is the quality that can distinguish exceptional essays from merely competent ones. Though the latter may be structured effectively and include supporting details, well-integrated quotes, and proper mechanics, if the style is dull or pedestrian, then the essay will not generate excitement or hold the readers' interest. Style is the difference between a plain turtleneck sweater and a handknit, designer one—both keep you warm, but one does it with added visual flair and textural appeal. The same principle is true of essays; the absence of gross error does not automatically result in the presence of genius. Style—once the fundamentals are taken care of—becomes a pivotal factor in the quality of the essay.

Don't despair if you think you haven't achieved a distinct **personal style** or **voice** in your writing. For many authors, it takes years to develop and perfect a distinct style. However, you can easily improve the style of the essay by reviewing your own attitude and feelings toward the topic, ensuring that your language

TIP

Stylistic Revisions

Each of the following tips will help you develop clear and concise writing, thereby contributing to an effective style. (For more details on style, refer to a good writing handbook, such as Finnbogason and Valleau's *A Canadian Writer's Guide,* 2nd edition.)

Tips on Word Choices

- Weed out any deadwood, or wordiness (words that simply fill space without contributing meaning).

- Choose words that reflect the tone and purpose of your essay. Check connotations of words; ensure that any use of figurative language conveys the tone you desire.

- Ensure that your words mean precisely what you intend them to mean; if you have any doubt about the meaning of a word, double-check it in the dictionary.

- Check your level of formality. Keeping your audience in mind, revise your word choices to reflect the level of formality and detail that's appropriate.

- Keep the writing crisp, active, and direct. Work to eliminate any passive structures that might weaken the impact of the writing, replacing them with active verbs and concrete terms.

Tips on Sentence Structure

- Check sentences to ensure that you don't repeat a particular structure too frequently (mix both compound and complex sentences).

- Vary the length of sentences (alternate between long and short).

Adhere to the conventions of style

To simplify your stylistic revision, become familiar with the following common conventions for essay writing:

- *Present-tense verbs.* When writing about a text (whether fiction or nonfiction), use the present tense throughout. In other words, write "Wayne Grady *describes* the polygraph machine in great detail," *not* "Wayne Grady *described* the polygraph machine in great detail."

- *References to the author.* The first time you mention an author's name, use both first and last names, without any title (that is, "Candace Savage" rather than "Ms. Savage"). Thereafter, use only the last name, also without any title (that is, "Savage," not "Ms. Savage" or "Candace"). After all, do total strangers greet you by your first name?

reflects your audience and purpose, and practising good writing. There's no reason why you couldn't create a strong and effective paper that reflects, at least to some extent, your own personality.

6. Edit to correct mechanics

Once you've completed revising for structure, contents, and style, tackle the particulars of mechanics (sentence structure, grammar, punctuation, spelling, and so on). You can find more help with these issues in any good grammar handbook.

Examine the following mechanical issues:

- *Quote integration.* Is each quote integrated smoothly and correctly into the text? (For more about quote integration, see Appendix 2.)

- *Sentence structure.* Is your writing free of fragments, run-on sentences, and awkward sentences?

- *Grammar.* Check your verbs, pronoun–antecedent agreement, tenses, and so on. Don't rely on grammar-check programs to highlight all errors.

- *Spelling.* If you don't have a spell-check program, pull out your dictionary and check spelling.

7. Proofread the essay carefully

When you proofread, you check the overall format of the paper. Format includes the title page, spacing, page numbering, and any other details that contribute to the visual correctness (including typographical accuracy) of the essay. Certain aspects of format are quite flexible, so be sure to check with your instructor for individual preferences.

SNAG

Expecting a spell checker to do it all

Don't make the same mistake many people do and assume that your paper is free of spelling errors just because you've run a spell check. You still need to proofread the paper carefully, with your own eyes, to catch errors that the spell checker misses. For instance, a quick typist will often transpose or replace letters in a word, writing "form" instead of "from" or "food" instead of "good." While these words will not be flagged as incorrect by a spell checker, they are, in fact, still wrong for the sentence in which they appear. Check carefully to ensure that all the words in your paper are those you *intended* to be there!

TIP

Revising under pressure

If you revise in an in-class situation or during an exam, you don't always have the time you'd like to review carefully and certainly can't set the essay aside for a day or two before revising. In this case, to use your time most efficiently, run through the types of revision in succession, moving from the most fundamental aspects of the essay (such as thesis and points of support) toward the more superficial points (such as format). This way, even if you run out of time, you'll be sure to cover the most important areas first. Here is a useful sequence to follow:

- *The foundation of the essay:* thesis, outline and order of points, and supporting details
- *Correctness of the language:* grammar, punctuation, sentence structure, spelling
- *Style of the language:* figures of speech, word choices, tone, wordiness, sentence combining for effect
- *Correctness of the format:* page numbering, spacing, title format, title page, pages in correct order, and so on

SAMPLE ESSAY QUESTIONS AND RESPONSES

In the following section, we'll present a sample of each of the three types of essay discussed earlier in the chapter and demonstrate how one student went about planning, writing, and revising it. For each question, assume that the first two pre-writing steps were dictated by the assignment itself: the general topic is indicated in the essay question, and the instructor has assigned the purpose (to persuade) and the audience (a group of the student's peers).

The first two questions (based on nonfiction) relate to Charles Gordon's "The Canadian Way" (see Chapter 1). The third question (based on fiction) relates to Kate Chopin's "The Story of an Hour" (see Chapter 12).

Sample Essay Based on Personal Experience

The student essay that follows is based on Question 1 from the sample reading in Chapter 1, "The Canadian Way," by Charles Gordon. As you read through the student's process of pre-writing, writing, and post-writing, think about what your own essay in response to this question might look like:

> *Essay question:* What is your view of the kinds of shopping that Gordon criticizes in "big-box stores"? Discuss your own approach to this aspect of Canadian culture.

Pre-writing

This writer chose to use freewriting as his brainstorming method. He used as his topic "shopping in big-box stores."

STUDENT'S PRE-WRITING

I like the fact that there's everything in one place when you shop at these big-box stores. I don't have to travel from store to store just to find an unusual CD that may not be stocked in a smaller place. And it's quick, there's variety, I can get it all! On one trip, I found both the Lenny Kravitz CDs I wanted, even though one was almost 10 years old. And they're all pretty modern and roomy, you can stroll around and take your time, which is a great way to shop. I like to be able to relax while I shop, not have the pressure of sales people all over me, like when they try to get into the dressing room with you! But what's good is that you can get help if you want it. One time I wanted to buy new software for my computer, and when I went to the Future Shop, the salesman was really knowledgeable and he was able to show me the differences between Adobe Illustrator and Corel Draw, and which was cheaper, and could still do all the things I wanted it to. It can also be so much faster going to one of those big stores. But it's true that in some ways, it's less personal. My mom shops at the same clothing store that she's gone to for decades, and the owner says, "Hey, Shari," when she walks in, and gives her special attention whenever she sets foot in there. And once, he let her take something home without paying, because he said he trusted that she'd come back the next day with her credit card! Well, at the big-box stores, I doubt that would happen, but you can still get some good perks, like lessons on how to regrout the shower at Home Depot, or a no-questions-asked return policy, and it's never a hassle if something goes wrong. And everybody knows what they're getting there; it's sort of like a TV show that everybody watches. Everybody I know goes to these stores. It's like a group activity sometimes, when me and the guys go pick up tools and have a coffee and Timbits. And boy, they are certainly doing good business. Even if you drop into one of these places at 2:30 on Saturday morning, they're always packed!

Writing and refining the thesis

After looking through his notes, the student attempted to narrow down his ideas to hit on something specific about this pastime. He realized that most of his comments were positive and that he appreciated the phenomenon of big-box stores. His tentative thesis was "Shopping at big-box stores is a very popular pursuit in our society."

On further reflection, however, he decided that this idea was too commonplace since most people already agree with this notion. (Obviously, these places are popular, or they wouldn't be so successful!) Ultimately, he modified the thesis so that it expressed a more interesting viewpoint and one with which some people might disagree: "There are many benefits to shopping at big-box stores." As a *tentative* thesis, this sentence meets all the necessary criteria; it can always be further refined later.

Choosing and ordering points of support

Next, the student reviewed his freewriting to find general points in support of the thesis and thought about any additional reasons why this type of shopping was a positive experience. He chose as his points the following: it's economical; there's a huge variety of items to choose from; there's lots of customer service; and there are added features in each store. The points, reworked in parallel form and ordered emphatically, made up the following outline:

Thesis: Shopping in big-box stores is actually a positive experience.

1. Big-box stores offer good customer service.
2. These stores have a huge variety of items for sale.
3. These stores offer added features.
4. These stores are the most economical.

Finally, before writing a first draft, the student jotted down some specific examples to illustrate and support each of the main points. Some of these were drawn from the initial freewriting; others were added as he wrote.

Writing

Below is the first draft of the student's essay. Notice that the student is not too concerned about grammar, spelling, or style at this point; these issues will be treated more carefully during post-writing (revising and editing).

STUDENT'S ESSAY DRAFT

Enjoyable Shopping at Big-Box Stores

Many people may find that shopping at "big-box" stores such as Home Depot or Wal-Mart is a negative experience, but I like to shop at these kinds of stores. I spent a lot of time recently in these places, and I found out that they offer much more than just the products. Shopping at big-box stores can actually be an enjoyable experience.

A big advantage of big-box stores are the customer service. There is always somebody there to answer a question or help you with your purchase. At Wal-Mart, you are even greeted at the door by a "greeter" who makes sure that you have a kart and know where you are going. If you want to return something, there is never any problem.

The variety at big-box stores is much greater than at smaller stores. They have a large selection of items in any one category.

For instance at Chapters, you can find rows and rows of self-help books, romance novels, cookbooks, or whatever you might be looking for. If there's a specific title you're searching for, you are more likely to find it in a big store that can order books in large quanties. You can also find a greater selection in general at big-box stores. They have more room to keep all the products, so they can keep them in stock. You don't have to worry that the one item you're looking for was just sold to someone else.

I really like the added features. Most of these places have Web sites, and you can even order online. You also can usually sit around or take your time; nobody is going to kick you out. In the bookstores, there is always comfy chairs and quite areas where you can sit and read the books, and usually there's also a coffee shop. At some of the other places, like Home Depot, there's sometimes a restaurant on site where you can stop. At IKEA, you can shop around most of the morning, then stop to have lunch at their cafeteria, which has really good food. Their meatballs are excellent. Then you can go on your way. They don't care how long you take or how much you browse.

The best part are the prices. They are usually cheaper than other stores, no matter what you are buying. When I went to Wal-Mart for my running shoes, I was able to get the same pair for $20 less than in a smaller shoe store. Sure, the smaller stores have sales once in a while, but what if you can't wait? At the big-box stores, you know what you are going to get, and they advertise so that you know the prices in advance.

I think big-box stores are here to stay. It's true that some of the smaller stores are having difficulty keeping up. But with everything getting bigger and more technological, the big-box stores are the wave of the future.

Before you read the critical comments that follow, think about your initial responses to the essay. What did the writer do well? What still needs work? What would you remove, change, or add?

Comments

This writer has a solid foundation with a good outline and includes some persuasive points. He also provides some examples to illustrate his ideas. He has a clear grasp of the topic and generally expresses himself comprehensibly. However, a few main areas could be improved.

In general, the essay needs more substantiation (concrete evidence) to back up the assertions. As is so often the case, this student's work lacks examples. For instance, after stating that big-box stores offer more variety than smaller stores, the writer should provide examples of the specific items being sold in the bigger stores. Because the topic is one with which the writer has personal experience, it should be easy for him to select a variety of concrete, vivid details to illustrate his points (it's okay to use examples from his own life, as long as they illustrate general points). These examples will serve to strengthen the argument.

The essay could also use more transitions between ideas. Without these cues to guide them, the readers will lose the logical thread of the argument. In addition, the writer should explain certain points more fully, expanding the explanations already included. Reminding the reader how each point relates to the thesis (explaining how each of these points illustrates a benefit of shopping there) will also add **coherence** and help guide the reader through the argument. In checking the logical connections between ideas, the writer will also notice that his **conclusion** veers off topic and should be revised to reflect the thesis more directly. While his **introduction** does present a clear thesis, it could also be revised to engage the reader's attention more.

Finally, the writer needs to check his grammar and spelling to clear up some common errors (subject–verb agreement, spelling of "a lot" and "quiet," and so on).

Revised essay

After working through the steps of post-writing, here's how the writer revised the original draft. As you can see, some of the changes are fairly substantial (the writer completely changed the conclusion), while others are fairly minor. Because the original thesis and outline were strong, none of the main points have been changed.

See if you agree with the changes. If not, what would you have done differently?

STUDENT'S ESSAY REVISION

<u>Something Good Is in Store</u>

Lately, the concept "bigger is better" seems to surround us everywhere: we've got bigger cars, bigger TV screens and now, "big-box" stores. These incredibly successful emporiums offer an all-in-one shopping experience, situated in huge buildings filled with rows upon rows of merchandise and store clerks all wearing identical brightly coloured uniforms. It's true, many people think these stores are too big, too impersonal, or that they steal sales from the smaller, independent stores. However, there's a good reason why the big-box stores are so successful: they offer shoppers a wide variety of benefits.

While customer service in big-box stores may not be as personal as in smaller stores, it offers other advantages. Because there are so many employees in these large stores, you'll always be able to find someone to help or answer your questions. Wal-Mart even takes its customer service one step further, employing "greeters" who smilingly offer to help you find a department or a cart as you enter the store. In addition, big-box stores deal smoothly with any customer complaints or returned items. You'll never have to argue about a refund for that broken desk lamp or blender at a big-box store. As a result, even returning items is no longer an unpleasant experience in a big-box store.

Another advantage of shopping at all-in-one stores is the unlimited variety of merchandise. Because they operate on a grand scale, these stores can afford to keep a huge inventory in stock at all times. Looking for a handsaw? No problem; Home Depot has fifteen brands. Music stores such as HMV are more likely to stock a full range of musical styles, from gospel to acid jazz or a specific period of rock and pop. Smaller stores simply can't store the same number of items. At big-box stores, it's great to know you won't be stuck after travelling all the way to the store, only to discover they just sold the last bag of charcoal or box of light bulbs to someone else.

In addition, the added features at these stores can enhance the shopping experience. Most of the big-box stores have their own Web sites that let you order on-line. As a result, you can check the Internet to see if they carry the product you want and what it will cost. If you prefer to browse in-store, they are happy to let you wander through the aisles at your leisure. Bookstores such as Chapters even offer comfy chairs and quiet areas to sit and read, encouraging you to take your time. You may almost forget you're in a store as you sink into a soft, cushy chair by the fireplace, reading a favourite book with the aroma of freshly brewed Starbucks coffee wafting through the air. In places like IKEA, the on-site restaurant lets you take a break from shopping without having to leave the store. You can stop for lunch and a beverage before continuing to look for beds, sofas, or wall units.

Of all the benefits of big-box stores, the best part is the prices. It's usually more economical to shop in big-box stores than in other stores. When I shopped at Wal-Mart for running shoes, I was able to get the same pair for $20 less than in a smaller shoe store. The big-box stores guarantee low prices all year round, not just during sales, and many offer to match any lower advertised prices. Since we all like to find a bargain, these lower prices are very appealing.

Once you've experienced the many benefits of big-box stores, you'll realize how enjoyable it can be to shop there. For service, variety, added features, and economic value, big-box stores are big winners.

Sample Essay Analyzing a Nonfiction Reading

Our second student writer is the one who already undertook the sample reading (Charles Gordon's "The Canadian Way") in Chapter 1. Think about your own reaction to the article and how you'd answer this question as you follow along with the student through the stages of pre-writing, writing, and post-writing:

> *Essay question:* In "The Canadian Way," Gordon suggests that Canadians' behaviour fails to promote or support Canadian culture. What does Gordon imply we can do to save our unique culture? Support your answer with examples from the article.

As you recall, our student had already formulated some clear ideas about Gordon's argument, as well as some of her own ideas about Canadian culture and shopping in particular, by the time she'd finished reading the selection. Next, she attacked the essay question, above.

Pre-writing

This student chose to use the cluster technique, with the topic "Canadian culture in 'The Canadian Way' " at the centre of the cluster. See Figure 2.2.

Writing and refining the thesis

As she looked over her list of points, the student realized that Gordon's indictment of Canadian culture centred on a few key ideas—the prevalence of "bland" American culture in Canada, the lack of financial support for "true" Canadian

FIGURE 2.2 Cluster Technique for "The Canadian Way"

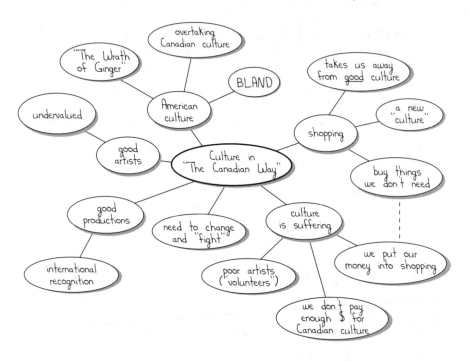

culture, the idea that we don't patronize Canadian cultural events enough, and the prominence of "shopping" as a substitute for genuine culture. With this in mind, she was able to construct the following working thesis statement: "In 'The Canadian Way,' Gordon suggests that there are several actions we can take to help save Canadian culture."

Choosing and ordering points of support

Armed with a working thesis, the student next reviewed her ideas and realized that she could reword them to represent actions Canadians can take to support our culture. She combined several of the ideas to come up with the following parallel points, placed in emphatic order in an outline:

> *Thesis:* In "The Canadian Way," Charles Gordon suggests that there are several actions we can take to help save Canadian culture.
>
> 1. Stop American cultural influence.
> 2. Put more time and energy into Canadian cultural activities.
> 3. Spend our money on Canadian culture.

For each of the points above, the student then added specific examples or details to her outline. Some of these she culled from her brainstorming notes; she also chose illustrative passages and quotes from Gordon's article.

Writing

Following is the student's first draft of her essay on "The Canadian Way." As you read through this early draft, consider which parts of the essay work well and which require further refinement.

STUDENT'S ESSAY DRAFT

Saving Our Culture

The idea that Canadian culture is in trouble is a valid one. If we think about it, most of us will feel ashamed about how little we support our Canadian culture. We can't just let our native culture die without a struggle.

Charles suggests that one problem with Canadian culture is that it's no longer really "Canadian," but has been influenced by the U.S. He uses sarcasm to suggest that many of us experience American culture all the time, at the expense of our own artists and writers. We'd rather "throw open the doors to the Americans" who give us garbage like Gilligan's Island VI: The Wrath of Ginger than watch our own TV shows and movies. American culture lowers the standards of all culture and keeps us from supporting Canadian cultural activities. But he tells us, "those who respect what Canadian artists and performers do" are not willing to "give up the fight."

Another major problem is that we are spending too much time doing other things, such as shopping. In fact, Charles even implies that the new culture we have created centres on shopping, especially for things we don't need. Instead of spending money on unnecessary items such as exotic birds, snakes and lizards or something that everyone else is getting, we should be supporting true Canadian culture. It's stupid to miss out on some high quality activities by ignoring our own products in our own back yard. We need to show appreciation for these people by recognizing their talent. By putting our time and energy into these admirable pursuits, we'll enjoy ourselves and also support our culture.

The most important thing we can do, though, is to "support the stuff, vote with our feet and our wallets." He says, "We have to support the stuff, vote with our feet and our wallets, buy the books, attend the theatres and the galleries, and yes, the ball parks and arenas." Without more money, Canadian culture will wilt and die, and we will be at fault. Many of the cultural performers don't get paid at all, and others are poor, and it's not fair to them for us to spend money on frivolous things. If we want them to be able to survive, we need to support them financially as well as emotionally.

Maybe we don't support our own culture as much as we should, but the culture is far from dead yet. As Charles says, the quality and output of Canadian artists is really improving, and Canadians are starting to gain recognition around the world. I think they'll make it on their own—but a little extra help from the audience wouldn't hurt.

Before you read the comments that follow, consider your own reactions to the essay: What works well in this essay? What are its weaknesses? What would you remove, change, or add?

Comments

In this case, the original thesis, while valid and well supported by the three main points, is never stated clearly in the introduction. As a result, it becomes difficult for the reader to follow along through the **body** of the paper without a single clear controlling idea (thesis) to direct the content. To clarify, the writer should begin by indicating the work to which she's responding (naming both author and title) and stating her interpretation of Gordon's message. The writer can also achieve more coherence by referring back to the thesis at various times throughout the body of the essay.

This writer should also pay attention to the logical progression of ideas in her paper. While she may know exactly why she chose the particular quotes she includes, she must make the reason clear to the reader, as well, by adding her own comments about these passages. It's quite possible that readers may interpret the quotes differently; by elaborating on the quotes, she renders the argument both clearer and more convincing. In addition, she must indicate each phrase that is quoted with quotation marks.

Finally, the writer must reexamine the tone in the essay. If she doesn't want to alienate readers, she needs to avoid making assumptions (Americans give us "garbage"; "Canadians are willing and able"), referring to her audience as "stupid," or telling the audience it's their "fault" that Canadian culture is struggling to survive.

Revised essay

Here is the writer's revised draft once she finished working through the steps of post-writing. In particular, the writer decided to redraft completely the introduction, including the thesis, and conclusion, making them more interesting to read. You'll also see that while the main points remain the same, the specific wording in places has been altered, and whole phrases at times have been removed, changed, or transferred to a more appropriate location.

See if you agree with the changes. If not, what would you have done differently?

STUDENT'S ESSAY REVISION

Canadian Culture: We Must Save It Ourselves

An internationally known stereotype of Canadians is that we're pleasant, polite and passive. Canadians tend to live and let live. But could this attitude be the cause of a cultural crisis in Canada? According to Charles Gordon in his article "The Canadian Way," Canadians themselves are the main reason that Canadian culture is in danger of extinction. Gordon uses his article to try to persuade the readers that we must take action to help preserve and promote Canadian culture. In his essay, he implies three actions we can take to save our culture.

One major problem with our culture, according to Gordon, is that it's no longer entirely "Canadian." He suggests that American influence in Canada is so pervasive that it has taken over, at the expense of our own artists and writers. Gordon's disapproval of U.S. culture is made clear through his sarcastic suggestion that some of us would rather "relax and enjoy Gilligan's Island VI: The Wrath of Ginger" than watch our own Canadian-made TV shows and movies. It's this "tidal wave of American blandness" that prevents us from enjoying Canadian cultural activities, he says. To counteract the wave of American culture, he suggests a remedy: we must "respect what Canadian artists and performers do," and not "give up the fight." In other words, Gordon believes we must reject the lower quality American culture and pay more attention to our own.

Another way we can support Canadian culture is to spend less time on pseudo-cultural pursuits, such as shopping. In fact, Gordon even suggests that "our true culture is shopping and everything else takes a back seat." Canadians don't spend enough time at the opera or ball game because "there is no time to do anything, and even if there was, we are tired." Yet Gordon suggests that being tired is just an excuse, since we manage well enough to do the things we find appealing (such as shopping). A better way to spend our time, he suggests, is on high quality activities created by Canadian "musicians, writers, actors, composers, and painters." The superior quality of Canadians' work is now gaining international recognition, but we must also recognize this quality here at home. We can help to support our own culture by showing appreciation for these artists and acknowledging their talent.

The most useful way Gordon thinks we can support Canadian culture, however, is to "vote with our feet and our wallets." Gordon advocates channelling more of our spending money into Canadian cultural products and activities. He advises us to "buy the books, attend the theatres and the galleries, and yes, the ball parks and arenas." Since many Canadian artists live at a subsistence level, they may not be able to continue producing without a better income. If we want them to survive, we need to support them with our dollars and cents as well as with our approval and appreciation. Instead of spending money on vanity items such as "exotic birds," "snakes and lizards" or "something you've never heard of but [something] everybody is getting," Gordon says we should be spending it on our own artists and performers.

The message of "The Canadian Way" is clear in its warning. If we don't learn to appreciate our own culture and support it economically, our culture will not survive. Despite its accusations and negative tone, Gordon's essay does imply that there is still hope if we start now to support Canadian culture. By developing and promoting our own culture from within our country, we'll save it from extinction—and we'll also be fostering a better image of Canadians around the world.

Writing Essays about Fiction

While the basic structure and major components of an essay are the same whether you're writing about nonfiction or fiction, there are some differences between the two kinds of readings that you should keep in mind as you structure your essay. (You'll find a reference chart in Appendix 1 highlighting the differences between a short story and a piece of nonfiction.)

Reading Fiction Critically

Students sometimes find it difficult to understand how critical reading applies to interpreting fiction. After all, what constitutes "facts" in short stories, if they are, by definition, nonfactual works of the imagination? Statistics, examples, and expert testimony are all very clear in nonfiction essays: what people say or do, actual events that took place, statistical data—these things are irrefutable. While the characters and events in short fiction are, indeed, fictional, you can think of them in a similar way: events described are inalterable on the page, as is what the characters say and do. These details constitute the "facts" of the story. Contrary to popular misconception, good responses to short fiction are not subjective (not simply based on gut feelings or emotional reactions). As with nonfiction, logical inferences must govern your interpretations of fiction. While it's true that good fiction provides us with a multitude of possible interpretations, to be valid each of these must still be supported by the content of the story. In other words, the events, dialogue, imagery, narrative, and other details within a story will serve as your supporting materials.

Here's a quick example of how important it is to base your interpretations of fiction on logical evidence. After reading Kate Chopin's "The Story of an Hour" (p. 411), how would you answer the question "Did Mrs. Mallard love her husband?" For most students, the immediate reaction to this question, based on an initial impression of the story, is a resounding *"No!"* Otherwise, they reason, how could she have rejoiced at his death? How could she be so disappointed at his return? In fact, the story itself provides the answer. To begin, reread paragraph 15. Notice the sentence "And yet she had loved him—sometimes." Clearly, even if she were not entirely happy with her spouse, she did in some way love him. Why do we assume otherwise? For many readers, their own emotional reaction to her behaviour influences their response; they assume any woman reacting with joy after the news of her husband's death couldn't possibly love him.

SNAG

When you're assigned an essay about a short story, the instructor is most likely looking for *your own* ideas about the story, rather than what a professional critic has written for a literary journal or magazine. While it can be helpful to do some research on what others have had to say about a particular story (especially if there is some historical context or useful information about the author), it's always best to come up with your own reactions *first,* and then use any research to back up or support what you say. What *you* have to say is most important.

Sample Essay Analyzing a Short Story (Fiction)

The student essay that follows is based on Kate Chopin's story "The Story of an Hour." Before you examine the essay, read the story (p. 411). Use the standard pre-reading, reading, and post-reading activities from Chapter 1, and start to formulate your own reaction to the story.

> *Essay question:* Discuss the theme of "freedom" in Kate Chopin's "The Story of an Hour."

Pre-writing

This student felt most comfortable using the journalist's method (asking questions). Her brainstorming notes on the topic "freedom in 'The Story of an Hour'" appear below.

STUDENT'S NOTES

Freedom:

WHAT does it say about freedom?

—freedom is fleeting—only an hour long

—freedom is difficult—she would have had a hard life if she'd been free, since life without her husband would be hard for a woman in the Victorian period

—freedom is a bit of an escape from her hard life—she was saying, "free! free! free!" because she felt that her husband's death was somehow letting her have her own life again

WHAT does freedom mean to her?
  —it means being her own person, having her own life to live forever more (can't do this with her husband alive)
  —it means she will be able to live alone and decide her own fate

WHAT did lack of freedom mean?
  —she hated living under her husband's thumb, even though he wasn't a bad man

WHAT does his return mean?
  —she loses her freedom

WHY is she happy to be free?
  —she didn't hate her husband, but she did hate her life with him; she hated her lack of freedom

  —lack of freedom was sort of like a prison to her

  —she felt that he kept her imprisoned (what right does another human have . . . etc.)

WHEN did she gain freedom?
  —the moment he died

WHEN did she lose freedom?
  —the moment she got married; because her whole life was controlled by him (but also when he returned, she was sent back to a state without freedom)

HOW does she deal with gaining freedom?
  —she's different from other women of the time; she likes it and doesn't feel threatened by it

HOW does she deal with losing her freedom again?

—she ends up dying—maybe because she can't stand having to lose the freedom

—she says before, when she thinks she'll be free for the rest of her life, "just yesterday she thought with a shudder that life might be long"—so she doesn't want to have to live with him without her freedom

—freedom means doing what you want, not having anyone tell you what to do

—she really had no freedom before he died

Writing and refining the thesis

At this point, the student had enough material to generate the tentative thesis "Mrs. Mallard would rather be dead than lose her freedom." With a little more thought, the student decided this thesis would be too difficult to prove and refined it, writing, "In 'The Story of an Hour,' by Kate Chopin, Mrs. Mallard can gain freedom only through death."

Choosing and ordering points of support in an outline

Her working thesis allows the student to discuss three time periods in the character's life: before her husband dies, after he supposedly dies, and after he returns. These three supporting points are arranged chronologically and in parallel form here in an outline:

> *Thesis:* In "The Story of an Hour," by Kate Chopin, Mrs. Mallard can gain freedom only through death.
>
> 1. Before Mr. Mallard's "death"
> 2. After Mr. Mallard's "death"
> 3. After Mr. Mallard's surprise return to life

For each point, the student examined both her notes and the story itself for supporting details to substantiate her ideas. She used both direct quotes and paraphrasing.

Writing

Below is the draft essay. As you read though it, see if you'd explain any points differently.

STUDENT'S ESSAY DRAFT

An Hour to Be Free

Mrs. Mallard is a woman who has no freedom. Her life is very controlled by her husband and by the society in which she lives. In Kate Chopin's "The Story of an Hour," the only way Mrs. Mallard can achieve freedom from her marriage is through death.

First of all, it's clear that Mrs. Mallard has no freedom, as long as her husband is alive. He controls her every move. She is dissatisfied with her marriage and unhappy with her husband. She wishes she could escape from the marriage.

Secondly, Mrs. Mallard finally gets a taste of freedom when her husband dies. She feels as if she's coming alive for the first time. She says, "free! free! free!" as she savours this newfound freedom. She imagines her new life far into the future, overcome with happiness at her new independence. She wishes she could live a long time.

Third, once Brently returns, Mrs. Mallard suddenly loses her newfound freedom. The thought of returning to her previous life with him has become unimaginable. Now, the only way to hold onto her freedom is by dying herself. Death seems preferable to a life without freedom. Once her husband comes back, she is unable to cope. She may not realize it, bur her escape from the marriage occurs at the moment of her own death. She can not have freedom within her marriage, so death is an escape.

Although she experienced a sense of freedom for only an hour, it was enough to convince Mrs. Mallard that she could no longer stay in a marriage without freedom. Death allows her to escape a life that has no happiness for her.

Comments

While the writer has developed a good thesis and supporting points, the essay is sorely lacking in details. In fact, it reads more like an extended outline than an essay. How can the writer substantiate what she says?

To begin with, the student needs to add detailed support. In other words, she must provide more examples and quotes from the story. Although many of the inferences in the essay are logical, they are not supported with specific evidence (quotes) from the story. Using quotes is particularly important when dealing with fiction, where interpretations can vary wildly; strong support will help to convince your audience of the validity of your viewpoint. Although the basic ideas in the essay need not change, the writer must add to them.

In addition, the writer should examine the essay's style. While transitions are a good idea, the specific transitions used could be more effective. Since she's not listing steps in a process, the writer should select transitions that illuminate the logical connection between paragraphs better than "first," "second," and "third." In examining her style, the writer should also attempt to find alternatives for the word "freedom," overused in this draft.

While the grammar and sentence structure here look fine, the main flaw of the essay is its superficial treatment of the topic. With a bit more thought and some carefully chosen quotes, the writer can produce a top-notch argument.

Revised essay

Here's how the student revised her draft after working through the steps of post-writing. For each of her major points, the writer ensured that she included a quote from or reference to the story to back up what she said; she also added further explanation and elaboration of her points. How would you evaluate this new essay? What, if anything, would you have done differently?

STUDENT'S ESSAY REVISION

A Fatal Freedom

Why does the main character, Louise Mallard, die at the end of Kate Chopin's story, "The Story of an Hour"? According to her doctors, Mrs. Mallard's weak heart fails her when she is over-joyed to see her husband alive again after he was presumed dead. In reality, she is reacting to the loss of freedom that his "death" brought to her. Throughout the story, the only way for Mrs. Mallard to achieve freedom from her marriage is through death, whether her husband's or her own.

Even before she learns the news of Brently's "death," it's clear that Mrs. Mallard can have no freedom as long as he's alive. As a woman living in the Victorian period, Mrs. Mallard is not permitted the kinds of freedom she would enjoy today. Her life is controlled and directed by her husband. The fact that he is "kind" and "tender" with her, or that he "never looked save with love upon her," doesn't change the fact that she is not in control of her own life. When Mrs. Mallard thinks about her marriage, she remembers that Brently had lived "for her" and that "[a] kind intention or a cruel intention made the act seem no less a crime." In other words, she feels that such restrictions on her life are unacceptable, even criminal. As long as they are both living, Mrs. Mallard cannot gain her freedom.

Once Brently is pronounced dead, Mrs. Mallard very quickly begins to taste her newfound freedom and her own transformation begins. Her husband's death prompts her rebirth. It is as if she starts a new life. Overjoyed, she cries, "free! free! free!" over and over. Suddenly, she's able to envision the future, thinking about "the long procession of years to come that would belong to her absolutely. And she spread her arms out to them in welcome." After all her years being subservient to someone else, her sudden independence liberates her. Even a moment of guilt is quickly brushed aside when she thinks, "What could love . . . count for in the face of this possession of self-assertion which she suddenly recognized as the strongest impulse of her being!" Brently's death has released the new, unfettered Mrs. Mallard.

Her joyful independence is quickly shattered, however, once her husband returns to the house, alive and well. After the transformation she has undergone, Mrs. Mallard is permanently changed and cannot return to her previous lifestyle. Just moments before Brently walked into the house, Mrs. Mallard "breathed a quick prayer that life might be long." Once he returns, however, she knows that life will revert to its previous routine, when she "had thought with a shudder that life might be long." She doesn't want a "long life" under her husband's domination. The shock of this realization is too much for Mrs. Mallard, and her weak heart gives out. By dying at this point, Mrs. Mallard escapes her marriage and dies a free woman.

At the end of the story, Mrs. Mallard's death serves to preserve her newfound freedom. Although she might not have consciously chosen to die, her death still releases Mrs. Mallard from living a miserable life she can no longer control.

As you can see, working through the process of pre-writing, writing, and post-writing will help you build on your ideas and ultimately improve the quality of your own writing. In each of the sample essays above, the writers' revisions resulted in stronger and more thoughtful essays that accomplished their purpose more effectively.

As you read through the remainder of this text and practise writing a variety of essays, you'll probably elect to combine two or more rhetorical modes in your own writing, as do most of the writers whose work provides the sample essays here. In the following chapters of this text, essays are arranged according to the predominant rhetorical mode in which they are written, though as you will see, professional writers rarely operate exclusively within one mode or another. This organization will help you pinpoint specific thinking and writing skills that may later be combined in other contexts. Like any skill set, it's best to learn the individual components one at a time before you combine them in a single operation.

Part 2

Readings

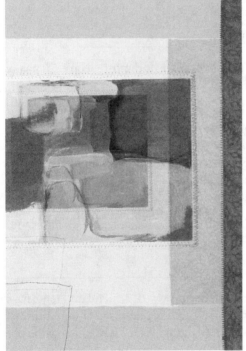

CHAPTER 3

Description

DESCRIPTION IN DAILY LIFE

Using description is a regular occurrence for most people. You already use description whenever you engage in activities such as the following:

- You send an e-mail message to your former roommate, proudly telling her/him what your new car looks like.
- You describe the boyfriend or girlfriend of your dreams to a friend.
- You relate to your sister how crowded the waiting room was as you waited for your annual checkup at the doctor's office last month.
- You write a letter to the dry cleaners describing the stain they left on your new white linen jacket, asking for some compensation.

WHAT IS DESCRIPTION?

Consider the following scenarios: You meet with a friend and tell her what your new boss looks like. You and your brother reminisce about your visit to the Louvre in Paris. You describe to a friend how the latest video game portrays its villains. Whenever you attempt to re-create for someone else the look, feel, or atmosphere of a person, place, or thing in words, you are using **description.** Description offers a picture in words for readers or listeners, allowing them to imagine the particular scene or person as if they had been there, or seen someone, themselves.

DEFINITION

Description: Description re-creates a person, thing, or scene in words so that someone else can imagine the subject.

A major trait of good descriptive writing is that it *shows* something directly to the reader, rather than just *telling* about it (think of the difference between watching a movie firsthand or having someone else tell you what happens). Description uses concrete, specific details rather than abstract terms and personal opinion. For example, the sentence "The dog appeared threatening" only *tells* us how the writer perceived the dog; we don't see it in our mind's eye. A better description is the following: "The pit bull darted in front of us, barking and growling. Its lips curled back over its nose, displaying a full mouth of sharp, shiny teeth." In this second passage, the readers can *see* the dog's movement and almost feel their flesh threatened by the "sharp, shiny teeth." By using specific, vivid language to *show* what the dog is like, the writer lets us draw our own conclusion.

There are two types of description: objective description and subjective description. In its most basic form, description is totally *objective;* that is, it presents information about how something looks, feels, sounds, smells, or tastes, without adding any of the writer's personal impressions or opinions. You'll find **objective description** in some textbooks (a description of the different parts of an atom, for instance), some journalism (the description of a murder weapon, the type and number of dents in a train wreck), and some commercial publications (the description in a cookbook of how to recognize a ripe papaya). The purpose of most objective descriptions is informative—to provide information to the reader without any additional value judgments.

DEFINITION

> **Objective description:** description that impartially re-creates objects, events, or people in words to provide information only

Here's an objective description of the floating islands on Lake Tagua-tagua, from Charles Darwin's journal of 1834. Notice that Darwin doesn't reveal his own feelings about the islands, but merely provides the physical details:

> They are composed of the stalks of various dead plants, intertwined together, and on the surface of which other living ones take root. Their form is generally circular, and their thickness from four to six feet, of which the greater part is immersed in the water. As the wind blows, they pass from one side of the lake to the other, and often carry cattle and horses as passengers.

In **subjective description** (the type you are most likely to read) the writer does intend to conjure a particular mood or create an emotional impact and uses details

Subjective description: description that re-creates a subject in words to establish an emotional tone or dominant impression

Dominant impression: a particular mood or feeling about the item, person, or place being described

and connotation to indicate her or his viewpoint on the subject being described. Subjective descriptions include such writing as a personal memoir describing favourite toys from childhood, an environmentalist's description of forests laid waste to make room for a condominium complex, or a newspaper's description of someone's botched plastic surgery (as a warning to avoid such operations). You'll find subjective descriptions in personal writing and fiction, as well as in many magazine and newspaper stories. In this case, the writer's objective is to establish a particular mood or feeling (called a **dominant impression**) that will elicit an emotional response from the reader.

Following is a subjective description of the wintry farmland from Sinclair Ross's short story "The Painted Door." In this excerpt, a lonely wife stares out a window at the snow-covered farmland outside:

> The sun was risen above the frost mists now, so keen and hard a glitter on the snow that instead of warmth its rays seemed shedding cold. One of the two-year-old colts that had cantered away when John turned the horses out for water stood covered with rime at the stable door again, head down and body hunched, each breath a little plume of steam against the frost air. She [the wife] shivered, but did not turn. In the clear, bitter light the long white miles of prairie landscape seemed a region strangely alien to life.

Notice how the writer conveys the notion that even the sun appears harsh and lifeless; it emits a "glitter" that is "keen and hard"; its light is "bitter"; and it is "alien to life." A different paragraph describing the same scene might establish a dominant impression through which the snow's feathery, white flakes and the morning sun emit an uplifting, bright light evoking happiness. The specific details and choice of words make the difference in each case.

WHY USE DESCRIPTION?

How often do you say things like "Describe it to me," "What did it look like?" "Really? I've never seen one," or "Can you picture it?" while talking to others?

These questions help to illuminate the purpose behind description. Description is useful when you wish to let another person have knowledge of a sensory experience. Description allows another to feel as if s/he has "seen what you see" or "been where you've been." Description, then, helps to create a *sense of shared experience,* even if the experience wasn't actually shared. It also makes something previously unknown understandable. With concrete details to spark sensory associations, description helps someone else identify with your subject. The experience is made tangible through the imagination.

How to Write a Description Essay

As with all essays, the process of writing description should be approached by working through pre-writing, writing, and post-writing stages (discussed in Chapter 2). However, you can strengthen your description essays by considering the additional points below. Keep in mind, however, that in reality most writers do not use exclusively descriptive writing; more often than not, description is a device used to support or reinforce some other purpose, such as making an argument or explaining a process.

Pre-Writing

1. Choose a general topic

You'll most likely be asked to write a subjective description for your professor, one that requires you to convey a particular emotion or dominant impression. Your best bet to ensure a lively, interesting, and effective description is to choose a subject that sparks your own interest, one you know to be multi-faceted or intriguing on more than one level. Tap into your natural tendencies to observe people and things, and see what catches your own imagination.

2. Consider your audience and purpose

Spend some time seriously contemplating your intended audience. Ask yourself who your intended readers are and whether they are familiar with the scene, item, or person you describe. Which details will you need to include so that the audience has a complete picture of your subject? The choice of audience also dictates whether the description is objective or subjective: your description of a serious car accident you witnessed will be quite different if you describe it to your best friend, compared to the (more objective) language you would use to describe it to the police officer writing up the accident report.

Equally important is having a clear idea of your intended purpose and the tone you will set. What is the dominant impression (emotional tone) you wish to

Add interest to everyday subjects

Don't automatically discount a simple or mundane subject as inappropriate for a description essay: with the right approach, almost any subject can be suitable for description. Your father's old oak desk chair, stained and worn to the user's shape with years of dedicated use, can become more than just a chair; viewed as an old friend or confidant, it suddenly holds infinite possibility for interesting details. Similarly, you can describe your nephew's three-day-old face, not yet touched by the thoughts and experiences of this world, in a way that emphasizes his uniqueness and innocence. Almost any subject can be used for description essays if you find a way to envision it imaginatively or in a new light.

express? The country cottage you visited last summer will be treated one way if you imply that its age made it a scary place to visit and quite another way if you think the place exudes warmth and comfort. Remember, the words you choose should reflect the particular tone or mood you wish to establish; this purpose will also determine which details you *don't* include in the essay.

3. Generate ideas about the topic

In addition to the standard methods for generating ideas described in Chapter 2, a particularly useful method for description essays is to focus on the five senses, one at a time: what does your subject look like? sound like? taste like? smell like? feel like? Similarly, if the topic immediately brings to mind any comparisons (for example, "My professor reminds me of Santa Claus"), these can also be useful to create a dominant impression.

4. Narrow to a thesis

Although it may feel as if strong description relies primarily on eliciting an emotional reaction, a good description must also have a clear thesis, even if it's not stated explicitly. Your thesis should let the reader know your subject and reflect the dominant impression in the essay. For instance, the thesis "My aunt's old cottage on Lake Simcoe is one of the spookiest houses I've ever seen" both tells the reader your topic (the cottage) and implies that you'll focus on scary details.

5. Organize your ideas in an outline

Although it's not a hard and fast rule, the most logical method to organize a description essay is spatial: the writer begins in one spot and moves logically to another, then another, in sequence. Unless your supporting points clearly suggest

> **Vantage point:** the point of view from which the writer describes a
> scene; all details and movement must follow logically from this point

a different method of organization (for instance, an essay describing how your
gymnastics teacher's appearance changes throughout the course of her pregnancy), spatial organization is a reliable choice.

Another task when organizing details for a description essay is establishing a
clear **vantage point.** The vantage point—or perspective from which you are
writing—will help to shape the dominant impression. To imagine your vantage
point, decide what position you wish to be in as you observe and describe the
scene or person. In other words, are you standing outside the house, slowly
moving inward? Are you sitting in a chair opposite the doorway, surveying the
room? Or are you in your car at the street corner, observing the action in the
intersection? Whatever the vantage point, it should remain consistent and not
bounce illogically from place to place.

Remember that good description follows a logical order, whether that order is
strictly spatial or not. For instance, to describe the cafeteria in your school, you
might begin at the entrance beside the food cases and move through the line to
the serving trays, beverages, salads, and so on. It would then make sense to finish
with an overall impression of the cafeteria's smells, sounds, or ambience, which
wouldn't necessarily fit into any specific step along the way.

6. Decide on specific support for the main points

To choose your specific details, focus on vivid, concrete, sense-related language.
Sensory details can awaken memories or create associations in the readers' minds:
ask yourself what you see, hear, smell, taste, or feel as you examine your subject.
Of course, the details you select will depend also on how well you know your subject matter and how clearly you can envision it.

TIP

Selecting details

Use brainstorming techniques to write down *all* the sensory details you
can muster about a particular scene or person. You'll then be better
equipped to exclude those that *don't* contribute to the dominant
impression you're attempting to create.

Going to extremes

Often, novice writers take one of two extreme approaches in descriptive writing: either they include too few details, rendering the writing vague and even boring, or they include too much obvious emotion in the description, providing a picture so heavily charged that the reader is ultimately put off. Resist both extremes, and ask yourself if there are any obvious gaps in the picture you create or if you have included too many emotionally charged details.

Writing

To strengthen your descriptive essay as you write, used **figurative language** (language that employs comparison to enhance meaning). Relying on the reader's emotional associations with particular words or images, figurative language is a valuable contribution to subjective description. A **simile** offers a comparison between two things linked by words such as "like," "as," or "similar to." A **metaphor** is a direct comparison that creates an equation between two things being described. Our student writer uses a simile when he writes, in "Disaster Office," "there were coffee stains like brown polka dots all over the shelf." When Emil Sher writes (in "Frozen Moment Serves as Reference Point in a Timeless Land"), "The sun was a faceless clock," he uses metaphor. For figurative language to be effective (as in these examples), it must provide an *original* comparison rather than relying on well-established **clichés,** such as "hungry as a horse" or "wolf in sheep's clothing."

DEFINITION

Figurative language: language that employs comparisons between two things as a means to illuminate the meaning of one. **Similes** use "as" or "like" to indicate comparisons, while **metaphors** imply the comparisons, creating direct equivalents between two things.

TIP

Say it like you mean it

Don't forget that sensory details include voices as well as other sounds. Using dialogue—the actual words that people utter—works to enhance the description and create a sense of immediacy for the readers. Readers can distinguish personality and even accent through the inclusion of some well-placed dialogue in the description.

Post-Writing

In addition to the usual steps in post-writing covered in Chapter 2, you can strengthen a description essay further by asking each of the following questions:

- Do I have a clear thesis, with a clear purpose?
- Is there a logical organizing principle to my description? Is the vantage point consistent?
- Have I included sensory details from all five senses if possible?
- Do all my details contribute to my dominant impression?

EXERCISES

1. Describe a common object to someone you imagine has never seen it. For example, what does a telephone look like? A glove? An orange? Focus on the sensory details that make the object unique.

2. Think of a place that is often emotionally charged for people. This could be a sports stadium, a tropical beach, a funeral parlour, a courtroom, or any other place you can think of. Next, decide which details you would include to create a positive or neutral tone in describing the place. Then, reexamine the location to choose which details you'd include if you intended a negative tone. (For example, a beach can be perceived as a relaxing or soothing place, but it may also be dangerous, rife with poisonous creatures or sharp objects. A courtroom can be a reassuring bastion of justice and retribution or a frightening place in which one receives punishment.)

3. Choose someone you know well, such as a relative, good friend, instructor, or even a cashier at the local supermarket. Create an objective portrait describing the person. Next, describe the person again, this time creating an emotional impression (for example, describe the person as someone who inspires fear, anger, pity, humour, and so on).

Model Student Essay: Description

The following description essay demonstrates how one student tackled this rhetorical mode. Highlighted are some key features that help to make the essay effective.

Disaster Office

thesis with dominant impression

I knew that Professor Cassidy was an excellent professor from the first day I attended one of his Chemistry classes. He was prompt, perfectly prepared for class and delivered a lecture that was organized, clear, and interesting. In fact, I tried to emulate his behaviour in my own studies. The first time I visited his office, however, I realized that these qualities of his didn't extend outside the classroom. To my surprise, his office environment seemed to reflect the very opposite of his classroom persona: it was a disorderly mess, and I felt as if I'd stumbled upon the aftermath of a natural disaster.

sensory detail: touch

When I arrived, the secretary told me to go ahead and wait in the office, since Professor Cassidy had stepped out for a few moments. I was soaked because there had been a downpour of rain earlier in the day, and it was still drizzling when I had arrived on campus. As I walked along the corridor, I could see a trail of muddy footprints leading down the hall, eventually stopping at Professor Cassidy's office door.

sensory detail: sight

sensory detail: touch

I peeked inside at the tiny room, so small it could barely accommodate a desk and extra chair. There was a metal coat rack just inside the door, its base surrounded by a fresh grey puddle flowing from a red umbrella propped against the rack. There was also a small collection of about six sneakers and rubber boots in disarray on a rubber mat. One orphan shoe, its brown leather scuffed and wrinkled, lay on its side in the puddle. The rack itself held a wet raincoat as well as a jean jacket and mass of assorted colourful sweaters, some barely hanging on by their sleeves. The musty smell emanating

sensory detail: sight

metaphor

from the damp wool made me feel as if I'd stumbled into a basement closet by mistake.

Suddenly I was assailed by another odour—a pungent, sour, acrid smell that wafted across the room. As I surveyed the room I noticed a coffee maker sitting on a ledge by the window—it was the smell of stale coffee that had been left on the warming element too long. The glass carafe contained a hard, black, glossy substance that had dried onto the bottom of the pot. In addition, there were coffee stains like brown polka dots all over the shelf on which the coffee maker stood. I found it hard to believe that Professor Cassidy could work in this kind of environment—but this was only the beginning of my enlightenment.

The rain continued to tap on the open window, which allowed some stray raindrops to enter the room through the screen at its bottom, spraying the assortment of cups and plates on the windowledge. Beside the mugs was a small potted plant, its thin, neglected leaves now yellowed and brown on the edges. It appeared as if it had barely made it through a drought.

Unfortunately, the desk was no better. Was this where Professor Cassidy wrote his brilliant lectures, I wondered? Its once-glossy wooden surface—except for the computer—was completely covered with stacks of books, journals, and papers, some so old that their edges were yellowed and brittle. Some were held open by other books that lay haphazardly across their spines, some were heaped in jagged piles on the desk or chair, some were piled on the floor, and others acted as coasters for cups in which there floated fuzzy green islands atop unidentifiable liquid leftovers. There was even a half-eaten slice of pizza on a greasy, yellowed paper plate, perched precariously on top of the computer screen. In between the books and papers was an accumulation of pens and pencils lying this way and that.

When I turned my attention to the walls of the small room, I noticed a collection of photos and prints on display. One of the photos—a youthful

Professor Cassidy smiling as he handed a diploma to a graduating student—had somehow survived a fall, and the glass was cracked into two triangles over the photo. Some of the posters on the walls illustrated famous scientific figures such as John Polanyi or Marie Curie. One of these was missing a tack on one corner so that the edge had curled downward like a stray lock of hair over Avogadro's forehead.

Just when I thought I must be in the wrong place—this was surely one of the greatest scenes of chaos I'd ever seen in my life—I heard Professor Cassidy's booming voice behind me: "Well hello, Mr. Carter! Welcome to my home away from home!" All I could think was, "How much worse could it be at home?"

sensory detail: sight

simile

reiterates thesis/ dominant impression

sensory detail: sound

A Street of Villages

by Mark Abley (b. 1955)

Mark Abley was born in England and grew up mostly in Saskatchewan, Alberta, and northern Ontario. Between 1975 and 1978, he studied English literature at Oxford University as a Rhodes Scholar from Saskatchewan. Apart from spending a year as a researcher for CBC-TV drama, Abley has worked as a writer and editor since leaving university. He has published two books of poetry, a literary travel book—Beyond Forget: Rediscovering the Prairies (1986)—and a book of fiction for young children. He also wrote the text for The Ice Storm *(1998), a photographic record of the weather crisis that devastated much of eastern Canada in 1998, and he edited a companion volume called* Stories from the Ice Storm *(1999). Since 1983, he has been a Montrealer, working much of that time as a feature writer for the* Montreal Gazette. *Abley has reported for the* Gazette *from such places as Ethiopia, Somalia, Croatia, Peru, Brazil, and Hong Kong. He won a National Newspaper Award in 1996. He lives with his wife, two daughters, and two cats in a suburb of Montreal.*

PRE-READING

Abley writes in this article (which originally appeared in *Canadian Geographic* magazine in 1998) about one of Montreal's most famous and busiest downtown venues. Before reading the selection, think about the title. What does it suggest about Sainte-Catherine Street? Does the article support this suggestion? What is the main street in your city or town like? What kinds of businesses or different cultures are represented by the stores or other buildings it houses?

Some streets are dominated by institutions of learning, others by commerce, others still by churches or banks.

Sainte-Catherine Street, which twines a narrow route from lower Westmount through downtown Montréal and into the heart of the city's east end, is none of these. Sure, it flanks a university and a few department stores, the odd bank, even a cathedral. But its purpose, its mission, is different. In the face of political stress and a perennially uncertain economy, Sainte-Catherine remains, first and foremost, a street devoted to pleasure.

Its presiding spirit—patron saint, you could almost say—is the woman whose sensuous, rouged, slightly open lips constitute an entire large photograph by the

Montréal artist Geneviève Cadieux. The lips are on top of the Musée d'art contemporain de Montréal, beside Place des arts, a few metres north of Sainte-
Catherine. In early summer, players of wind and brass bring the coolest jazz to
festive life in the plaza below these lips. No matter what the time of year, passersby
on their way to play at the Théâtre du Noveau Monde, a rock concert at the
Spectrum or a strip show at the Calèche du sexe glance up involuntarily to make
certain the lips are still beckoning.

4   Perhaps no other street in the country has such a rich and tangled history of
diverting, detaining, entertaining the public. For decades the Montreal Forum
seemed to define the western commercial limits of the street. But the Forum was
more than just a material landmark; it also became a mecca for hockey pilgrims
in a way that its replacement—the tall, steeply raked Centre Molson—will never
match. The Forum ensured that every time *le club de hockey Canadien* won a
Stanley Cup, Sainte-Catherine was the locus of celebration—and sometimes of
looting, too. For the moment, the Forum stands idle, its walls half-covered by
posters for events happening elsewhere.

5   Down the block lies the Seville Theatre, once one of Canada's finest atmos-
pheric cinemas, now an elegant shell threatened by demolition. The street's early
cinemas have not, in general, fared well. The York in the west end, the Electra and
Ouimetoscope in the east are boarded up. The System—a cinema that flouted
provincial law in the 1930s and '40s by allowing Quebec children in to watch a
movie—lingers only in the guise of a video store. The splendid Loews, it is
rumoured, may soon join the sorry ranks.

6   But on Sainte-Catherine, nostalgia would be unseemly, out of place. The street
is too vibrant, too rude, too "in your face" to make romanticism easy. Over the
years, it has kept on rejuvenating itself—a constant urban renewal that occurs
because the people of Montréal refuse to let the street wither and die. Between
1994 and 1997, the vacancy rate along Sainte-Catherine as it flows through the
heart of downtown fell from 19 percent to just five percent. Admittedly, "Picasso"
is but the name of a pizza joint. But who knows what irascible, obscure geniuses
might even now be at work in the numerous galleries and studios of the Belgo
Building, just down the street from Cadieux's provocative lips?

7   Sainte-Catherine has remarkably few vistas. It is a street of proximity. You enter
it on its own terms. Only occasionally—crossing the broad expanse of McGill-
College Avenue, for example—do you even glimpse the tree-covered mountain
that gives Montréal its name. For much of the street's length, the mountain and
the river are but rumours, irrelevant distractions to the serious pursuit of joy.

8   You can buy this joy in many ways, some of them illicit. Sainte-Catherine has
more than its share of strip joints and "tourist rooms"—the kind, you understand, that cater to tourists only by the hour. At midnight, parts of the street are
raucous with neon, fierce with desire. In the Gay Village, which surrounds Sainte-

Catherine just east of downtown, a sober-fronted building that use to contain Postal Station C became the home of a gay bar named K.O.X.

But dreams of a milder kind are also realized here: Bronzage Sunquest, Jacques 9 Cartier Hot Dog, Souvenirs Harmonie. One of the street's most trendy boutiques is named for the legendary tragic lovers Tristan and Iseut. The street understands cerebral pleasures as well as the hungers of the body. The owners of Café Cybermind chose to locate their computers and cappuccinos here. So did Chapters, the largest English-language bookstore in Montréal, which has been doing a roaring trade since its doors swung open in 1996. Though French is more dominant now than a generation or two ago, English is by no means invisible.

When you get to know Sainte-Catherine, what lingers most in the mind are its 10 people. The rural family, for example, that runs a fruit stall in Phillips Square, under the watchful eye of a bronzed King Edward VII. In the sharp days of fall, there is no better place in town to buy a basket of Lobo apples or a panier of ground cherries.

Or the old man who hauls a black stool and a small bag of doughnuts to his 11 regular scrap of sidewalk near the upscale boutiques of Ogilvy ("Ogilvy's" for most of its 132-year history). In December, while enthralled children and not a few adults watch the mechanical animals bobbing and weaving in the Christmas display window, the old man accompanies their wonder and solicits their cash by playing "Jingle Bells" on a Hohner accordion.

This is, in a sense, a street of villages. The tea-sipping ladies who grace one of 12 Westmount's retirement blocks on the far side of Greene Avenue might appear to share nothing with the leather-clad denizens of the Gay Village a few kilometres to the east. Yet both groups cling tenaciously to their identities and their homes in this ever-altering metropolis. The street's major commercial development in the 1980s—a complex of tiny cafés, boutiques and markets, along with a big new cinema and a pool bar called Sharx—was the Faubourg Sainte-Catherine: a self-conscious attempt to mold downtown, too, into the shape of a village.

People remake the street in their own image. As you head east—past what the 13 city, in a needless effort to emulate Paris, likes to call the *Quartier latin*, and on into the economically ravaged neighbourhood of Hochelaga-Maisonneuve—you find a growing Vietnamese presence. Give it another generation, and perhaps small businesses like Café Saigon Jr. and Pho Thanh Long will be seen as pioneers.

Even here, far from the money-changing temples of the glass and concrete 14 downtown, Sainte-Catherine goes on pursuing its mission. Hochelaga-Maisonneuve—an area that has been in steady, apparently inexorable decline for several decades—still boasts an artists' supply store, a boutique that sells nothing but dance shoes, and the dowager stone splendour of the Théâtre Denise-Pelletier. The grandeur has faded, not died.

Besides, Sainte-Catherine is up for another bout of renewal. The reason, 15 appropriately, is pleasure—in the form, once again, of celluloid. Idle for most of the past decade, the Art Deco building that housed Simpson's department store will be converted into a complex of 14 movie theatres. A similar fate awaits the Forum, at an expected cost of $75 million. The ghosts of Georges Vézina and Howie Morenz will soon be elbowing past no fewer than 30 screens.

16   In Montréal, as in every large city, some people live to shop. Sainte-Catherine welcomes them, of course. But they're outnumbered, I suspect, by those citizens who live to play. Sainte-Catherine is their home, too. For it's not only in Place des arts that performance has become an art. "Come closer," Cadieux's megalips are whispering. "Open your wallet, open your heart, open your mind."

QUESTIONS

Understanding the message: Comprehension

1. What does Abley mean when he writes that Sainte-Catherine Street is a "street of proximity"?
2. In what way does Sainte-Catherine Street cater to "cerebral pleasures" as well as those "of the body"?
3. Explain the meaning of the title.

Examining the structure and details: Analysis

1. Which method of organization does Abley use to organize his list of spots on Sainte-Catherine Street? What role does time play in this organization? Why do you think he chooses this approach?
2. What specific images does Abley invoke to help create a visual representation of the street? What method(s) does he use to create visual impressions: specific details, figures of speech, or both? Which other senses does he use in his descriptions? Provide examples.
3. How does Abley connect his introduction and conclusion? Do these two paragraphs effectively frame the essay?

Formulating a response: Inference and interpretation

1. Where does Abley state his thesis? Do you think he follows through with this thesis throughout the essay? How convincing is he in his support for the thesis?
2. How does Abley feel about Sainte-Catherine Street (in other words, what is the tone of the article)? Choose at least three or four words or sentences that contribute to this tone. Does he succeed in creating a consistent tone throughout the article?
3. After reading Abley's essay, do you feel that you "know" Sainte-Catherine Street? Why or why not?

Essay questions

1. Do you have a favourite street? What about it makes it special? Write an essay in which you describe the street, giving it a "purpose" or "mission" as Abley does to Sainte-Catherine Street.

2. Choose a spot in your city that has changed over time. In a descriptive essay, write about the place as it was before the changes. What impression did it give? What details will evoke the former atmosphere and impressions?

3. Abley suggests that the main purpose of Sainte-Catherine Street is that it is "devoted to pleasure." Does he follow through successfully with this impression through his article? How effectively does he convey the idea of "pleasure" as it's suggested on the street? Cite examples from the article to support your answer.

VOCABULARY

Musée d'art contemporain de Montréal: Montreal Museum of Contemporary Art

Place des arts: a complex of concert halls and theatres

Théâtre du Nouveau Monde: New World Theatre

Calèche du sexe: strip club

Montreal Forum: former home arena of the Montreal Canadiens hockey team

mecca: meeting place

locus: centre

irascible: moody, short-tempered

Bronzage Sunquest: Sunquest Tanning studio

Tristan and Iseut: tragic lovers in a medieval legend

Ogilvy: upscale department store

denizens: inhabitants

Quartier latin: Latin quarter, or student district

inexorable: inevitable, unalterable

dowager: elderly, upper-class woman

Georges Vézina and Howie Morenz: Hall of Fame players on early Montreal Canadiens hockey teams

Hesquiaht—a People, a Place and a Language

by Karen Charleson (b. 1957)

Karen Charleson is a mother of six and grandmother of two. A member through marriage of the Kiniqwastakumulth clan of the Hesquiaht First Nation, Charleson has lived at Hot Springs Cove on the west coast of Vancouver Island for the past 25 years. She has been heavily involved with Hesquiaht rediscovery camps since their inception in 1994. When political troubles within the Hesquiaht First Nation threatened to stop rediscovery activities, Charleson and her husband organized Hooksum Outdoor School. The school is based at Iusuk and dedicated to quality outdoor and environmental education through traditional Indigenous knowledge, modern skills, respect, and intimate connection to the natural world. Her writing has also appeared in a variety of Canadian magazines and newspapers.

PRE-READING

What do you know about First Nations peoples? When you think of reserves, what comes to mind? What are some of the stereotypes associated with reserves and their inhabitants? As you read Charleson's description (originally in *Canadian Geographic* magazine in 1998) of Iusuk, once a designated Hesquiaht Indian Reserve, think about these issues and your own encounters with nature and natural habitats. What effect does being in nature have on you?

1   There are no roads that can take us here. Not even the network of overgrown logging roads will lead us to this pristine place. We travel by boat, across miles made long by open Pacific water, to tuck ourselves behind the reefs and swells into the safety of this Vancouver Island harbour. Where once again the name of the territories before us and the name of a people coincide. Where people, place and language are all a single whole called Hesquiaht *(hesh'-kwi-aht)*.

2   No longer needing to hurry, we move more slowly inside the harbour, savouring the thrill of being here. Though we have made this voyage many times, the excitement of reaching our destination—a place named Iusuk *(i-yu'-sook)* near the head of the harbour—is always fresh and new, as if we were arriving for the first time.

My husband's father was born here, beside the river. The same river that still 3
meanders into the dark green of old forest cover and still teems with coho and
chum salmon each fall. A house once stood where the salal grows thick and tangled now, on a spit of land wedged between ocean beach and river bank. The past
is tangible enough to taste in the salt air, to blend inside our lungs with the
present. Across the low-tide beach, long lines of barnacle-encrusted stakes poke
out of the sand: the remains of fish fences that were embedded so deeply that generations of tides and children and storms have been unable to move them. In the
forest, cedar trees from which former residents stripped bark and planks continue
to grow taller and thicker.

We operate a rediscovery program here, a series of annual wilderness camps 4
for youths and adults from Hesquiaht and around the world. Iusuk gives them an
awareness of the natural world, the power of indigenous culture and a renewed
sense of themselves.

Such awareness comes easily here, in beauty that is obvious to the smallest 5
child: towering snags, trees where eagles perch, a river gliding from its forest
haven to meet the sea, a mountain looming behind the line of shore trees, a beach
of sand and gravel with massive rocks at the points. Camping here in summer, we
are bathed in shade until mid-morning, as the sun steadily climbs behind the
mountain and curtain of trees. Bald eagles scan our campsite from the treetops
then move around the nearest point for more privacy. Packs of harassing crows
dive at single ravens, forcing them to hop from tree to tree. Marbled murrelets
were here a few years ago; they have disappeared for the time being, but the sandpipers are back in greater numbers. When human activities quiet, they appear and
feed from the tide-bared sand. In the evening, softened light caresses us until,
across the expanse of harbour, the sun disappears beneath the flat lowland of
Hesquiaht Peninsula.

In late winter, schools of herring boil off Iusuk's shore, waiting to spawn on the 6
beds of kelp and eelgrass. Life is at its richest and most diverse: eagles, seagulls and
hosts of ducks arrive in such numbers that their bits of lost plumage dot the
waters. Steller's sea lions patrol the bay. Grey whales feed for weeks, fattening
themselves for their migration north.

Come spring, black bears traverse the beach and forest on regular routes. They 7
amble by us campers slowly, undisturbed by our presence on their way to overturn rocks at the ocean's edge to search for small crabs. They move quickly only
when startled by sudden noise or strange scents.

Iusuk was a designated Hesquiaht Indian Reserve until the 1960s. How it came 8
to be taken away from the Hesquiaht and transferred to provincial control, placed
within a logging licence and then within a provincial park, is a convoluted story.
Convoluted enough that the Hesquiaht First Nation is currently in court, suing
Canada for its return.

9   When we leave here, quiet descends. Not silence, but an absence of human noise. The bears and birds revert to routes and sites that they avoided in our presence. Iusuk has enriched and replenished us once again. As we pull out into the waters of the harbour, the place looks the same as when we arrived—serene and eternal.

QUESTIONS

Understanding the message: Comprehension

1. Charleson starts paragraph 2 with the phrase "No longer needing to hurry . . ." Why is the need to hurry absent here?
2. Charleson writes, "When we leave here, quiet descends. Not silence, but an absence of human noise." What is the difference between these two things?
3. Provide three examples of how "the past is tangible enough to taste the salt air," as Charleson presents it.

Examining the structure and details: Analysis

1. The first paragraph of the selection concludes with a series of short sentence fragments of information about Hesquiaht. What is the effect of these fragments? How do they relate to the subject matter that Charleson presents?
2. Charleson describes the area through all four seasons. What is the effect of this format? How does it help to convey Charleson's message about the nature of the island?
3. Charleson has chosen a first-person narrator for this description. How does this choice influence our understanding of the subject she treats? How would the effect of the description differ if it were written from a third-person point of view?

Formulating a response: Inference and interpretation

1. Why would Iusuk be the ideal place for a "rediscovery program" such as Charleson describes? In what way would such a program provide a sense of "the power of an indigenous culture" in addition to knowledge about nature?
2. What is the implicit thesis in this article? In what way does Charleson's use of descriptive language support the thesis?
3. Charleson's essay contrasts the modern world, "invaded" by human society and technology, with the natural world of Hesquiaht, where she and her companions can be "enriched and replenished." Do you see Charleson's position as contradictory? Why or why not? In what way can we say she participates in the very behaviour she criticizes?

4. Charleson is generally consistent in her tone, but the mood is broken at one point in the essay. Where does she abandon the descriptive style of writing that characterizes most of the reading? Do you think this departure is effective or not?

Essay questions

1. Do you know a place that has preserved its original pristine nature or one that allows the past to coexist with the present? In an essay, describe such a place and what makes it unique.
2. If you have ever been camping, describe the campgrounds and tents. If not, describe a scene that you think represents a natural environment, untouched by human industry or civilization.
3. Does Charleson effectively make clear her reverence for nature in this selection? Citing specific descriptions, explain how she conveys this tone throughout her essay.

VOCABULARY

salal: small flowering shrub with edible berries

tangible: palpable, concrete

indigenous: originating or growing in a certain area

snags: underwater tree stumps

marbled murrelet: small seabird

kelp and eelgrass: types of seaweed and seagrass

plumage: feathers

Frozen Moment Serves as Reference Point in a Timeless Land

by Emil Sher (b. 1959)

Emil Sher, who was born in Montreal and raised there, taught English at a secondary school in rural Botswana before returning to Montreal to pursue a degree in creative writing. He has written professionally ever since in a variety of genres, including stage plays, radio dramas, short fiction, essays, and children's television. He is particularly drawn to character-driven stories, narratives fuelled by individuals struggling to navigate their way through a world rarely of their own making. His works include Mourning Dove *(1996), a radio play about a father who kills his severely disabled daughter, now being adapted for the screen and stage. Several of his essays have been anthologized, and three of his radio plays were published in one volume titled* Making Waves *(1998).* Café Olé, *a romantic comedy filmed in Montreal, was released in 2001. A playwright-in-residence at Necessary Angel Theatre Company in Toronto, Sher is currently working on a book chronicling his first year as a father and* Bluenose, *a stage play for young audiences about three clumsy, colonizing pirates.*

PRE-READING

In this selection (originally in the *Montreal Gazette* in 1983), Sher writes about his temporary home in Botswana, where he lived and taught English to locals for a two-year period. Have you ever experienced homesickness while living in or visiting another country? What did you miss most about your home? Think about how our impressions of home change when we are away from it for some time. In what way are memories malleable?

---

1   "Africa, you were once just a name to me."

2   The words, like the continent, belong to poet Abioseh Nicol. The perspective, after two years in the land he calls "a concept," is mine.

3   Africa, you are many names to me.

4   Botswana, a landlocked country, a frontline state, peaceful and parched, often overlooked in portraits of southern Africa.

Bobonong, a sprawling village tucked into a dry corner of the country between 5
South Africa and Zimbabwe, the village I learned to call home.

Baboloki, a student with a puckish grin. Sam, displaced but committed, all pas- 6
sion and grace, who quoted South African poetry at school assemblies.

Gabadumele at the post office; a bowl of *mashi*, sour milk, with Peggy; a 7
weekend with Peninah at her cattlepost.

When there are no names, there are images. Once, on the way to a local shop, 8
I saw a young girl quietly clean her younger brother, his soiled pants bunched
around his ankles. No teasing, no fuss.

Or the old man whom I passed on my way to fetch water. Hair the color of ash, 9
shoes torn, he spent hours, tap, tap, tapping on a chain with a stone. That I never
quite understood just what he was doing never dulled the pleasure of watching him
work in the shadow of his hut or listening to the rhythmic chink of metal and stone.

He would have thrived in a Bessie Head novel. One of Africa's most eloquent 10
literary voices, she fled her native South Africa and embraced neighboring
Botswana as her own, settling in the village of Serowe.

"It was my habit," she wrote, "to walk slowly through the village and observe 11
the flow of everyday life—newly-cut thatch glowing like a golden haystack on a
round mud hut, children racing around, absorbed in their eternal games; a
woman busy pounding corn for the evening meal."

Some habits are worth picking up. 12

My thatched hut was by an open field on the fringe of Bobonong. During the 13
planting season I watched tired mules coax ploughs through stubborn soil. In the
hazy distance, a family on a donkey cart swayed to the rhythm of the rutted road.
Children slipped out of the bush, heads crowned with firewood.

Overhead, inevitably, was the watchful eye of the sun. 14

The sun was a faceless clock. Each morning it climbed over the horizon with 15
the unhurried patience of a village elder. By noon it straddled Bobonong from the
dry Motloutse River to the dusty road that snaked to Selebi-Phikwe, a mining
town some eighty kilometres away. At dusk, the sky was a celestial palette, one
gorgeous color bleeding into the next.

I had one of the best seats in the house. Perched on the tin roof of my brick 16
outhouse, I watched the sun dissolve and fade. Villagers looked at me with
bemused grins, and must have seen me for what I was: someone in the audience,
a spectator.

True, I had had my moments on stage. I bathed with a bucket and basin at sun- 17
rise. Some mornings I crawled into my chicken coop and returned triumphant,
two warm eggs palmed like a child's treasure. Fingers replaced forks at meals
where food was rolled, not speared. Every other day I steered my reluctant wheel-
barrow to the nearby communal tap. I read by candlelight and built fires beneath
a canopy of stars.

18   The everyday flow of life rarely ebbed despite the merciless drought. Rain is as valuable as currency in Botswana, and shares the same word: *pula*.

19   In weather where clothes dried almost as soon as they were hung, my hut offered shaded relief. Once inside, I sat by a picture of a small lake, a farewell gift from a friend. It's the type found on calendars of rural Quebec, idyllic shots that hang in insurance offices and banks. Autumn trees, postcard-perfect, colour the shore. A log slits the lake's empty, grey surface.

20   In the cool air of my thatched hut, I knew this was no anonymous lake. It's by a dirt road at Morin Heights, north of Montreal and Bobonong.

21   A large deck hugs one curve in the lake. Up from the deck is a house. I know its smells and sounds, the textures of each room. It's my parent's home in the Laurentians, a year-round retreat for three generations of one family, a house for all seasons.

22   From December until March we ski and stumble across the stone-hard lake. By April the ice relents, then graciously melts. Impassive all winter, the log transforms into an irresistible summer toy, dry on one side, delightfully slimy on the other.

23   And then fall arrives, and the calm lake, reflecting the autumn leaves above, becomes both mirror and canvas.

24   "In Botswana," Bessie Head wrote, "the presence of the timeless and immemorial is everywhere—in people, in animals, in everyday life and in custom and tradition."

25   Like the sun in Bobonong, the photograph of the lake at Morin Heights was a silent timepiece.

26   It never ticked, but hung quietly on a mud wall, a timeless moment in a Quebec autumn, oblivious to the village life that flowed beyond my crooked door. A reference point or a personal grid, it marked my point of departure and return.

27   I could have stayed forever despite all the signs. A small plant had sprouted from my mud floor. Goats had destroyed my garden: one green pepper, marble-sized tomatoes and something that, briefly, was once beans. Then my chicken died.

28   After two years, I was still hopelessly Caucasian. I was rarely homesick, not in spite of the photograph, but perhaps because of it.

29   Only once did I briefly pine to be back home. My mother had sent me an aerogram written at that time of year when the autumn trees in Morin Heights breathe a collective sigh. Tucked inside was a leaf.

QUESTIONS

Understanding the message: Comprehension

1. When Sher observes the sunset from atop the outhouse, he says, "Villagers looked at me with bemused grins, and must have seen me for what I was: someone in the audience, a spectator." What does he mean by this? What does he mean when he continues, "True, I had my moments on stage"? What are these moments?

2. Why is the leaf inserted in the letter from Canada the trigger to make Sher miss his home so much?

3. Why is the same word used in Botswana for "rain" and "currency"?

Examining the structure and details: Analysis

1. As a counterpoint to the opening line, Sher writes, "Africa, you are many names to me." How does he then go on to illustrate this point in the essay? What connects the illustrations to each other?

2. Sher includes smaller portraits of both individuals and places in his selection. How does he use figures of speech (both metaphors and similes) to help shape these descriptions?

3. What other rhetorical mode does Sher employ in his descriptions of both the village of Bobonong and Morin Heights in rural Quebec? According to Sher, what characteristics do the two places share? How does this part of the description help to support the general impression he's trying to convey?

4. Sher uses a variety of metaphors to enhance his description. Choose two metaphors and explain their effect on the reader.

Formulating a response: Inference and interpretation

1. The theme of timelessness and timekeeping dominates this piece. Does Sher succeed in evoking the timeless quality of the two places? If so, what contributes to this effect, in your opinion?

2. Is there a clear thesis in this essay? What do you think the main point is that Sher is trying to get across?

3. Sher describes both people and places in this selection. Which descriptions are most effective? Why do you think so?

Essay questions

1. Describe a place that could be considered timeless. This could be a historical landmark, a place that has not yet been touched by modern technology, a place that has been captured forever in a photograph, or an imaginary location, frozen in time in literature or film. What features of the place make it "eternal"?

2. Where does your family go for holidays? Do you have a regular place that you think of as yours? In a short essay, describe the place and the ways in which your family has left its impression there.
3. Sher describes his attempts to become a "local" in his village in Botswana. To what extent does he succeed? Can you see ways in which he sabotages his own effort to fit in with the local people? Provide examples from the selection to support your answer.

VOCABULARY

Abioseh Nicol: 19th-century poet from Sierra Leone; he wrote about blending Christian and African faiths

puckish: mischievous

celestial: heavenly

idyllic: charming, simple

Excess on the High Seas

by Andrew Pyper (b. 1968)

Andrew Pyper is the author of the novel Lost Girls *(1999), which was selected as a New York Times* Notable Book of the Year, *as well as* Kiss Me *(1996), a collection of short stories. He has also written essays and criticism for a number of publications, including the* Globe and Mail, Saturday Night, *and* Gear.

PRE-READING

Have you ever wanted to go on a cruise? In this article from the *Globe and Mail* (2000), Pyper describes his journey on a luxury cruise liner, "the biggest cruise ship in the world." As you read through the article, think about what amenities would be required to transform an all-inclusive vacation such as this into a spectacular journey. What would you want to do each day? What kinds of activities could occupy you as you float across the ocean?

1   One of the strangest things this strange new century has already witnessed is the Vegas-ization of the high seas. Where once tall ships and steamers purposefully struggled to find their ports, a regatta of floating four-star hotels known as cruise ships now flaunt and gleam, bearing cargoes of package-deal honeymooners, conventioneers and sweet-toothed retirees. As for Las Vegas, building 4,000-room pyramids, medieval castles and Manhattan skylines in the middle of the Nevada desert seems somehow proper, in the American tradition of making glittering "Somethings" out of absolute "Nothings" (think of Disney World, Britney Spears or the "difference" between Democrats and Republicans).

2   But the ocean is quite a different context from the desert. It is mysteriously deep, and storied with centuries of sailor lore, not to mention the shames and triumphs of military history and colonial takeover. The desert? Nothing but sand and mirages.

3   So it is that I board the spanking new Royal Caribbean liner Explorer of the Seas, the biggest cruise ship in the world, as it departs from New York on a special preview voyage.

4   A boat that has more in common with the West Edmonton Mall than a schooner, it offers 142,000 tons of recreational razzle and dazzle to fill the seven days out of 365 that those of a certain means can make themselves feel that all those extra hours and kissing up to that jerk boss was worth it. If your personal vacation philosophy is that bigger is better, then it doesn't get any better than this.

5   The Explorer is 310 metres and 14 decks of entertainment that is best sketched with numbers: 10 dining rooms (which serve 681 kilograms of beef tenderloin and 1.4 tonnes of chicken in a single week), 17 bars, a 1,350-seat theatre for "Broadway style" pageants, a four-storey shopping concourse, and a rock-climbing wall 60 metres above the ocean's waves, all staffed by a crew of 1,176 tending to the needs of yourself and 3,843 other guests. One feels the need for a calculator to appreciate the ship's splendours, and a detailed map in order to find them.

6   These are all facilities that, although on a much larger scale here, have been built into cruise ships for some years now. But the Explorer offers at least one thing that no other ship has, or that you'd ever think that it could have: a hockey arena. Okay, it's a little too small for a full 5-on-5 game, but if you brought your skates and stick down to the tropics with you, there's enough ice here to accommodate an afternoon of pickup shinny. In the evening, you could return to the rink to check out the figure-skating show, an excellent display of women wearing nothing but feathers being lifted, spun and tossed by men in sparkling tights.

7   Following this most unlikely sea-going spectacle, I make my way through the shopping concourse to my seat (among 1,919 other seats) in the dining complex, but not before first nipping in to the Champagne Bar for a glass of complimentary bubbly (drinks are included in the all-inclusive package, and you can't turn a corner without bumping up against a different booze venue, which was for me the ship's most thoughtful design feature).

8   Considering that the chef has to feed groups of people that many nations would consider fair-sized armies at each of two sittings, the food is superb.

9   Thankfully, there are no gluttonous buffets aboard the Explorer, nor an excess of all-you-can-eat masochism. Instead, service is at table, and the staff obviously well-trained, knowledgeable and courteous.

10   The dining rooms themselves are bedazzled with gleaming silver, crystal and white linens, but there is some evidence of restraint in the décor, even if the chandelier hanging in the middle of the atrium makes the Titanic's look like a rhinestone reading lamp.

11   After *petits fours*, it's time for a walk down the Promenade, an indoor shopping concourse that makes Planet Hollywood seem understated, complete with a Ye Olde-style English pub and zinc-tabled Parisian bistro about as convincing as those found in Saskatoon or Kitchener.

12   At midnight, however, the street scene is occupied by a parade of staff and performers dressed as tropical birds, clowns and even Santa Claus (how he finds the time to do these cruise gigs at this time of year is anyone's guess).

13   Then it's on to the casino (not surprisingly, the biggest at sea). Here you'll find the usual Vegas fixtures of blinding chrome and grim faced desperation, yet the blackjack tables were red-hot on the night I tested them. I left 30 bucks poorer although it could have been more if I hadn't split those eights towards the end—blame the martinis for that one.

To celebrate, I decide to shake a leg at the Chamber nightclub, the ship's "late 14 night hot spot." I'm wary. Nightclubs in such hermetically sealed environments are always a dodgy affair, as the designers' efforts to accommodate the broadest clientele often lead to airport-lounge décor and 10-year-old Madonna remixes. The Chamber does better than this: Gargoyles with red Christmas lights for eyes greet you upon entering the gothic dungeon, where a handful of the most brave jive to DJ house music as blue laser beams slice through them. The idea of a gothic castle built into a Finnish-made buoyant mall is more than a little absurd, but it's also appropriately creepy.

Finally, to bed, thinking on the elevator up how much fun having an Explorer 15 of my very own would be. I'd need a billionaire to go in on it though, as it costs around $600-million (U.S.) to build, champagne and soft-ice-cream dispenser not included. Oh well. You'd probably have a devil of a time hauling it up to the cottage behind the Volkswagen, anyway.

Back in my cabin, I take a nightcap of sea air on the balcony. The ocean is still 16 there, of course. But after all the special effects it is somehow diminished slightly, 17 as unlikely a sight as finding an ice rink on a ship.

QUESTIONS

Understanding the message: Comprehension

1. What does Pyper mean by "the Vegas-ization of the high seas"?
2. What feature of the cruise ship did Pyper most enjoy? How do you know?
3. What was Pyper's opinion of the décor on the ship? How do you know?

Examining the structure and details: Analysis

1. Where does Pyper employ objective description? Where does he use subjective description? What is the proportion of each type of description that he uses?
2. How effectively does Pyper convey the sheer magnitude of the ship? What helps to give his description more impact?
3. How does Pyper use comparisons to make his points?
4. What kinds of descriptive details does Pyper use in this essay? How much of the description is literal and how much is figurative?

Formulating a response: Inference and interpretation

1. What is Pyper's dominant impression in this piece? Choose examples from the text that support your answer.
2. After reading Pyper's article, did your ideas about cruise ships change? If so, in what way?

3. Reread the final paragraph of the article. Why do you think Pyper writes that the ocean "is somehow diminished slightly"? Do you agree? Why or why not?

Essay questions

1. What was the best vacation you ever had? In a descriptive essay, write about a vacation spot that still lingers in your memory.

2. Why are trips to Las Vegas or cruises such as the one Pyper describes so popular? Write an essay in which you discuss the appeal of what Pyper calls "the American tradition of making glittering 'Somethings' out of absolute 'Nothings.'"

3. Is Pyper's use of humour an effective means of expressing his views of the cruise liner? Write an essay in which you use examples from the text in a discussion of whether the use of humour helps or hinders the effectiveness of the article.

VOCABULARY

regatta: series of boats, as in a race

shinny: informal game of hockey

petits fours: small, individually iced cakes

gargoyles: usually grotesque-looking images of human or monster faces moulded to sides of buildings

CHAPTER 4

Narration

NARRATION IN DAILY LIFE

Whether you realize it or not, you most likely use narration on a regular basis. Real-life narration happens when you engage in activities such as the following:

- You relate to a co-worker how you spent the previous weekend, building a bookcase for your bedroom.
- You mail photos of your dog, Rocky, to your aunt and insert a note explaining how he saved your family from a fire.
- You send your boss a memo describing what happened at the refund desk when an irate customer threw a clock radio at your co-worker's head.
- You try to convince a friend to see a particular movie you enjoyed, by summarizing the plot.

WHAT IS NARRATION?

We all know someone who can "tell a good story": she's the person who regales us with tales of her new baby's antics; he's the one who commands a circle of intent listeners while recounting the events of the office barbecue; she's the one who can keep you on the telephone longer than you expected, listing the host of bad driving habits she observed while stuck in traffic the other night. What makes these storytellers more compelling, more interesting, more successful than others? It's simple: they know the secrets of good **narration.** Effective storytellers use colourful, entertaining language and know which details will best move the action along; they don't simply rattle off each and every detail as if all were of equal importance.

Telling stories is one of the first concepts we encounter, and master, in our lives. What would childhood be without bedtime stories? Stories teach us about linear development, attention, concentration, the connections among a series of events,

DEFINITION

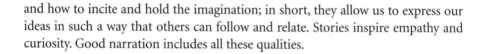

Narration: Narration tells a story from beginning to end and includes major events and characters.

and how to incite and hold the imagination; in short, they allow us to express our ideas in such a way that others can follow and relate. Stories inspire empathy and curiosity. Good narration includes all these qualities.

WHY USE NARRATION?

Like description, narration helps to provide a concrete illustration of your ideas, but one involving events and action rather than pure imagery. When we read stories, we also identify with the people or characters in the situation; this helps us to comprehend concepts more fully. We're able to empathize or imagine ourselves in a similar situation. When you want your readers to "put themselves in the picture," narration is the best way to accomplish your goal. For this reason, narration is often more personal than other modes of writing.

Narration is also used to clarify explanations or definitions. If you're asked to explain what friendship means to you, a short story can easily illustrate the point. A well-known use of narration in this fashion is Jesus' parables in the Bible. You, too, can use narrative writing to help clarify an idea through a living example.

HOW TO WRITE A NARRATION ESSAY

As you work through the stages of pre-writing, writing, and post-writing discussed in Chapter 2, pay attention to the following additional points that relate exclusively to narration.

Pre-Writing

1. Choose a general topic

If a topic hasn't been assigned by your professor, it's best to choose one that relates to something you yourself have experienced, witnessed, or know well. Writing a narration essay about someone else's life events can be more difficult, since you don't have access to all the details or specific emotional reactions. Of course, if you're composing a fictional narrative, you may simply create whatever details you'd like in your story. Even with fiction, however, it's easier to generate interesting and realistic details if you are already familiar with the topic.

2. Consider your audience and purpose

Ask yourself for whom you are writing the essay: what is their current level of knowledge about the topic? It's also important to determine your purpose: are you going to try to persuade your audience of something or merely entertain them? Your decisions here will help to shape the structure and details of the essay and the kind of language that you use.

3. Generate ideas about the topic

With your purpose and audience in mind, decide what event or series of events you'd like to write about. Narrow the topic down to one specific event or a few events that contribute to a larger occurrence. In this way, you will set clear boundaries for the narrative (a specific start and end point for the story). Even if you forgo a strictly chronological order of events (as when using flashbacks), the boundaries of the story's action should still be clear.

TIP

Tell the whole story

One way to generate ideas for narration essays is to run through all the events mentally, in sequence, in a particular narrative (even those considered irrelevant or redundant). For instance, if you tell a story about babysitting for your neighbour, revisit the events from the moment you arrived until you found yourself back in your own home. Specific details, such as what your neighbour said to you or his children before leaving the house, will jog your memory and help to produce a more complete list of details that will ultimately improve the quality of your essay. Later, you can remove those details that no longer mesh with your purpose or don't move the story along.

TIP

Borrow from the journalists

Newspaper articles traditionally employ a narrative technique in presenting their facts. In your own essays, take advantage of the journalist's questions to generate ideas about the topic. For instance, if you write an essay about how you won a chess competition, mention *who* else competed, *what* games you played, *when* the competition took place, *where* it was held, and so on. However, you must still ensure that the information is presented in a logical (usually chronological) fashion, fitting the background details into the narrative as you go.

At this point in the process, also consider your **point of view** (or narrator's perspective) for the essay. If you tell the story in the first person ("I"), for instance, the sequence of events and the details you include are determined by the limitations of your own perceptions, as you participate in or witness the action. A narrative in the third person ("he," "she," or "they"), on the other hand, places the narrator outside the action (but still requires a single vantage point from which the story is told if it's to sound logical).

DEFINITION

Point of view: the perspective from which a narrative is told; may be first-person (an "I" narrator, who is part of the narrative) or third-person (a narrator outside the action)

4. Narrow to a thesis

Your narration essay must have a thesis, even if it's not stated explicitly. In other words, your essay still needs to make a *point:* rather than simply telling what you did while babysitting, tell the story for a *reason.* Did the experience prompt you to discover your fear of being alone in a big, quiet house? Did the evening with your neighbour's children make you yearn for children of your own (or the opposite)? Your thesis will direct the details you choose as well as the organization of the narrative. You might, for instance, write about a volunteer experience cooking Christmas dinner for the homeless to show how you learned a valuable lesson in charity; alternately, you may simply wish to convey the notion "I had more fun than ever before in my life the first time I went scuba diving." Whatever your thesis, it must be clear to you before you begin to write.

5. Organize your ideas in an outline

For narration essays, the major points in your outline will generally coincide with the major events that move the action along. Choose a series of key events that will help to propel your narrative from beginning to end and omit those that don't contribute to the overall effect or thesis. For the most part, narratives use chronological order (since they relate a story in time), but this order is not mandatory (as when you use flashbacks, for example).

To keep a narrative interesting, pay close attention to your choice of events and details. When you relate the plot of a movie to a friend, you don't include every detail of every scene; if you did, your summary would take as long as viewing the

SNAG

Including too much

In trying to include all relevant details, students sometimes fall into the trap of including even irrelevant ones. To ensure that all your details are necessary, ask yourself what would happen if you removed them, one at a time. Can the readers still follow the action? Would there be any lapses in the logic of the story? If the narrative can still move along well without a particular detail and readers can still follow the thread of the action, that point may safely be removed.

film itself! Usually you repeat only those events that helped to move the story along, those that were central to the basic plot. Similarly, you should focus on details that serve to move the action along and retain the reader's interest in a narration essay. Notice, for instance, that Dan Yashinsky (in "Talking Him In") highlights those events that convey the seriousness of his infant son's traumatic illness and contributed to the bond between father and son. Even the stories Yashinsky learned to tell (narratives in themselves) were part of the healing and developing closeness between the two.

6. Decide on specific support for the main points

If you recall any good story you've heard, its most important element is invariably *what happens*. Selecting the specific events or details that add up to a story is a crucial skill to create a lively, interesting and effective narrative. In addition, descriptive elements such as dialogue, specific concrete examples, and figurative language are useful and effective in illustrating the details in your narrative. For this reason, narration and description are often considered in combination. It's almost impossible to tell a story without also describing the people, places, and sensory details that contribute to it. Good narrative uses the best elements of description to enhance the story and provide specific details that bring it to life.

Writing

As you write, keep in mind your outline and key events in the narrative. Remember that the paragraph length in your essay will be determined to some extent by the major events and may vary more than paragraphs in other types of essays. As long as you give equal attention to each of the major points in your outline, your narrative will be balanced, whether or not all paragraphs are the same length.

Keep the action moving

Using verbs—particularly, active verbs—will keep your narrative moving smoothly. Active verbs place the emphasis on the *doers* of an action (grammatical subjects) rather than the objects: you write, "Angela shot the intruder" rather than "The intruder was shot by Angela." Remember, a narrative is a story in which things should *happen*; verbs help to indicate action through a sense of events occurring.

Post-Writing

In addition to the usual tasks of post-writing covered in Chapter 2, when writing a narrative essay, you should also carefully consider the following points:

- Does your essay have a clear thesis, even if it's not stated directly? Is there a point to the narrative?
- Have you excluded any details that do not contribute directly to the overall purpose and action?
- Is your point of view consistent throughout (either first-person or third-person)?
- Have you used lively, active language including concrete, descriptive details?

As a form of writing, narration serves to create a sequence of events presented in a compelling fashion. Just like television soap operas that draw viewers back day after day, effective narration prompts its readers to continue reading in order to find out "what happens next." If a narrative is well organized, incorporates enough detail, and includes all the key events, it will be easy—and interesting—to read.

EXERCISES

1. Think of a well-known fairy tale, children's book, or movie. Write a list of all the plot events that are essential for someone to really understand the key points in the story.
2. Think of a common event that most people experience (going to the dentist for the first time, going grocery shopping, having an argument with someone, and so on). Write a list of all the details involved in this event. Then, decide how you'd tell the story from your own point of view; which of the details would you include? What if the story were told from another's point of view? Would you include the same list of details? Why or why not?

3. Choose an event in which you were involved with someone close to you. This can be something as simple as taking a trip to a department store with your sister, playing basketball with a friend, or sharing a new CD with someone. Which narrative details would you include if your point were to show the appeal of the activity itself? Which details would you include to show how sharing the activity deepened your relationship with the other person?

MODEL STUDENT ESSAY: NARRATION

The following narration essay demonstrates how one student handled this rhetorical mode. Highlighted are some key points that help to make the essay effective.

A Brush with Mortality

by Glenn Barron
(Grant MacEwan College)

introduction grabs reader's attention

Life is a precious gift, yet it is something we too often take for granted. In our lifetime, we may each have several brushes with death and not even know it. Other times, we may be fully aware of just how close we came to losing our life. One such instance happened to me, and I will never forget the experience. *thesis*

specific detail

It was approaching midnight. I had been working outdoors in a remote logging area. The thermometer mounted on my truck's rearview mirror displayed −40°C. In the area in which I worked, logging can only be carried out during winter months, as ice roads, constructed over miles of swampy land, are necessary to access the marketable timber. On that particular night, I was tired, hungry and freezing. I resented the fact that I was not at home in my nice warm bed.

specific dialogue

"How ya making out there?" Rob, a co-worker, asked, waking from the nap he was having in his truck's cab.

"Looks like I need some parts from town to fix the machine properly," I replied, as wisps of heat escaped from the open window of his truck.

"All right then. Let's go back to camp for the night. We can have the parts brought out first thing in the morning on a logging truck."

My mind raced. It was only a ninety-minute drive to town from the site, and I hadn't seen my wife in days.

"I think I'll head back to town tonight, get myself a fresh change of clothes, pick up the parts I need tomorrow morning and see you back here around noon," I said.

"Suit yourself. Just be careful driving this time of night. See ya tomorrow." With that, Rob pulled his truck into gear and headed back to camp.

key detail (connects to subsequent action)

Driving on ice roads, as I decided to do, requires complete attention. Speeds of up to 80 kilometres per hour are manageable with the help of grooves cut into the ice surface to provide some traction. Nevertheless, even a slight miscalculation will cause you to skid wildly out of control. In addition, ice roads are constructed only wide enough for one lane of traffic, and all traffic must be equipped with two-way radios to communicate the vehicle's position on the road. Pullouts, only large enough to park a logging truck, are built every four kilometres to allow opposing traffic to pass by.

At this point, I had been working outdoors since 7:00 AM, and the temperature rose to only −30°C during the warmest part of the day. Nothing I tried was helping me to warm up. Inhaling the freezing air through my nose, I felt a burning sensation after which my nostrils promptly froze over. The scarf wrapped around my face to prevent frostbite was already stiff with ice created by moisture from my warm breath, instantly freezing once I exhaled. As a result, I decided to leave on my insulated coveralls and boots for the drive home, anticipating that the clothes, combined with the hot air blasted by my truck heater, would help me warm up.

sensory detail

About thirty minutes into the drive, my truck emerged from a blanket of ice fog and I could see the Northern Lights through my windshield. Large columns of emerald and crimson light danced across the sky. I was struck by this beautiful display of nature and experienced a deep sense of peacefulness. The warm air in my truck eventually began to filter into my coveralls, finally allowing me to stop shivering.

I worked out the plan in my head: "Crawl into bed just after 2:00 AM. Manage six hours of sleep. Savour a nice hot shower and enjoy a leisurely breakfast with my wife. After breakfast, pick up the parts I need and be back at the job site by noon, as promised." It seemed perfect—so perfect, in fact, that my body and mind were now completely relaxed.

Unaware, I began to nod off as I raced down the ice road at speeds of up to 80 kilometres/hour. In an instant, I woke up realizing what had happened. Though I had made a pact with my wife that I would pull over and sleep in my truck if I ever felt sleepy while driving, this promise was not part of my plan that night. I was determined to get home before the night was through.

"Okay," I said aloud, "If I'm still tired by the next pullout, I'll stop and have a nap." I convinced myself that saying my thoughts out loud would help me to stay awake. Suddenly, I realized that the warm air was actually making me drowsy. I knew I could have stopped to remove the insulated coveralls, but that would have added more precious time to my trip. Instead, I told myself, "If I roll down the window and let some of the cold air in, it will help me stay awake."

The next time I nodded off, I woke with a start to find that my truck was skidding sideways, out of control. I jerked the steering wheel to try to straighten it out, but the truck veered off the ice road and into the deep snow that had been accumulating all winter. I slammed the brakes as hard as I could, but it was too late; my truck hit the snowbank at 75 kilometres/hour. The massive impact sent waves of snow flying over the windshield and into the cab through my truck's open window. Still steering wildly, I was headed directly for the tree-line, adrenaline racing through my veins. I was desperate to keep the truck straight, as turning sideways at this speed would likely flip the truck and possibly trap me underneath. Even if I did survive a rollover, I would likely freeze to death before the first morning traffic found me.

Realizing that my chances for survival were greater if I crashed into the trees, I wrestled with the steering wheel and kept the truck from rolling. Fortunately, the deep snow had a cushioning effect, slowly bringing the truck to a stop before it hit the trees.

Once stopped, I was enveloped by silence. I started to sweat profusely. My muscles, tense from the adrenaline rush, immediately began to ache. I became aware that my foot was still stubbornly pushed against the brake pedal, and my hands kept their firm grip around the steering wheel. The fear that had controlled my mind suddenly migrated to the pit of my stomach, making me feel queasy.

All at once it hit me: I had just narrowly escaped death. Shaking uncontrollably, I resolved to make the most of this second chance at life.

Up She Comes

by Silver Donald Cameron (b. 1937)

Silver Donald Cameron is one of Canada's most versatile and widely published authors. His essays and articles have appeared in numerous magazines, including Saturday Night, Maclean's, Reader's Digest, Nation, *and the* Atlantic Monthly. *He has received four National Magazine Awards and numerous other awards for work in radio, television, and the stage. His 15 books include* Wind, Whales and Whisky: A Cape Breton Voyage *(1991);* The Living Beach *(1998); and a collection of short pieces called* Sterling Silver: Rants, Raves and Revelations *(1994). He was formerly a columnist with the* Globe and Mail *and currently writes a weekly column for the* Halifax Sunday Herald. *Cameron has held teaching positions at Dalhousie University, the University of British Columbia, and the University of New Brunswick. He was the first dean of the School of Community Studies at the University College of Cape Breton in Sydney, Nova Scotia, and subsequently special assistant to the president of the university. He lives in D'Escousse, Isle Madame, where he was a founding director of Development Isle Madame and founding chair of Telile, the island's community television station. Cameron is also known from coast to coast as a speaker who uses humour and storytelling to enliven his provocative thought on a wide range of important issues.*

PRE-READING

In this amusing selection, Cameron tells the tale of dry-docking his 27-foot sailboat, and the trials and tribulations associated with the feat. Have you ever been on a sailboat? As you read through the article (originally published in *Canadian* magazine, 1999), try to imagine what it would be like to haul a three-tonne boat onto a ramp, with only a Jeep and some friends for aid. What might go wrong? Read on, and find out!

Boats are humbling things. Murphy's Law—"what can go wrong, will go wrong"—has two corollaries. First, Murphy was an optimist. Second, Murphy was a sailor. 1

Take our 27-foot sailboat, *Silversark.* Every spring she goes into the water. Every fall she comes out. Every year, things go wrong. 2

So here we are with the boat sitting on its trailer at the lip of the concrete launching ramp—three tons of slick wet boat, 13 feet high, waiting to come up 3 the ramp. A brutal old black Jeep pickup pulled it this far up, but now all four of the Jeep's wheels are slipping in seaweed and pebbles. It's a bitter October evening in Cape Breton, raw and damp, with a whistling wind slicing along the wharf. Friends and I have been at this all day and most of yesterday. And now here we are in the blackness, stuck. Can't move forward, can't go back.

4   Every year you think you've got the system down pat. Gonna be smooth as a buttered eel. Roll the trailer into the water, float the boat over it, pull them in together. Every year old Neptune chuckles, brooding on mischief, the white-bearded black-hearted old SOB. The trailer doesn't roll deep enough into the water. You've thought of that; you tied a rope to it. You clamber down on a floating dock and pull. Nope. A friend joins you. Nope. A third friend arrives. The rope lets go, and all three topple backwards into the water, plop-plop-plop, one on top of the other.

5   You really can hear laugher from underwater. You really can.

6   We use a long chain to pull the trailer back to the ramp once the boat is on it. My chain was old and rusty. Time for a new one. The expert at the rigging shop insisted I buy chain hooks, too. No, I said. I just tie the chain and use a shackle to keep it tied.

7   "Look, buddy," said the expert. "Somebody gets hurt, you get sued. You gotta use the right equipment. Can't go trustin' a shackle. Use a hook." Seemed to me a hook would slip off. No way, he said. And his talk about lawsuits and safety had rattled me.

8   Bought the chain hook. Tied the chain to the tongue, pushed the trailer in. It went too far. My buddy Bill tugged the chain. Up it came, rattling along, the empty hook trailing behind it. Now we had to haul the trailer back to reattach the chain. But the chain is what you use to haul the trailer back.

9   Rowed out in an inflatable dinghy and tried to hook a rope on the trailer's tongue. Nope. Tried to lasso it with a piece of chain. Nope. Finally dropped an anchor on the trailer, hooked a crossbar, hauled it back.

10   Sank the trailer again. Got the boat tied in place. Needed a backhoe to pull it out. We've got three backhoes on Isle Madame. One was broken down. Another was busy. Third fellow said he'd come at noon. He didn't. At 2:00 I hunted him down in Arichat, 11 kilometres away. He said he'd phoned at 1:00 to say he couldn't be there at 12:00, and nobody answered. (Naturally: I was down on the wharf, waiting for a backhoe.) But he could come at 4:00.

11   He didn't. At 5:00 I went to the service station. Sobbed on Russell's shoulder. Russell contemplated his beefy Jeep. Maybe . . .

12   At 6:00 Russell backed down the ramp. We hooked up the chain. The truck roared. The boat and trailer lurched, bucked and rose from the water. As the trailer reached the lip of the ramp, Russell's wheels spun helplessly.

13   "What if I hooked onto Russell?" Kevin said. We tied Kevin's little Tracker to the Jeep. More roaring engines. The boat came halfway up the ramp. Then both trucks spun.

What if I hooked onto Kevin? We tied my little Dodge pickup to the Tracker. 14
Bill directed us. I backed up, taking the strain, then Kevin, then Russell. Three
engines roared. The boat wobbled slowly up the ramp. Russell steered south.
Kevin slewed sideways, all four wheels spinning, heading west. I aimed southeast,
pulling Kevin straight. My wheels spun. Locked together, the three trucks skidded
and tugged, wheels churning, gravel flying in the darkness, dust whirling in the
headlight. The boat trundled forward.

My truck stopped abruptly, tailgate against a power pole. All hands were 15
choking and laughing. But the boat, tall and wet, stood on the dry land.

Every autumn, I think of the Newfoundland undertaker's threat to his delin- 16
quent client: "You're t'ree months behind payin' on yer mother's grave, now. If we
don't see the cash on Monday, b'y, up she comes."

Yes, b'y. One way or another, Up she comes. And that's it, thank God, for 17
another year.

QUESTIONS

Understanding the message: Comprehension

1. Why would Murphy have to be "an optimist" and "a sailor," according to Cameron?

2. Describe the steps that the men went through to eventually lift the boat to dry
   land.

3. What does Cameron mean when he writes, "You can really hear laughter from
   underwater. You really can"?

Examining the structure and details: Analysis

1. Examine Cameron's sentence structure. How often does he employ incomplete or fragmented sentences? What is the effect of these?

2. Writers are generally advised to avoid shifting person (from "I" to "you," for
   instance) because it is inconsistent and can be confusing to the readers.
   Where does Cameron shift person in this article? What do you think the effect
   of this shift is on the reader?

3. What kinds of descriptive details are included in this narrative? How many of
   the senses does Cameron evoke in his descriptions?

4. At what point does the author use a flashback to move the narrative along?
   Where does the flashback return to the present tense?

Formulating a response: Inference and interpretation

1. What is Cameron's tone in this article? How does his use of language contribute to this tone?

2. At the end of the article, Cameron says he is reminded of the undertaker's "threat to his delinquent client." In what way is the comparison between the buried corpse and the boat an apt one? Cameron is counting on the reader's associations between the buried corpse and the boat. What are these associations?

3. Who is the intended audience of this narrative? How do you know?

Essay questions

1. Write a humorous narrative in which you relate your own tale of a difficult task finally completed despite obstacles or hindrances.

2. Have you ever felt as if nature were conspiring against you? Write a narrative in which you describe the effects of some natural phenomenon (weather, earthquake, fire, and so on) on your life or that of someone you know well.

3. How does Cameron use language to express the narrator's increasing sense of exasperation while he and his friends try to haul up the boat? Write an essay in which you draw examples from the article to support your points.

VOCABULARY

Neptune: ancient Roman god of the seas

SOB: son of a bitch

slewed: turned sharply, skidded

trundled: rolled

Talking Him In

by Dan Yashinsky (b. 1950)

Dan Yashinsky is the founder of the Toronto Festival of Storytelling. He is the author of The Storyteller at Fault *(1990) and the editor of* Tales for an Unknown City *(1990),* Next Teller *(1994),* Ghostwise *(1998), and* At the Edge. *He travels to many countries as a storyteller. In 1999, he received the Jane Jacobs Prize for his work with storytelling in the community. He lives in Toronto and has two children.*

PRE-READING

A major worry for new parents is, "Will my baby be healthy?" In this piece (originally in *Elm Street* magazine, 1999), Yashinsky writes about the terrifying series of events that immediately followed the birth of his son, Jacob. How do you think you'd react if you found out that your newborn might not survive? In what ways would you try to bond with the child? What are the ways that people deal with illness over which they have no control?

We used to say his first language was *beep*. My second child spent his first 1
three weeks learning the mother tongue of intensive care, the beep-beep-beep of monitors tolling the electronic measure of his vital signs.

We entered the world of the neonatal intensive care unit (NICU) eight years 2
ago, when our baby was born near death. It is the bravest and newest of worlds, where human landmarks can be hard to find. Extreme hope and extreme dread rule the ward. You live for the doctor's rounds, the marks made on the charts, the slightest sign of progress. You treat each of the doctor's words like a pronouncement from the oracle. Yet in the midst of the NICU's medical miracles, one longs for some kind of old and tested wisdom. The ancient, affirming language of fate and tragedy has been replaced by medical test talk, genetic reports and the omnipresent beep.

Emergencies happen at two speeds: rush and reverie. The fast part started the 3
moment he was born. He was as white as paper, with an Apgar score of two. I found out later that seven is considered minimal for a healthy newborn. They hustled him to the examination table before his mother had a chance to hold him. He was too frail for holding.

4   He'd been born with his cord wrapped around a leg, blood draining out of his body faster than it was being replenished. The doctors had never seen a cord twisted like that. He was waxy-looking, his skin curiously uncreased; his eyes as bruised as if he'd gone 10 rounds in a dockside bar; his features hung on the tiny frame of his face with no animating force to pull them into proportion; his ears were abnormally low, his chin small. An alien baby too weak to give out a human cry.

5   The pediatrician chose his words carefully as he spoke to me out in the hall. Heart? Asphyxiation? There were "subtle signs"—I remember that phrase—of a mysterious syndrome. Or perhaps not. A transfusion would be done if there was no internal bleeding. Tests were needed. He might not live. If he did live . . . The doctor looked grim. The transfer team was on its way over from the Hospital for Sick Children.

6   As the medical crisis sped up, I fell into a reverie, the other, self-protective cadence of calamity. You focus on one simple thing at a time and leave all panic and fuss to the others. As the baby lay, perhaps dying, on the examination table in the corner, I went to my wife. Her fast, unanaesthetized labour had exhausted her, and there'd been no chance for the elation that should be part of the mother's healing from giving birth. I came to her and said, "We have to give him his name right away!" I had an urgent desire to name him, a feeling beyond any creed or ritual. You are less naked when you have a name. A name is a talisman. We had chosen a name earlier, one we'd inherited from her Quaker and my Jewish ancestry. We whispered it aloud to each other and agreed that it was still his name, no matter what happened next. I stepped back to the nurses, midwife and doctors and told them that the baby they were trying to save had a name. He was Jacob.

7   The transfer team arrived. They quickly began a transfusion, busying themselves with needles and tubes. I leaned over the wagon and, still in my centre-of-storm calm, put my hands on the baby's head and belly. The nurses were worried he was too weak to be handled, but I couldn't bear the thought he might leave this world untouched, unrocked. I moved him very gently from side to side, a millimetre each way, and hummed the lullaby I used to sing to his older brother. The nurses, with transfer team wisdom, took a snapshot of him as he lay there, slowly regaining colour, his eyes swollen shut with bruising. When they gave it to me I dimly registered that it might be the only picture we'd ever have of him.

8   We set out for the NICU, amazed by the subterranean system of passageways we followed to get to the Hospital for Sick Children. Later that night, when I returned to my wife's room, we weren't sure what to pray for—a mercifully quick leave-taking or the great luxury of hoping he'd pull through. I said to the doctors, "If he's going to die, give him back to us." They talked about the need for more tests. My own tears finally came when I told my wife that Jacob had danced, heard a song, been touched. I also threw things against the hospital wall.

9   And so began our vigil by his high-tech crib. For the next three weeks I sat next to him and talked non-stop. All intensive care parents find their own way to sur-

vive. I used storytelling. The doctors don't prescribe such things, and the nurses would sometimes look at me oddly, but talking was what came naturally. Apart from the incessant beeping and the occasional alarm, the NICU tends to be a quiet place. In the parents' lounge, a formal and sympathetic silence is observed. You don't ask many questions about one another's children, knowing the answers might be too painful to hear. There's a trend now to encourage parents to read aloud, sing lullabies and converse with their babies; but at the time I seemed to be the only one yakking away.

The first story I told him was *The Miller's Tale*, by Chaucer. I'd memorized the 10 whole thing on a bet with a friend from college, and it's one of the most useful things I've ever done. Reciting 600 verses of Middle English poetry is a soothing way to get out of tight spots—say, if you're having your teeth drilled or driving through rush-hour traffic on the highway. The baby didn't seem to mind hearing about Alisoun getting her unwanted suitor Absolon to kiss her in a place where the sun don't shine: "Aback he stirte, and thoughte it was amys, for wel he wiste a womman hath no berd. He felte a thyng al rough and long yherd."

From Chaucer I progressed to *The Jungle Book* and *Just So Stories*, by Kipling. 11 I thought that Jacob, still not sure he was ready for the world, was, like Mowgli, caught between two worlds. "His heart was heavy with the things he could not understand," Kipling writes of the human child raised by the wolf pack.

It was a long time before Jacob opened his eyes, and suckled, and made a bit of 12 noise. It took many days for him to gain strength. One of the doctors told me it was truly puzzling. All of his tests came back negative. Miraculously, no faculties or organs had been damaged by his horrendous experience. But the life force hadn't flared in him yet. There was another baby on the ward, massively brain-damaged, but suckling like a trooper. I asked Dr. Max Perlman, a neonatologist in the NICU, if we should prepare for life with a special-needs child, and he answered cryptically, "Not yet. Sometimes the things we don't understand are the ones that clear up by themselves." That was the hope we held onto. But meanwhile, where was Jacob?

I imagined our son at an immense distance from earth, a star boy balancing out 13 among the farthest and coldest constellations, loath to make the final jump into a human body. He'd expected warmth, succour, a pleasant shelter, sweet milk. Instead, there was this frail shell smelling of antiseptic, with formula running down a nasogastric tube and needles stuck in tender places. So I decided—or, more truthfully, felt compelled—to tell him stories, stories about the place he wasn't sure he wanted to touch down. Along with the tales written for other children in other lands, I told Jacob our own family ghost story.

His great-great-uncle Simon had been a soldier in the First World War. Simon 14 and his brother were arrested during the demobilization in Europe. They had tried to get food for their sick and hungry mother and been caught still in uniform.

For this crime they were shipped to northern Romania, to a garrison 800 kilometres from Bucharest. They were going to be judged by a military tribunal and most likely executed by firing squad. The morning of the trial, Simon's brother asked, "Do you ever think of Grandmother?" "No," said Simon, "she's been dead for so many years." "It's strange," said his brother. "I dreamed of her last night. She was lying on a couch looking very tired. I asked her why she was so exhausted, and she said, "If you knew how far I've come to save you today, you wouldn't ask that question!"

15   That morning, to their utter astonishment, the seven military judges declared them innocent and free. Their mother had somehow managed to catch a freight train and persuade the tribunal to save her sons. For the rest of his life Simon often marvelled at how their mother had miraculously rescued them; but he was even more amazed by the thought of where his grandmother had come from to appear in his brother's dream.

16   I imagined Jacob slowly led back from wherever he was by a host of ancestors, ghosts, even my late Chaucer teacher (who first inspired me to love *The Miller's Tale*). Perhaps the great-great-grandmother who helped Simon was still roaming within soul's range of earth, still able to companion a frightened star boy.

17   Perhaps we're born into story as much as we are into physical being. The stories he heard might have reminded Jacob, wherever he was, that human life was worth the terrible price of his traumatic birth. When Odysseus shipwrecks on the island of King Alcinous, he's only one stop from Ithaca, though he doesn't know it. Crafty as always, he doesn't tell anyone his true identity. One night, as the bard sings an epic tale about a famous Greek warrior named Odysseus, the cast-ashore cannot hold back his tears. The good king, seeing this, asks his name. Finally the wanderer reveals his true name, and takes over the telling of his own story. The king promises a magic voyage back home on ships that travel as swiftly as the dreams of their navigators: "Clear sailing shall you have now, homeward now, however painful all the past." Odysseus had to land on the shore of his story before he could finally sail dream-swift back to Ithaca.

18   There's a Jewish legend—and I told him this story near the end of Jacob's hospital stay—that says we each have a guardian angel. After we're conceived, the angel takes our soul on a world tour. We visit all the places we'll live in, see all the friends we'll make. And though this world is different from the celestial glory we've been accustomed to, it is also, in its way, beautiful and desirable. Then, just before we're born, God presses us in the middle of our upper lip. At that moment, we forget everything we have just witnessed. The legend says we still bear the mark of this touch, on our upper lips, under the nose. The dimple is strong on our son's lip. To survive such a rough beginning, perhaps an extra bit of angelic forgetfulness was necessary ahead of time. We left the ward after three weeks, the baby still a mystery to the doctors.

RESPOND IN WRITING   NE

Jacob is eight years old now. After breakfast and before school he likes to lie on 19
the couch, wave a huge toy sword in the air, and tell himself stories about a superhero named Jacob. I listen at the door and think of the immense distances heroes
travel, and the risks they take on their journeys. I remember how a star boy followed the signal of a human voice and chose to come all the way home.

QUESTIONS

Understanding the message: Comprehension

1. Why was Yashinsky's baby in the hospital? What was wrong with him?

2. What does Yashinsky mean by "Emergencies happen at two speeds: rush and reverie"?

3. What are the various unorthodox or nontraditional ways that Yahsinsky tries to help his baby?

4. Yashinsky claims that Jacob, like Mowgli in *The Jungle Book*, is "caught between two worlds." What are the two worlds between which Jacob is caught?

Examining the structure and details: Analysis

1. What different means of communication exist in the story? In what way do they relate to the events?

2. The story is written on two different planes of existence, corresponding with the distinction between "rush" and "reverie": the present reality (represented in the major narrative) and the "eternal" (represented by the classic stories and myths Yashinsky relates). How do these two realities counterbalance each other? How does each contribute to the overall effect of the narrative?

3. Which images of Jacob reinforce the writer's uncertainty that the baby will survive? Which different ways does Yashinsky represent his child (that is, to what or whom does he compare Jacob)? How does each comparison repre-sent where Jacob is in his recovery?

4. How do Yashinsky's stories change through the course of the narrative? Is there a logic to the progression?

5. At the end of the story, we learn that Jacob, at eight years old, tells himself sto-ries in which he is a superhero. In what way(s) did his father see this same connection between his son and superheroes? What are the similarities in the connection made by each?

Formulating a response: Inference and interpretation

1. Yashinsky narrates the events of his son's birth eight years after they have occurred. Why do you think he waits so long to tell the story?

2. At the time of his son's birth, Yashinsky is intent on naming his baby. Does this eagerness make a difference to how the baby is treated or how his parents feel about him? Why or why not?

3. Two different factors influence the child's recovery in Yashinsky's retelling of it: the author's own human, spiritual bond to his son, and medical technology. Which has the greater impact? Why?

4. How effectively does Yashinsky convey the sense of dread and helplessness that consumed him while he awaited his son's recovery? Cite examples of specific figures of speech, details, or dialogue and how they help to reinforce this impression.

Essay questions

1. If you have ever witnessed or been involved in a life-threatening situation that you are capable of writing about, write a narration essay in which you relate the series of events and how they were resolved.

2. Tell a story about a time in which you or someone you know overcame a great hardship and triumphed in the end. What allowed you (or the other person) to pull through? Include this underlying idea in your thesis as you tell the story.

3. In what ways is Yashinsky comparing his son to a superhero in the story, and how does this affect our understanding of the events in "Talking Him In"? Use examples from the text to support your answer.

VOCABULARY

Apgar score: number that rates the physical condition of a newborn infant

cadence: rhythm

elation: extreme happiness

talisman: good-luck charm

subterranean: underground

Geoffrey Chaucer: English poet (c.1340–1400)

"Aback he stirte . . . yherd": comic passage in which Absolon is startled by the realization of what, in the dark, he has been doing

Kipling: Rudyard Kipling (1865–1936), English writer

neonatologist: doctor specializing in newborn babies

nasogastric: from nose to stomach

tribunal: court

Odysseus, King Alcinous, Ithaca: hero of Homer's epic poem the *Odyssey*; king of the seafaring Phaecians; the city Odysseus tries to reach after the Trojan War

celestial: heavenly

Call of the Wild

by Charles Siebert (b. 1954)

Charles Siebert was born in Brooklyn, New York, where he currently resides. A graduate in 1981 of the Masters of Fine Arts Program at the University of Houston, he is the author of the recent novel Angus *(2000) and of the memoir* Wickerby: An Urban Pastoral *(1999). His poems have appeared in the* New Yorker *and in numerous anthologies, among them* New York: Poems, *edited by Howard Moss. His essays and articles have appeared in a variety of publications, including the* New Yorker, *the* New York Times Magazine, Harper's, Esquire, *and* Outside. *He is currently working toward the completion of a memoir about the inner workings and meanings of the human heart and a book of poems about New York City.*

PRE-READING

Siebert writes about a favourite pet and the uncertain source of its death (presumably a coyote) in this selection, originally published in *Saturday Night* magazine (1999). What kinds of feelings do people have for pets about which they care deeply? How would a pet's injury affect you? What do you know about coyotes? Have you ever felt threatened by a wild animal?

---

1   This is the time of day, near dusk, the dinner fire just lit at our cabin's outdoor cooking pit, when the coyotes start up. Their sounds vary so wildly that you think at first it might be a dog from a neighbouring farm, or a cow, or the hooting of an owl in the pine-tree tops, but soon the cries clamber up above all those benign referents, a frenzy of howls and yelps that instantly claims you and the night and whatever prey they've felled here within our isolate patch of Quebec woods.

2   My wife Bex and I have been coming here every summer for the past fifteen years, to Wickerby, a rundown old log cabin built by homesteaders back in the 1830s on a modest mountain overlooking the tiny town of Georgeville on Lake Memphremagog in the Eastern Townships. The place has been in Bex's family since she was a child growing up in Montreal. The cabin and its surrounding 150 acres long served her family as a summer and occasional winter getaway, but in the wake of the usual family upheavals and breakups, Bex and I, both writers based in New York City, have emerged as the only ones who have the time and will to come here on a regular basis.

I say "will" because Wickerby is in a state of disrepair so far beyond anyone's   3
current means to mend that it requires a good deal of will and courage to put up
at once with the place's lack of creature comforts—heat, hot water, toilet, stable
foundation and walls—and its ever-expanding creaturely onslaughts: the mice
and snakes and porcupine; the bats that swoop just above our bed each night in
the sleeping loft; and now, as never before, and with remarkable persistence, the
coyotes.

Stirring as their presence and their primordial calls may be, you'll forgive me if   4
I don't wax romantic about them. It was just last summer that coyotes killed our
eleven-month-old Jack Russell terrier, Angus.

It was a Sunday night in early July. Bex and I had just finished dinner and had   5
settled in to watch a movie on the VCR. (Wickerby gets only one English-
language TV channel, which features, of all things, nature shows.) Angus had been
inside the cabin with us but ventured out near dusk, as was his wont, to perform a
nightly perusal of what he'd established as his territory.

It had been a while since we'd heard any sign of him, and we began to get a bad   6
feeling. We took turns going outside to call for him. Eventually I decided to try the
start-up-the-car-engine trick. Still no sign of him. Then I turned on the head-
lights. Bex was standing just outside the cabin door. She looked left, away from the
glare, and spotted in its far reaches a small fleck of white in the grass of the north
field where we sometimes set a table out in the evenings to eat our dinner.

I could see her running and waving at me to come. Who knows how far Angus   7
had had to crawl to make it back to us, be he did and was still alive, though barely.
His eyes were fixed wide, unseeing, his jaw clenched as though still grabbing on to
whatever it was that had gotten to him. His coat was matted with saliva and dirt,
but there was hardly any blood. I ran to the cabin to get a pair of work gloves in
case Angus in his delirium attempted to bite. But he was too spent, in deep shock.
Even through the gloves I could feel the trapped air pockets under his coat. It
buckled and popped to the touch, like tinfoil.

In the days that followed, we'd hear all kinds of theories about what it was that   8
killed Angus. The farmer down the road from our place said a fox, but given
Angus's breeding, I think he could have handled a fox. Bear, bobcat, wolf—but
wolves, like bears and bobcats, are top predators that prey on other animals in the
forest food chain, tend to keep their distance from humans, and with the influx of
the latter to these parts in the form of tourism or the building of retirement homes,
have long since departed for more remote habitats.

We heard wolverine, a fisher, even a wolf-dog hybrid. A local handyman who   9
came up here a couple of weeks ago to help me fix the cabin's tin roof owns a 90
percent wolf. He says they instantly bond with immediate family members, but
that's as far as their loyalties and affections go. He said a friend of his came up the
front walk one day last winter looking for him. He usually kept the animal on a

chain in back, but it happened to be in the house this day. The friend unwittingly opened the front door and wound up in the hospital with 70 stitches in the forearm he used to keep his throat from getting ripped open.

10　　We initially ruled out coyotes. In all our years of coming here there'd never been trouble with coyotes, and if it had been them in this instance, no one could figure out why they wouldn't have carried Angus off. But the Sunday after the attack we got a fairly good idea of what had happened. We'd gone into Magog for dinner and arrived back here about 10 p.m., around the same time we'd found Angus. I walked out into the north field to get some air and look at the stars when the howling started. It was coming from just inside the treeline. At one point, amid the yips and howls and very dog-like woofs, I heard the yelping of pups. Right then a clear picture coalesced in my mind: the edges of Angus's territory suddenly claimed by a coyote pack with a pregnant or newly nursing mother, and Angus, being who he was, charging out to confront them. They were probably more concerned with protecting the pups than dragging Angus
11 off.

On and off for the rest of that summer we'd hear them, and have now nearly every night of this one. A few weeks ago, I overheard a woman down at the general store in Georgeville say that she'd lost eight cats to coyotes in the past two years. Coyotes, it appears, have taken up full-time residence in these parts and seem
12 intent on hanging around. That, after all, is what they're best at.

I've done some reading on coyotes. In the canine family, which includes the wolf, fox, coyote, and jackal, the coyote is a cousin of the dog, kind of a cross between the fox and the wolf. But it is the wolf, the dog's closest relative, sharing nearly 100 percent of the same DNA, which is now an endangered species in most parts of the world, while the coyote is thriving everywhere, literally in our own backyards. They troll the perimeters of airports, sunning themselves on runways. They pad about the swimming pools of Beverly Hills. Coyotes have migrated down to the Bronx. One recently crossed a bridge to Manhattan and
13 was seen dodging taxicabs before finally taking up residence in Central Park.

A major reason for their success is what might be called, in anthropocentric terms, their lack of preciousness. Wolves, precisely because they've always been a top predator, accustomed to ruling over their habitat, have never developed the kind of survival skills that would have enabled them to deal with the encroachment of other top predators, ourselves, for example. Wolves have either been subsumed into our world in the form of the dog, or chased out of it. Into their vacated niche, the coyote, one of the animals preyed upon by wolves, has vigorously stepped. Coyotes thrive in the margins, in the grey area between our stubbornly defended antipodes of civilization and wilderness. They're the flouters of that boundary, the ones who've retained their inherent wildness
14 while freely moving about and partaking of the fruits of our domesticity, even our pets.

Angus's fate was, in part, of his own making, the result of obeying his own wild instincts in a place where doing so brought him up against a far more formidable adversary than he could have ever encountered in his tamed and tilled native England. But it is, curiously, the chance nature and inevitability of the encounter that I take solace in now, the pure remorselessness of the wild and of Angus's fearful charge into it, into something at once of him and much greater than him, the jaws of his own ancestry, the part that never came along with us.

QUESTIONS

Understanding the message: Comprehension

1. Why do the author and his wife visit Wickerby more often than anyone else in their families?

2. Why does Siebert start his car engine as a way to find the lost Angus?

3. To what does the writer attribute the coyote's ability to survive, even in heavily populated areas?

4. What does Siebert mean in the final sentence? Paraphrase.

Examining the structure and details: Analysis

1. Why does the author take so long (he waits until the end of the third paragraph) to mention that the coyotes are something they must "put up with"? How does this deferral of information affect our response to the events?

2. In what ways is the coyote presented as being similar to other wild predators? In what ways is it different? What impression of the coyote is Siebert trying to achieve?

3. List the major events in "Call of the Wild." How many do we "see" in the narrative? How many are implied? Why do you think Siebert arranged his information this way?

Formulating a response: Inference and interpretation

1. How does the author feel about nature and wildlife in general? How do you know?

2. In discounting anything but a coyote as Angus's killer, is Siebert convincing? Why or why not?

3. How does the author feel about coyotes? How do you know?

Essay questions

1. Have you ever lost a favourite pet? Tell the story of the loss. Be sure that you include in your thesis the impact this event had, whether stated explicitly or not.

2. Do you agree that there are situations in which we encourage retaliation by encroaching on nature? Write a narration essay in which you tell about some natural threat that humans may ignore or overlook and how it will (or already does) affect us.

3. Is Siebert fair in his assessment of the coyote? Write an essay in which you explain why or why not. Cite examples from the selection in your response.

VOCABULARY

primordial: from the beginning of time; primitive

wont: habit

influx: inward flow

unwittingly: without knowing it, unintentionally

coalesced: took shape

troll: go fishing, try to catch prey

anthropocentric: seeing things in terms of human beings

antipodes: opposite poles, opposite ends

Duet for Wedding Belles
by Judith Golden (b. 1937)

Judith Golden has always lived and worked in Toronto. She is a social worker who conducts a private practice in marriage and family therapy and is Registrar of the Board of Examiners in Sex Therapy and Counselling in Ontario. She has a son and daughter who are lawyers and don't practise law and a daughter who is a social worker/theatre director. Her husband and life companion is a lawyer. She hosted the first Toronto radio phone-in show, Relationships, *at CFRB from 1987 to 1989 and is frequently asked to be a guest on a variety of TV interview shows. Golden was the script consultant to an award-winning short film,* The Best Kept Secret. *She has written for the* Canadian Women's Studies Journal, *the* Canadian Journal of Human Sexuality, Ontario Psychologist, *and* Bond, *a publication of the Ontario Association of Marriage and Family Therapists, and* Campus Canada.

PRE-READING

Golden writes in this article (published in the *Globe and Mail* in 1998) about how her lesbian daughter's marriage, because it is "traditional," is actually unconventional. What makes a marriage "traditional"? Is a lesbian couple capable of being traditional in this way? What are your own ideas about lesbian and homosexual couples? In recent years, images of lesbians and homosexuals have become commonplace in popular media, from magazine ads to television shows to major motion pictures. What kinds of ideas about this population are being promoted through the media?

When our daughter told me that she wanted to be married in a traditional 1
wedding ceremony, I gulped. Up to that time I had been very comfortable and happy with her arrangement with her partner. After all, hadn't they jointly bought a house? Wasn't that evidence of their commitment? And of their desire to be together? But they were adamant.

My daughter wanted all those who had been part of her life and had witnessed 2
all her important transitions, from her bat mitzvah to law-school graduation, to be present at the ceremony when she would declare her love to her beloved. And so, as we had done many times before in our lives, my husband and I decided to stretch ourselves to be supportive of our children.

3   I must admit that the wedding plans did not go as smoothly as they did for my other daughter's wedding. Alysa and I had had a lot of fun sharing time as we plotted the big day. It was a different scenario with this bridal party. This time, there were (not counting me) two political and strong-minded women who were both interested in all the wedding details. Amelia and Liz had to agree on all facets before I was included.

4   But what was my part? Their lesbian wedding books did not include scenarios for a wedding thrown by the parents, and there didn't seem to be a precedent. Was this because no parents would give their lesbian daughter a wedding?

5   I began to realize that we were on the cutting edge and that it was important for our community to witness such a public event, that it was important for other lesbian daughters who had not had the joy of a wedding. And although I sometimes had to fight for my wishes, I found that I was always respected; as three women together, we forged an even closer relationship.

6   The comments of friends and relatives were probably the most difficult part of going public with our plans. Did we have to call it a wedding and a marriage? It wasn't, we were told. It was merely a commitment ceremony. Why did they have to be so public? Why did they have to do something so traditional? Why couldn't they have something that was totally feminist? And why couldn't they devise something that was more earthy or crunchy-granola? I didn't realize at the beginning of this adventure that my husband and I would be experiencing the homophobia that our daughter is aware of every day of her life.

7   The beautiful wedding invitations, white with purple and pink flowers, declared that we, the families, were inviting our guests to attend the marriage of Amelia and Liz. Then we anxiously waited for the reply cards. Although a few people said they would definitely not attend and some wives accepted without husbands who were too uncomfortable to be present, the responses were warm and loving.

8   As the day approached, countless people told me how wonderful we were. At first I tended to agree with them. But after a while, I became irritated by the comment, realizing that every time someone applauded me for being a wonderful parent, they were saying that my beautiful daughter, my intelligent, loving and sensitive daughter, my golden ball of delicious fluff, somehow didn't deserve such a loving, traditional wedding because she was different. She was gay. If anyone was wonderful, it was the two of them.

9   The day of the wedding was absolutely perfect. A July day with brilliant sunshine. The setting was an estate on the grounds of Sunnybrook hospital in Toronto. An old, gracious, and elegant house where our older daughter had been married. The ceremony was outside on the lawn in front of the fountain. Amelia and Liz had commissioned a chuppah, the traditional Jewish bridal canopy. On it, in English and Hebrew, were the words, "You are my beloved and my friend."

RESPOND IN WRITING   NE

The ceremony combined their thoughts, the officiant's spiritual message, read- 10
ings, and the exchange of identical vows. I cried, as do most mothers of the bride.
And at the magic moment when the officiant made her pronouncement, everyone
held their breath. "And I now pronounce you . . . married."

In between the lunch and the dessert came the speeches. The love that was 11
present in the room for these two women could have launched a woman to the
moon. The joy and happiness that was wished for them overflowed. The love and
commitment, expressed to each other, was powerful and deep. Tears flowed. I was
so proud of my daughters and their spiritual depth, which had prompted their
desire to be married and in such a public way.

Most guests said it was the best wedding they had ever attended. Others said it 12
was a consciousness-raising event. And the only detail we missed, we were told,
was a pack of Kleenex that should have been on the tables, along with the one-use
wedding cameras. The next morning, my 80-year-old cousin called and said, "I
have never attended a wedding that had so much meaning." And to tell the truth,
neither have I.

QUESTIONS

Understanding the message: Comprehension

1. What obstacles faced the couple as they planned their wedding? How many of
   these would be present in planning a heterosexual wedding as well?

2. Why do you think the couple's "lesbian wedding books" did not contain "scenarios for a wedding thrown by the parents"?

3. What revelations does Golden experience during the wedding preparation? In
   what ways does the experience bring her closer to her daughter?

4. Why do some of the relatives and guests prefer not to call the union a "marriage"? In what ways is it different from a legal marriage? In what ways is it
   the same?

5. Explain the article's title.

Examining the structure and details: Analysis

1. The writer begins with an opening designed deliberately to steer us away from
   the actuality of the situation. What do we expect after reading the first paragraph? Why is the information surprising? How do we resolve the confusion?

2. Golden uses dialogue only twice in the selection: she quotes part of the couple's wedding vows and also quotes the officiant saying, "I now pronounce you . . . married." Why do you think she limits the dialogue this way? What effect does this have on the reader?

3. Although the topic is quite serious, Golden ended the original article with a humorous biographical note, "Judith Golden is the mother and mother-in-law of the bride." What impact does this sentence have at this point? How does it affect your response to the reading?

Formulating a response: Inference and interpretation

1. At one point, Golden becomes annoyed at a guest who calls her "wonderful," because the comment implies that her daughter is undeserving of her celebration. Do you agree with Golden's assessment? For whom do you think the situation would be more difficult, Golden or her daughter? Why?

2. What is Golden's implied thesis in this selection? Do you agree with it or not? Why or why not?

3. Golden questions of her daughter's wedding, "But what was my part?" How would you describe her role in the wedding? What "part" did she ultimately play?

Essay questions

1. Have you ever attended a public celebration such as a wedding, christening, anniversary party, or holiday dinner that held special meaning and seemed to touch people at a deeper level than usual? In a narration essay, tell the story of this event and what made it unique.

2. Tell the story of either the most beautiful or the most disastrous wedding you have ever attended. Include plenty of specific details to make the story come to life. Alternatively, write a narrative about what you think would be an ideal wedding.

3. What does Golden learn by the end of her experience? How is she changed by this event? Explain, using examples from the selection.

VOCABULARY

bat-mitzvah: Jewish ceremony welcoming girls into adulthood

homophobia: discomfort with gay and lesbian people or influences

CHAPTER 5

Example

EXAMPLE IN DAILY LIFE

Using examples is a common aspect of day-to-day interactions. You already use this technique whenever you engage in activities such as the following:

- You fill in your annual employee assessment form, explaining why you deserve a raise by citing all your accomplishments since the last assessment.
- You complain to your friend, listing all the traits about your boyfriend/ girlfriend that bug you.
- You describe all the cute expressions that your toddler said yesterday afternoon.
- You write a song for your ski club's holiday variety show in which you list all the ways that people are still generous today.

WHAT IS EXAMPLE?

Most of us use the phrase "give me an example" so frequently that we may not even realize when we say it. **Examples** are the basis for almost any idea or concept we wish to illustrate in a concrete form. Examples provide specific instances of general principles, as well as illustrations to help someone comprehend an abstract or difficult concept.

DEFINITION

Example: Examples provide concrete illustrations to demonstrate and clarify general ideas or abstract concepts.

Examples can be multiple (as when you explain a general concept or idea with several illustrations) or extended (as when you use only a single, long example to illustrate an idea or principle). For instance, if you wished to provide examples of challenges faced by new immigrants to Canada, you might include a large number of diverse examples, such as overcoming language barriers, learning new customs, adapting to the weather, or finding a job. In this instance, a variety of different examples works best to illustrate the concept. However, to illustrate the principle of "grace under fire" (maintaining one's dignity and calm even in extreme circumstances), one longer example about only one person might be preferable. A single narrative about a woman who acted quickly and calmly to save her child trapped in an overturned bus, even as the woman communicated with 911 operators and spoke with paramedics, would serve well as an extended example to illustrate the principle.

Why Use Example?

In explaining ideas or beliefs, most of us first turn to abstractions or generalizations: "Seaworld is a really fascinating place," "It's fun to play video games," or "The new mayor has really helped our city." In many cases, if the audience is already familiar with the concepts, they immediately understand what we mean or naturally imagine their own examples to illustrate a statement. If the concept is new to them, however, they will rely on examples to help clarify it in their minds. Most people need to encounter several examples of an abstract idea before they really feel they've grasped the concept.

You can help your readers to understand your ideas by using examples. Examples serve to illustrate for your readers exactly what you mean if you say, "Working as a sales associate at Canadian Tire is exciting." For some people, the excitement may not be immediately apparent. By providing examples, you help them comprehend the specific perks of the job.

Examples are also used to help clarify the meaning of abstract concepts. For instance, if you state, "Professor Singh is a man of great integrity," what, exactly, do you mean by "integrity"? Using examples to illustrate how Professor Singh acts will establish the meaning in a concrete way: he supports students who protest against the administration's unfair policies, even if it jeopardizes his job; he refuses to alter the results of a particular experiment, even when pressured by the government; he volunteers to help those less fortunate than himself. Each example brings the reader one step closer to a full understanding of exactly what "integrity" means to you.

Furthermore, examples can be used to explain a concept that would otherwise remain vague. In her article "Helping the Mind See," Augusta Dwyer writes,

"Pepin's ideas for simple maps for the blind emerged after consultation with those who deal with mobility issues every day." To clarify which people, exactly, "deal with mobility issues" daily, Dwyer then adds two examples: "his visually impaired staff and officials at various rehabilitation organizations."

Finally, examples, when chosen carefully, can also serve as persuasive support for your thesis. In "Canada, My Canada," Tomson Highway tries to persuade the reader that Canada is, indeed, one of the best places in which to live. He chooses his examples judiciously, including those that best represent Canada in a positive light.

HOW TO WRITE AN EXAMPLE ESSAY

It's quite common to see comments such as "Expand on this idea," "Add more details," or "Explain further" on graded essays. When instructors write such requests, they are really asking you to provide more examples in support of your ideas. Whether you generate your own illustrations or cite references from other texts, examples provide substantiation for what you say and help to convince your reader of your thesis. Examples serve to indicate that you understand the topic and can make it comprehensible to someone else.

To use examples well, you must also employ other techniques, such as description or narration. Many examples include descriptive details, using sensory perceptions to form concrete illustrations. When Katherine Govier describes bread as "sensual," she provides examples of its sensuality: "it smells yeasty and makes your mouth water in an indescribable way; its swollen golden crust looks beautiful; it fills, but doesn't overload the stomach." These sensory details are examples of *how* bread is "sensual," and help us to better understand this aspect of Govier's subject.

As with other rhetorical modes, example essays should be approached through the process of pre-writing, writing, and post-writing, discussed in Chapter 2. In addition, you can strengthen an example essay by considering the specific points below.

Pre-Writing

1. Choose a general topic

As with other types of essays, the best topics for example essays are those you already know something about. Choose topics that incorporate abstract concepts, state a general principle or observation, or can be viewed from a variety of angles. Your topic should have enough depth so that you can think of many ways to illustrate it.

At this point, you should also consider whether your topic would be better illustrated with one extended example or a series of shorter examples. The concept of a "loyal employee" might be more suited to one long example (a single employee could illustrate the point), while the concept of "friendship" may take many forms (and be explained through many examples).

2. Consider your audience and purpose

Knowing your audience will help you select appropriate examples and ensure that the audience can relate to what you write. Similarly, your purpose also helps you determine which examples to choose. If you intend to inform your audience about something, such as which medical services are free in Canada, you'd likely select a wide variety of services; if, however, your purpose is to persuade your audience that *all* health care should be free, then your selection might focus on only the very expensive services (such as surgeries or CAT scans).

3. Generate ideas about the topic

To generate ideas for example essays, think about (you guessed it) examples that illustrate the topic. Good sources include your own experience, the experience of others, facts or statistics, information from the media, history, culture—virtually any source can supply good examples, depending on your topic. You'll find both freewriting and the journalist's method especially useful to approach a single concept from a variety of angles. Remember that the examples you choose ultimately must not only clarify the topic, but also support your thesis.

4. Narrow to a thesis

The thesis in an example essay usually states either a general rule or principle ("Determination leads to success in business") or a viewpoint that includes an abstract concept requiring clarification ("The new Young Offenders Act is far too *punitive*").

As with other types of essays, an example essay requires a thesis that makes a point. Rather than writing "There are many kinds of dishonesty," turn your thesis into a statement *about* dishonesty in a particular situation: "Dishonesty has ruined many good relationships." This way, your examples serve a purpose (to support the thesis). As you think of examples to illustrate the thesis, you will also discover why you believe it to be true.

TIP

Start with a surplus

It's best to generate as many examples as you can *before* choosing those you'll use in the essay. Later, you can eliminate the irrelevant or inappropriate ones. You'll find this approach easier than having to come up with additional examples if you discover a deficit while writing the draft.

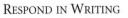

5. Organize your ideas in an outline

The method of organization you use depends on whether you've chosen a single (extended) example or a series of short examples to illustrate your point. If you use an extended example, your ideas will probably fall naturally into chronological order as you tell a story. For instance, to support the thesis "I improved my tennis game dramatically last summer," it would make sense to order the points from June through August, as your game improved.

However, if you've chosen to support your thesis with a collection of individual examples, it's usually best to order them emphatically, ending with the one you think will have the most impact. A thesis such as "Many factors contribute to the efficient kitchen at The Happy Diner restaurant" calls for an emphatic order.

6. Decide on specific support for the main points

Be sure that your examples are relevant and appropriate to your audience. As you select your specific details, keep your audience in mind. What do they already know? What must be explained in more detail? Throughout, vivid and specific details will help to make your examples more effective.

TIP

Choose support from different disciplines

When selecting examples, it's useful to consider a variety of subject areas or sources to illustrate the point. You may know of many successful athletes to illustrate the thesis "With hard work, even a disadvantage can lead to success." However, if your audience is not a group of sports fans, they'll want to read additional appropriate examples from other walks of life.

SNAG

Example overkill

While it's important to include a sufficient number of examples to support your thesis, a common problem is using *too many* examples to illustrate the same point. To determine whether you've gone overboard, check that you haven't repeated examples or used too many from only one subject area while ignoring others. The examples you use should provide your readers with several means of interpreting the topic without becoming redundant.

Writing

When writing example essays, it's easy to become so caught up in the examples themselves that you forget to include your own ideas or commentary as well. Remember, the examples should serve only as illustrations of the point you wish to make. If you've started with a clear thesis and keep it in mind as you write, you'll avoid ending up with just a long list of examples.

Post-Writing

In addition to the general steps in post-writing outlined in Chapter 2, think about the following important questions as you revise your example paper:

- Do I have a clear thesis that makes a point?
- Is my choice of one extended example or several shorter ones appropriate and clear?
- Is each of my examples relevant, appropriate, and in support of the thesis?
- Will my audience be able to understand and relate to each of my examples?
- Have I included enough examples without becoming repetitive?
- Have I included sufficient discussion or commentary about the examples in my essay?

EXERCISES

1. Think of a common personality trait. Next, generate a list of examples of each of the following: behaviours that illustrate it, animals that embody or suggest the same trait, colours that project the trait, and objects that might be seen to have the same trait. (For instance, "anger" could be represented by someone yelling, a tiger roaring, the colour red, and a whistling teakettle at full boil.)
2. Choose a statement of a general truth or a cliché about human behaviour, such as "Wealth makes people spoiled," "It's difficult to understand what someone's going through unless you've experienced it," "The love of someone special can change a person," or "Education provides people with more opportunities in life." Next, generate a list of examples that illustrate the point.
3. For each of the following statements, decide whether you'd illustrate it with an extended example or a series of examples; justify your answer.

- Being a parent can teach you a lot about generosity.
- Canadians are overly polite people.
- The view from our hotel room was spectacular.
- The ideal date must be prompt, respectful, and fun to be with.
- Multitasking is a way of life today.

The following example essay demonstrates how one student tackled this rhetorical mode. Highlighted are some key elements that help to make the essay effective.

Take This Job and Love It

creates connection to the reader

Most of us have heard the saying, "No one ever lay on their deathbed wishing they had spent more time at the office." The saying reflects how many people feel about their jobs: jobs are not a priority, and people perceive other aspects of their lives as more important or enjoyable. In fact, most people would prefer to avoid work altogether if they could. Truly fulfilling work—work that feels more like play, or work at which we can be consistently happy—eludes most people. After spending several summers doing a variety of boring jobs, I finally experienced this elusive kind of work. My position *thesis* as a summer tutor for third-graders made me realize that the ideal job really doesn't feel like work at all.

main point

As part of the team at Bayview Grade School, my day typically began on a high note. From the moment we first filed into the staff room for our daily 7:30 AM meetings, the tutors greeted each *example elaborates on main point* other warmly and chatted comfortably about the previous day's events. Eventually we came to know each other quite well and would insert jokes or personal comments about our hobbies or weekend activities into the conversation as well. We quickly discovered that many of us lived in the same neighbourhood, and several of the tutors became close *specific, concrete details* friends by the end of the summer. Over coffee and bagels, we'd discuss our planned class schedules for the day, teaching tools and equipment, or any special considerations for individual students. Often, the discussion continued later in the evenings, when we'd call each other to exchange ideas or review the day's events. The enthusiasm and professionalism created a sense of energy and camaraderie that made the job feel more like fun than responsibility.

Daytime activities were enjoyable and rewarding as well, and the time regularly flew by. My group began with English tutorials during which I read with the students. Re-reading classics such as *Anne of Green Gables, Charlotte's Web, Lord of the Rings*, or the Harry Potter series transported me back to my own childhood, and I found myself cheering for Harry, sympathizing with Charlotte, or dreaming along with Anne all over again. It was rewarding to see the kids' eyes open wide with surprise or to observe their enthralled faces as we unravelled the mysteries of the various plots. Their interest also stimulated great effort on their part, and students' reading skills inevitably improved, sometimes remarkably. When one boy, Cameron, was finally able to read complicated passages and mastered the word "sorcerer" by himself, I beamed with pride at his accomplishment and progress, a feeling I carried with me for days.

After English, we moved to math class, which provided a sort of refresher course for me. Although I've never excelled at math, I was easily able to master the grade-three level books. The challenge of finding creative, engaging methods to introduce concepts or complicated mathematical calculations kept me on my toes, involved and interested. On one occasion, I used piles of coloured stones to illustrate concepts of multiplication; another time, I had students share large bars of chocolate, breaking them into individual squares, to illustrate division. I became so focused on these tasks that I sometimes carried my work into other areas of my life. In fact, when my girlfriend and I went to see the movie *The Cell*, I missed most of the film because I was thinking about how to illustrate fractions in class the next day.

connection to thesis statement

specific, concrete details

second main point

further examples

third main point

reminder of thesis

specific illustration

RESPOND IN WRITING NEL

After classes, the students were given a recess
period during which they could play outside.
During these times, I truly forgot I was supposed to
be the adult and simply enjoyed playing with students. We organized a variety of sports such as
soccer, volleyball, softball, or badminton, or simply
sat outside and sang songs as we waited for parents
to pick up their children. During these outdoor
breaks, I got to know the students personally,
hearing about their plans for sleepover camp, visits
to grandparents' houses, pets, and favourite games
or toys. I hadn't realized how much eight-year-olds
would have to say on a whole range of subjects, or
how fascinating it would be to hear their ideas. I'd
often lose track of time during these afternoons and
was genuinely surprised to see cars pulling up
beside the schoolyard, the parents arriving to claim
their children for another day.

My summer job as a tutor gave me great satisfaction in a variety of ways, and it never felt like
"work." As I continue my education, I'll always
remember that summer of fun and learning. I know
that whatever career I ultimately choose, going to
work need not be drudgery or a chore, but can be a
challenging, rewarding, and highly enjoyable experience.

review of
thesis

specific
details

thesis,
summary

Helping the Mind See

by Augusta Dwyer (b. 1956)

A freelance journalist based in Canada, Augusta Dwyer travels frequently to Latin America to write about environmental, cultural, and political issues. She is the author of two nonfiction books, including Into the Amazon: Chico Mendes and The Struggle for the Rain Forest *(1990). She was the 1999 winner of the Canadian Association of Science Writers Journalism Award.*

PRE-READING

Try to imagine what it would be like to be blind. Would your home suddenly seem treacherous? How would you dress yourself? How would you find your way around city streets? In this article from *Canadian Geographic* magazine (2000), Dwyer describes a computerized device that helps blind people to navigate around cities and towns independently. What kinds of issues would such a device have to address? What functions would it have to have in order to be useful? Could a machine ever fully compensate for the help of another person or a Seeing Eye dog?

---

1 Jean-Marie Laperle is busy crunching code at his desk at VisuAide, a software company ensconced in a neatly manicured industrial park along Montréal's South Shore. Inside, the muggy mid-summer air is filtered and cooled, the walls painted in muted shades of grey and mauve. Littered with gadgets, Laperle's work area is unremarkable but for one detail: the monitor on his computer is switched off.

2 Laperle is blind. The 48-year-old programmer writes, reads and checks computer code by listening to a voice synthesizer and reading a row of Braille cells lining the bottom of his keypad. The software he and six visually impaired colleagues are perfecting is at the heart of several products aimed at giving the blind unprecedented confidence in moving around their hometowns.

3 Someday soon, Laperle may stroll the streets of Montréal using VisuAide's latest invention, a portable talking map. A receiver the size of a computer mouse will pick up signals from a constellation of 24 global positioning system (GPS) satellites and convey data to a computer that can fit inside a backpack. A database containing the city's geographic details—expressed in latitude and longitude—will then convert the information into the name of the street corner where

Laperle stands, or into a prominent landmark in front of him. A synthesized voice will then relay the information through earphones.

The talking map has life-changing potential, says Jim Sanders, vice-president 4 of client services and technology at the Toronto-based Canadian National Institute for the Blind (CNIB). "It's really rather exciting to think they're getting closer and closer to a breakthrough in solving one of the biggest problems blind people face—safe and efficient travel."

Then there is the crucial distinction between mobility and orientation. For 5 mobility, blind walkers use a cane or a Seeing Eye dog, says Gilles Pepin, VisuAide's owner. "They learn by heart their way around but use their cane or dog to avoid obstacles. Orientation is what's difficult. What tends to happen is that a lot of blind people stay at home or rely on someone to show them around because they don't have the orientation skills."

Affable and soft-spoken, Pepin, 40, grew up in Drummondville, Que., where he 6 still lives with his wife and two sons. Trained as an electrical engineer in Quebec and France, he longed to find a way to use his skills to help people. Leafing through a magazine one day, he came across an ad from Montréal's Institut Nazareth et Louis-Braille, which was looking for an engineering company to help improve computer equipment for the blind. He was assigned to the project by the company he worked for and soon realized the significant benefits technology could offer the blind. He founded VisuAide in 1988 and the company is now recognized as a pioneer in the field.

Since then, Pepin and his engineers have developed an impressive array of tools 7 for the blind. There is Victor, a digital talking book player the size of a small answering machine, with up to 50 hours of recording time. Users can skip chapters or quickly compare pages in disparate sections. Documents unavailable in Braille have been made accessible through Open Book: a scanner digitizes and translates text, which is communicated via a voice synthesizer. Then there is MouseCat, a virtual pointing device that enables the blind to "touch" something displayed on a computer screen. The user holds a computer mouse in hand and moves it until the pointer it is attached to "hits" an item on the screen and a resistive force is generated on the mouse (similar to two magnets repelling each other). The feedback allows the user to feel the length, height and shape of the object under the mouse pointer. There are also about 100 sounds associated with the icons, objects or menu—a door-opening sound, for example, when a file is opened.

Pepin is also working on a talking map for the blind. After joining forces in 1993 8 with Arkenstone, a California company with similar goals, Pepin decided to develop "a small, Walkman-sized system that you could carry around, that you could ask to guide you." The first step has been the invention of a talking map, called Atlas Speaks, usable on a desktop computer. Choosing from a collection of 20,000 digital maps on CDs, users enter a starting point or address into the computer and then the destination. A synthesized voice tells the user how to get there—which streets to take, where to cross and when to turn left or right. The information can be recorded or printed out in Braille to be taken along on the journey.

9   Pepin then turned his attention to exploiting navigational information provided by the United States military's GPS satellites, which allow for the use of on-ground receivers to determine the latitude and longitude of a location.

10   The current prototype, called Strider in the U.S., uses GPS and correction systems with digitized maps on a notebook computer. It includes an antenna, a GPS receiver, earphones and a keypad used to input questions. Weighing in at around four kilograms, it can be easily carried around.

11   Once the user has the position, it is translated into something they are familiar with, such as "library" or "Peel and Sainte-Catherine" [streets].

12   Theoretically, positions derived from GPS satellites are accurate to within metres. But because the U.S. military doesn't want the precise data GPS produces getting into the wrong hands, satellite signals are purposely distorted. In practice, therefore, information can be 50 to 100 metres off. The U.S. government has promised to descramble signals by 2002. In the meantime, correction systems, of which there are about half a dozen on the market, can improve accuracy to within a few metres. "We can accept accuracy within 10 metres in conjunction with the basic capability a blind person already has to get around," says Pepin, "to know, for example, that they're on one side of the street and not the other."

13   Orientation by satellite has one major obstacle: tall buildings can interrupt signals, forcing a user to move to an intersection or open plaza to regain contact. Charles LaPierre, a blind engineer in California, may have a solution. LaPierre did his master's thesis at Carleton University in Ottawa on how to combine GPS technology with a module that can determine dead reckoning. The module continues to track the user when the GPS signal is lost: an electronic compass (measuring direction) and a pedometer (measuring distance) kick in and tell the system where the user is. The module returns to standby when the GPS signal resumes. With this combination, a portable talking map would work even in a subway station or inside a building. VisuAide plans to integrate LaPierre's research into a Canadian product.

14   Pepin is not convinced that overly complex map models are necessary. If a blind person can already sense how far they are from an object by using a cane or guide dog, he says, why replicate such information on a sophisticated computer?

15   Pepin's ideas for simple maps for the blind emerged after consultation with those who deal with mobility issues every day—his visually impaired staff and officials at various rehabilitation organizations. When he demonstrated Strider recently to an international body, the experts had several recommendations.

16   "They told us, 'You're doing good work, but at the same time you're trying to make a product that is over-engineered, with too many functions,'" says Pepin.

They suggested a system of urban landmarks rather than conventional maps. The blind often don't need to know the exact street they are on to get to their destination he says. "If we can store enough landmarks, we don't need a complete map. We can go with the GPS to the corner of Sherbrooke and Peel streets, for instance, get the coordinates, and associate a message. It will reduce the price and the dimensions of the unit."

With only a small market for such products, Pepin and his partners are co- 17 operating with another company to develop a talking map for a potentially much larger audience—the tourism industry. After all, says Pepin, a tourist in a foreign city is almost like a blind person. Such thinking is the hallmark of an ideas man who also knows how to execute. "Gilles is truly a visionary," says the CNIB's Sanders, "but he's also an engineer, so he knows how to get from the idea to the practical."

And the practical is where the real story lies. To the undiscerning observer, 18 Laperle may be just another programmer debugging software. But for him, the work is much more than that.

In university, he says, computers became his link to the sighted world—to 19 technical or literary documents and to his fellow students. "If I had to work with someone, the other person could see what I was doing just by looking at my computer screen," says Laperle. The joy of that, and in being able to work independently on his studies and exams, is still palpable in Laperle's words. Now at VisuAide, he says, he works on bringing that same thrill to others.

QUESTIONS

Understanding the message: Comprehension

1. How does Laperle use a computer? How does his computer function differently from others?

2. What is the difference between mobility and orientation for blind people?

3. Why did Pepin decide to create VisuAide?

4. Why isn't the GPS system totally reliable? Why would a distortion of 10 metres in signals still be acceptable?

5. In what way(s) do the blind orient themselves differently from the sighted?

Examining the structure and details: Analysis

1. How does the introductory paragraph relate to the remainder of the selection? Does it effectively introduce the true subject of the essay? Why or why not?

2. Whom do you think Dwyer's intended audience is? What information must they already know?

3. What is Dwyer's purpose in "Helping the Mind See"?

4. The article opens and closes with a mention of Laperle, the blind programmer. In what way do the two paragraphs relate to each other? Does the conclusion serve effectively to create closure? Why or why not?

Formulating a response: Inference and interpretation

1. What drawbacks do you see to VisuAide's computer mapping system? Do you think it will work? Why or why not?

2. Jim Sanders of the CNIB says that the invention will help to provide "safe and efficient travel" for the blind. Do you agree with his assessment? If so, in what way(s) will Pepin's invention promote safer and more efficient modes of travel than are currently in use?

3. Do you think that Pepin is qualified to do the work he does? If not, how does he compensate?

Essay questions

1. Think of a variety of ways that you rely on technology to help you navigate through a normal day. Write an example essay in which you discuss the various gadgets or technological tools you could not do without, and why.

2. Most of us have experienced some form of impaired sensory perception, at least temporarily, at some point in our lives (for instance, decreased mobility due to a broken leg, a mouth frozen at the dentist's office, impaired hearing after swimming, impaired smell during a cold or flu, or even a diminished sense of feeling in a leg "asleep" from sitting too long in one position). Choose a situation in which one or more of your senses was (or might be) impaired, and think of the difficulties and disadvantages to functioning normally under those conditions.

3. Laperle admits that his system is not yet perfect. What are its flaws? Can you conceive of a system that would be better? Using examples from the reading, explain the weaknesses in Laperle's system and suggest how it might be improved.

VOCABULARY

ensconced: snug inside of

dead reckoning: estimation of position without using precise coordinates

pedometer: device to measure the distance someone has walked

palpable: clearly felt or experienced

Bread's Magic
by Katherine Govier (b. 1948)

A native of Edmonton, Katherine Govier was educated at the University of Alberta and York University. Her books include the short story collections Fables of Brunswick Avenue *(1985),* Before and After *(1989), and* The Immaculate Conception Photography Gallery *(1994), as well as the novels* Random Descent *(1979),* Going through the Motions *(1982),* Between Men *(1987),* Hearts of Flame *(1991),* Angel Walk *(1996), and* The Truth Teller *(2000). She also edited a travel anthology,* Without a Guide *(1994), and has contributed stories and nonfiction articles to anthologies, newspapers, and magazines. Govier has also been active in the writing community at large, serving as president of P.E.N. Canada from 1997 to 1998 and as coordinator of the Writers in Electronic Residence Program from 1988 to 1991. Her work has garnered many awards, including the Authors' Award and National Magazine Award in 1979, the City of Toronto Book Award in 1992, and the Marian Engel Award in 1997. She was also short listed for a Trillium Award in 1995 and 1997. Govier has lived in Calgary, Washington, D.C., and London, England, and now makes her home in Toronto.*

PRE-READING

What thoughts does the title of this selection evoke? Is bread "magic" to you? In what way? What aspects of this daily food might be considered "magic"? What are your own feelings about bread and how are they similar to the common notions we all share? In this article, published in *Canadian Geographic* magazine in 1999, Govier discusses how society views "the staff of life."

1   I don't bake bread any more. Two decades ago, even one decade ago I did bake it, the old fashioned way, with the yeast soaking in warm water, and then the ball of dough sitting in a bowl covered with a clean dishcloth. I loved the chemistry of yeast, the idea of it being alive. I liked the sight of dough puffing up in volume there on the warm radiator. Admiring the risen ball of dough, with its smug white satin surface and mysterious presence, was my favourite part of the process. My baked loaves were often a disappointment, flat or hard or with a huge air bubble in the centre.

2   The bread machine, when I got one for Christmas five years ago, briefly revived baking in my house. Before I went to bed at night, I would throw a couple of cups

of flour on top of a teaspoon of yeast into the strange little metal basket, add water and sugar and oil, and press a series of buttons. Sometime before dawn the machine would begin its curious churning; after the clock radio came on the electronic beeps signalling a baked loaf would sound.

I'd run expectantly down to the kitchen and lift the lid. On days when it all 3 went right, I was granted the golden mound of a perfect loaf, and of course the exquisite smell of bread fresh from the oven. We tore into the flesh of it for breakfast; the loaf would be gone within the hour. But all too often I'd find a hideous mass of hardened guck in the bottom: midnight was never my finest hour, and in a somnambulant state the night before I'd forgotten some key ingredient or pushed the wrong button.

And so I gave up electronic baking too. Kids left early for band practice, I had 4 breakfast meetings, even a good loaf might dry uneaten to become food for birds. Sometimes I wonder if bread has gone out of style. Even the most exquisite boutique-bought loaf may languish uneaten in my house these days. Nobody wants more than a couple of slices a day. The kids would rather take pasta salad than a sandwich in their school lunches. At dinner parties, everyone is on a diet.

I'm not dieting but some days I forget to have dinner; then I find myself having 5 a couple of slices of cinnamon toast before bed. It's great with tea and you don't have to stay awake to digest it. Sundays I might make melted cheese on toast, an old English nursery favourite, but none of this is enough to use up more than half a fresh loaf before it turns into a hard shell with a sandpaper face, or develops a lovely blue mould trim.

So, yes, I've given up baking along with fantasies of old-fashioned home- 6 making. But the desire to cut into a fragrant fresh loaf endures. I now buy bread, when I buy it, from one of a dozen chi-chi little establishments within a six-block walk of my central Toronto neighbourhood. After all, my mother bought bread and so did her mother, I imagine.

I have various handed-down recipes from that long-departed Yorkshire grand- 7 mother who immigrated to Vancouver in 1910. They include lemon curd and Irish potatoes, mostly delectables to satisfy the notorious sweet tooth of the English. I imagine that she had a breadman who delivered door-to-door in the cozy middle-class Kitsilano district in the 1920s. Such people still existed in the 1950s in Edmonton, where I grew up. I have dim recollections of a horse-drawn cart in the back lane; this was the milkman and with his glass bottles arrived each day a couple of commercial sandwich loaves wrapped in a strange waxy white paper.

Odd that we have a nostalgia for home-baked bread, even though many of us 8 rarely experienced it, never lived with a mother who stood at the kitchen counter with her arms up to elbows in flour, kneading dough. One of my favourite poems, by Irish poet Seamus Heaney, memorializes this mythic figure of a woman in a floury apron standing at a bakeboard near a stove:

9   *And here is love*
like a tinsmith's scoop
sunk past its gleam
in the meal-bin.

10   Why is it love? Clearly, bread is sensual—it smells yeasty and makes your mouth water in an indescribable way; its swollen gold crust looks beautiful; it fills, but doesn't overload the stomach. It also suggests the sexual, the warm glow of home fires, the magical power of yeast to make things rise. Bread is daily, which requires devotion, a part of the background, taken for granted, like mothers I suppose, until it makes itself screamingly obvious by its absence.

11   So much about bread lies in symbols. In reality, the cooling loaf has long departed the kitchen counter for the industrial rack. Dough is gone from women's hands into the hands of workers, mostly men, strangers to us. Baking bread is no longer a leisured, nurturing activity but a speedy process, involving hefty lifting, conveyor belts and giant vats. The tools are not modern. The ovens, the trays, the bowls date from the early industrial age. I can't be alone in having incorporated into my imagination the otherworldly bakers in Maurice Sendak's children's picture book, *In the Night Kitchen*. I think of them on a morning in a full bakery, strange little men in puffed white hats, sweating and cursing over burgeoning quantities of stubborn dough.

12   I still find that magical, that somewhere in this city, this is all happening every night. Strangers shape the glossy dough with their hands into myriad shapes. Fresh loaves come on with sunrise, like new-sprung mushrooms after rain, legions of them.

13   And what loaves! There is a mad variety, a dizzy choice. It seems almost profligate. And so specific! Perhaps I betray my Waspy, bread-poverished background here. I admit, I never saw a bagel until I was twenty-three. I admit, when I made the discovery I ate one every day for at least six months. But still, when I walk into a bakery I wonder why on earth whoever makes the stuff bothers with all those shapes and sizes. The sheer geometry makes my eyes roll: one can go with oval, long, circular (filled or hollow), square, in small, medium or large. One can take one's bread black, white, yellow, brown, diagonally scored, raisin-pocked or marked with a cross. And it is always fresh, baked early that morning.

14   Who eats all this bread? I wonder, standing at the counter. Exactly how many people will come in today and want one of those round, flat loaves with flax seeds? How many loaves will be left drying on the shelves tonight after the door of the bakery is closed? And what do the clerks do with it then? Throw it out? Feed it to the pigeons? The homeless? And of the loaves that go home with someone like me, how often is half a loaf left to go stale?

This bread is more than food for hungry people. It is a tradition, many tradi- 15
tions, we wish to honour, the idea that we are this close to grain, to hearth, to daily
baking. We are no longer so close. But we can buy a loaf and feel as if we are.
Maybe tomorrow we'll bake. Potential is the beauty of bread. It is there for us still,
the lively fizz of yeast, the mystery of dough rising, the intimate ritual of baking—
performed by strangers, but at least performed—and the way a warm slice of
bread dissolves in our mouth. We can have it new every day.

QUESTIONS

Understanding the message: Comprehension

1. What aspect(s) of baking bread by hand does Govier enjoy?

2. What were the problems Govier had with baking bread that contributed to
   her abandonment of the practice?

3. What aspects of bread are "magic" to Govier?

4. What does the writer mean when she says that the choices of breads available
   seem "almost profligate"?

Examining the structure and details: Analysis

1. Govier relates bread to nostalgia, which takes her into the history of bread and
   other foods. What examples of traditions gone by does she provide? How do
   they contribute to our understanding of why bread is appealing to most people?

2. The essay includes various examples of reasons why bread is so appealing to
   us. What kinds of examples does Govier include, and on what are they based?
   How do they differ from each other?

3. At various points in this essay, Govier employs figurative language to lend life to
   the topic and suggest that bread is a living organism rather than simply an inan-
   imate object. How does her choice of language contribute to this impression?

Formulating a response: Inference and interpretation

1. What is Govier's thesis in "Bread's Magic"? State it in one sentence.

2. Why do you think Govier focuses in her introduction on her own erstwhile
   failures with baking bread? Does this help to explain the focus later on in the
   reading?

3. A common expression about bread is that it is "the staff of life." Does Govier promote this idea in her article? If so, how does she imply that bread is vitally nourishing for us?

4. What is Govier saying about the role of bread in our modern society? How has this changed from its previous role a century ago?

Essay questions

1. Think of something traditional or something established as a large part of your daily life (for example, a personal computer, a pet, weekly meetings at work, the news on television, and so on). In an essay, provide examples to explain how this thing has become established in society.

2. In what way(s) does Govier suggest that bread is a living entity, rather than merely a foodstuff? Look at Govier's use of figurative language and the human reactions to bread's sensory characteristics in your response.

3. Govier suggests that our love of bread goes deeper than a mere love of the food; it's almost primal, something at the soul level, according to her. How does she impress on us that bread infiltrates our very psyches? In your answer, provide specific examples from the selection.

VOCABULARY

somnambulant: sleepwalking

languish: waste away

Yorkshire: county in England

lemon curd: custard-like lemon spread

Kitsilano: area of Vancouver

burgeoning: quickly expanding; growing

myriad: diverse, varied

profligate: excessive, wasteful

Dot-Com This!

by Stephanie Nolen (b. 1971)

Born in Montreal, Stephanie Nolen now makes her home in Toronto, where she is a reporter for the Globe and Mail. *Previously a writer in the arts and culture department, she now covers national and international issues at the* Globe.

PRE-READING

In "Dot-Com This!" (published in the *Globe and Mail* in 2000), Nolen discusses how our use of language is being transformed by e-mail and electronic media such as the Internet. How often do you use e-mail, if at all? How often do you surf in cyberspace? How are people's lives different today, as compared with several decades ago, due to the changes in these media? Do you think your own use of language has changed over the years?

It was inevitable, Jamie Reid says, that his love letters and his dinner-table chats 1
would show the effect.

Reid, 23, is what you might call a paid hacker—a self-taught network security 2
expert, hired by a desperate corporate world right out of his Toronto high school.
He lives totally immersed in the Internet world—and he knows it shows.

"You begin to look at things in a very logical and inductive way after working 3
with machines for a long time," he says. "You rely less on intuition. The problems
that computers solve have few variables; things add up. And you apply those same
ways of doing things to your everyday life. It only makes sense that people who
spend their days dealing with those sort of questions would attempt to quantize
everything from their shopping lists to their politics."

In truth, Reid didn't say that, he wrote it. As if to illustrate his own point, he 4
offered that observation via e-mail a couple of hours after I put the question to
him in a conversation. His reply, articulate and eloquent, was also a textbook
example of many of the other ways in which the Internet is changing the way we
use language. He wrote in one-sentence paragraphs. He listed points. He used
mathematical jargon ("quantize") in an everyday context. About the only thing he
didn't do was toy with capitaLetters.

It's all dot-com and network and i-this and e-that, these days, and so ubiqui- 5
tous are these words and symbols that we don't tend to give them much thought.
But in many subtle ways the Internet is dramatically altering the way we use language: How we write, how we speak, how we use words when we think.

6   "It was inevitable that our language would be affected because the Internet is not simply a technical phenomenon, it's a cultural phenomenon, and it doesn't even matter if you're on it or not, you are nonetheless affected by its presence in the culture."

7   So says Liss Jeffrey, adjunct professor at the McLuhan Program in Culture and Technology at the University of Toronto, and director of the byDesign eLab, an electronic lab engaged in the design of public space on-line. "New horizons open up and we, as human beings, have to find ways to describe those places. We create new things, we dream them up, and then we find ways to talk about them."

8   Take cyberspace. It's now a universally accepted idea that most of us spend part of each day there. We all know what it means. The term was coined by William Gibson in 1984; it is, Jeffrey says, something people have experiences of, an interactive participatory reality, and thus something for which we needed words.

9   There have been lots of other new words in the six years most of us have been visiting cyberspace. The Internet was invented in 1969, but didn't have public use until the early 1990s. The explosion came in early 1995, as service providers switched to flat-rate billing, instead of charging for volume of mail received. The 1994 edition of the *Canadian Internet Handbook* included two pages on the World Wide Web, predicting it might one day come into widespread use. A Nielson survey found that in 1996, 23 per cent of Canadians used the Internet; a year later, it was 31 per cent. Angus Reid found 55 per cent of us using it in 1999 and says this year, the number is up to 70 per cent.

10   But while much of the cultural analysis of the Internet is about the Web, Clive Thompson, editor-at-large at *Shift* magazine in New York, says the most significant factor has been e-mail, however pedestrian it may seem. "It's had by far the most immediate effects and more visceral effect," he says. "When people get to work, do they look at a groovy new site, or watch some streaming video, or something with generation-enhanced Flash content? Of course not. They check their e-mail."

11   And the often-overlooked result of our addiction to e-mail is that we write more. Much more.

12   "Before e-mail, the vast majority of people never wrote anything," Thompson says. "Their jobs didn't require it, their pastimes didn't require it, and it wasn't easy to do—before computers we didn't write a lot of text." Now people have a motive: "It's not that people want to write, but they want to talk to other people, and they have to write to do that."

13   But how are they writing?

14   Well, in English, for one thing. There has been an explosion in the number of people for whom English is a second language, even as the number of native speakers of English has steadily declined over the last 10 years. "English is changing its function in the world," says Eric McLuhan, author of *Electric*

Language, adding that English, as the language with the greatest flexibility and largest vocabulary, was the only language prepared for this shift.

But McLuhan, who is the son of the legendary communications theorist 15 Marshall McLuhan, says the 15 years of the computing era have had drastic effects on the building blocks of writing.

Attention spans have declined sharply, and with them, sentence length. Twenty 16 years ago, the average sentence length in a novel was 20 words; today it is 12 to 14 words. In mass-market books such as Harlequin Romance novels, the average sentence is only seven or eight words.

Paragraphs, too, have changed. Most prominently, one-sentence paragraphs 17 have become ubiquitous. That means, McLuhan says, that the traditional one-sentence paragraph has lost its role of transition or dramatic impact. In addition, he says, ideas are no longer developed in paragraphs. And all objective distance is lost. "It's all up front and in your face. That makes for high [reader] involvement and low detachment."

And the style of bullet-point writing, also a function of Internet communica- 18 tion, results in a compressed, discontinued presentation of information, heavy with parallelism—qualities once reserved for poetry, McLuhan observes. "We are reinventing poetics from the bottom up."

Robert Logan says all this should come as no surprise. A physicist at the 19 University of Toronto and the author of *The Sixth Language,* he uses chaos theory to argue that each time human society needs to deal with an information over-load, a new language emerges.

"Speech, writing, math, science, computing and the Internet form an evolu- 20 tionary chain of languages," he says. Writing and math emerged in 3300 BC in Sumer to keep track of tributes; then came science because of the need to teach how to organize that knowledge. Computing allowed people to organize the explosion of knowledge, and then, when everyone wanted to communicate with computers, the Internet emerged.

"To communicate, to operate in the 21st century, you must be fluent in all six 21 languages," says Logan, adding, "You can speak some with an accent."

Each language has its own grammar and syntax, evolving with the vestigial 22 structures of its predecessors. When writing emerged, it took the vocabulary of speech but added new words. Plato's Greek has many more words and grammat-ical structures than Homer's. With math came the grammar of logic; with science, the grammar of the scientific method; with the Internet, the grammar of hyper-text and search engines.

This is, in Logan's mind, the key contribution of the Internet era: We write, 23 speak and think in hypertext—the code in which text is written on the web—the links. It is tangential, not sequential.

24   "I am much more hypertext in my talking now," says Logan. "I jump off into something else, then return to where I was, to what I was talking about." It is the verbal equivalent of clicking on a blue-underlined link.

25   Reid hears something else, when his "geek" friends and colleagues are talking. "Knowledge is what's valued in this industry, and that's how people speak," he says. "There's a rapid-fire passing back and forth of facts, it's almost like a pissing contest, in the way it sounds. But it's just exchanging knowledge. There's no wisdom or value attached."

26   Jargon, of course, be it mathematical, scientific, computer-specific, has crept into everyday speech. Jeffrey calls it the democratizing of expert knowledge. And Thompson notes the binary influence on the spoken English of people who use programming languages. Take the use by geeks of "non"—as in the dry observation that a total system crash is a "non-trivial problem."

27   He also argues that the style of discourse has fundamentally changed.

28   "E-mail created an entirely new style of argument and discussion," he says, referring to the cut-and-paste back-and-forth. He compares it to the passing back and forth of illuminated manuscripts between medieval monks, who left wide margins for each other's comments—only that process took years. "This is: Here's what you said right back at you. You can't get away from your words."

QUESTIONS

Understanding the message: Comprehension

1. In what way does Jamie Reid's response in paragraph 3 "illustrate his own point" about the way the Internet world affects him?

2. Name three ways that the Internet has affected our use of written language.

3. What caused the "explosion" of Internet use in 1995?

4. Why are people writing more than they used to, according to Clive Thompson of *Shift* magazine?

5. What are the six "languages" in Robert Logan's book, *The Sixth Language*?

Examining the structure and details: Analysis

1. In what way(s) does Nolen's article prove Liss Jeffrey's point that "New horizons open up and we . . . have to find ways to describe those places. We create new things, we dream them up, and then we find ways to talk about them"?

2. Examine Nolen's writing in this article: look at the length of her paragraphs, the length and structure of her sentences, and her choice of vocabulary. Do you think her writing reflects the changes in language that she's talking about? Why or why not?

3. In what ways is the "Internet" language more immediate than previous languages? In what ways is it less logical?

Formulating a response: Inference and interpretation

1. Nolen suggests that the Internet is altering our use of language on a multitude of levels—writing, speaking, even thinking. Do you agree with this assessment? Why or why not?

2. Do you agree with Eric McLuhan that English was the only language capable of hosting this shift in the way we communicate?

3. Is thinking in the new "Internet" language an advantage or disadvantage? Why?

Essay questions

1. Write an e-mail message in which you provide examples of communication styles of people that you know well. How is each distinct?

2. Has the Internet or the use of e-mail had a significant impact on your own life? How? Provide specific examples to illustrate your point.

3. Find an example of writing in a newspaper or Web page that you think illustrates the principles being discussed in the article. What about this piece of writing reflects Nolen's ideas about how language has changed? What contradicts her ideas? Do you agree with her? Cite examples from both articles in your essay.

VOCABULARY

inductive: a method of logical reasoning, moving from specific instance to general rule

ubiquitous: everywhere at once, all the time

visceral: at an instinctive level

Marshall McLuhan: Canadian communications theorist (1911–1980)

Sumer: ancient Mesopotamian culture, often considered the birthplace of civilization

syntax: pattern of words or parts in a language

vestigial: trace; left over

discourse: communication in words

Canada, My Canada

by Tomson Highway (b. 1951)

Tomson Highway is a Cree from Brochet, in northern Manitoba. He is the celebrated author of the plays The Rez Sisters *(1986) and* Dry Lips Oughta Move to Kapuskasing *(1989), both of which won Dora Mavor Moore Awards and Floyd S. Chalmers Awards, and the novel* Kiss of the Fur Queen *(1998), which was nominated for both a Canadian Booksellers Association Libris Award and the Chapters/Books in Canada First Novel Award. His most recent novel is* Caribou Song *(2001). He holds three honorary degrees and is a member of the Order of Canada.*

PRE-READING

In this paean to Canada from the *Imperial Oil Review* (2000), Highway provides a series of examples as to why our country is great. Before reading the essay, think about what Canada means to you. When you think about our country, which of its characteristics do you feel are best? Which are worst? In what ways do you think the United Nations' assessment of Canada as "the best country in the world in which to live" is true?

Three summers back, a friend and I were being hurtled by bus through the heart of Australia, the desert flashing pink and red before our disbelieving eyes. It seemed never to end, this desert, so flat, so dry. The landscape was very unlike ours—scrub growth with some exotic cacti, no lakes, no river, just sand and rock forever. Beautiful, haunting even—*what the surface of the moon must look like,* I thought as I sat in the dusk in that almost empty bus. 1

I turned to look out the front of the bus and was suddenly taken completely by surprise. Screaming out at me in great black lettering were the words CANADA NO. 1 COUNTRY IN THE WORLD. My eyes lit up, my heart gave a heave, and I felt a pang of homesickness so acute I actually almost hurt. It was all I could do to keep myself from leaping out of my seat and grabbing the newspaper from its owner. 2

As I learned within minutes (I did indeed beg to borrow the paper), this pronouncement was based on information collected by the United Nations from studies comparing standards of living for 174 nations of the world. Some people may have doubted the finding, but I didn't, not for an instant. 3

Where else in the world can you travel by bus, automobile or train (and the odd ferry) for ten, 12 or 14 days straight and see a landscape that changes so spectacularly: 4

the Newfoundland coast with its white foam and roar; the red sand beaches of Prince Edward Island; the graceful curves and slopes of Cape Breton's Cabot Trail; the rolling dairy land of south-shore Quebec; the maple-bordered lakes of Ontario, the haunting north shore of Lake Superior; the wheat fields of Manitoba and Saskatchewan; the ranch land of Alberta; the mountain ranges and lush rain forests of the West Coast. The list could go on for pages and still cover only the southern section of the country, a sliver of land compared with the North, the immensity of which is almost unimaginable.

5   For six years in a row now the United Nations has designated Canada the No. 1 country in which to live.

6   We are so fortunate. We are water wealthy and forest rich. Minerals, fertile land, wild animals, plant life, the rhythm of four distinct, undeniable seasons—we have it all.

7   Of course, Canada has it problems. We'd like to lower the crime rate, but ours is a relatively safe country. We struggle with our health-care system, trying to find a balance between universality and affordability, but no person in this country is denied medical care for lack of money. Yes, we have our concerns, but in the global scheme of things we are well off.

8   Think of our history. For the greater part, the pain and violence, tragedy, horror and evil that have scarred forever the history of too many countries are largely absent from our past. There's no denying we've had our trials, but they pale by comparison with events that have shaped many other nations.

9   Our cities are gems. Take Toronto, where I have chosen to live. My adopted city never fails to thrill me with its racial, linguistic and cultural diversity. On any ordinary day on the city's streets and subway, in stores and restaurants, I can hear the muted ebb and flow of 20 different tongues. I can feast on food from different continents, from Greek souvlaki to Thai mango salad, from Italian prosciutto to Jamaican jerk chicken, from Indian lamb curry to Chinese lobster.

10   And do all these people get along? Well, they all enjoy a life of relative harmony, co-operation and peace. They certainly aren't terrorizing, torturing and mas-sacring one another. They're not igniting pubs, cars and schools with explosives that blind, cripple and maim. And they're not killing children with machetes, cleavers and axes. Dislike—rancour, even—may exist here and there, but not, I believe, hatred of the blistering intensity we see elsewhere.

11   Is Canada a successful experiment in racial harmony and peaceful coexistence? Yes, I would say so—and proudly.

12   When I, as an aboriginal citizen of this country, find myself thinking about all the people we've received into this beautiful homeland of mine, when I think of the mil-lions to whom we've given safe haven, following agony, terror, hunger and great sad-ness in their own home countries, well, my little Cree heart just puffs up with pride. And I walk the streets of Canada, the streets of my home, feeling tall as a maple.

QUESTIONS

Understanding the message: Comprehension

1. What are the specific characteristics that Highway loves best about Canada?

2. In what ways does Highway suggest that Canada is better than other nations?

3. For Highway, what is the most important factor that makes Canada great?

Examining the structure and details: Analysis

1. Discuss Highway's use of descriptive phrases in the opening of his essay. How does he emphasize his feelings about Australia?

2. Highway uses a broad array of sensory details and specific names in his many examples. Examine some of these details, and consider how they strengthen the point he's making.

3. How does Highway address the negative points in his essay? In what way does he try to minimize their impact?

Formulating a response: Inference and interpretation

1. In the sixth paragraph of his article, Highway tells why he believes Canadians are fortunate people and lists examples of the advantages our country offers us. Is his a fair assessment? What, if anything, does he leave out?

2. Does Highway convince you that Canada is a "successful experiment in racial harmony and peaceful coexistence"? Why or why not?

3. Are Highway's examples varied enough in their sources? Do you think he should have chosen other sources of information? Why or why not?

4. Who is Highway's audience in this essay? Do his language and choice of examples relate to this audience effectively?

Essay questions

1. Think about the place you live: this can be your home, your town, your city, or your province. What do you love most about living there? Provide a varied selection of examples to demonstrate what makes the place great.

2. Canada has often been voted "Number One Place to Live in the World" by the United Nations. Do you think this assessment is valid? Explain why or why not in a short essay.

3. Does Highway's article include all of the *most* important factors to consider when deciding what makes a place great to live in? Explain whether his assessment is comprehensive enough or what he may have left out and why. Refer to the article in your response.

VOCABULARY

hurtled: thrown with great force

cacti: plural of *cactus*

souvlaki: meat sandwich

prosciutto: kind of sliced ham

jerk: spicy Caribbean seasoning

rancour: bitter resentment or ill feelings

CHAPTER 6

Process

PROCESS IN DAILY LIFE

Like most people, you probably already use process in a typical day. Real-life use of process happens when you engage in activities such as the following:

- You leave a note for your grandmother explaining how to program the VCR.
- You explain to a friend how the Edmonton Oilers hockey team used teamwork to win their last game.
- You tutor your younger brother on how to beat the odds so that he can win at a particular video game.
- In an essay exam, you explain how friction works to help move your car when it's stuck in mud.

WHAT IS PROCESS?

If in your past you ever disassembled a radio or computer hard drive in an effort to understand how the various parts are connected and interact, you were conducting research on process. Process looks at the steps involved in something, whether they explain "how-to" (the steps you'd read in recipes or directions for building a model airplane) or "how does it work?" (how parts of a computer are linked to each other so that the whole machine functions or how the process of condensation works in a terrarium). **Process** separates a procedure or operation into disparate steps or segments, so that we can examine how these segments interrelate.

There are two basic types of process. The first is directive: it provides directions or instructions on *how to do something*. Presumably, **directive process** allows your reader to reproduce a process according to directions and accomplish an identical outcome to that being described: a recipe allows the reader to reproduce the same cake or meatloaf that the author made; the instructions for assembling a model Corvette allow each hobbyist to end up with a reproduction of the car.

The second type of process is purely informative: it provides information on *how something works* or *how something happens*. **Informative process** is directed at readers who don't intend to recreate the process, but simply wish to have an overall understanding of it. When you write about how a motorcycle engine works or how lightning is formed, you're writing an informational process.

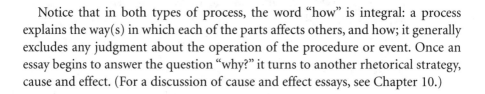
Notice that in both types of process, the word "how" is integral: a process explains the way(s) in which each of the parts affects others, and how; it generally excludes any judgment about the operation of the procedure or event. Once an essay begins to answer the question "why?" it turns to another rhetorical strategy, cause and effect. (For a discussion of cause and effect essays, see Chapter 10.)

WHY USE PROCESS?

People use process to help explain complex or multifaceted topics: when many steps are required to reach an outcome or an operation is too complex to be understood with a cursory examination, a process is called for. When you read a business magazine to find out how mutual funds function, for instance, you understand more fully why investing can be a risky business. When you read a pamphlet explaining how HIV spreads, you understand more fully the dangers of AIDS and why it's important to avoid sharing needles, to have protected sex, and to assume other precautions against spreading the virus.

A process may also allow someone to reproduce a set of actions or a final outcome. When you follow directions for a recipe, you expect the result to match that in the cookbook. When you follow your friend's instructions for downloading an MP3 file from the Internet, you expect to end up with a file that allows you, too, to listen to music on your computer.

HOW TO WRITE A PROCESS ESSAY

Unless the directive process is actually meant to appear in an instruction manual, providing instructions alone may not be enough to retain a reader's interest. When writing process essays, it's important to keep the language as lively and engaging as possible. Be sure to use lots of description, narration, or other techniques to help illustrate each of the steps. You can also increase interest through the organization or tone of your essay, as in a humorous piece on "how to choose a mate."

As you work through the pre-writing, writing, and post-writing stages discussed in Chapter 2, supplement the general steps with the following tips that apply specifically to process essays.

Pre-Writing

1. Choose a general topic

As with almost any kind of writing, the process essay will be more enjoyable to write, more interesting, and more effective if you choose a topic that you already know something about or in which you already have a great interest. In particular, if you've participated in or observed the process firsthand, you've already got a head start with your topic.

TIP

Stick to the familiar

Process essays needn't be overly complex or unique to be interesting; the topic "how to clean a house effectively" could conceivably be brimming with useful tips for readers, and "how to stay on your diet" will undoubtedly hold an audience's attention. What's most important is that your own knowledge of and interest in the process shine through in the writing.

2. Consider your audience and purpose

In thinking about your audience, ask yourself if they will perceive your topic as worthwhile. If you teach your readers something they wish to know, such as "how to build a deck," they will undoubtedly read on simply to learn the steps in the process. However, if the topic isn't one to which they are naturally drawn, the readers may not be willing to slog through a series of steps unless they are either well entertained or well informed. If you choose a topic such as "how to wash your hair," you'll need to infuse it with a healthy dose of humour to transform it into an engaging essay.

SNAG

Expecting the reader to read your mind

One of the differences between speaking and writing (and one that can make the latter more challenging) is that writing allows no immediate interaction between sender and receiver. If your listener doesn't understand something you say, s/he can simply ask, "Would you explain that again?" or "Can you clarify?" but a reader must make do with only your words on the page. As a result, it's often much easier simply to demonstrate to your audience how to do something than it is to explain the same technique in writing (this is why so many college and university "how-to" courses include lab sessions or hands-on components). If you're skeptical, just imagine telling someone how to make a bed, brew some coffee, tie shoelaces, or play a stereo *without* the benefit of an actual bed, shoe, coffeepot and coffee, or stereo and CDs in front of you—and using nothing but words! Clearly, a good process must include *very specific details* about time, movement, materials, actions, and so on. Determining your readers' current level of knowledge will help ensure that your essay conveys all the information the readers need to know.

3. Generate ideas about the topic

One of the best ways to generate ideas for process essays is the journalist's method: it allows you to run through all the steps, potential hazards, or unforeseen obstacles and to consider the audience as you answer the questions "Who?" "What?" "When?" "Where?" "Why?" and "How?" As you imagine each of the steps in the process, keep in mind any special considerations that might not be immediately obvious.

4. Narrow to a thesis

Whether you're writing a directive or informative essay, your thesis should provide a general sense of the major stages or phases of the process. This text, for instance, divides the process of writing into pre-writing, writing, and post-writing stages, although there are many more steps within each of the three major categories. A straightforward thesis for a directive process on this topic is "There are three major steps to writing a good essay." A thesis for an informative process essay, such as "performing CPR [cardiopulmonary resuscitation] requires knowledge, skill, and nerves of steel," also provides a general sense of the three main parts of the process, each of which can be transformed into a paragraph or more in the essay. Once you work through the steps or stages of the process in your own mind, determine the *major* divisions and formulate your thesis to include these.

5. *Organize your ideas in an outline*

Planning requires special attention in process essays, since one omission of even a small step can sabotage the entire process. Think through all the steps in a process to ensure that none is left out. Once you've determined a list of all steps, group them together into three or more larger steps or phases. For instance, in a paper explaining how to write a personal ad, you might find that the total number of steps can be further separated into three major phases: polling your friends for information, listing all your traits on paper, and revising the list so that you sound irresistible. By planning, you avoid the risk that you'll need to go back and insert extra steps or even rewrite portions of the essay.

While it's most common (and logical) to write a process in chronological order, there are some exceptions. If you write about "how to plan a wedding," for instance, some of the steps may overlap or occur simultaneously: you find the hall before sending out invitations but may be searching for a dress throughout the first few stages of the process. Similarly, an essay on "how to argue productively" also includes steps that may overlap (for example, try to empathize with the other person, state

TIP

Take an imaginary journey

Whether you write an informative or directive process, it's a good idea to start with a complete list of *every single step* by working through the process from beginning to end in your mind. This way, you'll guarantee that nothing essential is left out (you can always eliminate any unnecessary steps later on).

To test whether you've included enough, or appropriate, details in a directive process, try out the steps yourself. If possible, work through a directive process one step at a time, following the instructions *exactly* as written. Have you left out any essential information ("You mean you need to have a separate container for each of the salt and the acid?")? Are the steps clearly explained and easy to follow? Working through the process will help to uncover omissions or confusing areas that require more revision.

Keep your audience in mind

To determine which steps are *absolutely* necessary in a process, consider your audience's knowledge of the topic. If you address an audience of professional chefs, a process for making spaghetti sauce from scratch need not include specific details about how to blanch tomatoes, how to chop garlic, and so on; presumably, these culinary experts have already mastered such skills. If you are writing for novice cooks, however, you would need to start the process at an earlier stage and provide more details.

With steps, more is more

If you're uncertain about whether to include or exclude a detail, err on the side of excess; your readers would rather be reminded of a step they already know than be left in the dark because you omitted something they didn't know (which you assumed they did).

your own case unemotionally, really listen to what your partner says). In this second example, the overall structure is chronological, but there's some room for flexibility within each of the major steps. Seek an organization that works logically within the process you're explaining.

6. Decide on specific support for the main points

Because they often rely on a reader's ability to visualize the steps involved, process essays need specific, concrete details, particularly those that relate to the visual sense. Tell your readers exactly what size, what colour, what dimensions you are writing about. If you explain how to build a doghouse, you must indicate the length and width of boards, the specific style and length of nail, the particular type (or even brand) of glue, and so on; otherwise, your readers' result won't match their (or your) expectations.

As you flesh out the details of your essay, make sure that you indicate any difficulties, potential problems, or hurdles for the reader. Such indications will act both as warning (what to avoid) and motivation to let the reader know that others, too, have encountered such difficulties. For instance, if turning the steering wheel too quickly will cause the tires to squeal, let the reader know that fast turns should be avoided at this stage of the process. Even with a purely informative process, it's useful to highlight potential hazards or difficulties.

Notice that Marlane Press includes both the positive and the negative aspects of her conversion in "How I Converted from No Religion to Judaism," and Eileen Cahill discusses both the benefits and potentially negative responses to the process in "Pet Bereavement."

Writing

Transitional devices (cues to indicate time and sequence), useful in all essays, are indispensable tools when writing process papers. Imagine how confusing a process would be without cues such as "first," "next," or "finally"! Number the steps in the process, if you like, and add other cues for clarity and variety.

As you write about each step, be sure to define any unusual or new terms and to indicate any special materials or tools needed to complete the process. This way, the reader will have all the essential information to carry out the process *before* starting to read. You don't want your reader to undergo the all-too-common hassle of assembling some mechanism according to instructions, only to be struck with a glaring omission once the job is completed ("You mean the frame must be painted *before* the mirror is inserted?").

TIP

Keep it specific

The more exact your instructions in a process, the more easily it will be understood. For instance, rather than writing "stir" in your recipe, it's better to say, "stir for 30 seconds," or "stir until all lumps are removed and the mixture is perfectly smooth." If you can assign a number or measurement to the step, do so.

SNAG

Avoid tedious instructions

One of the most difficult aspects of process writing is to keep it engaging. Why don't people read the manuals that come with their VCRs? The answer is easy: they're often dry and boring to read. If you want your process to sustain the reader's interest, you must include vivid descriptive details, a variety of lively examples, and explanations that make the steps easily comprehensible to the reader. Process essays often use diagrams as well, to illustrate the instructions in a concrete way.

Post-Writing

In addition to the usual steps for post-writing (outlined in Chapter 2), you can strengthen a process essay by asking yourself the following questions:

- Does my thesis make clear what type of process I will write about and the steps involved?
- Have I included all the necessary steps required for my particular audience?
- Have I organized my process in the most effective manner?
- Have I defined all necessary terms and indicated any potential problems or obstacles?
- Have I made the process engaging enough to retain the reader's interest, especially if it's a procedure that might already be familiar?

EXERCISES

1. Following is a jumbled list of directions for an extremely commonplace process—making a peanut butter and jelly sandwich. After carefully examining the steps, put them in the correct order; then, add any steps that have been omitted. Remember, the reader must arrive at the desired goal by following these directions *exactly* as written!

   a. With one knife, spread peanut butter on one slice of the bread.
   b. Cut the sandwich in half.
   c. Get the jelly from the cupboard.
   d. Get another knife from the kitchen drawer.
   e. Put the slices together.
   f. Take two slices of bread out of the bag and place them on a plate, side by side.
   g. Open the jelly jar.
   h. Get the peanut butter from the cupboard.
   i. Be sure that the sides of bread with the peanut butter and jelly on them are on the inside of the sandwich.

2. Think of something habitual that you do and write a process that explains how to do it (imagine that your audience is completely ignorant of this process). Be sure to include *every* step. (Some examples: clean an aquarium, brush your teeth, send an e-mail message, park a car.)

3. Think about an informative process such as how different employees in a bank interact, how the parts in a television set work, or how the body digests food. Write a list of the steps or phases involved, and determine how you would organize them. Must your order be chronological? Why or why not?

The following process essay demonstrates how one student tackled this rhetorical mode. Highlighted are some key elements that help to make this humorous essay effective.

A Student's Guide to Procrastination (or How to Avoid Homework for a Day)

Introduction draws audience in

It's the end of term once again, and along with holiday cheer comes a familiar predicament: you're inundated with assignments, essays and exams, yet with absolutely no motivation to attend to any of them. How can you best deal with this dilemma? According to psychologists, a moderate level of stress can actually motivate people to reach their optimum levels of achievement. Therefore, the most logical recourse is to neglect your homework as long as possible, until you become so hysterically anxious that you can *really* work effectively.

thesis-- includes basic aspect of process

time indicatorj step one

Begin your evasive tactics first thing in the morning: it's important to remain in bed for as long as possible, without arousing the suspicion of your roommate. A good clock radio (one with a "snooze" button) is definitely a worthwhile investment. With this device, you can set the alarm to go off at a respectable hour (such as 7:30 AM) at which time music will softly play for approximately ten minutes before a buzzing noise sounds. When the "snooze" button is depressed, the radio reverts to music for another hour before the buzzer shrieks once more. This way, you make it appear as if you intend to

wake up at 7:30 AM, while repeatedly pressing the
snooze button once each hour for several hours.
Eventually, your roommate will become so annoyed
that she will disconnect the radio and wake you herself. At this point it is advisable to finally wake up
and get dressed. Your roommate does not come
equipped with a "snooze" mechanism, and any
attempts to shut her off could result in your own
bodily harm.

Next, you'll need nourishment for all the hard
work you intend to do. If you've followed the suggested wake-up routine, it will be almost noon
before you're finally ready to eat—but don't suc-
cumb to the temptation to skip breakfast altogether.
Eating only a "brunch" might be an effective
method to save time, but that's exactly what you're
trying to avoid. By enjoying a long, leisurely breakfast, then returning to the cafeteria to restock your
tray with a substantial lunch, you can extend your
mealtime to twice what it would normally be.

After a pleasant lunch, return to your room,
openly expressing a desire to begin studying in
earnest. Don't be misled by this declaration; it is
only a ploy to appease your classmates, for once you
enter your room, you'll discover the ideal excuse to
continue avoiding your studies.

You may suddenly notice that you abandoned
your room in too much of a hurry to make your bed
or tidy up; consequently, you must attend to this
task immediately. At this point, it's effective to
become indignant, declaring that you "absolutely
MUST" clean the entire room "RIGHT NOW,"
because you cannot function with any efficiency
when the room is such a mess. (Of course, the fact
that you habitually do all of your school work in the
library is irrelevant). This inspired urge to tidy up
will keep you engrossed for at least an hour or two.

If perchance you complete this task too quickly
(or if your room was clean to begin with), alternate
activities can be equally fruitless and wasteful. You
may be overwhelmed with the desire to perform

specific details

indicates potential problem

transition

indicates possible problem

transition

RESPOND IN WRITING   NE

one (or several) of the following actions: run to the corner store for a package of cigarettes (non-smokers may substitute gum, chocolate bars, pretzels or chips for the cigarettes); re-organize your desk drawers (otherwise, how would you know where your old movie stubs, rubber bands, half-empty matchbooks, extra coins or coloured markers were when you finally DID sit down to work?); finish that old needlepoint kit you bought two summers ago in Lake Louise; write a thank-you note to Aunt Ursula for last year's birthday present (or substitute your own relative); or any other innovative ideas you may have to complete a task you've been putting off.

By now it will be close to dinnertime. Since you could never immerse yourself completely in work while hungry, why not invite a friend over for dinner? If you are fortunate, the campus cafeteria will be serving its usual fare, and you'll decide to go to a pub off-campus. There, you can relish a delectable meal, along with numerous beers, so that by the time you return to your dorm (at 9:30 PM), you'll be in no condition to study. Consequently, you'll be obligated to watch *Friends* (or a similar television program) for a few hours until the effects of the alcohol diminish. (This also proves to be an entertaining activity, as Phoebe's funky clothes appear much more interesting through an inebriated haze).

Finally, at approximately 11:30 PM, stand up and announce loudly that you intend to set yourself seriously to work. Nevertheless, there still remain several alternatives if you feel you must squander away additional time. At this hour, there's bound to be something interesting on MuchMusic, and watching old rock videos is certainly more impressive than watching *Friends*. You could always decide to take a shower so you'll be fresh and clean before crawling into bed (since your bed is also fresh and clean, a result of your afternoon disinfection of the room).

conclusion

If none of these stratagems is available to you, it is, unfortunately, time to gather your books and head towards your bedroom with the aim of devoting some serious attention to your work. After all, you do have four final papers, three assignments, six lab reports and five tests to study for tomorrow—don't you think it's time to begin working on them?

The Art of a Lure
by Paul Quarrington (b. 1953)

Multitalented in a variety of creative disciplines, Paul Quarrington has been recognized for his work as a novelist, screenplay author, and musician; he is also an avid sports enthusiast and painter. Born in Toronto to parents who were both psychologists, Quarrington began his career as a musician, co-writing the best-selling single "Baby and the Blues" and touring with the Canadian band Joe Hall and the Continental Drift. He gained acclaim as a writer with his first popular novel, Home Game *(1983). Since then, he has published* The Life of Hope *(1985);* King Leary *(1987), which won the Stephen Leacock Medal for Humour;* Whale Music *(1989), which won the Governor General's Award and was also made into a successful motion picture;* Logan in Overtime *(1990);* Civilization and Its Part in My Downfall *(1994); and, most recently,* The Spirit Cabinet *(2000). He has also published nonfiction, such as* The Boy on the Back of the Turtle *(1997). In addition, his screenplay* Perfectly Normal *(1990) won a Genie Award. His love of sports has been incorporated into much of his writing, both fiction and nonfiction. Quarrington lives in Toronto with his wife and two children.*

PRE-READING

Have you ever been fishing? What is the appeal of the sport? What kinds of things do you do when you fish that help increase the catch? If you don't fish, what kinds of sports do you feel excited about? Quarrington's article is reprinted from *Cottage Life* magazine (1999). There is a pun in Quarrington's title. What is it, and how does it contribute to the article?

I find nothing so pleasurable as finishing an evening meal up at the Lodge (an ancient hinterland hotel that several friends and I have pressed into operation as a kind of co-op cottage), walking out to the end of the dock, and firing a fishing lure into the water. Granted, much of the pleasure derives from the fact that I am thereby absenting myself from dish-doing, but on some nights—when the water is absolutely calm and the sunlight toes off the surface—there really is nothing I'd rather be doing. Unless you care to count actually catching a fish. Because fishing with a lure is a dicey business, fraught with uncertainty and contradiction. A case in point: I once purchased a lure, a glowing green baby with fins like a '57 Chevy, designed to catch a huge aggressive piscivorous (don't worry, I'll get to it) specimen, such as the great northern pike. All I managed to catch was my buddy Jake, in the forearm, but that's a whole other story. On the other hand, I was once angling for bait fish, trying to catch shiners with a minuscule golden hook and a shred of worm. *Bang.* I got hit by a pike. Go figure.

2   Actually, though, you needn't go figure, at least not right away, because the editors of this fine periodical have asked me to investigate the subject of fishing with a lure. This is the second time the editors have asked me to investigate angling-related matters, so I thoroughly expect to be added to the masthead. (*Get back to the question, Quarrington: Why do lures work?—Ed.*)

3   All right, all right. Here goes. Everyone agrees that lures work, but, as Ed Crossman puts it, "No-one can conceive of why on earth they *do* work." This admission came as something of a shock, because if Crossman (the noted ichthyologist who co-wrote *Freshwater Fishes of Canada*) doesn't know, who does? "You might ask an angler," he suggested.

4   The trouble is, anglers haven't given the matter all that much thought. At least, most of their thoughts have been focused on specifics. Ask an angler, "Why do lures work?" and you're likely to receive this sort of answer: "Because they're green," or "Because they're red and black," or "Because if you splash this baby down on top of the weeds late in the afternoon in the month of August, it drives 'em nuts."

5   We might begin by wondering how they *might* work. Which is to say, let's consider the nature and acuity of a fish's senses. The subject of sight is the obvious place to start, because some lures have been fashioned in slavish duplication of nature. This is especially true of flies, which have been tied with great entomological care. A Grey Wulff, for example, looks exactly like a mayfly, except that it has a little hook protruding from its belly (and, if I tied it, is wearing a huge gummy turban of thread on its head). These lures are successful due to the manner in which trout (their primary designated target) feed. As mayflies hatch (and rise from the depths to the surface and into the air) the current pushes them downstream. This is like a conveyor belt of food, and trout sit in slower water (off to the side or in the eddy behind a rock) and nibble at their opportunistic pleasure. So the efficacy of a Grey Wulff lies not so much in its looking like a mayfly as in its not looking *unlike* a mayfly, if you see what I mean.

6   Most lures are designed to catch predatory piscivorous species, that is, fishes that are hunting for fishes. Some, therefore, resemble the prey; they are shaped and coloured like a minnow or some other bait fish. The most popular of such lures is the Rapala; the prototype was carved out of balsa wood and painted in realistic detail. It is important to realize that such lures would be fished near the surface. Although they now typically have plastic lips that force them downwards, most are still spied, by the fish, from underneath. What the fish responds to, therefore, is a silhouette.

So, you might wonder, why not just toss in a stick with a couple of hooks stuck 7
in it? From underneath a stick would possess the requisite minnow-like figure.
And, indeed, there exists such a thing as a "stick bait," a dowel with hooks in it that
merely lies on the surface. (The angler actually causes it to twitch, for reasons that
shall become clear.) You might also wonder if the elaborate paint jobs are for the
benefit of the fish or the angler?

For some time scientists bickered over the question of whether or not fish can 8
see colour, but it now seems apparent that in at least some species this is the case.
"There have been some experiments which suggest that they are able to do so,"
acknowledges Crossman. "But what is painted on a lure is not necessarily what
they see, because at depth much of the ambient light has been filtered out." This
might explain the very odd tints and hues you find in a tackle shop. A pink or a
blue lure, at depth, must possess, to the fish, a more natural sheen. I myself am
very partial to chartreuse lures, believing chartreuse to be a colour that, near the
bottom of the lake or in water of considerable murkiness, has the ability to suggest to a fish, "Come on, eat me . . . you know you want to."

If your inclination is to fish with an artificial that imitates the prey, the secret 9
lies in knowing what the fish off the end of your dock are eating. Is the primary
bait fish the silvery shiner or do the bigger fish tend to nibble on little perch, yel-
lowy-greenish and slashed with stripes? Or does the water contain bass on the
prowl for leeches or frogs? Replicas of both are available in the tackle shop, the
frog replicas being perforce more ornate than the leech replicas. Once you embark
on a stratagem of bait imitation, there seem to be no limits. I have seen a little
plastic duckling, powered by a tiny paddle wheel, a bath toy with an evil gang-
hook dangling from the rear. After all, ducklings are delicacies for big fish like the
muskellunge, so the deception does make a certain sense.

It is significant, however, that these types of lures—what we might call replica- 10
tors—are often nowhere near as effective as lures that have no analogue in nature.
What, exactly, is a "Five of Diamonds" imitating? For those of you who might be
unacquainted, let me describe it. It is a "spoon" (actually, you should imagine the
business end of a spoon with the handle cut away) rendered out of shiny painted
metal, and on the convex back there is a pattern of five red diamonds. It is among
the most popular lures in the world. How, exactly, does it work?

There are, I think, two factors to consider. One has to do with the subject we 11
touched on above, colour. While it's true that there are few fish marked by bright
red diamonds, their darkness against the lure makes for sharp contrast. Contrast,
in combination with movement, makes for what I'm going to term "flashing." In
the relatively static underwater world, flashing equals movement, and movement
equals significance. In the little anecdote I cited above, wherein I caught a pike
with a minuscule, barely adorned hook, I cunningly neglected to mention that
just prior to the pike-bang the sunlight had glinted off the metal, making it shine

momentarily like a jewel in the water. Another implication here is this: While anglers have their favourite colours, most would agree that it is a good idea to hedge your bets; get at least *two* colours, so that the contrast (in combination with movement) gives you a bit of flashing. I even employ this philosophy when purchasing lead-headed jigs for still fishing, purchasing ones that have been painted two disparate hues.

12   But all of the above is predicated on the assumption that a fish hunts mainly by sight. While this sense is definitely important to the fish, there is something else we have to consider: the lateral line system. Brian Coad, a research scientist at the Canadian Museum of Nature, notes that it's very hard to describe the lateral line system to a human being. "It's a sense that we don't have," he points out. "Basically, it's like touch at a distance. It would be as if someone entered a room and without seeing them or hearing them or anything like that, you'd just know they were there." So lures, by sending vibrations through the water, alert the fish of their presence.

13   The nature of these underwater vibrations is important. "There is a theory, for example," says Coad, "that sharks never want to eat human beings. But a human being swimming might register like a seal in distress." Which is to say, an erratic series of vibrations suggests to a fish that whatever is in the water is having difficulty getting about. Which is to say, injured. Which is to say, easy pickings.

14   And now we are getting close to an answer, at least a sound theory, of how lures work. And I found just the man to voice it. Noel Alfonso is a research assistant, a colleague of Coad's, but he is also a keen angler. Indeed, he guided at Great Bear Lake, an angling badge of some distinction. So here is his succinct summation: "Lures simulate the flashing, irregular movement of prey."

15   Now you can walk down to the end of your dock armed with scientific theory. First, you have to be reasonably certain that there are piscivorous predatory fish in the vicinity: pike, bass or trout, for example. You should know what the fish typically feed on, so that you can approximate the prey's size and coloration. Make sure that something about the lure flashes; it might be rendered out of metal, it might be bi- or tricoloured so that there is contrast. And—here is where our knowledge of the lateral line plays in—make sure it *moves*. Drag your lure near the dock so that you can actually see its action. A lure that swims surely through the water is not as likely to be effective as one that oscillates up and down or back and forth. I think highly of jointed, articulated lures—two halves linked together by a little swivel so that the bait sashays provocatively as it moves through the water. Vary your retrievals, that is, reel in spurts and starts, jerking the lure. Try different speeds, looking for the one that pushes the "attack" button in the fish's brain. Oh, and by the way, we shouldn't disregard the fish's other senses. Many people scent their lures (there are various malodorous unguents commercially available) and while there is disagreement over whether the new smell is an attractant, at least it

masks human residue (insect repellent, that sort of thing). And a fish can hear, so it's worth investing in a couple of those lures with a little rattle inside.

So I recommend you try this, some beautiful gloaming when the water is still 16 and the light is soft. Try casting a lure off the end of your dock. And always remember this: You could be doing the dishes.

QUESTIONS

Understanding the message: Comprehension

1. What are the reasons that Quarrington enjoys fishing?

2. In which sentence does Quarrington tell us the type of process he's writing?

3. What does Quarrington mean when he writes, "So the efficacy of a Grey Wulff lies not so much in its looking like a mayfly as in its not looking *unlike* a mayfly"?

4. What is the reason that the "Five of Diamonds" works, according to Quarrington?

Examining the structure and details: Analysis

1. What rhetorical mode(s) besides process does Quarrington use to a great degree in the article? How do they help to develop his ideas?

2. What three types of lures does Quarrington discuss?

3. At one point, the article inserts a comment from its editor, who writes, "Get back to the question, Quarrington: Why do lures work?" What effect does this intrusion have on the essay?

Formulating a response: Inference and interpretation

1. In what way(s) does Quarrington's relaxed style suit the subject matter? Provide examples.

2. Do you believe Quarrington's explanations of how lures work? What flaws might there be in his reasoning? Do you have any other theories as to how lures work?

3. By the time you finish reading "The Art of a Lure," do you feel that you understand how lures work? Why or why not?

Essay questions

1. Write an essay in which you discuss the process of using a particular tool or piece of equipment. You could focus on a sport (for example, how to shoot a puck, how to surf), a household task (for example, how to mow the lawn, how to load a dishwasher), or something work related (for example, how to operate a forklift, how to assemble a stereo speaker).

2. In what ways do sports enthusiasts or athletes artificially enhance or improve their performance? Apart from fishing, you might consider sports such as bird watching, hunting, wrestling, skiing, or others.

3. Although Quarrington is himself a fisherman, he consulted with a variety of experts in compiling his article and used information that he himself had picked up through the sport as well. Does he achieve an effective balance between personal anecdote and scientific evidence? Why or why not? Use specific references to the article to support your answer.

VOCABULARY

ichthyologist: zoologist specializing in fishes

acuity: sharpness

entomological: of or dealing with insects

piscivorous: eating primarily fish

balsa wood: lightweight wood often used in the building of models

ambient light: light contained in the natural surroundings

chartreuse: yellowish green

perforce: necessarily

analogue: match, something similar

unguents: ointments

gloaming: twilight or dusk

My Conversion from No Religion to Judaism

by Marlane Press (b. 1971)

Marlane Press is a journalist who lives with her husband on the east side of Vancouver. Since completing her studies at Langara College and the University of British Columbia and travelling the globe for 12 months, she has written for various publications, including the Vancouver Sun, *the* Globe and Mail, Western Living Magazine, *and the* Vancouver Courier. *She is also the Pacific correspondent for the* Canadian Jewish News. *After writing the following article, Press completed her conversion with a mikvah (ritual bath) and subsequently wrote about her first Christmas/Chanukah as a Jewish person.*

PRE-READING

In this piece (originally published in the *Globe and Mail* in 2000), Marlane Press discusses the process of adapting to a new religion. Can you imagine changing your religion? What circumstances might prompt such a shift? What are the challenges that would face someone who embraces a new religion? What about the challenges of an interfaith marriage? What is your opinion about people of different faiths marrying?

I will never forget the conversation I had with a rabbi soon after I made the decision 1
to convert to Judaism. I served him and his wife breakfast in the restaurant where I then worked. Don't ask me how we got onto the topic of my conversion, but he had an incredible impact on me. I don't usually have such a meaningful, memorable conversation before 8 a.m. Perhaps that's why his words have stayed with me for so long.

He told me that Judaism is fortunate to have someone like me who is enthusi- 2
astic and fascinated about committing to become a Jew. Flippantly, I asked him if Judaism is lucky because it is gaining a Jew in me or because it isn't losing one in my Jewish partner. He chuckled and took a sip of his decaffeinated non-fat latte. I held my breath, afraid that I had offended him.

An interesting question, he mused, and dove into his cholesterol-free omelette. 3
My breakfast-serving tact kicked in and I left him in mid-chew.

Unfortunately, I never received an answer. It's now more than 18 months later, 4
and I'm still pondering his comment and many larger questions: Does Judaism even want me? Will I ever truly identify as Jewish?

5   When I told my Jewish partner that I would convert, I could not have imagined how overwhelmed I would later feel. I did not take the decision lightly, but I never thought it would make me feel so confused. Since we began dating six years ago, I have endeavoured to learn more about Richard's religious and ethnic identification. Learning about a Jewish home, celebrating Shabbat, Pesach, Rosh Hashanah and the like are satisfying my lifelong curiosity about Judaism and my historical familial connection (my paternal great-great-grandmother was a Polish Jew).

6   There is no question that my imminent marriage in August prompted my conversion. While I realize Jewish law has always discouraged conversion for the sake of marriage, I believe my sincere conversion can actually serve to enrich the Jewish community and family that immediately surround us, and even perhaps on a larger scale.

7   I was not raised with any religious teachings. My mother is a Catholic who refused to bring my sister and me up in the same strict religious environment in which she was raised; my father is a non-practising Protestant. If anything, I thought it would be easy to convert since I had no religion to abandon.

8   And it's not as though I made a hasty decision, found a suitable synagogue and rabbi, and started the process immediately after deciding to convert. My fiancé and I have just returned from a one-year trip around the world. We've both had plenty of time to discuss and think. Easy. Hah. What an oversimplification.

9   The largest hurdle the conversion has erected is accepting the fact that many Jews will not recognize my Reform conversion. Despite the fact we will raise our children in the Jewish faith, Israel won't accept my children. I can now read Hebrew, have read most of the Five Books of Moses, innumerable Judaica books—the list goes on. Many of our Jewish friends are impressed that I know more about their history and religion than they do.

10   But it's not simply about reading and studying; it's about feeling Jewish and experiencing life Jewishly. My Reconstructionist rabbi, in his New Age way, tells me I must own a piece of Judaism to truly feel a part of it. Can I "feel" it before my July mikvah?

11   In the few months since my initial meeting with our rabbi, I've been in tears during the Shabbat candle lighting and prayers, and again during several meetings with our wonderfully understanding rabbi at Or Shalom Synagogue in Vancouver.

12   Fortunately, I have enrolled in an immersion and conversion class with some people who identify as Jews, some who identify as non-Jews—and some who feel they are in between, like me.

13   As we went around the circle introducing ourselves, a Jewish man divulged that he had wept bittersweet tears during his first prayers many years after he had renounced God and religion.

14   His experience gives me great hope and relief because it reaffirms that I'm not alone in feeling overwhelmed. Although I never renounced God, I felt—because of the omission of religion in my life—I had no right to a personal relationship with God.

I don't know exactly why I cry (and I write that in the present because it is 15
ongoing), but I know they aren't tears of sadness. I'm confident that I will soon
have a better understanding of where they originate. I've mentioned that my
paternal great-great-grandmother was Jewish. Could my tears be for her? Any
journey home is an emotional one.

I've read that, in the Bible, when the Israelites were given the Torah, their 16
response was: "We shall do and we shall hear." In other words, they promised to
act first and hear or understand second. To leap before looking. I feel that's what
I'm doing. I still don't have the answer to the questions I asked the rabbi nearly
two years ago, but perhaps I don't need it articulated by him. The answer to most
of my questions and initial doubts are within me. Eventually, they will surface.

For now, I'll just continue leaping.   17

QUESTIONS

Understanding the message: Comprehension

1. List the two ways in which Press's conversion is a benefit to the Jewish people.

2. What are the reasons Press gives that influenced her decision to convert? What were her links to Judaism before she made this decision?

3. What aspects of the experience surprised Press as she went through the conversion? What were the major problems she encountered?

Examining the structure and details: Analysis

1. In her account, Press does not separate the process into clearly discernible steps. Can you identify discrete stages that she writes about? Which type of process does she write?

2. How are the introduction and conclusion connected to each other in this essay? Do they create an effective framework for the body of the essay? Why or why not?

3. Which details does Press include to help convey the sense that religious conversion is more than following a series of steps, but also involves a spiritual and psychological component?

Formulating a response: Inference and interpretation

1. What is your reaction to Press's conversion? Do you finish reading the article with a sense that she made a good choice? Why or why not?

2. Which parts of the process seem illogical or unfair to you? Do you think these are insurmountable obstacles? Why or why not?

3. How does Press feel about her conversion at the time of the writing? Which details serve to express this feeling?

4. Who do you think is Press's intended audience for this selection? Why?

Essay questions

1. Discuss the challenges that would ensue if someone of your own religion or spiritual outlook were to marry someone of another religion (it need not be Jewish; choose any religion other than your own). In a process essay, write about how the two parties could overcome any potential difficulties they might face in such a union.

2. Have you or someone you know had to adapt after entering a new group (such as peers at a new school, co-workers at a new job, or in-laws in a new family)? Discuss the process of adapting to this new role and how you learned to fit in.

3. At the end of the essay, Press writes that she feels an affinity to the Israelites in the Bible, who "promised to act first and hear or understand second." Using specific examples from her essay, demonstrate how Press has also kept this promise in her own process of conversion.

VOCABULARY

Shabbat, Pesach, Rosh Hashanah: Jewish religious holidays: Sabbath, Passover, Hebrew New Year

Reform, Reconstructionist, Orthodox, or Conservative Judaism: different sects within the Jewish religion, with Reform and Reconstructionist being the most liberal

mikvah: ritual bath taken by Jews for purification on certain occasions

Murder, He Mapped

by Taras Grescoe (b. 1966)

Born in Toronto, raised in British Columbia and Alberta, Taras Grescoe spent four years living in Paris in the early 1990s, writing and teaching English. His journalistic career began in Vancouver where he contributed regularly to Georgia Straight, Vancouver Magazine, *the* Globe and Mail, *and* Beautiful British Columbia. *For the last three years, he has lived in Montreal and written articles for* National Geographic Traveler, *the* New York Times, *and* Delta Sky. *He's also a contributor to Quebec's most important French-language newsmagazine,* L'actualité. *As a freelancer, he's made a specialty of explaining foreign cultures to English-speaking readers, in publications such as* Sunday Review, Times of London, Salon *magazine,* Face, Condé Nast Traveler, *and the* L.A. Times. *He's also written for* Wired, Saveur, *and the* Chicago Tribune Magazine *and appeared as a substitute for William Safire, the* New York Times Magazine's *distinguished columnist. He won a Western Magazine Award in 1996 and has won two National Magazine Awards. His travel writing has been anthologized in two of the* Traveler's Tales *collections (*Paris *and* The Adventure of Food*), and his first book,* Sacre Blues: An Unsentimental Journey through Quebec *(2000), was nominated for two Quebec Writers' Federation Awards.*

PRE-READING

Think about how crime affects you. Is crime that affects a large city different from crime in other locations? What do the police do to unearth criminals who evade detection? Do you feel that your city is being safeguarded effectively against crime? Is the computer an effective tool for dealing with criminals? Consider these questions as you read Grescoe's article, which first appeared in *Canadian Geographic* magazine in 1996.

It started on the night shift in Vancouver's crime-ridden Downtown Eastside. Kim Rossmo, a beat cop juggling a full-time career and a full load of courses in criminology at Simon Fraser University, realized that the criminal activity he was witnessing every night wasn't completely random. There was a geographic logic to the choice of crime sites—not much different from the kinds of decisions people make when they're choosing a grocery store—and a lot of it could be explained, and even predicted, by new research in criminology. He began considering the possibility that what he was studying at school, along with advances in computer mapping, might help him and his colleagues become more effective criminal investigators.

2   Eight years later, Detective Inspector Rossmo, the first working cop in Canada with a doctorate in criminology, is getting a chance to test the investigative technique that he developed during his studies. On an overcast afternoon, Rossmo has left behind his police headquarters desk spread with street plans to re-visit the scenes of a series of murders, the last of which occurred six years ago. Over a two-year period, four women were found beaten and strangled to death, their bodies abandoned in back lanes throughout Vancouver. Rossmo pulls into a curving, unpaved alley in Shaughnessy, one of Vancouver's oldest, wealthiest neighbourhoods, and parks behind a sprawling stone mansion. "The body was found here, at this end of the lane," says Rossmo, leaning meditatively against the open door of his unmarked police car. "There's a hedge on one side, and a fence on the other. That gave the offender cover to take the body out of the vehicle, which was essentially a one-minute operation." Karen Taylor, a 19-year-old prostitute, was found on this spot, the killer's fourth and last victim. All the women were strangers to the killer, selected at random from street corners in the city's red-light districts. Then, just as suddenly as it started, the crime spree ended. There were no witnesses, no descriptions, no solid suspects. The only trace left by the killer: four agonizing points on a map.

3   This is the third body dump site Rossmo has visited this week, and he's still not exactly sure what he's looking for. More than anything, the inventor of geographic profiling—an innovative computer mapping technique that uses crime sites to predict the homes or workplaces of serial rapists, arsonists and murders—is hoping that by trading the map's two dimensions for the three in the real world, he'll be able to pick up on the kind of geographic details a simple street plan can't provide. Getting back into the car, he starts to think out loud: "Shaughnessy has an organic street layout, so I had trouble finding the alley, even though I knew exactly where it was located—its entrance was hidden by hedges. What this suggests to me is that the killer had some knowledge of the area. It's unlikely he lived in this neighbourhood—a psychological profile undertaken by an FBI-trained RCMP violent crime analyst suggested that the offender wasn't well-to-do—but this neighbourhood was part of his mental map of the city. He might have come here randomly, making deliveries, doing itinerant work." Half a block from the alley, Rossmo drives past a sign that reads "No Dumping." It's a detail that might not have any significance; on the other hand, there was an identical sign next to the place where a body was dumped in another back lane. "Which may mean we're dealing with an individual with a very twisted sense of humour." It's also the kind of detail that might eventually help Rossmo decide whether this murder was linked to other unsolved homicides. "Picking up on these kinds of things is the interpretive part of the technique, the art of geographic profiling."

The science, based on the emerging discipline of environmental criminology, 4
is what's attracting Rossmo attention worldwide. Until now, computer mapping's
applications in police work have been limited to better, faster ways of graphically
displaying the sites of crimes in a given city or neighbourhood. But these commercially available systems are little more than elaborate pin maps, good for
throwing simple crime patterns into relief and deciding where to allocate police
resources. In contrast, geographic profiling is a significant new investigative technique. By taking into account what criminologists know about how offenders use
urban geography, Rossmo has created a system that can provide detectives with a
crucial piece of information: the likely home base of a serial criminal.

Back at police headquarters, a sketch of a man in his 30s glowers across 5
Rossmo's desk—a police artist's rendition of a daring killer who taunted and ter-
rorized the Fraser Valley community of Abbotsford early this year. Rossmo nods
towards the drawing as he turns on his computer: "I was called in to do a profile
on that case, but that's about all I can say at this point because the matter is still
before the courts. I can confirm that the person who has been charged was living
within a 1.5-square-kilometre area identified in the profile that I prepared."

Nor can he discuss the details of his profile of the Vancouver prostitute mur- 6
derer. Even though the case has long been consigned to the filing cabinets of the
historical homicide division—along with 170 other unsolved Vancouver murders—it's likely that the killer is still at large.

To demonstrate his geographic profiling system, Rossmo calls on a colour map 7
of Greater Vancouver. Superimposed on the city grid is a graphic record of the
career of John Oughton, a notorious rapist who committed 150 sexual assaults
before he was convicted for 18 of them in 1985. "There are 79 crimes on this screen,"
says Rossmo, "committed over the better part of a decade. Oughton covered a huge
area." At first glance, the spots look as though they are randomly distributed. When
Oughton's apartment was searched, however, investigators found 28 coloured pins
stuck in similar maps of the Lower Mainland. Not only had the rapist been keeping
a record of some of his crimes, he'd been deliberately scattering them to prevent
investigators from finding his home.

Once all 79 spots have appeared on the screen, the computer draws a box 8
around the area of the crime sites, and then divides it into a grid. Starting with
any given point in the grid, it determines the distance from that point to the first
crime site. Using an equation that takes into account criminological research on
typical journeys to crime, the computer calculates the probability of that point
being the offender's home—and then repeats the process for every point on the
grid and every crime site. "In Oughton's case, there were 790,000 calculations to
do," says Rossmo, as the outlines of what looks like a relief map gradually appear
on the screen. "Now what this produces, at the end of the day, is a three-dimensional
space which expresses the probability of offender residence." That "space" is actually

an isopleth map, whose undulating ridges are typically seen illustrating levels of rainfall in a given area.

9   To more clearly display the data, Rossmo prints out a colour version of the same map on a transparency which he then lays over a street plan of Vancouver. The grey areas are the city blocks least likely to be Oughton's home; the red areas are the hot spots, the points of highest probability. "It turns out that because there were so many crimes, the program predicts the offender's home in under one percent of the area." And, in fact, a red dot appears at 37th Avenue and Cambie Street—the location of Oughton's basement suite in 1985. In other cases, it has picked out an offender's probation office or workplace. In situations like the Paul Bernardo case, which had a data base of 3,200 suspects, Rossmo's technique is a powerful winnowing tool, a means of sifting a handful of likely suspects from a vast field of names.

10   What distinguishes geographic profiling from other, simpler computer mapping techniques is its grounding in innovative research on the spatial behaviour of criminals. There's a whole body of literature, little known outside academic circles, that focuses on the geography of human movement at the level of the crime scene. Right-handed criminals, for example, tend to flee to the left, but move to the right when they encounter obstacles; they discard evidence to the right, and stay near outside walls when hiding in large buildings. In crime studies of urban geography, houses on corners are more likely to be burglarized than those in the middle of the street (corner houses offer criminals four, rather than two, escape routes), and neighbourhoods with grid-pattern streets have higher crime rates than those with organic street plans.

11   Rossmo first encountered these ideas while studying under Patricia and Paul Brantingham at Simon Fraser University. Pioneers in the field of environmental criminology, the husband-and-wife team put the emphasis on the geography of the criminal act, rather than the motivations of the criminals—the "where," rather than the "why" of the crime. "About 20 years ago," recalls Paul Brantingham, "Patricia and I were part of a group of geographers, criminologists and urban planners who got together to ask the question, 'What if criminals aren't pathological in a geographic sense?' And it turns out that what we know about the spatial patterns of normal people can be used to predict a lot about criminal behaviour."

12   For example, people are more likely to carry out their routine activities close to home, work or school, or within a set distance from the commuting routes between these points. "According to the least-effort people, if you're looking for a quart of milk," explains Brantingham, "you're more likely to go to the closest convenience store, rather than cross town and skip 27 intervening opportunities." For criminals whose activities include robbery or murder, fear of apprehension creates a buffer zone, with predictable dimensions, around the home. "When people

decide they're going to do a crime, they tend to notice opportunities in the course of doing routine, non-criminal stuff. When a serial killer is looking for a particular type of victim, he'll shape where he's going to look by where he usually goes in his day-to-day activities. And the distance he'll go to look isn't very far. Right around home, he'll have a tendency to go out a short distance, about 250 to 500 metres (several city blocks), so the immediate neighbours don't notice. The farther away he is, the less likely he'll be to look for victims or opportunities."

Not surprisingly, the shape of our activity space—how we choose to drive to 13 work, go shopping, or visit a friend—is related in predictable ways to where we live. What is surprising is how closely the spatial behaviour of criminals, even serial murderers, fits the norm. "There are only a few serial offenders who are so disconnected from humanity that they don't have any anchor points," says Brantingham. "The vast majority have homes and workplaces."

As a graduate student studying under the Brantinghams, Rossmo realized that 14 every time a serial criminal chose a new victim, burned down a warehouse, or dumped a body, he was leaving behind a new point on the map—and a more complete portrait of his own activity space. If the Brantingham model was correct—if criminal activity was governed by quantifiable spatial rules like the buffer zone and the least-effort principle—a few points on the map could help predict where a serial killer lived.

While still working the night patrol in Vancouver's skid row, Rossmo wrote 15 some of these rules into a computer program that could be adapted to the geography of any city. He tested it on several notorious historical cases, including the 11 murders committed by British Columbia serial killer Clifford Olson. The program produced a map that pin-pointed a four-square-block area around the child killer's home on Cottonwood Avenue in Coquitlam, just outside Vancouver, even though Olson had dumped bodies as far away as Golden Ears Provincial Park, 26 kilometres away.

Other police officers, getting wind of the new system, asked him to try it on 16 cases where the criminal was still at large. During a series of sexual assaults in Surrey in the early 1990s—the so-called tag team rapes—one of Rossmo's profiles narrowed the search to within less than a square kilometre. (In a subsequent limited-area mail-out, the rapists actually received police letters warning them to be on the lookout for suspicious characters.) Called in to investigate the Mahaffey/French murders in Ontario, Rossmo localized Paul Bernardo's neighbourhood, and was working on narrowing the focus when another sophisticated technique—DNA testing—led to Bernardo's arrest. Rossmo, who has demonstrated his system to Scotland Yard, the FBI's Behavioral Science Unit, and the Dutch police, spends much of his time these days fielding calls from investigators who want to know whether geographic profiling can help them crack both ongoing and long-stalled cases.

17   Rossmo cautions that the technique works in only about two-thirds of all serial crime cases. Although statistically rare, the geographically transient killer, who kills as he crosses the country, is particularly elusive: the murderer never establishes a home for the system to zero in on. "Sometimes there's a linkage analysis problem," says Rossmo. "You may have a number of crimes, and unless there's something really distinctive in the killer's modus operandi, you may not know which ones are connected." In other cases, the points on the map vital to the system are either lacking or unrevealing. Rossmo prefers to work with cases that have at least five or six crime sites, which will reduce the search to under 10 percent of the total area—in some cases a few city blocks. "Offenders often get caught before they commit enough crimes for the profile to work," points out Rossmo. "In other cases, a guy might keep on going back to the same park to dump a body, which gives us several murders but only one point on the map. And if prostitutes are being picked up and murdered in a red-light zone, that can limit the information as well."

18   In the Vancouver murders, the pick-up sites, limited to certain circumscribed districts, tell Rossmo more about where the victims worked than where the killer lived. In fact, according to Vancouver's historical homicide division, there are no firm suspects in the murders Rossmo is currently profiling. Which explains why Rossmo spent his afternoon seeking out a secluded back alley, poking around an old crime site. By selecting prostitutes as his victims, the killer covered his tracks well. Rossmo doesn't want him to think he can get away with it. "I was working patrol in the neighbourhood where one of these girls was working," he recalls. "We can place her on the street within five minutes. Then she just disappeared into thin air." Anything that Rossmo can find to link the crime to any of Vancouver's 170 other unsolved homicides—including a macabre detail like the presence of a "No Dumping" sign—may add another coordinate to his profile. Given enough such points on the map, Rossmo will be able to turn to his computer, narrow the search to a specific neighbourhood or a single block and help investigators close the net on a long-sought killer.

QUESTIONS

Understanding the message: Comprehension

1. In your own words, explain what "geographic profiling" is.

2. Why does Rossmo say that the killer who murdered Vancouver prostitutes has "a very twisted sense of humour"?

3. Explain the difference between the science (technical aspects) of geographic profiling and what Rossmo calls the "art" of it.

4. According to environmental criminologist Paul Brantingham, how does the "least-effort principle" apply to criminals?

5. What are some of the problems inherent in Rossmo's system?

Examining the structure and details: Analysis

1. Before he arrives at the specific and detailed description of how geographic profiling works, Grescoe offers us quite a bit of description and specific examples of other crimes. What effect do these accounts have on the reader?

2. Who is Grescoe's audience for this article? How do you know?

3. In providing information on geographic profiling, Grescoe also uses other rhetorical modes to expand on his subject. Name at least two other techniques that he uses. How do they help to strengthen his article?

4. In addition to describing the process of geographic profiling, what other process does Grescoe cover as he tells his story?

Formulating a response: Inference and interpretation

1. How effective is the geographic profiling that Rossmo uses? Would you feel confident relying on it? Why or why not?

2. Grescoe deals with a topic that is often fraught with strong emotion. Does he reveal his own feelings about the subject matter? How do you know?

3. In your opinion, is geographic profiling more an art or a science? Why?

4. What do you think Grescoe's purpose is in this essay? Do you think he succeeds in achieving it? Why or why not?

Essay questions

1. Write a process in which you describe how something technical or mechanical works. Possible topics include a computer, a CD player, a model train set, a video game, a motorcycle, an alarm clock, or a helicopter.

2. How would you solve a murder mystery? Think of an imaginary criminal being sought for murder (or use the facts about a real one), and describe the process the police went through in order to catch him or her.

3. Could Rossmo's system ever replace the current method of investigating crimes, having police officers attend a site personally and examine it individually? Citing examples from Grescoe's article, explain why or why not.

VOCABULARY

arsonist: someone who sets fires intentionally

organic: developed naturally; not logically planned

itinerant: moving about; not settled in one place

glowers: stares angrily

winnowing tool: tool to narrow down the information; tool to sort information

skid row: a city's run-down area

elusive: difficult to catch or pin down

modus operandi: method of working

macabre: gruesome or bizarre

Pet Bereavement

by Eileen Cahill (b. 1970)

Eileen Cahill graduated from York University in 1995 with a B.A. in Women's Studies and went on to earn a diploma in journalism (1998) from Humber College in Toronto. She is a devoted proponent of animal rights and has worked at the Ontario SPCA (Society for Prevention of Cruelty to Animals) as both a communications officer and a volunteer agent investigating cruelty to animals. She has also volunteered at various animal shelters and has completed an internship at PETA (People for Ethical Treatment of Animals). She is a vegan, currently living and working as an English teacher in Korea.

PRE-READING

Have you ever had a pet that meant a lot to you? What do you think you'd do to get over the pet's death? In this 1999 article from the SPCA's magazine, *Animal Voices,* Cahill outlines the steps that some people have taken to deal with the grief of losing a pet. How do people you know feel about their pets? Can we say that the relationship we have with our pets is similar to that we have with any loved one? How long would it take to recover from the grief of a pet's death?

1   Imagine waking up to find eight of your closest friends gone. That is what happened to Freda White, longtime animal friend and Agent for the Alliston and District Humane Society. In June 1998 she lost four dogs and four cats in a house fire that nearly took her own life as well. Only Freda, her husband and two animals survived: a cat named Gremlin, and a semi-wild cat who hadn't visited on the night of the fire.

2   "She must have had a premonition," Freda said.

3   Believing the dogs had followed her husband to safety, Freda risked her life in an attempt to rescue the cats. She was hospitalized for two months due to burns and smoke inhalation, and spent the first four and a half weeks unconscious and on life-support. Gremlin was badly burned and required seven months hospitalization. When Freda opened her eyes, she thought only a day had passed and didn't know the fate of her companion animals. If she had known, she believes she would have died too. "I still cry every day," said Freda, who never goes to bed without talking to her animals and is still grieving despite support from family and friends.

4   Juliana Thomas also suffered a devastating shock when her horse, Hyden, died in a fire only three days before Christmas 1997, when Juliana was 17 years old. The fire also killed 16 other horses.

5   Juliana's mother, Susan, received a phone call at 1:00 in the morning, and they immediately drove to the burning stable. The worst part, she remembers, was seeing the horses' charred bodies the next morning. Later, Juliana wouldn't let the family light a fire in the fireplace. "She couldn't look at fire," said Susan, who is still horrified when she thinks about what the horses went through. The fire changed not only Juliana's life, but the whole family's.

6   "There was a lot of sadness," Juliana said.

7   Julie Brooks, a social worker and bereavement counsellor who works with funeral homes in the Hamilton area, helps people cope with human deaths as her main responsibility. Through the Hamilton SPCA, she also runs a monthly support group for people who have experienced pet loss. Brooks believes there is "a complete parallel" between pet bereavement and human bereavement. In both cases, she stressed, grief lasts "as long as it takes," explaining that the length and severity of the process depends on the relationship, as well as the circumstances of the death. For example, those who lose pets suddenly may experience more severe, long-lasting grief than others. Brooks said it's normal to feel less emotionally stable for the first year or two after a pet dies, and to think about the pet from time to time for the rest of one's life.

8   Dr. Cindy Adams, Associate Professor at the University of Guelph's Ontario Veterinary College (OVC) and client relations specialist at the OVC Small Animal Hospital, has observed an important distinction between the experiences of bereaved pet guardians and those who have lost human friends or family members: Grief over a pet is less socially acceptable.

9   "I felt embarrassed that I was crying for animals when other people lose children, but they were children to us," Freda said, remembering how one of her dogs, Sasha May, had her own box of toys and wore boots in the winter.

10   Dr. Adams pointed out that unlike human death, few rituals accompany pet death. This means bereaved pet guardians are usually forced to grieve privately, and can benefit greatly from the support of a caring veterinarian. In light of the research she has conducted into this issue, Dr. Adams is currently integrating bereavement counselling into the college's curriculum, so future veterinarians will be better prepared to help their clients cope with grief.

11   The Hamilton SPCA's support group was initiated in response to a need for a safe, nonjudgmental environment where participants could talk about their feelings. Brooks encourages members to share their feelings and bring in pictures of their pets, and reassures them that what they're feeling is normal. She also offers written materials about the grief process as it relates to companion animals. In addition to those who have lost pets through death, the group also includes

people whose pets have disappeared, or been stolen or given away. Sometimes people anticipating the death of a pet will also attend the support group to prepare for the experience.

Kim-Marie Dallaire, an Aurora energy work practitioner who helps humans 12 and animals through Earth-centred practices such as Reiki and therapeutic touch, said guilt over the death of her cat, Mischief, will stay with her for some time. Kim had adopted a new kitten, Taz, as a companion for Mischief, unaware that Mischief had FIV, the virus associated with feline AIDS. Taz introduced worms and other illnesses into the household, which proved too much for Mischief's immune system. His liver started to fail, and Kim only learned about alternative treatments six months after his death.

Guilt is common among bereaved pet guardians, said Brooks. According to 13 Brooks, one of the worst things to say to a person in this situation is, "don't feel guilty." Instead, she suggests asking the bereaved guardian if he or she wants to talk about it, and offering support without judging. Some people, Brooks said, are overcome with guilt after the death of a companion animal—particularly in cases where the animal was "just sort of there" but didn't receive much attention, or has died in an avoidable accident. In cases like these, she suggests keeping a journal, writing a letter asking for the pet's forgiveness, or donating to a charity that helps animals. Kim said her spiritual practices have helped her "tremendously" in coping with Mischief's death, as well as the subsequent deaths of Taz and her dog, Amber. She advises others who have lost pets, "Allow yourself time to grieve and time to heal, and surround yourself with support people and support animals." Spirituality, as Kim understands it, is not limited to formal religious rites; she explained that for some people, "it can be walking in the woods."

When Kim's dog, Amber, died a year and a half ago after a long illness, Kim said 14 she had already done a great deal of anticipatory grieving. Intellectually, Kim knew Amber was free of pain, but still had trouble accepting "the loss of my companion and protector." Amber was severely abused and covered in motor oil when Kim adopted her, and the two had bonded immediately. Initially, Kim tried to cope with Amber's death by walking in the woods where they used to spend time together.

"I would remember the good things, like Amber chasing wild turkeys, squirrels 15 and hawks," Kim said. One day while walking in the woods, she asked to see Amber, and had a dream about her companion that night. "She was edged in light," Kim said. Amber was running, and looked back at Kim as if asking her to follow. Kim ran with Amber, their feet not touching the ground. Eventually they reached a big rock outcropping, and Amber ran ahead.

When she caught up, Kim saw Amber standing on the rocks, "the wind in her 16 hair." Hawks were circling in the air. Soon Kim realized Amber had a translucent appearance, and understood that this was more than a memory. "She was still looking out for me and knew I needed help," Kim explained. "When I woke up, my pillow was drenched in tears, but my heart felt lighter. I knew she was in a better place."

17 Brooks cautioned bereaved guardians against welcoming another animal too soon, especially as a way of trying to end the grieving process. Although this does help some people, she said, many others find it difficult to relate to a new animal when their attention is still focused on the one who died. When uncertain, Brooks advised taking more time rather than less.

18 One person who has benefited from the companionship of a new animal is Juliana Thomas, who now shares her life with another horse, Lambiek. After Hyden's death, Susan explained, "Juliana was an athlete who had lost her partner. She was lost." Lambiek, Juliana said, has helped her cope.

19 For Kim, animals have always been an important source of support. She explained that her companion animals are "far more than pets. They are family, friends and guides." Her animal friends grieved with her over the deaths of other animals in the household, and helped her function "because I had to feed them even if I didn't want to get out of bed."

20 Freda has adopted another dog and cat as companions for Gremlin, and they are helping her family come to terms with their grief. "But they can't replace the ones I lost," she added.

21 Many people choose to honour a pet's memory by holding a ritual, such as a funeral service, to celebrate the animal's life. Lisa Brooks, owner of the Muskoka Woodlands Cemetery in Huntsville, remembers how one family brought their four-year-old dog, Puppy, to visit the grounds the day before he was euthanized due to terminal cancer. The cemetery is located in a natural forest setting, she explained, with a canopied road where people and animals can walk peacefully. Brooks said the visit was part of the family's grieving process; after the dog's death, they dug his grave by hand and decorated it together. Some time later, another dog entered their lives and they returned to the cemetery to walk their new companion. "It's a nice place to take a walk," said Heather Green, Puppy's human companion, who is grateful to Brooks for providing this service.

22 Other people prefer to have their pets cremated and keep the ashes in a special place, or scatter them in the animal's favourite area. Many veterinarians and humane societies offer cremation services, including the Hamilton SPCA, the Oakville and District Humane Society and the Toronto Humane Society (all Ontario SPCA affiliates). And Dr. Cindy Adams has initiated a creative pilot project at the OVC Small Animal Hospital, which involves providing bereaved pet guardians with a way to remember their companions: A cement disc is set with the animal's paw print and given to the person as a souvenir.

23 Juliana and Susan were too distraught to attend Hyden's memorial service, as were many families who lost horses in the same fire. With permission from the

families, the stable's owner buried the horses on its grounds and Susan visited the grave some time later. Others have never been able to return. Although photographs are a comfort, the family is without other souvenirs of Hyden: Even the blanket she and Juliana had won in a recent competition was lost in the fire.

Freda was unconscious when her animals were buried; their graves are under a 24 tree on the property where the Whites still live. Freda intends to plant a garden in their memory, and said she will never sell the property. "We'll stay here until we die."

QUESTIONS

Understanding the message: Comprehension

1. What is the biggest obstacle for people who wish to engage in formal rituals to grieve for their pets?

2. List the parallels between pet bereavement and human bereavement.

3. What kinds of difficulties accompany pet death that are not part of the process of human bereavement?

Examining the structure and details: Analysis

1. Although Cahill doesn't outline a step-by-step, chronological process of bereavement, she does make clear the stages of the process. How does she identify the different stages so that the reader recognizes the process?

2. What other rhetorical devices does Cahill employ in describing pet bereavement? How do these devices help to make the process more understandable?

3. Cahill uses a fair number of direct quotations from both those who've experienced bereavement and those who are experts on the topic. What effect do these quotations have on the reader?

4. Who is Cahill's audience in "Pet Bereavement"? How do you know?

5. Why does Cahill include two examples about Kim-Marie Dallaire's pets? How do the examples differ from each other?

Formulating a response: Inference and interpretation

1. Why do you think that Cahill opens the article with two narratives of personal stories? How do these affect the reader?

2. What technique(s) does Cahill use to help people understand the intense impact that a pet's death can have on the pet guardian? Is she effective in trying to illustrate this bond and the pet guardian's response? Why or why not?

3. What labels or terms does Cahill introduce when referring to the people who own pets and the pets themselves? How do these terms affect our understanding of the relationship between the animal and the human?

Essay questions

1. Write about your own, or someone else's, experience with bereavement. What stages did the bereaved person experience, and how did s/he eventually overcome the grief?

2. Write an essay in which you support or argue against having formal funerals for pets. What are the benefits of such a ritual? What are the drawbacks?

3. Is Cahill successful in her depiction of animals as being parallel to humans? Does she convince us of this parallel? Would she convince someone who had not had a pet? Using examples from the text, discuss your answer in an essay.

VOCABULARY

euthanized: put to death to avoid suffering of terminal illness

Nature's Cling-Ons
by Candace Savage (b. 1949)

Candace Savage was born in northern Alberta and has spent her life in the west and north of Canada. She is the author of 18 books that span such subjects as wildlife, natural sciences, environmental issues, and women's history. She is a frequent guest at schools, conferences, and festivals. Her recent books include Witches: The Wild Ride from Wicked to Wicca *(2000),* Cowgirls *(1996),* The Nature of Wolves *(1996),* Bird Brains *(1995),* Aurora: The Mysterious Northern Lights *(1994), and* Trash Attack! *(1990). She has been shortlisted for the Bill Duthie Award and the B.C. Book Award for* Bird Brains *and the Science in Society Book Award and the Canadian Science Writers' Association Award for* Aurora *and* Bird Brains. *In addition, Savage has served as news editor of Sun Colour Press and public affairs officer for culture and communications for the Government of the Northwest Territories, Yellowknife, since 1984.*

PRE-READING

For many, the word "parasite" conjures a variety of awful and even horrifying images, such as those in the popular films *Invasion of the Body Snatchers* (parasites that take over our bodies and minds) or *Men in Black* (a parasitic alien that controls a corpse); we think of parasites as opportunistic, destructive creatures that drain us of our energy and very being. No wonder the idea of parasites is so revolting to so many people. In this article from *Canadian Geographic* magazine (1999), Candace Savage takes another look at these unusual creatures and explains how their lives are designed to be efficient and even ingenious. Is there anything positive about parasites? As you read on, draw your own conclusion.

Of all God's creations, few are less appealing to humans than parasites. Like a doctor offering a second opinion to an overweight patient ("all right, you're ugly too"), we pile on the invective: repulsive, revolting, harmful, useless. You know—parasitic. Yet get past the initial disgust and these lowly creatures begin to exert a perverse fascination. They even demand a grudging respect for the ingenuity with which they conspire against their hosts.

Take for example a humble worm known as the lancet fluke. Like many parasites, it passes through several stages in the course of its life, each of which requires a different host. At one juncture, the fluke must pass directly from the body of an ant into a sheep—a transition that would be a lot simpler if the two species ordinarily met. But ants generally stay near the ground, while sheep browse on the tips of vegetation. The fluke overcomes this difficulty by invading the ant in the form of larvae, which infest the nervous system. Under this foreign control, the ant suddenly and unaccountably decides to climb a tall blade of grass and lock its jaws shut on the tip. Unable to escape the lancet fluke's command, the ant has no choice but to await its ovine nemesis.

3   This bizarre plot was unravelled almost 40 years ago by Wilhelm Hohorst and colleagues in Frankfurt, Germany. Parasites, it seems, were not just unwelcome passengers in their hosts' bodies; they were a potent force with an unexpected impact on ecological networks. Who had ever heard of a sheep that ingested ants?

4   Since then, dozens of quirky variations on this alien-invasion theme have been documented by parasitologists. In the early 1970s, for example, William Bethel and John Holmes of the University of Alberta studied the behaviour of small aquatic crustaceans called amphipods. Healthy amphipods, they discovered, prefer to stay near the bottom of ponds, where they are relatively safe from predators. But if they become infected with *Polymorphus paradoxus,* a parasitic worm, they begin to seek the bright lights of the surface. This increases their chances of being eaten by surface-feeders like mallards, muskrats and beavers—the very species within which *P. paradoxus* must complete its life cycle. Amphipods infested with a different worm, *P. marilis,* are drawn only part way up, into the realm of that parasite's ultimate hosts, the diving ducks. And so it goes.

5   Even plants can be subject to hostile takeovers. Blueberries (both wild and cultivated) are afflicted by a disease called "mummy berry," which is caused by a fungus. The first symptoms appear in spring, when tender young leaves are infected by wind-borne spores. The foliage droops and turns brown and the leaves become coated with spores.

6   As unappealing as they are to human eyes, the leaves now attract insects, which crawl over the discoloured surfaces and lick them intently. Under the influence of the disease, the foliage has suddenly begun to produce sugars. What's more, the leaves have also developed ultraviolet markings—visible to insects—which mimic the "nectar-guides" on blueberry blossoms.

7   When the insects bumble off to visit the plant's real flowers, they deposit mummy-berry spores (picked up from the leaves) on the stigmas. As a result of this infection, the blueberry plant produces shrivelled, infertile fruit, within which the fungus survives the winter, ready to resume its dirty tricks next spring.

8   Only occasionally are victims able to shift the balance of power and defend their own interests. For example, bumblebees parasitized by a conopid fly often choose to spend nights out in the cold, rather than seek shelter within the communal nest. By letting their bodies cool, they slow the parasite's growth and may prevent it from maturing before their own, natural deaths. Recent research by

Murdoch McAllister and colleagues at Simon Fraser University suggests that pea aphids infected by wasps commit suicide to protect close relatives from coming in contact with the parasite. Death by desiccation—dropping to the parched earth—seems to be their preferred means of self-sacrifice.

Parasites are opportunists, with a cool, criminal disregard for the integrity of 9 their victims. "What's mine is mine and what's yours is mine" might be their motto. But far from being an ecological offence, this is the way of a world in which all lives interpenetrate each other. Working from the inside to complicate and subvert natural relationships, parasites are clever hackers in the worldwide web of life.

QUESTIONS

Understanding the message: Comprehension

1. In what way do parasites exhibit ingenuity against their hosts?

2. Does nature ever defeat the parasites? In what way(s)?

3. What does Savage mean in her last line, "parasites are clever hackers in the worldwide web of life"?

Examining the structure and details: Analysis

1. Examine Savage's opening to the article. How effective is the first line in drawing in the readers? Why?

2. Where does Savage begin and end the different processes of parasite life? Does she provide enough information for the reader to comprehend the processes?

3. How many different kinds of parasite does Savage include in her examination? Does she provide enough examples? Why or why not?

Formulating a response: Inference and interpretation

1. What makes parasites so repulsive to people?

2. Who is Savage's intended audience in this piece? How do you know?

3. At the end of the article, Savage writes, "But far from being an ecological offence, this is the way of a world in which all lives interpenetrate each other." Does she succeed in convincing the readers that there is value to the parasites? Why or why not?

Essay questions

1. Choose another natural creature considered to be distasteful or a nuisance by humans, and write an essay in which you discuss its usefulness in the greater ecological chain. (Some examples: mosquitoes, cockroaches, termites, snakes, coyotes, raccoons, squirrels, rats, mice.)

2. Discuss the concept of parasite as it applies to human behaviour. What kind of person is considered a parasite? In what ways do human parasites take over the lives of others?

3. What emotional effect does the article have on you? In what way(s) does Savage's presentation of the material contribute to this effect? Look at the ways in which Savage anthropomorphizes (attributes human characteristics to) parasites in forming your answer.

VOCABULARY

invective: insulting, abusive language

ovine: of or to do with sheep

nemesis: an agent of fate or doom; an unbeatable opponent or rival

crustaceans: aquatic beings with hard shells (for example, lobster, shrimp)

spores: reproductive part of organism, especially a fungus

stigmas: the part of a flower that receives the pollen and fertilizes it

aphids: small insects

desiccation: drying up

CHAPTER 7

Classification

CLASSIFICATION IN DAILY LIFE

Classification occurs on a daily basis for most people. Real-life classification happens when you engage in activities such as the following:

- You leave a note for your spouse about how to sort the laundry into different kinds of clothes.
- You organize the seating arrangement for a wedding based on the dining preferences of each guest (for example, chicken, fish, vegetarian).
- You write a proposal for the local community centre, explaining the many kinds of improvements that could be implemented within each area, including the building (refurbishing), the staff (hiring and training), and the programs.
- You tell your parents about different types of cell phones according to the features they have.

WHAT IS CLASSIFICATION?

Imagine a corporation's organizational chart, a hierarchy (such as a family tree), or a list arranged with different headings and subheadings, and you can master classification. If you start with a large number of ideas or items and organize them into similar categories or groups, you are classifying. For instance, if you thought about all the items for sale in a department store such as The Bay, you might decide they can be arranged according to three main categories: clothing, furniture, and appliances; this procedure is called **classification.** Later, you might look at each major category individually and divide it into subcategories, such as women's clothing, men's clothing, and children's clothing (under "clothing") or sofas, tables, chairs, and wall units (under "furniture"). This second operation (starting with a major category or subject area and dividing it into separate parts) is called **division.**

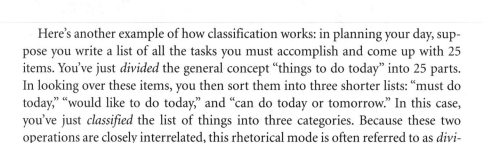

Here's another example of how classification works: in planning your day, suppose you write a list of all the tasks you must accomplish and come up with 25 items. You've just *divided* the general concept "things to do today" into 25 parts. In looking over these items, you then sort them into three shorter lists: "must do today," "would like to do today," and "can do today or tomorrow." In this case, you've just *classified* the list of things into three categories. Because these two operations are closely interrelated, this rhetorical mode is often referred to as *division and classification*. In this text, however, we will use the general term, *classification*, to encompass both these functions.

WHY USE CLASSIFICATION?

Classification can be used to help simplify large, unwieldy, or disorganized masses of information. A nurse with a list of complaints from patients in a walk-in clinic during December will find it easier to keep track of the illnesses if they're divided into categories: viral infections, bacterial infections, injuries, and so on. The once unruly list can then be made manageable and provide a framework through which the nurses and doctors respond: they know which treatment to apply according to the patient's type of complaint. Hospital emergency rooms regularly use such a system, classifying incoming patients as critical, urgent, nonurgent, or deferrable, for instance, to determine who must be seen first.

In classification essays, you organize information and narrow down a large amount of data into a manageable sum; by identifying similarities among items (placing several into the same category), you are also helping to clarify the meaning of something by drawing connections between ideas.

HOW TO WRITE A CLASSIFICATION ESSAY

When preparing classification essays, always work through the general stages of prewriting, writing, and post-writing discussed in Chapter 2. In addition, look at the following section, which contains pointers specific to classification essays.

Pre-Writing

1. Choose a general topic

As with other essays, the topic you choose for a classification essay should be something you know quite a bit about. Because you'll need to generate a list of individual items or parts and a series of different categories in which to organize them, you'll find that the more familiar you are with the topic, the easier the task will be.

To determine categories, select a single **basis of classification:** what principle or idea will govern the choice of categories? In the department store example that opened this chapter, the **classifying principle** was "types of merchandise sold in the store." In an essay about holiday tours, for instance, you could organize the types of tours according to "mode of travel": boat cruises, train tours, cycling tours, self-directed driving tours, and so on. The basis of classification will depend on the writer and her or his particular knowledge or interests. Another writer, for example, might classify the tours according to "how much they cost": under $500, $500 to $1000, over $1000, and so on. Both sets of categories work because each employs a single basis of classification.

DEFINITION

Classifying principle (or basis of classification): The classifying principle is the single concept on which your selection of categories is based; it is the means you use to develop category headings, and items are organized *according to* the classifying principle. The basis of classification ensures that separate categories are logically connected to each other, because each illustrates a different aspect of the same principle.

2. Consider your audience and purpose

Your audience and purpose influence the structure of your paper to a great extent. For instance, an essay about different concert venues will use different categories for an audience of music promoters compared with categories used for a group of concert-goers. The promoters would be more interested in the artist's point of view, reflected in the categories "potential income," " ticket prices," "number of seats," "backstage perks," and so on. In contrast, the audience members would more likely be concerned about their *own* enjoyment of the show, so categories such as "seating arrangements," "sound quality," and "stage effects" would apply.

Similarly, your purpose affects the categories you choose. For instance, a companion piece to Scott McKeen's "Time Thieves" (about types of procrastinators) with an entirely humourous, rather than serious, purpose would likely include headings very different from those in McKeen's article.

3. Generate ideas about the topic

Whether you begin with a whole and divide it into parts or with a group of items and classify them, try to examine your topic from a variety of angles. (In other words, there is more than one way to divide the contents of your dentist's office, just as there is more than one way to classify the list of movies starring Ben Affleck.) By looking at the topic in different ways, you give yourself more options for an interesting and effective essay.

Using the cluster technique (which graphically divides your topic into main ideas and subtopics) is particularly useful for classification, as are categories and lists, which allow you to look at the whole from a variety of angles.

TIP

Keep it logical

For best results, look for naturally occurring, rather than artificially imposed, categories or divisions. For instance, to write about different types of vehicles, you'd naturally consider *parts* of the vehicle as the means of classification: number of wheels (mopeds, motorcycles, cars, or trucks), fuel source (gas, diesel, electric, or solar), and so on. Similarly, you could use age as your means of classifying, with categories such as 1900 to 1950, 1950 to 2000, and 2000 and beyond. It wouldn't make sense to classify vehicles according to their colour, however, since this characteristic doesn't have much impact on the vehicle itself.

4. Narrow to a thesis

Even if the basis for classification seems obvious to you, a classification essay, like any other, should have a thesis that makes a point. In this case, your thesis should also indicate the basis of classification. Your goal is more than simply to provide a list of categories to do with a particular topic; you must also have a purpose in doing so. The statement "Madonna's career has produced five distinct kinds of music" isn't enough of a foundation for an interesting essay; you must have a *reason* for telling this to the reader. A better thesis would be "Over the course of her career, Madonna's musical output has evolved from vapid and superficial to spiritual and profound." Then, in describing the shift, you classify her music according to one of the five types. The purpose of the classification is to demonstrate how Madonna's music has matured over the years.

You do the math

For a stronger thesis and clearer essay structure, let your readers know the number of categories in advance, in the thesis statement. This way, you make the readers' job easier and help them follow along without having to keep track of major and minor divisions of the topic.

5. Organize your ideas in an outline

In this step, imagination can make the difference between a bland or obvious list of items and one that generates enthusiasm and interest. For instance, to classify "kinds of reading material," the most obvious classifying principle is "physical form": books, magazines, Web sites, comic books, and so on. A slightly more interesting approach is to delve into fiction, nonfiction, or reference categories. But what if you used as your classifying principle something atypical, such as the age at which people read it? You might end up with categories such as children's books, comic books, mystery novels, and science fiction (this list would change depending on the reader). Or what about reading material according to your mood as you reach for it? Here, the final categories could be Harlequin Romances (when you feel like pure entertainment), science magazines (when you're feeling contemplative), comic books (when you're stressed), or autobiographies (when you're feeling relaxed). The categories, then, correspond to your emotional states. In each case, you've chosen an organizing principle that develops naturally from the subject matter yet is, nevertheless, fresh and interesting to read.

Categories for classification essays should also be parallel: this means that all categories should illustrate the organizing principle and none should overlap (that is, cover material already included in another category). For instance, if you classify types of race cars, you could arrange these according to age: before 1940, 1940s to 1960s, post 1960s. If instead you chose to classify according to makes, such as Ferrari, Porsche, and McLaren, this also would work. A problem arises, however, if your categories are "cars that won at Le Mans," "cars that introduced new technology," and "Ferraris," since many Ferraris have won at Le Mans, and those with new technology can be included in either of the other two categories. In this case, the categories overlap.

The organization of a classification essay depends on the basis of classification. If you write about how the kinds of books you read change as you age, the obvious method of organization will be chronological. More often, however, the method of organization will be emphatic, since your categories will likely be independent of each other and not governed by any single time line.

Avoiding overlap

One way to ensure that your categories don't overlap is to cross-check the specific items you file into each category. If any item could *possibly* be included in two or more categories, you need to rethink the category headings.

6. Decide on specific support for the main points

As with other types of essays, the items in each category will be best supported with specific, concrete, vivid details.

SNAG

Drowning in details

While it's important to use lots of details to keep your essay interesting, don't overdo it. The details you include need not be exhaustive; that is, you don't necessarily have to include *every* type of country song in your category "country music." Providing a few representative examples is often enough to supply your reader with adequate information to fully understand the topic. Choose the best three or four examples, and make sure that you convey them with clear, vivid, descriptive language.

Writing

If you've chosen fresh, original category headings, you've already added interest to your essay. As you compose your draft, keep your reader engrossed with your writing style. Where appropriate, humour works well in classification essays. In fact, a few well-placed, amusing details or examples can persuade a reader that even the most mundane topic is worthy of attention. (Because he deals with a leisure pursuit, Clive Thompson in "Dead Space" feels free to introduce humour into his essay. On the other hand, Adele Weder's topic, women's prisons, in "A Woman's Place" discourages the use of humour because of its serious subject matter.)

Post-Writing

As you review your essay draft, work through the general steps of post-writing outlined in Chapter 2, and ask yourself the following questions:

- Are my audience and purpose clear? Is my basis of classification in harmony with these?

RESPOND IN WRITING NE

- Does my thesis state the main point and principle for classification?
- Have I included the essential categories needed to support my thesis? Are they independent of each other (don't overlap)?
- Are my categories ordered in the most effective fashion?
- Are my categories adequately developed with specific details and support?

EXERCISES

1. Choose one of the following topics for classification and think of three different means of classification by shifting the audience or purpose. (In the example below, the topic "pets" is used in each case, but the basis of classification changes according to audience or purpose.)

   Audience: parents
   Basis of classification: cost *or* amount of care required
   Audience: children
   Basis of classification: how exotic the pet is
   Purpose: informative
   Basis of classification: cost *or* type of care required
   Purpose: entertaining
   Basis of classification: type of care required *or* number of "human" traits exhibited

   Topics:

   - Types of clothing
   - Religious cults
   - E-mail messages
   - First dates
   - Doctors
   - Coaches
   - Holiday dinners

2. For each of the following places, make a list of everything you can think of that someone might find there. Then, classify the items into distinct categories.

   - A dentist's office
   - Your bedroom
   - A movie theatre
   - A public park
   - A rave
   - An electronics store

3. Choose *one* of the following topics and devise your own list of support with as many examples as you can think of for each. Next, decide how many of the details you'd need to best illustrate the category heading.

Topic: e-mail messages
Category heading: Urgent e-mail messages
Topic: sources of new vocabulary
Category heading: in-class lectures
Topic: sources of new vocabulary
Category heading: thesaurus
Topic: jokes
Category heading: practical jokes
Topic: jokes
Category heading: witticisms
Topic: banking services
Category heading: on-line banking

MODEL STUDENT ESSAY: CLASSIFICATION

The following classification essay demonstrates how one student tackled this rhetorical mode. Highlighted are some key features that help to make the essay effective.

Possession, Person, or Pet?

The dog as a pet is a staple of North American society. Our popular culture is full of canine icons such as Lassie, the Littlest Hobo, or Eddie on *Frasier*. Some say there are as many types of dog owners as there are dogs, and while this may be true, most owners fall into one of three major types: the Materialists, the Humanists, or the Traditionalists. Often, the category someone falls into reflects more about her or his personality than the dog s/he owns.

thesis; number of categories plus classifying principle

Materialists see their dogs as mere objects or status symbols, another possession to add to an *first category*

definition of "Materialists"

ever-growing collection. Always trying to improve their social position, these people buy whichever dog is trendy at the moment, regardless of price, personality, or whether the dog suits their lifestyle. For instance, after the movie, *One Hundred and One Dalmatians* used live animals on-screen in 1996,

specific detail

hordes of families purchased Dalmatian puppies, but then had to give them up months later once they recognized that these dogs are not always suitable for children, being somewhat hyperactive and temperamental. In addition, this type of dog owner strives to find the breed that is most rare at the time. In this way, the dog becomes a new toy that will be the envy of friends and neighbours, like a new Porsche or the latest DVD player. Materialists may

specific detail

purchase a Portuguese Water Dog, for instance, simply because it's not well known, paying no attention to whether the dog is suitable for the family's lifestyle, what kind of exercise or attention it needs, and so on.

Because they see their dogs as objects, Materialists focus more on the dog's appearance than its existence as a living being; in fact, it's not unusual for them to hire others to walk or feed their

second point about Materialists

key detail related to thesis (names)

animals. Materialists often assign their dogs names such as Ferrari, Paris, or Cashmere, to reflect the pet's elevated status. These owners frequently decorate their prized possessions with designer raincoats and booties, or buy "Doggie Perfumes" or "Gourmet Doggie Biscuits" from upscale boutiques and specialty stores. Marlen Cowpland, wife of Corel owner Michael Cowpland, is a prime example of a Materialist: she dyes the (naturally white) fur of her dogs fuchsia, chartreuse, or burgundy to match whatever outfit she's wearing at the time.

second category and definition of "Humanists"

At the opposite end of the spectrum are the Humanists, owners who perceive their pets as human surrogates. These dog owners take the saying, "A dog is a person's best friend" literally: they might not be speaking to their brother or cousins, but they are in constant contact with their dogs. In fact, Humanists often feel more affection for their animals than for real people. After all, they say, a dog will never yell at you, doesn't hold a grudge, and is always happy to see you. As a result, their dogs often sport names commonly used for people, such as "Joey," "Bradley" or "Sheila." Humanists also allow their dogs free reign in the house. Their dogs are usually permitted to sleep in the same bed as their owners, to eat the same food (often while sitting beside those at the dinner table), and can, basically, do anything the owners do. In addition, Humanists speak to their pets as if the dogs understand complicated English, asking questions such as "Well, now, Melissa, where would you like to go this Sunday? Shall it be the park or shall it be the school yard?" These types of owners are devastated when their dogs die, holding traditional funerals and burials for their pets, complete with announcements in the newspaper.

Finally, there are Traditionalists, individuals who take a balanced approach to their lives and dogs. Traditionalists treat their dogs the way dogs were meant to be treated—as pets. These owners train their dogs with consistency and discipline, acknowledging that dogs, though loved and cared for, are not permitted the same privileges as members of the family. Pets in Traditionalist homes usually have a designated spot of their own, such as a basket for sleeping or a mat on which their food bowls are placed. Traditionalists take full responsibility for the care and feeding of their pets. They also interact with their pets regularly, walking and playing with them on a daily basis. These dogs enjoy the typical activities of fetching, catching Frisbees, running, and chewing on bones. Accordingly, Traditionalists give their dogs conventional monikers such as Rover, Rags, or Buster. Children who live in homes with Traditionalist dog owners come to appreciate the animals as domestic pets that coexist with people and enrich family life. Dogs belonging to Traditionalists often display loyal, loving behaviour

key detail related to thesis (names)

specific detail

final category and definition of "Traditionalists"

specific detail

key detail related to thesis (names)

by fiercely guarding little children or warning families about fires that go undetected by the rest of the household.

Whether they're Materialists, Humanists, or Traditionalists, dog owners unwittingly reveal a lot about their own personalities by the pets they choose. Next time you decide to buy a puppy, beware of your own preferences—you may be telling the world more about yourself than you intended!

thesis
reiterated

Time Thieves
by Scott McKeen (b. 1959)

Scott McKeen began his writing career in the early 1980s at weekly newspapers in Alberta. He joined the Edmonton Journal *in 1986 and worked on several news beats, including crime, city hall, and the environment. McKeen has won a number of writing prizes in his career and was short-listed for both the Michener Prize for public service journalism and the National Newspaper Award for feature writing. In the fall of 2000, McKeen was the only Canadian recognized for feature writing by the American Association of Sunday and Feature Editors. His work runs regularly in newspapers across the country and has been published in magazines such as* Canadian Living *and* Reader's Digest. *He lives in Edmonton with his wife, Julie, and their three children.*

PRE-READING

In this article from *Canadian Living* magazine (2000), McKeen writes about different types of procrastinators. Think about your own behaviour: are you a procrastinator? If so, in what circumstances do you procrastinate? What kinds of things do you think might help you rid yourself of the procrastination habit? What are the disadvantages of procrastinating? Are there any advantages? Think, too, as you read about what McKeen means in his title. Who or what are the time thieves?

---

1 When psychologist Lenora Yuen describes herself as an expert in procrastination, it's not entirely a boast. Aside from her PhD and clinical work relating to procrastination, the thing that sets her apart from other academics is what a charitable person might call her "field experience."

2 Yuen, a self-labelled procrastinator, claims, these days, to be only moderately reformed. When she and coauthor Jane Burka sat down years ago to write a self-help book on procrastination called *Procrastination: Why You Do It, What to Do About It* (Addison-Wesley, 1983), they dawdled, they delayed and they digressed. Finally, as deadlines loomed, they scribbled with the intensity of hunted foxes. "There were times when we had a chapter due and we'd be working up until the very last minute" says Yuen. Once she even drove a completed chapter to the courier in her pyjamas. "We didn't have time to change!" she says.

3 If any of this sounds familiar, it's not surprising. All of us procrastinate from time to time, including—as Yuen's story shows—the experts.

RESPOND IN WRITING   NE

The ancient Romans, who created the word from *pro*, indicating forward 4
motion, and *crastinus*, meaning belonging to tomorrow, saw procrastination as a
positive thing. Better to pause and consider before rushing into a battle, they
believed. Today as well, of course, there are times when it's a good idea to delay a
decision until we've had time to think.

But for some people, putting things off grows beyond sober second thought to 5
become an unhappy condition that robs them of self-esteem, creative energy and
a personal sense of power. These inveterate procrastinators worry about unfinished business instead of finishing it or they try to distract themselves in an effort
to make the job or the problem go away—which, of course, it doesn't. Life becomes
a daily struggle under an overwhelming sense of burden. "It's like being late for
your own life," says Edmonton psychologist Paul Sussman.

Timothy Pychyl, an associate professor of psychology at Carleton University in 6
Ottawa and the head of its Procrastination Research Group, agrees.
"Procrastination exacts a huge price on our sense of well-being. If we delay things
unnecessarily again and again, it's like we live our lives under the guillotine's
blade, waiting for it to fall."

Though all procrastinators may share feelings of anxiety and powerlessness, not 7
all procrastination habits grow from the same roots. To tackle yours once and for all,
you need first to determine what type of procrastinator you are. Then you can start
learning how to make sure you're on time for life's appointments.

The Distractible Procrastinator

You're at home working on your tax return (or something equally scintillating). 8
It's time for a break; you head for the fridge. A practised procrastinator, you
immediately notice a spot of spilled milk on the crisper lid. Next thing you know,
you've cleaned the fridge and have moved on to the bathroom fixtures. Your
partner happens by and asks what you're up to. You say, "Oh, I'm doing my taxes."

Virtually all of us (understandably) avoid onerous tasks, even it if means 9
replacing them with only slightly less onerous alternatives. But Pychyl says new
research indicates that chronic procrastinators—people who never seem to get
going on a given job, never finish what they start or never stick with anything—
have trouble with "volitional skills." In other words, they may be exceptionally distractible or highly impulsive and have difficulty focusing on their first priority in
the face of competing priorities. According to Pychyl, the distractible procrastinator needs to learn to ignore the siren calls of other activities or interests and stay
focused on the task at hand.

The first step for any type of procrastinator, says Yuen, is to admit that you 10
have a tendency to put things off. Then consider some tried-and-true time-
management techniques. One method is to break projects down into bite-size
pieces. Take that income tax return, for example. Instead of thinking of it as one
mammoth project, tackle it in 15-minute chunks spread over consecutive days.

You might spend one session sorting bills and invoices into categories, one session adding up the totals, and so on. Continue to commit small amounts of time each day to the task until it's completed.

The Passive-Aggressive Procrastinator

11 Do the tasks that you are most likely to put off tend to be jobs other people want you to do? If so, you may be a passive-aggressive procrastinator.

12 Passive-aggressive procrastinators feel they have no control over decisions in their lives. In some cases they're people-pleasers who can't say no to anyone. They take on responsibilities they think others expect them to, but since these goals aren't their own they often resent them and delay completing them. In other cases they're power procrastinators who procrastinate in order to wield power over people they feel are controlling their lives. Both types resent this sense of lack of control and use procrastination as their revenge—only their styles differ.

13 Let's say your brother asks you for the second time in 10 days to pick him up at the airport miles from where you live. If you're a people-pleaser, you agree politely to do it even though you don't want to. So on the appointed day, you give yourself too little time to get to the airport and leave him waiting around long after his plane has landed. Or consider the teenager who, angry at being grounded, "forgets" to mow the lawn until it's too dark. Both of these procrastinators are really trying to gain some control or autonomy over their lives. Ironically their vengeance-by-delay only makes them appear unreliable and irresponsible.

14 Are power issues or buried resentments at the base of your procrastination habit? Look for patterns: Do you always say yes to people's requests yet resent doing so? Or do the projects on which you procrastinate all seem to revolve around the same person or persons? See if you can identify a negative pattern and deal with it in a more productive way.

The Fearful Procrastinator

15 "At the extreme, procrastination can be a deeply existential issue, a fear of engagement with life itself," says Pychyl, who compares it to standing nervously on the sidelines at a party while others dance and enjoy themselves. In fact, that's exactly where Pychyl found himself in Grade 7; that one memory motivated him to study procrastination as an adult. Just before the music ended, a teacher got all the non-participants up dancing—and inadvertently taught Pychyl a lifelong lesson. "I wondered why I hadn't started sooner," he remembers. "It was so much fun and such a profound thing—I had been afraid but I also knew I was missing out on something I really wanted to be doing."

16 Fear is the most frequent reason people procrastinate, and the fear itself has many faces: fear of rejection, fear of the unknown or fear of failure.

17 The person who puts off asking someone for a date, for instance, fears rejection. "Ask yourself, 'Why am I putting this off?' or 'What am I worried about?'" suggests

Yuen. She also recommends that you scale down your goal to make it less intimidating: ask the object of your affection to join you for coffee rather than for dinner.

Then there are procrastinators who fear the unknown. They peer into the 18 future but focus on the worst possible outcomes; they become paralysed by the what-ifs and end up never acting. Such a fearful procrastinator might never make a commitment to a relationship or leave a job that's unfulfilling for fear of landing in a position she likes even less.

Perhaps the most common breed of procrastinator, though, is the one who's 19 afraid of failure. "If I had to name one variable that was connected to people's procrastination, I'd start here," says Pychyl. These people, and most of us have experienced this at some time or other, worry that they can't meet standards that are considered acceptable. They're worried that they'll do badly on an exam, prepare a tasteless meal or deliver a mediocre report at work.

Yuen suggests the fear-of-failure procrastinators may have learned the habit— 20 or at least been rewarded for it—in grade school. If a child who constantly puts assignments off until the last minute gets decent marks, he may decide that he needs deadline adrenaline to do his best work.

For those who fear failure, Pychyl notes, procrastination can offer a built-in excuse. 21 Scramble to finish something at deadline and you can tell others—and more importantly yourself—that it wasn't your best work. "Gee, if I'd only had more time . . ."

The Perfectionist Procrastinator

Unlike self-motivated perfectionists, who don't procrastinate, says Pychyl, perfec- 22 tionist procrastinators set impossibly high standards for themselves and their work, not because they expect it but because they feel others expect it. Not surprisingly, they find their work onerous and joyless. Is it any wonder they put things off? If you're a perfectionist procrastinator, you [should] focus on doing things for yourself, not for other people. If you set your own goals, rather than ones you think others expect of you, you're more likely to stop procrastinating.

For Yuen and Burka, who procrastinated about writing their book, delaying 23 was a futile attempt at putting off the stress. "We talked a lot about our fears," says Yuen. "What if the book didn't live up to our hopes or expectations?" She can laugh about it now because the book went on to become a best-seller and went into reprint more than a dozen times. But the original manuscript was two years late getting to the editor! "Who else would write a book about procrastination?" says Yuen. Of course, if being a procrastinator were the only requirement, most of us would be published authors by now. When the two psychologists finally finished writing their book, they went out for a celebratory lunch with their editor. When they left the restaurant, Burka's car had disappeared. Then she realized why and blushed; her car had been towed. Why? She had unpaid parking tickets and an overdue registration. She had been meaning to pay them—but she'd kept putting it off.

QUESTIONS

Understanding the message: Comprehension

1. What does McKeen mean when he writes that Lenora Yuen has "field experience" as a procrastinator?

2. How does McKeen convey the intense psychological burden that is placed on people who procrastinate? What techniques does he use?

3. What is meant by "volitional skills"?

4. What is the most common reason why people procrastinate?

Examining the structure and details: Analysis

1. McKeen uses the device of *alliteration* in paragraph 2. How does his use actually parallel his meaning?

2. How does McKeen organize his list of procrastinators? What classifying principle do you think he uses to order them?

3. What method does McKeen use to tie together the opening and closing of his essay, even though he treats a variety of procrastinators within it?

Formulating a response: Inference and interpretation

1. In what way can procrastination be positive, according to McKeen? Do you agree or disagree?

2. Can all types of procrastinators be covered by McKeen's four categories? If not, what types has he overlooked?

3. What is McKeen's purpose in writing "Time Thieves"? Do you think he achieves this purpose?

4. What is McKeen's tone in the article? Is it appropriate for his subject matter? Why or why not?

Essay questions

1. Relate an incident in which you procrastinated about something important. Were the consequences dire or simply annoying? What, if anything, did you learn from the experience?

2. Think about other people whose behaviours can be classified according to types (for instance, studiers, gift-givers, hosts or hostesses, subway-riders, and so on). Write a classification essay in which you describe the various types and the differing ways they engage in the same activity.

3. Discuss the feasibility of McKeen's suggestions for procrastinators. Would his techniques work for you? Why or why not? In supporting your answer, use examples from McKeen's article.

VOCABULARY

mammoth: enormous, overwhelmingly large

existential: dealing with the ultimate meaning (or meaninglessness) of life

onerous: burdensome; unbearably heavy

futile: useless

A Woman's Place
by Adele Weder (b. 1961)

Adele Weder is a Vancouver-based writer specializing in architecture and design. She grew up in Saskatoon and later lived and studied in Quebec City, Halifax, Toronto, and Paris. She has been a staff writer at the Financial Times of Canada *and the editor of* Insite *magazine. Since moving to Vancouver in 1996, she has contributed regularly to national and international periodicals, including the* Globe and Mail, *the* National Post, Azure *magazine,* Canadian Architect, *and* Metropolis, *writing mostly on design but also on languages, art, and film. She is particularly interested in the social, environmental, and political aspects of design and its manifestation in other cultures. In 2000, she spent a month in Japan undertaking design-journalism research with assistance from the Asia-Pacific Foundation. She has served as a guest critic at the architecture schools of the University of Waterloo and the University of British Columbia, and as a juror at British Columbia's Lieutenant-Governor's Awards in Architecture. She is currently a member of the League for Studies in Architecture and the Environment.*

PRE-READING

In "A Woman's Place" (published in *Azure* magazine in 1999), Weder examines different approaches to the architecture of women's prisons. What preconceptions or emotional reactions do you have to the idea of women in prison? Do you think prisons should try to emulate a "natural" home environment, or should they feel like punitive institutions? If you could design an ideal prison for women, what would it be like?

---

1 "That's bullshit, I don't believe it," Marianne McKenna snapped at her colleagues. She didn't think anyone could be capable of the depravity her colleagues were describing—and certainly no woman. At the time—the tense and humid summer of 1993—McKenna was leading the design team on a new prison for women in Kitchener. A group of her male co-workers at Kuwabara Payne McKenna Blumberg [KPMB] was muttering angrily about one of the facility's potential residents: a first-time offender named Karla Homolka, freshly convicted of manslaughter in the abduction, torture and murder of two teenage girls.

2 "The guys shoved the newspaper under my nose and said, 'Look, this is who we're housing here,'" recalls McKenna. "I didn't even read the gory details. I just shot back, 'Look, these are *women*.'" McKenna now says she was "quite wrong" to

RESPOND IN WRITING   NE

assume that women were incapable of such monstrosities. But she never lost sight of her goal: to provide a humane environment for incarcerated women, many who come from marginalized and abusive backgrounds. "You can't judge the whole by the few," she says.

Grand Valley Institution for Women is the product of an idea, a classically lib- 3 eral belief in a humane response to wrongdoing and in rehabilitation over revenge. Since the federal government released a seminal 1990 task force report called *Creating Choices,* four other new complexes have opened: the Okimaw Ohci Healing Lodge in southwest Saskatchewan, by the Architects Collaborative; Nova Institute in Nova Scotia, by Sperry & Partners; the Edmonton Institution for Women, by Wood, O'Neil, O'Neil; and the Joliette Institution for Women, by Pierre Hetu and Belzile Gallienne Martin Moisan Plante. In the spirit of the task force, the words "penitentiary" and "prison" are noticeably absent from their names, but that's what they all are. They just don't look the part—or at least not in the way we've come to expect.

Unique among building types, prison architecture has traditionally been delib- 4 erately inhospitable to its occupants, either for revenge purposes or to make inmates terrified of returning. More recent currents of thought maintain that any hope of rehab depends on inmates being able to access treatment and career-training programs, maintain family ties, and learn to live in something that approximates a normal residential environment.

One of the systemic problems for female offenders is that there are just too few of 5 them: of Canada's federal inmates, just 2.5%—about 300 prisoners in recent years—are women. They have been a "correctional afterthought," concluded the task force.

Until recently, the Kingston Prison for Women, or P4W, was the only federal 6 penitentiary in the country for female offenders. Because their numbers are so few, female inmates have usually served their time far away from home and family, and with virtually no alternative regarding the kind of facility they'd be housed in. Hard-core inmates rubbed shoulders with young first-timers in on relatively minor drug offenses.

And surely, argued the reformers, female offenders have different needs from 7 their male counterparts. Incarcerated women often have more pressing childcare responsibilities. Many come from physically and sexually abusive backgrounds. And women, more than men, tend to rely on their friends during the recovery process.

However contentious the issue may be in the popular media, people who work 8 with female offenders adamantly maintain that as a group, even the most violent of them are vastly less inclined to commit random or predatory crimes and more likely to have been convicted of "familial" violence stemming from past abuse. The difference might not comfort the family of a husband slain by a wife who happened to be neglected and abused as a child, but it does suggest that a different kind of incarceration might be in order.

9   The gist of *Creating Choices* is this: people respond to their environment. If they're treated with respect and serve their time in a milieu that fosters self-esteem, the chances of rehabilitation are better. And if their architectural environment resembles a home and a neighbourhood more than a cell and a prison yard, they'll take pride in it, be able to socialize in a more traditional manner, and reintegrate better with the outside world when their time's up. The task force stipulated that the new prisons provide inmates with small cottage units, natural light, colour, more discreet security equipment, play areas for visiting children, units where mothers can reside with their babies, a facility to accommodate Aboriginal spiritual ceremonies, and opportunities for contact with nature.

10   Can architecture assist in rehabilitation? The authors of *Creating Choices* think so, although it's difficult to measure. Brenda, a former inmate of both Kingston Prison for Women and the new Healing Lodge, is full of praise for the latter. The Maple Creek complex was designed on the premise that aboriginal women, more than any other group in Canadian society, suffer from violence, victimization and abuse, which has led to their over-representation in the prison population. Okimaw Ohci's facilities—a main lodge based on the form of an eagle and a wigwam-shaped spiritual building—conform to aboriginal design values (which eschew harsh rectilinear layouts) and reflect the mandate to focus not only on confronting past criminal activities, but also on fostering self-esteem. Yet the Healing Lodge's design wasn't as critical to Brenda as the fact that "when you first enter the place, they're very polite and the guards don't wear uniforms." For her, the physical environment was secondary to the human response.

11   But Heather, a former inmate of both pre-task-force Burnaby Correctional Centre (a provincial institution which also houses some federal inmates) and post-task-force Nova, points out that women can be subconsciously affected by their physical environment. After months of marching down long, bare corridors, hearing heavy clanging doors and gates and staring at cinder-block walls and fences, says Heather, "you start to feel like an animal. You identify with your surroundings. And they're telling you, you're just a criminal: that's all you are and all you'll ever be." She recalls lying in bed at night in her cell at Burnaby and running her hand up the wall—"like I was reaching out for some warmth, any warmth, any sign of humanity that could help me." All she felt was cold cinder block. Later, she was transferred to Nova. There, she worked with other inmates to fix meals and take care of her living space. Most critically, she was able to meet regularly with her six-year-old daughter. And at night, when she slid her hand up, she touched "warm walls," literally and figuratively.

12   Yet for some former inmates, the very notion of a "humane prison" is an oxymoron. Kim Pate, executive director of the Canadian Association of Elizabeth Fry Societies, an advocacy group for incarcerated women, recalls an inmate's blunt assessment of Grand Valley Institution for Women: "She told me, 'It's like being

mind-fucked, because we've got all the crap we had at P4W, but it's all cloaked in this pretty pink packaging.'"

From certain angles, Grand Valley reads like signature KPMB architecture: 13 emphatic angular forms juxtaposed gracefully with a central rotunda, generous glazing, rich colours, fine birch-veneer millwork. Soon enough, of course, you'll encounter the irrefutable evidence that we aren't in Kitchener City Hall anymore. To get past the main foyer, you have to pass through an array of airport-type screening booths and gizmos, one of which scans your i.d. card for microscopic traces of drugs—which they tell you after you've handed it over. On the bulkhead above the screening booth hangs a gilt-framed photograph of a man in a gray suit. Our guide reports that he's the commissioner of Correctional Service Canada and that he's a really nice guy. But it still seems weird that a prison supposedly premised on building women's self-esteem would have its entrance marked by a clichéd image of patriarchy.

Beyond the main building is a series of porched clapboard houses that bring to 14 mind Florida's new urbanist town of Seaside. As you approach, you notice the fake-wood vinyl siding, which stands in for the originally designated wood clapboard. But McKenna says it was "war" just to get these prisons built. Myriad design compromises—from cladding the houses in vinyl to shrinking the size of the spiritual buildings—were needed to quell public disapproval of inmates residing in environments that were too "nice."

Inside the inmates' residences, the white walls and sloped ceilings recall a mid- 15 dlebrow ski lodge. In fact, very little in the residences suggests incarceration, except for those details not ordained by the architects: a velveteen curtain over a small window in each bedroom door for the nightly bed-check, for instance; and the occasional glimpse through the window of razor-wire chain-link fence. And also the more subtle design features based on the premise that if the physical surroundings can affect an inmate's character, the reverse is also true: the inmates can transform hardware and millwork into lethal weapons. The original metal towel hooks have been replaced with rounded plastic ones so that in a fight they couldn't be ripped out and used as weapons. Drawers at the far left of the bathroom counters were sealed shut after prison officials ascertained inmates could use them to effectively lock others into the adjoining toilet room.

For all its innovation, Grand Valley suffers the same glaring omission as Joliette and 16 other penitentiaries: a conspicuous absence of art. The corridors sport stretches of blank walls that would be perfect for thought-provoking and inspiring images. But prison officials deem posters maintenance problems and framed works fire and security hazards because of the complicated wiring systems the walls conceal. "That's totally ridiculous," responds Pate. "It's standard residential construction," says McKenna.

Spartan landscaping and razor-wire chain-link fencing are fixtures at all five 17 places, thanks to a spate of escapes at Edmonton soon after its opening. As I ride up the road to the Joliette Institute for Women with Pierre Hetu and Michel Gallienne, they utter a shared grumble. "The barbed wire," groans Gallienne. "We didn't want it there." Nor did they specify the vinyl siding on the inmate residences, which make them look a lot like army barracks. Some of the locals decried their original homey brick-clad design, howling that it was too luxurious for felons. The architects' concept of several small houses also got scrunched into just a few larger units. Government officials ordained these changes to the design not for budgetary reasons, sighs Joliette's warden Marie Andrée Cyrenne, but because of "public perception."

18   Inside one of these vinyl-clad houses, an attractive, smiling young inmate shows us around the home that she shares with a half-dozen other inmates, with the poise and aplomb of someone who's undoubtedly been hand-picked for the task. Every room appears impeccably clean and tidy (which, to this visitor, is not home-like at all.) The doors, window frames and other detailing are painted ashen pink, a shade too close to the sickly and ubiquitous pink trim in modern hospitals.

19   Across the way is the building that contains the segregation or isolation units— what's known colloquially as "the Hole," or "Seg." Here, there's no pretense of home, even in the new innovative institutions. There can't be, by definition: it's for removing an inmate as a last-ditch effort to save her from herself or others. Inmates in Seg are especially prone to self-destruction, so the primary design challenge is to disarm the room. The Hole in Joliette is much like the Hole in all other institutions. No blinds. No protruding hardware. A sleek stainless-steel toilet instead of a porcelain one that could be smashed. A single light, recessed and sealed into the ceiling. A tiny rectangular slot to pass a dinner tray from the corridor to the cell.

20   There may be some women already so oppressed by bad luck and social injustice that all the enlightened architecture and rehab programs in the world can't save them. There may even be a few women whose apparent capacity for violence and evil weakens the case of the inmates from truly abusive and disadvantaged backgrounds. But, says the Elizabeth Fry society's Kim Pate, "Our system is supposed to be set up so that we don't decide policy on the basis of one individual. These prisons would look a lot different if all prisoners were like Homolka."

21   Karla Homolka is currently serving her sentence quietly in Joliette, where she was transferred after Kitchener residents protested her expected arrival at Grand Valley. Joliette's warden, Cyrenne, insists that the very concept of punishment is archaic, for every inmate. "They have lost their liberty. That's punishment enough."

22   Brenda, who's served time for killing her lover and for kidnapping and beating up an acquaintance, agrees with that assessment, adding that her own feelings of remorse augment her punishment, and that she's "definitely" reformed now. "What scares me most is not what other people think but what will happen to me after I die. There will be Judgment Day."

QUESTIONS

Understanding the message: Comprehension

1. How do the names of the four prisons Weder describes reflect the new approach to incarcerated women that is presented in the government's 1990 task force report, *Creating Choices?*

2. What were the disadvantages of having only one prison, P4W in Kingston, for Canadian female criminals?

3. According to the article, why do prisons built for females need to be different from those built for males?

Examining the structure and details: Analysis

1. What common features exist in all the prisons Weder describes? What is the classifying principle she uses to classify the new women's prisons? What category headings would you use to distinguish the prisons from each other?

2. What purpose is served by the direct quotations that Weder uses? Do you think the quotes are essential for her to convey the personalities of the women who are housed in these prisons? Why or why not?

3. Examine the language Weder uses when discussing both the inmates and the prison administrators (What verbs does she use in association with prison guards or administrators? What modifiers does she use to describe the inmates?). What words are used to identify the inmates themselves, and how do these word choices differ depending on who is using them—Weder or the prison administrators? What patterns do you find?

Formulating a response: Inference and interpretation

1. Reexamine the opening two paragraphs of Weder's article. What method does she use to introduce her topic? In what way does the opening paragraph shape the reader's response? Do you think this is an effective opening?

2. What do you think is Weder's purpose in writing this article? Do you think she succeeds? Why or why not?

3. At one point, Weder quotes Marianne McKenna saying that it was "war" getting the prisons built, because of "public disapproval of inmates residing in environments that were too 'nice.'" Do you think that the prisons have succeeded in

balancing a "humane" environment with one that still acts as punishment for crimes? Do you agree with Kim Pate that, since the inmates "have lost their liberty," that is "punishment enough"?

Essay questions

1. Think of four places that belong to the same general category, such as four fast-food restaurants, four movie theatres, four ski hills, four dance clubs, or four mobile homes. Write an essay in which you classify the places to indicate the differences among them.

2. What would be an ideal prison for women? In an essay, outline the different aspects of a woman's prison that you think would be important to consider when designing such an institution.

3. Over the years, many people have voiced the opinion that Canadian prison inmates, women in particular, have been treated too lightly and that their prison stays have not acted as enough of a punishment to deter future behaviour (in one famous incident, Karla Homolka, notorious ex-wife of serial-killer Paul Bernardo, was shown cavorting at a party with friends, wearing a stylish evening dress). Does Weder's article convince you that these new prisons will serve their purpose of punishing the inmates? Write an essay in which you explain why or why not. Cite examples from the text to support your points.

VOCABULARY

contentious: controversial

milieu: environment

eschew: reject

rectilinear: built in straight lines

oxymoron: a statement that contains its own opposite; apparent contradiction

juxtaposed: contrasted, side by side

irrefutable: unable to deny; proven to be true

Dead Space

by Clive Thompson (b. 1968)

Clive Thompson is a writer who covers the social, political, and business implications of high tech and the Internet. He is the weekly high-tech columnist for Newsday *in New York and the monthly high-tech columnist for the* Report on Business, *Canada's main business magazine. He also writes regularly for publications including the* New York Times, Fortune, *the* Washington Post, Worth, Elle, Shift, New York, Lingua Franca, Raygun, *the* Globe and Mail, *the* Toronto Star, *and many others. Thompson won a 1999 Canadian National Magazine Award for reporting on the workplace implications of high-tech culture. He is also the host of* ShiftTV—*a weekly show about technology on the Life Channel. He is a regular media commentator on high-tech issues for various CBC radio and TV shows, as well as NBC, the Fox network, National Public Radio, ABC, and New York 9.*

PRE-READING

Thompson's article first appeared in *Shift* magazine in 2000. What does the title of his article suggest to you? Once you know that Thompson is writing about violent video games, does your impression change? How often do you associate the word "dead" with video games? In what way(s) is it related to them? Consider your reactions to death in video games as you read the following selection.

1   Videogame designers have to deal with some peculiar aesthetic issues. Put yourself in their shoes for a moment. Pretend that you're crafting a first-person shooter—one of those ultraviolet bits of eye candy. Pretend, say, that you're creating *Kiss Psycho Circus: The Nightmare Child,* that gory shooter starring the boys of Kiss that hit stores recently.

2   Obviously, you have to invent some wildly overpowered weapons—such as *KPC*'s rocket launchers and chain guns. Then, you have to design some eerie dungeons, complete with realistic shadow movement (as with the game's vaguely Goth, postapocalyptic setting). You fashion a few dozen gruesome monsters to kill, as well as the orange fractal explosions that will leave them lying in blood-drenched bits on the ground. Finally, you throw in some moist sound effects—such as the appropriately gut-wrenching *hurk!* produced when a Kiss grenade splashes an unwitting opponent all over the ceiling. Another one bites the dust! Nice work, comrade!

3   Ah, but then comes a more subtle, and rather unexpected, question: What do you do with the dead bodies?

4   This is not a simple problem. Five minutes into any self-respecting shooter, the average player has probably slaughtered twenty or thirty adversaries. Those body counts tally up pretty quickly. So what do you do with all that fresh meat? Leave it lying around? Sweep it up?

5   It sounds silly, but this question is easily one of the most politically sensitive issues in game design today. Because this is when you, Mr. or Ms. Game Designer, have to meditate on what your game says about the repercussions of violence. You begin to think about what all this wanton firepower really means. OK, sure, yeah, we all know It's Just A Game, but when it's predicated on disemboweling endless rows of opponents with hollow-point bullets, designers are inadvertently forced into making some philosophical decisions. What will society regard as a tolerable, entertainment-based display of death?

6   If you look at it historically, the methods of body disposal in videogames form a rather polished mirror of social attitudes toward media violence. As we changed, so did our games. We could even map it out into a few discrete periods:

7   **The cold war zap:** The earliest videogames to grapple with immolation were the wacky, lo-fi galaxy shooters like *Space Invaders*. The little hieroglyphic aliens crept lower and lower, thud-thud-thudding along, while you fired ICBM-style missiles at them. But when you hit an alien, there was no protracted flameout, no dramatic fall from the sky. They just sort of vanished. In a sterile little blink.

8   Partly, you could say that this was a technical limitation of game chips at the time. An arcade machine couldn't render a much more complicated death. But when you consider that *Space Invaders* debuted in the frigid depths of the cold war—with hundreds of thousands of stockpiled missiles, a Soviet menace and a nearly senile, Dirty Harry–quoting American president—it's hard not to view the game's explosions as an elegant expression of nuclear dread. Yeah, that was death in the atom bomb age. A sudden blink, and you're gone—leaving only your shadow on the side of a building.

9   **Death and videotape:** The next big shift in dead-enemy disposal took place with the advent of photo-realistic images. In gun-shooter games like *Lethal Enforcers,* suddenly you weren't targeting goofy, low-rez graphics: The bad guys were bitmapped photos of real people. As a result, the games took on an unsettling Rodney King-like visual quality, as if they'd been shot on a cheap surveillance camera. The age of mediated, meta-TV reality was blooming, and so our dead bodies vanished like a video signal. In *Lethal Enforcers,* a murdered criminal would flicker once or twice and then vanish, as though a camera cord had been accidentally tugged loose.

10   Fighting games like *Mortal Kombat* and *Killer Instinct* took it one step further, adding an element that had hitherto been oddly missing from videogame car-

nage: geysering blood. Even the lamest combo move (like Sindel's weird little hair grab in *Mortal Kombat*) would produce a spurting fountain of hemoglobin. Yet, when it came to dead bodies, squeamishness still reigned. Each game started off with a clean slate—and all that blood evaporated, gone without a trace.

Flying chunks of flesh: Aesthetically, *Quake* stunned the gaming world with its 11 first-person style. But almost as significant was its innovative approach to body disposal. For the first time in any game, after you shot somebody, their corpse actually hung around. For hours. You could blow someone to bits, leave the room and wander around, and come back to find it still lying in a pool of gore. And the game physics were alarmingly precise when it came to simulating the trajectory of body parts when a grenade whacked a monster. At one point, I blew a grunt's head off and watched it go flying up onto a castle bridge. Half an hour later, I came along the bridge and, sure enough, there was the head. You don't find programming this precise in Microsoft Explorer.

Critics lambasted *Quake* for its loving attention to corpses and body chunks. 12 But this very attention to detail was precisely what made the game so funny, witty and more than just a gorefest. By taking body disposal to its logical extremes, *Quake* had an aesthetic and narrative effect not unlike the over-the-top violence of Quentin Tarantino's *Pulp Fiction*. Recall the ghastly scene where Jules and Vince, having accidentally shot their friend, must mop up the bits of brain in the back of the car. When you take it as far as absurdity, the physics of death becomes not merely an enactment of violence, but a grim comment on it. (What a human tragedy. But man, what a pain in the ass to clean up!)

Two-headed gaming: These days, games are of a mind divided. In the post- 13 Columbine era, the subject of videogame death is as politicized as ever, with some kids actually being thrown out of school for admitting they play violent games. Public scrutiny has provoked a sort of schizoid reaction in designers' aesthetics.

Half of today's battle games actually soft-pedal the bodies, trying to dispose of 14 them as tastefully as possible. In the recent *MDK 2*—"MDK" standing for "Murder, Death, Kill"—the blown-away remains of your enemies sort of crumple up in a curiously bloodless fashion. (I'm still trying to figure out how they make it look so sterile.) Or consider *Pokémon*, where the vanquished monsters merely "faint." Meanwhile, self-avowed bad-boy designers like Gathering of Developers just smirk and grind our faces in the body count, with games that feature not only big-ass guns, but big-ass guns carried by Kiss members, for God's sake. Or look at a game like *Soldier of Fortune*, where felled soldiers lie around with *Monty Python and the Holy Grail*-style gushing arm stumps and spilled guts.

One could hardly ask for a better reflection of our intractable attitudes toward 15 violence in the media. Cannons to the left of us, cannons to the right—and a lot of collateral damage in the middle.

QUESTIONS

Understanding the message: Comprehension

1. What does Thompson mean when he writes, "you throw in some moist sound effects"? In what way are the sound effects "moist"?

2. Why is the method of "body disposal" one of the most politically sensitive issues in game design today?

3. In what way(s) are the changes in violent video games directly related to advances in technology, according to Thompson?

4. In what way(s) was the game *Quake* innovative, the first to include a particular feature?

Examining the structure and details: Analysis

1. How does Thompson introduce his topic? Why do you think he begins by asking us to put ourselves in the video game designer's shoes?

2. What principle does Thompson use to classify the "methods of body disposal" in video games? How would you label the different categories he uses?

3. What parallels does Thompson draw between each shift in the video game and the societal values or political climate at the time? Does he veer from this arrangement at any point? If so, where?

Formulating a response: Inference and interpretation

1. What do the changes in body disposal say about society's attitudes toward violence? How do they reflect what's changed in society itself?

2. Do you agree with Thompson's assessment of *Quake* as being "funny, witty and more than just a gorefest"? If you've seen the film *Pulp Fiction*, do you think the analogy is apt? Why or why not?

3. What is Thompson's tone in this article? Why do you think he chose to write it this way?

Essay questions

1. Choose another broad category of game (board games, card games, children's games, and so on), and write an essay in which you classify the different types of this game.

RESPOND IN WRITING   NE

2. Write your own classification essay about how video games have changed over time. What other aspect of video games (besides how they deal with violence and death) can you classify according to different time periods?

3. What is Thompson's underlying thesis about the attitude toward killing in violent videogames? Write an essay in which you answer this question, citing examples from the selection to support your points.

VOCABULARY

eye candy: something with visual appeal but little intellectual value

immolation: sacrificial death

low-rez: low resolution

bitmapped: digitally represented, as on a computer monitor

Rodney King: Los Angeles resident who became famous when police beat him after stopping him on the highway

Columbine: U.S. high school in which two teens killed fellow students and themselves

Monty Python and the Holy Grail: British comedy troupe's movie

intractable: stubborn, hard to change

Mother Tongue

by Amy Tan (b. 1952)

Amy Tan was born in Oakland, California, and grew up in the San Francisco Bay Area. She moved with her mother to Switzerland in 1968, where she completed high school before returning to California. She received a B.A. in English and linguistics and an M.A. in linguistics from San Jose University. She worked as a consultant for disabled children and as a reporter, an editor, a publisher, and a technical writer before publishing her first novel, The Joy Luck Club *(1989), which won the Bay Area Book Reviewers Award and was nominated for the National Book Critics Circle Award. When the story was made into a Hollywood film in 1993, Tan co-wrote the screenplay. She also wrote* The Kitchen God's Wife *(1991),* The Hundred Secret Senses *(1993), and* The Bonesetter's Daughter *(2001). Tan's work has been translated into 20 languages worldwide. She is married to Lou DeMattei, an attorney; they live in San Francisco and New York with their cat and dog.*

PRE-READING

Tan's sensational first novel, *The Joy Luck Club*, brought her critical acclaim and introduced the Asian-American community to a mainstream, white, audience in the United States. In this essay from the *Threepenny Review* (1989), she examines how her immigrant mother's command of English shaped Tan's own use of language and her views about it. Think about how you use language every day: would you say that you speak more than one English? What difficulties are faced when someone learns a new language? How does one's command of language influence others' perceptions of a person?

1   I am not a scholar of English or literature. I cannot give you much more than personal opinions on the English language and its variations in this country or others.

2   I am a writer. And by that definition, I am someone who has always loved language. I am fascinated by language in daily life. I spend a great deal of my time thinking about the power of language—the way it can evoke an emotion, a visual image, a complex idea, or a simple truth. Language is the tool of my trade. And I use them all—all the Englishes I grew up with.

3   Recently, I was made keenly aware of the different Englishes I do use. I was giving a talk to a large group of people, the same talk I had already given to half a

dozen other groups. The nature of the talk was about my writing, my life, and my book, *The Joy Luck Club*. The talk was going along well enough, until I remembered one major difference that made the whole talk sound wrong. My mother was in the room. And it was perhaps the first time she had heard me give a lengthy speech, using the kind of English I have never used with her. I was saying things like, "The intersection of memory upon imagination" and "There is an aspect of my fiction that relates to thus-and-thus"—a speech filled with carefully wrought grammatical phrases, burdened, it suddenly seemed to me, with nominalized forms, past perfect tenses, conditional phrases, all the forms of standard English that I had learned in school and through books, the forms of English I did not use at home with my mother.

Just last week, I was walking down the street with my mother, and I again 4 found myself conscious of the English I was using, the English I do use with her. We were talking about the price of new and used furniture and I heard myself saying this: "Not waste money that way." My husband was with us as well, and he didn't notice any switch in my English. And then I realized why. It's because over the twenty years we've been together I've often used that same kind of English with him, and sometimes he even uses it with me. It has become our language of intimacy, a different sort of English that relates to family talk, the language I grew up with.

So you'll have some idea of what this family talk I heard sounds like, I'll quote 5 what my mother said during a recent conversation which I videotaped and then transcribed. During this conversation, my mother was talking about a political gangster in Shanghai who had the same last name as her family's, Du, and how the gangster in his early years wanted to be adopted by her family, which was rich by comparison. Later, the gangster became more powerful, far richer than my mother's family, and one day showed up at my mother's wedding to pay his respects. Here's what she said in part:

"Du Yusong having business like fruit stand. Like off the street kind. He is Du 6 like Du Zong—but not Tsung-ming Island people. The local people call putong, the river east side, he belong to that side local people. That man want to ask Du Zong father take him in like become own family. Du Zong father wasn't look down on him, but didn't take seriously, until that man big like become a mafia. Now important person, very hard to inviting him. Chinese way, came only to show respect, don't stay for dinner. Respect for making big celebration, he shows up. Mean gives lots of respect. Chinese custom. Chinese social life that way. If too important won't have to stay too long. He come to my wedding. I didn't see, I heard it. I gone to boy's side, they have YMCA dinner. Chinese age I was nineteen."

You should know that my mother's expressive command of English belies how 7 much she actually understands. She reads the *Forbes* report, listens to *Wall Street Week*, converses daily with her stockbroker, reads all of Shirley MacLaine's books with ease—all kinds of things I can't begin to understand. Yet some of my friends tell me they understand 50 percent of what my mother says. Some say they understand 80 to 90 percent. Some say they understand none of it, as if she were speaking pure Chinese. But to me, my mother's English is perfectly clear, perfectly natural. It's my mother tongue. Her language, as I hear it, is vivid, direct, full of observation and imagery. That was the language that helped shape the way I saw things, expressed things, made sense of the world.

8   Lately, I've been giving more thought to the kind of English my mother speaks. Like others, I have described it to people as "broken" or "fractured" English. But I wince when I say that. It has always bothered me that I can think of no way to describe it other than "broken," as if it were damaged and needed to be fixed, as if it lacked a certain wholeness and soundness. I've heard other terms used, "limited English," for example. But they seem just as bad, as if everything is limited, including people's perceptions of the limited English speaker.

9   I know this for a fact, because when I was growing up, my mother's "limited" English limited *my* perception of her. I was ashamed of her English. I believed that her English reflected the quality of what she had to say. That is, because she expressed them imperfectly her thoughts were imperfect. And I had plenty of empirical evidence to support me: the fact that people in the department stores, at banks, and at restaurants did not take her seriously, did not give her good service, pretended not to understand her, or even acted as if they did not hear her.

10   My mother has long realized the limitations of her English as well. When I was fifteen, she used to have me call people on the phone to pretend I was she. In this guise, I was forced to ask for information or even to complain and yell at people who had been rude to her. One time it was a call to her stockbroker in New York. She had cashed out her small portfolio and it just so happened we were going to go to New York the next week, our very first trip outside California. I had to get on the phone and say in an adolescent voice that was not very convincing, "This is Mrs. Tan."

11   And my mother was standing in the back whispering loudly, "Why he don't send me check, already two weeks late. So mad he lie to me, losing me money."

12   And then I said in perfect English, "Yes, I'm getting rather concerned. You had agreed to send the check two weeks ago, but it hasn't arrived."

13   Then she began to talk more loudly. "What he want, I come to New York tell him front of his boss, you cheating me?" And I was trying to calm her down, make her be quiet, while telling the stockbroker, "I can't tolerate any more excuses. If I don't receive the check immediately, I am going to have to speak to your manager when I'm in New York next week." And sure enough, the following week there we were in front of this astonished stockbroker, and I was sitting there red-faced and quiet, and my mother, the real Mrs. Tan, was shouting at his boss in her impeccable broken English.

We used a similar routine just five days ago, for a situation that was far less 14 humorous. My mother had gone to the hospital for an appointment, to find out about a benign brain tumor a CAT scan had revealed a month ago. She said she had spoken very good English, her best English, no mistakes. Still, she said, the hospital did not apologize when they said they had lost the CAT scan and she had come for nothing. She said they did not seem to have any sympathy when she told them she was anxious to know the exact diagnosis, since her husband and son had both died of brain tumors. She said they would not give her any more information until the next time and she would have to make another appointment for that. So she said she would not leave until the doctor called her daughter. She wouldn't budge. And when the doctor finally called her daughter, me, who spoke in perfect English—lo and behold—we had assurances the CAT scan would be found, promises that a conference call on Monday would be held, and apologies for any suffering my mother had gone through for a most regrettable mistake.

I think my mother's English almost had an effect on limiting my possibilities 15 in life as well. Sociologists and linguists probably will tell you that a person's developing language skills are more influenced by peers. But I do think that the language spoken in the family, especially in immigrant families which are more insular, plays a large role in shaping the language of the child. And I believe that it affected my results on achievement tests, IQ tests, and the SAT. While my English skills were never judged as poor, compared to math, English could not be considered my strong suit. In grade school I did moderately well, getting perhaps B's, sometimes B-pluses, in English and scoring perhaps in the sixtieth or seventieth percentile on achievement tests. But those scores were not good enough to override the opinion that my true abilities lay in math and science, because in those areas I achieved A's and scored in the ninetieth percentile or higher.

This was understandable. Math is precise; there is only one correct answer. 16 Whereas, for me at least, the answers on English tests were always a judgment call, a matter of opinion and personal experience. Those tests were constructed around items like fill-in-the-blank sentence completion, such as, "Even though Tom was _____, Mary thought he was _____." And the correct answer always seemed to be the most bland combinations of thoughts, for example, "Even though Tom was shy, Mary thought he was charming," with the grammatical structure "even though" limiting the correct answer to some sort of semantic opposites, so you wouldn't get answers like, "Even though Tom was foolish, Mary thought he was ridiculous." Well, according to my mother, there were very few limitations as to what Tom could have been and what Mary might have thought of him. So I never did well on tests like that.

The same was true with word analogies, pairs of words in which you were sup- 17 posed to find some sort of logical, semantic relationship—for example, "*Sunset* is to *nightfall* as _____ is to _____." And here you would be presented with a list of four possible pairs, one of which showed the same kind of relationship: *red* is to *stoplight, bus* is to *arrival, chills* is to *fever, yawn* is to *boring.* Well, I could never think that way. I knew what the tests were asking, but I could not block out of my mind the images already created by the first pair, *"sunset* is to *nightfall"*—and I would see a burst of colors against a darkening sky, the moon rising, the lowering of a curtain of stars. And all the other pairs of words—*red, bus, stoplight, boring*— just threw up a mass of confusing images, making it impossible for me to sort out something as logical as saying: "A sunset precedes nightfall" is the same as "a chill precedes a fever." The only way I would have gotten that answer right would have been to imagine an associative situation, for example, my being disobedient and staying out past sunset, catching a chill at night, which turns into feverish pneumonia as punishment, which indeed did happen to me.

18   I have been thinking about all this lately, about my mother's English, about achievement tests. Because lately I've been asked, as a writer, why there are not more Asian-Americans represented in American literature. Why are there few Asian-Americans enrolled in creative writing programs? Why do so many Chinese students go into engineering? Well, these are broad sociological questions I can't begin to answer. But I have noticed in surveys—in fact, just last week—that Asian students, as a whole, always do significantly better on math achievement tests than in English. And this makes me think that there are other Asian-American students whose English spoken in the home might also be described as "broken" or "limited." And perhaps they also have teachers who are steering them away from writing and into math and science, which is what happened to me.

19   Fortunately, I happen to be rebellious in nature and enjoy the challenge of disproving assumptions made about me. I became an English major my first year in college, after being enrolled as pre-med. I started writing nonfiction as a freelancer the week after I was told by my former boss that writing was my worst skill and I should hone my talents toward account management.

20   But it wasn't until 1985 that I finally began to write fiction. And at first I wrote using what I thought to be wittily crafted sentences, sentences that would finally prove I had mastery over the English language. Here's an example from the first draft of a story that later made its way into *The Joy Luck Club,* but without this line: "That was my mental quandary in its nascent state." A terrible line, which I can barely pronounce.

21   Fortunately, for reasons I won't get into today, I later decided I should envision a reader for the stories I would write. And the reader I decided upon was my mother, because these were stories about mothers. So with this reader in mind— and in fact she did read my early drafts—I began to write stories using all the Englishes I grew up with: the English I spoke to my mother, which for lack of a better term might be described as "simple"; the English she used with me, which for lack of a better term might be described as "broken"; my translation of her

Chinese, which could certainly be described as "watered down"; and what I imagined to be her translation of her Chinese if she could speak in perfect English, her internal language, and for that I sought to preserve the essence, but neither an English nor a Chinese structure. I wanted to capture what language ability tests can never reveal: her intent, her passion, her imagery, the rhythms of her speech and the nature of her thoughts.

Apart from what any critic had to say about my writing, I knew I had succeeded where it counted when my mother finished reading my book and gave me her verdict: "So easy to read." 22

QUESTIONS

Understanding the message: Comprehension

1. Why does the presence of Tan's mother at the writer's talk make "the whole talk sound wrong"?

2. What are the different types of English that Tan speaks?

3. In what way(s) is the language Tan uses with her mother different from Standard English? What have the differences come to mean to her?

4. What kind of impact did Tan's mother's English have on others? How did it shape their impressions of the elder Tan?

5. In what ways did Tan's mother's use of English affect Tan's own impression of others? How did it affect her own language development?

Examining the structure and details: Analysis

1. Tan begins with a personal note and a disclaimer, "I am not a scholar of English or literature. I cannot give you much more than personal opinions on the English language and its variations in this country or others." How does this shift to the personal affect the readers? In what way(s) does Tan contradict this disclaimer by the end of the selection?

2. How does Tan characterize those who react to her mother's broken English? How does her use of details support this impression?

3. How does Tan convey the notion that her mother's thoughts are far more sophisticated than her language?

4. What principle does Tan use to classify the kinds of English? Cite an example she provides for each category.

Formulating a response: Inference and interpretation

1. How effective is the title "Mother Tongue"? Think of the different associations with this title in formulating your answer.

2. Does Tan convince you that others were unfair in their assessment of her mother? Why or why not?

3. Is Tan fair in her representation of people's reactions to her mother? Do you think her portrait of others is biased? Why or why not?

4. Who is Tan's intended audience in this essay? Do you think that her details within each category of English are appropriate for this audience?

Essay questions

1. We've all had experiences in which we were misunderstood by a listener, even though we assumed we were being perfectly clear. Write an essay in which you classify "kinds of misunderstandings" between people, according to the underlying reasons (for example, lack of understanding, lack of attention, and so on).

2. What types of problems do second language speakers have in a new country? Imagine yourself in another country, with a national language that is different from your first language. What would be the most frustrating occurrences in day-to-day life? List these, and then classify them according to the principle of "most frustrating language problems." Write an essay about these problems.

3. Tan ends her article by assuming she is successful as a writer if her mother finds the writing "easy to read." Does Tan succeed in crafting something easy to read here as well? What makes the writing easy to understand, or not? Cite examples from the article to support your answer.

VOCABULARY

Forbes report, Wall Street Week: business journal and TV show on business news

empirical: measurable, scientific

benign: not malignant; not life-threatening

linguists: specialists who study the science of language

semantic: meaning-related

quandary: uncertainty

nascent: developing

Notes That Resonate for a Lifetime

by Robyn Sarah (b. 1949)

Robyn Sarah was born in New York to Canadian parents and grew up in Montreal, where she still lives. She is a graduate of the Conservatoire de Musique et d'Art Dramatique du Québec and of McGill University, where she completed an honours degree in philosophy. Her poems began appearing in Canadian periodicals in the early 1970s, while she completed an M.A. in English. Subsequently she taught English at Champlain Regional College for 20 years. She is the author of several poetry collections, including The Touchstone: Poems New and Selected *(1992) and* Questions about the Stars *(1998), and two collections of short stories, most recently* Promise of Shelter *(1997). Since the mid-1990s she has been a frequent contributor to the* Globe and Mail *and the* Montreal Gazette, *writing on education, literacy, poetry, and a variety of other topics. Her poems, stories, and essays have been published widely in Canadian literary quarterlies, as well as in the United States in such publications as the* Threepenny Review, *the* New England Review, *the* Antioch Review, Prairie Schooner, *and others.*

PRE-READING

Think back to your early days of grade school. What do you remember about the teachers you had then? What characteristics or behaviours make a "great" teacher? Also, think about what makes someone inspiring to others: which of your teachers over the years has had the greatest impact on you today? In this article from the *Globe and Mail* (1997), Sarah writes about the teachers who left a lasting impression in her life.

Among my teachers over the years I look back upon a few duds, but mostly I 1 remember good teaching. Not that all of my teachers were inspired or inspiring: only a few were that. But teaching doesn't have to levitate to be good, just as a meal doesn't have to meet gourmet standards to nourish.

I remember all kinds of good teaching. I remember meat-and-potatoes 2 teaching—experienced, conscientious teaching backed by a solid knowledge of the subject. I remember teachers who subdued their personalities in order to become the purest possible conduit for a beloved subject—and teachers who used their personalities to enliven a subject they did not particularly love. I remember stern teachers, grumpy teachers, patient teachers, funny teachers, eccentric teachers—all of them basically good teachers, giving what they knew in the style that was theirs, giving it daily, year after year, without fanfare.

3   Such teachers are the backbone of the profession. Years after, even if we cannot remember a single individual lesson, we remember the ambiance of their classes and know that we learned from them. But most of us remember best one or two teachers who played us a note that has gone on resonating, in different ways and contexts, long beyond the time we spent in their classes. We carry their gifts with us for a lifetime.

4   My fifth grade teacher, at the time she taught me, was already beloved of two generations—because she never yelled, kids would say; because she didn't load us with homework; because she explained things in a way you could understand. But what I remember is how she brought her own life's interests into our classroom. Back in the days when "opening exercises" included five or ten minutes of hymn singing, this teacher—a barbershop singer—graced those minutes by teaching us the hymns in four-part harmony. (She had founded her own chapter of barbershoppers, quitting her original group in protest when it barred a black singer from joining: this story, too, she shared with us. And I think it was no accident, seeing we were an overwhelmingly Jewish class in a Protestant school, that she chose from the school's Protestant hymnbook those hymns based on Psalms of our own scriptures, and never, ever made us sing "Onward Christian Soldiers.")

5   I have still got all those descant melodies in my head: the remembered beauty of their blending, and the comical picture of us ten-year-olds at our desks, frowning in concentration and at first covering our ears, so as to be able to sing our own line without being confused by hearing the others. As I have also the example of our teacher's stand against racism, and her personal sensitivity.

6   One day when I was twelve and tearful at my own ineptitude, my piano teacher told me this story: Two men tried repeatedly to accomplish a task neither found himself able to do. After the third try, one man said, "I'm a failure"; the other said, "I failed three times." It's a story that, in the years since, has buttressed me through every kind of disheartenment. I'm sure it didn't originate with my piano teacher, who drew upon great teachings wherever he found them (sources ranging from Socrates to Lao Tse) and usually passed them on without attribution. Never mind: the point is, he passed them on—and always in a context where they lit up like neon for me, and sang.

7   Moreover, he gave me a couple of lifelong tools that I've found applicable in contexts far removed from music. Here's one from a time when I was having trouble making myself practice a difficult passage: Put an alarm clock on the piano—set the alarm to ring in ten minutes—tell yourself you're going to work on the hard part just until the alarm rings and then quit. (What happens, of course, is that in those ten minutes, having let yourself off the hook in advance,

you are free to get involved. Nine times on ten, when the alarm rings, you are annoyed at the interruption and want to go on working.)

Another: When you're playing something badly, don't "practice" by playing it 8 doggedly over and over in the hope that the mistakes will magically iron themselves out. Repetition reinforces: you are teaching yourself your own mistakes. Instead, play it differently: slow it down, or break it into segments, or alter the rhythm—or leave it alone and play something else for a while. The time to play over and over is when you are playing something well: at such a time, repetition reinforces what you're doing right, even if you aren't entirely conscious of what it is.

As a university undergraduate, I studied philosophy with an Orthodox rabbi 9 whose classes were so fabled that students who weren't registered for his course would turn up regularly to hear him lecture—sometimes standing at the back of the hall for the duration. When it came time for our first assignment, he explained the topic in detail, then gave us our deadline. "But sir," a chorus of voices, a waving of hands, "how many words? how many pages? How long does it have to be?"

The question made him wince; he seemed not to have thought about it in those 10 terms, and to find them somehow inappropriate. I heard in his answer—in its gentleness, and the absolute clarity of its import—something to carry with me through life: "Look, don't worry about it. Just hand in something you can respect." A small but profound revelation: we were to hand in, not something *he* would respect, not something to impress *him*—but something *we* could respect. The onus was on us—as indeed it always is—to make the assignment our own.

Often years pass before we realize what we have been given by our teachers. 11 How then to acknowledge the gift? I can think of no better way than to pass it on.

QUESTIONS

Understanding the message: Comprehension

1. Explain the title: in what way can it contain more than one meaning?

2. Why is it significant that Sarah's fifth grade teacher "never, ever" made the class sing "Onward Christian Soldiers" in her class?

3. What did Sarah learn from her piano teacher that's not related to music?

Examining the structure and details: Analysis

1. What are the different classes of teachers that Sarah presents in this article? How many categories does she use? How do her categories differ from what you might expect of a list of teaching types?

2. What is the most important aspect of teaching, according to Sarah? How do you know?

3. Sarah compares teaching to other activities in the article (the most obvious being playing an instrument, with "notes that resonate"). What other activity is mentioned in comparison with teaching? How do these metaphors contribute to the thesis of the article?

Formulating a response: Inference and interpretation

1. Sarah writes in the first person, even though she describes others in the article. Why do you think she uses a first-person narrator? How does it affect our understanding of the selection? How would it have been different with a third-person narrator?

2. How have Sarah's teachers over the years had an impact on her personal life? What emotional or psychological impact have they each had?

3. Although she is classifying "good" teachers, Sarah concentrates on stories about only three. Does she provide sufficient details in each category? Do her examples limit her argument? Why or why not?

4. Do Sarah's beloved teachers fit the common assessment of what makes a good teacher? In which ways? In which ways are her good teachers distinctive or outside the norm?

Essay questions

1. Write an essay in which you include your own list of kinds of teachers, using your own experience at school.

2. Choose another group from a particular profession or career and classify the members into types (some possibilities: doctors, waiters, telemarketers, writers).

3. What trait do all of Sarah's good teachers have in common? What techniques does she employ to convey this similarity? Support your answer with examples from Sarah's essay.

VOCABULARY

descant: singing

ineptitude: awkward inability; lack of talent

CHAPTER 8

Comparison and Contrast

COMPARISON AND CONTRAST IN DAILY LIFE

How common is the skill of comparison and contrast? You probably engage in comparison and contrast regularly, when you participate in activities such as the following:

- You date two people concurrently and try to decide which one you'd like to continue seeing by comparing them with each other.
- You tell your cousin how your maternal grandmother is different from your paternal grandmother.
- You write a letter to your parents from your new residence at school, informing them how the city in which your college is located differs from the town in which you grew up.
- You write a report for your boss advising a change in how the office furniture is organized, pointing out the ways your arrangement will be more efficient than the previous one.

WHAT IS COMPARISON AND CONTRAST?

When you write a comparison and contrast essay, you pinpoint similarities and differences between two like things: two restaurants, two science fiction films, two swimming coaches. Strictly speaking, a **comparison** looks only at similarities, while a **contrast** examines only differences, but in reality, most essays that compare or contrast will include both operations under the term *comparison*. Accordingly, we'll use *comparison* to refer to essays that use one or both methods.

All good comparisons focus on a pair of subjects from within a single class or category, those that already share something significant in common; your audience won't gain much from a paper that compares two topics so different that there is no connection between them. Likewise, if the two subjects are so similar

DEFINITION

Comparison and contrast: Comparison and contrast examines similarities, differences, or both between two related things.

as to be almost identical, there's also little reason to compare them (what could readers learn that's new about either one?).

For instance, you might compare two diets from the category "fad diets" (such as the High-Protein Diet and the Cabbage Soup Diet). You could compare these according to foods allowed on the diet, the rate of weight loss, and the health problems that may occur as a result of the diet. Alternatively, you might select two diets from two different life stages, such as a recommended diet for women in early adulthood compared with the diet recommended during pregnancy, to show how the concept of healthy eating changes once a woman "eats for two." It wouldn't make sense, however, to compare a pregnant woman's diet with one of the fad diets, since there is no common ground between them (one is for healthy women who don't wish to lose weight; the other is for people who wish to lose weight quickly).

WHY USE COMPARISON AND CONTRAST?

Whenever you need to select between two, or from among many, choices that are in some ways similar, comparison and contrast can help. For instance, imagine you'd been accepted to four different colleges; how would you decide which to attend? Often, people look at pros and cons (simply another form of comparison and contrast) when making decisions. You might consider, for example, that Northlands College in Saskatchewan offers a wide variety of forestry courses in conjunction with government and business agencies, whereas Quebec's CEGEP L'Abitibi-Témiscamingue offers a forestry program entirely in French (an advantage if you wish to improve your command of that language). One institution may boast renowned instructors, while another is lauded for its state-of-the-art equipment. By isolating the similarities and differences between two things, you can evaluate their relative merits and drawbacks.

Comparison and contrast is also useful to determine which of many available choices is superior or preferable. For instance, you might use comparison and contrast to convince your dinner companion that your first choice of restaurant is better than the greasy diner s/he suggested.

How to Write a Comparison and Contrast Essay

The general guidelines for pre-writing, writing and post-writing in Chapter 2 will help you to write your comparison and contrast essay. In addition, the following steps will provide further pointers specific to comparison and contrast.

Pre-Writing

1. Choose a general topic

It's a good idea to deal with only two items or subjects at a time when you examine topics for comparison. While it's possible to compare a larger number of items, focusing on two keeps the essay a manageable size and usually makes it easier for your audience to follow.

TIP

Pick a category, any category

One way to ensure that your general subjects are chosen from the same category or class (and, therefore, furnish a reasonable basis for comparison) is to select topics that already share something major in common. For instance, you might pick two entertainers because both are actors (or, even more specifically, Academy Award–winning actors); or two television comedies because both are ensemble acts, such as *Saturday Night Live* and the CBC hit *This Hour Has 22 Minutes*. What about MuchMusic versus MTV? Both are television stations airing popular music videos. Two homes might be chosen because both are country getaway cottages. As long as there's a reasonable basis for similarity, you'll have plenty of room to develop individual points of comparison that make sense and add interest.

---

2. Consider your audience and purpose

As stated earlier, the purpose of a comparison essay is often to persuade: you show which of two choices you prefer, and you expect your audience to concur. However, a purely entertaining purpose also works in comparison essays, as when you compare which task is *less* appealing, washing the dishes or dusting the living room; which soap opera has better love scenes, *The Young and the Restless* or *Days of Our Lives;* which pet triggers more phobias, a tarantula or a boa constrictor; and so on. Clearly, authors Robert Patterson and Charles Weijer, both physicians, intend their comparison between Doctors Julius Hibbert and Nick Riviera (from the cartoon *The Simpsons)* to be taken in jest. Finally, you may elect to use comparison and contrast as a means to understand the similarities or differences between two items more completely, even if they are equally worthwhile; in this case, your purpose is to inform (see the Model Student Essay in this chapter for a comparison and contrast essay the purpose of which is to inform).

3. Generate ideas about the topic

Because your essay examines points of similarity, difference, or both, you must consider every aspect of the subjects as thoroughly as you can. Uncovering less obvious similarities or differences might ultimately lead to more interesting and informative essays. Use a variety of brainstorming techniques to examine your topic from many different perspectives.

4. Narrow to a thesis

Two aspects of the comparison should be included in the thesis statement of your essay: the basis of comparison (what significant thing do they have in common?) and an indication of your purpose. You may, for instance, decide to compare two Web sites for popular newspapers in your city; your basis for comparison is the fact that both newspapers are published in your home town. If you decide that the Web site for the *Daily News* is more user-friendly than that for the *Daily Times,* your purpose, to persuade your audience that one is preferable, should be obvious in the thesis statement. The thesis statement "When surfing the Web for local news, I always choose the *Daily News* over the *Daily Times*" lets your readers know, first, that you are comparing two *local* papers' sites (the basis for comparison); and, second, that you *prefer* the site for the *Daily News.*

5. Organize your ideas in an outline

Once you've decided on your basis of comparison, your main points should all refer back to that principle. In the comparison between two daily newspapers, above, the point is to demonstrate that one is more user-friendly than the other. Consequently, each point should indicate one trait that contributes to (or detracts from) how user-friendly the site is. Comparing the contents of the two sites (whether hard news or fluff pieces) does not contribute to our understanding of how user-friendly each is.

Comparison essays are generally organized according to one of two methods; the method you choose usually depends on the length of the essay. For shorter essays, the block method is generally preferable; for longer essays, you may elect a point-by-point method.

Block method. In the block method, you organize your essay in two "blocks" of information, one for each of the two main subjects being compared. Then, under each subject heading, you include several points of support—and use the same points for each of the two subjects. Let's say you've decided to compare two local fitness clubs, your local community centre and the Fit N Toned Club, in order to decide which you'll join. Consequently, your main points of support must each relate to this concept—what makes a health club appealing, one that you're likely to use regularly? Assuming that you can afford to join both places, you could then choose as your main points the services offered (such as equipment, instruction, fitness classes, and so on); the location (whether it's convenient and close to your home, whether it has adequate parking, and so on); and the social aspects (whether the other members are people you can imagine as friends, whether the club offers any social meetings, whether the neighbourhood encourages social gatherings with nearby restaurants or bars, and so on). In block format, these points would be organized as follows:

A. Community Centre
  1. Location
  2. Social aspects
  3. Services

B. Fit N Toned
  1. Location
  2. Social aspects
  3. Services

Under each of the main points, you then add specific supporting examples.

The block method suits short essays in which the reader can remember all the points about the first subject even while reading about the second.

SNAG

Subjects become separate essays

While the block (or subject-by-subject) method of organizing is useful for shorter papers, you must beware of the tendency to separate subjects so much that they become two distinct "mini essays." One way to avoid this potential hazard is to keep the transition between ideas clear when you begin your discussion of the second subject; refer back to the first subject occasionally throughout your discussion of the second as you move on to examine each of your key points.

Point-by-point method. In the point-by-point method, you organize the essay according to each of the main points of comparison, discussing first one subject, then the other, under each point. The numbered points, then, become the essay's main headings, and the subjects themselves are treated side by side under each of these. In the essay about the two fitness facilities, here's how this type of outline would look:

A. Location
   1. Community centre
   2. Fit N Toned

B. Social Aspects
   1. Community centre
   2. Fit N Toned

C. Services
   1. Community centre
   2. Fit N Toned

Notice that whichever method you choose, *both outlines ultimately cover identical points*. That is, each essay discusses the club's location, its social aspects, and the services it offers, whichever method of organization is used. The point-by-point method works nicely with longer essays covering several points because it allows readers to examine each similarity or difference side by side. They don't exhaust their memories in an attempt to recall everything already mentioned about the first subject as they move through the second. Finally, the main points themselves can be ordered spatially, chronologically, or emphatically in a comparison and contrast essay, depending on the subject matter.

TIP

Arm yourself with a surplus

As with other topics, starting with more points than you need will make writing a comparison and contrast easier. This way, you'll be able to select only the three to five very best points to support your thesis.

SNAG

Mismatched points

Be scrupulous when outlining a comparison and contrast essay to ensure that the specific points of comparison remain the same for both subjects, particularly if you use the block method. It's easy to begin writing about one subject (say, your English professor) and examine one list of details, then move to a second subject and mention others that come to mind more readily. Discussing your English professor's humour, extensive knowledge, and patience is fine, but not if you then compare her to your chemistry professor, whose punctuality, adherence to rules, and stern temperament are examined.

6. Decide on specific support for the main points

Both the choice and presentation of details contribute to the overall effectiveness of comparison essays. In looking at the same issues for two separate subjects, find examples that really illustrate the similarities and differences you wish to evince. Once again, concrete examples and specific, vivid language will strengthen the writing.

SNAG

Telling readers what they already know

A common pitfall in writing comparisons is to repeat what is really just the basis of comparison—the obvious similarities or differences between two things. For instance, if you compare Céline Dion and Barbra Streisand as singers, you need not tell your audience that both have amazing vocal range and power; these defining characteristics are already clear to anyone who has ever heard, or heard of, the two. It would be more interesting to focus on what these divas *do* with their incredible voices.

SNAG

Confusing analogy with comparison

A common error in writing a comparison and contrast essay is to write an analogy instead. Like comparison and contrast, **analogy** compares two subjects, but two subjects we would never normally consider to be similar. The purpose of analogy is to help elucidate one subject by comparing it with the other. For instance, a student may write an essay based on the thesis "Working in my office is like being stranded on a desert island." This thesis does, indeed, allow the writer to draw similarities between the two experiences (lack of resources, sense of isolation, need to work independently, and so on) and serves to illuminate what it's like to work in the office; however, the basis for comparison is not valid, since one is a real work situation and the other is an imaginary notion. Furthermore, analogy is used to highlight the first subject (what it's like to work in your office); the desert island is used only to help convey that idea and is not examined in any detail as a subject in its own right. A true comparison, on the other hand, would examine two like work environments (working in your current office compared with working in a previous building, for instance).

Writing

In order to keep the comparison at the forefront and to prevent confusion on the part of your readers, pay close attention to the use of transitions while writing your draft. Transitions ensure that connections between the various subjects and points are clear. As you discuss your second subject, don't be afraid to relate the main points to those same ideas as they were treated in the first subject. Using transitional devices such as "similarly," "in the same way as," "in contrast," or "on the other hand" can all serve to link the main points of the first subject to those in the second subject when the essay is organized using the block method, for instance.

Post-Writing

Once again, using the general guidelines in Chapter 2 will help you to revise your comparison and contrast essay. In addition, consider the following questions that apply specifically to this type of essay:

- Is it clear in what way my two subjects are similar? Have I made the basis of comparison clear? Is this evident in my thesis?
- Have I decided on a clear purpose, and is this evident in my thesis?
- Have I included all the necessary main points of comparison?
- Have I covered the same points for each subject, regardless of my method of organization?
- Is the order of points logical given my thesis and purpose?
- Have I included a good variety of support in my essay?

EXERCISES

1. Think of two things that are at first glance very similar—for example, a pair of twins, two running shoes, two row houses, two copies of the same book. Next, find as many differences between the two as you possibly can.
2. Choose two people who fascinate you, whether from your own life, fiction, or history. Compare their good and bad qualities.
3. Choose two items or people who have many similarities (two economy cars, two teachers, two parents, two movie theatres, two Italian restaurants, and so on). Next, try to come up with at least three *different* bases of comparison of the two (for example, you could compare teachers according to marking styles, ability to keep lectures interesting, or willingness to help students beyond the boundaries of the classroom).

The following comparison and contrast essay demonstrates how one student tackled this rhetorical mode. Highlighted is how the writer incorporated key aspects of comparison and contrast to make the essay effective.

Two Unique "I Do's"

Last summer, it seemed as if everyone I knew decided to get married at once. After attending six weddings (and being a bridesmaid at three of them), I now consider myself a "wedding expert." Of all the nuptials I attended, two stand out most in my mind: Carla's and Bob's. Their weddings differed in almost every way, yet despite all the differences, I realized that these two celebrations shared one very important trait.

thesis-- includes basis for comparison

subject A, point #1

Carla wanted a traditional June wedding, and that's exactly what she planned. The ceremony took place on a perfectly sunny summer day, on the fairy-tale grounds of a historic inn. Over 200 chairs were placed in parallel rows on the manicured grass, with a red carpet laid down the middle aisle. In front of the seats, decorated with flowing arrangements of white roses, tulips and orchids, was a white canopy built just for the occasion. Beneath it, Carla, John (the groom), and the minister stood while the couple exchanged traditional vows.

specific sensory details

more about point #1

After the ceremony, the guests were invited to be seated in the lavish dining room, arranged on the patio under a massive tent. Inside, the linen-covered tables were adorned with more flowers, candles, fine china and crystal. The atmosphere was so formal, in fact, we forgot we were actually outdoors! As we dined, we were able to peek out at the lush green lawns and foliage around the inn. The atmosphere was truly magical.

Bob's wedding, on the other hand, was completely unconventional. The location, like Carla's,
was outdoors—but in this case, "outdoors" meant a
provincial park! The ceremony took place at a
campground where guests were invited to camp
overnight. With the forest and sounds of wildlife
surrounding us, we sat cross-legged on the grass or
perched on rocks and hillocks overseeing the ceremony, which took place in a small clearing between
the tents and communal washrooms. The minister,
too, was camping overnight, and brought along her
dog, a golden retriever that barked through most of
the ceremony. About halfway through the vows
(which, of course, Bob and Karen had written
themselves), it began to drizzle, and guests were
quickly enlisted to shield the bride and groom with
oversized umbrellas, creating a human canopy over
the couple.

Clothing was another feature that distinguished
the two weddings. At Carla's, it was "formal attire
only." We bridesmaids were fitted for custom-made
dresses, sleek and sophisticated satin gowns in
"seafoam green." Even our silk pumps were professionally dyed to match the dress colour perfectly.
When Carla walked down the aisle, she could have
been modeling for *Brides* magazine. Her designer
gown, flowing in silk and tulle, was beaded all over
the bodice with tiny, sparkling pearls and sequins.
John's tuxedo matched perfectly, with a cummer-
bund and bow tie in cream-coloured satin.

The dress code at Bob's wedding, in contrast, was
decidedly more relaxed. Nevertheless, there was also
a unique style to the clothing at this wedding.
Guests were cautioned to wear something "comfortable," since we'd be erecting tents, setting out food,
or, as it turned out, holding umbrellas! Most people
arrived in shorts and T-shirts. The bride and groom
ingeniously managed to be equally casual. At first,
Karen breezed in wearing a loose, flowing Laura
Ashley frock, a light cotton print of tiny mauve and
white flowers. Bob, as always the iconoclast, wore

RESPOND IN WRITING

black cotton slacks and a T-shirt painted to look like a shirt and tie. Even the minister wore shorts and a T-shirt under her robes, and her dog sported a bandana on its collar. Once the ceremony ended, however, Karen pulled off the dress to reveal a tank top and shorts, and Bob exchanged his slacks for cut-off jeans.

The meal itself was another memorable aspect of the two weddings. Carla's dinner, a six-course affair, started with avocado and shrimp soup, followed by caviar and hearts of palm salad, a main course of salmon Wellington and dessert of chocolate mousse and cherries jubilee. Guests were offered champagne cocktails before dinner and a choice of wines throughout the meal. Between courses, waiters brought "palate cleansers" of lemon and mint sorbet.

subject A, point #3

specific
details

On the other hand, the fare at Bob's wedding offered no surprises, since the guests themselves had prepared it. At this pot luck wedding, everyone brought a dish to the campsite, where the food was arranged on platters on a picnic table. Guests then descended, paper plates and plastic cutlery in hand, to help themselves from the communal buffet. Chomping on salads, quiches and pastas, guests mingled and chatted as we ate. Someone even brought a case of homemade wine, its label boasting, "Karen and Bob: 2001."

subject B, point #3 with appropriate transition

thesis
reiterated

Although they were very different in their approach and individual details, my two friends' weddings shared some important features. Each one offered a great party: Carla's live band played on into the wee hours of the morning, when people decided to kick off their shoes and keep dancing. At Bob and Karen's wedding, we danced outdoors, lanterns flickering and the portable CD players at maximum volume, keeping the raccoons and bears at bay as we boogied. In the end both weddings seemed to overflow with love, friendship and feelings of joy for the happy couples; in that respect, they were exactly the same.

conclusion brings both subjects together

Gender Gap in Cyberspace

by Deborah Tannen (b. 1945)

Deborah Tannen is a university professor, researcher, and writer who has published 16 books and over 85 articles, many of which focus on differences between male and female communication styles. Her most famous book, You Just Don't Understand: Men and Women in Conversation *(1990), was on the* New York Times *Bestseller List for four years. In recent years she wrote* I Only Say This Because I Love You: How the Way We Talk Can Make or Break Family Relationships throughout Our Lives *(2001),* The Argument Culture: Moving from Debate to Dialogue *(1998), and* Talking from 9 to 5: Women and Men in the Workplace *(1995). She has published a variety of periodical and magazine articles and essays in publications such as the* New York Times, Newsweek, Time, *the* Harvard Business Review, *and* People *magazine. In addition, she writes short stories, plays, and poetry; her first play,* An Act of Devotion, *was included in* The Best American Short Plays: 1993–1994. *Tannen also lectures to corporations and universities around the world and is a frequent guest on television news and talk shows, such as* Oprah, Larry King Live, 20/20, *and* ABC World News Tonight. *She received her Ph.D. from the University of California, Berkeley, and is a professor of linguistics in Georgetown University's Linguistics Department. Tannen was born in Brooklyn, New York.*

PRE-READING

This article originally appeared in a 1994 issue of *Newsweek* magazine. In it, Tannen compares the way men and women she knows use computers, specifically e-mail. Think about your own experience using computers: for what purposes do you use them? How difficult was it for you to learn? Are you completely comfortable with the technology? What differences (if any) do you see between the way women and men approach new technologies?

1   I was a computer pioneer, but I'm still something of a novice. That paradox is telling.

2   I was the second person on my block to get a computer. The first was my colleague Ralph. It was 1980. Ralph got a Radio Shack TRS-80, I got a used Apple II+. He helped me get started and went on to become a maven, reading computer magazines, hungering for the new technology he read about, and buying and mastering it as quickly as he could afford. I hung on to old equipment far too long

because I dislike giving up what I'm used to, fear making the wrong decision about what to buy, and resent the time it takes me to install and learn a new system.

My first Apple came with videogames; I gave them away. Playing games on the computer didn't interest me. If I had free time I'd spend it talking on the telephone to friends.

Ralph got hooked. His wife was often annoyed by the hours he spent at his computer and the money he spent upgrading it. My marriage had no such strains—until I discovered E-mail. Then I got hooked. E-mail draws me the same way the phone does: it's a souped-up conversation.

E-mail deepened my friendship with Ralph. Though his office was next to mine, we rarely had extended conversations because he is shy. Face to face he mumbled, so I could barely tell he was speaking. But when we both got on E-mail, I started receiving long, self-revealing messages: we poured our hearts out to each other. A friend discovered that E-mail opened up that kind of communication with her father. He would never talk much on the phone (as her mother would), but they have become close since they both got on line.

Why, I wondered, would some men find it easier to open up on E-mail? It's a combination of the technology (which they enjoy) and the obliqueness of the written word, just as many men will reveal feelings in dribs and drabs while riding in the car or doing something, which they'd never talk about sitting face to face. It's too intense, too bearing-down on them, and once you start you have to keep going. With a computer in between, it's safer.

It was on E-mail, in fact, that I described to Ralph how boys in groups often struggle to get the upper hand whereas girls tend to maintain an appearance of cooperation. And he pointed out that this explained why boys are more likely to be captivated by computers than girls are. Boys are typically motivated by a social structure that says if you don't dominate you will be dominated. Computers, by their nature, balk; you type a perfectly appropriate command and it refuses to do what it should. Many boys and men are incited by this defiance: "I'm going to whip this into line and teach it who's boss! I'll get it to do what I say!" (and if they work hard enough, they always can). Girls and women are more likely to respond, "This thing won't cooperate. Get it away from me!"

Although no one wants to think of herself as "typical"—how much nicer to be *sui generis*—my relationship to my computer is—gulp—fairly typical for a woman. Most women (with plenty of exceptions) aren't excited by tinkering with the technology, grappling with the challenge of eliminating bugs or getting the biggest and best computer. These dynamics appeal to many men's interest in making sure they're on the top side of the inevitable who's-up-who's-down struggle that life is for them. E-mail appeals to my view of life as a contest for connections to others. When I see that I have fifteen messages, I feel loved.

9   I once posted a technical question on a computer network for linguists and was flooded with long disquisitions, some pages long. I was staggered by the generosity and the expertise, but wondered where these guys found the time—and why all the answers I got were from men.

10   Like coed classrooms and meetings, discussions on E-mail networks tend to be dominated by male voices, unless they're specifically women-only, like single-sex schools. On line, women don't have to worry about getting the floor (you just send a message when you feel like it), but, according to linguists Susan Herring and Laurel Sutton, who have studied this, they have the usual problems of having their messages ignored or attacked. The anonymity of public networks frees a small number of men to send long, vituperative, sarcastic messages that many other men either can tolerate or actually enjoy, but that turn most women off.

11   The anonymity of networks leads to another sad part of the E-mail story: there are men who deluge women with questions about their appearance and invitations to sex. On college campuses, as soon as women students log on, they are bombarded by references to sex, like going to work and finding pornographic

12   posters adorning the walls.
     Most women want one thing from a computer—to work. This is significant counterevidence to the claim that men want to focus on information while women are interested in rapport. That claim I found was often true in casual conversation, in which there is no particular information to be conveyed. But with computers, it is often women who are more focused on information, because they

13   don't respond to the challenge of getting equipment to submit.
     Once I had learned the basics, my interest in computers waned. I use it to write books (though I never mastered having it do bibliographies or tables of contents) and write checks (but not balance my checkbook). Much as I'd like to use it to do

14   more, I begrudge the time it would take to learn.
     Ralph's computer expertise costs him a lot of time. Chivalry requires that he rescue novices in need, and he is called upon by damsel novices far more often than knaves. More men would rather study the instruction booklet than ask directions, as it were, from another person. "When I do help men," Ralph wrote (on E-mail, of course), "they want to be more involved. I once installed a hard drive for a guy, and he wanted to be there with me, wielding the screwdriver and giving his own advice where he could." Women, he finds, usually are not interested in what he's doing; they

15   just want him to get the computer to the point where they can do what they want.
     Which pretty much explains how I managed to be a pioneer without becoming an expert.

QUESTIONS

Understanding the message: Comprehension

1. What is the similarity between writing e-mail and speaking in a car for men, according to Tannen?

2. How do computers appeal to boys' desire for dominance, according to Tannen?

3. What does the author mean when she writes, "E-mail appeals to my view of life as a contest for connections to others"?

4. Explain the last line of the article.

Examining the structure and details: Analysis

1. What method does Tannen use to introduce her essay? How does it relate to the rest of the essay?

2. What types of examples does Tannen provide to support her points? How effective are they? Cite examples from the article in your answer.

3. In the second to last paragraph, Tannen uses metaphor to express her point. What is the metaphor she uses? What effect does it have on the reader?

Formulating a response: Inference and interpretation

1. What is Tannen's tone in this essay? How does she convey this tone? Which expressions, in particular, support it?

2. Discuss Tannen's logic in suggesting that women are "ignored" or "attacked" for their e-mail messages in on-line discussions or that female students on-line are harassed by anonymous correspondents. Does she prove the point effectively? Why or why not?

3. Why do you think Tannen chose a first-person ("I") point of view? How does this affect the reader?

4. How appropriate is the title of this piece? Explain your answer.

Essay questions

1. Think of a technology or machine besides personal computers that people use on a daily basis (for example a car, a washing machine, a VCR, or voice mail). Write a comparison or contrast essay in which you examine the differences between how men and women treat this technology or machine.

2. Do you know anyone who is computer phobic? Write an essay in which you explain his or her difficulty with computers and how this compares with the behaviour of someone at ease with the technology.

3. Tannen's assessment of how men and women respond to computers is partially based on theories derived from her research. Do you agree with her assessment in this essay? Using specific examples from the article, explain why or why not.

VOCABULARY

paradox: an apparent contradiction, but one that is actually true

maven: expert

obliqueness: indirect nature

sui generis: unique

disquisitions: formal discourses, usually in writing

vituperative: abusive

chivalry: courteousness; gallantry

novices: beginners

damsel: woman (literally, a maiden)

knaves: men (literally, a soldier)

Cheapskates
by Rod McQueen (b. 1944)

Born in Guelph, Ontario, Rod McQueen graduated from the University of Western Ontario with an honours degree in English language and literature in 1967. He worked as a general reporter for the London Free Press *and was an editor in Maclean Hunter's business publication division. From 1970 to 1976 he was press secretary to Robert Stanfield, leader of the Progressive Conservative Party, and then he spent two years as director of public affairs at the Bank of Nova Scotia. In 1978, he joined* Maclean's *magazine as business editor and in 1979 was named managing editor. In 1982, McQueen became a freelance writer and broadcaster; his work has appeared in most major Canadian magazines, as well as several American and British publications. From 1987 to 1988, he and his wife, Sandy, lived in London, England, where he continued to freelance for Canadian and British periodicals. From 1989 to 1993 McQueen was bureau chief for the* Financial Post *in Washington, D.C. He continued to work for that publication when he returned to Toronto and is now a columnist and senior writer at the* National Post. *He has won numerous awards for his writing, including the National Business Book Award for* Who Killed Confederation Life? The Inside Story *(1996) and the Canadian Authors Association Award in history for* The Eatons: The Rise and Fall of Canada's Royal Family *(1998). His other books are* The Moneyspinners, Risky Business, Leap of Faith, Both My Houses *(in conjunction with Father Sean O'Sullivan),* Blind Trust, *and* The Last Best Hope—How to Start and Grow Your Own Business.

PRE-READING

What do you consider to be the major differences between Canadians and Americans? If you think of the United States as a richer country than Canada, what distinguishes the way Americans and Canadians handle money? In this essay from the *National Post Business Magazine* (2000), McQueen looks at the differences between Canadian and American patterns of donation. Do you consider yourself charitable? If so, what makes you think so?

Canadians are a stingy bunch. Our parsimonious nature is particularly odious 1 when charitable donations by Canadians are compared to giving by our American cousins. Philanthropy in the U.S. increased by 17% in 1999 over the previous year while donations by Canadians remained unchanged. Worse, overall philanthropic giving in the U.S. is consistently 35 to 40 times greater than in Canada.

2   American foundations spill more than their Canadian counterparts drink. During the last 100 years, many of America's famous families have established foundations with massive endowments: Ford, Rockefeller, Carnegie, Mellon and Getty. In modern times, more multi-billionaire Medicis have come forward with cash, including CNN's Ted Turner and Microsoft's Bill Gates.

3   An American family foundation with a billion-dollar nest egg is not uncommon. In Canada, a modest $50-million fund is the more likely size. Our biggest foundation, the J. W. McConnell Family Foundation of Montreal, controls $500 million, only 2% the size of the foundation established by Bill Gates.

4   Even volunteerism is higher in the U.S., where 51% of the citizens donate their time to the community compared to 27% of Canadians. As for gifts-in-kind, the ratio is more than 100-1 in favour of U.S. donors. However the matter of money on the move is measured, Canadians are tighter than two coats of paint.

5   Canada's most charitable couple must surely be Izaak Walton Killam, a Nova Scotia–born entrepreneur who died in 1955, and his wife, Dorothy, who passed on a decade later. Between them, they gave $125 million to hospitals, universities and the Canada Council, an amount that is equivalent to more than $700-million in today's dollars. In the 35 years since their bequests, no other Canadian individual, couple or family has come even close to matching that largesse, a sad commentary on our selfish nature.

6   The attitudinal chasm between the cultures in the U.S. and Canada is rooted in history. Americans are a revolutionary people while Canadians clung to colonialism. So while Americans hungered for the wilder ways of life, liberty and the pursuit of happiness, Canadians believed in a more straight-laced existence founded on peace, order and good government. The result has been to make Canadians feel so conservative and conniving that we somehow think we'll need to keep every penny we have all to ourselves. Charity not only begins at home, it ends there, too.

7   Corporate Canada has provided little leadership. Powerful executives and major employers count heavily on governments to feed the homeless and aid the helpless. No surprise there. Business has relied on the crutch of government succour for both itself and its social responsibilities ever since the so-called free-enterprise builders of the Lachine Canal went bankrupt in the 1820s and sought a public-sector bailout.

8   As a result, Canada now suffers from the worst of both worlds, a debt-encumbered state with little money for good works and a largely indifferent ruling class with no history of giving.

9   To be sure, there have been a few munificent Canadians. Joey Tanenbaum, a former steel magnate turned Toronto land developer, and his wife, Toby, have given $100 million to various causes including the opera, art galleries, and medical research. In May, scientist Richard Tomlinson donated $64 million for

research in medicine and technology to his alma mater, McGill University, much to the chagrin of McMaster University in Hamilton, Ont., where he had taught. That same month the University of Toronto received $50 million from the R. S. McLaughlin Foundation, in memory of Sam McLaughlin, who founded the motorcar company that became part of General Motors Corp.

But that's about it when it comes to the big money. Most other Canadian dona- 10 tions are modestly in the $1-million to $5-million range. Perhaps Izzy Asper, chairman of Can-West Global Communications Corp., of Winnipeg, spoke for many of his fellow entrepreneurs when he said, "It's tougher to give away money effectively than it is to make it. There's a tendency for people to say, 'Give me your money and shut up.'" The dilemma often involves control over the money once it's given to the deserving cause. Should the donor have final say or should the organization be in charge? This is a difficult question that often gets in the way of giving.

There are, however, some welcome signs that Canadian tight-fistedness may be 11 diminishing. The dot-com economy is creating vast new reservoirs of sudden money for many who, unlike their old-economy equivalents, seem far more eager and willing to share what they have. When Robert Young was raising funds to start what became the software company Red Hat Inc., his aunt, Joyce Young of Hamilton, Ont., invested a few thousand dollars. After the company went public last year, her holdings became worth $40 million and she promptly gave the entire amount to the Hamilton Community Foundation.

Such recent and bountiful bequests seemed to spur Ted Rogers, chief executive 12 officer of Rogers Communications Inc. In June he and his wife, Loretta, gave $25 million to the University of Toronto and $10 million to Ryerson Polytechnic University, the largest single donation that Toronto's Ryerson has ever received. "Gifts inspire others to make gifts," he said, "which inspires others to make gifts."

Let's hope he's right. Let's hope he and countless others give away much more 13 than they have in the past. After all, Rogers is worth more than $2 billion and his wealth has been generated in a regulated environment through winning cable TV licences, thus creating local monopolies.

Moreover, the rich and powerful should be much more financially forth- 14 coming now that changes in federal tax rules encourage giving. For example, individuals are now allowed a more favourable deduction on donations of company shares to charities.

"American-style" philanthropy is what some observers have called this year's 15 flurry of charitable activity as if this were just another example of how more like them we Canadians are becoming as part of the free trade economy.

Perhaps. So far, one thing is certain. Former prime minister Pierre Trudeau 16 famously said that living next door to the U.S. is like sleeping with an elephant. Maybe that's why we've always given peanuts.

QUESTIONS

Understanding the message: Comprehension

1. Why do Americans contribute so much more than Canadians to charitable organizations, according to McQueen?

2. What are some of the issues that "get in the way" of sizable corporate donations?

3. What factors may contribute to Canadians donating more money in the future?

Examining the structure and details: Analysis

1. Find examples of figurative language in the article. How does McQueen use simile and metaphor to support his argument?

2. What are the different reasons that McQueen cites to explain the differences between American and Canadian charitable habits? What kind(s) of evidence does he supply for each?

3. How much attention does McQueen give to each of his major subjects (Americans and Canadians)? Why do you think he structures the essay this way?

4. If we assume that McQueen's basis of comparison is between the past and present Canadian habits instead of between American and Canadian habits, how do his points change?

Formulating a response: Inference and interpretation

1. What is McQueen's tone in this article? Cite examples of particular words or expressions that support your answer.

2. Does McQueen convince you that Canadians are less charitable than Americans? Why or why not?

3. On whom or what does McQueen blame Canadians' parsimonious behaviour? Is his reasoning convincing? Why or why not?

Essay questions

1. Are some causes or charities more worthy of your donations than others? Write an essay in which you compare people or organizations that you think legitimately deserve charitable donations, versus those you feel don't warrant the help of others.

2. There are many more differences between Americans and Canadians than their patterns of philanthropy. Think of another major area in which the two populations differ (for example, patriotism, attitude toward government, ideas about medicine, sexual habits, tolerance of others, and so on) and write an essay in which you compare American to Canadian behaviour in that area.

3. If McQueen's purpose is to convince Canadians to give more to charitable donations, do you think he succeeds? Write an essay in which you support your answer by citing examples from the text.

VOCABULARY

parsimonious: extremely economical; frugal

odious: offensive

philanthropy: giving (money, goods, and so on) to others in order to help those in need

Rockefeller, Carnegie, Mellon, Getty: wealthy American industrialists and philanthropists who endowed major foundations

Medicis: members of the wealthy and influential Florentine family of the Italian Renaissance; patrons of the arts and sciences

bequests: money for a particular organization, left in a will

largesse: generosity

chasm: gulf or large gap

succour: comfort or aid

free-enterprise builders of the Lachine Canal: historic canal near Montreal, opened in 1825, built largely as a result of the efforts of a group of Montreal merchants

D'oh! An Analysis of the Medical Care Provided to the Family of Homer J. Simpson

by Robert Patterson and Charles Weijer

Robert Patterson, M.D., and Charles Weijer, M.D., Ph.D., are both Canadian physicians and authors. Dr. Patterson currently runs a medical practice as general surgeon in Leamington, Ontario, while Dr. Weijer is assistant professor and bioethicist at Dalhousie University in Halifax. Both are also avid fans of cartoons on television.

PRE-READING

This article originally appeared in the December 1998 issue of the *Canadian Medical Association Journal (CMAJ)*. What does the article's title suggest to you? Are you familiar with the television cartoon show *The Simpsons*? If so, what do you know about its portrayal of doctors and patients? Traditionally, the *CMAJ* reserves space in its holiday issue for humourous or satiric pieces that poke fun at both the medical profession and some of its practices. Does this fact change your approach to pre-reading?

1   These are hard times for physicians. Governments blame doctors for spiralling health care costs as they slash spending. Ethicists decry medical paternalism. Our patients—sorry, our clients—demand to be treated like consumers. And political correctness has changed the way we speak. It's enough to give your average doctor an identity crisis. Who are we? Who should we aspire to be?

2   Working on the premise that life imitates art, we searched for and found a role model for physicians to follow in these difficult times. We found him in a long-running cartoon series, *The Simpsons,* and spent many hard hours in front of the television, collecting and collating data for analysis. We hope readers will give our conclusions the attention they deserve.

3   In the quiet town of Springfield,[1] noted for its substandard nuclear power plant and eccentric citizenry, Drs. Julius Hibbert and Nick Riviera frequently come in

---

[1] It is unclear where Springfield is located. According to *Webster's Ninth New Collegiate Dictionary,* it could be in Illinois, Massachusetts, Ohio, Missouri or Oregon.

contact with Springfield's everyman, Homer J. Simpson, and his family. Homer, who works at the power plant, is known for his love of donuts and Duff's beer.

Like the forces of good and evil battling for the soul of medicine itself, these 2 physicians are polar opposites. Julius Hibbert is an experienced family physician with a pleasant, easygoing manner, while Nick Riviera is an ill-trained upstart who is more interested in money than medicine. Knowing that appearances can be deceiving (and first impressions rarely correct), we explored this question: Which of these 2 physicians should Canada's future physicians emulate? 4

We briefly entertained Hibbert as a potential role model. He is a trusted family physician who provides care not only to Homer but also to his spouse Marge and their 3 children: Bart, Lisa and Maggie. He delivered all of the children and has weathered many a Simpson medical crisis, from Bart's broken leg to Lisa's primary depression. 5

Generally the quality of care he provides is solid, although there was an incident when he accidentally left the keys to his Porsche inside a patient. We decided to ignore this incident, since such a mishap can befall any physician. 6

Hibbert has diagnostic acumen of Oslerian proportions. He uses this regularly to identify a variety of baffling conditions, from Marge's alopecia areata to Homer's unique form of hydrocephalus. 7

"Don't worry, it's quite beneficial," he told Homer about the latter condition. "Your brain is cushioned by a layer of fluid one-eighth of an inch thicker than normal. It's almost as if you're wearing a football helmet inside your own head. Why, I could wallop you all day with this surgical 2-by-4, without ever knocking you down."[2] 8

Another positive trait is Hibbert's sense of humour, which he uses to put patients and their families at ease. When Homer was critically injured and rushed to hospital after opening a can of beer that spent some time in a paint mixer thanks to Bart, Hibbert's levity helped relieve an otherwise tense situation. 9

"Mrs. Simpson, I'm afraid your husband is dead," he said. 10

"Oh my god!" Marge responded. 11

"April Fools!" 12

Deeper analysis, however, reveals that Hibbert is no Semmelweiss. He treats the health care system like his personal cash cow by taking time to talk to his patients and distributing lollipops to children. No wonder the U.S. system is so expensive. Worse yet, he stocks his office with patient education materials that either contain value judgements or are poorly written. 13

When Homer first courted his bride-to-be, Hibbert gave a pamphlet entitled *So You've Ruined Your Life* to a pregnant but unmarried Marge. Fair enough. But 14

---

[2] All quotations taken from our TV screens were checked against those from Ray Richmond (ed.), *The Simpsons: A complete guide to our favorite family* (New York: HarperCollins Publishers, 1997).

later on, when Homer was poisoned after eating an incorrectly prepared blowfish at a Japanese restaurant, Hibbert handed him another brochure, *So You're Going to Die*. By giving away the conclusion in the title, Hibbert ruined the surprise ending. What fun is that?

15 Another gross violation of ethics occurred when Bart stuck various objects to his skin with Crazy Glue. In a scene reminiscent of the Spanish Inquisition, Dr. Hibbert showed him the instruments of surgery, thereby frightening the poor youngster so badly that he began to sweat, causing the objects to fall off.

16 Obviously, informed consent and truth-telling mean little or nothing to this medical Machiavelli. Any ethicist worth her salt would flail him for such an act of unbridled paternalism. Perhaps worst of all, Hibbert shows about as much sensitivity to politically correct language as Howard Stern, as demonstrated by this conversation with Lisa.

17 "Yes, I remember Bart's birth well," he said. "You don't forget a thing like Siamese twins!"

18 "I believe they prefer to be called 'conjoined twins,'" Lisa replied.

19 "And hillbillies prefer to be called 'sons of the soil,'" Hibbert responded, "but it ain't gonna happen."

20 No, the true medical hero for whom we search is Julius Hibbert's foil, the enterprising Dr. Nick Riviera, an international medical graduate who attended the Club Med School. He practises with an enthusiasm that is matched only by his showmanship. Unfortunately, this has led to 160 complaints from Springfield's narrow-minded Malpractice Committee, but artists like Riviera are rarely understood in their time. Dr. Nick, as he is known, may be a tad weak on anatomy. "What the hell is that?" he asked after making an incision for Homer's coronary artery bypass. However, he does possess all the requisite traits for the doctor of tomorrow: he is resource conscious and he gives the customer what she wants.

21 Ever resourceful, Dr. Nick finds innovative new uses for underutilized medical materials, such as cadavers. By placing several of them in his vehicle, he can drive in the car-pool lane and get to work more quickly. This commendable behaviour is also environmentally conscious.

22 And he's no shill for the medical establishment. Knowing that physicians' fees are the real cause of the health care funding crisis, Dr. Nick produced a TV ad in which he offered to do any surgical procedure for just $129.95 (Can$193.95 at time of writing). Cost-effective and consumer conscious, Riviera would never let quality of care interfere with discount-rate fees.

23 His greatest asset, though, is his willingness—no, his mission—to satisfy every whim and fancy of his patients.

24 He is acutely aware that many patients actually want to be sick and, like Albert Schweitzer, he compassionately helps them. When Bart was run over by a car but appeared unhurt, his parents considered a lawsuit against the driver. Dr. Nick was

very eager to assist them. "Your son is a very sick boy," he said. "Just look at these x-rays! You see that dark spot there? Whiplash. And this smudge here that looks like my fingerprint? That's trauma."

In another touching moment, Homer discovered that he would qualify for dis- 25 abled benefits and be able to work at home if he weighed more than 300 pounds, and immediately sought a way to increase his weight. Dr. Nick was there in his time of need.

"You'll want to focus on the neglected food groups, such as the whipped group, the 26 congealed group and the choc-o-tastic," he advised. "Be creative. Instead of making sandwiches with bread, use Pop-Tarts. Instead of chewing gum, chew bacon."

Being so burdened with his patients' wishes, Riviera often sacrifices his per- 27 sonal needs. Every now and then, however, he manages to think of his own well-being. "The coroner—I'm so sick of that guy," he told Homer as he prepared to perform cardiac surgery on him. "Now if something should go wrong, let's not get the law involved. One hand washes the other."

In these turbulent times, we need a hero to guide us into the next millennium. 28 As a profession, we must shed the dark past embodied by Dr. Hibbert—a wasteful, paternalistic and politically incorrect physician. Instead, the physician of the future must cut corners to cut costs, accede to the patient's every whim and always strive to avoid the coroner. All hail Dr. Nick Riviera, the very model of a 21st-century healer.

"See you at the operating place!" 29

QUESTIONS

Understanding the message: Comprehension

1. What are the two ways to interpret the sentence "We hope the readers will give our conclusions the attention they deserve"?

2. In what way does Dr. Hibbert treat "the health care system like his personal cash cow"? Explain.

3. Which actual practices of potentially dedicated and competent doctors are being lampooned in this article? Cite examples.

Examining the structure and details: Analysis

1. Which style of organization did the authors use in this comparison? How is it appropriate?

2. At which point in the article do the authors first indicate that they are not approaching their subject in a serious vein?

3. Do the authors use both comparison and contrast in their essay? If so, on which do they rely more to make their point?

4. Are the specific points of comparison used for each subject balanced (that is, do the writers cover the same points with each subject)? What impact does this approach have?

5. Why did the authors include the use of footnotes in this article? What effect does it have on the reader?

Formulating a response: Inference and interpretation

1. Find at least three examples from the article that demonstrate the authors' use of humour and explain what makes those examples humorous.

2. Do the authors succeed in presenting one doctor as "superior" to the other? Why or why not?

3. What is the underlying, serious, message that the authors are sending with this article? What is their thesis? Is it stated? If so, where?

4. The intended audience of *CMAJ*, where this article originally appeared, is physicians. Given this audience, what do you think is the purpose of the piece? How do you know?

Essay questions

1. Think of two people you know who perform the same job (for example, two family doctors, two dentists, two plumbers, two sales clerks in clothing stores, two waiters, two babysitters) and write a humorous essay comparing them, with the purpose of identifying which person is better at her or his job.

2. Have you ever received less-than-perfect treatment in a serious situation? If so, compare the actual treatment you received to your own ideal of treatment.

3. Although the article is clearly humorous, in what way is it also a serious indictment of the Canadian system of health care? Write an essay in which you explain the more serious message being conveyed in the article, by citing specific examples.

VOCABULARY

medical paternalism: doctors treating patients as inferior or in a patronizing way

emulate: imitate; try to be like

acumen: insight; keen perception

Oslerian proportions: of great proportions; named for Sir William Osler (1849–1919), famous Canadian doctor and teacher

alopecia areata: hair loss in clumps

hydrocephalus: excess fluid around the brain, leading to unusual swelling of the head

levity: humour, ability to make light of a situation

Semmelweiss: Ignaz Semmelweiss (1818–65), physicist who revolutionized surgical hygiene when he made the connection between illness and not washing the hands

cash cow: source of income

Spanish Inquisition: historical period of investigation for religious and politcal reasons to suppress heresy; notorious for its use of torture

Machiavelli: Niccolò Machiavelli, Florentine political theorist who claimed that the ends justify the means

foil: opposite

cadavers: dead bodies

shill: person who cons others (usually by posing as a customer so others will be drawn in)

Albert Schweitzer: Nobel Prize–winning doctor (1875–1965), humanitarian, theologian who devoted much of his life to helping others

One Good Turn
by Witold Rybczynski

Educated as an architect, Witold Rybczynski is a professor of urbanism and director of the Urban Design Program at the University of Pennsylvania; he is also a professor at the Wharton School of the University of Pennsylvania. He has won a number of awards for academic excellence, including the Alfred Jurzykowski Award (1993); the Progressive Architecture Award (1991); and the Athenaeum of Philadelphia Award (1997). He is an Honorary Fellow of the American Institute of Architects. He also serves on the Advisory Board for Encyclopedia Americana *and is co-editor,* Wharton Real Estate Review. *After he began writing in his 40s, he achieved fame with his book* Home: A Short History of an Idea *(1986). In addition, he wrote* The Most Beautiful House in the World *(1989),* City Life: Urban Expectations in a New World *(1995),* A Clearing in the Distance *(1999), and* One Good Turn: A History of the Screwdriver and the Screw *(2000), from which the following excerpt is taken. His most recent book is* The Look of Architecture *(2001).*

PRE-READING

How much do you know about screwdrivers? Can you imagine being fascinated with one? In this excerpt from *One Good Turn*, Rybczynski examines three common kinds of metal screw and screwdriver and discusses why he thinks the screw is "the biggest little invention of the twentieth century." Think about the screw and screwdriver as modern tools. Are there other tools that even come close to the same simplicity and usefulness? What kinds of tools are indispensable to you?

---

1   Take a close look at a modern screw. It is a remarkable little object. The thread begins at a gimlet point, sharp as a pin. This point gently tapers into the body of the screw, whose core is cylindrical. At the top, the core tapers into a smooth shank, the thread running out to nothing.

2   From the time of their invention in the Middle Ages until the beginning of the twentieth century, all screws had either square or octagonal heads, or slots. The former were turned by a wrench, the latter by a screwdriver. There is no mystery as to the origin of the slot. A square head had to be accurate to fit the wrench; a slot was a shape that could be roughly filed or cut by hand. Screws with slotted heads could also be countersunk so that they would not protrude beyond the surface.

Yet a slotted screw has several drawbacks. It is easy to "cam out," that is, to push ₃ the screwdriver out of the slot; the result is often damage to the material that is being fastened or injury to one's fingers—or both. The slot offers a tenuous purchase on the screw, and it is not uncommon to strip the slot when trying to tighten a new screw or loosen an old one. Finally, there are awkward situations—balancing on a stepladder, for example, or working in confined quarters—when one has to drive the screw with one hand. This is almost impossible to do with a slotted screw. The screw wobbles, the screwdriver slips, the screw falls to the ground and rolls away, the handyman curses—not for the first time—the inventor of this maddening device.

American screw manufacturers were well aware of these shortcomings. ₄ Between 1860 and 1890, there was a flurry of patents for magnetic screwdrivers, screw-holding gadgets, slots that did not extend across the face of the screw, double slots, and a variety of square, triangular, and hexagonal sockets or recesses. The last held the most promise. Replacing the slot by a socket held the screwdriver snugly and prevented cam-out. The difficulty—once more—lay in manufacturing. Screw heads are formed by mechanically stamping a cold-steel rod; punching a socket sufficiently deep to hold the screwdriver tended to either weaken the screw or deform the head.

The solution was discovered by a twenty-seven-year-old Canadian, Peter L. ₅ Robertson. Robertson was a so-called "high-pitch man" for a Philadelphia tool company, a travelling salesman who plied his wares on street corners and at country fairs in eastern Canada. He spent his spare time in his workshop, dabbling in mechanical inventions. He invented and promoted "Robertson's 20th Century Wrench-Brace," a combination tool that could be used as a brace, a monkey wrench, a screwdriver, a bench vise, and a rivet-maker. He vainly patented an improved corkscrew, a new type of cufflink, even a better mousetrap. Then, in 1906, he applied for a patent for a socket-head screw.

Robertson later said that he got the idea for the socket head while demon- ₆ strating a spring-loaded screwdriver to a group of sidewalk gawkers in Montreal—the blade slipped out of the slot and injured his hand. The secret of his invention was the exact shape of the recess, which was square with chamfered edges, slightly tapering sides, and a pyramidal bottom. Later, he rather grandly explained his invention: "It was discovered early by the use of this form of punch, constructed with the exact angles indicated, cold metal would flow to the sides, and not be driven ahead of the tools, resulting beneficially in knitting the atoms into greater strength, and also assisting in the work of lateral extension, and without a waste or cutting away of any of the metal so treated, as is the case in the manufacture of the ordinary slotted head screw."

An enthusiastic promoter, Robertson found financial backers, talked a small ₇ Ontario town, Milton, into giving him a loan and other concessions, and established his own screw factory. "The big fortunes are in the small inventions," he trumpeted to prospective investors. "This is considered by many as the biggest little invention of the twentieth century so far." In truth, the square socket really was a big improvement. The special square-headed screwdriver fitted snugly—Robertson claimed an accuracy within one one-thousandth of an inch—and never cammed out. Craftsmen, especially furniture-makers and boat builders, appreciated the convenience of screws that were self-centring and could be driven with one hand. Industry liked socket-head screws, too, since they reduced product damage and speeded up production. The Fisher Body Company, which made wood bodies in Canada for Ford cars, became a large Robertson customer; so did the new Ford Model T plant in Windsor, Ontario, which soon accounted for a third of Robertson's output. Within five years, he was employing seventy-five workers and had built his own powerhouse and a plant to draw the cold-steel rod used in making the screws.

8   In 1913, Robertson decided to expand his business outside Canada. His father had been a Scottish immigrant, so Robertson turned his attention to Britain. He established an independent English company to serve as a base for exporting to Germany and Russia. The venture was not a success. He was thwarted by a combination of undercapitalization, the First World War, the defeat of Germany, and the Russian Revolution. Moreover, it proved difficult to run businesses on two continents. After seven years, unhappy English shareholders replaced Robertson as managing director. The English company struggled along until it was liquidated in 1926.

9   Meanwhile, Robertson turned to the United States. Negotiations with a large screw manufacturer in Buffalo broke down after it became clear that Robertson was unwilling to share control over production decisions. Henry Ford was interested, since his Canadian plants were reputedly saving as much as $2.60 per car using Robertson screws. However, Ford, too, wanted a measure of control that the stubborn Robertson was unwilling to grant. They met, but no deal was struck. It was Robertson's last attempt to export his product. A life-long bachelor, he spent the rest of his life in Milton, a big fish in a decidedly small pond.

10   Meanwhile, American automobile manufacturers followed Ford's lead and stuck to slotted screws. Yet the success of the new Robertson screw did not go unnoticed. In 1936 alone, there were more than twenty American patents for improved screws and screwdrivers.

11   Several of these were granted to Henry F. Phillips, a forty-six-year-old businessman in Portland, Oregon. Like Robertson, Phillips had been a travelling salesman. He was also a promoter of new inventions and acquired patents from a Portland inventor, John P. Thompson, for a socket screw. Thompson's socket was too deep to be practicable, but Phillips incorporated its distinctive shape—a cruciform—into an improved design of his own. Like Robertson, Phillips claimed that the socket was "particularly adapted for firm engagement with a corre-

spondingly shaped driving tool or screwdriver, and in such a way that there will be no tendency of the driver to cam out of the recess." Unlike Robertson, however, Phillips did not start his own company but planned to license his patent to screw manufacturers.

All the major screw companies turned him down. "The manufacture and mar- 12 keting of these articles do not promise sufficient commercial success," was a typical response. Phillips did not give up. Several years later the president of the giant American Screw Company agreed to undertake the industrial development of the innovative socket screw. In his patents, Phillips emphasized that the screw was particularly suited to power-driven operations, which at the time chiefly meant automobile assembly lines. The American Screw Company convinced General Motors to test the new screw; it was used first in the 1936 Cadillac. The trial proved so effective that within two years all automobile companies save one had switched to socket screws, and by 1939 most screw manufacturers produced what were now called Phillips screws.

The Phillips screw has many of the same benefits as the Robertson screw (and 13 the added advantage that it can be driven with a slotted screwdriver if necessary). "We estimate that our operators save between thirty and sixty percent of their time by using Phillips screws," wrote a satisfied builder of boats and gliders. "Our men claim they can accomplish at least seventy-five percent more work than with the old-fashioned type," maintained a manufacturer of garden furniture. Phillips screws—and the familiar cross-tipped screwdrivers—were now everywhere. The First World War had stymied Robertson; the Second Word War ensured that the Phillips screw became an industry standard as it was widely adopted by wartime manufacturers. By the mid-1960s, when Phillips's patents expired, there were more than 160 domestic, and eighty foreign, licensees.

The Phillips screw became the international socket screw; the Robertson screw 14 is used only in Canada and by a select number of American woodworkers. (Starting in the 1950s, Robertson screws began to be used by some American furniture manufacturers, by the mobile-home industry, and eventually by a growing number of craftsmen and hobbyists. The Robertson company itself was purchased by an American conglomerate in 1968.) A few years ago, *Consumer Reports* tested Robertson and Phillips screwdrivers. "After driving hundreds of screws by hand and with a cordless drill fitted with a Robertson tip, we're convinced. Compared with slotted and Phillips-head screwdrivers, the Robertson worked faster, with less cam-out."

The explanation is simple. Although Phillips designed his screw to have "firm 15 engagement" with the screwdriver, in fact a cruciform recess is a less perfect fit than a square socket. Paradoxically, this very quality is what attracted automobile manufacturers to the Phillips screw; the point of an automated driver turning the screw with increasing force would pop out of the recess when the screw was fully set, preventing overscrewing. Thus, a certain degree of cam-out was incorporated into the design from the beginning. However, what worked on the assembly line has bedevilled handymen ever since. Phillips screws are notorious for slippage, cam-out, and stripped sockets (especially if the screw or the screwdriver is improperly made).

16   Here I must confess myself to be a confirmed Robertson user. The square-headed screwdriver sits snugly in the socket; you can shake a Robertson screwdriver, and the screw on the end will not fall off; drive a Robertson screw with a power drill and the fully set screw simply stops the drill dead; no matter how old, rusty, or painted over, a Robertson screw can always be unscrewed. The "biggest little invention of the twentieth century"? Why not.

QUESTIONS

Understanding the message: Comprehension

1. What are the problems that plagued builders who used slotted screws? What are the advantages of the Robertson screw?

2. What are the reasons for the Robertson screw's failure in England?

3. What are the advantages of the Phillips screw? What are the disadvantages? In what way was one apparent disadvantage used as an asset?

Examining the structure and details: Analysis

1. Which paragraphs constitute the introduction to this article? What is their subject matter? Why do you think Rybczynski starts it this way?

2. Rybczynski uses a variety of other rhetorical modes in his comparison and contrast essay. What are these? How do they help to advance his ideas?

3. Does Rybczynski cover the same points about each of the types of screwdriver? If not, which one(s) are given more emphasis? How does this influence the reader's interpretation of the subject matter?

Formulating a response: Inference and interpretation

1. Who do you think Rybczynski's intended audience is in this essay? How do you know?

2. At the end of the article, Rybczynski writes, "I must confess myself to be a confirmed Robertson user." Does he convince you that the Robertson is the superior screwdriver? Why or why not?

4. What do you think is the author's purpose in writing this essay? How well does he achieve this purpose?

Essay questions

1. Is there an object (it need not be a tool) that, once you discovered it, you could no longer do without? Write a comparison essay in which you explain why it is superior to other similar objects.

2. Compare two methods of achieving the same outcome (for example, cooking pizza versus ordering in, attending a lecture versus reading a textbook, watching a video versus watching a film in a theatre).

3. To what do you attribute the failure of the Robertson screw outside of Canada? In writing your essay, consider the product, the countries to which Robertson tried to sell, and Robertson himself. Rely on specific examples from the text to support your ideas.

VOCABULARY

gimlet point: the sharp point of a screw used as a tool to bore holes

tenuous: weak or uncertain

purchase: hold or grip

bench vise: tool that clamps together to hold some object in place while someone is working on it

rivet-maker: machine to make rivets, metal pins that hold several layers together

chamfered: having a solid face in some shape (for example, a square)

thwarted: frustrated or hindered

undercapitalization: the state of having insufficient capital to achieve desired results

cruciform: in the shape of a cross

paradoxically: with a seeming contradiction

From Stone Orchard

by Timothy Findley (b. 1930)

One of Canada's best-known and "most cherished writers," Timothy Findley has won virtually every major award in Canadian literature (and some more than once). He has received the Governor General's Award for both fiction and drama, the City of Toronto Book Award, the ANIK Award for television documentary, the Canadian Booksellers Association Award, the Canadian Authors Association Award for fiction, the Trillium Award, the National Radio Award, the Edgar Allan Poe Award for best original paperback, the Crime Writers of Canada Award for best play, a Gemini award, and is an Officer of the Order of Canada, as well as a Knight of the Order of Arts and Letters (France). Findley began his career as an actor with the Stratford Shakespeare Festival (Ontario) before turning to writing. His works include fiction (both novels and short stories); drama for stage, screen, and radio; and nonfiction. From his first novel, The Last of the Crazy People *(1967), through the highly acclaimed* The Wars *(1977) until his most recent works,* Elizabeth Rex *(2000) and* Pilgrim: A Novel *(2000), Findley's work has been consistently lauded by critics for its forceful themes, imagination, felicitous language, and a style infused "with the pageantry of the stage." Findley and his longtime companion, William Whitehead, now divide their time between living in rural Ontario and Cotignac, France.*

PRE-READING

This excerpt is taken from Findley's book, *From Stone Orchard: A Collection of Memories* (1998), a collection of essays about his beloved Ontario farm, Stone Orchard. Before leaving Ontario to live in France, Findley wrote the essay "From Stone Orchard" in which he compared his two homes. Have you ever spent time in a small town in the country? If so, what did you like about it? If not, what do you imagine life would be like there? Think about the daily routines, the people, and the environment in general. How is country life different from city life? What do people find particularly appealing about the former?

1   Across the road, the field through which I sometimes walk on my way to town rolls up gently to a crest, sliding away on the other side towards the old railroad bed and the Beaver River. Mornings and evenings, I sit at the kitchen window and watch Len Collins's cattle grazing there with their calves. When they stand against the skyline at dusk, they create a pastoral image that, for me, tells why we live where we do. *Here* would not be *here* without that field.

Most of one recent summer, however, Bill and I were not watching cattle—we 2 were watching goats. They were browsing on scrub brush in an abandoned olive grove beside a vineyard. Clearly, we were not at Stone Orchard.

We were in France—on the outskirts of the Provençal village of Cotignac— 3 having gone there in order to escape the phone and the FAX while a book got finished. Evenings, we sat looking down the terraced hillside at the scene below us. The *chevrier* was the classic goatherd: carrying a crook, wearing a wide, white hat, with a wineskin slung on his back. His constant companions—aside from the bearded flock—were a tanned young woman and a lame black dog. This, then, became the pastoral image of where we were. *There* would not have been *there* without it.

Two small communities, two unique countrysides—each in its way a stand-in for 4 paradise. But paradise tempered with a healthy dose of reality. In Provence, there is often merciless heat and drought—in southern Ontario, merciless cold and damp. The essence of both these places lies in the word *survival*.

Being in Cotignac gave me distance enough and perspective with which to 5 view my home community, and a deeper appreciation of what it offers—and what it demands in terms of survival. The trip abroad also revealed surprising parallels between these two distinctive places, and confirmed our decision, thirty years ago, to put down roots in a rural setting.

Across the road, I watched a calf being born one spring. Then I saw all the 6 other members of the herd—including Len's pony, Dolly—approach the newborn and give it a good nosing. Finally, I watched the cow eating most of the afterbirth—sensing instinctively what to do, without, as far as I can tell, knowing that the hormones it contained would stimulate the flow of the right kind of milk for her offspring. As she urged the calf to its feet and guided it to her udder, some crows flew down from the trees and finished what remained of the afterbirth. In half an hour there was not a trace of evidence—no telltale signs for predators. Nature's efficiency more often than not can take your breath away.

At Cotignac, one evening, we watched a kid being born in the abandoned vine- 7 yard below our house. This was a difficult birth, accompanied by a fair amount of vocalization from the nanny. The goatherd knew what to do and went to her aid. When he finally stood up, he removed his shirt and wrapped it around the newborn. Clutching the kid to his chest, he led a procession away from the field towards the home pasture. He and the newborn were followed closely by the nanny. Then came the rest of the herd, in single file—and bringing up the rear, the beautiful young woman and the lame black dog. As we watched them disappear from view, we almost expected music—pan pipes, perhaps—and a final curtain descending slowly over the scene. It was pure theatrical magic.

Cannington and Cotignac—each with a population of fewer than two thou- 8 sand—each with its individual anchor in history—each with its future in question. Their merchants must now compete with the giant malls and supermarkets of neighbouring towns; their surrounding countrysides face the threat—still distant,

I'm glad to say—of urban sprawl. Still, the early signs are there in both cases, and it's worrying.

9   Both communities have their special festivals. Early every winter, Cannington musters local talent and pizazz to mount a Santa Claus parade. This event can be glorious. And hilarious. Over time, Saint Nick's padding swells and thins—as tall men, short men, fat men and skinny men put on the suit. One year, Saint Nick himself rode down Cameron Street. It must have been him, because all the local red-and-whites were still in mothballs. No one ever tracked him down, the North Pole being too distant. On another occasion, Nora Joyce, our miracle of a housekeeper, donned the suit and rode the sleigh. The only trace of Nora was her merry eyes. She was the best Saint Nick we've seen.

10   Late every summer, Cotignac stages a wine festival, during which an enormous papier-mâché Bacchus is paraded round the *cours*—the central square where all the café tables sit under the plane trees. His appearance is preceded by locals in musketeer costume, firing their ancient muskets into the air. All the dogs go mad when the guns go off and they tear around the streets barking up a storm. As Bacchus passes, the whole population is there to cheer him on with a stirring anthem and a raised glass. An exhilarating, heady climax.

11   On the banks of the Beaver River, which passes through Cannington, there is a park laid out beneath maple trees. Here, the War Memorial stands, and a benevolent fountain offers a wading pool to dogs and children. Picnic tables and tennis courts compete for attention—as does the nearby baseball diamond. Every summer weekend sees a boisterous community or family celebration. And there's a bowling green, with Edwardian echoes of white-clad players and a green-and-white pavilion.

12   All of this has its counterpart in Cotignac, where the *cours* spreads its welcome beneath its canopy of trees. In their shade, the several cafés, bars and restaurants compete for our attention and, on market day, music is provided by strolling guitarists and singers. Even, time to time, by violinists. Down on the sandy flats beyond the square, old and young alike play at boule—a unique and lovely game to watch, demanding skill and panache. The *thwack* of metal balls punctuates the evening's conversation. Boule is a social game, and the sense of civilized camaraderie is one of its great pleasures.

13   The War memorial in Cotignac sits in front of the *mairie*—the town hall. You reach it by climbing up through winding streets, passing old fountains set in tiny, green parks. The water from their stone spouts has flowed all the way from the Alps and is clear and cold and pure. Citizens bring their jugs and fill them there while they gossip. The memorial itself depicts a helmeted infantryman peering from his trench and beneath him, on the marble, are printed the names of *les enfants de Cotignac*—the children of Cotignac—who gave up their lives in both world wars. It is the same at Cannington, and what is saddest in both locations is the repetition of family names—the same, again and again.

RESPOND IN WRITING   N

Each village, too, has its local volunteer fire brigade. In Cotignac, its members 14
are called *les pompiers*—and, like their Cannington counterparts, they are also on
call to help with medical emergencies and road accidents. Survival depends on all
these services. There can be no security without them.

If there is a notable difference, it is in the strength of tradition. In France—in 15
the villages, at least, businesses have resisted consolidation. Yes, there are huge
supermarkets in the nearby towns—also dotting the autoroutes between the
towns—but in the smallest places, you buy your magazines at the *presse* and your
cigarettes at the *tabac* and—apart from market day—your vegetables at the *alimentaire*,
your meat at the *boucherie*, your bread at the *boulangerie* and your
desserts at the *pâtisserie* . . . etc.

This helps account for the fact that—unlike Cannington—there is hardly any 16
unemployment in Cotignac.

As for the pleasures of the weekly market—and of café tables in the open air— 17
we kept asking ourselves: *why not in Cannington?* Ontario farms grow vegetables;
our summers are almost as warm and sunny for outdoor dining. The only answer
we've ever found is: *Canada chose something else.* And, as we watch how difficult
it is for Cannington, itself, to survive as a community, we wonder if the choice was
right. We even wonder if it was conscious, or if it was simply the sum total of a
whole series of minor, day-to-day decisions that didn't seem important at the
time. As examples of these choices, Cotignac has three bakeries plus the pastry
shop; Cannington has none. And while Cotignac has eight cafés and bars,
Cannington barely supports two, plus a small pizza palace. Enough said.

Still, the rest of what these two villages share is still present—a strong sense of 18
place—a keen awareness of tradition—a neighbourly society—and a setting of
haunting beauty. These are the ongoing legacies of rural life—both there, and here.

As for Cotignac, now that we have bought the house we originally stayed in, we 19
will go back there once or twice every year. It is where the writing now gets done,
and so we call it *Mots Maison*. Word House. And we will always return to
Cannington—even if only in our dreams—and to Stone Orchard. We will always
live there in our hearts. There is no escaping the pull of home, with its sight of
Len's cattle standing on their hill, the cries of the killdeer and the moonlit silence
of the pond.

QUESTIONS

Understanding the message: Comprehension

1. What are the defining characteristics for Findley that distinguish the
   Canadian setting as "here" and the French setting as "there"?

2. In what way does the "essence of both these places" lie in the word "survival"?

3. Why does Findley refer to the birth of a calf in Cannington as an example of "[N]ature's efficiency," while the similar birth of a kid in Cotignac is "pure theatrical magic"? What is the major difference between the two events?

Examining the structure and details: Analysis

1. At what point does Findley introduce the two subjects he is comparing? Why do you think he waits as long as he does?

2. Where does Findley's essay switch from a purely descriptive approach to a more analytical one? At what point in the essay does he make this transition?

3. Does Findley's approach to the two places focus more on comparison or contrast? In what way does this choice support his ultimate thesis? Provide examples to support your answer.

4. Does Findley use a block or a point-by-point method of organization? How is it appropriate for his subject matter?

Formulating a response: Inference and interpretation

1. Findley says that his trip to Cotignac "confirmed [his] decision, thirty years ago, to put down roots in a rural setting." After reading "From Stone Orchard," what characteristics of each of the two places do you think contributed to this decision?

2. Is one town in "From Stone Orchard" presented as being superior to the other? If so, which one? Support your answer with specific references to the text.

3. Findley tells us that each town is "in its way a stand-in for paradise. But paradise tempered with a healthy dose of reality." After reading the essay, do you agree with Findley? What aspects of both "paradise" and "reality" does he include?

4. Which part of the essay is more effective in your opinion, Findley's description of the similarities between the two towns or his description of the differences? Why?

5. What is the main point (thesis) of Findley's essay? Which sentence best expresses it?

Essay questions

1. Choose two similar places that you know well, such as two cities or towns, two schools, or even two supermarkets. Then, write your own comparison essay in which you describe the similarities and differences between the two. Be sure to include parallel points for the two places, whichever format you choose for your comparison.

2. Write an essay in which you argue that *either* a rural *or* an urban lifestyle is preferable, by comparing the two. Choose a sufficient range of points of comparison (such as living space, cost of living, leisure activities, medical care, and so on) to make the argument convincing.

3. Write an essay in which you explain why you think Findley and his partner have chosen to move from Cannington to Cotignac. Are there clues in his essay that explain this choice? Include examples in your essay.

VOCABULARY

pastoral: rural; part of country life

chevrier: goatherd

nanny: mother goat

Bacchus: Greek or Roman god of wine

musketeer: 17th-century soldier

musket: large gun used by soldiers

Edwardian: during the reign of King Edward VIII in England, 1901–1910

presse: newspaper stand

tabac: tobacco store

alimentaire: grocery store

boucherie: butcher shop

boulangerie: bakery for breads, rolls, and so on

pâtisserie: bakery for fine desserts (such as pastries and cakes)

CHAPTER 9

Definition

DEFINITION IN DAILY LIFE

Definition is a skill you probably already use fairly often. Real-life definition is used when you engage in activities such as the following:

- You give a speech as valedictorian for your high school graduation ceremonies about what success means to you.
- You write a report outlining "patient compliance" by defining the term as it relates to patients taking prescribed drugs.
- You write an essay for your college-entrance application form, explaining what learning means to you.
- You explain the concept of death to your six-year-old niece after her goldfish dies.

WHAT IS DEFINITION?

Imagine this all-too-common scenario: a mother asks her kids to help clear up the kitchen after dinner. When she returns to the room several hours later, the table is cleared and the dishes are neatly stacked in the sink—still dirty and covered with dried food. To her (rather vocal) expression of dismay, the plaintive kids reply, "You said 'clear up'—we didn't know you meant *wash the dishes,* too!" Whether genuine or intentional, a misunderstanding has occurred; this mother should have ensured that her **definition** of "clear up" was, itself, clear.

DEFINITION

Definition: Definition explains what something means or is in a particular context.

Definitions can range from a simple, dictionary-style definition (also called a **formal definition** or **denotation**) that provides a short, direct explanation of something, to a more complex definition (also called an **extended definition**) that clarifies abstract concepts (such as "love" or "prejudice") or complicated, multidimensional concepts (such as "dress-down Fridays," "rock and roll," or "the Internet"). While short, formal definitions may serve in a variety of situations, most definition essays present an extended definition. This second type of definition is the focus of this chapter.

DEFINITION

formal definition: A formal definition provides a general explanation of what something means in its most basic, common form.

extended definition: An extended definition provides a multifaceted, longer explanation of a complex concept or term, often as it applies to a particular situation or context.

WHY USE DEFINITION?

Imagine how chaotic life would be if we assumed that others always knew what we meant, when in fact their definitions of words and concepts differed from our own. Definition helps to prevent such chaos by clarifying the unfamiliar; it creates shared meaning when one person looks at a term or idea in one particular way (from among many possible ways). If you explain how to play the card game bridge, you need to define the key term "trump" as well as "bid," "suit," and so on. Similarly, the mother in our scenario, above, should have made certain that her children knew exactly which activities she included in the concept of "clear up."

With familiar terms that may have a variety of meanings, definition clarifies your own interpretation of the term so as to differentiate it from the other possible interpretations. For instance, the concept of "basic needs for survival" will be defined differently by someone accustomed to a luxurious lifestyle (such as the wealthy president of a large corporation) versus someone living in dire straits (such as a homeless teenager living on the streets). Similarly, if your friend purports to be religiously devout but then treats others disrespectfully or uncharitably, you may decide that your respective definitions of "devout" are not compatible. When he was president of the United States, Bill Clinton unwittingly furnished reporters with endless copy by taking the definition of "sexual relations" to an absurd extreme, insisting that oral sex was not included in a literal definition of "sexual relations." Clearly, specific, detailed, unequivocal definitions are necessary in our society so that people can operate from a common standpoint.

As well as clarifying what we mean, definition also eliminates those aspects of an idea that *don't* apply to our individual interpretation; it serves to let others know both what is included in, and excluded from, our meaning.

How to Write a Definition Essay

In addition to the standard steps for writing an essay outlined in Chapter 2, some specific considerations apply to writing definition papers. Here are some pointers to ensure that your definition essay is strong and effective.

Pre-Writing

1. Choose a general topic

To be useful, a definition must relate to a topic for which there is some possibility of misunderstanding or misinterpretation if you don't define the term. Look for general topics that are familiar to you, for which you feel you could help to clarify otherwise nebulous or potentially confusing concepts. If you know a lot about the Internet, for example, you could search for a common term that some might misunderstand (such as "portal"), or you could define a common concept as you see it ("surf the Net," for instance).

Generally, less complicated topics or those without any shades of grey are not practical material for definition essays. If we all agree on what farming means or what a car is, then another definition will add nothing to our knowledge or experience (unless, of course, it's written in an amusing or tongue-in-cheek fashion, solely for entertainment value). However, certain terms remain vague or are so multidimensional that's it's difficult to reach consensus on their meaning. Examples such as "love," "punishment," "mentor," and "relaxation" fit into this category. In these cases and with other terms like them, the meaning will be different no matter whom you ask—so they offer perfect topics for definition essays.

2. Consider your audience and purpose

Ask yourself how much information you need to provide in order to clarify your term or concept for your chosen audience. If the idea is totally foreign to the readers (the concept, "geisha," for instance, doesn't exist in North American culture; consequently, North Americans often think that a geisha is a prostitute, which is not the case), you must find a similar concept, something familiar that possesses some of the same characteristics so that your audience has a starting point for the definition. In an essay about geisha, for instance, you might begin by stating that they are similar to professional hostesses or escorts but also undergo additional cultural training. You would then outline more specific traits.

Whichever type of definition you write, your purpose is to delineate the term or idea sufficiently so that your readers won't get it mixed up with something else that's similar, yet not quite the same; you limit the meaning, narrowing it down from all possible meanings to the very one you intend.

3. Generate ideas about the topic

In generating ideas for your essay, decide which aspects of the term or concept are necessary for your definition to be clear. Must you provide a denotative (dictionary) definition? What about placing the term or idea within a larger category? Or should you explain how the term or idea is different from other similar terms or ideas? Depending on whether your definition deals with an abstract or concrete term, something relatively familiar or completely foreign, you should alter the approach accordingly. In this case, freewriting about all the potential meanings applied to a term or using the journalist's method to examine your concept from a variety of angles can be helpful.

4. Narrow to a thesis

While it's possible to have a purely expository thesis in a definition essay (for example, "A keener is a highly conscientious, over-zealous student"), your thesis, as with any of the rhetorical modes, will be more interesting and lead to a more engaging essay if it contains an argument. Defining a keener as "an overly zealous, conscientious student who inevitably annoys the rest of us" can provide both a definition and some entertainment value.

TIP

Create your own meaning

Remember that your purpose in a definition essay is often to distinguish how you interpret a particular concept or idea as opposed to the standard or traditional meaning. Consequently, resist the temptation to use the dictionary alone to define your term, though you may start with a dictionary to grasp the concept yourself or help you decide in which direction you wish to take it. Think instead of how your own meaning may differ from the commonly accepted one.

5. Organize your ideas in an outline

Unlike most other essays, a definition does not fall easily into one of the three major types of organization. Most definitions use a kind of emphatic order, moving from the general (the meaning already shared between you and the audience) to the specific (what makes your own definition of this term or concept unique).

The traditional method for organizing a definition is to first place it within the larger class of similar objects or ideas, then distinguish it from those by explaining its differentiating features. In other words, you tell the reader what it is by relating it to something familiar, then explain why it is different from that familiar thing. Here's an example:

> *Neglect* is a form of abuse involving the failure to provide adequate attention, supervision, nutrition, hygiene, health care and a safe and clean living environment for a minor child or a dependent elderly individual. [Linda A. Mooney et al., *Understanding Social Problems*, Scarborough, Ontario: Nelson Thomson Learning, 2001: 523]

First, the definition classes neglect as one form of abuse, but then illustrates how it differs from other kinds of abuse, such as sexual or psychological.

Another common way to begin a definition essay is to provide the dictionary (denotative) definition, then expand on it to demonstrate your own unique interpretation of the term.

Use logic when determining the order of points for your essay. If you define a term that has changed in meaning over the years (such as "awesome"), then you might wish to order the information chronologically, from earlier meanings to the most recent.

6. Decide on specific support for the main points

More than any other mode, definition writing requires you to make use of the other rhetorical modes in fleshing out your essay. In other words, you can define something through examples, by providing comparisons, by classifying it, by describing it, and so on. The more different and varied the examples you use, the more likely is your definition to be clear and successful.

Writing

There are many ways to build a specific definition. Here are some of the most common:

- *Compare your term or object to something similar, then point out the differences.* For instance, to build a definition of what a tutor is, you might liken her or him to an instructor or teacher. You could go on to indicate all the ways that a tutor functions like a teacher, pointing out the differences as you go (a tutor is hired privately; a tutor usually readdresses subject matter that has already been covered in a classroom setting; and so on).

- *Explain how the concept is part of a larger concept or category.* For example, to define what a helicopter is, you could place it in the class of aircraft in general. Once the reader knows that airplanes, rockets, hot-air balloons, and

Use nouns for concepts and their general categories

To ensure that you choose effective categories in which to place your concepts, use a noun or noun phrase for both the concept and the category; you can even follow the concept being defined with the wording "is a type of" or "is a kind of" to be certain you use this format. Some examples are "An ocelot is a type of cat," "Overeaters Anonymous is a kind of self-help group," and "Yuk-Yuk's is a type of comedy club." This way, you avoid vague or misleading statements such as "Overeaters anonymous is where you go to talk about problems with overeating," which would apply equally to a self-help group, your therapist's office, your best friend's bedroom, and so on.

so on are all vehicles that fly through air, seeing the helicopter as one of these helps her or him to understand the concept more clearly and pinpoint the unique traits of the helicopter as it differs from the rest of the class.

• *Explain what the item or object does or how it functions.* If you try to define what an investment consortium is, you might explain that it's a group of people who confer with each other and work together to contribute money for investment purposes, the profits of which are then shared. You would expand more specifically on the operation of the group in the remainder of your essay.

• *Use other rhetorical modes to define terms.* As with all your writing, definition essays may call upon other **rhetorical modes** to help flesh out the essay. One good way to define something is to provide examples of it, of course; you can also compare or contrast it to other similar items or explain the

Defining a term with itself

One pitfall writers encounter when they attempt to compare new terms or concepts to similar terms is that they use the new term itself as part of the definition. For instance, writing "A forensic police officer is an officer who helps to solve violent or mysterious crimes by using forensics" still does not let the reader know what, exactly, the officer does to solve crimes. To avoid this problem, ensure that you don't repeat the word you are defining or its derivatives (other forms of the word) in your definition.

process through which something works. Notice how Diane Francis provides several examples in "Depression Can Strike Anyone," as well as a paragraph explaining the causes of depression. In "Science, Scientists, and Society," John Polanyi compares the term "science" with "pseudoscience."

Make use of the full range of choices available to you when writing your definition. The goal is to ensure that your reader has a clear understanding of the concept itself, the way in which it is unique, and how it is different from other ostensibly similar items.

- *Explain what the term is not or what it does not do.* Anticipating your readers' assumptions, you can explain that your term may not meet standard expectations or explain which usual concepts or characteristics are *not* included in your definition. For example, if you're defining "love," you may tell what love is *not*, as in this famous Biblical excerpt from 1 Corinthians 13:

> *Love is patient; love is kind and envies no one. Love is never boastful, nor conceited, nor rude; never selfish, not quick to take offence. Love keeps no score of wrongs, does not gloat over other people's sins, but delights in the truth. There is nothing love cannot face; there is no limit to its faith, its hope, and its endurance.*

Similarly, if you define what a money market mutual fund is, you could distinguish it from a bank account since the money is not insured by the government, nor is it guaranteed a particular interest rate, for example.

SNAG

Forgetting the exclusions

Anyone who has ever had to learn a second language knows the embarrassment of using a word exactly as it is defined in the dictionary and then finding that the usage—one of many listed—is inappropriate in the current context. Be careful that you don't encourage such misunderstanding in your own definition essay: think of all the possible interpretations of your term, and distinguish between those that apply to your definition and those that don't.

Post-Writing

Once again, you should follow the standard steps in post-writing (outlined in Chapter 2) as you approach your definition essay for revision. In addition, consider the following questions that are specific to definition:

- Have I defined my audience and purpose clearly and tailored my specific definition appropriately?
- Have I chosen a term or concept that is open to interpretation?
- Have I organized my points in a logical and effective manner?
- Have I made use of a variety of other rhetorical modes in building my definition paper?
- Are my supporting details in line with my purpose?
- Have I indicated what my concept or term is not, if necessary?

EXERCISES

1. Choose a common word that can be interpreted in a variety of ways (some examples are "faith," "assertiveness," "pampering," "dishonesty," "achievement"). Think of at least three different definitions that could be applied to each word.
2. Examine each of the following terms. Next, think about how you would define each term in an extended definition for each of the following audiences. How would the definition of "intimate relationship" change if it were presented to a four year-old versus a police officer, for instance? Which aspects of the definition could remain the same for different audiences?

   Terms: (1) intimate physical relationship, (2) stressed out, (3) criminal behaviour, (4) intoxicated

   Audiences: (1) a four year-old child, (2) a teenager, (3) a doctor, (4) a police officer

3. For each of the following concepts or terms, think of at least three types of support, using different rhetorical strategies such as comparison, description, narration, example, process, and so on:

   - frozen yogurt
   - water skiing
   - wisdom
   - root canal

MODEL STUDENT ESSAY: DEFINITION

The following definition essay demonstrates how one student handled this rhetorical mode. Highlighted are some key points that help to make the essay effective.

Trekkies: An Alien Species

setting context for definition (placing "Trekkie" within larger category of "fan" and then distinguishing it from "fan")

Even if you've never been a fan of the television series *Star Trek,* you're probably familiar with the show and its multiple spin-offs, such as *The Next Generation, Deep Space Nine* or *Voyager,* as well as numerous films. Some people, however, have taken the notion of "fan" where no one has gone before, and live, breathe, eat, or even dream *Star Trek.* These people, known affectionately as "Trekkies," are obsessed with all things *Star Trek,* but especially with the early 1960s series starring William Shatner and Leonard Nimoy.

thesis

The well-known stereotype of a classic Trekkie is a somewhat awkward, nerdy, science whiz—the type of person who probably earned all As in her or his science courses in high school, spent Saturday evenings reading science fiction or physics, and can never get a date to the prom. Classic Trekkies wear their pants too short, their shirts buttoned too high, and perpetually have pen protectors in their breast pockets. This image is so pervasive that it has been successfully lampooned in many forms of media, from *Mad Magazine* to *Saturday Night Live* to the 1999 comedy hit movie starring Tim Allen, *Galaxy Quest.* To some extent, Trekkies themselves perpetuate this stereotype with their single-minded focus on *Star Trek,* sometimes to the exclusion of other aspects of their lives.

first defining characteristic of "Trekkies"

specific details

Unlike other types of fans who may admire a singer or actor from afar, Trekkies are so obsessed with their idealized images of the fictional Captains Kirk, Picard, Sisko and Janeway or the Starships Enterprise and Voyager that they allow the show to infiltrate their daily lives, and the thin line between fact and science fiction becomes blurred. For instance, one Trekkie I know named each of his three children after *Star Trek* characters, resulting in the unique and somewhat bizarre monikers Data,

distinguishing "Trekkies" from other fans

2nd defining characteristic

specific detail

Odo, and Neelix McHugh. Others may decorate their homes with *Star Trek* memorabilia or plaster the walls with posters of Mr. Spock, Counsellor Troy, or Seven of Nine. Devoted Trekkies own *Star Trek* uniforms, wear Bejoran earclips and rings, or paint Native American Indian symbols on their foreheads to imitate Commander Chicotay. Even further, many Trekkies have made the fantasy more tangible by attempting to build warp-speed engines or to reproduce a cloaking device. After a while, people begin to wonder whether these starry-eyed fans still have their feet firmly planted on Planet Earth.

specific detail

Authentic Trekkies also faithfully attend conferences devoted to *Star Trek* memorabilia and information, taking place across North America. There, they approach the topic with a somewhat religious zeal, endlessly hashing over old episodes, vying for autographs from the show's stars, or listening to actors reminisce about experiences filming the shows. As the shows become older and the "crews" also age, the event is less an opportunity to share in the magic of *Star Trek* than it is to view aging stars who've done precious little since they last flew through the Delta Quadrant. None of this matters to Trekkies, who are thrilled simply to be in the same vicinity as Captain James T. Kirk or Dr. Julian Bashir, along with thousands of other eager Trekkies crammed into huge auditoriums, of course.

3rd defining characteristic

specific examples

More than anything else, however, Trekkies are renowned for their vast storehouses of trivial knowledge about the shows and films. A die-hard Trekkie can tell you not only the first name of Spock's mother, but also the number of Tribbles that invaded the Enterprise, the precise location of Data's on/off switch, the exact dimensions of the Holodeck, or the more than 300 Ferengi Rules of Acquisition. Many Trekkies hold contests to see who can relate the most obscure facts about the show, or who has memorized more dialogue from shows already aired. An alarming number of Trekkies maintain Web pages devoted to the shows as well.

final (key) defining characteristic

specific details

conclusion and
final thought
about
"Trekkies"

With the incredible success of the many *Star Trek* series and the clones that emerged after them, the enthusiasm about this timeless show is not about to die down any time soon. Even if they are somewhat biased in their adoration of *Star Trek*, Trekkies enlighten the rest of us about the positive attributes of these shows and characters, and introduce many people to the joys of life in the science-fiction future. May they live long, and prosper.

Science, Scientists, and Society
by John Polanyi (b. 1929)

John C. Polanyi is a Nobel Prize–winning scientist (1986) and professor of chemistry. Born in Germany, Polanyi came to Canada from England as a child and returned there to obtain his B.Sc., M.Sc., and Ph.D., all from the University of Manchester. His experiments on chemiluminescence of molecules helped to predict and elucidate energy relationships in chemical reactions and eventually led to the discovery of the most powerful sources of infrared radiation that have ever been developed. He has won a variety of awards and honours, among them the Royal Medal of the Royal Society of London and the Order of Canada.

PRE-READING

Polanyi here expresses his own interpretation, first published in *Queen's Quarterly* (2000), of what science is (or should be). Before you read the essay, think about your own experiences with science, either in class at school or elsewhere. What are your feelings about practising science? Do you enjoy it? If so, why? If not, why not? What is the value of science in everyday life? How can we make the study of, and interest in, science more common in our society?

I am passionate about the civilizing effects of science. That does not make me 1
insensible to the dangers of science, but they pale beside the dangers of pseudoscience. Think of the fascist and the communist movements, so much intertwined. One claimed the authority of science because it had a theory of race, the other because it had a theory of class. Yet neither was science, both pseudoscience. They did not celebrate inquiry; they suppressed it. They were the enemies of science and, not coincidentally, of humanity.

Real science is different. It never gives up searching for truth, since it never 2
claims to have achieved it. And it is civilizing because it puts the truth ahead of all else, including personal interests. These are grand claims, but so is the enterprise in which scientists share. How do we encourage the civilizing effects of science? First, we have to understand science.

Scientia is knowledge. It is only in the popular mind that it is equated with 3
facts. That is, of course, flattering, since facts are incontrovertible. But it is also demeaning, since facts are meaningless. They contain no narrative.

4   Science, by contrast, is story-telling. That is evident in the way we use our primary scientific instrument, the eye. The eye searches for shapes. It searches for a beginning, a middle, and an end. We sense this from personal experience, and we know it from experiments. When a light beam is reflected from the human eye, it can be seen to scan a person's profile while paying special attention to those features it judges significant. It does not simply point; it paints. Since painting is a skill, so too is seeing.

5   What we see is, as a consequence, culturally conditioned. That is, of course, open to misunderstanding. It might be construed to mean that our conclusions are simply a matter of taste. But that is untrue. Though we explore in a culturally conditioned way, the reality we sketch is universal. It is this, at its most basic, that makes science a humane pursuit; it acknowledges the commonality of people's experience.

6   This, in turn, implies a commonality of human worth. If we treasure our own experience, and regard it as real, we must treasure the experience of others. Reality is none the less precious if it presents itself to someone else. All are discoverers, and if we disenfranchise any, all suffer.

7   It is true that we do science competitively, but to succeed we also do it cooperatively. The history of science, in which discoveries ricochet from mind to mind, makes this clear.

8   What is happening, then, in the process of discovery? It would be better to admit that we do not know; the act of knowing remains unknowable. Of course, we know that the mainspring of discovery is reason.

9   The first prophet of this Age of Reason was not Descartes, but Lucretius. He excoriated mysticism as the foe, and exalted the progressive revelations achieved by the application of logic: "Little by little, time brings each thing into view, and reason raises it up into the coasts of light."

10   The fact that Lucretius wrote about reason in verse indicates that he was also aware of the need for aesthetics as a guide when, as ultimately happens, logic fails. If reason brings us to a result that is ugly, we must reason again. For reason is supreme but not alone.

11   It is important that we reflect as best we can upon our craft, since our understanding of science will inform public policy towards it—"science policy," as it is called. For example, if seeing is a skill, then we should rely on those who have that skill to determine what science we do.

12   In Canada we routinely offend against that principle. We have, for example, numerous "Centres of Excellence" because we recognize that the skill on which discovery depends is possessed by few. But then we proceed, in evaluating such centres, to give only a legislated 20 per cent weight to "excellence." A preposterous 80 per cent is reserved for considerations having to do with "socio-economic worth."

This includes guesses as to the probable contribution of the academic science 13 to job creation and wealth-creation. Also included in this 80 per cent are marks for "style," defined as quality of management, extent of networking, and degree of interdisciplinarity. Excellence is trampled underfoot in the pursuit of what are thought to be the distinguishing marks of efficiency and relevance—but are, in fact, unreliable guides to either.

Compulsion to micromanage science in this fashion, evident today in many 14 market-economy countries, is surprising. In these same countries it is anathema to have governments pick winners in the marketplace for goods. Yet this is a relatively transparent marketplace compared with that for ideas, the marketplace that characterizes science. Nonetheless, when it comes to science, governments believe themselves qualified to select the most worthwhile projects on the basis of utility and "style."

This selection procedure is largely a sham, and we scientists should not lend 15 ourselves to it (though we routinely do so). We should, instead, insist on applying the criterion of quality. That this criterion is real is evidenced by the awesome success of science—peer-reviewed science—in this century.

Have we failed, as scientists, to explain science? Seemingly. Have we too often 16 kept silent because we thought it expedient? Undoubtedly.

Though neglectful of their responsibility to protect science, scientists are 17 increasingly aware of their responsibility to society. But what is that? Some dreamers demand that scientists only discover things that can be used for good. That is impossible. Science gives us a powerful vocabulary, and it is impossible to produce a vocabulary with which one can only say nice things.

Others think it the responsibility of scientists to coerce the rest of society, 18 because they have the power that derives from special knowledge. But scientists, like any other group, are not permitted to seize the levers of power. Nor should they be blamed for failing to do so. They must work through democratic channels. Anything else would be incredible arrogance.

What responsibilities remain? Plenty. Scientists are only beginning to come to 19 terms with them.

In the time that I have been a scientist I have seen huge changes in our per- 20 ception of these responsibilities. Let me give some examples.

In the late 1950s a major topic under discussion was whether Canada should 21 acquire nuclear weapons. The United States was trying to get Canada to do the decent thing, and arm itself with nukes. The weapons were, after all, to be for the defence of North America.

Individual scientists like myself—and many more conspicuous—pointed to 22 the dangers of radioactive fallout over Canada if we were to launch nuclear weapons to intercept incoming bombers. On the face of it, this was technical advice. But more truthfully it was a philosophical position. We chose to make our calculations concerning fallout because we were opposed to the acquisition of nuclear weapons, not the reverse.

23 I do not mean to discount the technical element. I merely want to stress (as I did in the context of discovery) that what the scientist sees is influenced by what he believes.

24 Much the same applied to the next public debate, which had to do with nuclear fallout shelters. Technical arguments were once more advanced (by myself, among others) to illustrate the absurdity of sheltering a nation from a determined nuclear attack. At a deeper level, however, we were objecting to an outlook according to which security was to be found in the life of a troglodyte.

25 We were appalled by the abandonment of attempts at coexistence in favour of the life of a mole. Better to die in the pursuit of civilized values, we believed, than in a flight underground. We were offering a value system couched in the language of science.

26 Around 1970 my scientist friends in the US indoctrinated me in a fresh question of policy. In the war in Vietnam, the United States was using herbicides (Agent Orange) and a tear gas (CS_2). This could well be construed as being in contravention of the Geneva Protocol, which for almost half a century had banned the use of chemical weapons. It was, at that date, one of the few instruments of international law regulating the use of weapons, and was correspondingly precious.

27 I went off to see our ministers of defence and of foreign affairs, as well as the prime minister. God knows how I got into their offices, but I did. They gave me a hard time—as was proper—protesting, "These things are used for killing weeds and for riot control; how can you say they are weapons of war?" The answer was that when employed to prosecute a war, they had become weapons of war. They were being used to expose the enemy, so as to kill him.

28 One does not need to be a chemist to make that point. But it helps to come from a community with a commitment to objectivity, and a degree of independence from special interests. Under this scientific and moral pressure the Canadian government conceded publicly that the use of these weapons in Vietnam was, in their view, a contravention of the Geneva Protocol. The government of the United States was not pleased.

29 What we in the scientific community were seeking, in our idealism, was a world ruled by law. The moral force that we brought to this debate derived from our membership in an international community ruled by law—albeit unwritten law. For without the acceptance and enforcement of standards of probity, there would be no functioning scientific community.

30 And without steps being taken to widen this realm of rule-based cooperation, beyond the narrow bounds of science and similar professions, there will be anarchy leading ultimately to all-out war. But technology has made such war intolerable. The solution is to be found not in more technology, but in less war.

When in March 1983 President Reagan announced the Strategic Defense 31
Initiative (SDI), popularly known as Star Wars, this issue was clearly joined.
President Reagan was offering a technical fix to the threat of nuclear war. The SDI,
he made it clear, was to be the scientist's antidote to the nuclear poison. However,
in the process of distributing this illusory antidote we were to abandon the only
genuine defence against nuclear missiles, which lay, as it still lies, in institutional-
ized restraint.

The SDI was an invitation to a new arms race, one in nuclear shields which 32
would proceed in parallel to the continuing arms race in swords. With missile
defences back in the news today, this is a lesson to remember.

In the course of these political struggles, the scientists became increasingly 33
aware of themselves as an international non-governmental organization. This
NGO bases itself, I claim, not primarily on its technical expertise but on its moral
tenets. In science we have a group of individuals supporting one another, worldwide, in an endeavour whose success depends upon placing the truth ahead of
personal advantage.

Not all succeed in doing this, but all are agreed as to the necessity. In science, 34
truth must take precedence not only over individual advantage, but also over
"group advantage"—sectional interests such as nationality, creed, or ethnicity.

This assertion of higher purpose has made scientists (and all scholars) sup- 35
porters of human rights. Our championing of human rights puts to rest the
notion that what we are offering is primarily technical expertise. Technical
expertise has nothing, directly, to do with human rights. It is once more the moral
force of science—evident in such individuals as Einstein, Russell, Pauling, and
Sakharov—that makes it effective.

Our community's voyage of self-discovery is not over. I believe that it will lead 36
us to a more active support of democracy, wherever it is threatened. That notion
would have seemed preposterous when I began my life as a scientist. But no
longer. Today Academies of Science use their influence, around the world, in support of human rights. They should do the same for democracy, for the death of
democracy is the end of free enquiry. The bell tolls for us.

QUESTIONS

Understanding the message: Comprehension

1. At the same time that he defines "science," Polanyi succeeds in defining "pseudoscience" as well. In your own words, explain the meaning of each term.

2. What are the key characteristics of true science, according to Polanyi?

3. What does Polanyi mean when he writes, "facts are meaningless" because "They contain no narrative"?

4. In what ways does Polanyi distinguish how we manage "the marketplace that characterizes science" from the "the marketplace for goods"?

Examining the structure and details: Analysis

1. What method does Polanyi use to open his definition essay? How does he organize the remainder of the essay?

2. What are the various rhetorical techniques that Polanyi uses to define the term "science"? Cite examples.

3. Describe the essay's general structure. How is it organized? What effect does this have on the reader's understanding of "science"?

Formulating a response: Inference and interpretation

1. Do you agree that the evaluation scheme used by the "Centres of Excellence" Polanyi describes is unfair? Why or why not?

2. Would you say that Polanyi is, in fact, defining the term "scientist" rather than "science"? Why or why not?

3. Do you think Polanyi had an ulterior motive in writing this essay? What other issue does he address? In what way is his definition of "science" biased?

4. How would you state the thesis of this essay? Explain.

5. In his last line, Polanyi makes an **allusion** to a famous poem by John Donne, "For Whom the Bell Tolls" (1621). Find a copy of the poem and read it carefully. How does this allusion relate to Polanyi's subject matter? Is Polanyi's use of this reference appropriate? Why or why not?

Essay questions

1. Write your own definition of what science means to you, or choose another major discipline, such as history, literature, politics, or medicine. Begin, as does Polanyi, by comparing your definition to the general public's preconceived notions about the discipline.

2. Think of a subject or group that is often misunderstood or stereotyped (for example, punk rockers, attendees at raves, Christian Scientists, participants at

motorcycle conventions, lawyers, wrestlers) and write an essay in which you present a clear explanation of how they truly operate or what they truly believe.

3. Reexamine Polanyi's essay and determine what you think is the key trait, according to Polanyi, that characterizes science. In an essay, explain how the various examples he provides serve to support this key trait.

VOCABULARY

fascist and communist movements: totalitarian regimes in which people have few individual rights

disenfranchise: to deprive of rights or privileges

Descartes: René Descartes (1596–1650), French philosopher and mathematician, often called the father of modern philosophy

Lucretius: Roman poet and philosopher (c. 99–55 B.C.)

excoriated: denounced

aesthetics: philosophical study of the beautiful qualities in artistic creations

anathema: something that is detested

expedient: most advantageous

troglodyte: recluse; someone who dwells in caves or below ground

herbicides: poisonous substances, usually applied by spraying, used for killing plants or weeds

conceded: acknowledged

probity: integrity; honesty

anarchy: chaos or confusion

tenets: principles

Einstein, Russell, Pauling, Sakharov: German-American scientist, British philosopher, American scientist, and Russian scientist and human-rights activist; all were active in the 20th century

Where the Truth Lies

by Wayne Grady (b. 1948)

Wayne Grady was born in Windsor, Ontario. He earned his B.A. in English from Carleton University in 1971 and is currently a writer of magazine articles and books, an anthologist, and a translator (from French to English). His books include The Bone Museum: Travels in the Lost Worlds of Dinosaurs and Birds *(2000);* Chasing the Chinook: On the Trail of Canadian Words and Culture *(1998), from which this selection is taken;* The Quiet Limit of the World: A Journey to the North Pole to Investigate Global Warming *(1997), shortlisted for the Governor General's Award;* Vulture: Nature's Ghastly Gourmet *(1997); and* Toronto the Wild: Field Notes of an Urban Naturalist *(1995), shortlisted for the Toronto Book Award. Among his translations are* Black Squirrel, *by Daniel Poliquin (1996);* On the Eighth Day, *by Antonine Maillet (1989), which won the Governor General's Award for translation; and* Christopher Cartier of Hazelnut, *by Antonine Maillet (1985), winner of the John Glassco Prize for Literary Translation. Grady has won two Science in Society Awards and has served as the editor of* Harrowsmith *magazine and as the science editor of* Equinox *magazine. He lives north of Kingston, Ontario, with his wife, Merilyn Simonds, and has two children.*

PRE-READING

Although most of us consider honesty to be important, nearly all of us have told a "little white lie" at some point in our lives. In this essay, one of many from his book *Chasing the Chinook*, Grady discusses the polygraph machine and the notion of lying. Is it ever necessary to lie? How do you feel when you know that you've been lied to? Is there really any way to ensure that someone is telling the truth? Finally, how much should we rely on machines such as polygraphs when we try to determine if an alleged criminal is lying?

---

1   *Polygraph (psy) An apparatus for recording, simultaneously, a number of physiological processes: the lie detector.*
            —1968, The Gulf Dictionary of Business and Science

2   In Thomas Malory's *Morte d'Arthur*, there is a scene I always think of when I think of lying. Arthur is removing his court to Tintagel, travelling slowly through dark woods. He suspects that his wife, Guinevere, is having an affair with

his favourite knight, Sir Lancelot, as indeed she is. In order to be near Guinevere, Lancelot has disguised himself as a monk and is part of Arthur's entourage. When they come to a raging stream, Guinevere is afraid to ford it, and Lancelot (in his monk's robe and cowl) offers to carry her across. That evening Arthur, unable to contain his suspicions about his wife's conduct, asks her point-blank if she has been unfaithful to him. Guinevere hesitates, then with queenly sang-froid replies: "The only other man who has held me in his arms except you, my lord, is that monk who carried me across the river this afternoon." Arthur is satisfied. So would a polygraph have been.

The polygraph, or lie detector, was invented by John Augustus Larson in the 1920s. Larson (who was born on December 11, 1892, in Shelburne, Nova Scotia) had graduated from Boston University in 1914 and received a Ph.D. in psychiatry from the University of California in 1920. In the years between then and his appointment in 1928 as medical director of criminology at Rush Medical College, he perfected a machine that he believed would catch people who told lies. 3

The word "polygraph" had been around for a long time. It simply means "multiple writings," and was first applied to an invention patented in France in 1763 that made mechanical copies of handwritten letters. The writer wrote a letter using a pen attached to a system of jointed rods, and a second pen, attached to the other end of the rods, moved exactly as the first pen. Later developments involved various liquids and viscous plates; the Gestetner machine is a polygraph, as is the Xerox machine and its clones. In fact, clones are polygraphs, because the word came by extension to refer not only to the machine but also to the copy made by the machine, and hence to any person who copies or apes another, or is himself a copy of an original. Sir Lancelot, in his hooded robe, was a polygraph of a monk. 4

In his 1925 satire *Heart of a Dog*, the Russian writer Mikhail Bulgakov creates a Frankenstein-like doctor who specializes in "rejuvenation operations," usually of a sexual nature. The doctor transplants a man's pituitary gland and testicles onto a dog, and the dog thus becomes intellectually and sexually human (he is the narrator of the story) while remaining physically a dog—a dog who is a human copy and makes copies of humans. Bulgakov names him Poligraf Poligrafovich, after the famous Moscow publishing house Mospoligraf. A 1996 stage version of *Heart of a Dog*, by Canadian playwright Robert Astle, keeps the hero's name, Polygraph Polygraphovich, but since a polygraph is now better known as a lie detector than as a publishing company (thank goodness), Astle might have made Bulgakov's original point better had he changed the named to Xerox Xeroxovich. 5

The connection between Bulgakov and Larson's lie detector is hidden in the word "duplicity." A lie detector detects duplicity by duplicating a subject's inner reactions on a scroll of paper. Larson's polygraph produces "multiple graphs," each one recording a particular aspect of the subject's reaction to certain yes–no questions. In looking for a foolproof way of determining whether or not a person 6 was being duplicitous, Larson reasoned that lying took more effort than telling the truth, because the lying subject had to remember two things—the truth and the lie—whereas an honest subject only had to remember the truth. This effort, he believed, could be measured. Larson also knew that fear (in this case, of being found out) triggers adrenalin surges that produce detectable changes in heart and respiratory rates, blood pressure and perspiration. Attach sensors to the right spots on a subject's body, monitor what happens when the subject is asked a series of questions—some straightforward and some loaded—and you have an exact duplicate of the inner state of the subject's innocence or guilt.

7   Maybe. Polygraph tests are still not admissible in court. Many people— including members of the Society for Psychophysiological Research and Fellows of the American Psychological Association, when they were surveyed by the *Journal of American Psychology* in 1995—believe that "polygraphic lie detection is not theoretically sound." Polygraphs cannot provide reliable proof of innocence or guilt, they say, because some people behave guiltily when asked innocent questions, while others remain perfectly unperturbed when grilled on the most gruesome crimes. In other words, while honest people have only to remember the truth, there are dishonest or deluded people who remember their lie, or who, like Guinevere, so phrase the lie that they believe it to be the truth. For them, a polygraph is little better than a stack of Bibles.

8   Polygraphs are used by police, but only to weed out unlikely suspects, and then with sometimes ambiguous results. O.J. Simpson failed two polygraph tests a few days after being arrested for the murder of Nicole Simpson, for example, and yet was acquitted by a jury of his peers. Did the polygraph lie? General Jean Boyle, former Chief of Defence Staff, passed a polygraph test concerning his role in tampering with documents relating to the conduct of the First Airborne Division in Somalia, but later admitted that he had violated "the spirit" of the Access to Information Act by telling a CBC reporter that certain documents no longer existed when in fact they existed under a new name. Perhaps General Boyle had read *Morte d'Arthur*. Or he may have read Douglas Williams's best-selling book *How to Sting the Polygraph*, which proclaims on the jacket: "If you are scheduled to take a polygraph, relax! It can be beaten rather easily."

9   The Canadian Bar Association agrees that polygraph tests cannot be relied upon. "The polygraph is not sufficiently sophisticated," says Sheldon Pinx, chair of the CBA's National Criminal Justice Sector. "The machine does not, at the end of the day, say whether you're being truthful or dishonest. It simply provides certain information to a polygraphist, who then has to interpret those readings and come up with an opinion. It's really opinion justice."

10   Not so, according to RCMP polygraphist Robert Russell. In 1996, Russell was called in to polygraphically test Al McLean, Speaker of the Ontario Legislative Assembly, who had been accused by his assistant, Sandi Thompson, and two other

female employees of sexual harassment in the workplace. The tests cleared McLean. Russell says polygraph tests are "95 percent reliable in the hands of experts." But 95 percent reliable still means that one of every twenty people in prison might be there because they break out into a cold sweat whenever anyone asks them their name, and one out of twenty criminals are at large because they can coolly deny any knowledge of how their landlady got into a dumpster.

Outside the courtroom, polygraphs are being used more and more for ordi- 11 nary industrial security and routine surveillance. For $500, a company like Paragon Investigations and Polygraph Services Ltd. will come to your home or office and tell you if your partner is having it off with your favourite knight, or whether your trusted employee is selling preliminary lab results to your competitor. Some people find this an invasion of privacy: with enforced polygraph testing, the whole notion of presumed innocence flies out the window.

In the end, as the author of *Morte d'Arthur* knew, the best lie detector is one's 12 own conscience, and a polygraph cannot distinguish among subjects who are cold-blooded, or unconvinced they have committed a crime, or merely innocent. Which was Guinevere? Such ambiguity lies behind Quebec filmmaker Robert Lepage's 1996 movie *Le polygraphe,* in which François, a waiter in Quebec City, is suspected of having murdered his girlfriend, Lucille. While the police are investigating, François's friend decides to make a film based on the case and asks François to play the part of (i.e. to duplicate) the murderer. The film's title refers to a surrealist twist in which François's confessor is not a priest but one of Larson's little machines. The film, like a good polygraphist, poses some disturbing questions about the nature of guilt and innocence, lies and equivocations—and, like a good confessor, leaves it to us to puzzle the answers out for ourselves.

QUESTIONS

Understanding the message: Comprehension

1. What is the pun in the title?

2. Grady begins his definition essay with a short narrative from Malory's *Morte d'Arthur.* What does this narrative tell us about the polygraph and how it works?

3. Why is lying more difficult than telling the truth?

4. What does Grady mean when he writes, in paragraph 6, "For them [people who phrase the lie so they believe it is the truth], a polygraph is little better than a stack of Bibles"?

Examining the structure and details: Analysis

1. Grady prefaces the essay with a quote from the *Gulf Dictionary of Business and Science*. What methods does he use in his extended definition to prevent the essay from becoming too dry and factual?

2. How does Grady's first paragraph pique the readers' interest and keep them reading? How effective is his return to this subject at the end of the essay?

3. Find several examples of Grady's use of humour in the essay. What purpose does the humour serve? How is it related to the topic?

Formulating a response: Inference and interpretation

1. Does Grady indicate his opinion about whether polygraphs are useful? If so, for what purpose(s) does he think they should be used?

2. Do you agree that polygraph evidence should not be admissible in court? Why or why not?

3. Does Grady include a sufficient number of examples and rhetorical devices to make his definition clear? Why or why not?

4. What is Grady's tone in this essay? Does it suit the topic? Why or why not?

Essay questions

1. Choose one of the following terms and create your own extended definition of it in essay form: white lie, misrepresentation, diplomacy, exaggeration, fraud, impersonation, hypocrisy, con.

2. Do you believe that it pays to be honest and that liars don't prosper in our society? Write an essay in which you argue either that honesty pays off in the end, or that honesty is, in fact, a quaint, old-fashioned concept with no place in the real world today.

3. What do you think Grady's underlying message (thesis) is in this article? Using examples from the text, explain Grady's point and whether he conveys it effectively.

VOCABULARY

Morte d'Arthur: Sir Thomas Malory's 1485 treatment of the legend of King Arthur of Britain and the Knights of the Round Table

ford: to cross over a river or stream

sang-froid: composure in tough situations (literally, "cold blood")

viscous: thick, sticky; gooey

duplicity: deceitfulness

having it off: having an affair

equivocations: deliberately misleading statements; statements that can be interpreted in more than one way

Depression Can Strike Anyone
by Diane Francis (b. 1946)

One of the most prominent—and, at times, controversial—financial writers in Canada, Diane Francis was born in Chicago, Illinois, where she dreamed of being a novelist before turning her talents to nonfiction writing. After taking a newspaper feature writing course at Sheridan College in Toronto, she began freelancing and has contributed to a large variety of newspapers and magazines, including Canadian Business, Quest, *the* Toronto Star, Maclean's, *the* Toronto Sun, *the* Financial Post, *and, currently, the* National Post. *She has also published a number of books, including* Bre-X: The Inside Story *(1997)*, Fighting for Canada *(1996)*, Underground Nation: The Secret Economy and the Future of Canada *(1994)*, A Matter of Survival: Canada in the Twenty-first Century *(1993)*, Contrepreneurs *(1988)*, and Controlling Interest: Who Owns Canada? *(1986)*. She was named* Chatelaine *magazine's Woman of the Year in 1992. She is also the director for the Canadian Foundation for AIDS Research.*

PRE-READING

What does depression mean to you? In this essay from *Maclean's* magazine (2000), Francis dispels some popular myths about what true clinical depression is. Have you ever known someone who was truly depressed? What was s/he like? If you have experienced depression, how would you describe it? In what ways are depressed people different from the rest of us? How do you think you would deal with severe depression?

---

1   People routinely use the word "depressed" colloquially, thus changing the real medical definition of the term. They say they are "depressed" about the weather. They say a movie is "depressing." But those usages are what some mental health professionals would label as "small-d" depression, describing a slight mood shift or a negative topic.

2   Such moods, however, should not be confused with clinical depression, or "Big-D" depression. Some experts say that as many as one out of every five persons will be afflicted with this debilitating and painful syndrome in their lifetime. And as those of us who have an afflicted loved one know only too well, "Big-D" depression involves severe mood changes, and loss of self-esteem and vitality.

Clinical depression is a diagnosis applied to any individual who is immobilized 3
by mood for a period of at least two weeks. To some in the medical profession,
depression is the number 1 health problem. "It's a prevalent, costly and deadly
disease, and about seven per cent of the world's population suffers [all the time]
from severe depression," explains Raymond DePaulo, professor of psychiatry at
Johns Hopkins University in Baltimore, Md., and an international expert on the
disease. "It's widely distributed throughout the world's population and the genes
involved are ancient genes, not mutated more recent ones. This means that when
we were all living in caves, these were part of everyone's gene pool."

It is a physiological condition, not a character flaw as many people mistakenly 4
believe. It is this basic misunderstanding that stigmatizes those with the disease,
making it worse. This also prevents proper diagnosis because victims and their
friends and relatives often zero in only on the symptoms. It is said that women go
to their doctors when depressed, but men go to their bartenders. Indeed, those
suffering from depression are at a greater risk of becoming alcoholics—a mis-
guided attempt at a kind of self-medication to numb psychic pain. Loved ones
tend to deal with the alcohol issue rather than the underlying depression. So does
the alcoholic.

The same misdiagnosis can apply in cases involving drug abuse. Depression's 5
victims are at a greater risk of turning to cocaine or heroin, and then crime in
order to afford the expensive, illegal narcotics they have become addicted to as a
means of reducing their depression.

Such symptoms—substance abuse, self-destructive behaviour and nega- 6
tivity—are not widely understood as depression's manifestations. Even family
physicians sometimes send away patients with physical complaints who are, in
fact, depressed, when they should be referring them instead to psychiatrists who
can prescribe antidepressant medications, or they should prescribe those drugs
themselves.

Clinically depressed people are all around: many of the homeless are depres- 7
sion's victims. So can be the maladjusted teenager, that cranky colleague or that
unkempt neighbour who shuffles along the street. Depression is a hideous disease
characterized by the inability to feel joy, be optimistic or take care of oneself. "Big-
D" people populate our prisons. "Big-D" people populate our high schools and
often remain undiagnosed until they kill themselves or others. On the other hand,
depression can also be found among some of the world's most gifted people.
"Mozart, Van Gogh and others suffered from depressions and were absolutely
unable to produce when they were afflicted," says Dr. DePaulo.

Depressed brains do not function properly—they are plagued by chemical 8
imbalances. One prominent theory is that depressives suffer the effect of seratonin inhibition. Seratonin is an enzyme that facilitates the transmission of signals within the brain, and the brains of many biochemically depressed people

have little or no seratonin compared with the general population. For some unknown reason, inhibitors devour most of the seratonin. The result is that their brain wires are cut, impeding the wires from transmitting emotions and rational thoughts. This is why victims feel empty, confused and unable to think clearly. Prevented from functioning normally, they then develop psychological problems because they are disabled when it comes to work or interpersonal relationships.

9   The good news about depression is that most cases are treatable with medication. Victims also require therapy to deal with the psychological problems acquired along the way. But for most of the afflicted, the cause is not an unhappy or neurotic childhood or a nasty family. The cause is physiological, initially. But if depression remains unrecognized, scorned or heckled, it can singlehandedly guarantee an unhappy and neurotic childhood and miserable adulthood.

10   We should declare medical war against depression's debilitating and damaging impact. One psychiatrist has even said that Paxil (a popular antidepressant) should be put in the drinking water, like fluoride. While such fixes may be unrealistic, the fact is everyone from teachers to physicians, parents, grandparents and friends must learn to differentiate between "Big-D" and "small-d." It is just as insensitive and unhelpful to bark at a clinically depressed person to "get out of bed and get on with life" as it would be to say the same thing to someone with breast cancer or serious heart disease. Depression is probably the biggest single medical cause behind most human suffering. That's why we should be less judgmental about people around us who are miserable, and, instead, try to encourage them to seek help.

QUESTIONS

Understanding the message: Comprehension

1. What do most people mean when they use the terms "depressed" or "depressing"?

2. What do most people assume is the cause of depression? What is the actual cause?

3. Why does Francis refer to clinical depression as "'Big-D' depression"?

4. Why are depressed individuals at greater risk than normal of becoming alcoholics or drug addicts?

Examining the structure and details: Analysis

1. One of the ways to help establish a definition is to explain what the topic is *not*. How often does Francis use this technique? Cite examples.

2. Go over the essay to determine how Francis organizes her material. What technique(s) does she use throughout to create coherence?

3. How much of Francis's definition is based on fact and how much on personal interpretation? Why do you think she wrote it this way?

Formulating a response: Inference and interpretation

1. Who is Francis's intended audience in "Depression Can Strike Anyone"? How do you know? Does she provide an adequate definition for this audience?

2. Where is Francis's thesis stated? How does her evidence serve to support the thesis?

3. How does Francis convey her attitude about people who suffer from depression? What specific words or phrases does she use to let the reader know how she feels?

Essay questions

1. Many people who have physical or psychological conditions are judged unfairly by the general population. Using Francis's essay as a model, write your own definition essay to alter the preconceived notions about one of the following: people with eating disorders (such as anorexia, bulimia, obesity); the physically challenged (people in wheelchairs, blind individuals, and so on); people with drug or alcohol addictions; or another group of which you are aware.

2. Near the end of her essay, Francis quotes one psychiatrist who recommends that a popular antidepressant "should be put in the drinking water, like fluoride." Do you think that as a society we are becoming too dependent on drugs as a "quick fix" for any psychological ill? Why or why not?

3. Does Francis succeed in convincing the reader that depression "is a hideous disease"? Write an essay in which you argue one way or the other, citing examples from the article to support your argument.

VOCABULARY

colloquially: of common, everyday speech

physiological: related to body functions

stigmatizes: ruins the reputation of; ostracizes

Cowboy Culture

by Ian Tyson (b. 1933)

Known as a country singer who began his career in partnership with his ex-wife, Sylvia, Ian Tyson has also enjoyed a solo career as both singer and ranch operator. Originally from British Columbia, Tyson moved to Toronto at age 24, where he met and partnered with Sylvia Fricker, whom he later married. The two formed the legendary duo Ian and Sylvia, turning out hits such as "Four Strong Winds," "Someday Soon," and "You Were on My Mind." After his marriage broke up, Tyson returned to the ranch country of southern Alberta to raise and train horses. His first solo album, Old Corrals and Sagebrush *(1983), consisted of cowboy songs, both traditional and new, and launched his second musical career. His latest album,* Lost Herd, *won the Prairie Music Award for Outstanding Country Recording for 1999. Tyson, a recipient of the Order of Canada, currently makes music and raises horses with his second wife, Twylla, and daughter, Adelita, in Alberta's Rocky Mountains.*

PRE-READING

What's a real-life cowboy's life like? In this selection from *Equinox* magazine (1998), Tyson explains. In present-day Alberta, cowboys are alive and well. What associations come to mind when you think of cowboys? How have cowboys traditionally been represented on television, in films, or in other media? Why would someone wish to *become* a cowboy? What do you think accounts for our culture's fascination with cowboys?

1   In Alberta these days, there is a plethora of cowboys. Not all of them ride the range. There are doctor-cowboys, lawyer-cowboys—weekend warriors in big hats and fancy trailers going down the road, back to the office on Monday morning. But the cowboys in these photographs [the original article was accompanied by photographs] are real cowboys, working cowboys, custodians of the Spanish horseback tradition that goes back 400 years in the Americas.

2   Along the eastern slopes of the Alberta Rockies, the cow-calf operations still have to be handled by people on horseback. Cattle must be rounded up from the hills and driven with precision and skill. The ranges are still vast enough to require a day or two of hard riding just to locate the herd. Young people are drawn to the life by an affinity for livestock and the love of horses, but the reality of ranching on the northern plains is the thankless job of putting up enough winter

feed. Down in New Mexico, they think we're crazy up here. "Hell, you can ranch with two saddle horses down here. Up north, it's a tractor deal!" Yes, frequently it is a tractor deal. However, there are still plenty of times when the old skills are trotted out and the horse once more is king.

It has always been important for cowboys not only to perform their duties well 3 but to look good doing it. Spanish tradition again, vaquero-style. Some kid will practise his hip shot all winter on the roping dummy just for a moment of glory at the local rodeo. But, of course, a real cowboy's life isn't like that. That kind of romance reached its zenith along the shallow shores of the Milk River in the late 1880s, when a typical roundup would see 150 fiercely competitive riders doing mind-blowing things with rawhide riatas on unruly broncs. By the turn of the century, the open range was seriously overstocked with cattle. Then came the brutal winter of 1906–07, the "Great Die-up," and open-range cattle drives would live on only in the haunting photographs of L.A. Huffman and the paintings of Charlie Russell. From then on, it was stock raising, barbed-wire fences, and the manufacture of winter feed—more and more winter feed. The homestead era followed, dominated and directed by the railways, ploughing under the great grasslands forever. The homesteads failed; the grass was ruined. Today there are virtually no large native grasslands intact on the Canadian prairies.

Still, in the foothills, cowboy culture lives on. Indeed, its visceral appeal seems 4 stronger than ever, especially now that most people live a long way from the land. But when I was growing up in British Columbia in the 1950s, cowboys were considered shiftless and no-account. Actually, they were a true subculture. They lived and worked on those huge ranches of the Nicola Valley and Cariboo, moving from one to another wherever they could find work. Many of the top hands I remember were native riders. The last time I rode out with the crews at Douglas Lake was in the late 1980s, and I met only one native cowboy. I wonder how many I would encounter today.

These photos were taken along Alberta's front range of the Rockies from 5 Longview down through Pincher Creek country. The 1990s have been wet years, and in those green hills, you can find an eclectic mix of two cow puncher styles: west of the Rockies, it's vaquero; east of the Rockies, it's Texas. The merits of each are the topic of endless bunkhouse debates, but suffice to say that the West Coast style is more leisurely, with emphasis on pretty throws and ornate horsemanship. Texas style is harder, split rein, more pragmatic. The two cattle cultures developed different saddles and gear, and when the range-cattle industry came to Alberta in the 1880s, both were accepted. Hands that came with the herds from Oregon adopted the vaquero style, while those with the herds that arrived from Texas took the Texas cow-puncher style. For 120 years, the two ideologies have coexisted in southern Alberta.

Still and all, beyond the styles, ranch life on the northern plains remains one 6 of hard work, endless winter feeding, and the stress of spring calving. Toss in the violent mood swings of an Alberta March, and cowboy life doesn't sound very romantic at all. Yet the legend lives on. About mid-August, nature's gears change. You can almost hear them. There's a different hum: Gardeners look to their bedding plants with concern, and the first frost is just over the hill. The biting bugs are gone, and the mountains turn hazy blue with golden flanks. It's roundup time once again, and the boys will be in the saddle for a month. If he's lucky enough to be mounted on a good 'un with his "foot in the stirrup and his hand on the horn, he'll be the best damn cowboy ever was born."

QUESTIONS

Understanding the message: Comprehension

1. What does Tyson mean by the term "weekend warriors"?

2. Why do people become cowboys, according to Tyson?

3. What are the "old skills" of cowboys that Tyson refers to?

4. What is the appeal of "cowboy culture" now that so many people no longer live close to the land?

Examining the structure and details: Analysis

1. What methods does Tyson employ to distinguish his interpretation of "cowboy" from the commonly held stereotype?

2. Which strategy for definition that is *not* one of the other rhetorical modes does Tyson use in this article?

3. How does Tyson's style in the article match his subject matter? Provide examples to support your answer.

Formulating a response: Inference and interpretation

1. In what way(s) does Tyson exhibit the breadth of his knowledge on the subject? Does he qualify as an expert on cowboys? Why or why not?

2. What do you suppose is Tyson's purpose in this essay? Provide examples to support your answer.

3. Does Tyson provide enough support for his definition to create a well-rounded and clear picture of cowboy culture? Why or why not?

4. Tyson examines both the stereotype (romantic view) of cowboys and the harsher reality of cowboy life in Alberta. Do you think his view is biased? Why or why not?

Essay questions

1. Many professions are idealized by those outside of them, yet the reality may not jibe with our romanticized versions. Choose a profession that has such a stereotype (such as doctor, actor, athlete) and write an essay in which you explain what the true life of such a professional is like.

2. Create your own definition for a distinct culture that you know of. This could be the "culture" of the dormitory, in a particular classroom, of a particular company, of your family, or any other you might think of.

3. How does Tyson's definition of what a cowboy is contradict the common perception? Using specific references to the selection, explain how Tyson's cowboy differs from the stereotype.

VOCABULARY

plethora: large number

affinity for: a liking of

vaquero: Spanish term for cowboy or cattle driver

zenith: highest point

Milk River: a river that flows through southern Alberta from and to Montana

riatas: long, braided leather whips used on horses

visceral: on a physical, instinctive level

Nicola Valley and Cariboo: farming regions in central British Columbia

eclectic: diverse; varied

pragmatic: practical

We've Lost Our Homing Instincts

by Catherine Gildiner (b. 1948)

Catherine Gildiner is a psychologist in private practice and a published writer who has written essays, screenplays, a memoir, and a novel. She has a Ph.D. in psychology and an M.A. in English literature. She has attended universities in the United States, Canada, and Oxford, England, and has taught at the University of Toronto and York University. Over the years she has written articles on both Freud and Darwin for psychology journals, book reviews for the Globe and Mail, *and several CBC* Ideas *radio shows. She has written a psychological advice column for* Chatelaine *magazine for a number of years and has appeared on radio and television as a psychologist dealing with topical psychological issues. Over the last 10 years she has published dozens of humorous essays, most of which have appeared in the* Globe and Mail. *She has recently written a best-selling, Trillium Award–nominated memoir entitled* Too Close to the Falls *(1999), about her unusual childhood when she worked full-time from the age of four delivering medicine from her father's drugstore. She has also published sport essays, had screenplays optioned, and currently has a novel,* Murder in the Freud Archives, *in progress. Gildiner lives with her husband, Michael, and three sons in Toronto. In her spare time she has been training on a masters' competitive rowing team for a number of years, and her crew has won several gold medals in both national and international competitions.*

PRE-READING

What defines "home" for people? In this humorous article from the *Globe and Mail* (2000), Gildiner muses on some of the changes our conception of "home" has undergone in recent decades. When you think of "home," what comes to mind? Do you spend a lot of time at home with your family, or is your home a place defined in a different way? What makes people decide that a certain place is a home?

1   A funny thing happened last week at the gym. Some people had heard me on CBC Radio talking about Cheryl Mendelson's *Home Comforts*—a brand new, hotly marketed, 900-page bible of laundry techniques, stain-removal and other housekeeping, home-making skills. When I started talking about it again at the

gym, the other obsessive-compulsives paused their machines and gathered around my "Butt Buster" (that's the brand name) as though it were a pulpit. Women who have never spoken in six years of perpetual motion could not stop themselves from soliloquizing on the state of their mouldy humidifiers and how, although some of their husbands have come out of the closet, the moths are still firmly ensconced.

Home. The word plunges a red-hot poker through the no-longer-aproned 2 hearts of women. Who's minding the house now that most women are working outside of it? I'm a therapist, and for a lot of my clients—professional couples and teenagers—it seems that the very concept of the home, the nest, the family base is one big blur on our collective mental window.

The disagreement is not whether the art of housekeeping has declined— 3 everyone agrees it has—but what impact that has had. Back at the gym, some of the women sprayed their domestic frustration around the room like rogue Windex. They raged against what they interpreted to be feminist ideals that drove them out to work in the first place ("Why am I sorting out some legal file when I could be sorting the family photos at home and getting some satisfaction from it?")

Others got mad at their men: "After all, I went out and learned how to com- 4 pete, why can't he learn to vacuum? He doesn't see the dirt and never will." And there were others who wanted to sweep the idea of "home" under the carpet with the other debris; they basically said, "Who cares about housework? Who cares about 'home'?"

But people do care. The famed psychotherapist Erik Erikson—the man who 5 coined the term "identity crisis"—once said that whenever he embarked on any therapy with a patient he would eat dinner with his patient's family to understand their relationships. In some of our 21st-century homes, Mr. Erikson would be hard-pressed to know where to begin.

Recently, I suggested to one of my client families that they discuss a problem over 6 family dinner. The 11-year-old son looked mystified. His lawyer mother reminded him that a family dinner was what they used to do at Grandma's house—before she died. Then the boy's lawyer father explained that everyone in the household gets home late. For meals, they fend for themselves.

This wasn't an isolated incident. In another session with different clients, I saw 7 a 14-year-old girl similarly baffled by the term. Her father helped her out by telling her that "family dinner" meant "holiday dinner." The light bulb went on. "Oh," she said, "like when we all eat together on Christmas."

In Mr. Erikson's seminal book *Childhood and Society,* he delineated a psychosocial 8 theory of development that describes crucial steps in the person's relation to the social world. The child's first and most important experience of the world happens at home. That's where the child learns the rules, becomes attached.

9   If one buys Mr. Erikson's epigenetic principle—that development occurs in sequential stages, and we become fixated at whatever stage our needs fail to be met—then it may be time for a heads-up. How does the infant sort out the chaos of the world if the first home-world he or she enters is also chaotic? How influential is a sense of domestic order?

10   I'm not sure myself. So I've been polling some of the perceptive teenagers I meet in my work and I've asked more than 20 of them about family dinners. About half told me they eat with their parents and siblings three days a week; the other half reported that they rarely ate together. Yet asked if they missed shared mealtimes, they seemed nonplussed, as though I had asked if they missed having a pet elephant.

11   The consensus seemed to be that the benefits of both parents working outweighed the drawbacks. Their parents were able to buy them bigger bedrooms, their own video games, their own TVs (a majority had one in their room). I pointed out that all these luxuries made them more isolated from their families. One boy said candidly that no one wants to be more together than that.

12   But several others said that they would experience not eating together at least half the time as a rip in the fabric of an already threadbare family existence. (This is significant. The rule of thumb with teenage groups is that they usually have three times as intense feelings as they express. Teenager emotion is like the hunt for cockroaches; for every sentiment you see there are dozens you miss.) As Judith Martin says in her book *Miss Manners' Guide to Domestic Tranquility,* "A household where the members don't sit down at dinner together nearly every night is a convenience store, not a home."

13   Ah, that word again. What makes a home? Are we in danger of losing the skills that build and keep one together? Homemaking is not just about shared mealtimes. It is also about paying care and attention to a physical space.

14   This was brought home to me last month [when] I gave a talk to real-estate agents from across Canada. We were supposed to be talking about how they could motivate themselves through sales slumps; however, the agents were far more concerned about how to motivate the people whose houses they were selling to clean and spruce up their residences before that all-important open house. The agents even debated the question of who should foot the bill for the professional cleaning teams that too often had to be sent in before the doors could be opened to potential buyers.

15   The agents knew you can't sell a house unless someone has taken the time to remove the rotten food from the fridge and change the mouldering sheets in the unaired bedrooms. They knew that saleable children's bedrooms should be equipped with bed linens, not sleeping bags. Lest we forget, these real-estate agents were not talking about instructing the unwashed poor. They were talking about advising middle-class "home"-owners.

I am not suggesting that women must give up their day jobs and go back to home-making. Such sentiments have been championed by a new coterie of young journalist damsels-in-dissent such as Danielle Crittenden, Wendy Shalit and Amity Shales, who claim to have cast off the shackles of feminism—the same movement, I might add, that allowed them to become journalists in the first place. 16

But I do think we—men and women—have to look at what's at stake for all of us. Many of us try to ignore the challenge of domestic order, or as they say in my field, we lower the bar. Some hire a once-a-week cleaning lady to keep the chaos at bay. Some of us who don't have that luxury simply beat little paths to and from the fridge and hope for the best. 17

But the attention drawn by Ms. Mendelson's hefty tome on homemaking skills—and by Martha Stewart, and Judith Martin and perhaps even Ms. Crittenden—suggests a yearning out there for old experiences of domesticity, and a need to hear from new authorities on the subject. 18

Ms. Mendleson is particularly intriguing. She has a PhD in philosophy and a Harvard law degree. Clearly she isn't cleaning the house because she couldn't do anything else. She made a choice to put her energy into home care. That Ms. Stewart has built a multimillion-dollar empire on domestic advice is yet another sign of our longing. 19

Charles Darwin noted that nesting is part of the maternal instinct in most animals. (The day before my son was born I had an overwhelming desire to line my kitchen cupboards with contact paper, something I never did before—nor since.) It occurs to me that we are now thwarting our nesting instincts, in effect repressing them because we no longer give ourselves the time or the energy to nest. This repression would explain the feelings of anxiety and longing we're currently feeling around the notion of home. Who knows? Champions of freer expression of domestic instincts such as Mendelson and Martha may be to the 21st century what Sigmund Freud was to the 20th. 20

QUESTIONS

Understanding the message: Comprehension

1. What does Gildiner mean when she says, "although some of their husbands have come out of the closet, the moths are still firmly ensconced"?

2. What are the different views about women's situations at work and at home that Gildiner encounters at her gym?

3. What psychological problems does Gildiner foresee if families continue to operate in the manner in which they now live?

4. At what expression is Gildiner poking fun when she writes, "damsels-in-dissent"? How appropriate is her adaptation?

5. Reread the final paragraph of the article. What does Gildiner mean when she says, "Champions of freer expression of domestic instincts such as Mendelson and Martha may be to the 21st century what Sigmund Freud was to the 20th"?

Examining the structure and details: Analysis

1. Examine Gildiner's diction (word choices) in this article. Does the level of formality suit the subject matter? Why or why not?

2. How many different methods does Gildiner use to define the concept of "home"? At what point does the definition tell the readers what a home is *not*?

3. Gildiner's article is divided into three sections. What is the main concern of each section? Why does she divide it this way?

Formulating a response: Inference and interpretation

1. Find two or three examples of humour in this article. Does the humour help to strengthen the point being made or diminish it? Why?

2. Do you see the impact of our society's shift away from a focus on "home" as negative? Why or why not? Does Gildiner let us know her own feelings about this issue? If so, what are they?

3. What has been the psychological result of this shift away from "home," according to Gildiner? Do you agree with her assessment? Why or why not?

Essay questions

1. Do you recognize any of the changes that Gildiner describes in your own family or home? Write an essay in which you explain what "home" means to you and your family and how it may be different from the traditional definition.

2. The home has traditionally represented a place in which a family shares their experiences and enjoys security as a unit. If "home" is a disappearing concept, what other activities or places will replace it? In what other ways can families grow, share and feel close to each other? Write an essay in which you answer this question.

3. Does Gildiner convince you that the idea of "home" is an essential one for people to be psychologically well adjusted? By using examples from the article, explain why or why not.

VOCABULARY

soliloquizing: delivering a solo speech

ensconced: settled in snugly or securely

epigenetic: based upon heredity or genes

nonplussed: baffled, perplexed

mouldering: decaying, dusty

coterie: group of people with common interests

Danielle Crittenden, Wendy Shalit, Amity Shales: authors of, respectively, *What Mothers Didn't Tell Us: Why Happiness Eludes the Modern Woman, A Return to Modesty: Discovering the Lost Virtue,* and *The Greedy Hand: How Taxes Drive Americans Crazy and What to Do About It.*

CHAPTER 10

Cause and Effect

CAUSE AND EFFECT IN DAILY LIFE

You are most likely already familiar with cause and effect. Real-life use of cause and effect happens when you engage in activities such as the following:

- You explain to your parents why it's difficult to get all your studying done with a part-time job that takes 22 hours per week.
- You write a proposal to your municipal government asking for more frequent garbage pickup and explain how the excess garbage is ruining the neighbourhood.
- You explain to your niece why Aunt Charlotte is so much happier than she used to be.
- You explain to your eight-year-old son why using compost in your garden will help the plants to flourish.

WHAT IS CAUSE AND EFFECT?

A common refrain of parents is that their children don't always consider the future consequences of their actions. How many adults have said, "If only I knew then—when I was sixteen—what I know now! Boy, would I have behaved differently!" What these people lament is a previous inability to project the effects of their actions. **Cause and effect** essays look at what makes things happen, as well as the ramifications of actions.

DEFINITION

Cause and effect: Cause and effect examines what makes things happen and/or what results ensue from particular factors or events.

Cause and effect relates to why things happen (what causes some result, and what effects will ensue after a particular cause or causes). If you pinpoint effects, you look to the future or to the end of a series of events: what *will happen* or what *did happen* as a result of certain circumstances or events. If you examine causes, you begin with an effect (outcome or situation) and look backward in time to see what made it happen or contributed to it. Many writers include both causes and effects in their writing because they are so closely intertwined.

Cause and effect essays may be based on actual events that have already occurred (factual) or based on assumptions drawn from existing data (hypothetical). For instance, if a social worker writes a report about his 35-year-old client whose parents divorced when the client was 5, the report is based on effects in the present; any impact the divorce has had on the client's behaviour is already apparent. On the other hand, an environmentalist's paper about the effects of ozone depletion is, at present, still to some degree speculative; we won't know all the possible effects until the ozone layer is, in fact, depleted.

Here's an example of a passage in which the final effect (the financial recovery in Southeast Asia after World War II) is established before the writer then traces the causes:

> What explains the striking ability of Japan and the four little tigers [South Korea, Taiwan, Singapore, and Hong Kong] to follow the Western example and transform themselves into export-oriented societies capable of competing with the advanced nations of Europe and the Western Hemisphere? Some point to the traditional character traits of Confucian societies, such as thrift, a work ethic, respect for education, and obedience to authority. In a recent poll of Asian executives, more than 80 per cent expressed the belief that Asian values differ from those of the West, and most add that these values have contributed significantly to the region's recent success. Others place more emphasis on deliberate steps taken by government and economic leaders to meet the political, economic, and social challenges faced by their societies. [William J. Duiker, *Twentieth Century World History*, Belmont, California: West/Wadsworth, 1999: 324]

The author makes clear two major causes of the economic success: the traditional Asian character and culture, and the moves made by Southeast Asian government and economic leaders.

In this next example, the writers begin with a particular circumstance or pre-existing condition (the use of a V-chip in televisions to prevent youth from watching violent or sexually explicit programming) and then determine the ultimate effects of this circumstance:

One concern some people have with this device is that it may stifle innovation in television, by promoting the idea that bland is better. It remains to be seen whether many adults will take the trouble to use the device, given that many do not even program the date into their VCRs. As well, children might tape contentious programming on an unblocked TV [one without a V-chip] and play the tape on a VCR. In general, in the wired world, censorship is extremely difficult both for technical and political reasons. [Shirley Biagi and Craig McKie, *Mass Media and Social Issues,* Scarborough, Ontario: ITP Nelson, 1999: 262]

Clearly, the authors of this passage do not predict a positive effect resulting from availability of V-chips. Notice that the effects in this paragraph—bland programming, parents' apathy, and children's ingenuity—are all hypothetical projections of what *could* happen should the V-chip become widely available.

Causes and effects are inextricably linked to each other; what is a cause in one logical thread may serve as an effect in another, and one effect may later become a cause of something that follows it. For this reason, cause and effect essays often move back and forth between causes and effects, and rarely focus only on one side of the issue.

WHY USE CAUSE AND EFFECT?

In addition to helping us understand events and situations in our world, cause and effect also helps us to make important decisions that depend on an understanding of these elements. The classic Christmas film starring Jimmy Stewart, *It's a Wonderful Life,* traces the effect one man, George Bailey, has on all the people he has touched in his life, by showing him how their lives would have been different without his influence. After learning how much of an impact he's exerted on others, George reconsiders a major decision he's made, and the film ends happily. Like George, many of us weigh important decisions with great care when we know the effects may be irreversible. Should you take the new dream job, even though the salary is a step down? Should you train for a marathon? Should you ask the person of your dreams out on a date? Each of these decisions brings with it a multitude of possible outcomes. Examining the potential consequences of actions or events helps you to predict future outcomes and make important decisions.

In contrast, you may wish to examine how a certain situation developed: How did you reach your credit card limit in only two weeks? Why was your progress report three days late? Why are you afraid of cats? In these cases, an examination of the causes—which factors contributed to a conclusion or current situation—will help to illuminate the reasons why things are as they are.

How to Write a Cause and Effect Essay

Writing a cause and effect essay is a fairly complicated endeavour, and one that requires careful, critical thought and excellent planning. A good way to approach the task is to think of writing it as a way to solve a mystery: What made this event happen? What will happen if this action is taken? What if this second action is taken? The same patterns of thought that help you unravel murder-mystery plots or determine your own opinions about court cases in the news are also used in cause and effect writing, and serve to make it one of the most challenging rhetorical modes.

SNAG

Confusing coincidence or correlation with cause

Just because something *follows* something else does not necessarily mean that the second thing was *caused* by the first. If you find a $20 bill on the sidewalk and subsequently get a job offer, finding the bill did not cause the employer to call you; the sequence of events is just a coincidence.

Similarly, if you do well on your biology lab test every time you wear your favourite pair of jeans but fail the test the one day you wear sweat pants instead, it would be illogical to assume that wearing jeans *caused* you to do well on the tests; the connection between the two events is simply a correlation (a pattern of two things occurring together with regularity). With more complex situations, it is imperative to question whether two correlated events (those that appear side by side) are actually *causally* related.

TIP

Give each cause its due

Be sure to give all causes equal attention; just because one cause is more obvious than another, it may not be more important. For instance, in asking "What caused the cafeteria to close?" the most obvious answer might be "The profits were too low to keep it open any longer." However, further investigation may illuminate a series of causes leading to the loss of revenue: the food was neither fresh nor tasty, customer service was poor, the location was off in the nether reaches of the building. Often, one cause stems from another. A thorough writer examines all interrelated causes before deciding which of them contribute directly to an effect.

Pre-Writing

1. Choose a general topic

In choosing your topic, you can begin with a current state of affairs and delve into the various causes, or look at a situation or event and project the effects. In the former, you state the final effect, and then trace the causes that led up to it. In the latter, beginning with the causes and projecting effects that ensue as a result, you deal with unknowns and will, to some extent, need to forecast the future.

2. Consider your audience and purpose

As with other types of essays, ask yourself for whom you are writing the cause and effect essay. How much does your audience already know about the topic? The answer to this question will determine the kinds of details you include and how far back in the cause-effect chain you wish to begin the essay. Consider your purpose as well: will you try to convince the audience that a certain sequence of events is causally related or simply inform them about something that has already occurred? Your decisions about audience and purpose influence the structure, details, and language of the essay.

3. Generate ideas about the topic

Because cause and effect analysis uses advanced critical thinking, you may need extra time to generate ideas about the topic or to conduct further research (see Chapter 13 for more information on research and documentation). Specific causes are not always as clear as they may first appear, and only with a little more careful examination can you ensure that the causes you identify truly are those implicated in an effect. In the infamous Walkerton, Ontario, water scandal that gained national prominence in 2000, seven people died and thousands were ill after drinking tainted water. The most obvious cause of the deaths was the E. coli bacteria in the water; however, once the case went to court and testimony was given, it became clear that the tainted water was made possible only by a series of events that occurred over many years (falsified results of water tests, a waterworks manager with inappropriate training, and a doctor whose early warning about potential water poisoning was ignored). All of these factors permitted a proliferation of E. coli bacteria to the point that people became ill.

Similarly, we may not always be able to predict effects with great accuracy. For instance, before the turn of the millennium, many professionals in the computer industry predicted a drastic effect as a result of hasty computer programming practices through the late 20th century (many computer systems used two digits rather than four to represent dates). These experts cautioned that when the date shifted from 1999 to 2000, computers would misread the two-digit "00" as "1900," leading to utter mayhem on January 1, 2000. The predicted effects of the so-called

Oversimplifying causes and effects

While something may appear to be the only cause or effect in a situation, it's important to consider *all* relevant outcomes or sources, and then decide which are more or less important. For instance, enthusiastic parents may decide that buying a puppy for their child will increase the child's sense of responsibility and ability to express love and caring (an effect). However, they may also overlook the facts that their own workload will increase, they'll have less flexibility to go out spontaneously after work or to take vacations, or they may have to deal with potential health problems if they or their child is allergic to the pet. All of these effects must be considered before making a decision.

Let it flow

Like a flow chart that indicates the major and minor steps in a process, a modified flow chart for describing causes and effects can also be useful to examine how certain steps along the way influence one or more others and how steps are interrelated. For instance, if you were to diagram the effects of drinking alcohol before driving, you could consider the various steps in a flow chart such as the one in Figure 10.1.

Y2K bug included everything from the obliteration of all bank records to the failure of electricity and other power sources to the malfunctioning (or complete breakdown) of elevators and hospital equipment. In reality, almost none of the projected chaos ensued—to the great embarrassment of doomsayers everywhere.

Ultimately, the impact of subsequent effects might spread through years, affecting both the driver and others.

Using a flow chart will help you to examine carefully which causes contribute to which effects and the relative strength and importance of each cause (how much it impacts later effects); it will also help to uncover any "missing links" (overlooked causes or effects) in the list.

4. Narrow to a thesis

A thesis for a cause and effect essay should limit the extent to which you examine the causes and effects. It's impossible to begin at the inception of any series of

FIGURE 10.1 Flow Chart on Effects of Drinking and Driving

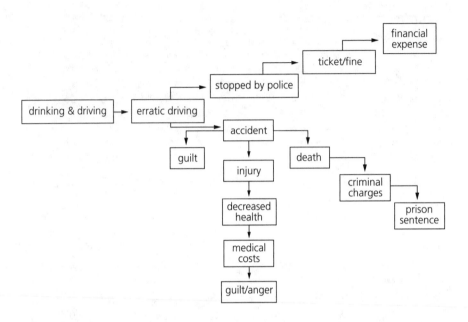

events—you'd likely be travelling back in time to the dawn of creation (after all, *anything* that has ever happened is related to something before it). In a short paper examining a current economic decline, for instance, you might think to revisit the "Great Crash" of 1929; however, to do so would necessitate a long and complicated paper. If your time and resources are limited, delineate key boundaries for your cause and effect essay; choose an appropriate starting point and deal with the most important causes or effects from that point onward. In discussing current economic trends, for instance, it might make more sense to return to a more recent recession in the 1970s. If you keep your thesis focused on something specific and manageable in scope, you will produce a better essay, one that can conceivably examine the topic in its entirety.

5. Organize your ideas in an outline

Whether you begin with a specific situation (the effect) and trace back the different causes that contributed to it, or start with a particular situation (the cause) and predict which effects will ensue as a result, the most obvious method to organize a cause and effect essay is chronological. However, in many cases, the causes or effects coexist in time (such as several poor lifestyle factors that all contribute to heart disease concurrently). In these cases, an emphatic order, or a combination of chronological and emphatic order, will serve you better.

6. Decide on specific support for the main points

Because cause and effect relies on logic, it is reinforced greatly by adding specific, factual details and statistics. Whenever possible, include empirical (objective, factual) evidence in your cause and effect writing, even if it means doing some research to find out more about the topic (for more about research and documentation, see Chapter 13). Be sure that you provide sufficient support for every assertion you make.

Cause and effect is one type of writing where other rhetorical modes may come into play for support or interest, but they do not provide the foundation of the essay, since concrete, factual evidence must be at its core. You may include a narration or description only if it relates to the reality that you are discussing in the cause and effect essay.

Writing

Keeping logical connections in mind should be paramount as you write. You may have figured out how the three causes you mention all contribute to a final outcome, but make sure that your readers understand these logical links as well. (For more about logic, see Chapter 11.)

Another aspect of logical reasoning is to ensure that you have concrete evidence for each of your inferences. If you say that eating disorders are caused by low self-esteem, can you cite some studies that have proven the link? Do you have a concrete example to back up each of your conclusions?

SNAG

Listing without clear causal links

Once you've indicated a series of causes for a particular effect, or effects following particular causes, it's easy to lapse into writing *only* a list of these points without making the causal connections clear. Be sure that you don't omit important connections, the *why* that links these points together. More than simply providing information about what affects something else, you must explain *how* and *why* it has that effect. Transitional devices and phrases such as "because" or "the reason that" generally serve to clarify these connections. For example, Krista Foss in the article "How Young Is Too Old?" shows both the factors that led to an effect (toxins, broken homes, better food and environment) and the reasons for which they did so (toxins trigger chemicals that initiate puberty; the bodies of girls raised by men other than their fathers have no chemical inhibitors for early puberty; and better health in general allows the body to reach a critical mass sooner).

Post-Writing

As with your other types of essays, revising a cause and effect paper should rely on the post-writing steps discussed in Chapter 2. In addition, make use of the following questions to sharpen your cause and effect paper:

- Am I focusing on causes that led to an effect, or effects that followed (or will follow) a cause?
- Does my thesis clearly state the relationship I'm examining? Does it delineate the boundaries of my discussion?
- Have I used an appropriate method to organize my points?
- Have I included all of the essential causes or effects?
- Is my reasoning clear and logical? Do I have concrete examples to support each of my logical conclusions?
- Have I made the logical connections between causes and effects clear?

EXERCISES

1. Think of three major decisions you have made in your life and outline the effects of each; for instance, your choice of college, your choice of automobile, your choice of boyfriend or girlfriend, your choice of apartment or residence. Then, examine what effects might have ensued if you had decided differently.
2. Think of someone with whom you have a good relationship and another person with whom you do not get along. What causes you to get along well with the first person, but not with the second?
3. Think of a habit or fear that you have or a superstition you believe. What might be the causes of this behaviour or belief? Be sure to look as far back as possible into your personal history to trace the causes.

MODEL STUDENT ESSAY: CAUSE AND EFFECT

The following cause and effect essay demonstrates how one student tackled this rhetorical mode. Highlighted are some key elements that help to make the essay effective.

A Remarkable Change

Sigmund Freud believed our personalities are formed by the time we're five years old. His theory certainly seemed to apply to my older sister, Robin, who'd completed her teens and early twenties without changing her attitudes or behaviours in any discernible way. Focused on herself and her friends, Robin's greatest concern of the day was whether her tights matched her miniskirt or whether she'd suffer a Bad Hair Day. When her college program required her to volunteer for six months at a local telephone crisis line, I was sure she'd hate the job and drop out. To my surprise, the work had an enormous impact on her outlook toward life, and eventually prompted remarkable changes in her personality. Because of her volunteer work, my formerly shallow, self-absorbed sister was *thesis* transformed into a role model I deeply admire.

first effect   The first change I noticed in Robin after she started volunteering was an increased interest in the people she spoke to on the crisis line. She began to talk animatedly about how the callers affected her personally. Many of her callers were lonely, isolated, or poor people with problems that my family couldn't imagine dealing with. She was openly sympathetic to *specific* the plight of a single mother, now living in a shelter, *illustrations* who'd been abused by her common-law husband, and the elderly man who called each night because he was too ill to leave his apartment, yet feared he might not wake the next morning. For the first time, Robin *explanation of* began to take an interest in people outside her social *effect* circle, and really appreciated how lucky she was. She took a serious interest in the welfare of others, something she'd never really done before.

second effect   After about a month on the job, her attitude shifted further; she became less interested in looks or appearances. Although she still took care to dress neatly and appropriately, she pared down her wardrobe considerably and changed its contents dramatically. Previously, the clothes in Robin's closet could have supplied all the costumes for a fashion shoot in any high-fashion magazine from *Glamour* to *Elle*. At this point, however, she began to wear simpler, more comfortable, practical clothing, trading in miniskirts and high heels for cotton slacks, loafers, and T shirts; she even donated many of her old things to charity. She started pulling back her straight, blonde hair in a no-nonsense ponytail rather than spending 45 minutes blow-drying it each morning. Moreover, she chastised me for judging people according to first impressions, telling me, "People are more than their appearances—it's what's inside that counts." What's more, she really meant it.

[margin: contrast to previous behaviour]

[margin: specific example of effect]

As she continued to expand her knowledge of others, Robin also took an interest in people beyond Canada and learned about global issues of human rights, legal injustices, and world poverty. Whereas her previous knowledge of the world had been restricted to details of television sitcoms, soap operas, or reality game shows, now Robin began to read the daily newspapers diligently, and her new-found concerns were expressed through questions to my parents about their own philanthropic activities. Did they send money to help the starving children in other countries? Did they donate to the MS society's annual fundraising telethon? Did they give food to the homeless or clothes to the Salvation Army? As she pressed each of us, her genuine concern to see some good done prompted further awareness and generosity in the rest of the family as well. We began to appreciate our privileged positions living in a middle-class Canadian family, and we initiated a family tradition of donating food to a local food bank.

[margin: third effect]

[margin: specific details]

[margin: secondary effect (Robin's impact on others)]

The final phase of my sister's transformation came about after she completed her internship at the crisis line. Rather than pursue the career she'd originally chosen, Robin announced at the dinner

[margin: final effect]

table one evening that she would, instead, be travelling to Africa to teach disadvantaged children for a year. Truly, we were all amazed. I looked over at my sister and marvelled at the sincere, dedicated, and enthusiastic person sitting in front of me, completely different from the one who'd sat at this same table a year before. That night, Robin decided that she wanted to pursue a career helping others.

reiteration of thesis and final thought

Perhaps the changes in my sister were simply due to the process of maturation, and would have occurred in any case; or maybe Robin finally grew up. I believe, however, that her experience at the crisis line is what initiated the change. Learning about and getting to know people less fortunate than herself prompted my sister to recognize how much she had in her own life and encouraged a willingness to help others. Today, my once self-centred older sibling is studying to become a doctor who will practise medicine in the Northwest Territories. I can honestly say I admire her more than anyone else I know, and her determination and good work have been an inspiration to me.

How Old Is Too Young?

by Krista Foss (b. 1964)

Krista Foss is a reporter for the Globe and Mail. *She has written extensively on health matters and more recently on controversies and crime. She is a two-time recipient of a Canadian Business Press Award for her writing and research. She lives in Toronto.*

PRE-READING

Parents often worry that their children are growing up too fast or that childhood is no longer the same period of innocence it used to be. In this article from the *Globe and Mail* (2000), Foss discusses the reasons why young girls are reaching physical maturity at an earlier age than in our parents' generations. Are young girls forced into behaviours and situations they are not emotionally ready for simply because they exhibit signs of physical maturity? What are the repercussions of girls having to grow up too fast?

1   Dana, a Toronto teenager, started to menstruate when she was in Grade 5, and on the cusp of turning 10 years old.

2   "It was embarrassing, sort of weird," the now 14-year-old remembers. "There was only one other friend at the time who had started, too."

3   To Dana's mother, Jane, a busy single parent of two daughters, it was more than a little weird, it was worrisome—especially when she saw her grade-school girl being chatted up by a hulking, smirking teenager at a bus stop one day.

4   "I felt her physical development was happening sooner than her emotional and social development," said Jane. "There are also worries about health risks." But when is it normal for a young girl to start sexually maturing and when is it just too darn early?

5   Currently, it's a question of heated scientific debate and parental nightmares. While today's preteens may be aping the vampy Britney Spears and using glitter gel, most parents and grandparents want to think of them as little girls.

6   Recent research is robbing us of some of that security.

7   In 1997, the journal *Pediatrics* published research that made a lot of reverberations. A huge study of 17,077 girls, age 3 to 12, done throughout the United States by a network of pediatricians reporting from their offices, came to the conclusion that young girls were showing significant breast and pubic-hair development one year earlier than previous studies had shown.

Significantly, about 27 per cent of African-American girls and 6.7 per cent of their white counterparts had evidence of pubic hair and breast development at 7. By age 8, nearly half of the African-American girls had such signs of sexual maturation, and almost 15 per cent of white girls. (Breast development usually precedes menstruation by about two years.)

Some read the 1997 study as further evidence that today's North American girls are reaching puberty much sooner than they would, or should—and they blame environmental and social factors as the culprits for pushing each successive generation of females toward sexual maturity at uncomfortably young ages.

Recent research has brought to light intriguing evidence to support possible causes of North America's epidemic of "precocious puberty"—the medical term for sexual maturity that arrives abnormally early.

One of the most controversial theories is that environmental toxins are triggering a physiological rite of passage ahead of time: These toxins flood the bodies of girls while in utero with estrogen-like chemicals that have leached into their mother's food and water from plastics and pesticides.

In October, the science journal *Nature* published a study by University of Missouri researchers that gave that argument some credibility. They exposed mice fetuses to estrogenic endocrine-disrupting chemicals, a fancy name for the suspected compounds widely used in an array of products, at the same level that a pregnant woman might encounter. When the mice matured, the rodents exposed to the chemicals reached puberty much earlier than the mice not exposed. The researchers made the tentative conclusion that human fetal exposure to these same environmental toxins may be damaging a developing child's hormonal clock, putting them on the path toward precocious puberty.

But the science around endocrine-disrupting chemicals is as yet incomplete, and others argue that the environmental exposure is far too low to produce such damning consequences.

Another provocative idea about why young girls may be entering puberty prematurely was published in the *Journal of Personality and Social Psychology* last August. In this study, researchers studied 150 young girls and the relationship with their fathers. Their hypothesis was that young girls who have good relationships with their biological fathers in the first five years of life would reach puberty at normal ages—because the scent of a biologically related male was an evolutionary signal to inhibit maturity.

The flip side to that hypothesis was that those girls who were exposed to a lot of unrelated adult men, especially in their first five years of life, would achieve puberty sooner. And in fact, when the researchers rated each girl's relationship with her father, they found a strong association between age of puberty and ties with a biological dad. The stronger the relationship with the father, the more likely puberty was to occur at a normal age.

16   "Something like premature puberty has to have a genetic component," says Stephen McFadyen-Ketchum, a lecturer at Vanderbilt University and one of the study's authors. "But we suspected a different social environment could trigger those genes earlier than others."

17   Of course, it was just an association, warns Dr. McFadyen-Ketchum. Right now, he and his colleagues are trying to repeat the study.

18   But most doctors suspect something less esoteric, and more obvious, is causing precocious puberty: Today's girls eat better, and often too much, when compared to girls 100 years ago.

19   "A critical body mass has to be reached before a girl will menustrate," said Dr. Denis Daneman, chief of the division of endocrinology at the Hospital for Sick Children in Toronto. That is why, he explains, it is more likely that a chubby girl will reach puberty sooner than an athletic one.

20   Data used to support the medical textbooks' guidelines of the normal ages of puberty come largely from small studies of specific populations of girls, including undernourished children from a British orphanage. Today's young females are better fed, and often overfed, given the much-documented rise in childhood obesity. As a result, Dr. Daneman says, it's not surprising that girls are reaching puberty sooner.

21   And in fact, most pediatricians are adjusting downward their notions of when it is normal for puberty to start.

22   Last October, two years after the 1997 study of 17,077 U.S. girls, a review of the research was published in the journal *Pediatrics* by the U.S.-based Lawson-Wilkins Pediatric Endocrine Society.

23   The society's review concluded that the textbooks had overshot normal puberty estimates and this newer study brought more accuracy to the picture. Therefore, not all girls who were showing breast development before the age of eight had precocious puberty.

24   "New guidelines propose that girls with either breast development or pubic hair should be evaluated if this occurs before age seven in white girls and before age six in African-American girls," said the society's new recommendation.

25   The society still recommended that boys should be investigated for precocious puberty if they exhibit rapid growth, acne, [and] penile and scrotal enlargement before the age of nine, because none of the new research has changed the picture for boys. (About 90 per cent of precocious puberty occurs in girls, according to Dr. Daneman).

26   The new recommendations have important implications for the decision to medically treat a young girl should she exhibit unusually early signs of puberty.

27   For the past 20 years, pediatric endocrinologists have used a drug called a GnRH analogue or agonist, which essentially blocks, or slows down, the hormonal onset of pubescent growth. The rationale for using the drug is that girls

who undergo puberty too soon will end up as shorter adults than they could or should have been, had they gone through puberty normally. A rapid, early puberty means their bones start to age faster than their chronological age, the end result being a shortened growth period.

The drug allows them to achieve a more normal height and, not incidentally, a 28 more normal adolescence.

"If you have a child who is very young and has rapidly advanced into puberty, 29 then it is easy to make the decision to treat her," said Dr. Daneman. "You can slow down the sexual development, slow the bone maturation and linear growth and allow them to grow more like their peers. Then you can stop the medication in time to allow them to complete puberty at the same time as their peers."

But the Lawson-Wilkins review suggests that not as many girls are candidates 30 for the drug therapy as may have been previously assumed, and that the concern that girls with moderately precocious puberty will be unusually short adults is overstated. Most end up within a normal height range. It also indicates that the drug therapy is not useful for little girls who start puberty-like changes between the ages six to eight.

The bottom line seems to be that puberty arrives earlier for the well-fed North 31 American girls than was previously thought. And that early arrival is indeed normal.

Jane, the Toronto mother, never did consult a doctor about Dana's early onset 32 of puberty. Jane had started menstruating at the same age. At that time, she remembers it being excruciatingly lonely. So, in her household there has been a lot of discussion about puberty, how it feels and how friends react. That didn't prevent her daughter Dana's near instantaneous transition from child to modest young woman—"One day I was bathing her and the next the bathroom door was closed on me." But it has meant that mother and daughter can share a laugh about it together. As a result, Jane's younger daughter thinks that whenever she goes through the same changes as her sister, it will be normal and healthy.

QUESTIONS

Understanding the message: Comprehension

1. Why would the early development of girls cause "parental nightmares"?

2. According to the controversial findings reported in the science journal *Nature,* how is our lifestyle part of the problem of "precocious puberty"?

3. Explain why a girl living with her biological father until age five should reach puberty at a normal age.

Examining the structure and details: Analysis

1. What method does Foss use to introduce her article? How does it relate to the conclusion? Do you think her method is effective?

2. What different types of evidence does Foss include in her article?

3. Does Foss deal with causes, effects, or both? What are they?

4. What other rhetorical strategies does Foss employ in discussing the causes of "precocious puberty"?

Formulating a response: Inference and interpretation

1. Do you find Foss's statistics shocking? Do you agree that girls are maturing at too young an age? Why or why not?

2. Which of the various causes do you think is most likely? Why?

3. What is the tone of this article? How does the language used contribute to this tone?

4. Does Foss ever reveal her own opinion on the issue? If so, what is it, and where is it indicated?

Essay questions

1. What do you think are the effects of the "precocious puberty" that Foss describes? Write an essay in which you discuss the potential ramifications of children maturing too quickly.

2. Some people believe the opposite of what Foss discusses—that adults in our society often refuse to grow up and become fully functioning adults. In a cause and effect essay, discuss some of the reasons why adults might wish to prolong their youth and avoid embracing the challenges, responsibilities, and obstacles of maturity.

3. Does Foss provide enough breadth in the areas she examines to find causes for precocious puberty? What other kinds of evidence might she have included? After examining the number and sources of the causes she cites, write an essay in which you answer this question, using examples from the text.

VOCABULARY

reverberations: repeated, small waves

precocious: ahead in development

in utero: in the uterus; before birth

estrogen: female hormone

endocrine: having to do with the body's glandular system

esoteric: unusual or mysterious; understood or known only by a select group

An Insatiable Emptiness

by Evelyn Lau (b. 1971)

Evelyn Lau was born in Vancouver. Her first book, Runaway: Diary of a Street Kid *(1989), a chronicle of her teenage experiences with drugs and prostitution, was a Canadian bestseller and was made into a CBC-TV movie. She is also the author of two short story collections,* Fresh Girls *(1993) and* Choose Me *(1999); a novel,* Other Women *(1995); and three books of poetry,* You Are Not Who You Claim *(1990),* Oedipal Dreams *(1992), and* In the House of Slaves *(1994).* You Are Not Who You Claim *won the Milton Acorn Poetry Award and* Oedipal Dreams *was nominated for the Governor General's Award. Her latest book,* Inside Out: Reflections on a Life So Far, *was published in 2001.*

PRE-READING

In this personal essay, which appeared in *Georgia Straight* (1995), Lau chronicles her experiences with bulimia, an eating disorder in which someone "binges and purges" (overeats and then rids the body of food, either through use of enemas or vomiting) in order to prevent weight gain. What do you know about dieting in our culture and eating disorders in general? How important is body image? Have you ever had any experiences in which health was put second to image?

1   I no longer clearly remember the first time I forced myself to throw up. What I do remember is how inexpert I was and how long it took before I succeeded in actually vomiting instead of just gagging and retching. I began by sticking my finger down my throat and wiggling it around, but this produced few results; it wasn't until articles about bulimia appeared in women's magazines that I finally thought to use the handle of a toothbrush instead of my forefinger. It became easy after that.

2   In my mid-teens, I was too young to believe I was anything but immortal. It didn't occur to me what I was doing was dangerous—instead, it seemed a smart and practical way of coping with things. I went through months of throwing up once or twice a day, then brief periods when I did not throw up at all, when I seemed to have broken the pattern. Surely this meant I was in control. But by the time I turned 18, the months of not throwing up had diminished to weeks, and when I *was* vomiting I was doing it four, five, six times a day. I had become addicted to the sensation. It was no longer a penance I had to perform after eating, but the reward at the end of a binge. I loved the feeling I had after purging,

of being clean and shiny inside like a scrubbed machine, superhuman. I would rise from the bathroom floor, splash my face with cold water, vigorously brush the acid from my mouth. I would take a wet cloth, wipe off the vomit that had spattered my arms, and feel as energized as someone who had just woken from a nap or returned from an invigorating jog around the block. I felt as if everything disgusting inside me had been displaced so that it was now outside myself. Not only all the food I had eaten, but my entire past.

No one could tell me to stop, not even my friends who eventually knew what I 3 was doing. They could not control this part of my life or any other. This was mine alone—the chemical flower smell of the blue water in the toilet, the vomit that shot out as a burning liquid, drenching the sides of the bowl. After a session in the bathroom, a certain emptiness would sing inside me, a sensation of having become a cage of bones with air rushing through it. I craved this feeling so much I no longer cared what I had to eat in order to vomit—I would cram clusters of bananas into my mouth, or tubs of ice cream that lurched back up my throat in a thin and startlingly sweet projectile.

When I left the bathroom, I felt like someone who had achieved some great 4 thing—climbed a mountain, written a book—and survived. I was overweight by only 10 pounds or so, but when I looked in the mirror all I saw was buttery flesh covering my body. My stomach had become swollen and globular from the gorging and purging; I had earned it the way other women earn washboard stomachs and lean waists from hours of sit-ups and crunches at the gym.

As a child, I had been thin and healthy, with a flat belly and limbs that turned 5 brown in the summer. I had my first period when I was 11, and for the next several years the blood welled out of me in thick, rust-coloured gouts that no tampons or pads could contain. My body had somehow become a vessel filled with secret, terrible workings, and I longed to make it translucent, pared-down, clean as a whistle. But the blood spread in the shapes of clouds on my skirts and pants, for 10 or 12 days each month, and my hips and breasts pressed outwards. I hated what was happening to my body, once so straight and uninflected. I attracted the attention of one of my parents' friends, who stared at the fuzzy-dark crook at the top of my thighs when I sat cross-legged in front of him, who asked me to perform somersaults and splits while his thick lips hung open with desire. My own father grew awkward around me, refusing to touch me or meet my eyes, driven away by this growing body that forced him out like a giant balloon expanding in a small room. I was in despair. I wanted to trick my body back into childhood by starving it, but I was hungry all the time; I craved food during the week prior to my traumatic periods. Sometimes I would consume a whole bag of shortbread cookies or three chocolate bars; the sugar and fat would induce a heavy, mucousy lethargy.

My breasts continued to develop, horrifying my mother, who frequently made 6 me undress in front of her so she could ridicule them. Her actions convinced me there was something wrong with my body. She decided to put the whole family on a diet, serving small portions of steamed fish and vegetables, chicken with the skin removed. During dinner, and in the hungry hours of the evening that followed, she would say over and over again, "It's because of you we didn't get enough to eat, that we're going to bed hungry. Look at the sacrifices we're making for you." I would sit at the dinner table, staring down at my plate with tears in my eyes, grief forming a hot, choking knot in my throat. I would watch my father slowly raise his fork to his mouth while my eagle-eyed mother watched me triumphantly, eating only half of what was on her plate in order to set an example.

7   My mother was so thin and white that whenever I glimpsed her undressing behind a half-closed door, her thighs looked like those of the Holocaust survivors I examined in photographs in history class at school. Meanwhile, I began to put on weight, growing chubby beneath sweatshirts and loose jeans. I stole chocolates from the drugstore, bought greasy bags of day-old cookies from the bakery, consumed candies in a blind rush on the mile-long walk from school to home. I crammed myself with food, yet I hated food: its veils of grease, its sauces like paste. I hated its fragility beneath my hands, could not bear the delicacy of pastry. But once I started eating, I could not stop, and after I gave in I would again have to cope with the horrible feeling of satiation—a feeling so uncomfortable and guilt-ridden it threatened to annihilate me.

8   I hated the unaccustomed thickness of my body, yet I took a secret, perverse pride in the space I was filling up, the air I was pushing aside in the family home in order to make room for myself. I looked in scorn upon my mother, who wore tiny pink sweaters with pearl buttons, size XS. Her legs were like bleached sticks, the skin white and crepey; her hipbones jutted visibly beneath her skirts, and she reminded me of a starving cow, its ribs and hips holding up the tent of skin. At 13, I had grown to match my father's weight. But at 130 pounds, he was small for a man, his arms straight, the biceps undefined. He was weak, useless in the battle that had sprung up between my mother and myself. He would not protect me, he took no sides in the daily tug-of-war for power. He merely absented himself, took the coward's way out. For this, I knew, one day I would make him suffer.

9   I thought that if I were to physically fight my mother I could break her dry arms like twigs. I could twist her skeleton between my hands; I could sit on her and suffocate her. But it never came to that. Instead, with each pound I gained, my mother became more controlling. I felt that in my entire world there was only one thing my mother could not take away from me: my body. She was trying, of course, with her diets and carefully calibrated meals and calorie counters set up around the kitchen. She wanted to watch me day and night, but in this she inevitably encountered frustration and failure: she could not see the junk food I snuck between meals and hid between textbooks and in my locker at school.

And it was driving my mother crazy, I began to realize. She turned to the only 10 thing she could control 24 hours a day: her own body. For every pound I gained, she lost one. In Grade 9, when I came home from school I found her doing jumping jacks and skipping rope in the living room, or following an aerobics show on television. She had virtually stopped eating, complaining that I was doing enough eating for us both. Her eyes grew large in her face, and her hair began to fall out in swirls that clogged up the drain in the sink and the shower. When I stood up from the table and looked down at my mother's skull, I could see the wide, white swathe of the part in her hair.

For a while, my father insisted that she eat, but he soon gave up and came 11 home less and less, always too late for the dinner hour, fraught as it was with its agonizing tensions: my mother staring at me with fascination as I ate, her eyes transfixed with hunger. I thought I could no longer stand it; I was as guilty as a murderer with every bite. At night, I lay in my room contemplating suicide and listening to the footsteps of my father pacing his study, waiting for his wife to fall asleep before daring to enter their bedroom. When I trespassed there, I saw pink walls, pink curtains, a pink throw on the queen-sized bed. The bedroom faced south, and all day the sun shone relentlessly through the gauze curtains, revealing the motes of dust in the air. When I opened the dresser drawers, I found beautiful, tiny clothes, beaded and jewelled, carefully folded and wrapped in plastic, as if their owner had already died. I knew these clothes would never again be worn by my mother, and I would never be small enough to wear them. I knew this was a source of bitterness in my mother's life—she could not pass herself on to me; she could not live her life again through me. In order to survive, I would have to deny my mother this second life and claim my own.

In the en suite bathroom I found orange lipsticks dried to hard, wax nubs, 12 cakes of powder that crumbled at a touch, an old tube of KY Jelly squeezed from the bottom like toothpaste. All of it seemed a shrine to my mother's glamorous past. She had been a beauty in her youth, with thick hair that hung down to her waist, so much hair it was almost impossible to bind into ponytails. She had pale skin and pink cheeks like apple blossoms, and she wore short skirts and high heels to work.

What my mother didn't know was that I was already beginning to incorporate 13 her inside me. She didn't know that she was winning and that for the rest of my life I would contain aspects of her—both the young beauty turning men's heads and the wasted figure doing sit-ups on the living room floor. I would grow up to wear contact lenses and to put a wave in my hair; I would admire myself in mirrors and spend small fortunes on clothes and cosmetics. Beneath this evidence of self-esteem, though, I would learn to cultivate a parallel self-hatred: my thoughts would repeat themselves obsessively; I would become compulsive in my behaviour, desperate for control; I would avoid other women because I was afraid they would be like my mother; and I would live at the mercy of my emotions, the endless stream of hatred that poured out of my mouth when I bent over the toilet.

14   "You will never succeed at anything," my mother told me day after day. "You're like your father—spineless, weak, good for nothing."

15   The last time I saw them, when I was 17 and they were in their 50s, he seemed bewildered by what had happened to our family. She had become a confused, agitated women who plucked ceaselessly at the strap of her purse with an anguished tic. She had become powerless to control me, this piece of herself that had separated from her. She had lost me in her attempt to keep me forever.

16   I was 20 years old when I began to lose the feeling of immortality. I thought my body would regenerate itself in time, that once again everything would be new and resilient. But it only got worse. My body began showing signs of wear—my throat constantly ached from throwing up, and when I opened my mouth I saw in the mirror a red, inflamed pendulum dangling behind rows of teeth softened and eroded by acid. My own teeth, once so enamel white—the sort of teeth parents thank God for; the sort of teeth a man meeting me for the first time would go away remembering—had, overnight it seemed, turned pitted and yellow, the back ones worn down to shrunken saddles. When I looked in the mirror, they were translucent as X-rays, made, it seemed, of water and putty. I began to brush more vigorously after each purge, not knowing then that I was accelerating the process, scrubbing my teeth with my own stomach acid.

17   I waited for the day when I would throw up blood. Already I could taste it at the back of my throat, inching farther upward with each heartbeat. Now after vomiting, I would rise shakily from my knees, gripping the edge of the counter for balance, my heart knocking wildly in my chest. A column of flame speared me from my stomach to my throat—my esophagus a two-edged blade in my chest, a tunnel set on fire, a steel pole thrust through me.

18   Now when I threw up, I reeled from the pain. I was not throwing up half-digested food, as I had for years, but what felt like complete objects—plastic balls, pieces of Lego, nuts and bolts that tore at me as they came out of my body. Afterwards, my stomach would hurt so much that for the rest of the evening any sustenance I sought would have to be the sort given to a convalescent or a starvation victim: thin porridge, vegetable soup, herbal tea.

19   I no longer thought of myself as a girl or a woman. I no longer felt sexual desire. I was an "it," a conduit for a constant stream of ugliness that had to pass through it in order for me to stay pure.

20   In some dim part of me, I knew that when I left my apartment to go out into the street, other people did not see me as I saw myself. They did not recoil from me in horror, as I expected. I knew I was a reasonably attractive young woman, like so many young women in the city, neither fat nor thin. But I felt somehow grotesque and abnormal. Strangers knew nothing of my secret; friends were help-

less; my dentist would only shake his head over my open mouth and tap his pencil along my teeth to track the path of corrosion the vomit had left in its wake.

Once, in a determined moment, I called the Eating Disorders Clinic at St. Paul's 21 Hospital, but the waiting list meant I would not get in for a year. At that time, a year seemed forever, so I did not add my name to the list. Surely in a year's time everything would change, resolve itself. Twelve months later I called again, but by this time the list was even longer, and again I did not add my name.

I finally stopped being bulimic nearly two years ago, when I was 22. It ended not 22 because of willpower or therapy or something so banal as an increased sense of self-esteem. It ended because the pain from throwing up rendered the pleasure slight by comparison. It ended when my softened teeth cringed at every mouthful and when I woke several times each night with cramps racking my stomach from one side of my waist to the other. It ended when I arrived at the point where I could no longer feel my feet. Months later, when I went to the doctor, he would diagnose it as an electrolyte imbalance caused by the vomiting up of so many vitamins and minerals. But for a long time, I didn't know what it was, and it frightened me—sometimes when I stood up, I nearly fell over. My feet were like dead fish, cold and clammy, disconnected from the rest of my body. Once in a while they flared suddenly to life, a constellation of pins and needles, so that I could not bear to press my soles to the floor. When I tried to go to the bathroom in the middle of the night, I felt in the underwater light of that hour as if I had transformed into the fairy-tale mermaid who had chosen her lover over the sea: with each step, I landed on knife points.

By then I had also developed a hiatus hernia—a portion of my stomach pro- 23 truded through my esophagus—and my teeth became so compromised that one day one of them simply disintegrated under pressure.

"Your tooth isn't going to grow back," the dentist said flatly, and it was then I 24 understood for the first time that my body did not possess some secret store of replacement parts, that physical damage, like its psychological counterpart, left marks that could remain a lifetime.

The last time I forced myself to throw up, it felt like internal surgery. Grief, 25 love, rage, pain—it all came pouring out, yet afterwards it was still there inside me. I had been bulimic off and on for eight years, and in all that vomiting I had not purged myself of any of the things that were making me sick.

QUESTIONS

Understanding the message: Comprehension

1. Why does Lau's mother curb her own eating?

2. Explain the title. What is the "emptiness" to which Lau refers?

3. What are the physical symptoms and bodily changes that occur because of bulimia?

4. Why does Lau finally stop her bingeing and purging?

Examining the structure and details: Analysis

1. Lau begins her essay with a vivid description of the process of forced vomiting. How do the explicit details affect us as readers? Why do you think she begins this way?

2. Although the subject matter is quite disturbing, Lau's use of language is often poetic: she uses figures of speech quite frequently and applies positive connotations to the descriptions she includes. Find two or three examples of positive descriptions of her bulimia. How does this affect the impact of her article?

3. What are the positive effects of continuing to be bulimic, according to Lau?

4. What is the cause of Lau's bulimia, according to this article?

Formulating a response: Inference and interpretation

1. Most bulimics use vomiting as a means to an end: they vomit so that they can remain slim, so that they don't gain weight. Presumably, this was Lau's initial motivation as well. What ends up being her motivation after a while?

2. In what way(s) did Lau suffer as a result of her bulimia? In what way(s) did she benefit? Which effect seems to be the stronger force in this essay? Why?

3. In this essay, Lau begins by discussing the effect of her bingeing and purging and ends by reviewing the causes. What effect does this order of the information have? Would it have been more or less effective to present the story chronologically, moving from cause to effect? Why?

4. Lau's essay returns again and again to the notion of emptiness, both literal and figurative. Do you think she succeeds in her quest to fill this emptiness, both physical and emotional? Why or why not?

5. Lau says her bulimia ended "not because of willpower or therapy or something so banal as an increased sense of self-esteem." Why does she say that an increased sense of self-esteem is "banal"?

Essay questions

1. Write an essay in which you explain the cause or effect of a negative habit.

RESPOND IN WRITING NE

What prompted the habit to develop? Alternatively, what was the outcome of the habit, and how was it resolved?

2. Write about a close relationship, either positive or negative, in which another person affected you strongly and influenced your life or behaviour. What was the effect of your contact with that person?

3. Lau indicates the impact her mother had on her development of bulimia and its outcome. However, Lau herself affected her mother's behaviour as well, perhaps more than she acknowledges in this essay. Using examples from the selection, discuss the relationship between the two women and how they may have influenced each other.

VOCABULARY

translucent: thin enough that one can almost see through it

lethargy: sluggishness or drowsiness

calibrated: measured

electrolyte: the ions needed by cells to regulate the electric charge and flow of water molecules across the cell membrane

Hockey Night in Port Hawkesbury

by Lynn Coady (b. 1970)

Born and raised in Cape Breton, Nova Scotia, Lynn Coady obtained her B.A. from Carleton University in Ottawa and studied creative writing at the University of British Columbia in Vancouver, where she now lives. She was nominated for the 1998 Governor General's Award for Fiction and the Thomas Raddall Atlantic Fiction Award for her first novel, Strange Heaven, *which won the Canadian Authors Association/Air Canada Award for the best writer under 30 and the Dartmouth Book and Writing Award for fiction. Coady's second book,* Play the Monster Blind, *was published to rave reviews in 2000. She has also written award-winning plays and a screenplay. A new novel will be published in 2002. Her nonfiction articles and reviews have appeared in several publications, including* Saturday Night, This Magazine, *and* Chatelaine.

PRE-READING

To many of us, hockey is the quintessential Canadian sport; it almost defines who we are. In this essay, originally in *This Magazine* (1999), Coady explains the impact that hockey had on her as a girl growing up in the Maritimes and the lasting impact of the sport. What are your opinions about hockey? Can you be truly "Canadian" and know nothing about it? How many people that you know are hockey fans? What is the enormous attraction of this sport to so many Canadians?

1   My hometown's hockey team was called the Port Hawkesbury Pirates. Their colours were maroon and white and they had a fierce pirate's-head eyepatch emblazoned in the center of their jerseys. Their greatest rivals were the Antigonish Bulldogs. I remember one particular playoff where the entire town was mobilized against the mainland village of Antigonish. My dad owned the Dairy Queen, and used its towering sign to denigrate everything about our neighbours on the other side of the causeway. *Ho ho Shebo,* he used to have up there, to the befuddlement of tourists looking for a deal on Brazier Burgers. Shebo was the name of the opposing team's coach. It was a chant the town liked to use whenever our team was ahead. Another day it was *Port Hawkesbury Pirates versus the Antigonish Poodles.* I thought that up. Dad was tickled, and thrilled me by enshrining it beneath the DQ logo for a whole two weeks.

I went to the big game with my dad. I was attired that evening in a Port 2
Hawkesbury Pirates jacket zipped up over a Pirates jersey. Perched on my head
was a Pirates cap. Clutched in my hand, a Go Pirates pennant. I loved everything
about that night. Listening to Dad holler the most eloquent of personal insults at
the nefarious Shebo, the guffaws of the surrounding adults. A woman swaddled
head to toe in fox-fur cursing a blue streak like I had never heard. The hard
benches. My brother's hand-me-down longjohns bunching underneath my
clothes. The insane excitement all around me such as I had never experienced in
that town before or after.

But I can't relate to you a single thing about the actual game. Because I didn't 3
understand a goddamn thing that was going on. When the crowd screamed, I
screamed. When the crowd booed, I booed. When the crowd threatened to disembowel the referee, I too became a mindless, homicidal maniac. I was having the
time of my life. But when the actual game was going on, and the crowd sat in rapt
awe, this is approximately what was going on in my head: *Guy skating, guy skating,
guy skating. Another guy. Skate, skate, skate. Guy from the other team. Skate, skate.
Who has it now?*

Oh. Fat guy. Skating, skating . . . 4

There you have, summed up, my eternally ambivalent relationship with the 5
game of hockey and everything it represents. And it represents a lot, let's not kid
ourselves. To grow up anywhere in small-town Canada is to grow up with the
conviction that hockey is, if not the only thing that matters, one of the things
that definitely matters most. In memories of my family, my town, my youth,
hockey is always front and center. My dad coached, and my two older brothers
played. Hockey-related pictures, trophies, plaques galore adorn my parents'
home.

As a teenager, I was not permitted to be off in my room "sulking" when a Leafs 6
game was on. It was a sacred time that I was expected to participate in, like when
we said the rosary. Dad and the boys would eat chips with dip, drink pop, yell and
bounce up and down in their seats. My mother would commandeer the couch and
sneak in little naps between goals and intermission, when she would play Ron
MacLean to Dad's Don Cherry. A Toronto game is the only thing I have ever seen
my father stay up past 11 for. I would sit at the very back of the living room with
a selection of magazines on the table beside me.

You think I am not aware of what I sound like: Miss Priss, brimming with lofty 7
notions and a hearty disdain for anything involving protective cups. "Really, faw-
tha, another Leafs game? Can't you see I'm reading Joyce? If only we had an alternative cinema, I'd be so out of here." But it's not true. I was an adolescent,
remember, and even more than screening the occasional Fassbinder film, what I
really wanted was to fit in. Hockey wasn't merely my Dad's trip. It was everybody's.
People spoke hockey, do you see? It was like a club, or a religion, and if you understood it, everybody else could understand you. You made sense to them. You fit.

8   Here are some terms and expressions I don't understand to this day.

9   Blue line.

10 Sudden death.

11 De-*fense!* De-*fense!* (I know what the word means, but why do people yell it over and over again?)

12 And what's with the octopi?

13 I have alternated my whole life from a fierce resentment of hockey to a wistful longing I can't quite put my finger on. The resentment is simple enough. It comes from having the overriding importance of hockey burned into me my entire life while at the same time understanding that someone like me (female) should never expect to have anything to do with such a vastly significant phenomenon. It comes from the fact that were I to admit this to any of my brothers they would assume I had not received enough oxygen to my brain as a baby.

14 So off I went into the world of books and English departments, where nary a taint of hockey fever could be felt—or so I thought. (Bill Gaston's newest novel is about a former pro-hockey player who becomes an English undergrad. The comedy writes itself.) Imagine my chagrin when I discovered that my own patron saint of Maritime Lit despised such stuffy havens for precisely the reason I sought them out. In *Hockey Dreams,* a veritable hymn to the gods of the rink, David Adams Richards tells of a variety of literary snotties who think it terribly impish to root for the Russians because "Wayne Gretzky's just so Canadian." Then there is the woman from Penguin Books who becomes awfully confused when Richards and a Czech writer strike up an animated conversation about the (Pittsburgh) Penguins. That would be me, I can't help but think. Desperately veering the conversation toward Kafka, praying no one discovered my pathetic ignorance about what really mattered—who made the big save, who got the most assists.

15 But what confounds me even more is how much I relate to this book. I understand, whether I want to or not. It is not so much the games Richards is remembering, but the way his friends floated in their oversized jerseys, the smell of wet wool, sub-zero Saturdays gathered around *Hockey Night in Canada.* The feeling. Throughout the book, Richards struggles to explain the unexplainable, the mystery of hockey. There are those who understand and those who will never understand, he intimates. I know what he means, because I am both.

16 So that wistful longing makes sense, I suppose, when I look back on that Pirates versus Bulldogs game. I grew up with the understanding that hockey was all-important, hockey players were gods, and to be a hockey fan was to enter into some kind of enchanted circle that bestowed instant community and good fellowship upon you. That's what I was feeling that night. I was sitting on the Port Hawkesbury side of the rink, *our* rink, screaming for *our* team, on behalf of *our* town. I was 12 years old, sexually invisible, my days of artsy alienation far off in the inconceivable future. For a moment, I belonged. Because of hockey.

QUESTIONS

Understanding the message: Comprehension

1. Coady's title is an allusion. To what is she alluding? How does her allusion help to enrich our understanding of the essay?

2. In what way is Coady's "relationship with hockey" ambivalent?

3. How is Coady different from her brothers?

4. Why is Coady disappointed in her "patron saint of Maritime Lit [author David Adams Richards]"?

Examining the structure and details: Analysis

1. Ultimately, what are the effects on Coady of growing up immersed in a hockey-oriented culture?

2. Throughout her essay, Coady uses unconventional sentence structures, such as fragments or extremely short lines instead of paragraphs. Re-examine some of these structures, in paragraph 2 or paragraphs 9 to 13. What is the impact of these structures? Are they appropriate for the subject matter? Why or why not?

3. Where does Coady first reveal her feelings about hockey? How is this information surprising to the reader? How does it relate to what follows?

4. In what way does the conclusion clarify the introduction? What new detail does Coady reveal in the final paragraph that throws the introduction into a new light?

Formulating a response: Inference and interpretation

1. What are the reasons for Coady's dislike of hockey? What are the reasons for her "wistful longing"? Are the two feelings contradictory? Why or why not?

2. To what extent does Coady explain the logical links between her causes and effects? Do you think she leaves too much for the reader to figure out? Why or why not?

3. What is Coady's tone? How does she use language to help convey the tone in this essay? Cite examples to support your answer.

Essay questions

1. If you have siblings, write a cause and effect essay to explain why you are different from them. Alternately, write a similar essay to explain why any two siblings (for example, your mother and your aunt, your father and your uncle, two cousins, two friends) are different from each other.

2. One of the criticisms of modern hockey teams is that they are too violent. What causes the players to be this violent? In what ways are they encouraged to behave violently? Write an essay in which you discuss either the causes or the effects of violence in children's hockey games.

3. What are the different ways that Coady indicates her disdain of hockey? In addition to the examples she uses, look at her tone, word choices, and sentence structure in your answer.

VOCABULARY

Port Hawkesbury, Antigonish: Nova Scotia towns

denigrate: belittle, attack the reputation of

eloquent: well-worded

nefarious: wicked or evil

disembowel: cut out the guts of

commandeer: take control of

Ron MacLean, Don Cherry: hockey broadcast announcers

Fassbinder film: Rainer W. Fassbinder (1945–1982), New Wave German film director

chagrin: disappointment

Kafka: Franz Kafka (1883–1924), Czech writer

alienation: feeling of being rejected or excluded by others

Saving the Earth
by David Suzuki (b. 1936)

David Suzuki is the internationally known geneticist and environmentalist who has successfully popularized science for general audiences, particularly through the CBC television series The Nature of Things, *which he hosts. In addition, Suzuki is a prolific writer, broadcast journalist, and civil rights activist. Born in Vancouver, Suzuki began his career in the United States after receiving his B.A. from Amherst College and Ph.D. from the University of Chicago. He returned to Canada in 1963 and began to work at the University of British Columbia. He is a two-time winner of the E.W.R. Steacie award (given annually to an outstanding Canadian scientist under 35) for his work on mutations in fruit flies, which garnered an international reputation. In 1990, he and his wife, Dr. Tara E. Cullis, founded the David Suzuki Foundation, which promotes environmental issues. Suzuki has also been honoured as a member of the Royal Society of Canada, was named an Officer of the Order of Canada, and has received the United Nations Environmental Medal. He has written more than 28 books.*

PRE-READING

Suzuki's writings often deal with how modern society can avoid pollution or harming the environment. The following essay was published in *Maclean's* magazine in 1999 as part of a premillennial examination. What kinds of environmental hazards do you believe threaten our planet? In what ways does our earth need to be "saved"? Do you practise environmentally friendly behaviours in your daily life? What kinds of activities come to mind when you think of environmentalists?

In recent years, if you've been able to look beyond the media obsession with celebrity, violence and sex, you may have begun to realize that the planet is undergoing cataclysmic and unprecedented change. Ironically, in 1992, the year the largest gathering of heads of state in human history met at the Earth Summit in Rio de Janeiro to take concrete steps towards a sustainable future, the Canadian government was forced to acknowledge the unthinkable: the vast shoals of northern cod that had supported people for hundreds of years had all but disappeared. Since then, record floods have hit Quebec and Manitoba, flash fires spread across Alberta, and an ice storm ravaged parts of Ontario and Quebec, knocking out electricity for weeks. Rates of breast and testicular cancer, asthma and lymphoma have reached epidemic levels and continue to rise. Hurricane Mitch wiped out thousands of people in Central America while heat waves killed 700 people in Chicago and thousands in India. Insurance companies have paid in the 1990s close to four times the weather-related claims in the entire decade of the 1980s. Can we continue to believe these are all just random, isolated events?

2   But the media have been mesmerized by the spectacular rise in Dow Jones averages, megamergers and record profits, as well as the catastrophic disintegration of economies from Japan to Brazil. Rachel Carson's seminal 1962 book *Silent Spring* created an enormous wave of awareness and concern about the environment that grew to a peak in Rio in 1992. But since then, the economy has become our dominant preoccupation. We are bludgeoned by the relentless mantra of buzzwords like globalization and free trade, debt and deficit, competitiveness, profitability, inflation and interest rates. So where are we heading? As we approach the end of a millennium, the only way we can gain an intimation of where we are going is by reflecting on where we have come from.

3   I was born in 1936, when the human population of the entire planet was around 2 billion. In my lifetime, the number of human beings has tripled. In the year of my birth, the population of Vancouver was 253,000, of Calgary 83,000, and Toronto 645,000. Back then, more than 95 per cent of the world's forests were still intact and pristine while vast areas of Africa, the Amazon and Papua New Guinea were yet to be penetrated by people from the industrialized world. As a child in British Columbia, I hiked through virgin forests, drank from any creek without a second thought and ate raw food pulled directly from the soil or off a tree.

4   My family moved to London, Ont., in 1949 when the city had a population of 70,000. We had been impoverished by the war and I spent a lot of time fishing in the Thames River to help feed the family. For me, it wasn't work. Walking the banks of the Thames, I had some of my most memorable experiences with nature. My grandparents owned a farm just outside the city where I spent many happy days hunting freshwater clams or turtles in their creek or watching foxes and pheasants in the fields. Often, I would stop off at a nearby swamp where I would find salamander eggs, catch frogs or collect insects. Those were magical times, imprinting an indelible love of nature that led to a career in biology.

5   Today, I return to a very different London, a rapidly growing, vibrant city that boasts more than 300,000 inhabitants. But the Thames River is so polluted, people recoil in horror at the notion of eating a fish from it. The only things my grandparents' farm now grows are highrise apartments, while the creek runs invisibly through underground culverts. The magical swamp that captivated me as a boy is covered over with an enormous shopping centre and large parking lot. So where do London's youth find their inspiration today? From grazing through malls filled with consumer items, playing Nintendo games or surfing the Net? The world of young people now is a human-created one that celebrates the inventive-

ness and productivity of human beings. But there is no way that human ingenuity can match the incredible wonder, magnificence and inspiration of the natural world four billion years in the making. That is not a put-down of our species, it is simply a recognition of the complexity and interconnectedness in nature that we barely comprehend.

Human beings are a remarkable species. We emerged along the Rift Valley in 6 Africa a mere quarter of a million years ago. In evolutionary terms, we are an infant species gifted with a complex brain that is our major survival attribute. That brain conferred curiosity, memory and inventiveness, which more than compensated for our lack of speed, strength or sensory acuity. Today, we have become the most numerous and ubiquitous mammal on the planet.

In this century, our species has undergone explosive change. Not only are we 7 adding a quarter of a million people to our numbers every day, we have vastly amplified our technological muscle power. When I was born, there were no computers, televisions, jet planes, oral contraceptives, transoceanic phone calls, satellites, transistors or xerography, just to mention a few. Children today look at typewriters, vinyl records and black-and-white televisions as ancient curiosities. Taken together, this technology has dramatically increased the impact of each human being on the earth.

In the second part of this century, one of the great insights from biology 8 resulted from the application of molecular techniques to examine specific genes within individuals. To our amazement, when a creature such as a fruit fly was studied, genes were found to exist in many different forms. Even though such species were highly evolved to occupy specific environmental niches, they did not become homogeneous; instead, they maintained a wide array of gene forms. The phenomenon is known as genetic polymorphism, and we now understand that this is the key to a species' resilience. Over the broad sweep of evolutionary time, the environment is constantly changing. A genetic combination that might be well-suited for one environment might not do as well when conditions change, while other, less favorable gene forms might flourish under the altered conditions. So long as the species as a whole carries diverse genes, combinations better suited to the new circumstances can be selected out when conditions change.

In the same way, it is thought that species diversity within ecosystems, and 9 ecosystem diversity around the world, help to explain life's incredible tenacity under different conditions and volatile surroundings. Planetary conditions have changed tremendously over the four billion years that life has existed—the sun is 25 per cent hotter, poles have reversed and then changed back, continents have moved and smashed together, ice ages have come and gone—yet species have not only survived, they have flourished, and much of that is due to diversity. The converse of genetic polymorphism is monoculture; that is, the spreading of a single genetic stock or species over a broad area. We have learned expensively in fisheries, forestry and agriculture that monoculture creates vulnerability to new infections, disease or altered environmental conditions.

10   Human beings have added another level of diversity, namely culture, to the equation of adaptability. It is diverse cultures that have enabled our species to survive in so many ecosystems, from the Arctic to the equator. In this wonderful array of cultures, there were many different notions of wealth, purpose in life and cosmic meaning. Today, that has changed dramatically: one kind of economics has become the dominant preoccupation of societies around the world and globalization of that economy is hailed as a source of all wealth and material well-being. This notion is based on perceiving the entire planet as the source of resources while all people in the world form a potential market. But if we live in a finite world, then all resources have limits and prudence demands that we recognize the existence and extent of those limits.

11   No one person, company or government sets out to deliberately trash our surroundings, yet the collective effect of human numbers, technology and consumption is corroding the life-support systems of the planet. That pronouncement is not the rant of an eco-catastrophist; it is the conclusion reached by leading members of the scientific profession. In November, 1992, more than half of all living Nobel Prize winners signed a document called "World Scientists' Warning to Humanity" that began with this stark statement:

12   "Human beings and the natural world are on a collision course. Human activities inflict harsh and often irreversible damage on the environment and on critical resources. If not checked, many of our current practices put at serious risk the future we wish for human society."

13   Scientists are extremely cautious when making pronouncements to the general public, so this was a most unusual alarm call. The warning went on to list the areas where the crises exist and the measures needed to avoid a catastrophe. The document then grew more ominous and urgent: "No more than one or a few decades remain before the chance to avert the threats we now confront will be lost and the prospects for humanity immeasurably diminished." It is puzzling to me that we seem frantic to know the most intimate details about O.J. Simpson, Diana, Princess of Wales, or Monica Lewinsky and consume pronouncements by Bill Gates, Larry King or Oprah Winfrey as if they are gospel. But when more than half of all Nobel laureates warn of an impending but avoidable disaster, we are too busy to take notice.

14   Humanity has repeatedly demonstrated a capacity to respond heroically and immediately to a crisis. Hurricanes, floods, fire or earthquakes elicit remarkable responses. After Pearl Harbor, there was only one choice in North America, to respond and win. There was no debate about whether we could afford an all-out war effort or what the results of not responding might be. In biological terms, the globe is experiencing an eco-holocaust, as more than 50,000 species vanish annu-

ally and air, water and soil are poisoned with civilization's effluents. The great challenge of the millennium is recognizing the reality of impending ecological collapse, and the urgent need to get on with taking the steps to avoid it.

But our obsession with economics has become an impediment to taking 15 appropriate action. I have often been told, "Listen, Suzuki, we have to pay for all those parks and environmental cleanups. We can't afford to protect the environment if we don't have a strong, growing economy," or words to that effect. That sentiment flows from a belief that the economy provides us with all of our products, from food to oil to manufactured goods. This is nonsense, of course. Everything that we depend on, whether it is cars, popcorn or computers, comes from the earth and will eventually end up coming back to it. It is the biosphere, that thin layer of air, water and soil within which life exists, that creates the earth's productivity and abundance that, in turn, make economies and our lives possible.

But now, ignoring evolution's priceless lesson about the value of diversity, we 16 are monoculturing the planet with a single notion of progress and development that is embodied in the globalized economy. As all nations rush to carve out a place in this construct, we tie our entire future on it. But what if, as many believe, it's based on mistaken notions or assumptions? What will we have to fall back on?

It is widely believed that trade enables human beings to exceed the ability of a 17 certain region to support its inhabitants. Thus, Canadians can acquire Panamanian bananas, Turkish rugs or Japanese electronic products by trading for them with resources or products that are plentiful in Canada. But the reality is that we still require the earth to generate our food, clothing and shelter and to absorb and detoxify our wastes. Trade enables us to co-opt someone else's land to provide goods for us. Adding up the total amount of land (and ocean) required to provide our annual needs, ecologist Bill Rees of the University of British Columbia has calculated that every Canadian (and inhabitant of an industrialized country) now requires the production from seven to eight hectares. If every human being on the planet aspired to a comparable level of prosperity, it would take between five and six more planets! Even if we ignored the entire developing world, we in the wealthy nations already consume more than the earth can provide sustainably. We are blinded from seeing the alternate ecological imperative that demands that we pull back and slow down.

I suggest the following thought exercise can help to get our priorities in order. 18 Imagine that you have lived a full and rich life and are now on your deathbed. As you reflect back on life, what memories fill you with happiness, pride and satisfaction? I suspect it will not be the latest designer clothing, a huge house, a sport utility vehicle or a Sony entertainment centre. In fact, what makes life worthwhile and joyful is not "stuff" that can be bought with money. The most important things are family, friends, community and the sharing, caring and cooperating together that enhance the quality of all of our lives.

19   There are several reasons we are failing to see the urgency of what is happening. A few of them are:

20 1) Most people alive today were born after 1950 and thus have lived all their lives during a period of spectacular, unprecedented and unsustainable growth and change. But for most of us, this is all we've ever known and it seems normal. Rapid change also brings rapid collective forgetfulness, and memories of what the world once was quickly fade.

21 2) Most people now live in the human-created environment of big cities where it's easy to believe the illusion that we have escaped our biological dependence on the natural world.

22 3) The explosive increase in information shatters the world into fragments devoid of the history or context that might explain their relevance, importance or significance. In order to attract attention, stories or reports become shorter and increasingly shrill, sensational or violent.

23 4) Political "vision" is focused on re-election and fulfilling the special demands of campaign funders. Political promises are contradicted with little fear of reprisal amid the cacophony of immediate crisis and short-term electoral memory.

24 5) In a global economy freed from the constraints of national boundaries or regulations, the search for maximal profit in minimal time has little allowance for long-term sustainability of local communities and local ecosystems.

25 6) The great public faith that "they"—scientists and technologists—will resolve our problems is simply unwarranted. While technology can be impressive, our knowledge of the complexity and interconnectivity in the real world is so limited, our "solutions" have little hope of long-term success. For example, we have no idea how to replace or mitigate thousands of species now extinct, substitute for pollination once done by insects killed by pesticides, or repair the ozone layer.

26   We can't carry on with business as usual if we wish to avoid an increasingly uncertain and volatile world. The signs are everywhere. But if "experts" lack credibility, try talking to any elder about what fish, birds or woods were like when they were young. Then extrapolate ahead from the changes they have lived through to the kind of world our children and grandchildren will have if we continue along the same path.

27   What are our real basic needs in order to live rich and fulfilling lives? I believe there is no dichotomy between environmental and social needs. Hungry people will not care if their actions endanger an edible species or an important habitat. Unemployment, injustice or insecurity lead to desperation and the need to sur-

vive at all costs. To protect an environment for future generations, we have to build a society on a foundation of clean air, water, soil and energy and rich biodiversity to fulfil our biological needs; we have to ensure full employment, justice and security for all communities to serve our social needs; and we have to retain sacred places, a sense of belonging and connectedness with nature and a knowledge that there are cosmic forces beyond our comprehension or control, to satisfy our spiritual requirements. Then, we can work on the best kind of economy to construct from there. Right now, we seem to be trying to shoehorn everything into the constraints dictated by the economy without establishing the fundamental bottom line.

QUESTIONS

Understanding the contents: Comprehension

1. What has been preoccupying us instead of the environment, according to Suzuki?

2. What has been the relationship between the environment and the population of Canada, according to Suzuki? How has our focus changed since Suzuki was a boy?

3. Explain how "genetic polymorphism" works.

4. Why would a monoculture be more susceptible to diseases or infection, according to Suzuki's explanation? How are we "monoculturing the planet," according to Suzuki?

Examining the structure and details: Analysis

1. How does Suzuki use his introduction to convey the magnitude of the topic he's discussing? What is Suzuki's attitude toward the media? How do you know?

2. What is the effect of changes in our culture, according to Suzuki? What rhetorical mode does he use in addition to cause and effect as a way to impress this effect upon us?

3. Suzuki deals with the effects of our environmental apathy, but he also addresses the causes of it. What, according to him, has contributed to our ignoring the environmental emergency in which we live? Why do you think he places the causes after the effects in the essay?

Formulating a response: Inference and interpretation

1. Do you think that Suzuki is being overly dramatic or overreacting in his description of the environmental problems as an "eco-holocaust"? Is his approach to the subject justified? In other words, does his tone suit the subject matter? Why or why not?

2. In what ways has the world of technology changed since Suzuki was a child? Do you agree that "this technology has dramatically increased the impact of each human being on the earth"? Why or why not?

3. Do you agree with Suzuki that those of us in developed countries are more culpable than others when it comes to diminishing the earth? Justify your answer.

4. What is Suzuki's thesis? Why do you think he places it where he does?

5. Is Suzuki's conclusion effective, or anticlimactic? Why? Why do you think he ends this way?

Essay questions

1. Imagine that you work for an environmental agency and your task is to write a proposal for cleaning up your town or city. What kinds of solutions might you propose that would help to make your city more environmentally friendly?

2. Think of a specific technology that has a regular impact on your life, and write an essay in which you discuss the effects of that technology (for example, cell phones, pagers, ATM machines, on-line shopping, and so on).

3. In proving his point about the environment, Suzuki uses a variety of sources and examples. Do his examples further the intent of his argument or hinder it? As a reader, were you spurred to action or simply offended by the writer's indictment of you? Discuss the effects of these examples and why you think they either work or don't work.

VOCABULARY

culverts: drains or channels under a road or sidewalk

acuity: sharpness

ubiquitous: present everywhere

tenacity: strong hold, ability to hold on firmly

effluents: flowing waste matter

extrapolate: draw a conclusion based on known facts or information

dichotomy: split into two

biodiversity: the variety of plant and animal species in the world or in a particular habitat

Bad Girls

by Shari Graydon (b. 1958)

Shari Graydon is a writer, educator, and media analyst. Prior to becoming press secretary to Ujjal Dosanjh, premier of British Columbia, she taught media analysis and women's studies at Simon Fraser University and communications at Kwantlen University College. From 1995 to 1997 she wrote a regular column for the Vancouver Sun, *and in 1996 she produced a 13-part television series about women and media for WTN. She served for eight years as the president of MediaWatch, a national feminist organization concerned about the portrayal and representation of women and girls in the media. In this capacity she gave hundreds of presentations and guest lectures to a variety of health, education, business, and community groups across Canada. She has provided media analysis commentary to CBC radio and television and contributed to a variety of print publications. In addition to her volunteer work with MediaWatch, she has served on the boards of Capilano College and the BC Centre for Excellence in Women's Health and as a judge with the BC Newspaper Awards. She lives in Vancouver.*

PRE-READING

Did you follow the news reports about the violent murder of Reena Virk, the B.C. teen who was brutally murdered by a group of her classmates? Do you think that teenaged violence is on the increase? In this article from *Homemaker's* magazine (1999), Graydon examines these topics. Is the media representation of teens today unbiased? How much of a threat do teenagers face from their peers?

1   Dressed in a baggy T-shirt, cotton pants and runners, her long, wavy hair gelled and falling around her shoulders, she looks like an ordinary teenager. The stories she tells me about being spoiled as a child, rebelling as a young teen against her mom and hanging out at the mall with her friends sound like pretty common teenage experiences. Yet she spent her "Sweet 16" birthday behind bars, locked up in one of British Columbia's closed custody units for youth. "Janice" (the Young Offenders Act prohibits publication of her real name) is in jail for her part in the brutal murder of 14-year-old Reena Virk in November, 1997, an event that stunned the nation and prompted "Bad Girl" headlines coast to coast. About life in the detention centre, she says, "It's not so bad; I already knew lots of the kids."

The vicious attack leading to Virk's murder by a group of teenagers in a middle- 2
class suburb of Victoria wasn't the first such incident to make headlines. In recent
years stories of teen violence—usually involving testosterone-pumped boys carried
away by their own misplaced machismo—have disturbed us all.

What made Reena Virk's case so shocking was that seven out of eight of the 3
kids who participated in butting out a cigarette on her forehead, and punching
and kicking her until she was dazed and bleeding, were girls. And one of them is
alleged to have returned to the scene of the initial attack with a male friend, battered Virk unconscious and thrown her in the river, where she drowned, her body
discovered a week later.

In the wake of burgeoning news reports about girl-to-girl violence, the case 4
galvanized growing concerns across the country about just what young women
are up to these days. The answer appears to be "No good." Statistics Canada
reported in July that while the overall crime rate fell for the sixth consecutive year,
it escalated among teenage girls by five per cent. The big picture seems to be even
more alarming: from 1987 to 1997 the number of young women charged with
violent crime grew from about 900 to 4,800, a staggering five-fold increase and
twice that of same-aged boys.

Despite these figures and sensational Bad Girl headlines, the jury's still out on 5
how widespread the problem is. For one thing, the actual numbers are relatively
small: 1997's five per cent increase brought the rate to 472 offences per 100,000
population. That compares with 1,328 per 100,000 among male offenders, which
represents a four per cent drop from the previous year. For another, two-thirds of
those charges were for minor assault, involving hitting or shoving that didn't
result in bodily harm. The aggravated assault charges laid against the girls who
attacked Reena Virk represented less than one per cent of the violent offence
charges in that year.

Experts also point out that the numbers have risen because more charges are 6
being laid. Alan Markwart, director of the Youth Justice team with the B.C.
Ministry for Children and Families, attributes this in part to the "zero tolerance"
policies now popular in schools struggling to deal with student violence. "Cases
formerly dealt with by school principals are now more likely to result in legal
charges," he says. He also speculates that police may be less inclined today to dismiss physical aggression between two girls as merely a "cat fight." Instead, they've
begun to apply to girls the same standards used to determine the seriousness of
crimes committed by boys.

Mitigating factors notwithstanding, criminologists and youth workers say 7
that teenage girls are much more likely these days to express their anger over
trivial things—and in increasingly physical ways. Once-persistent "sugar and
spice" cultural stereotypes are dying hard as researchers point to evidence
showing that girls have always felt just as much anger as boys; they've just been

encouraged to channel their aggression into more socially acceptable "feminine" behaviors—like gossiping, name-calling and excluding the kids they want to punish. That girls are now expressing their anger physically is largely a sign of the times, attributable to the growing acceptance of violence in the teenage subculture. Studies have shown that exposure to violence can lead to increased violent behavior on the part of girls, desensitizing them to the point where they no longer feel emotional distress.

8   But the attack on Reena Virk was so frenzied—the girl's skull was fractured, her back broken—the issue takes on confounding proportions. How can young girls be capable of such shocking cruelty? What's going on in their heads?

9   Prying answers out of Janice isn't easy. Throughout our conversation, she is distracted by the comings and goings of people on the other side of the Plexiglas wall. At one point she interrupts herself to declare with pride, "That was my boyfriend who just walked by."

10   When I ask her about the night that Reena Virk died, I can tell that she doesn't really want to think—let alone talk—about what happened. But she does tell me that the source of the conflict was her belief that Virk had spread rumors about her and messed around with her boyfriend.

11   She says that the testimony and news stories describing her and a friend as "luring" Reena Virk to the site of a planned attack were false. "Fights happen every day," she says. "It just got out of hand."

12   Judging by the experiences of Stacey and Camille (pseudonyms), two Vancouver-area girls who have been on both the delivery and receiving ends of teen violence, the circumstances leading to Reena Virk's death were chillingly common. Rumors, jealousy, competition over boyfriends, they say, are the issues most likely to ignite a fight among teenage girls. As to why more and more of those fights seem to be escalating into physical aggression, Stacey says: "You want to look big in front of your friends, to have a 'Don't mess with me' attitude. And if someone goes after you, you can't just sit there and take it."

13   Dr. Sibylle Artz, director of the School of Child and Youth Care at the University of Victoria, has authored one of the few studies of violence among teenage girls. Her book, *Sex, Power and the Violent School Girl* (Trifolium Books, 1998), provides insights into the profile of the "typical" violent teenage girl.

14   Violent girls often emerge from home lives in which they've been physically, sexually and/or emotionally abused, experienced significant alienation from at least one parent and observed chronic drug or alcohol misuse.

15   Not surprisingly, staying focused in school and fitting in generally are often a challenge for these kids, who quickly gravitate towards other teenagers with similar backgrounds. The subculture that develops reflects the same kinds of conflict and substance abuse that they see at home. And belonging to the rebel group becomes a desperate survival issue.

As Camille sees it, "If you're not getting attention at home, your friends—and 16 belonging—are really important. You basically do whatever's necessary to get talked about"—including violence—"because attention, even if it's negative, is better than nothing."

This sounds perverse to most adults—and indeed, to most teenagers. But for 17 the kids involved, says Shawn McNabb, a Youth Services worker in Burnaby, B.C., "Social interaction built around a constant battle for dominance is often consistent with what they experience at home."

The rites of passage required for acceptance into the tough crowd still include 18 the traditional sources of peer pressure: smoking, drinking, taking drugs. Stacey explains that these are now accompanied by the expectation that girls, like boys, will demonstrate their worth in the gang by "beating up someone who has called you down." The ethic of revenge is often accompanied by the assumption that the victims "deserve" their treatment. Camille describes the coveted male attention won by "defending your rep" with fists and feet: "You get talked about and you get respect."

Some experts have suggested that girls are becoming more violent because they 19 want to be more like boys, leading to speculation that feminism factors into the issue. By encouraging young women to seize power and go after what they want, the theory goes, we've created a monster—transforming girls into aggressive, insensitive takers.

Reality tells a different story. Youth workers say that girls who use violence as a 20 means of resolving conflict typically have much more emotional investment in the traditional female goals of getting married and having a family than pursuing independence and a career. They are also more prone to seek validation through men than compete with them. The icons of popular culture—from the bikini-clad "warrior babes" to the ubiquitous Spice Girls—reinforce this notion. Although lip service is paid to female power, the images of women predominating in the media send overwhelmingly sexist and misogynist messages, says Dr. Artz, teaching that "females are inferior to males and, in the last analysis, sexual objects."

Dr. Artz believes that understanding this dynamic is crucial to resolving vio- 21 lence among teenage girls. "The extent to which girls from troubled homes buy into messages about women's inferiority and see status as something to be gained through male attention supports their inclination to judge each other harshly."

Most experts agree that solutions do not include tightening up the Young 22 Offenders Act. "The research is pretty clear," says Alan Markwart: "Get-tough approaches won't solve youth crime." Instead, training and education are paramount. Markwart stresses the importance of identifying kids in troubled homes at a young age. Then, he says, "there are two components: strong support for and training of parents, and enhanced early education to encourage kids' success in school."

23   Violence-prevention programs in the schools are useful too, says Dr. Artz, as long as they're geared to those they're intended to help. An antiviolence initiative she and project partner Dr. Ted Riecken, acting associate dean of education at the University of Victoria, introduced into B.C.'s Sooke school district underscores the need for gender-specific training programs.

24   This particular program, whose initiatives range from installing playground equipment to "bully-proofing" courses involving role-playing, was prompted by a University of Victoria 1993 survey of 1,500 grade 8 to 10 students, which revealed that 51 per cent of boys and 21 per cent of girls had admitted to beating up another person in the previous year. A sampling of the same age group taken last spring, five years into the project, showed a decrease in physical aggression of over 20 per cent among males and of 50 per cent among females. "Girls are clearly more ready to respond to this type of program," says Dr. Artz. Adds Dr. Riecken, "Girls respond to programs that focus on social skills training and desire to build positive relationships."

25   Angst among teenage girls is often provoked by the difficulty in forming trusting relationships with peers. When this is compounded by parental neglect and feelings of worthlessness—especially in the context of society's profoundly contradictory messages about female power, the importance of male attention and acceptable sexual behavior for women—the situation is ripe for violent behavior.

26   Violence begets violence. It also creates victims, who could be our daughters. If the price Reena Virk paid with her life has any meaning at all, it has at least sounded a wake-up call to the pressing need for more research into the real lives of teenage girls today.

QUESTIONS

Understanding the message: Comprehension

1. Why was the murder of Reena Virk so shocking?

2. Explain the relationship between crime rates in general and those for teenage girls.

3. Even though the crime rate for teenage girls has increased "five-fold," Graydon tells us that some experts are not as concerned as others. Why not?

4. In what way are teenage girls today different from those of the past?

Examining the structure and details: Analysis

1. What are two of the causes Graydon mentions for the increased crime rate among teenage girls? How does her use of comparison help to explain these?

2. Graydon's article can be divided into two sections, one looking at the effects of violence among teenage girls and one examining the causes. Where does she make this shift in the article? Why do you think she structures it this way?

3. How many different causes of aggressive behaviour among teenage girls does Graydon include? Does she offer enough to create a convincing argument?

4. What different kinds of evidence does Graydon use to support her points?

Formulating a response: Inference and interpretation

1. Reread paragraph 3. Does the paragraph convey the horrific nature of the crime effectively? Why or why not? What kind of effect does it have on the reader?

2. Were you surprised by the increase in violence among teenage girls? Do the reasons Graydon provides for this increase convince you? Why or why not? If not, what do you think accounts for this increase?

3. As Graydon writes in her introductory paragraph, many of the female young offenders she describes look and sound like "ordinary" teenagers. If what "Janice" says is true and "fights happen every day," what distinguishes these girls from the average?

4. At one point in her article, Graydon writes, "Despite these figures and sensational Bad Girl headlines, the jury's still out on how widespread the problem [of teen violence] is." Is her use of the phrase "the jury's still out" appropriate, given the content of her article? Why or why not?

Essay questions

1. In 1965, psychologist Albert Bandura was one of the first to demonstrate that children who regularly observe violent behaviour (such as on television or video games) are more likely to model this behaviour themselves. Since then, many studies have reproduced Bandura's results. Write an essay in which you discuss the effects that increased violence will have on our society as a whole.

2. Do you agree that the predominant images in media today indicate that "females are inferior to males and, in the last analysis, sexual objects"? Respond to this question by selecting some popular media representations of women (either from film, television, or magazines) and use them in your response.

3. Graydon ends her article with an exhortation, emphasizing "the pressing need for more research into the real lives of teenage girls today." The sentence reflects her general approach in which she implies that the "reality" of the

girls' lives is quite different from the appearance or expectation that society has. Discuss how Graydon contrasts the two images of teenage girls in her essay. How does the reality measure up against the expectation or stereotypes? Use examples from the essay in your answer.

VOCABULARY

machismo: exaggerated expression of masculinity

burgeoning: quickly growing or multiplying

galvanized: stimulated

coveted: desired, sought-after

misogynist: antiwomen

CHAPTER 11

Argument

ARGUMENT IN DAILY LIFE

Argument is an extremely useful skill that you may already use in a variety of day-to-day situations. Real-life use of argument happens when you engage in activities such as the following:

- You write a memo to your boss, convincing her you're the perfect person to take on the company's new project in Barbados.
- You try to persuade your son to eat all of his vegetables because they are good for him.
- You write a letter to the editor of your local newspaper, refuting the previous day's editorial about the premier's stand on welfare reform.
- You challenge your roommate's statement that Arnold Schwarzenegger is a better actor than Sylvester Stallone.

WHAT IS ARGUMENT?

When people think of the word "argument," they often equate it with "fight." In terms of rhetorical strategies, however, an argument is nothing of the sort: it's more like the invigorating, engrossing discussion you have when you debate with a friend whether the latest rap star is an astute yet satiric commentator on society's foibles, or a blatant misogynist and racist; when you convince your friend that he shouldn't drop out of the firefighting program, despite personal setbacks; or when you persuade your boyfriend that it's worthwhile to spend a month's income on a week in Florida during Study Break.

Strictly speaking, there is a distinction between **argument** and **persuasion.** Traditionally, argument is considered to be one aspect of the larger strategy, persuasion; persuasion must both convince readers of the truth of some statement or thesis and also persuade them to action, while argument alone attempts to convince

DEFINITION

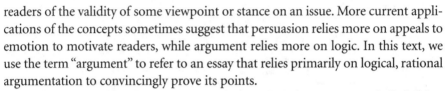

Argument: Argument defends or promotes a viewpoint through logical reasoning and clear evidence in order to convince readers that the viewpoint is worth adopting.

Persuasion: Persuasion works to convince readers that something is true or to incite readers to action, often through the use of emotional appeals.

readers of the validity of some viewpoint or stance on an issue. More current applications of the concepts sometimes suggest that persuasion relies more on appeals to emotion to motivate readers, while argument relies more on logic. In this text, we use the term "argument" to refer to an essay that relies primarily on logical, rational argumentation to convincingly prove its points.

Argument uses logical reasoning to alter someone's opinions or beliefs or to incite someone to action. By arguing that young adults should enter into marriage only after achieving financial independence, a writer might influence some readers to change their plans. Similarly, if you convince your readers that the organization for which you volunteer is worthy of their support, you expect that several will then donate money to the charity. Most advertising campaigns hope to persuade you to act—that is, to buy their products.

Logic and reason are the fundamental tools of argument. Because the most airtight arguments are based on logical reasoning rather than purely emotional influence, they require all of the skills you've developed in practising the other rhetorical techniques. You must use rational thought and specific evidence to support your ideas, even if they are reinforced with some emotional appeals. After all, most readers find it extremely difficult to refute established facts.

WHY USE ARGUMENT?

Do you ever wonder how some people accomplish what they do? As you look around you or read the news, you may ask yourself questions such as, "How did that CEO convince his current financial officer to leave her previous employer and join MegaWealth Enterprises?" or "How did those workers achieve a 12 percent pay raise without ever going on strike?" Even in your day-to-day experiences, you may occasionally wonder about questions such as, "How did that real estate agent convince me to buy this house when it's out of my price range?" or "How did my spouse ever get me to buy a Volvo instead of a BMW?" or "How did my friend Alison convince her school board to purchase 1500 new computers?"

RESPOND IN WRITING

What these successful types all share is skill in the art of argument and persuasion. Not only do they present their own, well-supported ideas, but they also convince others that their point of view is the best one, and one worth adopting. In addition, they may appeal to their audience's emotions or known biases as a way to convince them. (When you consider someone else's arguments, however, as a well-informed reader you must take care to identify any emotional manipulation in your assessment of an argument's validity). A good argument, then, is one of the most effective means of changing others' opinions or behaviour.

You can use argument to educate others as well as to convince them. A good argument includes a clear set of evidence and can inform readers about issues that they may not understand completely or with which they may not be familiar.

Finally, your skills in constructing arguments will help to reinforce and strengthen your own critical thinking so that you can better evaluate and assess the arguments you encounter in your own life—thereby improving the judgments you make.

HOW TO WRITE AN ARGUMENT ESSAY

In a sense, all the essays you write are to some extent argumentative since you try to prove a point and present it in a way that your reader accepts the message. Even when you write a descriptive essay, you create a dominant impression to convince your reader that the location or person you describe can be interpreted according to your perception. Even those who have never visited Botswana may be impressed by Emil Sher's description of the land where he once taught (see "Frozen Moment Serves as Reference Point in a Timeless Land," on page 92). When you write an argument essay, however, you try to convince your reader that your particular perspective on some issue, usually controversial, is the best one.

As you work through the usual pre-writing, writing, and post-writing stages of your essay, outlined in Chapter 2, keep in mind the following specific points as well in fashioning your argument.

Pre-Writing

1. Choose a general topic

To find a suitable topic for an argument paper, think about those subjects or topics that generate debate or those that create a bit of controversy; issues about which two or more distinct opinions already exist are ideal subjects for this kind of paper. Note, however, that any issue that can be decided *purely* on personal

The nays have it

If you find yourself stumped while trying to generate topics for argument essays, think of people with whom you have disagreed (whether they are people in your own life or people from the news or other media). Ask yourself, for instance, why you don't get along with your manager. What's the difference between her viewpoint and yours? The relationship could provide the germ for your essay on ideal management techniques. Why did you disagree with your friend who supports Napster and the notion that all music should be available for free on the Internet? Your stance on the issue is the perfect starting point for an essay on why current copyright laws are unfair to artists. If the fees at your local fitness club bring out your fighting spirit, you might consider a paper on why such facilities should be subsidized by the government. Cull those negative experiences for some positive material!

preference (without requiring factual evidence) is not suitable for argument. For instance, the question "Is the taste of milk chocolate preferable to that of dark chocolate?" can be decided only by the individual taste buds of those answering the question; the *taste* of one is not inherently better than the taste of the other. The question "Is dark chocolate better for your health than milk chocolate?" however, can be answered by referring to scientific studies (the Heart and Stroke Foundation of Canada cites various studies confirming that dark chocolate has more flavonoids, compounds in foods that increase heart health), as well as other logical appeals. The best topics for argument essays provide factual evidence that could be used to support a number of different viewpoints.

A good way to find suitable material for an argument essay is to examine what you already believe. Do you have any strong convictions or theories that have been reinforced over the years? If so, start with these. Remember, however, that the beliefs must be supported by impartial evidence, so get ready to examine the source of the belief very carefully.

2. Consider your audience and purpose

Because you're writing an argument essay, the purpose is predetermined: you will attempt to persuade your readers that your viewpoint is valid or true; alternatively, you may seek to incite your audience to action.

When considering your audience, think carefully about their existing beliefs and knowledge. Is the issue you discuss important to them? Do they have any pre-existing biases? If you try to convince a group of students that tuition fees should

SNAG

be lowered, you will probably not meet much (if any) resistance. Convincing the administration, however, will take a bit more hard evidence and reasoning. Typically, if your audience is neutral (they haven't yet made up their minds about the issue) or already agree with you, you will need less empirical evidence to convince them than if you address an audience that disagrees with your idea or is openly opposed to it.

3. Generate ideas about the topic

Looking at opposing views is one of the best ways to generate ideas for argument essays. By doing so, you not only determine the opposition, but also uncover your own true feelings and beliefs about the issue. Using the journalist's method, category headings to list opposing viewpoints, or the cluster technique can all be highly useful in this task.

The most important aspect of any argument is the logic on which it is based. This means you must ensure that your premises are correct (see more on logical premises under "Writing," below) and that the evidence you choose is both abundant and well chosen. As you think about aspects of your topic, consider whether current, reliable evidence is available. Remember, experts in any field have the knowledge and expertise to draw conclusions about or provide information on their topics of interest; by examining your topic in detail and perhaps conducting outside research, you effectively attempt to become an "expert" with the authority to write about the topic persuasively. (For more information on research, see Chapter 13.)

4. Narrow to a thesis

Since a good thesis is debatable, remember that there can be *many* effective thesis statements in response to any one reading or about one particular issue. There is no single "correct" thesis; the power of your thesis depends on how well it is expressed and how well you can support it with evidence to convince your readers that it's valid. As you devise your thesis, assess it critically, as you would any thesis you read. Are the assumptions logical? Is the idea based on fact rather than emotion or opinion? Can you back up what you say with enough convincing evidence?

TIP

Look at both sides of an issue

One of the most straightforward methods to construct a thesis is simply to disagree with what has been said by someone else or to critique an existing argument or idea. For instance, many Canadians resent paying taxes and would like to lose less of their paycheques. A thesis such as "The Canadian government should lower taxes for everyone" will provide plenty of material and certainly allows you to criticize the current system. At the same time, however, don't forget to examine the reasons why we have the taxes in the first place. What would be lost by decreasing taxes? Would cities receive fewer free services? Would maintenance of federally funded highways decline? Would our health care system deteriorate? For your argument to be both logical and convincing, you need to make it clear to your readers that you are aware of, and have considered, all sides of the issue.

5. Organize your ideas in an outline

Because your aim in an argument essay is to convince readers, it makes most sense to organize your points using emphatic order. A typical outline for an argument essay includes, first, an acknowledgment of the opposing viewpoint(s), followed by your own points of support, in order of increasing strength. This structure works best to convince others for several reasons:

- *It proves that you did your homework.* An acknowledgment of opposing views will prove to your audience that you thoroughly understand the issues and have chosen your particular thesis with full knowledge of *all* choices available to you. It tells the readers that, after carefully considering all possibilities, you have, nevertheless, chosen the one in your essay. If you don't include opposing viewpoints here, your readers may conclude that your information is incomplete, and your argument, therefore, invalid.

- *It ensures that no readers are alienated by a viewpoint that ignores their beliefs.* By acknowledging the opposition, you draw in readers who might otherwise be reluctant to read your essay. Particularly with more controversial topics, acknowledging other views will prevent readers who already hold those views from dismissing your argument out of hand; by admitting their standpoint has some credence, you indicate that you respect their intelligence and choices, but that you simply wish to offer a *better* alternative.

- *It works to draw in readers slowly, convincing them of your ideas in incremental steps.* A common psychological ploy used by salespeople is called the "foot in the door" technique: a salesperson convinces you to buy something small at first, paving the way for an even larger purchase afterward. (Once you've agreed to purchase a new sweater, you're more likely also to purchase the pair of pants to go with it.) Similarly, it's easier for readers who are initially opposed to your perspective to accept a small concession at first. As your argument progresses, you ask the readers to accept more and more of your ideas. For instance, if your essay tries to prove that final exams should be abolished, you won't convince anyone unless you first acknowledge that *some* assessment of students' skills and abilities is essential, whatever system is used. You may then move on to the disadvantages of exams, ultimately gaining power as you prove your thesis.

- *It retains the readers' interest right up to the end.* As mentioned in the discussion of pre-writing in Chapter 2, ideas presented in emphatic order become progressively more interesting and, therefore, will keep the readers attuned to the essay. If you begin with your strongest point, the remainder of the essay will seem anticlimactic, and the readers simply may not bother to read on.

Use a variation of emphatic order for persuasive essays in which you think you might encounter strong opposition (for example, when you're dealing with more controversial topics). For instance, if you try to prove that all domestic cats and dogs should be spayed or neutered, you would have a very hard time convincing those animal rights activists who believe that animals should never undergo *any* nonemergency surgery. Of all your potential readers, those who already agree with you will need no convincing, and those who are neutral on the issue will probably be willing to continue reading. Those opposed, however, must somehow be made to believe that your argument is worth pursuing. To convince them, begin by acknowledging their viewpoint before moving on to your own ideas (which ultimately contradict theirs).

By acknowledging the opposition first in your essay, you not only provide a piece of information with which they can identify, but you also let them know you are aware of all sides of the issue and are willing to concede some merit in their position. Subsequently, you suggest that, despite their good ideas, you have nevertheless decided that another route is preferable. This technique is employed by Jamie O'Meara in "Guns, Sex, and Education." After first acknowledging the dangerous models and influence of guns in our society, he turns the argument on its head, saying, "Which is why guns belong in our schools." By this point, however, his readers already believe he's a reasonable individual worthy of their attention.

6. Decide on specific support for the main points

In argument essays, the specific support you choose to bolster your ideas is crucial. As stated earlier, without logical premises or valid examples, your argument won't convince anyone; it must be supported by factual evidence, whether testimonials from experts in a particular field, statistics, cultural trends, or any other objective information that serves to strengthen the thesis. Once you've decided on the reasons why you believe something, you may need to dig further into the topic to unearth other, already documented, proof or experts' previously published results.

In many cases, you will need to conduct research (whether your own studies or an examination of others' materials) to find enough evidence to support your argument (for more information on using research sources in essays, see Chapter 13). Obviously, a thesis such as "My mom is the most generous person I know" would require specific examples of her generosity, all of which could be drawn from your own experience. A thesis such as "All college students could benefit from working part-time during their years of study," however, would require more substantial evidence, such as reports from students who have worked, statistics about how students could or could not benefit (Are their marks affected? Do they acquire skills that transfer to their professional careers?), and so on, most of which would need to be gathered from other sources.

TIP

Use a variety of support

It's a good idea to use a variety of methods as specific support for your ideas. Any factual evidence will strengthen your argument and make it more credible, but the facts themselves can be taken from statistics, news reports, experts' statements, historical data, and other sources. Using other rhetorical modes—a brief definition, examples, comparisons, or cause and effect examinations—is also effective in an argument paper. The more varied the types of evidence you amass to prove the same idea, the more convincing your argument will be.

Writing

As you write, keep in mind the logic of each and every one of your inferences. It will help to examine two common forms of reasoning, inductive and deductive, used in logical arguments. In **inductive reasoning,** you begin by examining many different situations or specific cases and then base your conclusion on the patterns you see. Medical research, for instance, often draws conclusions based on inductive reasoning: after observing thousands of instances of low birth weights among babies born to women who consume caffeine while pregnant, medical scientists conclude that caffeine consumption during pregnancy may result in low birth weight. Similarly, many mysteries are solved through inductive reasoning: a series of burglaries is examined for common features, and the police investigators then draw a conclusion about the criminal's motives or procedures. To be correct, inductive reasoning must be based on a representative number of cases (not just two or three) and rock-solid evidence (observing the correct details in drawing conclusions).

In **deductive reasoning,** you begin with a general situation or case (a major premise) and then show how individual cases or specific situations (minor premises) illustrate the first, general statement. You draw your conclusion based on the connection between the two. For instance, a researcher suggests that most people today are overweight because we engage in less physical activity than people did 50 years ago. She examines a variety of people at different ages and in different socioeconomic classes and uses these as examples to prove her point.

This process of reasoning can be illustrated in the following three-part example, called a *syllogism:*

Major premise:	All Manitobans must attend school until they are 16.
Minor premise:	Masayo is a Manitoban.
Conclusion:	Masayo must attend school until she is 16.

Notice that the minor premise matches its subject (Masayo) with the subject (Manitobans) and not the predicate (must attend school until age 16) of the major premise. The conclusion, then, connects the subject of the minor premise (Masayo) to the predicate of the major premise (must attend school until age 16). A change in the order of the statements changes the logic of the premises:

Major premise:	All Manitobans must attend school until age 16.
Minor premise:	Masayo must attend school until age 16.
Conclusion:	Masayo is a Manitoban.

In this second instance, the logic is unsound, because Masayo could be a resident of any province that requires its students to attend school until age 16. As you can see, the reliability and correctness of the major and minor assumptions are essential for your logic to be sound. If the major premise is not true, the conclusion will inevitably be false—even if the proper order of statements is observed. Always ensure that the premises on which you base your conclusions are solidly rooted in fact and reality.

Remember, too, that good arguments may sometimes effectively appeal to emotions, as long as the major points are supported with facts as well. If you know that your audience is interested in charitable pursuits, there is nothing wrong with taking advantage of the associations people may have with certain words or phrases as a way to convey your idea. Using descriptive language, as well, can drive home a point with emotional impact. For instance, in "Homeless in Paradise," Lawrence Solomon paints a picture of the homeless as victims of our society, employing descriptors such as "these vulnerable people" when referring to them. You must ensure, however, that even emotional appeals are grounded in a larger, logical argument.

SNAG

Leaving logic behind

Lapses in logic (or **logical fallacies**) sometimes occur when presenting evidence in argument essays. Because your thesis is a strongly held belief, your own devotion to the thesis may sometimes eclipse the reasoning necessary to prove this point to others. Check your writing to ensure that you're not seduced by one of the following common errors in logic:

- *Non sequitur.* Literally, this Latin phrase means "it does not follow." A non sequitur is a conclusion that doesn't really relate to the evidence that precedes it. Here's an example: "People everywhere are becoming more and more rude in day-to-day interactions, and we must reduce the amount of impolite behaviour in our society. Therefore, anyone who is rude in public should be jailed." Even if the premise (first sentence) is true, it doesn't necessarily follow that an appropriate action to combat rudeness is prison time! Similarly, if your accountant announces that you owe the government an extra $5000 in taxes this year, it doesn't necessarily follow that he's incompetent (there may be other reasons why your tax rate is higher this year than last).

- *Either/or reasoning.* This problem occurs when someone assumes that there are only two alternatives in a situation, and if alternative A is incorrect, then alternative B must be the "right" choice. Students who lack self-esteem often fall into this trap when they berate themselves for work that falls short of their expectations. "I failed the test, so I'm a total failure" goes one train of thought. This conclusion is based on the assumption that there are only two choices: "success" or "complete

(continued)

failure." In fact, there is an entire spectrum of possibilities in between: you may be highly successful in one area even if you lack skill in another; you may fail one test in a course yet still pass the course. A mother who warns her child, "Put on a scarf or you'll catch a cold," is also falling into this trap.

- *Post hoc, ergo propter hoc.* This phrase, which literally means "after this, therefore because of this," is another way to introduce the error of confusing coincidence with causation, discussed in Chapter 10. Just because one event or situation succeeds another, it doesn't always follow that the first *caused* the second.

- *Circular reasoning.* This error (also referred to as "begging the question") occurs when a person implies that the *reason* something exists is because it already exists. Circular reasoning takes for granted that the major premise (the idea on which the argument is based) is already true and does not have to be proved. Here's an example: "Our school produces top-performing swimmers because we always rank highest in swim meets" just tells us in two different ways that the school's swimmers are above average in ability. The writer needs to examine what causes them to do well. Similarly, writing "Buttery Battered Chicken sells the best fried chicken because it is superior to everyone else's" also repeats the concept—the chicken is better than other brands—without delving into what, specifically, contributes to that assessment.

- *Ad hominem.* This fallacy occurs when someone looks at the *source* of the argument, instead of the argument itself; s/he judges the conclusion depending on who is presenting it. For example, saying "My doctor has no right to tell me to quit smoking because he's a smoker himself" suggests that the *idea itself* of quitting smoking is invalidated simply because it's been presented by someone who smokes.

- *Hasty generalization.* With this fallacy, a conclusion is based on either far too few examples or those that don't directly relate to it. For example, you may catch a cold after walking in the rain without an umbrella. Just because you discover that two of your friends have also had this experience, it's not logical to conclude that walking in the rain causes colds. Three samples are not enough to prove a point unequivocally. (If you delve further into the subject, you'll find that there are all kinds of factors at play, not the least of which is the cold virus itself—a precondition to catching a cold, rain or shine.)

- *Oversimplification.* Sometimes, what appears to be the most obvious conclusion is not always the truth; this fallacy ignores other alternatives. Mr. Smith is caught holding a revolver over his dead wife's body; the police automatically assume he is the murderer. This conclusion assumes that the killer must be the person holding the weapon. However, anyone who has ever watched *Law and Order* (or any crime-based television show) knows that we should never jump to the first conclusion that occurs to us.

(continued)

- *Stereotyping.* This fallacy occurs when a person assumes that a given stereotype—generalized characteristics attributed to a group of people or person within a group—is applied as "proof" of some point. Since stereotypes are often based on hearsay or unsupported assumptions, they are never suitable for argument; they neglect the uniqueness and individuality of each member within the group. Saying "All plastic surgeons work to get rich" or "Obese people are lazy" is not only insulting and prejudiced, it's also inaccurate. Even positive stereotypes ("All Asians excel at math") disregard the reality and are not suitable as support.

- *Misplaced analogy instead of argument.* As you learned in Chapter 8, analogy is an extended comparison between two things. However, you must be very careful in using an analogy to prove a point since the defining trait of analogies is a comparison between two *unlike* things; the analogy may fall short at one or more points of comparison. For example, the statement "Raising children is like contributing to a bank account; the more you put into it, the more valuable it becomes" assumes some similarities between children and bank accounts. Even if we ignore this distasteful association between children and money, the analogy doesn't work on all levels; what about children who *don't* "increase in value"? Furthermore, how would we measure such an increase? Ultimately, most people withdraw money from their bank accounts; does this mean that parents should expect some sort of payment from their children? The two subjects are simply too different, and the issue of raising children too complex, for this analogy to prove the argument. While you may add analogies to your essay as further illustration of your point(s), an analogy alone is never enough to clinch an argument.

Post-Writing

As with your earlier efforts, you should follow the strategies for revision and editing outlined in Chapter 2. In addition, argument essays present unique challenges that can be addressed by the following questions:

- Is my thesis logical?

- Have I considered all of the opposition in forming my argument?

- Have I considered my audience and purpose?

- Are my points organized in a manner that will most effectively draw in the reader, retain her or his interest, and lead to a convincing case for my viewpoint?

- Have I included a wide variety of support, particularly factual details and statistics that can prove my thesis?

- Have I ensured that my argument is free of logical fallacies?

- Have I included appeals to emotion only if appropriate?

EXERCISES

1. Choose a commonly held belief or truth, and see how many cases you can think of in which it's *not* true. For example, "It's a good idea to save money" might be an invalid statement to those who have more than they could ever spend, to those who have so little money that they'd starve if they didn't spend what they have, or to those whose lives are at an end. Here are some other examples:

   - It's important to lose weight if you're overweight.

   - Parents must support their children in every way.

   - A good education is necessary for a good job.

   - People should not steal.

2. Try to determine more than four different types of evidence to prove each of the following statements:

   - It's important to give to charity.

   - It's not a good idea to stay out partying until 3:30 a.m. the night before an exam.

   - Pets are beneficial to their owners.

   - Students need to take more of an active role in the way their schools are run.

   - We should have tougher laws against drunk drivers.

3. Watch some television infomercials. What techniques of argument and persuasion do they use? How often do they employ logical fallacies? How much do they appeal to emotion?

MODEL STUDENT ESSAY: ARGUMENT

The following argument essay demonstrates how one student tackled this rhetorical mode. Highlighted is how the writer incorporated key aspects of argument to make the essay effective.

What's in a Name?

establishes relationship with audience

Some people believe that sharing our lives with others is what makes life truly worthwhile, and most of us in Canada still choose to sanctify this belief within marriage. Marriage signifies a commitment to share "for better or for worse," perhaps even to have a family. And for most people—even in 2002—it also means that one partner will have to change her name after the ceremony. Since changing her name bestows no benefits to either a woman or her family, a better choice is for women to behave as their husbands do after marriage, and retain their birth names.

thesis

acknowledges the opposition

One of the most common arguments made by proponents of same-name marriages is that a shared surname fosters a sense of consistency and reflects the partnership and commitment of the two people in the marriage. These advocates neglect to mention, however, that this same consistency and commitment could easily be achieved if both partners took on *the woman's* last name, or even if both changed their names to a third, entirely different, surname. Same-name supporters also argue that two different last names might prove confusing for children in the family (especially if the children's last name is different from their mother's).

specific details and statistics to support argument

However, if we consider that almost half of all marriages end in divorce and approximately 75% of all divorced persons eventually remarry, we know that there are already many children (living in step families) who carry different surnames from their siblings or a parent. In these blended families, children born of different parents coexist and function effectively without becoming confused about their identities or forgetting which is their birth parent. Similarly, it makes sense to assume that children in families with parents sporting different surnames could function equally well.

highlights weaknesses in opposition; proposes alternatives

Many people consider that changing a woman's name after marriage is a well-established conven-

second
acknowledg-
ment of
opposition and
contradictory
response to
it

more evidence
to support
the thesis

point in
support of
thesis

tion, and comply without giving much thought to the matter. But our society has forgone many other traditions related to marriage, so this one could equally undergo revision. For example, the institution of marriage itself has been evolving as common-law unions proliferate. Similarly, the traditional husband–wife roles in any conjugal union have already shifted significantly with so many women working full-time outside the home. Furthermore, there have always been women who rejected this tradition of changing names at marriage. From the early days of filmmaking, most actors have retained their own names even after marrying, as have most published writers. Other professionals, such as doctors or lawyers, also frequently keep their names once a professional practice has been established, to avoid confusion and provide consistency to their clients. These women recognize that clients might interpret a change negatively, resulting in loss of work.

offers alter-
natives

specific
details

Women in the general population may also experience drawbacks associated with changing their names. By the time a woman reaches adulthood, she has established a solid sense of self-identity, reflected in, and reinforced significantly by, her name (for this reason, prisoners are commonly made to wear identifying numbers rather than their names, thereby denying them a sense of individuality). Furthermore, there are very few circumstances outside of marriage in which people voluntarily change their names, unless they find themselves in danger (as in a witness protection program) or they already despise the name they were given at birth. And since marriages are occurring later and later in life (most first-time brides are almost 28, according to StatsCan), a strong sense of self, connected to a specific name, will need to be reconstructed after a woman marries. In what other circumstances would a person reach the mature age of 30, 40, or even 50, and then be asked to shift her sense of self so dramatically?

specific
statistic to
support
argument

When a woman changes her name, she not only loses her own, individual, identity, but becomes almost an adjunct to her husband; even her title changes in most cases from "Miss" to "Mrs." No doubt, we've all seen cards or envelopes addressed to couples in which only the man's name is included, as in "Mr. and Mrs. Jim Smith." In this case, the woman's own, unique name—what's left of it—has been completely obliterated. In extreme circumstances, a woman may find herself carrying the name of a loathed or estranged individual (her ex-husband) for the rest of her life after divorce.

Most importantly, however, it is impractical for women to change their names after having established lives and careers, and once their birth names have been registered in a plethora of government, business, or medical files. It is both time consuming and tedious to track down every single bank, dentist's office, credit card company, or school board in order to request a change of name. While no province *requires* a woman to change her name, some, such as Quebec, establish as their standard practice that women retain their names upon marriage. In this way, one unified, consistent record of a woman's existence spans all of her professional, legal, medical, or personal contacts, and can be maintained without interruption or error from birth to death.

It's time we realized that asking women to change their names at marriage serves no real purpose except to indicate that they are attached to a man. In today's world, the majority of families include *both* husband and wife working outside the home; women contribute almost equally to the workforce, and in fact do more than their male counterparts at home. It no longer makes sense for them to be treated as a mere appendage of their husbands. By retaining their names, women not only assert their equality with men, but also preserve their identities as unique, valuable individuals in society.

The Myth of Cottage Life
by Russell Smith (b. 1963)

Russell Smith was born in Johannesburg, South Africa, and grew up in Halifax. He studied French literature at Queen's University and at the Universities of Paris and Poitiers in France. He is the author of the novels How Insensitive *(1994) and* Noise *(1998) and of the collection of short stories* Young Men *(1999). His articles have been published in a variety of newspapers and magazines in Canada and the United States. He now lives in Toronto, where he writes a weekly column on the arts and culture for the* Globe and Mail.

PRE-READING

Have you ever been to a country cottage? Is it true that the summertime cottage or camp "really defines the Canadian summer"? In this article from the *Globe and Mail* (2000), Smith writes about the common Canadian practice of heading to the country during the summer. What makes these country homes special and desired? What is the appeal of going to live in a more natural setting for a weekend or a month? In what ways has cottage life changed over the past few decades?

E nough about how wonderful the cottage is. I'm sick of reading about how 1
everybody has one. I can't open a newspaper without hitting another misty-eyed paean to the joys of the lake, the dock, the laziness and health that comes from tranquility. Well, *duh*. I'm sure it's lovely to be rich. This newspaper [the *Globe and Mail*] in particular has been especially convinced of the relevance of wealthy pleasures to everybody's life, publishing endless reminiscences of children and dogs by campfires, and how big American ships swamp our little canoes.

But we are far from being the only propagandists: CBC radio keeps playing a cute 2
song about cottages by Martha and the Muffins, and there is a whole magazine devoted to cottage life, with its own TV show. It's the time of year when well-paid TV producers think: "Hmm, summer stories . . . Well, everybody *I* know is off to a cottage—this is what really defines the Canadian summer, right?"

Well, no, actually. It's the time of year when most of us, trapped in the heat and 3
noise of cities, can only dream of cool and quiet and a lake to swim in.

Hey, I'm happy for people with cottages, I really am. There's nothing wrong with 4
all these pleasures; I would boast about them too. There's nothing wrong with

wealth either, whether inherited or earned. What I object to is the total uncon-sciousness of such boasting. Imagine if every newspaper decided, around the first long weekend of spring, that it was Porsche season, and asked their most poetic writers to write essays on the joys of driving their Porsches. ("We all know the feeling, that gripping high whine as the tach spikes 5,000 . . . and who hasn't noticed the smell of new leather, that nostalgic reminder of all the Porsches you've driven?")

5   Maybe it's easier in the rest of Canada to own or rent a summer cottage. In the largest city, there are two, and only two, ways of having your own summer resi-dence: 1) be wealthy, or 2) inherit one from your family. Again, there is nothing wrong with either of these options. (If I inherited a cottage, I probably would not give it to the poor.) But most of us do not qualify for either category.

6   I have done my best to participate in this primarily Ontarian tradition. I am open to any and all invitations by people with summer places. And I have tried to rent one. You do this by buying a book of listings, or going online, and you start to make your calls in January. You make 10 phone calls. The people who answer the phone are usually amused that you are trying at all. They have the whole summer booked to regular clients. It's like trying to get tickets to Leafs games: The whole place is booked up by season-ticket holders.

7   This year, my partner and I got a booking on our 15th phone call. The place was more expensive than any of our top choices, and advertised as "secluded." Overjoyed, we deposited our vast cash advance in the owner's bank account. Finally, we were going to experience the whole lazy dock-and-canoe shebang, read novels and listen to the sad cry of the loon, as all the newspapers tell us you can do.

8   Unfortunately, when you're down at the bottom of the barrel like us, you don't get a rustic experience at all. You get a more proletarian holiday: cottages like sub-urban houses crammed together around a lake roaring with motorboats and Jet Skis. You are 10 feet from your neighbour's barbecue, and their wailing top-40 radio. Pop beats—variously anthemic, saccharine, hackneyed and violent—boom from stereos placed all around the lake, echoing across the oily water. One after-noon, we listened, trying to read on the slab of concrete that passed for a dock, to a 15-minute radio ad for M and M's Meat Market in Peterborough ("We have spe-cial deals on chicken breasts, and Marla will be here for the next hour . . ."). One friendly neighbour called to us from her dock, worried that we didn't have any-thing to do, since we had no motorboat.

9   These people were recreating, with as many machines as they had at their dis-posal, an urban environment. Noise was actually what they were on holiday *for*. The experience confirmed that the mass of urban people either can't afford the wilderness, like me, or don't even want it, like our cottage neighbours. It also con-firmed my view that suburban culture is the truly dominant one everywhere.

10   The myth of the wilderness as a common Canadian experience is, of course, not the newspapers' creation. Since Atwood's *Survival* and Northrop Frye's "garrison

mentality" idea, it has dominated our cultural commentary, as persistent and tenacious as zebra mussels. I was once on a panel discussion about the bloody Canadian identity with Peter Gzowski (who else?) and he asked another panelist, who had just mentioned Whitehorse, if she had ever been there. It was a very proud, pointed and indeed aggressive question: "Have you ever *been* to Whitehorse?"

At which point all the panelists were driven to reflect, I'm sure, that they would   11
be delighted to go to Whitehorse *if the CBC would pay for it.*

Pierre Berton once wrote, in the preface to *Klondike:* "The experience of naked   12
rock and brooding forest . . . of the wolf's haunting howl and the loon's ghostly
call, is one that is still shared by the majority of Canadians . . ." This would come
as a surprise to the Portuguese teenagers listening to stereos in the alley outside
my window, or to the Vietnamese businessmen in darkened karaoke bars down
the street. They have no experience of any wilderness at all. *(The wolf's haunting
call?)* Of course they would love to see it.

I said this once in Berton's presence, and he laughed good-naturedly (for   13
Berton is, above all, a good sport). He conceded that perhaps Canada has changed
somewhat since he wrote that.

Canada has changed. But you wouldn't know it from reading the newspapers.   14

QUESTIONS

Understanding the message: Comprehension

1. In what way(s) does Smith say going to the cottage has changed since it was first a place to hear "the sad cry of the loon"?

2. Explain the last two sentences of the article.

3. What *is* "the myth of cottage life"?

Examining the structure and details: Analysis

1. Reread the opening paragraph of Smith's article. What technique does Smith use to introduce his topic? How does it draw in the reader?

2. What other rhetorical modes does Smith use to support his argument? What kinds of examples does he use?

3. What are the premises on which Smith bases his argument? List them. How logical is his reasoning?

Formulating a response: Inference and interpretation

1. Do you agree with Smith that propounding the joys of cottages is akin to deciding that "the first long weekend of spring . . . was Porsche season"? Why or why not? In what way is the comparison relevant?

2. How does Smith create an emotional rapport between himself and his readers? Does this connection help to make his argument more convincing? Why or why not?

3. Does Smith include enough evidence to make his argument convincing? Why or why not?

4. What is Smith's thesis? Where is it stated?

Essay questions

1. Does your family have a country retreat or cottage? If not, have you ever been to someone else's cottage or spent time in the country? Write an essay in which you argue that either country life or city life is superior to the other. Be sure to use specific evidence to support your thesis.

2. Are there other Canadian rituals that people feel compelled to engage in, simply because they are practised by the majority? Think of another commonly practised behaviour besides "heading to the cottage" (for example, parents spending huge sums on their children's weddings, traditional holiday dinners, owning a car). Write an argument essay in which you argue against this particular ritual, uncovering why it is something people should not feel compelled to do.

3. How does Smith use comparison and contrast to make his point about cottage life? Using examples from the article, write an essay in which you discuss Smith's use of this technique.

VOCABULARY

paean: song or poem praising something

propagandists: people whose goal is to promote something

tach: tachometer, the gauge in a car that indicates the engine's speed of rotation

proletarian: working class

anthemic: a style of rock music with a strong, repetitive refrain that aims for a certain grandeur

saccharine: cloyingly sweet

hackneyed: trite; commonplace

Atwood's *Survival:* the book in which Margaret Atwood (b. 1939) argues that the Canadian psyche, as reflected in Canadian literature, is shaped by the struggle against a hostile environment

Northrop Frye's "garrison mentality": the noted Canadian critic (1906–1991) spoke of the early settlers of British North America huddled against the wilderness as though in a beleaguered garrison

Peter Gzowski: Canadian broadcaster and author (1934–2002)

Pierre Berton, *Klondike*: Canadian journalist and historian (b. 1920) whose *Klondike* recounted the Klondike gold rush of 1898

Guns, Sex, and Education

by Jamie O'Meara (b. 1967)

Jamie O'Meara is senior editor at the Montreal news and entertainment weekly
Hour, *where he has worked as a music journalist for seven years. Educated at the*
University of Western Ontario in London, Ontario, and at Concordia University in
Montreal, he was nonetheless raised in the rural backwaters of southwestern Ontario
where, at a very young age, his parents plied him with firearms as a means of
"keeping him out of trouble." These rural experiences, combined with an unlikely yet
long-lasting love affair with punk rock, have informed his later writing in ways that
even he couldn't anticipate. O'Meara has also written for Saturday Night,
Alternative Press, *and the CBC; his band, Rise, has a new album out called* Freezer
Burn. *He is currently unarmed.*

PRE-READING

With the Canadian government's recent move to require registration for all
firearms, the issue of guns was once again brought to prominence. In this
essay from *Saturday Night* magazine (2000), O'Meara asks whether the issue
of guns should be treated in the same way as the issue of sex in schools. What
are the dangers of informing students about guns? What are your personal
feelings about guns in our society?

1   The first thing I noticed was its weight. It wasn't just cold, it was heavy, like the
rock you pick up when you're six years old, with visions of windowpanes
dancing in your head. By itself, it's just a rock. In your hand, it has power. That's
how the gun felt.

2   It was a 9-mm military-issue Browning semi-automatic, I think, obtained from a
friend who had joined the army cadets. Because of its weight, I had a hard time lev-
elling it at the car battery we'd put halfway up the slope of the abandoned gravel pit
at the back of our rural Ontario farm. This was where my brother and I spent a good
part of our summers, with our .22-calibre rifles and .177 pellet guns, keeping the
pop-bottle population under control. This gun, though, felt different than the ones
we'd been shooting since we were kids. Fascinatingly so.

3   Borrowing my stance from every cop show ever made, I lined up my plastic
prey and squeezed the trigger five times in quick succession. The first shot hit the

battery and the next four thumped into the earth about twenty feet in front of me. A box of fifty rounds later, I was no closer to hitting my target with any regularity and, frankly, my hand was beginning to hurt. I packed the gun away and returned it to my buddy. (He, after exhausting its cachet among our friends, tossed it in a local river.)

All in all: boring.   4

And that may be a hard concept to grasp if, like most North Americans, you 5 were raised on a steady diet of *Rambo, The Terminator,* and *Mad Max:* they showed that guns are fun, the implements of adventure. If you're holding one, people do what you want them to do. All of that's pretty attractive to young people, for whom power and control often seem in scarce supply. So why would a kid voluntarily give up the chance to play with a handgun?

Certainly not because of parental warnings. Lock the booze cabinet with 6 double-plated armour and that's not going to save your Smirnoff. Threaten blindness and the wrath of all saints and that's not going to stop adolescents from masturbating. And tell children that guns are dangerous and that's not going to stop them from wanting to use one if it's accessible—in the gun cabinet, from a store, or in the schoolyard. All you can hope to do is teach them to act responsibly if the occasion arises.

Which is why guns belong in our schools.   7

Any parent knows that the best way to defuse the curiosity of a child is to 8 address it head on, to transform the mysterious into the mundane. If memory serves, there is no place more mundane than school. Adding a firearm component to the current curricula in regions where guns are prevalent would achieve two things: it would satisfy the inherent inquisitiveness that children have about guns; and it would allow educators to monitor the reactions children have to the weapons—something that might have been of inestimable value to the faculty at Columbine High School in Colorado.

In Canada, it may be argued that guns aren't prevalent enough—in homes or 9 on the streets—to warrant a proactive approach to gun education. Tragedies such as the one last year in Taber, Alberta, and the recent spate of youth shootings in Toronto indicate otherwise.

Put a kid on a firing range under strict controls, oblige him to fire hundreds of 10 rounds at a circular target over lengthy periods of time, and what happens? Dirty Harry becomes a junior biathlete, without the skis. The kids who maintain an interest can be funnelled into gun clubs, where they can work through their attraction under the watchful eyes of trainers adept at spotting potential problems.

As long as guns have a mystique, they'll seem powerful. As long as kids feel 11 there's power in guns, they'll be tempted to get their hands on them. And sooner or later someone who possesses a gun is going to want to use it. The solution is to address this desire early on and supply children with the rules of conduct. It's the same principle that lies behind sex education.

12   Think about it: sex education is taught so that kids will have a better understanding of how their bodies work, why they feel sexual desires, and how to act (or not) on those desires. Basically, we equip our kids with sexual knowledge so that they'll have the confidence to act responsibly. The same argument holds true for gun education: that, armed with knowledge and familiarity, kids will be better equipped to think about guns in a responsible manner. (In fact, the classic argument against sex education—that by providing kids with dangerous information they can't handle, we're encouraging them to run out and recklessly try it for themselves—is exactly the objection you're likely to hear raised against gun instruction.)

13   We accept the natural sexual curiosity of children and teenagers, and have legislated protection for them in the form of education, rather than pretending that the curiosity doesn't exist. Children are also curious about guns. We should give them the same protection. We don't want our kids shooting first and asking questions later.

QUESTIONS

Understanding the message: Comprehension

1. How is it that guns are "boring," according to O'Meara?

2. What common images of guns in the media are mentioned? List them.

3. What is the main motivation for kids wanting guns, according to O'Meara?

Examining the structure and details: Analysis

1. How does O'Meara attract the interest of his readers at the beginning of the essay?

2. How does O'Meara acknowledge and draw in those who may be opposed to his argument? With which point(s) does he "acknowledge the opposition"?

3. What are the various reasons that O'Meara provides for allowing gun education in schools? How many different kinds of evidence does he provide?

4. What comparison does O'Meara employ to make his point? Is it a valid comparison? Why or why not?

Formulating a response: Inference and interpretation

1. Do you agree with O'Meara's belief that "watchful eyes of trainers adept at spotting potential problems" at gun clubs work to weed out potential trigger-happy teens? Why or why not?

2. What is O'Meara's tone in this piece? Is it appropriate for the subject matter? Why or why not?

3. Does O'Meara appeal more to logic or emotion in this essay? Explain your answer.

Essay questions

1. Is the use of guns among teens or children in Canadian society a threat? How do we in Canada compare to those in the United States? In an argument essay, explain your viewpoint on this issue.

2. How effective is sex education in our schools? Does it achieve its intended purpose? In an argument essay, argue either to retain the system as it is or for changes that you think will improve sex education in schools.

3. Could O'Meara have included any other evidence to make his argument more convincing? In an essay that uses examples from O'Meara's article, explain how he might have structured it differently to be even more convincing.

VOCABULARY

cachet: distinguished position; appeal

Columbine High School: Colorado high school at which, in 1999, two teenage outcasts shot and murdered 14 other teens and one teacher before shooting themselves

Taber, Alberta: the town in which a 14-year-old boy killed one high-school student and wounded another in an apparent copycat crime a week after the Columbine shootings

Dirty Harry: the San Francisco police officer portrayed by Clint Eastwood, in the film of the same name (1971), who seldom shrinks from the use of violence to achieve his goals

biathlete: athlete who competes in a sports competition (biathlon) that combines rifle shooting with cross-country skiing

Should We Need a Licence to Be a Parent?

by Janice Turner

Janice Turner is a journalist who wrote for the Toronto Star *through the 1990s. Her articles focused mainly on life and health issues.*

PRE-READING

Most people would never drive a car or shoot a gun without a licence. In this article from the *Toronto Star* (1999), Turner introduces the notion of a licence for parents. What would change in our current understanding of the family unit if parents were required to have a licence before they could have children? Do you think it's too easy for people to have children today? Are there some parents who should be deemed unfit to raise children?

---

1   You need a licence to drive a car, serve liquor, go on a deer hunt; heck, you need a licence to call yourself a barber.

2   Why not to raise a child?

3   Why is it that society demands so very little of prospective parents?

4   That's what two Nova Scotia academics want to know. They suggest would-be moms and dads be required to get a "parenting" licence.

5   Their idea has attracted much attention, not all of it flattering.

6   They call the concept pro-active. Some call the idea elitist and authoritarian.

7   They insist they have only the best interests of children in mind. Parents would be more respectful of their obligations if they had to earn the privilege, they say. A licence would set some minimum requirements, symbolize the importance of parenting and underscore the notion of children's rights.

8   Child abuse and child abandonment hit the headlines with depressing frequency. Most recently, a 5-year-old girl was found wandering barefoot in the snow in the middle of the night while her mother was at a karaoke bar. The Toronto Children's Aid Society said it deals with 10 cases each week in which children have been left unattended.

9   A *Toronto Star* investigation two years ago looked at 70 cases between 1991 and 1996 in which a parent (or other caregiver such as a mother's boyfriend) was charged criminally after a child died of abuse.

Katherine Covell, an associate professor of psychology, and husband Brian 10 Howe, an associate political science professor, are directors of the Children's Rights Centre at the University College of Cape Breton. They maintain that family life and parental freedoms are already regulated. The trouble is, they say, the rules deal with problems *after* the fact.

By that time, too often, irreparable damage has been done.　　　　　　11

It can take years, Covell and Howe say, for any action to be taken after a family 12 is brought to the attention of children's aid officials.

Aside from such problems, there is no method of preparing people, especially 13 teenagers, for parenthood and little to discourage them from having babies in the first place, they say. A teenager who completes high school may be less likely to choose parenthood as a route to adulthood.

Covell and Howe recommend parents be compelled to complete high school, 14 pass a certified course on infant development, obtain a licence, sign a contract agreeing not to abuse or neglect the child and take upgrade courses throughout the child's life and when there are major family changes, such as divorce, death of a spouse or sibling.

Children have rights and parents have responsibilities, the researchers say, yet 15 many people who have children have no interest in raising them. (Howe has no children of his own but considers himself a father to Covell's two grown children.)

Requiring parents to have a high school diploma, they concede, is arbitrary and 16 intended as a starting point for discussion. It has drawn criticism for being elitist.

Earlier this month, Ontario announced it will require 16- and 17-year-old wel- 17 fare mothers to complete high school and take a 35-hour parenting course, or lose their benefits. A teen who complies will get $500 toward her education or her child's. Critics say the policy is punitive and assumes that low-income parents are less capable than those who are well-off.

Stan Shapiro, a Richmond Hill psychotherapist who has worked with parents 18 and families for more than 30 years, says that, as a symbol, a licence could do much to raise the profile of parenting.

"Perhaps the job of parenting would be taken more seriously," he says. "The 19 idea is you have to have skills, which parenting does require. Too often it's seen as 'natural.' A licence would bring it to another level and would make people aware that there maybe are things that they could learn."

Shapiro is director of the Ontario Parenting Education Centre, a private, non- 20 profit organization that runs practical parenting courses throughout Greater Toronto.

He points to a recent Statistics Canada study that concluded parenting style 21 has a larger impact on a child's behaviour than any other factor.

"Parenting matters a heck of a lot," Ivan Fellegi, Canada's chief statistician, said 22 on the study's release in October.

23   "It's not true [your kids are] doomed for life if you're a single parent or you're poor. You have a big chance of not doing well, but being a positive parent is a far bigger factor."

24   Thousands of parents take prenatal classes but most of them would never think of taking a parenting course, Fellegi said.

25   Kim Swigger, a parent of two children, aged 7 and 10, and school council chairperson at Sir Samuel B. Steele junior public school, calls the idea of licensing parents "extreme."

26   "It's a simplistic approach to a really complicated problem," says Swigger, a former public health nurse. "It implies that passing some kind of test will guarantee a certain level of performance. I don't think you can apply that to parenting."

27   Mary Gordon, administrator of parenting programs for the Toronto District School Board, says the state should be in "the parent-enabling business, not the licensing business."

28   It would be far more effective to give people, in a non-threatening and non-judgmental way, information that they could filter through their own value systems, she says.

29   Bob Glossop, co-ordinator of programs and research at the Vanier Institute of the Family, doesn't dismiss Covell and Howe's concerns. But he'd caution against any mandatory measures that suggest all parents are ill-equipped.

30   "The majority of parents are not falling down in doing their jobs," says Glossop. "Most parents are deeply committed to doing their best."

31   The issue of licensing parents arises every few years, Glossop says, but never seems to get very far.

32   "My sense is that the majority would not welcome that kind of intrusive involvement of the state."

33   Glossop acknowledges that many parents today feel stressed and could use some form of educational support. Society has changed, yet many people simply parent as they were parented.

34   Glossop suggests a major public awareness campaign might help to prepare prospective parents for the awesome changes and responsibilities they'll face.

35   "I respect the concern out of which the [licensing] suggestion is raised," Glossop says. "We need enhanced parenting skills."

36   But certification goes too far.

37   "I'm not sure I even understand *how* licensing could be effectively introduced," Glossop says.

38   Who would set the standards and what would be the sanctions for those in violation?

39   Regrettably, many parents shy away from parenting courses, thinking they don't need them or that it might make them stand out in an unfavourable way, Shapiro says.

                                                      Respond in Writing   NE

Having mandatory instruction might remove the hesitancy. 40

After all, "if you're going to have the job, you ought to be serious about it and 41 be trained at it," Shapiro says.

Although Shapiro doesn't have a problem with the concept of licensing, he says 42 it's a non-starter.

Licensing is an authoritarian response to the deeply troubling issues of abuse 43 and neglect, Gordon says.

"Knowledge and empathy will enhance positive parenting, appropriate and 44 joyful parenting, much more than any silly licence will," she says.

"Children who are parented well bring so much to the world." 45

Helping to educate parents about the stages of child development and other 46 basic health and welfare issues should be at least as important as our efforts to support the environment, she says.

"When we gave people information and support, they bought into [home and 47 office] recycling programs. That's the way to go, rather than the Big Brother way," she says.

QUESTIONS

Understanding the message: Comprehension

1. What are the benefits of "parenting" licences, according to the two Nova Scotia academics who introduced the idea?

2. Why do professors Covell and Howe advocate mandatory completion of high school for parents?

3. Would all parents be required to get a licence under Covell and Howe's system? If not, for which parents would a licence be mandatory?

4. What kinds of resistance to parenting licences is predicted in the article?

5. What does Mary Gordon mean when she says that providing information is "the way to go, rather than the Big Brother way"?

Examining the structure and details: Analysis

1. How much of Turner's information is based on factual evidence? How much is unsubstantiated by experts or statistics?

2. At what point in her essay does Turner acknowledge the opposition?

3. List the main points that Turner makes in this argument. What is her method of organization?

Formulating a response: Inference and interpretation

1. At which points does Turner appeal to the readers' emotions? How effective are these instances?

2. Do you think Turner's purpose is to change only beliefs, or behaviour as well? Why?

3. In paragraph 15, Turner tells us, "Howe has no children of his own but considers himself a father to Covell's two children." Why do you think she mentions this fact? What impact does it have?

Essay questions

1. Would requiring parents to obtain a licence serve to diminish poor parenting and potential abuse? Write an argument essay in which you explain why or why not.

2. What makes a perfect parent? In an essay, describe the qualities required to be an ideal parent.

3. Is Turner's approach to her topic extensive enough to convince readers? If not, what other kinds of evidence might she have included to make the argument more sound? Cite examples from the text in your response.

VOCABULARY

elitist: reserved only for a select few

Big Brother: a character (a government-controlled entity) that spies on people in *1984* (1949), a novel by George Orwell (1903–50); the government's slogan in the novel is "Big Brother Is Watching You."

Homeless in Paradise

by Lawrence Solomon (b. 1948)

Lawrence Solomon is one of Canada's leading environmentalists, is an authority on public utilities, public–private partnerships, and regulation, and is a prolific writer. He is the author of several books on environmental issues, including The Conserver Solution *(1978), which became a guidebook for those interested in incorporating environmental factors into economic life. In the early 1980s, he turned to writing about energy deregulation, publishing* Energy Shock *(1980),* Breaking Up Ontario Hydro's Monopoly *(1982) and* Power at What Cost? *(1984). Subsequently, the United Kingdom adopted his model for deregulation in its 1989 reforms, and this model later became the dominant pattern for electricity restructuring reform in the world. Solomon is currently a columnist with the* National Post *and has written for a variety of publications, including the* Globe and Mail, *the* Wall Street Journal, *and the award-winning* Next City, *of which he was both editor and publisher.*

PRE-READING

How much do you know about the homeless population in Canada? What programs or initiatives exist in your community to combat homelessness? Under what circumstances do you imagine someone might end up living on the streets?

In the 1960s and 1970s, homelessness was virtually unknown in North America, 1 the term not even in public parlance. In 1964, Columbia University researchers scoured four Manhattan parks to count those sleeping there: they found one man. Likewise, in Chicago, Vancouver, Los Angeles, Montreal, and other major cities, homelessness was the exception and not the rule. In the 1960s, big city newspapers rarely ran stories on the homeless, unlike the last decade when they averaged one homeless story every two days. Until the 1980s, the homeless were not part of a widespread phenomenon; they were exceptional hard-luck cases.

Then these exceptions became the rule. Not because poverty suddenly 2 increased—it didn't. Not because welfare was drastically reduced—generally welfare became more generous. Not much because mental institutions suddenly released their patients—the deinstitutionalization of mental patients that took place in the 1960s and early 1970s explains a small fraction, perhaps one-tenth or one-twentieth, of the torrent of homelessness that engulfed our major cities in the 1980s.

3   One factor, and one factor alone—changes in housing policy—accounts for the immense rise of homelessness: Governments outlawed much of what was then the bottom end of the housing market—the derelict apartment buildings, seedy hotels, and rooming houses—while legalizing vagrancy. In this way, and with only the best of intentions, governments replaced a vast supply of substandard, but low-cost, housing with a much vaster, much more substandard, and much lower-cost supply of housing in the form of our streets, back alleys, and parks.

4   Before the government inadvertently converted our public spaces into sleeping quarters, poor people—including alcoholics and the mentally ill—lived in low-rent districts, muddling along as best they could. Those poorer still doubled up with them, or sublet rooms in exchange for cash or household services, typically babysitting for women, odd jobs for men. There was nothing particularly noble about most of these arrangements: The poor who put up still needier relatives on their living room couches would have preferred the space for themselves; those put up often felt dependent and unwelcome, and, had they the wherewithal, many would have left their position of servitude. Nevertheless, they made do, keeping up appearances and maintaining relations, however poorly. Relatively few people relied on shelters.

5   Then came urban renewal, a euphemism for slum clearance that levelled much of the low-quality housing stock across the continent. Newark and New York City lost almost half of their low-rent housing between 1970 and 1990; New York City's Bowery, with 10,000 beds in 1965, had but 3,000 in 1980. In the 1970s and 1980s, Chicago lost 20 percent of its low-rent housing; of the 10,000 spaces in the Loop area's cubicle hotels, 600 remained. By the early 1980s, Toronto lost virtually all of its 500 flophouse beds; by the end of the decade, it had lost one-third of its rooming houses. Between the mid-1970s and the late 1980s, the number of unsubsidized low-cost units fell 54 per cent in the typical large U.S. metropolitan area. Public housing—once a shining hope—failed utterly in housing the very poor.

6   While the stock of low-cost housing declined, the cost and difficulty of living on the cheap increased. Welfare recipients who doubled up with family members faced benefit reductions, giving them and their families reasons to drift apart. Rent control legislation, which stopped apartment building construction, backfired on the poor. While it kept rents low, a surplus of apartment seekers gave landlords the luxury of picking and choosing tenants: In competition with stable tenants able to pay rent on time and unlikely to damage property, the down-and-out had no chance. The housing shortage and rising land prices also spurred gentrification of old neighborhoods that housed the destitute, leading to their eviction. Even tenant rights legislation backfired. Because it prevented landlords from evicting the prostitutes, drug dealers, and rowdy tenants who caused good tenants to leave, they stopped renting to anyone with the potential to be troublesome. When governments extended rent control and tenant rights to rooming

houses and single-room occupancy hotels, and tightened housing regulations to force landlords to better maintain the dwindling stock of decaying housing, the landlords themselves vacated. Much of the low-income housing was lost to fires; often arson was suspected.

With so much low-rent housing demolished, and so much of the balance 7 reserved for respectable tenants, the poorest of the poor had no place to go but the streets, newly freed up through the repeal of vagrancy laws. To those with addictions, this dark cloud had a silver lining: Without accommodation costs, they could devote more of their meagre income to their habit.

Those we call homeless are not a homogeneous lot and, often, not even home- 8 less. In many cities, the majority of panhandlers, squeegee kids, and other street people that we come across have fairly conventional abodes. Meanwhile, the majority of the truly homeless escape our view: In a 1989 study of Chicago's homeless, interviewers found most to be "neat and clean" and only 20 per cent to panhandle or take handouts. Most homeless do not make a career of it: They find themselves on the street following some unmanageable stress—the death or ill-ness of a loved one, the breakup of a relationship, debt, and legal problems top the list—and then they pull out of it. Yet most remain deeply disturbed. According to a recent study of Toronto's homeless by the Clarke Institute of Psychiatry, two-thirds have a lifetime diagnosis of mental illness, and two-thirds suffer from alcohol and substance abuse. Only one homeless person in seven in this highly vulnerable population suffers from neither.

Although most are mentally ill, few are seriously so. Only about 10 per cent of 9 the homeless population has suffered from some severe mental illness, most often not the schizophrenia we associate with the homeless but a dark depression. While most of the severely ill lack proper treatment, few belong in institutions. The vast majority of mentally ill people, today as before deinstitutionalization, live in the community. Only today we've made the pavement the only practical housing choice for all too many of them.

The more important characteristics of the homeless—whether or not they're 10 mentally ill—are that they have fewer work skills, fewer social skills, and less resourcefulness than the housed population. They have difficulty maintaining relationships with friends and family. Almost half reported that they could rely on "no one" in their lives. Only four per cent were married or in common-law rela-tionships. All this speaks to their lack of community and numbing sense of isola-tion—conditions that, above all, explain much of the social pathology that is homelessness. Being society's least valued members, they are the first to be fired, the last to be hired, those most shunned in civil society, modern lepers.

Those who live on the streets do not appear as a line item in government 11 books, except for the odd outreach program. Neither do taxpayers take a direct hit. Some resent, others pity, the panhandlers; some fear the talkers and ravers that they encounter, but most see the homeless as an unsettling but cost-free fixture on the urban landscape.

12   Failing to deal with homelessness is a false economy, quite apart from the great moral costs of turning our backs on this defenceless population. The homeless cast a pall on our use of our cities, prompting parents and their children to abandon the public parks they frequent, pedestrians to avoid places they might be accosted, and merchants to relocate. The homeless show up big time in our penal system—30 per cent have spent time in police stations or jail in the previous year—and in our health care budget.

13   As shown in a study published in June in the *New England Journal of Medicine*—the first extensive documentation of the impact of homelessness on the health care system—the homeless have been exacting a silent toll on a society that ignores their plight. The homeless at New York City's public hospitals stayed an average of 4.1 days longer, and cost an average of $2,414 more per admission, than low-income patients who had homes. One group of psychiatric patients, whom clinicians believed couldn't be discharged safely, averaged 70 days more than otherwise called for. At the city's flagship Bellevue Hospital, nearly half the admissions were homeless. "The homeless account for less than one-half of one per cent of the city's population, but they are having a huge impact on the health care system," said Sharon Salit, the report's lead author. "The extra costs for a single hospital admission are as much as the annual welfare rental allowance for a single individual in New York."

14   About half the homeless admissions required treatment for mental illness or substance abuse, and half for skin disorders, respiratory complaints, trauma, and parasites—problems generally regarded as preventable among other populations. "For want of a place to clean between their toes, change their shoes and socks, and elevate their feet when they get swollen, homeless patients get infections in their feet" that often become a chronic condition called cellulitis, said Dr. Lewis Goldfrank, Bellevue's director of emergency medicine. "We almost never see that among people who have homes." A 1996 study of Los Angeles's homeless warned that TB could reach epidemic proportions.

15   The homeless need medical care, especially psychiatric care. We must generously fund outpatient programs: Just as nobody would release Alzheimer's patients onto the streets without adequate treatment and supervision, we cannot let these vulnerable people fend for themselves. We must also ensure that those few who are a danger to themselves or to the public receive compassionate care inside an institution. But most of all, the homeless need homes and an end to their alienation, without which their condition cannot improve. Most homeless advocates, while understanding the need for more housing, too often seek quick-fix solutions in government housing, forgetting that the last thing the homeless need is to be warehoused in anonymous public housing supervised by a faceless government bureaucracy. We must require the homeless to engage the rest of us.

The way out of homelessness begins by backing out of the same path that cre- 16
ated it. We must restore vagrancy laws, both to safeguard the public sphere for us
all and to require housing for those unable to properly look after themselves. To
shelter those evicted from the streets, welfare must provide the down-and-out with
housing vouchers that can be used anywhere, not just in shelters but in exchange
for that couch in a relative's living room. (To discourage a black market, each
voucher should identify its recipient and be dated, and the landlords, rooming
houses, and others who accept vouchers without housing the voucher recipient
should be liable to fines.) Generous vouchers will minimize substandard housing.

To encourage friends and relatives to take the homeless in and other landlords 17
to re-enter the business, we must throw out rules preventing easy evictions of tenants who disturb the peace or otherwise fail to meet their obligations to their
neighbours and the landlord (even publicly funded hostels and shelters routinely
evict or refuse to admit disorderly occupants). This accountability will prod some
of today's homeless—whom the Clark Institute found to be more aggressive, anti-
social, moody, irritable, and less open to taking responsibility for change—to get
along with those around them, as their counterparts once did.

While the government re-regulates the use of public spaces, it should deregu- 18
late the housing market to let the homeless find inexpensive housing niches for
themselves. The largest sources of appropriate housing—ones that many munic-
ipalities wrongly ban—are basement apartments and other occupancies in residential districts.

Because most homeless individuals are neat, clean, and nonviolent, many 19
would find shelter in middle- and lower-class residences willing to set aside some
space in exchange for the housing voucher. Such a relationship would especially
appeal to homeowners on fixed incomes, who find themselves single and perhaps
frail in a large home, and who themselves need a little income and an occasional
helping hand with household chores.

We live in times of plenty, with the means and the obligation to humanely look 20
after our most unfortunate members of society. In helping others, we will also
help ourselves through more hospitable streets, a healthier society, and the personal gratification of doing our share to help people who have fallen on hard
times, and not always from sins of their own making.

QUESTIONS

Understanding the message: Comprehension

1. Prior to the 1980s, where did the poorest people live, according to the article?

2. What did the term "urban renewal" mean?

3. Why couldn't the very poor continue to rent in low-rent buildings, even after urban renewal had taken place?

4. In what way is Solomon's portrayal of the homeless population different from the stereotype of the homeless?

Examining the structure and details: Analysis

1. What method of organization does Solomon use in his argument? In what way does it differ from the typical order for this type of essay?

2. Does Solomon use inductive reasoning, deductive reasoning, or both? Where?

3. Which other rhetorical modes does Solomon use in his argument?

Formulating a response: Inference and interpretation

1. Re-read paragraph 5. What is the effect of this barrage of statistics on the reader? Do you think this technique is successful? Why or why not?

2. Who is Solomon's audience for this article?

3. How does Solomon use appeals to emotion as a means to gain sympathy for the homeless? Look at his use of adjectives and figurative language. How effective is he in gaining your sympathy?

4. Examine the various reference sources that Solomon cites in his essay. How effective are his sources? Are there any important sources of information you think are lacking in this argument?

5. Solomon waits until paragraph 16 of a 20-paragraph essay to outline his plan to reduce homelessness. Why does he wait so long?

Essay questions

1. What is your own solution to the homeless problem that plagues big cities? Is there a way to reduce homelessness that won't cost taxpayers even more money?

2. How much of our personality and sense of self is determined by the home in which we live? Write an essay in which you examine the impact that living in different types of dwellings might have on people.

3. What is Solomon's plan to reduce homelessness? Is it feasible? Explain why or why not in an essay that draws examples from the article.

VOCABULARY

euphemism: polite or vague term used to replace one that is considered harsh, rude, or inappropriate

gentrification: raising the value of a neighbourhood through renovations, new housing, cleaning up, and so on

pall: shadow, gloominess

At Play in the Fields of the Savage God: The Art of Suicide in Popular Culture

by Moira Farr (b. 1958)

Moira Farr has been a writer and editor since 1985, when she completed the graduate journalism program at Ryerson University. Her feature articles, essays, and reviews have appeared in a variety of publications, including Toronto Life, *the* Globe and Mail, Utne Reader, This Magazine, *and* Chatelaine. *Formerly, she served as managing editor of* This Magazine *and senior editor of* Equinox. *Her first book,* After Daniel: A Suicide Survivor's Tale, *was published in 1999. She's currently doing freelance writing and working on another book.*

PRE-READING

Farr begins her article by discussing the 1994 suicide of rock star Kurt Cobain. Did you read or hear about Cobain's suicide? If so, how did the rock star's death affect you? Are you aware of any other influential public figures who have committed suicide? Most of us have some knowledge of suicide even if we haven't been touched by it directly. What causes people to commit suicide? Is the impulse something genetically ingrained? This excerpt is taken from Farr's book, *After Daniel: A Suicide Survivor's Tale*, in which she examines her own reaction to the suicide of her lover, Daniel Jones, and the larger issue of suicide in society. In this article, she discusses what she perceives to be a self-destructive impulse within us all.

---

1   April 1996. Sitting in a movie theatre at the Carlton Cinema in Toronto, watching director Bruce McDonald's darkly comic rock' n' road film *Hard Core Logo*. The mock documentary traces the archetypal rise and fall of a punk band, complete with clashing egos, artistic dissonance, chaotic if-it's-Tuesday-it-must-be-Saskatoon life style, sleazy music-business double-crosses, and drug and alcohol abuse. It's scuzzy territory, similar to what Daniel explored in his novel *1978*. Indeed, we are told in the film that the fictional band Hard Core Logo, originally the creation of Vancouver author Michael Turner, whose novel bears the same name, launched itself that year. Depending on how you view it, it was punk's zenith, or nadir.

The film seems like the mother of all Daniel sightings to me. The band's 2
Mohawk-hairstyled, ear-pierced lead singer, Joe Dick—played by Hugh Dillon,
real-life lead singer of The Headstones—bears an extraordinary resemblance to
Daniel, or so it seemed to me at the time. It's partly projection on my part; with a
full head of hair, Dillon's likeness would probably fade.

By the end of the film, I've acclimatized somewhat to the look-alike effect and 3
have become absorbed in the plot. Then, in the film's final scene, the camera
tracks a jumpy, plastered Joe Dick out to the sidewalk in front of the hall where
he and the band have just performed, apparently for the last time, having ended
the show with a violent onstage explosion of hostilities that have festered for years
between Dick and his best-buddy guitarist Billy Tallent. The latter has announced
he is jumping ship (a ship that is sinking anyway, if only Dick would grow up and
admit it) to pursue fame and fortune with a high-profile American band. In the
middle of being interviewed, Dick pulls a handgun from the pocket of his coat,
shoots himself in the head, and falls, blood pouring onto the sidewalk, to the
gasps, groans, and "oh my gods" of the film's faux documentarians and members
of the live audience.

The whole thing leaves me spooked. My friend Karen and I walk silently out of 4
the theatre. "That guy really looked like Daniel," I finally say. "Yeah," Karen replies
in a solemn, I-wish-it-wasn't-true tone, "I know." Obviously, the suicide packed a
mean punch that I, and most of the audience, had not anticipated—though foreshadowing details are in fact littered throughout the film, as I discovered when,
out of curiosity, I rented the video recently. Unlike life, you can view a movie
again, fast-forwarding and rewinding to your heart's content, seeing what you
may have missed, confirming or discarding your suspicions.

Dick makes at least two references to Kurt Cobain in the course of the film. 5
One song on the soundtrack is called "Suicide Club," another, "Something Is
Gonna Die Tonight." During an over-the-top group acid trip at the secluded
country house of a burnt-out punk icon named Bucky Haight, there's a half-
second flash of Dick putting a gun to his head, and during the final performance,
he makes the gesture again. Hard to imagine that the final outcome of all this
would be such a surprise, but suicide can really be like that. Besides, the world of
punk—and a good portion of modern and postmodern art, music, and literature
aimed at and emanating from people under 30—are utterly ruled by the poses
and attitudes of despair. It's part of the general cultural blur, the barely noticed
psychological wallpaper that adorns youthful waking lives *en masse*. That it might
be more than a pose in some cases is cause for denial.

Yet it is unrealistic to imagine that out of all that stylized anger and aggression, 6
there would not be casualties, and there are. We may want to hope that everyone
can leave their fuck-the-world attitudes behind at the bar or concert venue and go
off to happy, harmonious lives, wholesome hobbies, unperturbed relationships,

purposeful work. We don't particularly want to face the fact that many come to these gatherings to let off steam precisely because they do not lead such lives. Young people are naturally drawn to music that channels the tempestuous emotions they feel or, conversely, jump-starts them out of their protective numbness, and ideally transcends it. But in much of punk, and other newer incarnations of alternative music, it can amount to just revelling in those potentially dangerous emotions.

7   Where did this notion that self-destruction is cool originate? It goes a long way back: The contemporary incarnation, from the "heroin chic" of high-fashion photo spreads to the proliferation of rock bands that glory in depression and suicide, has its roots in the Romantic era. Goethe's *The Sorrows of Young Werther* sparked a notorious spate of suicides among the poetically disposed youth of Europe in the early nineteenth century; the widely observed phenomenon of similar "contagion"-style suicides in the generations since has thus been labelled "the Werther effect."

8   With the end of official Romanticism in the early twentieth century, argues Alfred Alvarez in *The Savage God*, "suicide did not disappear from the arts; instead it became a part of their fabric. . . . Because it threw a sharp, narrow, intensely dramatic light on life at its extreme moments, suicide became the preoccupation of certain kinds of post-Romantic writers, like Dostoevsky, who were the forerunners of twentieth-century art." Fast-forward to the post-, or semi-, or techno-literate end of the century, and find that despair-fuelled rock musicians and other assorted film or TV-celebrities have supplanted writers as the Werthers of our age. Their deaths by suicide or other forms of violence can spark mass response. After the suicide of Kurt Cobain in 1994, public mourning among young people reached fever pitch, and a handful of youth suicides was documented throughout North America. However, it is interesting to note that the youth suicide rate in the Seattle area where he lived and died never skyrocketed as feared. Experts who studied the statistics have since speculated that the large-scale mobilization of crisis teams in high schools, and suicide-prevention measures such as distress phone lines exclusively for young people, may actually have had the intended preventative effect.

9   From the zealots of Masada to the kamikaze pilots of Japan; from today's Arab suicide bombers to Jonestown's spiked-Kool-Aid drinkers and the Heaven's Gate cult members following the Hale-Bopp comet to a better life aboard a spaceship— the inspirations and rationales may change, but the paradoxical human impulse to immortalize oneself through an early and exalted death has probably always been with us. The history of human culture is littered with ample evidence of a collective self-destructive instinct, a drive that impels us to enact our own deaths for various glorified reasons, or at least, to fantasize about doing so. As a species, we also groom certain individuals for self-sacrifice to quell the group's disturbing urges. Anyone writing about human psychology from Freud and Jung on has explored one or another aspect of this disturbing truth.

Respond in Writing   NE

The connection between such aggressive urges and suicidality, from ancient 10 times to the present, cannot be overlooked. Many well-preserved, millennia-old bodies exhumed from boggy graves throughout Europe appear to have met their deaths in some kind of ritual sacrifice. Some are young, strong specimens of humanity, wearing the garb of royalty or at least nobility, and surrounded by valuable, symbolic objects; they bear no marks of having struggled in their final moments. They have lain peacefully for centuries, on grounds that appear to have borne sacred significance for the tribal groups to which they belonged. In their resplendent clothing and jewellery, they keep the secrets of their lives and deaths, but scientists speculate that at least some of these people died their apparently ritualized deaths willingly. Perhaps if they lived today, they'd pursue careers as poets or rock musicians.

It is a powerful force, this curious and largely unconscious desire to live and die 11 nobly and famously, and to be remembered into eternity, one that may well be the collective emotional backdrop against which many an individual suicidal drama or fantasy is played out. In our age, the psychological mechanisms at work in these fantasies may also have to do with imagining how one will look to the living— heroic, forever young—après one's own self-styled entry into *rigor mortis*, rather than with any belief in a halcyon afterlife.

And so the famous, in their untimely deaths, provide some unconscious grat- 12 ification to us. Even as the unfamous fans vicariously grieve, they plug into a kind of electrical surge of feeling that make them feel more alive, at one somehow with large and powerful forces beyond anyone's control. Perhaps the Kurt Cobains of the world hook themselves and their personal confusions, their depressions, and addictions, to this same charge, creating a gateway through which to usher in their own suicides. The individual circumstances of each death may be unique, bearing all the hallmarks of contemporary culture—guns, street drugs, antidepressants, familial chaos, dissolute celebrity lifestyles—but the impulse comes from a primal place in the human psyche.

I can't say to what degree these kinds of unconscious motives operated in 13 Daniel's case. He was familiar with the culture of suicide, read about it as extensively as he did other subjects, might even be said to have possessed an aesthete's refined appreciation of it and the nihilistic, existentialist ideas that have somehow justified it in this century. I maintain my view that these "philosophies" and "principles" are no useful guides to a depressed individual, that they merely mask underlying savage, self-destructive impulses that cannot be successfully explained or rationalized intellectually. This of course hasn't stopped a great many writers from attempting to do so, in the wake of wars, holocausts, pogroms, and other social cataclysms that traumatize, depress, and have historically given rise to such ideas.

Is it really any wonder then, that when it comes to suicide, we like to watch? 14 *Hard Core Logo* wasn't the first or the last depiction of suicide in films, TV, theatre, books, and elsewhere to catch me off guard. Only a few weeks after Daniel's death, a well-meaning friend invited me to see a play with her, obviously hoping to take my mind off my troubles for a few hours. Not long into the performance we realized that suicide was a major subplot. I think it upset my friend more than it did me. "Are you okay?" she whispered, holding my arm as though she would lift me from my seat and briskly escort me out of the theatre if I answered no. It was almost funny. I assured her that I was fine. I think I was still too numb to care what the play had to say about anything, let alone suicide.

15 Later, in April, when I was visiting my sister in London, England, she set me up one evening with a plate of comfort food in front of the TV, to watch an episode of the BBC police drama *Inside the Line*. Midway through the episode, a young policewoman leaps to her death from a Thames River tour boat; I laughed to see my sister practically lunge across the living room for the off button. In the 1990s, there's clearly little point trying to protect a mourner from reminders of suicide and its awful prevalence.

16 The problems of navigating the outside world in the middle of your grief, without stepping on any landmines that could rip uninvited into your private emotional life, is more pressing and real than it has ever been, precisely because of the inescapability of these dime-a-dozen references. For better or worse, individuals in contemporary society have a relationship with the mass media; we bond and respond according to our own personality and prevailing mood. This multiple-personality Media can be a breezy, entertaining buddy, a concerned and thorough teacher bent on enlightening and informing, a shameless manipulator, a brainless twit, an overbearing nuisance, and worse, an insensitive, torturing bully.

17 Based on my own experience, I'm tempted to counsel anyone who is going through the early stages of such grief to avoid films, newspapers, and TV altogether. Although unaffected by my sister's television show or the play, I *was* stunned to find my own private mourning suddenly overlaid by mass public shock at the violent, self-inflicted death of Kurt Cobain. I winced and looked away from large close-ups of his haunted face staring from the covers of magazines everywhere. I could barely listen to news clips of Courtney Love's raw, excoriating public reading of his suicide note; I'd already read one too many, and didn't think I had any more to learn, or any more I could take, of the genre. (Now, I hear it is possible to buy T-shirts with Cobain's suicide note printed on them.)

18 It's not that exploring suicide, even facetiously, is inherently wrong or dangerous. Studies on the links between fictional, filmed, or televised treatments of suicide and its actual incidence have yielded contradictory results. Some artists do seriously explore or touch on the subject. Our death instincts, in the form of self-destructive impulses, are real, and often denied in our day-to-day lives, sometimes astonishingly so, given how prevalent random violence has become. So why not

explore these impulses and the circumstances that surround them, this dangerous real terrain?

I've noted my own feelings and reactions too, for as with *Hard Core Logo*, I 19 found as I watched other films that I rarely saw it coming, and yet couldn't believe that was the case, once it had happened. My emotional response varied greatly. When I watched the film *Carrington*, based on the real life story of Dora Carrington, a Bloomsbury denizen who had a long and curiously intense relationship with the homosexual Lytton Strachey, I felt as though the wind had been kicked out of me when the scene came in which the painter Carrington, played by Emma Thompson, calmly prepares to shoot herself. My heart sank as she briskly gathered up her brushes, paints, and palette and threw them into a garbage can in her studio, moments before she matter-of-factly positions the long-barreled gun against her chest and, still standing, pulls the trigger.

Something about this image of the artist simply giving up, saying, "To hell with 20 it, I can't do it anymore," resonated in a terrible way for me. How difficult it seems for so many of the gifted to find the conditions in which they can make their art without destroying themselves. How many great creations in images, music, and words have been lost to the world because of suicide? Naturally, I was thinking of Daniel, and all of his lost words.

More than anything, beyond the particular, personal ways I have come to view 21 Daniel's suicide, I have been perplexed as I contemplated all the stories about suicide, in a riot of forms, that have sped past me on the hectic currents of popular culture over the past five years. Why is it, I have wanted to know, that while we seem immersed in images of suicide and attitudes of despair, we are stunned, disbelieving, at a complete loss to understand what happened when a real suicide is forced upon us? Something still just doesn't add up.

QUESTIONS

Understanding the message: Comprehension

1. What are the connections between Farr's own life and the film *Hard Core Logo*?

2. How many different models for suicide does Farr present? What (or who) are they?

3. Explain in your own words why certain individuals in society are groomed "for self sacrifice," according to Farr. How is ritual sacrifice connected to suicide in her theory?

4. Why are there so many media depictions of suicide, according to Farr?

5. Do media depictions of suicide increase real-life suicides?

Examining the structure and details: Analysis

1. What different types of evidence does Farr provide to prove her points? Which rhetorical techniques does she use to support her ideas?

2. How does Farr link her introduction and conclusion?

3. How much of Farr's evidence is based on personal experience? How much is based on factual evidence? Is the balance effective? Why or why not?

4. Is Farr's reasoning more inductive or deductive? Explain.

Formulating a response: Inference and interpretation

1. Why do you think Farr begins with a personal recollection before moving to a larger examination of suicide in society? What effect does this opening have?

2. What is Farr's thesis in this essay? Do you agree with it? Why or why not?

3. Who do you think is Farr's intended audience in this article? Is her tone appropriate for this audience? Why or why not?

4. Does Farr suggest that suicide is caused more often by some instinctive impulse (nature) or circumstances within society (nurture)? Defend your answer with examples from the text.

Essay questions

1. How much of a problem among teenagers today is the self-destructive impulse that Farr writes about? Write an argument essay in which you discuss different ways to reduce or eliminate these self-destructive behaviours.

2. Think of a film, television program, or book you know that deals with the issue of violence or suicide. Write a critique of the portrayal, discussing how realistic the characters and situations are that lead to the violent or suicidal behaviour.

3. In what ways is Farr's own experience with suicide reflected in the various other examples she provides? How is her personal situation an illustration of her theory about suicide? Provide examples from the selection in formulating your essay response.

VOCABULARY

Bruce McDonald's *Hard Core Logo*: 1996 film that documents a reunion tour of a Vancouver punk rock band

archetypal: serving as a model or pattern for all

dissonance: lack of harmony

zenith: highest possible point; peak

nadir: lowest possible point

faux: fake, fictional

foreshadowing: predicting, warning

en masse: as a group; collectively

incarnation: representation; embodiment

Dostoevsky: Russian novelist (1821–81), author of *Crime and Punishment*

supplanted: replaced

Masada: Jewish fortress where in 73 A.D. about 1000 people chose suicide over capture by Russian forcres

kamikaze pilots of Japan: suicide pilots of World War II who crashed their planes into targets

Jonestown: site in Guyana where in 1978 913 members of a utopian community under Jim Jones committed suicide

Heaven's Gate cult members: 39 people who in 1997 committed suicide at a site in New Mexico

exalted: raised in status; praised

Freud, Jung: Sigmund Freud (1856–1939), Austrian psychologist, often called the father of psychoanalysis; Carl Jung (1875–1961), Swiss psychologist known for his work on the collective unconscious

après: after

rigor mortis: bodily stiffness that occurs after death

dissolute: causing death or disintegration

primal: basic, instinctive

aesthete: someone highly aware of the beauty in art, literature, etc.

nihilistic: an attitude of negativism, one that rejects norms

existentialist: believing life has no meaning

pogroms: organized massacres

excoriating: critical, berating

facetiously: amusingly, frivolously

CHAPTER 12

Fiction Readings and Questions

The Story of an Hour
by Kate Chopin (1851–1904)

Born in St. Louis, Missouri, Kate Chopin is known today as one of the most signifi-cant figures in the American women's movement. She was a typical Southern mother and wife who lived with her husband and family in New Orleans and on a cotton plantation. In 1882, after her husband's death, she turned to writing fiction, begin-ning with children's stories and eventually moving to the feminist stories for which she is famous, in Bayou Folk *(1884) and* A Night in Acadie *(1897). Perhaps her most acclaimed work is* The Awakening *(1899), a novella that traces a married woman's inner turmoil when she is sexually attracted to, and falls in love with, a man other than her husband. The book created a stir and was greeted with such moral outrage at the time of publication that it virtually ended Chopin's career. Today, it is renowned as one of the quintessential stories reflecting women's struggles.*

PRE-READING

In the following story (published in 1894) Chopin writes about a woman's reaction after she learns that her husband has been killed in a train crash. As you read through, think about the different ways that people cope with dev-astating news and personal tragedy. What kind of behaviour would you expect to see from someone who'd just lost a spouse?

1   Knowing that Mrs. Mallard was afflicted with a heart trouble, great care was taken to break to her as gently as possible the news of her husband's death.

2   It was her sister Josephine who told her, in broken sentences; veiled hints that revealed in half concealing. Her husband's friend Richards was there, too, near her. It was he who had been in the newspaper office when intelligence of the railroad disaster was received with Brently Mallard's name leading the list of "killed." He had only taken the time to assure himself of its truth by a second telegram, and had hastened to forestall any less careful, less tender friend in bearing the sad message.

3   She did not hear the story as many women have heard the same, with a paralyzed inability to accept its significance. She wept at once, with sudden, wild abandonment, in her sister's arms. When the storm of grief had spent itself she went away to her room alone. She would have no one follow her.

4   There stood, facing the open window, a comfortable, roomy armchair. Into this she sank, pressed down by a physical exhaustion that haunted her body and seemed to reach into her soul.

5   She could see in the open square before her house the tops of trees that were all aquiver with the new spring life. The delicious breath of rain was in the air. In the street below a peddler was crying his wares. The notes of a distant song which some one was singing reached her faintly, and countless sparrows were twittering in the eaves.

6   There were patches of blue sky showing here and there through the clouds that had met and piled one above the other in the west facing her window.

7   She sat with her head thrown back upon the cushion of the chair, quite motionless, except when a sob came up into her throat and shook her, as a child who has cried itself to sleep continues to sob in its dreams.

8   She was young, with a fair, calm face, whose lines bespoke repression and even a certain strength. But now there was a dull stare in her eyes, whose gaze was fixed away off yonder on one of those patches of blue sky. It was not a glance of reflection, but rather indicated a suspension of intelligent thought.

9   There was something coming to her and she was waiting for it, fearfully. What was it? She did not know; it was too subtle and elusive to name. But she felt it, creeping out of the sky, reaching toward her through the sounds, the scents, the color that filled the air.

10   Now her bosom rose and fell tumultuously. She was beginning to recognize this thing that was approaching to possess her, and she was striving to beat it back with her will—as powerless as her two white slender hands would have been.

11   When she abandoned herself a little whispered word escaped her slightly parted lips. She said it over and over under her breath: "free, free, free!" The vacant stare and the look of terror that had followed it went from her eyes. They stayed keen and bright. Her pulses beat fast, and the coursing blood warmed and relaxed every inch of her body.

                                        RESPOND IN WRITING   N

She did not stop to ask if it were or were not a monstrous joy that held her. A 12
clear and exalted perception enabled her to dismiss the suggestion as trivial.

She knew that she would weep again when she saw the kind, tender hands 13
folded in death; the face that had never looked save with love upon her, fixed and
gray and dead. But she saw beyond that bitter moment a long procession of years
to come that would belong to her absolutely. And she opened and spread her arms
out to them in welcome.

There would be no one to live for her during those coming years; she would 14
live for herself. There would be no powerful will bending hers in that blind persistence with which men and women believe they have a right to impose a private
will upon a fellow-creature. A kind intention or a cruel intention made the act
seem no less a crime as she looked upon it in that brief moment of illumination.

And yet she had loved him—sometimes. Often she had not. What did it 15
matter! What could love, the unsolved mystery, count for in face of this possession of self-assertion which she suddenly recognized as the strongest impulse of
her being!

"Free! Body and soul free!" she kept whispering.   16

Josephine was kneeling before the closed door with her lips to the keyhole, 17
imploring for admission. "Louise, open the door! I beg; open the door—you will
make yourself ill. What are you doing, Louise? For heaven's sake open the door."

"Go away. I am not making myself ill." No; she was drinking in a very elixir of 18
life through that open window.

Her fancy was running riot along those days ahead of her. Spring days, and 19
summer days, and all sorts of days that would be her own. She breathed a quick
prayer that life might be long. It was only yesterday she had thought with a
shudder that life might be long.

She arose at length and opened the door to her sister's importunities. There 20
was a feverish triumph in her eyes, and she carried herself unwittingly like a god-
dess of Victory. She clasped her sister's waist, and together they descended the
stairs. Richards stood waiting for them at the bottom.

Some one was opening the front door with a latchkey. It was Brently Mallard 21
who entered, a little travel-stained, composedly carrying his gripsack and
umbrella. He had been far from the scene of the accident, and did not even know
there had been one. He stood amazed at Josephine's piercing cry; at Richards'
quick motion to screen him from the view of his wife.

But Richards was too late.   22

When the doctors came they said she had died of heart disease—of joy that kills. 23

QUESTIONS

Understanding the message: Comprehension

1. What are two possible ways to interpret the story's opening sentence?

2. Why did Richards, Mr. Mallard's friend, rush to tell Mrs. Mallard the news of her husband's death?

3. What is unusual about Mrs. Mallard's initial reaction to the news of her husband's death? In what way(s) is her reaction different from that of a typical Victorian wife?

4. Why might Mrs. Mallard think that her newfound joy was monstrous (paragraph 12)?

5. Explain the title.

Examining the writer's craft: Analysis and interpretation

1. Reread paragraphs 5 and 6. List the different things that Mrs. Mallard notices as she looks out the window. What is unusual about this list of items? What is the strongest sentiment being conveyed in these paragraphs? What do they suggest about Mrs. Mallard at this point?

2. In paragraph 9, Chopin writes, "There was something coming to her and she was waiting for it, fearfully." What do you think was coming to her? Why was she fearful of it?

3. What kind of relationship did Brently and Louise Mallard have? How would you describe their marriage? Refer to specific details from the story in your answer.

4. Did Mrs. Mallard love her husband? Why or why not?

5. Was Brently a good husband? How do you know?

6. Once her husband "dies," the descriptions of Mrs. Mallard suggest that she has taken on a new life. Look at the descriptions after her "change," in paragraphs 18 and 20 in particular. To what is Louise being compared?

7. What is the irony of the last line of the story? In what way is the line actually true?

Essay questions

1. In what way(s) has Mrs. Mallard been transformed by the end of the story? Using details from the story to support your contentions, describe how she changes from the beginning to the end of the story.

2. How is Mrs. Mallard's death foreshadowed in the story? Write an essay in which you discuss how her death is predicted through the details in the story.

3. Discuss the theme of freedom in "The Story of an Hour." Use specific references to the text in your essay.

VOCABULARY

intelligence: information

spent: completed, worn out

elusive: difficult to perceive or grasp

tumultuously: wildly agitated or disturbed

exalted: raised or increased in power or effect

save with love: except with love

elixir: potion (sometimes, a magic potion that confers immortality)

fancy: imagination, fantasies

importunities: insistent requests

unwittingly: unknowingly

The Loons

by Margaret Laurence (1926–87)

Firmly established as one of Canada's best-loved and most influential writers, Margaret Laurence was born in Neepawa, Manitoba, and her Prairie roots influenced her writing throughout her life. In fact, four of her major works (The Stone Angel, 1964; A Jest of God, 1966, which won the Governor General's Award; The Diviners, 1974; and A Bird in the House, 1970, from which this selection is taken) were set in Manawaka, the fictional counterpart to her home town. Once a reporter at the Winnipeg Citizen, *Laurence hit her stride with fiction writing. Other works include* This Side Jordan *(1960), which won the First Novel Award;* The Tomorrow-Tamer and Other Stories *(1964), and* The Fire-Dwellers *(1969). Laurence died of cancer at the age of 61, in Lakefield, Ontario.*

PRE-READING

In this selection from Laurence's collection of related stories, *A Bird in the House*, the narrator, a girl named Vanessa, remembers one summer at her family's cottage when the family took in a poor neighbour named Piquette. As you read, notice Vanessa's initial conflicted feelings and how they compare with her feelings once she gets to know Piquette, once Vanessa is a teenager, and finally, once she encounters Piquette years later. Have you ever experienced a change of heart after forming a first impression of someone? In what ways can superficial assessments of people be dangerous?

---

1   Just below Manawaka, where the Wachakwa River ran brown and noisy over the pebbles, the scrub oak and grey-green willow and chokecherry bushes grew in a dense thicket. In a clearing at the centre of the thicket stood the Tonnerre family's shack. The basis of this dwelling was a small square cabin made of poplar poles and chinked with mud, which had been built by Jules Tonnerre some fifty years before, when he came back from Batoche with a bullet in his thigh, the year that Riel was hung and the voices of the Metis entered their long silence. Jules had only intended to stay the winter in the Wachakwa Valley, but the family was still there in the thirties, when I was a child. As the Tonnerres had increased, their settlement had been added to, until the clearing at the foot of the town hill was a chaos of lean-tos, wooden packing cases, warped lumber, discarded car tires, ramshackle chicken coops, tangled strands of barbed wire and rusty tin cans.

RESPOND IN WRITING

The Tonnerres were French half-breeds, and among themselves they spoke a 2
patois that was neither Cree nor French. Their English was broken and full of
obscenities. They did not belong among the Cree of the Galloping Mountain
reservation, further north, and they did not belong among the Scots-Irish and
Ukrainians of Manawaka, either. They were, as my Grandmother MacLeod would
have put it, neither flesh, fowl, nor good salt herring. When their men were not
working at odd jobs or as section hands on the C.P.R., they lived on relief. In the
summers, one of the Tonnerre youngsters, with a face that seemed totally unfamiliar with laughter, would knock at the doors of the town's brick houses and
offer for sale a lard-pail full of bruised wild strawberries, and if he got as much as
a quarter he would grab the coin and run before the customer had time to change
her mind. Sometimes old Jules, or his son Lazarus, would get mixed up in a
Saturday-night brawl, and would hit out at whoever was nearest, or howl drunk-
enly among the offended shoppers on Main Street, and then the Mountie would
put them for the night in the barred cell underneath the Court House, and the
next morning they would be quiet again.

Piquette Tonnerre, the daughter of Lazarus, was in my class at school. She was 3
older than I, but she had failed several grades, perhaps because her attendance
had always been sporadic and her interest in schoolwork negligible. Part of the
reason she had missed a lot of school was that she had had tuberculosis of the
bone, and had once spent months in hospital. I knew this because my father was
the doctor who had looked after her. Her sickness was almost the only thing I
knew about her, however. Otherwise, she existed for me only as a vaguely embarrassing presence, with her hoarse voice and her clumsy limping walk and her
grimy cotton dresses that were always miles too long. I was neither friendly nor
unfriendly towards her. She dwelt and moved somewhere within my scope of
vision, but I did not actually notice her very much until that peculiar summer
when I was eleven.

"I don't know what to do about that kid," my father said at dinner one evening. 4
"Piquette Tonnerre, I mean. The damn bone's flared up again. I've had her in hospital for quite a while now, and it's under control all right, but I hate like the
dickens to send her home again."

"Couldn't you explain to her mother that she has to rest a lot?" my mother said. 5

"The mother's not there," my father replied. "She took off a few years back. 6
Can't say I blame her. Piquette cooks for them, and she says Lazarus would never
do anything for himself as long as she's there. Anyway, I don't think she'd take
much care of herself, once she got back. She's only thirteen, after all. Beth, I was
thinking—what about taking her up to Diamond Lake with us this summer? A
couple of months rest would give that bone a much better chance."

My mother looked stunned. 7

"But Ewen—what about Roddie and Vanessa?" 8

9   "She's not contagious," my father said. "And it would be company for Vanessa."

10   "Oh dear," my mother said in distress, "I'll bet anything she has nits in her hair."

11   "For Pete's sake," my father said crossly, "do you think Matron would let her stay in the hospital for all this time like that? Don't be silly, Beth."

12   Grandmother MacLeod, her delicately featured face as rigid as a cameo, now brought her mauve-veined hands together as though she were about to begin a prayer.

13   "Ewen, if that half-breed youngster comes along to Diamond Lake, I'm not going," she announced. "I'll go to Morag's for the summer."

14   I had trouble in stifling my urge to laugh, for my mother brightened visibly and quickly tried to hide it. If it came to a choice between Grandmother MacLeod and Piquette, Piquette would win hands down, nits or not.

15   "It might be quite nice for you, at that," she mused. "You haven't seen Morag for over a year, and you might enjoy being in the city for a while. Well, Ewen dear, you do what you think best. If you think it would do Piquette some good, then we'll be glad to have her, as long as she behaves herself."

16   So it happened that several weeks later, when we all piled into my father's old Nash, surrounded by suitcases and boxes of provisions and toys for my ten-month-old brother, Piquette was with us and Grandmother MacLeod, miraculously, was not. My father would only be staying at the cottage for a couple of weeks, for he had to get back to his practice, but the rest of us would stay at Diamond Lake until the end of August.

17   Our cottage was not named, as many were, "Dew Drop Inn" or "Bide-a-Wee," or "Bonnie Doon." The sign on the roadway bore in austere letters only our name, MacLeod. It was not a large cottage, but it was on the lakefront. You could look out the windows and see, through the filigree of the spruce trees, the water glistening greenly as the sun caught it. All around the cottage were ferns, and sharp-branched raspberry bushes, and moss that had grown over fallen tree trunks. If you looked carefully among the weeds and grass, you could find wild strawberry plants which were in white flower now and in another month would bear fruit, the fragrant globes hanging like miniature scarlet lanterns on the thin hairy stems. The two grey squirrels were still there, gossiping at us from the tall spruce beside the cottage, and by the end of the summer they would again be tame enough to take pieces of crust from my hands. The broad moose antlers that hung above the back door were a little more bleached and fissured after the winter, but otherwise everything was the same. I raced joyfully around my kingdom, greeting all the places I had not seen for a year. My brother, Roderick, who had not been born when we were here last summer, sat on the car rug in the sunshine and examined a brown spruce cone, meticulously turning it round and round in his small and curious hands. My mother and father toted the luggage from car to cottage, exclaiming over how well the place had wintered, no broken windows, thank goodness, no apparent damage from storm-felled branches or snow.

Only after I had finished looking around did I notice Piquette. She was sitting 18 on the swing, her lame leg held stiffly out, and her other foot scuffing the ground as she swung slowly back and forth. Her long hair hung black and straight around her shoulders, and her broad coarse-featured face bore no expression—it was blank, as though she no longer dwelt within her own skull, as though she had gone elsewhere. I approached her very hesitantly.

"Want to come and play?" 19

Piquette looked at me with a sudden flash of scorn. 20

"I ain't a kid," she said. 21

Wounded, I stamped angrily away, swearing I would not speak to her for the 22 rest of the summer. In the days that followed, however, Piquette began to interest me, and I began to want to interest her. My reasons did not appear bizarre to me. Unlikely as it may seem, I had only just realized that the Tonnerre family, whom I had always heard called half-breeds, were actually Indians, or as near as made no difference. My acquaintance with Indians was not extensive. I did not remember ever having seen a real Indian, and my new awareness that Piquette sprang from the people of Big Bear and Poundmaker, of Tecumseh, of the Iroquois who had eaten Father Brebeuf's heart—all this gave her an instant attraction in my eyes. I was a devoted reader of Pauline Johnson at this age, and sometimes would orate aloud and in an exalted voice, *West Wind, blow from your prairie nest; Blow from the mountains, blow from the west*—and so on. It seemed to me that Piquette must be in some way a daughter of the forest, a kind of junior prophetess of the wilds, who might impart to me, if I took the right approach, some of the secrets which she undoubtedly knew—where the whippoorwill made her nest, how the coyote reared her young, or whatever it was that it said in Hiawatha.

I set about gaining Piquette's trust. She was not allowed to go swimming, with 23 her bad leg, but I managed to lure her down to the beach—or rather, she came because there was nothing else to do. The water was always icy, for the lake was fed by springs, but I swam like a dog, thrashing my arms and legs around at such speed and with such an output of energy that I never grew cold. Finally, when I had had enough, I came out and sat beside Piquette on the sand. When she saw me approaching, her hand squashed flat the sand castle she had been building, and she looked at me sullenly, without speaking.

"Do you like this place?" I asked, after a while, intending to lead on from there 24 into the question of forest lore.

Piquette shrugged. "It's okay. Good as anywhere." 25

"I love it," I said. "We come here every summer." 26

"So what?" Her voice was distant, and I glanced at her uncertainly, wondering 27 what I could have said wrong.

"Do you want to come for a walk?" I asked her. "We wouldn't need to go far. If 28 you walk just around the point there, you come to a bay where great big reeds grow in the water, and all kinds of fish hang around there. Want to? Come on."

29   She shook her head.

30   "Your dad said I ain't supposed to do no more walking than I got to."

31   I tried another line.

32   "I bet you know a lot about the woods and all that, eh?" I began respectfully.

33   Piquette looked at me from her large dark unsmiling eyes.

34   "I don't know what in hell you're talkin' about," she replied. "You nuts or some-thin'? If you mean where my old man, and me, and all them live, you better shut up, by Jesus, you hear?"

35   I was startled and my feelings were hurt, but I had a kind of dogged persever-ance. I ignored her rebuff.

36   "You know something, Piquette? There's loons here, on this lake. You can see their nests just up the shore there, behind those logs. At night, you can hear them even from the cottage, but it's better to listen from the beach. My dad says we should listen and try to remember how they sound, because in a few years when more cottages are built at Diamond Lake and more people come to it, the loons will go away."

37   Piquette was picking up stones and snail shells and then dropping them again.

38   "Who gives a good goddamn?" she said.

39   It became increasingly obvious that, as an Indian, Piquette was a dead loss. That evening I went out by myself, scrambling through the bushes that overhung the steep path, my feet slipping on the fallen spruce needles that covered the ground. When I reached the shore, I walked along the firm damp sand to the small pier that my father had built, and sat down there. I heard someone else crashing through the undergrowth and the bracken, and for a moment I thought Piquette had changed her mind, but it turned out to be my father. He sat beside me on the pier and we waited, without speaking.

40   At night the lake was like black glass with a streak of amber which was the path of the moon. All around, the spruce trees grew tall and close-set, branches blackly sharp against the sky, which was lightened by a cold flickering of stars. Then the loons began their calling. They rose like phantom birds from the nests on the shore, and flew out onto the dark still surface of the water.

41   No one can ever describe that ululating sound, the crying of the loons, and no one who has heard it can ever forget it. Plaintive, and yet with a quality of chilling mockery, those voices belonged to a world separated by aeons from our neat world of summer cottages and the lighted lamps of home.

42   "They must have sounded just like that," my father remarked, "before any person ever set foot here."

43   Then he laughed. "You could say the same, of course, of sparrows, or chip-munks, but somehow it only strikes you that way with the loons."

44   "I know," I said.

45   Neither of us suspected that this would be the last time we would ever sit here together on the shore, listening. We stayed for perhaps half an hour, and then we

went back to the cottage. My mother was reading beside the fireplace. Piquette was looking at the burning birch log, and not doing anything.

"You should have come along," I said, although in fact I was glad she had not. 46

"Not me," Piquette said. "You wouldn' catch me walkin' way down there jus' for 47 a bunch of squawkin' birds."

Piquette and I remained ill at ease with one another. I felt I had somehow failed 48 my father, but I did not know what was the matter, nor why she would not or could not respond when I suggested exploring the woods or playing house. I thought it was probably her slow and difficult walking that held her back. She stayed most of the time in the cottage with my mother, helping her with the dishes or with Roddie, but hardly ever talking. Then the Duncans arrived at their cottage, and I spent my days with Mavis, who was my best friend. I could not reach Piquette at all, and I soon lost interest in trying. But all that summer she remained as both a reproach and a mystery to me.

That winter my father died of pneumonia, after less than a week's illness. For 49 some time I saw nothing around me, being completely immersed in my own pain and my mother's. When I looked outward once more, I scarcely noticed that Piquette Tonnerre was no longer at school. I do not remember seeing her at all until four years later, one Saturday night when Mavis and I were having Cokes in the Regal Café. The jukebox was booming like tuneful thunder, and beside it, leaning lightly on its chrome and its rainbow glass, was a girl.

Piquette must have been seventeen then, although she looked about twenty. I 50 stared at her, astounded that anyone could have changed so much. Her face, so stolid and expressionless before, was animated now with a gaiety that was almost violent. She laughed and talked very loudly with the boys around her. Her lipstick was bright carmine, and her hair was cut short and frizzily permed. She had not been pretty as a child, and she was not pretty now, for her features were still heavy and blunt. But her dark and slightly slanted eyes were beautiful, and her skin-tight skirt and orange sweater displayed to enviable advantage a soft and slender body.

She saw me, and walked over. She teetered a little, but it was not due to her 51 once-tubercular leg, for her limp was almost gone.

"Hi, Vanessa." Her voice still had the same hoarseness. "Long time no see, eh?" 52

"Hi," I said. "Where've you been keeping yourself, Piquette?" 53

"Oh, I been around," she said. "I been away almost two years now. Been all over 54 the place—Winnipeg, Regina, Saskatoon. Jesus, what I could tell you! I come back this summer, but I ain't stayin'. You kids goin' to the dance?"

"No," I said abruptly, for this was a sore point with me. I was fifteen, and 55 thought I was old enough to go to the Saturday-night dances at the Flamingo. My mother, however, thought otherwise.

"Y'oughta come," Piquette said. "I never miss one. It's just about the on'y thing 56 in this jerkwater town that's any fun. Boy, you couldn' catch me stayin' here. I don' give a shit about this place. It stinks."

57   She sat down beside me, and I caught the harsh oversweetness of her perfume.

58   "Listen, you wanna know something, Vanessa?" she confided, her voice only slightly blurred. "Your dad was the only person in Manawaka that ever done anything good to me."

59   I nodded speechlessly. I was certain she was speaking the truth. I knew a little more than I had that summer at Diamond Lake, but I could not reach her now any more than I had then. I was ashamed, ashamed of my own timidity, the frightened tendency to look the other way. Yet I felt no real warmth towards her— I only felt that I ought to, because of that distant summer and because my father had hoped she would be company for me, or perhaps that I would be for her, but it had not happened that way. At this moment, meeting her again, I had to admit that she repelled and embarrassed me, and I could not help despising the self-pity in her voice. I wished she would go away. I did not want to see her. I did not know what to say to her. It seemed that we had nothing to say to one another.

60   "I'll tell you something else," Piquette went on. "All the old bitches an' biddies in this town will sure be surprised. I'm gettin' married this fall—my boyfriend, he's an English fella, works in the stockyards in the city there, a very tall guy, got blond wavy hair. Gee, is he ever handsome. Got this real classy name. Alvin Gerald Cummings—some handle eh? They call him Al."

61   For the merest instant, then, I saw her. I really did see her, for the first and only time in all the years we had both lived in the same town. Her defiant face, momentarily, became unguarded and unmasked, and in her eyes there was a terrifying hope.

62   "Gee, Piquette—" I burst out awkwardly, "that's swell. That's really wonderful. Congratulations—good luck—I hope you'll be happy—"

63   As I mouthed the conventional phrases, I could only guess how great her need must have been, that she had been forced to seek the very things she so bitterly rejected.

64   When I was eighteen, I left Manawaka and went away to college. At the end of my first year, I came back home for the summer. I spent the first few days in talking non-stop with my mother, as we exchanged all the news that somehow had not found its way into letters—what had happened in my life and what had happened here in Manawaka while I was away. My mother searched her memory for events that concerned people I knew.

65   "Did I ever write you about Piquette Tonnerre, Vanessa?" she asked one morning.

66   "No, I don't think so," I replied. "Last I heard of her, she was going to marry some guy in the city. Is she still there?"

67   My mother looked perturbed, and it was a moment before she spoke, as though she did not know how to express what she had to tell and wished she did not need to try.

"She's dead," she said at last. Then, as I stared at her, "Oh, Vanessa, when it hap- 68
pened, I couldn't help thinking of her as she was that summer—so sullen and
gauche and badly dressed. I couldn't help wondering if we could have done something more at that time—but what could we do? She used to be around in the cottage there with me all day, and honestly, it was all I could do to get a word out of
her. She didn't even talk to your father very much, although I think she liked him,
in her way."

"What happened?" I asked. 69

"Either her husband left her, or she left him," my mother said. "I don't know 70
which. Anyway, she came back here with two youngsters, both only babies—they
must have been born very close together. She kept house, I guess, for Lazarus and
her brothers, down in the valley there, in the old Tonnerre place. I used to see her
on the street sometimes, but she never spoke to me. She'd put on an awful lot of
weight, and she looked a mess, to tell you the truth, a real slattern, dressed any old
how. She was up in court a couple of times—drunk and disorderly, of course. One
Saturday night last winter, during the coldest weather, Piquette was alone in the
shack with the children. The Tonnerres made home brew all the time, so I've
heard, and Lazarus said later she'd been drinking most of the day when he and the
boys went out that evening. They had an old woodstove there—you know the
kind, with exposed pipes. The shack caught fire. Piquette didn't get out, and neither did the children."

I did not say anything. As so often with Piquette, there did not seem to be any- 71
thing to say. There was a kind of silence around the image in my mind of the fire
and the snow, and I wished I could put from my memory the look that I had seen
once in Piquette's eyes.

I went up to Diamond Lake for a few days that summer, with Mavis and her 72
family. The MacLeod cottage had been sold after my father's death, and I did not
even go to look at it, not wanting to witness my long-ago kingdom possessed now
by strangers. But one evening I went down to the shore by myself.

The small pier which my father had built was gone, and in its place there was 73
a large and solid pier built by the government, for Galloping Mountain was now
a national park, and Diamond Lake had been re-named Lake Wapakata, for it was
felt than an Indian name would have a greater appeal to tourists. The one store
had become several dozen, and the settlement had all the attributes of a flourishing resort—hotels, a dance-hall, cafés with neon signs, the penetrating odours
of potato chips and hot dogs.

I sat on the government pier and looked out across the water. At night the lake 74
at least was the same as it had always been, darkly shining and bearing within its
black glass the streak of amber that was the path of the moon. There was no wind
that evening, and everything was quiet all around me. It seemed too quiet, and
then I realized that the loons were no longer here. I listened for some time, to

make sure, but never once did I hear that long-drawn call, half mocking and half plaintive, spearing through the stillness across the lake.

75   I did not know what had happened to the birds. Perhaps they had gone away to some far place of belonging. Perhaps they had been unable to find such a place, and had simply died out, having ceased to care any longer whether they lived or not.

76   I remember how Piquette had scorned to come along, when my father and I sat there and listened to the lake birds. It seemed to me now that in some unconscious and totally unrecognized way, Piquette might have been the only one, after all, who had heard the crying of the loons.

QUESTIONS

Understanding the message: Comprehension

1. What is Vanessa's initial expectation of how Piquette should be once they arrive at the cottage? Why is Vanessa disappointed?

2. What are the four distinct images of Piquette that Vanessa describes, first, at the beginning of the story (paragraph 3); next, at the cottage; next, when she meets Piquette four years after Vanessa's father dies; and finally, after Piquette has died?

3. Why does Vanessa's mother change her mind about allowing Piquette to join the family at the cottage?

4. Why is Piquette offended by Vanessa's question at the cottage, "I bet you know a lot about the woods and all that, eh?"

5. Does anyone in the story (including Piquette herself) have an accurate sense of Piquette's true self? In what way(s) does Piquette prevent people from getting to know the real person she is?

6. What does Vanessa mean when she says of the summer with Piqette at the family's cottage, "But all that summer she remained as both a reproach and a mystery to me"?

7. Why does Piquette marry Alvin Gerald Cummings?

Examining the writer's craft: Analysis and interpretation

1. In what way do Laurence's introductory paragraphs prepare us for Piquette's ultimate downfall? What message about Piquette's family history is Laurence conveying here?

2. Trace the different family members' reactions to the news that Piquette will be joining them at the cottage for the summer. How does each person perceive Piquette? What does each reaction tell us about the personality of the character?

3. In what way can we see Piquette as a symbol, and what does she symbolize? Why is it significant that Piquette's children die with her?

4. After Piquette refuses to engage in conversation with Vanessa at Diamond Lake, Vanessa comments, "It became increasingly obvious that, as an Indian, Piquette was a dead loss." What is the irony of this statement?

5. At the end of the story, Vanessa tells us that the name "Diamond Lake" had been changed to "Lake Wapakata." What is the significance of this change? In what way is it ironic?

6. Do you think that the fire that killed Piquette was deliberate (that perhaps she set it herself)? Why or why not? What evidence does the story provide to support either conclusion?

7. Reread the last paragraph of the story. In what way would Piquette have been "the only one, after all, who had heard the crying of the loons"? What is the connection between Piquette and the loons? In what way(s) are they similar?

Essay questions

1. Was Piquette's inability to fit comfortably into society caused more by the society in which she lived or by Piquette herself? Write an essay in which you use references to the story in your answer to this question.

2. Write an essay in which you discuss one of the following themes in this story: cultural identity, heritage, the past versus the present, or modern technology.

3. What is Piquette seeking throughout the story? How do her various transformations illustrate her quest? Why do you think she fails to achieve her goal?

VOCABULARY

Manawaka, Wachakwa River, Wachakwa Valley, Diamond Lake, Lake Wapakata: fictional locations in Manitoba

Batoche: site of a battle in 1885, near Prince Albert, Saskatchewan

Riel: Louis Riel, Metis leader of the Red River rebellion (1869–70) and Member of Parliament, executed in 1885 for his part in the Northwest Rebellion

Metis: a person of mixed European and Native Canadian ancestry

tyres: tires

patois: a French dialect

C.P.R.: Canadian Pacific Railway

relief: Employment Insurance

Nash: type of car

fissured: covered with thin lines, cracks, or grooves

Big Bear and Poundmaker: 19th-century Cree chiefs

Tecumseh: Shawnee chief

Father Brebeuf: Jesuit missionary who was killed by the Iroquois Indians in 1649

Pauline Johnson: early Native Canadian writer

Hiawatha: Iroquois chief, about whom Henry Wadsworth Longfellow wrote the poem *Song of Hiawatha* (1855)

ululating: howling, lamenting

stolid: impassive, not easily stirred

gauche: awkward, out of place

slattern: messy, slovenly woman

The Lost Salt Gift of Blood
by Alistair MacLeod (b. 1936)

Despite a fairly small output of fiction, Alistair MacLeod has from the beginning of his career been considered one of Canada's foremost writers of fiction. With the highly anticipated and universally acclaimed publication of his first novel, No Great Mischief, *in 2000, his reputation was secured for good. Born in North Battleford, Saskatchewan, MacLeod grew up in Nova Scotia. He worked in a variety of jobs (miner, logger, farmhand) before turning to teaching. After receiving his education at St. Francis Xavier University in 1960, he began a career in teaching that eventually led to his long-term professorship in English at the University of Windsor, from 1969 until his retirement in 2000. Most of his stories (as well as his novel) are set in Cape Breton, and he has been called one of the "most important chronicler[s] in fiction of the landscape and folkways of Cape Breton to appear on the Canadian literary scene." His collections include* The Lost Salt Gift of Blood *(1976),* As Birds Bring Forth the Sun and Other Stories *(1986), and* Island *(collected and new stories, 2000). He is married and has six children.*

PRE-READING

In this story from MacLeod's collection of the same name, a man returns to Newfoundland from western Canada. As the story progresses, we learn more about the narrator and the people he visits. Are there places from your past you'd like to revisit? What draws people back to places they left long ago? What connects people to others in ways that transcend time or space?

Now in the early evening the sun is flashing everything in gold. It bathes the blunt grey rocks that loom yearningly out toward Europe and it touches upon the stunted spruce and the low-lying lichens and the delicate hardy ferns and the ganglia-rooted moss and the tiny tough rock cranberries. The grey and slanting rain squalls have swept in from the sea and then departed with all the suddenness of surprise marauders. Everything before them and beneath them has been rapidly, briefly, and thoroughly drenched and now the clear droplets catch and hold the sun's infusion in a myriad of rainbow colours. Far beyond the harbour's mouth more tiny squalls seem to be forming, moving rapidly across the surface of the sea out there beyond land's end where the blue ocean turns to grey in rain and distance and the strain of eyes. Even farther out, somewhere beyond

1

Cape Spear lies Dublin and the Irish coast; far away but still the nearest land and closer now than is Toronto or Detroit to say nothing of North America's more western cities; seeming almost hazily visible now in imagination's mist.

2   Overhead the ivory white gulls wheel and cry, flashing also in the purity of the sun and the clean, freshly washed air. Sometimes they glide to the blue-green surface of the harbour, squawking and garbling; at times almost standing on their pink webbed feet as if they would walk on water, flapping their wings pompously against their breasts like over-conditioned he-men who have successfully passed their body-building courses. At other times they gather in lazy groups on the rocks above the harbour's entrance murmuring softly to themselves or looking also quietly out toward what must be Ireland and the vastness of the sea.

3   The harbour itself is very small and softly curving, seeming like a tiny, peaceful womb nurturing the life that now lies within it but which originated from without; came from without and through the narrow, rock-tight channel that admits the entering and withdrawing sea. That sea is entering again now, forcing itself gently but inevitably through the tightness of the opening and laving the rocky walls and rising and rolling into the harbour's inner cove. The dories rise at their moorings and the tide laps higher on the piles and advances upward toward the high-water marks upon the land; the running moon-drawn tides of spring.

4   Around the edges of the harbour brightly coloured houses dot the wet and glistening rocks. In some ways they seem almost like defiantly optimistic horseshoe nails; yellow and scarlet and green and pink; buoyantly yet firmly permanent in the grey unsundered rock.

5   At the harbour's entrance the small boys are jigging for the beautifully speckled salmon-pink sea trout. Barefootedly they stand on the tide-wet rocks flicking their wrists and sending their glistening lines in shimmering golden arcs out into the rising tide. Their voices mount excitedly as they shout to one another encouragement, advice, consolation. The trout fleck dazzlingly on their sides as they are drawn toward the rocks, turning to seeming silver as they flash within the sea.

6   It is all of this that I see now, standing at the final road's end of my twenty-five-hundred-mile journey. The road ends here—quite literally ends at the door of a now abandoned fishing shanty some six brief yards in front of where I stand. The shanty is grey and weather beaten with two boarded-up windows, vanishing wind-whipped shingles and a heavy rusted padlock chained fast to a twisted door. Piled before the twisted door and its equally twisted frame are some marker buoys, a small pile of rotted rope, a broken oar and an old and rust-flaked anchor.

7   The option of driving my small rented Volkswagen the remaining six yards and then negotiating a tight many-twists-of-the-steering-wheel turn still exists. I

would be then facing toward the west and could simply retrace the manner of my coming. I could easily drive away before anything might begin.

Instead I walk beyond the road's end and the fishing shanty and begin to 8 descend the rocky path that winds tortuously and narrowly along and down the cliff's edge to the sea. The small stones roll and turn and scrape beside and beneath my shoes and after only a few steps the leather is nicked and scratched. My toes press hard against its straining surface.

As I approach the actual water's edge four small boys are jumping excitedly 9 upon the glistening rocks. One of them has made a strike and is attempting to reel in his silver-turning prize. The other three have laid down their rods in their enthusiasm and are shouting encouragement and giving almost physical moral support: "Don't let him get away, John," they say. "Keep the line steady." "Hold the end of the rod up." "Reel in the slack." "Good." "What a dandy!"

Across the harbour's clear water another six or seven shout the same delirious 10 messages. The silver-turning fish is drawn toward the rock. In the shallows he flips and arcs, his flashing body breaking the water's surface as he walks upon his tail. The small fisherman has now his rod almost completely vertical. Its tip sings and vibrates high above his head while at his feet the trout spins and curves. Both of his hands are clenched around the rod and his knuckles strain white through the water-roughened redness of small-boy hands. He does not know whether he should relinquish the rod and grasp at the lurching trout or merely heave the rod backward and flip the fish behind him. Suddenly he decides upon the latter but even as he heaves his bare feet slide out from beneath him on the smooth wetness of the rock and he slips down into the water. With a pirouetting leap the trout turns glisteningly and tears itself free. In a darting flash of darkened greenness it rights itself with the regained water and is gone. "Oh damn!" says the small fisherman, struggling upright onto his rock. He bites his lower lip to hold back the tears welling within his eyes. There is a small trickle of blood coursing down from a tiny scratch on the inside of his wrist and he is wet up to his knees. I reach down to retrieve the rod and return it to him.

Suddenly a shout rises from the opposite shore. Another line zings tautly 11 through the water throwing off fine showers of iridescent droplets. The shouts and contagious excitement spread anew. "Don't let him get away!" "Good for you." "Hang on!" "Hang on!"

I am caught up in it myself and wish also to shout some enthusiastic advice but 12 I do not know what to say. The trout curves up from the water in a wriggling arch and lands behind the boys in the moss and lichen that grow down to the sea-washed rocks. They race to free it from the line and proclaim about its size.

On our side of the harbour the boys begin to talk. "Where do you live?" they 13 ask me and is it far away and is it bigger than St. John's? Awkwardly I try to tell them the nature of the North American midwest. In turn I ask them if they go to school. "Yes," they say. Some of them go to St. Bonaventure's which is the Catholic school and others to go Twilling Memorial. They are all in either grade four or grade five. All of them say that they like school and that they like their teachers.

14   The fishing is good they say and they come here almost every evening. "Yesterday I caught me a nine-pounder," says John. Eagerly they show me all of their simple equipment. The rods are of all varieties as are the lines. At the lines' ends the leaders are thin transparencies terminating in grotesque three-clustered hooks. A foot or so from each hook there is a silver spike knotted into the leader. Some of the boys say the trout are attracted by the flashing of the spike; others say that it acts only as a weight or sinker. No line is without one.

15   "Here, sir," says John, "have a go. Don't get your shoes wet." Standing on the slippery rocks in my smooth-soled shoes I twice attempt awkward casts. Both times the line loops up too high and the spike splashes down far short of the running, rising life of the channel.

16   "Just a flick of the wrist, sir," he says, "just a flick of the wrist. You'll soon get the hang of it." His hair is red and curly and his face is splashed with freckles and his eyes are clear and blue. I attempt three or four more casts and then pass the rod back to the hands where it belongs.

17   And now it is time for supper. The calls float down from the women standing in the doorways of the multi-coloured houses and obediently the small fishermen gather up their equipment and their catches and prepare to ascend the narrow upward-winding paths. The sun has descended deeper into the sea and the evening has become quite cool. I recognize this with surprise and a slight shiver. In spite of the advice given to me and my own precautions my feet are wet and chilled within my shoes. No place to be unless barefooted or in rubber boots. Perhaps for me no place at all.

18   As we lean into the steepness of the path my young companions continue to talk, their accents broad and Irish. One of them used to have a tame sea gull at his house, had it for seven years. His older brother found it on the rocks and brought it home. His grandfather called it Joey. "Because it talked so much," explains John. It died last week and they held a funeral about a mile away from the shore where there was enough soil to dig a grave. Along the shore itself it is almost solid rock and there is no ground for a grave. It's the same with people they say. All week they have been hopefully looking along the base of the cliffs for another sea gull but have not found one. You cannot kill a sea gull they say, the government protects them because they are scavengers and keep the harbours clean.

19   The path is narrow and we walk in single file. By the time we reach the shanty and my rented car I am wheezing and badly out of breath. So badly out of shape for a man of thirty-three; sauna baths do nothing for your wind. The boys walk easily, laughing and talking beside me. With polite enthusiasm they comment upon my car. Again there exists the possibility of restarting the car's engine and driving back

the road that I have come. After all, I have not seen a single adult except for the women calling down the news of supper. I stand and fiddle with my keys.

The appearance of the man and the dog is sudden and unexpected. We have 20 been so casual and unaware in front of the small automobile that we have neither seen nor heard their approach along the rock-worn road. The dog is short, stocky and black and white. White hair floats and feathers freely from his sturdy legs and paws as he trots along the rock looking expectantly out into the harbour. He takes no notice of me. The man is short and stocky as well and he also appears as black and white. His rubber boots are black and his dark heavy worsted trousers are supported by a broadly scarred and blackened belt. The buckle is shaped like a dory with a fisherman standing in the bow. Above the belt there is a dark navy woolen jersey and upon his head a toque of the same material. His hair beneath the toque is white as is the three-or-four-day stubble on his face. His eyes are blue and his hands heavy, gnarled, and misshapen. It is hard to tell from looking at him whether he is in his sixties, seventies, or eighties.

"Well, it is a nice evening tonight," he says, looking first at John and then to me. 21 "The barometer has not dropped so perhaps fair weather will continue for a day or two. It will be good for the fishing."

He picks a piece of gnarled grey driftwood from the roadside and swings it 22 slowly back and forth in his right hand. With desperate anticipation the dog dances back and forth before him, his intense eyes glittering at the stick. When it is thrown into the harbour he barks joyously and disappears, hurling himself down the bank in a scrambling avalanche of small stones. In seconds he reappears with only his head visible, cutting a silent but rapidly advancing *V* through the quiet serenity of the harbour. The boys run to the bank's edge and shout encouragement to him— much as they had been doing earlier for one another. "It's farther out," they cry, "to the right, to the right." Almost totally submerged, he cannot see the stick he swims to find. The boys toss stones in its general direction and he raises himself out of the water to see their landing splashdowns and to change his wide-waked course.

"How have you been?" asks the old man, reaching for a pipe and a pouch of 23 tobacco and then without waiting for an answer, "perhaps you'll stay for supper. There are just the three of us now."

We begin to walk along the road in the direction that he has come. Before long 24 the boys rejoin us accompanied by the dripping dog with the recovered stick. He waits for the old man to take it from him and then showers us all with a spray of water from his shaggy coat. The man pats and scratches the damp head and the dripping ears. He keeps the returned stick and thwacks it against his rubber boots as we continue to walk along the rocky road I have so recently travelled in my Volkswagen.

Within a few yards the houses begin to appear upon our left. Frame and flat- 25 roofed, they cling to the rocks looking down into the harbour. In storms their windows are splashed by the sea but now their bright colours are buoyantly brave in the shadows of the descending dusk. At the third gate, John, the man, and the dog turn in. I follow them. The remaining boys continue on; they wave and say, "So long."

26   The path that leads through the narrow whitewashed gate has had its stone worn smooth by the passing of countless feet. On either side there is a row of small, smooth stones, also neatly whitewashed, and seeming like a procession of large white eggs or tiny unbaked loaves of bread. Beyond these stones and also on either side, there are some cast-off tires also whitewashed and serving as flower beds. Within each whitened circumference the colourful low-lying flowers nod; some hardy strain of pansies or perhaps marigolds. The path leads on to the square green house, with its white borders and shutters. On one side of the wooden doorstep a skate blade has been nailed, for the wiping off of feet, and beyond the swinging screen door there is a porch which smells saltily of the sea. A variety of sou'westers and rubber boots and mitts and caps hang from the driven nails or lie at the base of the wooden walls.

27   Beyond the porch there is the kitchen where the woman is at work. All of us enter. The dog walks across the linoleum-covered floor, his nails clacking, and flings himself with a contented sigh beneath the wooden table. Almost instantly he is asleep, his coat still wet from his swim within the sea.

28   The kitchen is small. It has an iron cookstove, a table against one wall and three or four handmade chairs of wood. There is also a wooden rocking-chair covered by a cushion. The rockers are so thin from years of use that it is hard to believe they still function. Close by the table there is a wash-stand with two pails of water upon it. A wash-basin hangs from a driven nail in its side and above it is an old-fashioned mirrored medicine cabinet. There is also a large cupboard, a low-lying couch, and a window facing upon the sea. On the walls a barometer hangs as well as two pictures, one of a rather jaunty young couple taken many years ago. It is yellowed and rather indistinct; the woman in a long dress with her hair done up in ringlets, the man in a serge suit that is slightly too large for him and with a tweed cap pulled rakishly over his right eye. He has an accordion strapped over his shoulders and his hands are fanned out on the buttons and keys. The other picture is of the Christ-child. Beneath it is written, "Sweet Heart of Jesus Pray for Us."

29   The woman at the stove is tall and fine featured. Her grey hair is combed briskly back from her forehead and neatly coiled with a large pin at the base of her neck. Her eyes are as grey as the storm scud of the sea. Her age, like her husband's, is difficult to guess. She wears a blue print dress, a plain blue apron and low-heeled brown shoes. She is turning fish within a frying pan when we enter.

30   Her eyes contain only mild surprise as she first regards me. Then with recognition they glow in open hostility which in turn subsides and yields to self-control. She continues at the stove while the rest of us sit upon the chairs.

During the meal that follows we are reserved and shy in our lonely adult ways; 31 groping for and protecting what perhaps may be the only awful dignity we possess. John, unheedingly, talks on and on. He is in the fifth grade and is doing well. They are learning percentages and the mysteries of decimals; to change a percent to a decimal fraction you move the decimal point two places to the left and drop the percent sign. You always, always do so. They are learning the different breeds of domestic animals: the four main breeds of dairy cattle are Holstein, Ayrshire, Guernsey, and Jersey. He can play the mouth organ and will demonstrate after supper. He has twelve lobster traps of his own. They were originally broken ones thrown up on the rocky shore by storms. Ira, he says nodding toward the old man, helped him fix them, nailing on new lathes [sic] and knitting new headings. Now they are set along the rocks near the harbour's entrance. He is averaging a pound a trap and the "big" fishermen say that that is better than some of them are doing. He is saving his money in a little imitation keg that was also washed up on the shore. He would like to buy an outboard motor for the small reconditioned skiff he now uses to visit his traps. At present he has only oars.

"John here has the makings of a good fisherman," says the old man. "He's up 32 at five most every morning when I am putting on the fire. He and the dog are already out along the shore and back before I've made tea."

"When I was in Toronto," says John, "no one was ever up before seven. I would 33 make my own tea and wait. It was wonderful sad. There were gulls there though, flying over Toronto harbour. We went to see them on two Sundays."

After the supper we move the chairs back from the table. The woman clears 34 away the dishes and the old man turns on the radio. First he listens to the weather forecast and then turns to short wave where he picks up the conversations from the offshore fishing boats. They are conversations of catches and winds and tides and of the women left behind on the rocky shores. John appears with his mouth organ, standing at a respectful distance. The old man notices him, nods, and shuts off the radio. Rising, he goes upstairs, the sound of his feet echoing down to us. Returning he carries an old and battered accordion. "My fingers have so much rheumatism," he says, "that I find it hard to play anymore."

Seated, he slips his arms through the straps and begins the squeezing accordion 35 motions. His wife takes off her apron and stands behind him with one hand upon his shoulder. For a moment they take on the essence of the once young people in the photograph. They begin to sing:

Come all ye fair and tender ladies 36
Take warning how you court your men
They're like the stars on a summer's morning
First they'll appear and then they're gone.

37   *I wish I were a tiny sparrow*
And I had wings and I could fly
I'd fly away to my own true lover
And all he'd ask I would deny.

38   *Alas I'm not a tiny sparrow*
I have not wings nor can I fly
And on this earth in grief and sorrow
I am bound until I die.

39   John sits on one of the home-made chairs playing his mouth organ. He seems as all mouth-organ players the world over: his right foot tapping out the measures and his small shoulders now round and hunched above the cupped hand instrument.

40   "Come now and sing with us, John," says he old man.

41   Obediently he takes the mouth organ from his mouth and shakes the moisture drops upon his sleeve. All three of them begin to sing, spanning easily the half century of time that touches their extremes. The old and the young singing now their songs of loss in different comprehensions. Stranded here, alien of my middle generation, I tap my leather foot self-consciously upon the linoleum. The words sweep up and swirl about my head. Fog does not touch like snow yet it is more heavy and more dense. Oh moisture comes in many forms!

42   *All alone as I strayed by the banks of the river*
Watching the moonbeams at evening of day
All alone as I wandered I spied a young stranger
Weeping and wailing with many a sigh.

43   *Weeping for one who is now lying lonely*
Weeping for one who no mortal can save
As the foaming dark waters flow silently past him
Onward they flow over young Jenny's grave.

44   *Oh Jenny my darling come tarry here with me*
Don't leave me alone, love, distracted in pain
For as death is the dagger that plied us asunder
Wide is the gulf, love, between you and I.

45   After the singing stops we all sit rather uncomfortably for a moment, the mood seeming to hang heavily upon our shoulders. Then with my single exception all come suddenly to action. John gets up and takes his battered school books to the kitchen table. The dog jumps up on a chair beside him and watches solemnly in a supervisory manner. The woman takes some navy yarn the colour of her hus-

band's jersey and begins to knit. She is making another jersey and is working on the sleeve. The old man rises and beckons me to follow him into the tiny parlour. The stuffed furniture is old and worn. There is a tiny wood-burning heater in the centre of the room. It stands on a square of galvanized metal which protects the floor from falling, burning coals. The stovepipe rises and vanishes into the wall on its way to the upstairs. There is an old-fashioned mantelpiece on the wall behind the stove. It is covered with odd shapes of driftwood from the shore and a variety of exotically shaped bottles, blue and green and red, which are from the shore as well. There are pictures here too: of the couple in the other picture; and one of them with their five daughters; and one of the five daughters by themselves. In that far-off picture time all of the daughters seem roughly between the ages of ten and eighteen. The youngest has the reddest hair of all. So red that it seems to triumph over the non-photographic colours of lonely black and white. The pictures are in standard wooden frames.

From behind the ancient chesterfield the old man pulls a collapsible card table 46 and pulls down its warped and shaky legs. Also from behind the chesterfield he takes a faded checkerboard and a large old-fashioned matchbox of rattling wooden checkers. The spine of the board is almost cracked through and is strengthened by layers of adhesive tape. The checkers are circumferences of wood sawed from a length of broom handle. They are about three quarters of an inch thick. Half of them are painted a very bright blue and the other half an equally eyecatching red. "John made these," says the old man, "all of them are not really the same thickness but they are good enough. He gave it a good try."

We begin to play checkers. He takes the blue and I the red. The house is silent 47 with only the click-clack of the knitting needles sounding through the quiet rooms. From time to time the old man lights his pipe, digging out the old ashes with a flattened nail and tamping in the fresh tobacco with the same nail's head. The blue smoke winds lazily and haphazardly toward the low-beamed ceiling. The game is solemn as is the next and then the next. Neither of us loses all of the time.

"It is time for some of us to be in bed," says the old woman after a while. She 48 gathers up her knitting and rises from her chair. In the kitchen John neatly stacks his school books on one corner of the table in anticipation of the morning. He goes outside for a moment and then returns. Saying good-night very formally he goes up the stairs to bed. In a short while the old woman follows, her footsteps travelling the same route.

We continue to play our checkers, wreathed in smoke and only partially aware 49 of the muffled footfalls sounding softly above our heads.

When the old man gets up to go outside I am not really surprised, any more 50 than I am when he returns with the brown, ostensible vinegar jug. Poking at the declining kitchen fire, he moves the kettle about, seeking the warmest spot on the cooling stove. He takes two glasses from the cupboard, a sugar bowl and two spoons. The kettle begins to boil.

51   Even before tasting it, I know the rum to be strong and overproof. It comes at night and in fog from the French islands of St. Pierre and Miquelon. Coming over in the low-throttled fishing boats, riding in imitation gas cans. He mixes the rum and the sugar first, watching them marry and dissolve. Then to prevent the breakage of the glasses he places a teaspoon in each and ads the boiling water. The odour rises richly, its sweetness hung in steam. He brings the glasses to the table, holding them by their tops so that his fingers will not burn.

52   We do not say anything for some time, sitting upon the chairs, while the sweetened, heated richness moves warmly through and from our stomachs and spreads upward to our brains. Outside the wind begins to blow, moaning and faintly rattling the window's whitened shutters. He rises and brings refills. We are warm within the dark and still within the wind. A clock strikes regularly the strokes of ten.

53   It is difficult to talk at times with or without liquor; difficult to achieve the actual act of saying. Sitting still we listen further to the rattle of the wind; not knowing where nor how we should begin. Again the glasses are refilled.

54   "When she married in Toronto," he says at last, "we figured that maybe John should be with her and with her husband. That maybe he would be having more of a chance there in the city. But we would be putting it off and it weren't until nigh on two years that he went. Went with a woman from down the cove going to visit her daughter. Well, what was wrong was that we missed him wonderful awful. More fearful than we ever thought. Even the dog. Just pacing the floor and looking out the window and walking along the rocks of the shore. Like us had no moorings, lost in the fog or on the ice-floes in a snow squall. Nigh sick unto our hearts we was. Even the grandmother who before that was maybe thinking small to herself that he was trouble in her old age. Ourselves having never had no sons only daughters."

55   He pauses, then rising goes upstairs and returns with an envelope. From it he takes a picture which shows two young people standing self-consciously before a half-ton pickup with a wooden extension ladder fastened to its side. They appear to be in their middle twenties. The door of the truck has the information: "Jim Farrell, Toronto: Housepainting, Eavestroughing, Aluminum Siding, Phone 535-3484," lettered on its surface.

56   "This was in the last letter," he says. "That Farrell I guess was a nice enough fellow, from Heartsick Bay he was.

57   "Anyway they could have no more peace with John than we could without him. Like I says he was here too long before his going and it all took ahold of us the way it will. They sent word that he was coming on the plane to St. John's with a woman they'd met through a Newfoundland club. I was to go to St. John's to meet him. Well, it was all wrong the night before the going. The signs all bad; the grandmother knocked off the lampshade and it broke in a hunnerd pieces—the sign of death; and the window blind fell and clattered there on the floor and then lied

still. And the dog runned around like he was crazy, moanen and cryen worse than the swiles does out on the ice, and throwen hisself against the walls and jumpen on the table and at the window where the blind fell until we would have to be letten him out. But it be no better for he runned and throwed hisself in the sea and then come back and howled outside the same window and jumped against the wall, splashen the water from his coat all over it. Then he be runnen back to the sea again. All the neighbours heard him and said I should bide at home and not go to St. John's at all. We be all wonderful scared and not know what to do and the next mornen, first thing I drops me knife.

"But still I feels I has to go. It be foggy all the day and everyone be thinken the plane won't come or be able to land. And I says, small to myself, now here in the fog be the bad luck and the questions and the death but then there the plane be, almost like a ghost ship comen out the fog with all its lights shinen. I think maybe he won't be on it but soon he comen through the fog, first with the woman and then see'n me and starten to run, closer and closer till I can feel him in me arms and the tears on both our cheeks. Powerful strange how things will take one. That night they be killed." 58

From the envelope that contained the picture he draws forth a tattered clipping: 59

> *Jennifer Farrell of Roncesvalles Avenue was instantly killed early this* 60
> *morning and her husband James died later in emergency at St.*
> *Joseph's Hospital. The accident occurred about 2 A.M. when the*
> *pickup truck in which they were travelling went out of control on*
> *Queen St. W. and struck a utility pole. It is thought that bad visibility*
> *caused by a heavy fog may have contributed to the accident. The*
> *Farrells were originally from Newfoundland.*

Again he moves to refill the glasses. "We be all alone," he says. "All our other 61 daughters married and far away in Montreal, Toronto, or the States. Hard for them to come back here, even to visit; they comes only every three years or so for perhaps a week. So we be hav'n only him."

And now my head begins to reel even as I move to the filling of my own glass. 62 Not waiting this time for the courtesy of his offer. Making myself perhaps too much at home with this man's glass and this man's rum and this man's house and all the feelings of his love. Even as I did before. Still locked again for words.

Outside we stand and urinate, turning our backs to the seeming gale so as not 63 to splash our wind-snapped trousers. We are almost driven forward to rock upon our toes and settle on our heels, so blow the gusts. Yet in spite of all, the stars shine clearly down. It will indeed be a good day for the fishing and this wind eventually will calm. The salt hangs heavy in the air and the water booms against the rugged rocks. I take a stone and throw it against the wind into the sea.

64   Going up the stairs we clutch the wooden bannister unsteadily and say good-night.

65   The room has changed very little. The window rattles in the wind and the unfinished beams sway and creak. The room is full of sound. Like a foolish Lockwood I approach the window although I hear no voice. There is no Catherine who cries to be let in. Standing unsteadily on one foot when required I manage to undress, draping my trousers across the wooden chair. The bed is clean. It makes no sound. It is plain and wooden, its mattress stuffed with hay or kelp. I feel it with my hand and pull back the heavy patchwork quilts. Still I do not go into it. Instead I go back to the door which has no knob but only an ingenious latch formed from a twisted nail. Turning it, I go out into the hallway. All is dark and the house seems even more inclined to creak where there is no window. Feeling along the wall with my outstretched hand I find the door quite easily. It is closed with the same kind of latch and not difficult to open. But no one waits on the other side. I stand and bend my ear to hear the even sound of my one son's sleeping. He does not beckon any more than the nonexistent voice in the outside wind. I hesitate to touch the latch for fear that I may waken him and disturb his dreams. And if I did what would I say? Yet I would like to see him in his sleep this once and see the room with the quiet bed once more and the wooden chair beside it from off an old wrecked trawler. There is no boiled egg or shaker of salt or glass of water waiting on the chair within this closed room's darkness.

66   Once though there was a belief held in the outports, that if a girl would see her own true lover she should boil an egg and scoop out half the shell and fill it with salt. Then she should take it to bed with her and eat it, leaving a glass of water by her bedside. In the night her future husband or a vision of him would appear and offer her the glass. But she must only do it once.

67   It is the type of belief that bright young graduate students were collecting eleven years ago for the theses and archives of North America and also, they hoped, for their own fame. Even as they sought the near-Elizabethan songs and ballads that had sailed from County Kerry and from Devon and Cornwall. All about the wild, wide sea and the flashing silver dagger and the lost and faithless lover. Echoes to and from the lovely, lonely hills and glens of West Virginia and the standing stones of Tennessee.

68   Across the hall the old people are asleep. The old man's snoring rattles as do the windows; except that now and then there are catching gasps within his breath. In three or four short hours he will be awake and will go down to light his fire. I turn and walk back softly to my room.

69   Within the bed the warm sweetness of the rum is heavy and intense. The darkness presses down upon me but still it brings no sleep. There are no voices and no shadows that are real. There are only walls of memory touched restlessly by flickers of imagination.

Oh I would like to see my way more clearly. I, who have never understood the 70
mystery of fog. I would perhaps like to capture it in a jar like the beautiful childhood butterflies that always die in spite of the airholes punched with nails in the
covers of their captivity—leaving behind the vapours of their lives and deaths; or
perhaps as the unknowing child who collects the grey moist condoms from the
lovers' lanes only to have them taken from him and to be told to wash his hands.
Oh I have collected many things I did not understand.

And perhaps now I should go and say, oh son of my *summa cum laude* loins, 71
come away from the lonely gulls and the silver trout and I will take you to the land
of the Tastee Freeze where you may sleep till ten of nine. And I will show you the
elevator to the apartment on the sixteenth floor and introduce you to the buzzer
system and the yards of the wrought-iron fences where the Doberman pinscher
runs silently at night. Or may I offer you the money that is the fruit of my collecting and my most successful life? Or shall I wait to meet you in some known or
unknown bitterness like Yeats's Cuchulain by the wind-whipped sea or as a
Sohrab and Rustum by the future flowing river?

Again I collect dreams. For I do not know enough of the fog on Toronto's 72
Queen St. West and the grinding crash of the pickup and of lost and misplaced
love.

I am up early in the morning as the man kindles the fire from the driftwood 73
splinters. The outside light is breaking and the wind is calm. John tumbles down
the stairs. Scarcely stopping to splash his face and pull on his jacket, he is gone,
accompanied by the dog. The old man smokes his pipe and waits for the water to
boil. When it does he pours some into the teapot then passes the kettle to me. I
take it to the wash-stand and fill the small tin basin in readiness for my shaving.
My face looks back from the mirrored cabinet. The woman softly descends the
stairs.

"I think I will go back today," I say while looking into the mirror at my face and 74
at those in the room behind me. I try to emphasize the "I." "I just thought I would
like to make this trip—again. I think I can leave the car in St. John's and fly back
directly." The woman begins to move about the table, setting out the round white
plates. The man quietly tamps his pipe.

The door opens and John and the dog return. They have been down along the 75
shore to see what has happened throughout the night. "Well, John," says the old
man, "what did you find?"

He opens his hand to reveal a smooth round stone. It is of the deepest green 76
inlaid with veins of darkest ebony. It has been worn and polished by the unre-
lenting restlessness of the sea and buffed and burnished by the gravelled sand. All
of its inadequacies have been removed and it glows with the lustre of near per-
fection.

"It is very beautiful," I say. 77

78   "Yes," he says, "I like to collect them." Suddenly he looks up to my eyes and thrusts the stone toward me. "Here," he says, "would you like to have it?"

79   Even as I reach out my hand I turn my head to the others in the room. They are both looking out through the window to the sea.

80   "Why, thank you," I say. "Thank you very much. Yes, I would. Thank you. Thanks." I take it from his outstretched hand and place it in my pocket.

81   We eat our breakfast in near silence. After it is finished the boy and dog go out once more. I prepare to leave.

82   "Well, I must go," I say, hesitating at the door. "It will take me a while to get to St. John's." I offer my hand to the man. He takes it in his strong fingers and shakes it firmly.

83   "Thank you," says the woman. "I don't know if you know what I mean but thank you."

84   "I think I do," I say. I stand and fiddle with the keys. "I would somehow like to help or keep in touch but . . ."

85   "But there is no phone," he says, "and both of us can hardly write. Perhaps that's why we never told you. John is getting to be a pretty good hand at it though."

86   "Good-bye," we say again, "good-bye, good-bye."

87   The sun is shining clearly now and the small boats are putt-putting about the harbour. I enter my unlocked car and start its engine. The gravel turns beneath the wheels. I pass the house and wave to the man and woman standing in the yard.

88   On a distant cliff the children are shouting. Their voices carol down through the sun-washed air and the dogs are curving and dancing about them in excited circles. They are carrying something that looks like a crippled gull. Perhaps they will make it well. I toot the horn. "Good-bye," they shout and wave, "good-bye, good-bye."

89   The airport terminal is strangely familiar. A symbol of impermanence, it is itself glisteningly permanent. Its formica surfaces have been designed to stay. At the counter a middle-aged man in mock exasperation is explaining to the girl that it is Newark he wishes to go to, *not* New York.

90   There are not many of us and soon we are ticketed and lifting through and above the sun-shot fog. The meals are served in tinfoil and in plastic. We eat above the clouds looking at the tips of wings.

91   The man beside me is a heavy-equipment salesman who has been trying to make a sale to the developers of Labrador's resources. He has been away a week and is returning to his wife and children.

92   Later in the day we land in the middle of the continent. Because of the changing time zones the distance we have come seems eerily unreal. The heat shimmers in little waves upon the runway. This is the equipment salesman's final destination while for me it is but the place where I must change flights to continue even farther into the heartland. Still we go down the wheeled-up stairs together,

donning our sunglasses, and stepping across the heated concrete and through the terminal's electronic doors. The salesman's wife stands waiting along with two small children who are the first to see him. They race toward him with their arms outstretched. "Daddy, Daddy," they cry, "what did you bring me? What did you bring me?"

QUESTIONS

Understanding the message: Comprehension

1. At the beginning of the story, why is the narrator so reluctant about being there and so close to leaving?

2. What is the relationship between the narrator and the elderly couple?

3. How is John connected to both the narrator and the elderly couple?

4. What does the old man mean when he says, at the end of the story, "Perhaps that's why we never told you"? What is it they "never told" the narrator?

Examining the writer's craft: Analysis and interpretation

1. The first five paragraphs of the story are devoted to pure description; there are no characters or dialogue introduced. What is the tone of this subjective description? Identify examples of the author's use of figurative language in these paragraphs. How do they contribute to the tone?

2. At the beginning of the story, why is it significant that John teaches the narrator how to fish?

3. Why do you think the narrator refers to the older couple as "the woman" and "the man," even though he knows them? What effect does referring to them this way have on the reader?

4. How do the two songs relate to the story?

5. How does the last line relate to what the narrator has just gone through in the story?

6. Did the narrator go to Newfoundland to retrieve his son? How do you know?

Essay questions

1. What role does fog play in this story? In discussing this image, refer to the various associations it conjures.

2. Discuss the theme of uncertainty in this story. In particular, how does it shape the narrator's thoughts and actions?

3. In this story, it can be said that MacLeod's narrator and John reverse the usual roles of father and son. In what way(s) do these characters embody this reversal? Why do you think MacLeod presents them this way?

VOCABULARY

lichens: mossy plants that grow on rocks

ganglia: nerve cells; plural of *ganglion*

marauders: raiders

myriad: large number

laving: washing

dories: small boats

jigging: moving jerkily

iridescent: colourfully glimmering

Joey: Joey Smallwood (1900–91), former premier of Newfoundland

worsted: heavy, wooly fabric

sou'westers: raincoats

serge: heavy, twill fabric

rakishly: dashingly, jauntily

scud: clouds

lathes (laths), headings: strips of wood and netting used to make lobster traps

skiff: small boat

ostensible: seeming or appearing to be

hunnerd: hundred

swiles: seals

Lockwood: narrator in Emily Bronte's novel, *Wuthering Heights* (1847); in a dream, he turns away the ghost of the story's heroine, Catherine, as she calls to him at the window of her childhood bedroom

trawler: fishing boat

summa cum laude: with great distinction; designation given to university graduates with the highest grades

Cuchulain: hero from Celtic myth who goes mad because he killed his son; subject of Yeats's poem "Cuchulain's Fight with the Sea"

Sohrab and Rustum: title of a poem by Matthew Arnold (1822–88), in which Rustum, a Persian hero, unknowingly slays his own son

tamps: packs (tobacco) into

Little Green Monster

by Haruki Murakami (b. 1949)

(Translated from the Japanese by Jay Rubin)

Haruki Murakami was born in Kyoto, Japan, and grew up in Kobe. His most recent novel, The Wind-up Bird Chronicle *(1998), won the Borders Original Voices Book of the Year Award for fiction and was named an Editor's Choice by* Booklist *and a Notable Book by the* New York Times Book Review. *Other works include* Dance Dance Dance *(1995),* Hard-Boiled Wonderland and the End of the World *(1993), and* The Elephant Vanishes *(1994), from which this selection is taken. His most recent books are* South of the Border, West of the Sun *(2000), a collection of stories, and* Underground: The Tokyo Gas Attack and the Japanese Psyche *(2001), a non-fiction examination of a Japanese cult's gas attack on the Tokyo subway system in 1995. He lives with his wife outside Tokyo.*

PRE-READING

This story is told by a female narrator who, while sitting and staring at her favourite oak tree in the backyard one day, encounters a little green monster. As you read the story, think about what loneliness does to people. Does the narrator's behaviour surprise you? What would you have done?

1   My husband left for work as usual, and I couldn't think of anything to do. I sat alone in the chair by the window, staring out at the garden through the gap between the curtains. Not that I had any reason to be looking at the garden: There was nothing else for me to do. And I thought that sooner or later, if I sat there looking, I might think of something. Of all the many things in the garden, the one I looked at most was the oak tree. It was my special favorite. I had planted it when I was a little girl, and watched it grow. I thought of it as my old friend. I talked to it all the time in my head.

2   That day, too, I was probably talking to the oak tree—I don't remember what about. And I don't know how long I was sitting there. The time slips by when I'm looking at the garden. It was dark before I knew it: I must have been there quite a while. Then, all at once, I heard a sound. It came from somewhere far away—a funny, muffled sort of rubbing sort of sound. At first I thought it was coming from a place deep inside me, that I was hearing things—a warning from the dark cocoon my body was spinning within. I held my breath and listened. Yes. No

RESPOND IN WRITING

doubt about it. Little by little, the sound was moving closer to me. What was it? I had no idea. But it made my flesh creep.

The ground near the base of the tree began to bulge upward as if some thick, 3 heavy liquid were rising to the surface. Again I caught my breath. Then the ground broke open and the mounded earth crumbled away to reveal a set of sharp claws. My eyes locked onto them, and my hands turned into clenched fists. Something's going to happen, I said to myself. It's starting now. The claws scraped hard at the soil, and soon the break in the earth was an open hole, from which there crawled a little green monster.

Its body was covered with shining green scales. As soon as it emerged from the 4 hole, it shook itself until the bits of soil clinging to it dropped away. It had a long, funny nose, the green of which gradually deepened toward the tip. The very end was narrow and pointed as a whip, but the beast's eyes were exactly like a human's. The sight of them sent a shiver through me. They showed feelings, just like your eyes or mine.

Without hesitation, but moving slowly and deliberately, the monster 5 approached my front door, on which it began to knock with the slender tip of its nose. The dry, rapping sound echoed through the house. I tiptoed to the back room, hoping the beast would not realize I was there. I couldn't scream. Ours is the only house in the area, and my husband wouldn't be coming back from work until late at night. I couldn't run out the back door, either, since my house has only the one door, the very one on which a horrible green monster was now knocking. I breathed as quietly as I could, pretending not to be there, hoping the thing would give up and go away. But it didn't give up. Its nose went from knocking to groping at the lock. It seemed to have no trouble at all clicking the lock open, and then the door itself opened a crack. Around the edge of the door crept the nose, and then it stopped. For a long time it stayed still, like a snake with its head raised, checking conditions in the house. If I had known this was going to happen, I could have stayed by the door and cut the nose off, I told myself: The kitchen had plenty of sharp knives. No sooner had the thought occurred to me than the creature moved past the edge of the door, smiling, as it if had read my mind. Then it spoke, not with a stutter, but repeating certain words as if it were still trying to learn them. It wouldn't have done you any good, any good, the little green monster said. My nose is like a lizard's tail. It always grows back—stronger and longer, stronger and longer. You'd get just the opposite of what what you want want. Then it spun its eyes for a long time, like two weird tops.

Oh, no, I thought to myself. Can it read people's minds? I hate to have anyone 6 know what I'm thinking—especially when that someone is a horrid and inscrutable little creature like this. I broke out in a cold sweat from head to foot. What was this thing going to do to me? Eat me? Take me down into the earth? Oh, well, at least it wasn't so ugly that I couldn't stand looking at it. That was good. It had slender, pink little arms and legs jutting out from its green-scaled body and long claws at the ends of its hands and feet. They were almost darling, the more I looked at them. And I could see, too, that the creature meant me no harm.

7   Of course not, it said to me, cocking its head. Its scales clicked against one another when it moved—like crammed-together coffee cups rattling on a table when you nudge it. What a terrible thought, madam: Of course I wouldn't eat you. No no no. I mean you no harm, no harm, no harm. So I was right: It knew exactly what I was thinking.

8   Madam madam madam, don't you see? Don't you see? I've come here to propose to you. From deep deep deep down deep down deep. I had to crawl all the way up here up here up. Awful, it was awful, I had to dig and dig and dig. Look at how it ruined my claws! I could never have done this if I meant you any harm, any harm, any harm. I love you. I love you so much I couldn't stand it anymore down deep down deep. I crawled my way up to you, I had to, I had to. They all tried to stop me, but I couldn't stand it anymore. And think of the courage that it took, please, took. What if you thought it was rude and presumptuous, rude and presumptuous, for a creature like me to propose to you?

9   But it *is* rude and presumptuous, I said in my mind. What a rude little creature you are to come seeking my love!

10   A look of sadness came over the monster's face as soon as I thought this, and its scales took on a purple tinge, as if to express what it was feeling. Its entire body seemed to shrink a little, too. I folded my arms to watch these changes occurring. Maybe something like this would happen whenever its feelings altered. And maybe its awful-looking exterior masked a heart that was as soft and vulnerable as a brand-new marshmallow. If so, I knew I could win. I decided to give it a try. Your *are* an ugly little monster, you know, I shouted in my mind's loudest voice— so loud it made my heart reverberate. You *are* an ugly little monster! The purple of the scales grew deeper and the thing's eyes began to bulge as if they were sucking in all the hatred I was sending them. They protruded from the creature's face like ripe green figs, and tears like red juice ran down from them, splattering on the floor.

11   I wasn't afraid of the monster anymore. I painted pictures in my mind of all the cruel things I wanted to do to it. I tied it down to a heavy chair with thick wires, and with a needle-nose pliers I began ripping out its scales at the roots, one by one. I heated the point of a sharp knife, and with it I cut deep grooves in the soft pink flesh of its calves. Over and over, I stabbed a hot soldering iron into the bulging figs of its eyes. With each new torture I imagined for it, the monster would lurch and writhe and wail in agony as if those things were actually happening to it. It wept its colored tears and oozed thick gobs of liquid onto the floor, emitting a gray vapor from its ears that had the fragrance of roses. Its eyes sent an unnerving glare of reproach at me. Please, madam, oh please, I beg of you, don't

think such terrible thoughts! it cried. I have no evil thoughts for you. I would never harm you. All I feel for you is love, is love. But I refused to listen. In my mind, I said, Don't be ridiculous! You crawled out of my garden. You unlocked my door without permission. You came inside my house. I never asked you here. I have the right to think anything I want to. And I continued to do exactly that—thinking at the creature increasingly terrible thoughts. I cut and tormented its flesh with every machine and tool I could think of, overlooking no method that might exist to torture a living being and make it writhe in pain. See, then, you little monster, you have no idea what a woman is. There's no end to the number of things I can think of to do to you. But soon the monster's outlines began to fade, and even its strong green nose shriveled up until it was no bigger than a worm. Writhing on the floor, the monster tried to move its mouth and speak to me, struggling to open its lips as if it wanted to leave me some final message, to convey some ancient wisdom, some crucial bit of knowledge that it had forgotten to impart to me. Before that could happen, the mouth attained a painful stillness, and soon it went out of focus and disappeared. The monster now looked like nothing more than a pale evening shadow. All that remained, suspended in the air, were its mournful, bloated eyes. That won't do any good, I thought to it. You can look all you want, but you can't say a thing. You can't do a thing. Your existence is over, finished, done. Soon the eyes dissolved into emptiness, and the room filled with the darkness of night.

QUESTIONS

Understanding the message: Comprehension

1. How do the narrator's feelings about the little green monster change throughout the story?

2. In what ways is the monster like a human? In what ways is it different?

3. What do we know about the circumstances of the narrator's life? Describe the day-to-day existence of her life as you know it. What does this reveal about her personality?

Examining the writer's craft: Analysis and interpretation

1. Reread the first paragraph. What concept is repeated? What does the paragraph tell us about the narrator's state of mind?

2. Why does the monster appear? What function does it serve for the woman?

3. The monster has a very distinct speech pattern that is almost childish in its use of language. Why does the author use the childish style he does? How does it relate to the meaning of the story?

4. With whom do your sympathies lie, the woman or the monster? Why? Do your sympathies shift from one character to the other at any point? If so, where?

5. Why do you think the narrator reacts to the monster as she does? Could her reaction be prompted by something other than the monster? What makes her feel such hatred?

Essay questions

1. What does the little green monster symbolize? Write an essay in which you discuss the meaning of the monster.

2. Discuss the theme of love (or hatred) in this story. What is the story telling us about love and how it works?

3. Are the events of the story humorous or horrifying? Why?

VOCABULARY

inscrutable: difficult to know or understand

The Jimi Hendrix Experience

by Guy Vanderhaeghe (b. 1951)

Born in Esterhazy, Saskatchewan, Guy Vanderhaeghe is the author of three collections of short stories, three novels, and two plays. His book Man Descending *(1982) won the Governor General's Award and the Geoffrey Faber Memorial Prize in Great Britain. His novel* Homesick *(1989) was co-winner of the City of Toronto Book Award. His latest novel,* The Englishman's Boy *(1996), won the Governor General's Award, the Saskatchewan Book Award for Fiction, and the Saskatchewan Book of the Year Award. He currently lives and writes in Saskatoon.*

PRE-READING

In this story from the book *Turn of the Story: Canadian Fiction on the Eve of the Millennium* (1999), three teenagers looking for excitement pull pranks on stuffy middle-aged adults in a small town. As you read the story, think about yourself at fourteen or fifteen: what was "fun"? Think about what the boys go through and how their ideas may change by the end of the story. How has your own definition of "fun" changed over the years?

It's the summer of 1970 and I've got one lovely ambition. I want to have been 1 born in Seattle, to be black, to be Jimi Hendrix. I want a burst of Afro ablaze in a bank of stage lights, to own a corona of genius. I ache in bed listening to "Purple Haze" over and over again on my record player; the next night it's "All along the Watchtower." I'm fourteen and I want to be one of the chosen, one of the possessed. To soak a guitar in lighter fluid, burn baby burn, to smash it to bits to the howl of thousands. I want to be a crazy man like Jimi Hendrix.

What I didn't know then is that before my man, Jimi, flamed his guitar at 2 Monterey, he warned the cameraman to be sure to load plenty of film. This I learn much later, after he's dead.

It's not a good time for me; my father moves us to a new city when school fin- 3 ishes in Winnipeg; all I have is Jimi Hendrix, Conrad, and Finty. I don't know what I am doing with these last two, except that with school out for the summer I lack opportunities to widen my circle of acquaintances. Beggars can't be choosers.

Finty I meet outside a convenience store. He introduces me to Conrad. There's 4 not much wrong with Finty; born into a normal family, he'd have had a chance. But Conrad is a different story. Finty proudly informs me that Conrad's been known to set fire to garbage cans and heave them up on garage roofs, to prowl a car lot with a rusty nail and do ten thousand dollars' worth of damage in the wink of an eye. He's a sniffer of model-airplane glue, gasoline. That stuff I don't touch. It's impossible to imagine the great Jimi Hendrix with his head in a plastic bag. Occasionally, I'll pinch a little grass from my big sister Corinne's stash in her panty drawer, have my own private Woodstock while Jimi looks down on me approvingly from the poster on my bedroom wall. I tell myself this is who I am. Finty and Conrad are just temporary way stations on the big journey.

5   Conrad scares me. His long hair isn't a statement, just a poverty shag. His broken knuckles weep from hitting walls; he's an accident willing itself to happen. The only person who comes close to scaring me as much is my father, a night janitor who works the graveyard shift in a deadly office complex downtown, midnight to eight in the morning. A vampire who sleeps while the sun is up, sinks his teeth into my neck at the supper table, goes off to work with a satisfied, bloody, grey smile on his lips. As far as he's concerned, there's only one lesson I need to learn—don't be dumb when it comes to life. I hear it every night, complete with illustrations.

6   I'm not dumb. It's my brilliant idea to entertain ourselves annoying people because that's less dangerous than anything Conrad is likely to suggest. The same principle as substituting methadone for heroin.

7   The three of us go around knocking on people's doors. I tell whoever answers that we've come about the Jimi Hendrix album.

8   "What?"

9   "The Jimi Hendrix album you advertised for sale in the classifieds in the newspaper."

10   "I didn't advertise nothing of any description in any newspaper."

11   "Isn't this 1102 Maitland Crescent?"

12   "What does it look like? What does the number say?"

13   "Well, we must have the right house then. Maybe it was your wife. Did your wife advertise a Jimi Hendrix album?"

14   "Nobody advertised nothing. There is no wife any more. I live alone."

15   After my warm-up act, Finty jumps in all pathetic with misery and disappointment like I've coached him. "This isn't too funny, you ask me. Changing your mind at the last minute. I promised my sister I'd buy your album for her birthday. A buck is all I got to buy her a lousy secondhand birthday present, and then you go and do this. We had to transfer twice on the bus just to get here."

16   "His sister's got polio, mister." I tilt my head like I can't believe what he's doing to the poor girl.

17   Conrad says to Finty, "I got fifty cents. It's yours. Offer him a buck and a half. He'll take a buck and a half."

18   "I ain't going to take anything because I don't have no Jimmy Henson record. I don't even own a record player."

"I've got thirty-five cents. That makes a buck eighty-five. He *needs* the album 19 for his sister. Music is all she has in life," I tell the man.

"She can't go out on dates or nothing," Finty says, voice cracking. "It's the 20 wheelchair."

"Look, I'm sorry about your sister, kid. But I'm swearing to you—on a stack of 21 Bibles, I'm swearing to you—I don't have this record."

"Maybe you've forgotten you have it," I say. "Does this ring a bell? Sound 22 familiar?" And I start cranking air guitar, doing "Purple Haze," no way the poor wiener can stop me until I'm done screaming hard enough to make your ears bleed.

One afternoon we're cruising the suburbs, courtesy of three bikes we helped 23 ourselves to from a rack outside a city swimming pool. Conrad's been sniffing. You can feel the heat coming off the asphalt into your face when you lean over the handlebars to pump the pedals. This is steaming the glue and producing dangerous vapours in Conrad's skull. Already he's yelled some nasty, rude remarks at a woman pushing a baby carriage; now he's lighting matches and flicking them at a yappy Pekingese on somebody's lawn, driving the dog out of its tiny mind. The lady of the house is watching him out her front window, and I know that when she lets the drapes fall closed it'll be to call the cops.

Conrad is badly in need of structure, a sense of purpose at this particular 24 moment, so I point to a bungalow across the street, a bungalow where every shrub in the yard has been trimmed to look like something else. For instance, a rooster. I definitely recall a rooster. It's easy to guess what sort of person will live in a house of that description. Prime territory for the Jimi Hendrix experience. Finty and Conrad are off their bikes in a flash; no explanation needed.

There's a sign on the front door, red crayon on cardboard, Entrance Alarmed. 25 Please Enter at Rear. The old man who comes to the door is dressed like a bank manager on his day off. White shirt, striped tie, bright yellow alpaca cardigan. He's a very tall, spruce old guy with a glamour tan, and he's just wet-combed his white hair. You can see the teethmarks of the comb in it.

"We came to inquire about the album," I say. 26

"Yes, yes. Come in. Come in. I've been expecting you," he says, eyes fixed on 27 something above my head. But when I turn to see what's caught his interest, there's nothing there.

"This way, this way," he urges us, eyes blinking up into a cloudless sky. For a 28 second I wonder if he might be blind, but then he begins herding us through the porch, through the kitchen, into the living room, pushing air away from his knees palms out like he's shooing chickens. Finty and Conrad are giggling and snorting. "Too rich," I hear Conrad say.

The old man points and mutters, "Have a seat. Have a seat," before he evapo- 29 rates off into the back of the bungalow. Conrad and Finty start horsing around, scuffling over ownership of a recliner, but it's already a done deal who's going to end up with it. Like the big dog with the puppy, Conrad lets Finty nip a bit before he shoots him the stare, red little eyes like glazed maraschino cherries left in the jar too long, and Finty settles for the chesterfield. Big dog flops in the recliner, pops the footrest, grins at me over the toes of his sneakers. "Right on," he says.

30   I don't like it when Conrad says things like "Right on." He's not entitled. He and Finty aren't on the same wavelength as people like me and Jimi Hendrix. Conrad would just as soon have been asking people for Elvis Presley albums if I hadn't explained that the types whose doorbells we ring are likely to own them.

31   Finty is into a bowl of peanuts on the end table. He starts flicking them at Conrad. Conrad snaps at them like a dog trying to catch flies, snaps so hard you can hear his teeth click. The ones he misses rattle off the wall, skitter and spin on the hardwood floor.

32   I'm wondering where the old guy's gone. My ear is cocked in case he might be on the phone to the police. I don't appreciate the unexpected turn this has taken, the welcome mat he spread for us. I'm trying to figure out what's going on here, but there's this strange odour in the house that is worming into my nostrils and interfering with my thoughts. When I caught the first whiff of it, I thought it was the glue on Conrad's breath, but now I'm not so sure. A weird, gloomy smell. Like somebody's popped the door on a long-abandoned, derelict fridge, and dead oxygen and stale chemical coolant are fogging my brain.

33   I'm thinking all this weird stuff when Finty suddenly freezes on the chesterfield with a peanut between his thumb and middle finger, cocked to fire. His lips give a nervous, rabbity nibble to the air. I scoot a look over my shoulder, and there's the old man blocking the entrance to the living room. With a rifle clutched across his chest.

34   Conrad's heels do a little dance of joy on the footrest.

35   The old gentleman pops the rifle over his head like he's fording a stream, takes a couple of long, plunging strides into the room, and crisply snaps the gun back down on a diagonal across his shirt front, announcing, "My son carried a Lee-Enfield like this clear across Holland in the last war. He's no longer with us. I thought you boys would like to see a piece of history." He smiles, and the Lee-Enfield starts moving like it has a mind of its own, the muzzle sliding slowly over to Finty on the chesterfield. One of the old guy's eyes is puckered shut; the other stares down the barrel straight into Finty's chest. "JFK," he says. Then the barrel makes a lazy sweep over to Conrad in the recliner. "Bobby. Bobby Kennedy."

36   Some nights I turn on the TV at four in the morning when all the stations have signed off the air. I like how the television fizzles in my ears, how my brain drifts over the electric blue and grey snow, how the phantom sparkles of light are blips on a radar screen tracking spaceships from distant planets. Similar things are happening in my head right now, but they feel bad instead of good.

"Get that out of my face," Conrad orders him.   37

The old man doesn't move. "I could feel John and Bobby giving off copper 38
right through the television screen. Lee Harvey could feel it and Sirhan Sirhan
could feel it. I think, as far as North America goes, we were the only three."

Conrad squints suspiciously. "What kind of bullshit are you talking?"   39

"And you," says the old man, voice rising. "You give off copper, and so does 40
your friend by the peanut bowl. Chemistry is destiny. Too much copper in the
human system attracts the lightning bolt. Don't blame me. I'm not responsible."

There's a long silence. Conrad's heels jitter angrily up and down on the 41
footrest.

"Do you understand?" the old man demands. "Am I making myself clear?"   42

The question is for Conrad, but I'm the one who answers. I feel the old man 43
requires something quick. "Sure. Right. We get it."

He sends me a thoughtful nod as he lays the gun down at his feet. A second 44
later he's rummaging in his pockets, tearing out handfuls of change, spilling it
down on the coffee-table top like metal hail, talking fast. "Of course, there are
always exceptions to the rule. Me for one, I'm immune to the thunderbolt. I could
walk clear through a mob of assassins with a pound of copper in my belly and no
harm, no harm. Untouchable." His fingers jerk through the coins, shoving the
pennies to one side. Suddenly his neck goes rigid, his tongue slowly pokes
between his lips. A narrow, grey, furry trough. He picks up a penny and shows it
to each of us in turn. Presses the penny carefully down on the tongue like he's
sticking a stamp on an envelope. Squeezes his eyes tightly shut. Draws the penny
slowly back into his mouth and swallows. We watch him standing there, swaying
back and forth, a pulse beating in his eyelids.

Conrad's had enough of this. "Hey, you!" he shouts. "Hey, you, I'm talking to you!" 45

The old man's eyes flutter open. It's like watching a baby wake up.   46

"We don't give a shit how many pennies you can swallow," Conrad says. "We're 47
here about the album. The famous album."

"Right, the album. Of course," says the old man, springing to the footstool, flip- 48
ping up the lid.

"And another thing," Conrad warns him, winking at me. "Don't try to pass any 49
golden oldies off on us. Troy here is a hippie. He's got standards. You know what
a hippie is?"

"Yeah," says Flinty, taking heart from Conrad. "You know what a hippie is?"   50

The old man drags a bulging photograph album out of the footstool, drops it 51
on the coffee table, sinks to his knees on the hardwood beside it. You'd think it was
story time at Pooh Corner in the children's room at the library the way he turns
the pages for us.

The pictures are black and white, each one a snapshot of a road under construc- 52
tion. All of them taken just as the sun was rising or setting, the camera aimed

straight down the highway to where it disappears into a haze of pale light riding the horizon. There are no people in any of the pictures, only occasional pieces of old-fashioned earth-moving equipment parked in the ditches, looking like they were abandoned when everybody fled from the aliens, from the plague, or whatever.

53   Conrad grunts, "What the hell is this?"

54   "An example of the law of diminishing returns," the old man answers, dreamily turning the pages. "In a former life I was a highway contractor. Unrecognized for my excellence."

55   "How come there's nobody in these pictures?" Conrad wants to know. Pictures without people in them don't make any sense to him.

56   "Oh, but there is," the old man corrects him. "Identify the *person*. I think it's evident who he is, although there has been argument. If you would confirm his identity, it would be very much appreciated."

57   Conrad and Finty peer down hard at the snapshots. As if there really might be a human being lurking in them. After a minute, Conrad irritably declares, "There's nobody in any picture here."

58   "He fades in and fades out; sometimes he's there and sometimes he's not. But he's very definitely there now. You'll recognize him," the old man assures us.

59   By now Conrad suspects the old man is pulling something, a senior citizen variation on the Jimi Hendrix experience. "Oh, yeah, I see him now. Jimi Hendrix peeking around that big machine in the ditch. That's him, isn't it, Finty? The nigger in the woodpile." He jabs Finty in the ribs with his elbow, hard enough to make him squeak.

60   "Wrong. The person in question is definitely in the middle of the road. Walking towards us. Look again."

61   This only pisses Conrad off. "Right. I ain't stupid. Don't try to pull this crap on me."

62   "Please describe him," the old man says calmly.

63   "Here's a description for you. An empty road. Get a pair of fucking glasses, you old prick."

64   "So that's your line." The old man's voice has started to tremble; it sounds like Finty's when he talks about his sister in the wheelchair, only genuine. "Just a road. Just an *empty* road." He stabs his forefinger down on the photograph so hard it crinkles. "You, sir. Describe him," he says, turning to Finty.

65   "Huh?" Finty looks over at Conrad for help. Conrad's eyes are slits, glassy with the glue oozing out of his brain.

66   "Knock, knock. Who's there?" The old man's finger taps the photograph urgently, bouncing like a telegraph key. "Who's there? Who's there? Knock, knock."

67   Conrad juts his jaw at Finty, a warning. "Don't you say nothing."

68   The old man slaps his knee. "There, you've given it away!" he shouts. "Not

thinking, were you? Telling him not to give it away—but that's an admission by the back door, isn't it?"

He snatches the album, shoves it into my hands. Tiny points of chilly sweat 69 break out on his forehead. They make me think of liquefying freon, or whatever gas they pump into refrigerators to keep them cold. The chemical smell is industrial strength. It's coming from him.

"The truth now," he whispers to me. "Tell me what you see." 70

I feel Conrad staring at me. I hear him say, "Nothing there, Troy. Nothing." 71

I gaze down at an empty road, scraped raw by grader blades, patches of greasy 72 earth shining like freshly picked scabs. A burr of foggy light bristles on the horizon.

"Just a road," I say. 73

"But roads don't just happen," says the old man gently. 74

"No." 75

"So tell me, who else is in the photograph?" 76

It's no different from staring into a blank television screen. The snow shifting, 77 forming the faces of famous people locked in the circuitry from old programs. The hiss of static turning into favourite songs, guitar chords whining and dying.

"He's playing head games with us, Troy," Conrad warns. "Fuck him. Fucking 78 lunatic."

The old man leans in very close to me; I feel his alpaca sweater brushing the 79 hairs on my bare arm. "Tell the truth," he murmurs. "Who do you see?"

I hold my breath, and then I say it. "You." 80

"Yes," says the old man. When he does, I sense Conrad rising to his feet, sense 81 his shadow lurching down on the two of us.

"And my head. What do you see above my head?" the old man coaxes. 82

"Enough of this shit, Troy," Conrad says. 83

I look at the picture, the old man's finger guiding me to the pale grey froth on 84 the horizon. He rests it there, the phantom light crowning his nail.

"Light." 85

"The aura." 86

"The aura," I repeat numbly after him. 87

All at once, Conrad boots the album out of my hand, sends it flying across the 88 room, pages flapping. The old man and I dare not lift our heads; we just sit there, looking at the floor, listening to the ragged whistle of Conrad's breathing. It goes on for a long time before he says, "You think I don't know what you're up to, Troy? But you don't fuck with me, man. Just don't try to fuck with me. Just don't."

The old man and I sit with bowed heads, listening to Conrad and Finty pass 89 through the house, their voices getting louder the closer they get to the door. Then it slams, and the old man's head jerks up as if it were attached to it by a wire. Conrad and Finty hoot outside. I listen to their voices fade away, and then I realize the old man is talking to me.

90   "I knew you were the one to tell the truth. I knew it at the back door when I saw all the generous light . . ." He pauses, touches my head. "Here."

91   And I'm up and running through the house, colliding with a lamp, moving so fast that the sound of breaking glass seems to have nothing to do with me. Out the screen door, hurdling my stolen bike, clearing the broken spokes, the twisted wheel rims that Finty and Conrad have stomped. I'm running, my scalp prickling with tiny flames, I feel them, the flames creeping down the nape of my neck, licking at my collar, breathing hotly in my ears.

92   And Jimi, two months from being dead, is out there in front of me, stage lights snared in his hair, a burning bush. And a young road builder is standing alone on a blank, unfinished road, his head blooming with a pale grey fire.

93   And here I am, running through the late afternoon stillness of an empty suburban street, sucked down it faster than my legs can carry me, this hollow, throaty roar of fire in my head, that tiny point on the horizon drawing me to where the sun is either coming up or going down.

94   Which?

QUESTIONS

Understanding the message: Comprehension

1. Why is it significant that Jimi Hendrix "warned the cameraman to be sure to load plenty of film" at Monterey?

2. What does the narrator mean when he says that his father "sinks his teeth into my neck at the supper table, goes off to work with a satisfied, bloody, grey smile on his lips"?

3. Why do the three boys choose the old man's house as their target?

4. What causes the smell in the old man's house?

Examining the writer's craft: Analysis and interpretation

1. At the beginning of the story, Troy says, "I want to be a crazy man like Jimi Hendrix." How has this wish come true by the end of the story?

2. The story is written in the present tense, even though the narrator is clearly older, looking back on the events. What effect does this choice of tense have on the reader's experience of the story? How does it relate to the narrator's relationship to the action?

3. In what ways are Conrad and Jimi Hendrix similar in the narrator's mind? By the end of the story, how does the narrator himself become associated with Hendrix?

4. Reread paragraph 4. At the end of the paragraph, the narrator says, "I tell myself this is who I am." How is this statement different from simply saying, "This is who I am"? What does this tell us about the narrator?

5. The narrator describes the old man's house as "a bungalow where every shrub in the yard has been trimmed to look like something else . . . It's easy to guess what sort of person will live in a house of that description." Given this description, what are the boys expecting the man to be like? In what ways are they wrong?

6. In what ways does the narrator see himself as different from Finty and Conrad? In what ways does the old man see him as being different from the other two?

7. What do you make of the old man? What "album" does he believe the boys are there to inquire about? Discuss why he behaves the way he does. Do you think he's crazy? If not, why not?

8. In what way is Troy telling the truth when he says it's the old man in the picture? In what way can he be in the picture?

9. In what ways can the title be interpreted by the end of the story? Describe more than one "Jimi Hendrix experience" that takes place in the story.

Essay questions

1. Discuss the images of light and fire in this story. What do they represent? How do they reflect changes in the narrator?

2. Compare the narrator's personality at the beginning of the story to that at the end. How is he different? What lesson has he learned?

3. At the beginning of the story, the narrator says, "I'm fourteen and I want to be one of the chosen, one of the possessed." In what way does this wish come true by the end of the story? In what way is he both "chosen" and "possessed"?

VOCABULARY

Jimi Hendrix: legendary rock guitarist (1942–70) with the group the Jimi Hendrix Experience, and later a solo act, Hendrix was notorious for his destructive antics onstage. He died of a drug overdose at the height of his career, an event that forever immortalized him as a rock icon. For more information, see the official Hendrix Web site at http://www.jimi-hendrix.com.

alpaca: soft, wooly fabric

JFK, Bobby Kennedy: John F. Kennedy (1917–63), 35th president of the United States, assassinated in 1963; Bobby Kennedy (1925–68), his brother, assassinated during his campaign for the presidency in 1968

Lee Harvey: Lee Harvey Oswald, accused assassin of President John F. Kennedy

Sirhan Sirhan: convicted assassin of Senator Robert Kennedy

burning bush: bush through which God presented himself to Moses in the Bible

Falling

by Robert Boyczuk (b. 1956)

Robert Boyczuk is a Toronto writer and college professor. Most of his work falls into the genre of speculative fiction (which includes science fiction, fantasy, horror, and magic realism). He has published short stories in several magazines, including On Spec, Transversions, *and* Prairie Fire, *and in the anthologies* On Spec: The First Five Years *(1995),* Erotica Vampirica *(1996),* Northern Frights 4 *(1997),* Tesseracts[7] *(1998),* Northern Suns *(1999), and* Queer Fears *(2000). His story "Assassination and the New World Order" won first prize in* Prairie Fire's *1995 Speculative Writing Fiction Contest, as well as Honourable Mention in the 1995* Year's Best Fantasy and Horror. *"Falling" received Honourable Mention in the 1993* Year's Best Fantasy and Horror.

PRE-READING

Boyczuk's story (originally published in *On Spec*, 1993) is told by the narrator, Adrian, as he relates events while falling to the ground from the window of his high-rise apartment building. Think about the notion of suicide as you read through the story, and what might go through one's mind in this situation.

23.

A good clean fall is what Adrian hoped for. 1
One step out from the ledge, a quick plummet and— 2
No fuss, no muss. 3
At least none for him. 4

22.

Disconcerted, Adrian hangs above the crowd, stuck between earth and sky, his 5 progress arrested ten stories too soon. He cannot move, or even blink, only float before curious eyes like a half-formed thought. At first, he finds his suicide a source of profound embarrassment; later he comes to regard it as simply another banal fact of his life.

21.

Adrian soon realizes that, no, he is not exactly suspended. Careful observation 6 shows that he is indeed falling: objects at the top of his field of vision have inched upwards and out of sight while new ones have slowly crept in at the bottom.

Certainly he is falling, not quickly, perhaps as little as a centimetre every hour, but falling all the same. Moreover, he notes that the tableau below grows slightly smaller with each passing day, the scope of his vision narrowing as he approaches his death.

20.

7   Adrian is neither comfortable nor uncomfortable.

8   He simply *is*.

9   He can, if he strains, make out the blurred contour of what he believes to be his right arm. Further away, somewhat more in focus, is the tip of his right foot, still covered with its frayed work sock. Many stories below lies the familiar corner of Market Street and East Avenue, the gathering crowd pressed against police cordons. It is as if he is looking through a circular plate of glass whose focal point is at the centre, and whose image becomes increasingly distorted towards the edges like a funhouse mirror.

10 Physical sensation has vanished. He feels neither heartbeat nor breath, senses no breeze stirring on his skin even when he can see litter scudding energetically across the street below, has no bodily aches or pains, not even the familiar ones to which he's grown accustomed.

11 As for the other aches, he knows these too will disappear in the course of time.

19.

12 Falling is not a particularly bad thing, he thinks in these early days. It gives one time to reflect.

13 For instance: he hadn't found her especially beautiful. Her mother was native Indian and her father Asian giving her skin a curious hue that he had never seen before. Her nose was too large for her face, her teeth crooked and slightly yellow. But it was the way she had cut her hair, raggedly short, the stubble dyed an alarming red, that caught his eye with its improbability. "Take me home," she had whispered that first evening, unexpectedly, startling and exciting him at the same time. They had only known each other three hours, he reluctantly attending a client's dinner party, she a friend of a friend.

18.

14 For a span of days after his leap he recalls events clearly: first the commotion, the sidewalk and street crowded with onlookers, curiosity seekers, officials. To the side were parked several vehicles—a fire truck, an ambulance, three police cars— lights flashing, doors ajar, serious men leaning on the roofs of their vehicles and speaking quietly amongst themselves with an occasional nod in his direction.

15 Not long after came the media.

16 They arrived all at once, surging like angry insects, hauling cameras and recorders, dragging dishes and antennas, scrambling over one another, pushing

and shoving, some even ludicrously shouting questions as if they thought Adrian might answer, though he can no more speak than he can stop his descent.

What, he wonders often, can they find so compelling in one man's death?   17

17.

She was, he believes, somewhat vain, though this he can easily forgive her. She 18 would sit for hours before the gilt framed mirror in his bathroom, naked and beautiful against white tile, snipping meticulously at the tiny hairs that had become too long, or those that seemed to have grown into too regular a pattern, as if she viewed any kind of uniformity with the same kind of embarrassment he felt in an ill-fitting suit. Afterwards, he would sweep the floor, filling the dust pan with those small, bright red strands of hair, sometimes rolling them between his thumb and forefinger before letting them drop into the garbage.

16.

All rescue attempts fail.   19

Nets cannot hold him, both fibre and metal twines stretch then tear, snapping 20 violently back when the last strands finally part under his inescapable weight. Platforms are anchored with thick bolts to the side of his apartment building to cradle him, but these too splinter and tumble to the ground taking with them part of the dirty yellow brickwork of the wall. And once, as if they had forgotten previous attempts, spiderwork scaffolding is erected till its rough boards almost touch his buttocks, but this too he pushes through, his creeping momentum bending and twisting the thin metal tubes supporting the platform until the whole structure suddenly explodes and showers the terrified crowd, injuring several.

He feels a stab of anger at their stupidity, and wonders why no one has thought to ask him if he wants to be saved, why no one has even tried to question him 21 about his wishes?

But the anger passes, and what follows is an overwhelming guilt at the suffering others endure at his expense.   22

15.

Adrian's apartment is nearly bare.   23

Over the years he has reduced those objects surrounding him until he has only 24 the essentials he needs for a day-to-day existence. His living room is spartan, holding a few necessary furnishings: a drafting table he purchased at an art supplies store and on which his computer sits, an office swivel chair he discovered at a yard sale, his mother's small worn leather couch and battered end table, a large-screen TV with remote control.

His bedroom contains a bed, a dresser, and a small night table with an old lamp he 25 has kept from his childhood. The fridge and cupboards in his kitchen are nearly bare.

26   There are no pictures or decorations of any sort on the walls, with the exception of an old photograph of his father—a thin, sombre looking man wearing a dark suit—that sits in a wooden frame atop his fridge.

14.

27   There are periods Adrian cannot remember clearly, and he believes during these times his mind *sleeps,* as it did in that other life, for the various states accompanying sleep remain. One difference, however, is that he remembers wisps of dreams, half-formed visions, although until now he has retained almost none since childhood. He dreams outlines of hard, unforgiving geometric patterns, squares and triangles, cubes and blocks against a brilliant white background that leave burning afterimages when he returns to consciousness.

28   For some reason this makes him sad.

13.

29   *Adrian, We Understand,* reads one sign. *Hang in there, Adrian,* says another. *Don't Do it!* implores a third absurdly, as if he had not already made his decision.

30   He reads these signs with detachment, knowing that most who watch him do not share these sentiments. He senses their distaste for the melodramatic, can imagine their resentment of what they see as his huge conceit. But this is not all. He also believes he can see the longing in their eyes, watching hungrily and imagining their own varied ends, feeling frustration at this upsetting of the proper order of things. Sometimes he believes it is they who hold him here, that it is their appetite that denies him his peace. In his death they see all the small deaths they die each day, a metaphor, he thinks, for their own gradual disintegrations.

31   But he discards this notion as too obvious.

12.

32   Adrian has lived in this neighbourhood all his life, although its character has taken a turn for the worse in the last few years. Why he has remained he cannot say. He recalls long summer days spent playing in the streets, his parents watching from the stoop of the red-brick rowhouse on East Avenue. His family lived three houses from the corner until his father had failed to come home one night in August. Adrian remembers that night for its particular humidity and the movement of his mother, who hummed and sweated and cooked porridge as if nothing in the world was more important. The following week he and his mother moved in with his aunt's family twelve doors down the street.

33   Sometimes Adrian wonders what might have happened to his father, wonders if he is still alive, wonders if he sees his son suspended on the screen of his television on the six o'clock news.

11.

And sometimes, when he is not careful, he catches himself wondering where 34
she is now.

10.

A memory: 35

It is late, and Adrian stares at the screen, having just finished his final contractual 36
obligation. Adrian does not work in an office, at least not the same one every day. He
is a freelance programmer, his specialty the C programming language. Often he works
from his small, one bedroom apartment. In this he considers himself lucky. Though
his work does not afford him the security he would like, he tells acquaintances that he
enjoys the variety of jobs it brings him. With his career, as with all other things, he is
careful and cautious, fearful of the consequences of ill-considered actions.

He leans back in his chair and rubs his eyes. 37

For the last three months he has taken on no new clients, leaving behind in 38
each company's file the small discreet business cards of competitors whose work
he feels is reliable. His decision is not a rash one. Adrian is not a rash man.

Before her he had lost himself in the thrum of his work, the long hours of code 39
that strolled out on the screen before him like elegant flamingoes.

When she left she took even this. 40

Perhaps, he thinks, she was only an excuse, a last chance, realizing the process 41
of his isolation had begun long before he met her.

He pushes himself out of his swivel chair and walks into the kitchen where he 42
leans against the fridge. Looking at the dusty picture of his father he thinks of her.

9.

Adrian considers falling. He counts off mentally the meanings and phrases of 43
falling in his life: to fall asleep, to have a falling out, falling through the cracks, deals
falling through, falling flat on his face, falling into line, falling all over himself, to
fall short of his goals, to fall out a window, to fall in love, to fall from grace, the fall
of man.

8. 44

Exactly what attracted him Adrian could not say. 45

Her temperament was contradictory and difficult, her emotional swings wild
and unpredictable. She dressed and acted aggressively and with confidence, yet in
private moments betrayed to him fears of weakness and self-doubt; her anger rose
suddenly and without warning, but passed quickly, leaving a tenderness and com-
passion so complete Adrian feared that he might weep; she was moved by beggars
on the street and almost always stopped to give them money, but would fly into a

rage when appeals were made on TV. It was as if only in this tension of opposites she found her momentum.

46   To Adrian her behaviour was nerve-racking.

47   But then he remembers a family wedding, when, for a time, she seemed at peace, free of these constantly warring complexities. She was transformed, a serenity he had not seen before settling on her features, and she became almost beautiful. Adrian watched this metamorphosis with amazement, as she moved from cousin to uncle in light, carefree steps; then, later, as she whirled past him on the dance floor in the arms of her father, bestowing a warm smile on him that made his heart skip a beat. He smiled back, but it was too late, for she has already turned.

48   And at that moment he thought that should he ever be capable of loving someone, it might be her.

7.

49   The crowd, Adrian notes, has taken to wearing long overcoats, hats and scarves. Dead leaves skitter through the streets.

50   How long has he been falling, Adrian wonders. Days? Weeks? Years? Forever? Or no time at all?

51   Although he knows this should bother him, it does not, for he now recognizes that his fall is a gift, his momentum a revelation, his leap one of faith. This prolonged tumble has presented him with an opportunity few are given: a chance to rewrite his story.

52   Adrian rejoices in falling.

6.

53   When he thinks of her it is her eyes he thinks of first: big, brown and luminous, impassioned, lively eyes. He recognizes that this is only a fancy, knowing eyes cannot express emotion, that they are anything but expressive, changing little from the time of birth. Why then, he wonders, did his chest constrict each time he looked directly into hers, or now, when he merely recalls them? Why did he talk to her so often with his eyes averted, lest she see how foolish and irrevocable his own belief had become?

54   She was erratic, an enigma, unknowable, and perhaps this is what, in part, attracted him. Each time she left he had no way of knowing if she would return.

55   "I love you," he had once ventured at her moment of departure, quietly, uncertain, not sure she had even heard. She paused, one hand on the door, then turned and walked back to where he sat on the end of his old couch.

56   "Almost forgot," she said as he watched her long narrow fingers snatch sunglasses from the end table before she walked out the door.

5.

57   Though still caught in his fall, Adrian tries to imagine possible futures with her, considering them living together in his little apartment. But each scene he

envisages does not work, suffering from some subtle dissonance which will not allow him to enjoy the moment. He can't help wondering, for instance, what she would do as he works at his computer. Certainly she can't stay in the room, for then he'd never accomplish anything, her presence a distraction too great for him to bear. Would she sit quietly on the edge of the bed until he is finished? Perhaps she could busy herself about the kitchen preparing his meals? Or would she leave without saying a word to him, returning to the cafes and bars and clubs where she keeps friends?

So he makes up a larger apartment for them, and safer friends for her, and 58 though she looks and sounds the same, she also changes in these visions, becomes more understanding, less demanding, unpredictable and vulnerable enough to excite his curiosity without making him overly anxious. At these times he is convinced she waits for him below, amongst the crowd, where she keeps her vigil night and day, waiting patiently for the end of his descent.

4.

It had happened again. 59

"Shit," she said, in that small, angry voice, shaking her head. She said it as if she 60 was not even talking to him, as if he was not even there in bed next to her.

Adrian followed her stare down to where her hand rested uselessly between his 61 thighs, where she had for the last half hour tried without success to revive his ardour.

"Sorry," was all he could think to say. 62

"Why can't you just relax? Huh? There's just no in between for you, is there? Christ, 63 you're either too fast or not at all. I don't know how much longer I can take this."

"Sorry," he said again, listening to the sound of the word, wondering if perhaps 64 there was not some small part of him that willed it to happen this way, that wanted to push things to their limit, to see how far they could be stretched before they broke.

3.

It is night, and a solitary figure stands below in the circle of lamplight. Snow 65 continues to fall, and Adrian watches as the man's breath slips out in small white clouds, the only sign that he is alive.

Adrian feels alone, as if he has been abandoned. 66

In some future history, Adrian thinks, I will be forgotten, the text will disappear, 67 the historical notes vanish, a loose page torn from the book to fall, unnoticed, to the floor; and this thought, more than anything else, frightens him.

2.

Real memories have become increasingly elusive. Many are now only vague 68 afterthoughts, a feeling that something once happened, that something was once important, but now has no meaning. Thus diminished, Adrian feels them slip away like the strings of helium filled balloons from between his fingers. But no matter how much of his life has eroded in this manner he cannot free himself from the one image he would if it were in his power: the contempt that twists her features as she speaks.

69   "You have no feelings." Her words are clipped and cruelly direct. "You pretend you feel, but there is nothing there. Only self-interest. Sometimes I'm not sure there is even that. You're so lost in yourself you can't even see how desperately lonely you are."

70   Adrian ventures nothing this time, not even his usual denials.

71   "There's no room in your universe for anyone else. We are all creations that live and die as we enter and leave your sight. So I'll make it easy for you, and leave."

72   Adrian sits alone in his apartment.

73   Did she really say all that?

74   Could she have said all that?

75   But she was wrong, had misinterpreted. He did feel, but could not express it. He couldn't do otherwise. It wasn't in the nature of the character he had created for himself.

1.

76   Alone, Adrian hangs far above the street, caught between endless planes of earth and sky, bit-by-bit becoming aware of a small thought that worries away at the edge of his resolve.

77   He wonders, did she ever care?

78   But yes, he must believe, has to believe, for that is all that carries him towards a final resolution.

79   He knows the weight of her love will bear him down like a stone.

QUESTIONS

Understanding the message: Comprehension

1. For what reason does Adrian tell us he committed suicide?

2. Describe Adrian's lifestyle before he met his girlfriend.

3. What kind of person is Adrian? Describe his character.

4. What kind of person is Adrian's girlfriend? Describe her character.

Examining the writer's craft: Analysis and interpretation

1. Do we feel sorry for Adrian? Why or why not?

2. Section 21 suggests that Adrian is in a sort of suspended animation, "falling, not quickly, perhaps as little as a centimetre every hour, but falling all the same." In what way is this movement symbolic of Adrian's thoughts? Since he cannot, literally, be falling at this pace, what is meant by the statement?

3. Why is the story arranged in sections the way it is? How does this contribute to the overall meaning?

4. Reread section 9. Is there a particular sequence to the list? In what way does it relate to Adrian's life?

5. Describe the relationship between Adrian and his girlfriend. What role does each play in the relationship? How does this help to illuminate Adrian's personality?

6. What is Adrian's true motivation for committing suicide?

Essay questions

1. In section 20, we read: "Adrian is neither comfortable nor uncomfortable. He simply *is*." In what way can we say that Adrian truly experiences his life—"being"—at the point that he is about to end it? What else in the story suggests that Adrian finally appreciates the value of life?

2. Discuss the symbolism of the title. In what ways is Adrian "falling" in a symbolic sense?

3. Is it possible to know how much of what Adrian remembers or does is reality and how much fantasy? Discuss the theme of reality versus fantasy in the story and how it helps to elucidate what Adrian experiences.

VOCABULARY

irrevocable: unable to recall or take back

enigma: something mysterious or baffling

dissonance: lack of harmony

By the Edge of the Sea

by Anita Rau Badami (b. 1961)

Anita Rau Badami was born in India. In 1991, she moved to Calgary, where her first novel, Tamarind Mem *(1996), was her M.A. creative writing thesis at the University of Calgary. Her second novel,* The Hero's Walk *(2000), was published to even greater acclaim. In 2000, Badami received the Marian Engel Award given to a writer in mid-career, and in 2001, she won the Commonwealth Writers Prize for Best Book (Caribbean and Canada region). She, her husband, and their son have made Vancouver their home since 1995. Badami is currently at work on her third novel.*

PRE-READING

This story is an adaptation of part of Badami's latest novel, *The Hero's Walk*. In it, the protagonist, Sripathi Rao, lives in the town of Toturpuram on the Bay of Bengal, with his family. Even in this short excerpt, the reader gains insight into Rao's character and the interrelationships among family members. As you read through this excerpt, consider how Rao interacts with his wife and the relationship he has with his children.

1 It was only five o'clock on a July morning in Toturpuram, and already every trace of night had disappeared. The sun swelled, molten, from the far edge of the sea. Waves shuddered against the sand and left curving lines of golden froth that dried almost instantly. All along the beach, fishermen towed their boats ashore and emptied their nets of the night's catch. Their mothers and wives, daughters and sisters, piled the prawn and the crab, the lobster and the fish, into large, damp baskets still redolent of the previous day's load, and then, leaving the shimmering scales and cracked shells for the crows to fight over, they caught the first bus to the market, laughing as other passengers hastily moved to the front and made way for them and their odorous wares.

2 In a few hours the heat would hang over the town in long, wet sheets, puddle behind people's knees, in their armpits and in the hollows of their necks. Sweaty thighs would stick to chairs and make rude sucking sounds when contact was broken. Only idiots ventured out to work and, once there, sat stunned and idle at their desks because the power had gone off and the ceiling fans were still. It was impossible to bat an eyelash without feeling faint. The more sensible folk stayed at home, clad only in underwear, with moist cloths draped over their heads and

RESPOND IN WRITING

chests, drinking coconut water by the litre and fanning themselves with folded newspapers.

Even though it was the middle of July in this small town that crouched on the 3 shores of the Bay of Bengal, the southwest monsoons that provided a minor interlude between periods of heat had not appeared. So all of Toturpuram longed for December when the northeast monsoons would roar in. The memory of those cool, wet mornings was so appealing that everyone forgot that December was also the beginning of the cyclone season, when winds blew at 150 kilometres per hour, smashing everything that stood in their way. They did not remember the torrential rains that knocked out the power lines and plunged the town into stinking, liquid darkness. And they utterly forgot how the sea became a towering green wall of water that dissolved the beach and flooded the streets, turning roadways into drains and bringing dysentery and diarrhea in its wake.

Today the morning light touched the squalid little town with a tenuous beauty. 4 Even the dozens of angular apartment blocks that marched stolidly from the beach up to Big House on Brahmin Street were softened by the early glow. Sheaves of television antennae bristled up from the roofs of those apartments and caught fire as the sun rose. Big House was the only building on the street that did not flaunt one. Sripathi Rao, the owner, had reluctantly bought a television set a few years ago, but it was an old model that only had an internal antenna. His mother, Ammayya, had been disappointed.

"Nobody will even know we have a television," she protested. "What is the use 5 of having something if nobody *knows* about it?"

Sripathi would not be swayed. "So long as you get your programs, why does it 6 matter who knows what we have? Besides, this is all I can afford."

"If you had listened to me and become a big doctor you wouldn't have been 7 talking about affording and not affording at all," grumbled his mother. She never missed an opportunity to remind him how much of a disappointment he was to her.

"Even if I was one of the Birlas, I would have bought only this television," 8 Sripathi had argued. Or the Tatas or the Ambanis or, for that matter, any of India's mighty business tycoons. He did not believe in ostentatious displays—of possessions or of emotions.

When the phone rang for the first time that day, Sripathi was out sitting on the 9 balcony of his house. As usual, he had woken at four in the morning and was now reading the newspaper, ticking off interesting items with a red marker. He stopped when he heard the high, fractured trill, but made no move to go down to the landing halfway between the first and ground floors to the phone. He waited for someone else to get it. There were enough people around, including—he thought with some annoyance—his son, Arun, asleep in the room across the corridor from his own.

10   Afterwards Sripathi wondered why he had felt no twinge of premonition. He remembered other times when tragedy had occurred: how uneasy he had been the day before his father's lifeless body was discovered on Andaal Street, and how strange the coincidence that had taken him there the next morning where he had joined the curious crowd gathered around it. And before his beloved grand-mother, Shantamma, was finally claimed by the Lord of Death, his nights had been full of restless dreams. Weren't disasters always heralded by a moment of immense clarity or a nightmare that rocked you, weeping, out of sleep? This time, however, he experienced nothing.

11   The phone continued to ring, grating on Sripathi's nerves. "Arun!" he shouted, leaning back in his chair so that he could see the length of his bedroom through the balcony door. "Get the phone! Can't you hear it?" There was no reply. "Idiot, sleeps all his life," he muttered. He pushed the chair away from the square iron table on which he had arranged his writing material, and stood up, flexing his rounded shoulders.

12   As a youth, Sripathi had found that he was taller than all his friends and, because he hated to be different or conspicuous in any way, developed a stoop. His thick grey hair was cut as short as possible by Shakespeare Kuppalloor, the barber on Tagore Street. An expression of permanent disappointment had settled on a face dominated by a beaky nose and large, moist eyes. After the softness of the eyes, the thin, austere line of his mouth came as a surprise. Once during an argu-ment, his wife, Nirmala, had remarked that it looked like a zippered purse. He remembered being taken aback by the comparison. He had always found her to be like a bar of Lifebuoy soap—functional but devoid of all imagination.

13   The phone stopped ringing, and silence draped itself around the house once more. Sripathi went back to the balcony and settled down in the faded cane chair that had survived at least twenty years of ferocious sun and rain.

14   Nirmala rustled in, fresh in a crisp pink cotton sari, her black hair a sliding knot at the nape of her neck. She had a smooth, sweet-tempered face that belied her fifty-two years, and she looked much younger than Sripathi, even though there was only five years between them. On her broad forehead she had a round, red sticker-bindi. Sripathi remembered that in the past she had used powdered vermilion. She would lean over the sink in the bathroom after her ablutions, her body still warm and damp, her buttocks outlined heavily against the straight cotton of her petticoat, creating a stir of desire in Sripathi, and with the ball of her middle finger would apply a dot of Boroline cream to the centre of her forehead. Then, just as carefully, she would dip the same finger into a small silver pot of ver-milion and press it against the creamy circle. But a few years ago she, too, had yielded to modernity and abandoned her ritual of cream and red powder for the packs of felt stickers that came in a huge variety of shapes, sizes, and colours. Ever since, Sripathi had had a running argument with her about the bindis that she left stuck to the bathroom mirror like chicken-pox marks on the glass.

She handed him a stainless-steel tumbler of steaming coffee. "Why didn't you 15 answer the phone?" she wanted to know.

"Why didn't you?" 16

"I was busy emptying out the vessels in the kitchen. Today is water day, 17 remember? In between I was trying to make breakfast before your mother started shouting that she was hungry. And you want me to run up to get the phone also? Enh? What were *you* doing that couldn't be stopped for one moment?"

She began to remove the towels from the balcony wall, where they had been 18 spread out to dry the previous night. Sripathi caught a glimpse of her bare waist as she leaned forward and the sari pallu fell away. There were extra folds of soft flesh there now, although he remembered how, when Nirmala was young, that waist used to arch deeply inwards before joining her hips. He couldn't resist pinching a fold of her waist gently, and she jumped, startled, before slapping his hand away.

"*Chhee!* Old man, doing such nonsense first thing in the morning!" she 19 exclaimed.

"What nonsense? I was just administering the pinch test." He had read in the 20 Thursday health section about a test that fitness instructors used to determine the amount of fat their clients had to shed.

"I forgot to tell you," Nirmala said, ignoring his teasing, "yesterday evening at 21 the temple I saw Prakash Bhat and his wife. So uncomfortable it felt. They pretended not to see me. Can you imagine?"

Tilting his tumbler, Sripathi poured a stream of milky coffee into a small bowl on 22 the table, stopping just before it frothed out. Then he poured it back into the tumbler. To and fro he went, expertly, until he had created a hillock of foam over his coffee.

"Maybe they really *didn't* see you," he told Nirmala. "You imagine all sorts of 23 things."

"I don't imagine. I know they ignored me. I'm not a fool, even though I don't 24 have big-big degrees in this and that. That Prakash used to call me Mamma, do you remember? He was almost married to our Maya and now see how little respect he shows me. And I thought that he was a decent boy!"

Nirmala carried the towels into the bedroom but continued to talk. "Prakash's 25 wife is very plain-looking," she said. "A potato nose and tiny eyes. Lots of jewellery, but. As if shining stones can blind one to her face. She was wearing the diamond necklace. Do you remember how lovely it looked on our Maya? And now that lumpy creature has it. *Tchah!*"

Sripathi scowled at Nirmala's back. She was bent over the bed now, straight- 26 ening out the wrinkled sheets. "I told you, stop going on and on about forgotten things. I don't want to hear them."

She patted the pillows briskly and stretched, her palm pressed into the small of 27 her back, rubbing the tension away. "Yes-yes, it is all right for me to listen to your boring office stories every day," she protested. "But the minute I open my mouth, you tell me to keep quiet. Anyway, what I wanted to say was that the girl is pregnant, and they were talking to Krishna Acharye about performing the bangle ceremony."

28 "Why do you have to listen to other people's private conversations? Eavesdroppers never hear anything good."

29 Nirmala came back to the balcony to take Sripathi's empty tumbler and looked indignantly at him. "I didn't listen. Krishna Acharye himself told me. How bad I felt, you can't imagine."

30 "Why should you feel bad about some stranger's bangle ceremony?"

31 "Don't pretend you don't understand. That girl could well have been Maya, and I would have been the one talking to Krishna Acharye about buying green bangles and saris and all. What an unfortunate woman I am!"

32 Past the house with the petunias that looked like a storybook picture, past the row of cherry trees without cherries and the small store that said *Vancouver Buns,* to the crossing where she would have to decide whether to run right or left. Nandana was going home. She was nervous about being alone on the road, but she knew it was only a hop, a skip, and a jump away. She also kept a watchful eye out for strangers and killer bees. The first, both her mother and father had warned her about. *Never* talk to strangers, they had said. If a stranger approaches, start screaming or run away. *Never* accept anything from someone you do not know. "Even if they offer you a Mars bar, you *have* to say no," her mother had cautioned, looking very solemn. She knew it was her favourite treat.

33 Not that they would ever let her go out alone. No *way.*

34 As for killer bees, Nandana was more worried about those. She had seen a nature program about Africa on television last week. Killer bees were dangerous. They could kill with a single sting and travel long distances without getting tired. Nandana wasn't sure where Africa was in relation to Vancouver, but on the world map in her room it didn't look far at all. She and Molly McNaughton had discussed it and agreed that it was ab-SO-lute-ly possible for those bees to fly to Canada.

35 Why had her parents left her for almost three whole days in Anjali's house? It occurred to Nandana that maybe she had done something to annoy her parents. She tried to think what it could be. She had taken her favourite green pyjamas with the yellow frogs for this sleepover. They were too small, and her father had wanted her to take her red ones instead. Guiltily she remembered that she hadn't put her toys away before Aunty Kiran had come to pick her up. Perhaps *that* had made her father mad.

36 She was standing at the crossing, trying to decide which was her left hand and which her right, when she saw Aunty Kiran running down the street after her.

37 "Oh Nandu, you silly girl, I was so worried," she started to cry. Then she insisted on carrying Nandana back part of the way, even though she was a big girl

and far too heavy. She let herself be carried, so as not to upset Aunty Kiran further, but she stuck her legs out as stiff as two sticks because she felt stupid. Finally, she was allowed to slide down to the ground, and that was better, she thought. But she still had to hold Aunty's hand until they reached the white house behind Safeway.

"Oh God, oh God, this is terrible," Aunty Kiran wailed as soon as she shut the 38 door. "What is this poor child going to do?"

Why, thought Nandana, is she getting so agitated about me going home? 39

Uncle Sunny took the backpack from her and looked grim. "We should tell 40 her," he said to his wife. "It isn't good to keep it from her. Sooner or later she will have to be told. Better soon."

"I want my mom," said Nandana firmly. She was getting a funny feeling in her 41 stomach, as if there were beetles crawling around inside. "I told my daddy I would help him recycle the newspapers. I want to go home. Please."

Aunty Kiran blew her nose on a tissue that she pulled from the pocket of her 42 jeans. She took Nandana into the living room with the big sofas.

"Those sofas look like fat tourists in Hawaiian shirts," her father had com- 43 mented once.

Her mother had poked him in the side and giggled. "Don't say things like that 44 in front of Miss Big Ears. She will go and blurt it out for sure."

As if. She knew all about not hurting people's feelings. It was called being 45 diplomatic.

"Honey, I have something to tell you," Aunty Kiran began, holding Nandana 46 very close.

The thought crossed Sripathi's mind that the call might have been from Maya, his 47 daughter in Vancouver, and he paused in his passage across the bedroom. His eyes fell on a photograph of Maya, with her foreign husband and their child, on the windowsill next to Nirmala's side of the bed, and immediately his mood became tinged with bitterness.

It was nine years since Sripathi had heard Maya's voice. She had phoned often, 48 begging to speak to him, but he had refused. Her letters arrived regularly in the mail in thick aerogram envelopes with foreign stamps. Only Nirmala read them, though, over and over, storing them under her pillow so that she could examine the fine writing before she went to sleep. Often he was tempted to ask her what Maya had to say in those missives, but hurt, pride, and anger intervened and silenced him. Later on, even that brief curiosity died, and with it he buried all memory of Maya. Sometimes, however, from force of habit, Nirmala would still read bits aloud to Sripathi. "She went skiing in the snow, she says. I hope it is not too dangerous. Why does she want to try such things?"

Or, "Alan is teaching this year. They have to leave the child in daycare. The poor 49 little baby. I wish I was there, then no problem they would have." And he would snap at her. "I don't want to hear. If you want to keep babbling, go somewhere else and let me sleep."

50   He had chosen the name for her when she was born, for he could hardly believe that he had fathered this beautiful, perfectly formed creature. He had stayed awake all night in the small room where Nirmala and the baby lay, alert to the smallest whimper, certain that if he slept the child would slip away like a breath. Every time he peered into the cradle at the crumpled red face, the eyes squeezed shut, the curled hands like pale shells, he thought of yet another name for her. Latha. No, too ordinary. Sumitra? No, that was the youngest of King Dasharatha's wives. His daughter would be second to none. At two in the morning he had had a brilliant idea. He would christen her Yuri after the Russian astronaut who had gone into space that year, the first human to leave the grip of earth's gravity and wander among the stars. My daughter will be like him, she will reach for the skies, nothing less.

51   When Nirmala heard the name, she had burst into tears. "Yuri, Yuri? What kind of nonsense name is that?" she sobbed, jerking her nipple out of the baby's mouth and setting her bawling as well.

52   "What's wrong with it?" Sripathi demanded. She would probably want to give his daughter a name that every other child in India had, just to conform.

53   "What's wrong? It means nothing, that's what. We can't give her a meaningless name."

54   "How do you know it means nothing? Do you know Russian?"

55   "Russian?"

56   "It is the name of a Russian astronaut," explained Sripathi in the patient voice of one talking to a child.

57   "Are you crazy? We have a million Indian names, good Hindu ones with auspicious alphabets, and you go and choose a foreign one. And from a Communist country too!"

58   "I believe in the Communist philosophy," argued Sripathi aggrievedly. His first child, and he couldn't even give her a name without an argument.

59   "No, no, no! I don't care if you are a Turk who believes in Buddhist philosophy," declared Nirmala, "Yuri sounds horrible. Besides, when she goes to school other children are sure to call her 'urine.' Poor thing. No child of mine is going to have such a ridiculous name. That is final. You call her whatever you want. I will call her something else."

60   Sripathi had to agree. Children could be cruel, and the last thing he wanted was to saddle his precious daughter with a name that would hurt her. And so he had eventually settled on Maya and Nirmala had agreed, insisting only on Lalitha as a second name after her own dead mother.

61   Maya: illusion. The name was singularly appropriate for a daughter who had disappeared their lives like foam from the shoulder of a wave.

RESPOND IN WRITING N

The telephone started to ring again. This time Sripathi slapped his letter pad 62
down and hurried across the room, his heels touching the cold floor over the
worn ends of his rubber slippers.

"As if we cannot even afford a twenty-rupee pair of slippers," Nirmala 63
remarked. "You might as well not wear anything on your feet!"

"Why should I waste money? These are okay for the house for another year or 64
two. If I am comfortable, why should you be bothered?" Sripathi argued over his
shoulder.

He went down the stairs to the landing and picked up the receiver. "Yes? 65
Sripathi Rao here," he said.

QUESTIONS

Understanding the message: Comprehension

1. What kind of personality does Sripathi Rao have? Describe his character traits
   as they are presented in the selection.

2. Why is Sripathi's mother disappointed that their television set has no
   antenna?

3. What is the relationship between Nandu (Nandana, the little girl) and
   Sripathi and Nirmala? How do you know?

4. Who is calling Sripathi at the end of the story? How do you know?

Examining the writer's craft: Analysis and interpretation

1. Reexamine the opening paragraphs of the story. How does the author use
   descriptive details and figurative language to create tone? What is the tone
   being evoked?

2. The story opens with a contrast between the unbearable heat and the
   impending monsoons. What other contrasts occur in the story?

3. Describe the relationship between Sripathi and Nirmala.

4. In what way does the use of dialogue enhance our appreciation of the story?
   What effect does the dialect have on the reader?

5. Reread the third section of the story, beginning at paragraph 32, in which we
   see events from Nandu's point of view. In what way(s) does Badami convey
   the child's perspective? How well does she accomplish this?

6. At one point, Sripathi Rau says to his wife, "I told you, stop going on and on about forgotten things. I don't want to hear them." In what way might this notion haunt him at the end of the story?

7. Examine the writer's use of figurative language in this story: choose two or three similes or metaphors and discuss their effectiveness.

Essay questions

1. Discuss the use of foreshadowing in the story. What events or details help to predict the story's final outcome?

2. Discuss the theme of family in this story. How does it relate to the main characters' lives?

3. What role does the past play in this story? What message does the story convey about the value and meaning of the past in our lives?

VOCABULARY

redolent: having an odour or smell

dysentery: disease of the colon that produces painful diarrhea

squalid: repulsively filthy and degraded

tenuous: thin or weak

stolidly: without emotion, impassively

red sticker-bindi: red dot on the forehead of a married woman

vermilion: brilliant red

ablutions: washing

sari pallu: the part of a sari (dress worn by Indian women) thrown over the shoulder

rupee: Indian currency

RESPOND IN WRITING N

ID Me

by Camilla Gibb (b. 1968)

Camilla Gibb's first novel, Mouthing the Words *(1999), was selected as one of the best books of the year by the* Globe and Mail *and won the City of Toronto Book Award. The book is now being translated into seven other languages. Her second novel,* The Petty Details of So-and-so's Life, *will be published in 2002. Her short stories, essays, and reviews have appeared in the* Globe and Mail, *the* National Post, *the* Ottawa Citizen, Quill and Quire, Fireweed, Descant, Canadian Forum, Geist, Write, Lazy Writer, *and* Xtra *and in the anthologies* Bad Jobs, Carnal Nation, Brazen Femme, The IV Lounge Reader, *and* ReVisions: Feminist and Gender Theory at the Turn of the Century. *Gibb was born in 1968 in London, England, has a Ph.D. in social anthropology from Oxford University, and lives in Toronto.*

PRE-READING

This story, which originally appeared in *Canadian Forum* (2000) is narrated by a young woman who muses on her relationship with her younger brother, a tattoo artist who has a variety of tattoos himself. As you read the story, think about what brings siblings close to each other, even when they are different types of people with different goals in life. Do you know anyone who is very different from you, yet to whom you are very close?

I can still make out the initials. The ones he carved into his arm with a home- 1
made tattoo gun made from the broken needles of our mother's old Singer. He is 9 and I am 10 and we are in the basement by the furnace with a face like a monster, and I cannot stand to watch as he pulls the needle downward through his skin. I would cry out, but I am afraid, because we're already in trouble. It is the middle of the afternoon and it is Tuesday and we prefer being in the basement to being in grades three and four. We prefer being in the basement to a lot of things. In any case, it's my brother's first tattoo and I don't ask what he's thinking, etching his own initials into his skin.

But I do wonder about it later. I wonder if he was afraid to forget his name. I 2
wonder if he was afraid of getting lost in the street. I picture some kind stranger in a suit and a white hat approaching and saying in a voice out of a black and white movie, "Why, you look lost, son. What's your name, son?" and then, "What the dickens?" as my brother pulls up his sleeve to consult his bicep.

3   If it was the fear of being lost and not found that motivated him I would have suggested a different set of initials. Ones which would lead you back to a house with a swimming pool, or a family with twelve kids, or a mother who would buy you skates and take you to hockey practice.

4   Now the initials are obscured by later tattoos. The worst one is the airbrushed Jesus: all blood and thorns. "Reading a porno," he tells me proudly. It begins just below the elbow and swims laps around a fleshy, undefined bicep. I'm beginning to lose sight, as I move close enough to brush my lips against the hair on his arm. The initials are lost in a sea of overlapping blues and greens, but it doesn't seem to matter to the boy disguised as a biker daddy who is my baby brother.

5   He is Big Lou to the guys loitering in the tattoo shop. Llewellyn to his distressed mother, and Baby Blue to his sister, me. I am Tamsen to my proud mother, Timmy to my Baby Blue and Tam to just about everybody else. At times Blue and I are indistinguishable. His jeans are too tight and sit just underneath the belly of his appetite. He is balding with the rest of his hair pulled back into a black ponytail, a scruffy goatee on his face and sideburns. The tattoos are gradually creeping up his neck, threatening to strangle his face like jungle vines wrapped tight around a tree which they are slowly suffocating. He is six foot four and two hundred and twenty pounds and virtually indistinguishable from me at five foot three, with curly red hair and pale freckled skin, and nothing in my stomach except consommé and popcorn for days.

6   The smaller I feel, the more I am sure I am nothing more than a barnacle stuck to his leg. He carries me round like that, round and round his shop where he is posturing and tattooing and piercing, and avoiding paying GST, and doing the occasional drug deal on the side. He carries me round like that all summer, every summer, when I am home from Barnard and I seem to cry too much to ever hold on to a summer job.

7   Summers begin with prostrating myself before employers who want to pay me Commission Only to call up people and sell newspaper subscriptions over the phone. They hire me because I can do a good imitation of perky and well mannered and I go to school in a big city everybody dreams about and fears. But I can only do perky for so long. Not long enough, I'm afraid, to make it to my first pay cheque. It's a fast slippery slope from "you're hired" to misery, self-pity and indiscriminate loathing.

8   This year I attempt to ward off impending doom by daydreaming that I am an anthropologist observing life in the workplace, doing research for a book called *Corporate Culture and the Greatest of Apes.* I quickly begin to lose the Meaning and Purpose of my observations of human behaviour, however, and decide that I want to apply myself in a way that makes a Real Difference. So I pretend I am a therapist and I get into long intimate discussions with women who tell me that they cannot possibly subscribe to another paper because their husbands get a kick out of the Sunshine Girl.

Sometimes I haven't got it in me to do anything but cry. To put my forehead 9
down on the plastic countertop of my work station and try and stop myself by
holding my breath and letting the blood rush into my head until my ears are
pounding. I am crying about nothing and everything in particular, and I have
been doing this every summer since I got too old to go to day camp.

This summer I get fired for acting like I belong in a Woody Allen movie. 10
Actually, I get fired because my calls were being monitored.

"Do you think this is a phone sex chat line?" my boss yelled at me. 11

It was mortifying really. I had spent the better part of an hour talking with a 12
Mrs. Randy Picard and we were on the verge of some real therapeutic intimacy
where she had just told me this horrible story about how her husband wanted her
to have breast implants but they could only afford to have one done a year. I was
about to ask her whether she thought that was wise, considering the fact that her
husband was employed on a contractual basis and she had no independent
income, when in burst Big and Important Mr. McGillivary shouting vulgarly.

I stammered to apologize to Mrs. Randy Picard but she was already screaming, 13
"What? Are you broadcasting this around your office? Do you think this is a
fucking joke?" and slammed the phone down before I had a chance to explain that
I was really a therapist posing as a telemarketer and that my colleague was clearly
threatened by women.

Last summer I got fired for wearing black every day to my job at a children's 14
bookstore. That usually included big black circles under my eyes from crying on
the bus to work and smudging my mascara. Anita started subtly by saying, "It's
not a very *happy* colour, is it." On Wednesday it was, "Don't you own any pastels?"
By Friday she had moved on to increasingly hostile and cutting remarks like,
"Don't you *like* life? Our company strives to promote learning as a key to happiness. Your wardrobe and demeanour do not convey Happiness."

She tried to help by giving me a gift certificate for Laura Ashley. I complied 15
over the weekend and bought myself a rather lovely navy slip with black lace trim
which looked great with my Docs. On Monday morning, though, she accused me
of blatantly rejecting authority and I was out the door again. One slip the richer
though.

The summer before that I got fired for not wearing my shoes properly. Not 16
inserting my heels where they apparently belonged and shuffling my way to clear
tables where women wearing pantyhose in hues with names like Perfect Pearl and
Crown Jewel lunched on little bits of green with dressing on the side. Whatever.

I clearly have an attitude problem or lack a work ethic, or maybe I am missing 17
some essential gene which processes the potential of income as incentive. I marvel
as I watch Baby Blue talk savvy and lucrative street talk and use the right combination of charm and intimidation to develop a reputation for being the maker of
cool in our sleazy summer town. He is the first of a New Tribe of tattoo artists in

Niagara Falls. His work appeals to the newlyweds from small Canadian towns who come to honeymoon and cement their union with snapshots of falling water and his and hers tattoos. He does cops and cocaine dealers in adjacent chairs. He pierces the nipples, clits and labia of all the strippers in town and spends nights with the cops and the cocaine dealers in strip clubs admiring his own work.

18   He is my baby brother and we are indistinguishable.

19   I am hanging in the humid stick of August in the purple plastic dental chair. Fiddling with the lever and clasping a Diet Coke between my thighs.

20   "Dude, that's my sis," Blue yells at the greasy haired biker. "Don't fuckin' look at her like that." He is proud and protective of me. He says, "She's getting her fuckin' BA, asshole, so treat her with a little respect."

21   It's been three summers now of him saying, "Let me ID you. Let me do some ink on you." I've never objected, I just haven't put my mind to designing anything. It's also occurred to me that if I do this I will be giving up the right to die anonymously. I will, with a tattoo, have an identifying mark on an otherwise unremarkable body. If I chose to disappear or do myself in I will thus be branded as myself rather than a more glamorous someone like the selves in some of my more elaborate fantasies. A sacrificial virgin who has just escaped near death at the hands of the Reverend Moon. A minor movie star whose meteoric rise to fame and fortune is struck down with the prognosis of a fatal illness. In all the fantasies, I am bound to die, but I would still like to retain the option of provoking a nationwide search and being an unsolved mystery. I hate limiting my options.

22   I love my Baby Blue, love him more than anyone and I never want to upset him. No one else in my family is going for the free tattoo deal offered routinely in lieu of actual tangible Christmas and Birthday presents. So finally, on the stickiest day in August I say lethargically, "Ok. How about a cool Celtic band just above my bicep."

23   "Not cool," he says, shaking his head. "Stupid cliché. And besides, it's gonna look Real Stupid when you're an old lady and your arm is all saggy."

24   It's never occurred to me that I'm going to be an old lady one day. I mean, I marvel every year that I am still alive and it's hard to imagine much beyond that. But he's grossing me out. Saying, "Remember Grandma? Remember the underneath bit flapping like chicken skin?"

25   "Ok, Blue. So do whatever. Ok? Whatever."

26   And so he's telling me about the band of thorns he's going to do around my wrist. I don't care really. I don't care what he does. It's sort of not the point. The point is I am his sister and he's going to mark me in his particular way. Even if I only live for another year. He's going to give me an identity, take away my anonymity. He's going to carve his initials into my arm.

QUESTIONS

Understanding the message: Comprehension

1. What kind of voice is "a voice out of a black and white movie"?

2. What does the narrator mean when she says, "I get fired for acting like I belong in a Woody Allen movie"?

3. What types of summer jobs has the narrator had? In what ways have they all been similar?

Examining the writer's craft: Analysis and interpretation

1. The word "ID" in the title refers, of course, to the abbreviation for "identify" or "identity" as in "the ID number for a specific model car." The word, "id," however, is also a psychological term coined by psychologist Sigmund Freud. Find out the meaning of the term. In what ways is this second meaning appropriate in the story?

2. Reread the opening paragraph of the story. What do we learn about the relationship between the narrator and her brother? What do we learn about the family life of the two siblings? In what way is this information relevant to the rest of the story?

3. Which aspects of her brother does the narrator relate to herself? In what way does she believe she is "indistinguishable" from him?

4. In paragraph 8, the narrator describes how she attempts "to ward off impending doom" by daydreaming that she is an anthropologist. Why does she capitalize certain words in the paragraph?

5. The narrator describes in some detail how she was fired from successive summer jobs. What is the tone of these paragraphs? In what way is the tone in opposition to their content? What do we learn about the narrator's personality from these paragraphs?

6. Think of the stereotypes that generally are associated with tattoos and those who sport them. In what way(s) do the characters in "ID Me" either fit into or depart from these stereotypes?

7. Why does the narrator say that her brother is "going to carve his initials into my arm" at the end of the story? What do his initials represent for her?

8. Her brother tells the narrator that he will tattoo a "band of thorns" on her wrist. What are the associations with this image? How do they fit the narrator's personality?

Essay questions

1. What does this story say about the nature of identity? How do people know themselves? In an essay, discuss this theme of identity in the story.

2. Is the narrator of this story a victim? Why or why not? Write an argument essay in which you answer these questions.

3. On the surface, the narrator and her brother are polar opposites. In what ways, however, are they alike? Compare the two characters.

VOCABULARY

Singer: brand of sewing machine

barnacle: hard-shelled marine creature that sticks to bottoms of ships

Barnard: Barnard College, prestigious U.S. university

Sunshine Girl: photo feature in the *Toronto Sun* newspaper, in which a woman poses seductively

Woody Allen: U.S. film director, best known for his early comic works that depicted him as a neurotic, sex-starved New York nerd

Laura Ashley: women's clothing store known for pretty floral prints

Docs: Doc Marten's shoes or boots, chunky and thick-soled, popularized by the punks in England around 1980

Reverend Moon: Christian minister from Korea who founded the Unification Church, considered by some to be a religious cult

CHAPTER 13

Research and Documentation

Some of the essays you are asked to write may call for research. In these cases, you'll need to know where to find additional materials to back up your ideas, as well as how to incorporate them into your essay, whether through quotation or paraphrase. This chapter discusses these issues of research and documentation. For each potential source of information, we'll explain what it is, the advantages and disadvantages associated with using the source, and how to locate it. In the second half of the chapter, we'll discuss how to incorporate this material into the body of your essay (using in-text citations) and at the end (in a Works Cited or References list).

SOURCES OF INFORMATION

Sources of information fall into two basic categories: traditional (mostly print media) and contemporary (mostly electronic media). Traditional sources are found in the library and are usually available in "hard copy." They include card catalogues, books, periodical indexes, biographies, and other reference sources. Contemporary sources can be found either at libraries or by using a computer with access to on-line databases. These sources include the Internet and electronic databases (for example, CD-ROMs).

Whenever you find a promising source, remember to write down *all* of the bibliographic information about that source to use in your Works Cited or References list. It's best to record this information as you take notes, so you won't be forced to rush back to the library the evening before the paper is due for one small piece of missing information.

The most common sources of information and how to find each one are described below.

Encyclopedias

Encyclopedias are multivolume works that provide basic, general information about a wealth of topics. Encyclopedias can be very broad in scope, such as *The World Book* or *Collier's Encyclopedia*, or focused on very specific fields or topic areas, from art or science to cooking to the military to jokes. Usually arranged alphabetically by subject, encyclopedias provide short to medium-length general articles about many topics. Most articles are written by professionals or experts on the topic.

Information for Bibliographic References

When you take notes from an encyclopedia, jot down the following information, as much as is available, to use later in your Works Cited or References list:

- Author of article (if provided)
- Title of article
- Title of encyclopedia
- Editor of encyclopedia
- Number of volumes in the set
- Place of publication
- Year of publication

For electronic encyclopedias, also include the following information, as available:

- Publication medium (for example, CD-ROM, database, Internet)
- Name of vendor
- Name of electronic publication
- Date of issue

Advantages

Encyclopedias provide a great starting point for most topics, especially if you are unfamiliar with the topic and want an overview of the major issues.

Disadvantages

Encyclopedias are far too general for most research papers and should not be used as main sources of information. In addition, print encyclopedias are updated infrequently, sometimes once a year or less, which means some of the information could be out of date.

How to find encyclopedias

Encyclopedias, either in bound volumes, on CD-ROMs, or in databases on-line, can all be found in the reference area of a library. Some encyclopedias (such as *Encyclopedia Britannica*) are also available free through the Internet; others require a subscription for access.

Books

If you conduct research in the library, books are both the most obvious and the most accessible resource. A book contains a vast amount of information on a single topic, and often cover this topic in depth.

Information for Bibliographic References

When you take notes from a book, jot down the following information to use later in your Works Cited or References list. Include all of the following that are available:

- Name(s) of author(s)
- Name(s) of editor(s) (if mentioned)
- Name(s) of translator(s) (if mentioned)
- Title of book
- Edition used (if not the first)
- Title of part of the book (if you are using only one part of the book, such as a short story in.a larger collection, a preface, or only one chapter in a larger book)
- Volume used (if one of several) and total number of volumes
- Publisher (if more than one is mentioned, note them all)
- Place of publication (the city only; if the city is not commonly known, then include the country)
- Year of publication (copyright date; if there is more than one volume and the volumes were published in different years, take down all the dates)

It's also a good idea to write down the library call number for the book in case you wish to retrieve it later on.

Advantages

If you seek an explanation of how the universe began, for instance, physicist Stephen Hawking's *A Brief History of Time* certainly provides in-depth coverage.

In fact, well-researched books often rely on many sources of information for their data, and offer a certain level of expertise and detail about the topic (leafing through the bibliography at the back of the book may supply additional sources for your research). If you want a multifaceted, extended view of a topic, a book may be the perfect source.

Disadvantages

Even in today's fast-paced publishing world, it still takes approximately two years from the time a book is written to the time it appears in print. Clearly, any material in a book is dated by the time you see it. Particularly for topics related to science and technology, two years may be too long. Books can provide good, detailed background information, but don't rely on them for up-to-the minute data.

A second disadvantage of books is the flip side of the major advantage: because they contain so much information, books take a long time to read. If your essay concerns only one small aspect of accounting systems within large corporations, for example, it's not practical to wade through an entire book on general accounting in order to find the three paragraphs related to your essay. If you can, pinpoint specific chapters or passages in books most relevant to your topic.

How to find books

Most library catalogues today are computerized and many are available on-line (enabling you to search the catalogue at home through the Internet). In a few cases, a library may use a card catalogue, cataloguing its holdings on small cards stored in filing cases.

The easiest way to search for a book is if you already know the name(s) of the author(s) or exact title. However, most library catalogues also allow you to search by subject, so that you can type in a general subject (such as "low-cost housing") and browse through the resulting list of titles returned to you. Once you have information about a particular book, seek the appropriate library branch to check out the book. If you have trouble finding a book on your particular subject, review the subject listing you've used; sometimes a synonym will elicit different titles. For instance, you might key in "subsidized housing" as an alternative to "low-cost housing." Finally, you could also consult the standard list of subjects by which books are catalogued, called *The Library of Congress Subject Headings*. This book can be found at most library reference desks.

Periodicals

A periodical is published on a regular basis (that is, "periodically"), either once per month, once per week, once per day, or less frequently (some are published quarterly or biannually). For instance, *Chatelaine* magazine is published monthly, *Newsweek* magazine is published weekly, and the *Winnipeg Free Press* is published daily.

Advantages

Because they are published regularly and frequently, the information in periodicals is usually current and up-to-date. If you write about a recent political situation, you will obviously want to use periodicals rather than books to obtain information that is as immediate as possible. In addition, good periodicals employ reliable, professional writers who are often experts in their field.

Disadvantages

Some periodicals (such as magazines) may afford only superficial coverage of a topic because they cater to a large, popular audience (for example, even though *O: The Oprah Magazine* hires many experts to write its columns, these articles are almost always quite short and provide only a cursory examination of any one topic). On the other hand, others (such as professional journals) may delve *too* deeply into a topic for your purposes, or target a very specialized audience and may not be appropriate for your particular paper.

How to find periodicals

In a library, the current periodicals (most often those published within the last year) are usually available on shelves in a designated area. At the end of each year, libraries gather the year's issues of each periodical and bind these in a single hardcover volume to be shelved in the reference area. (Some libraries store old periodicals on microfiche as well.) You can also find some full-text periodicals on databases at the library; many others are available on-line through the Internet.

Rather than search through individual issues or Web pages of any particular periodical in the hopes of finding something applicable to your topic, a much faster method is to use periodical indexes, either those printed on paper or those stored electronically at the library (called databases).

PERIODICAL INDEXES (PRINT). Periodical indexes are designed to collect and catalogue information about periodical articles as they are published. Many periodical indexes are published on a monthly or weekly basis, updating lists of topics and articles that have appeared in the periodicals during that time period. About once per year, the individual volumes are collected into a larger, bound volume, in which researchers can check all periodical articles published in that year. Some indexes are specialized, dealing only with a particular subject area (such as business or literature), while others, such as the *Reader's Guide to Periodical Literature*, cover a broad range of interests and publications.

To use a periodical index, you search for a particular topic. The index will indicate relevant articles, the periodical in which they've been published, the author, the page number, and other pertinent information. Your task, then, is to seek out the actual magazine, newspaper, or journal article mentioned in the index, and see if its information is relevant to your paper. Of course, not every periodical mentioned in an index will be available in your library, so while scouring the indexes you must find more sources than you'll actually need.

PERIODICAL DATABASES AND ON-LINE SOURCES. If you use a database or on-line index, you may also have access to abstracts (summaries) of the articles; a few will include full-text versions of the articles as well, so that you won't need to find the original magazine, newspaper, or journal. Some popular databases in Canada are ERIC (Educational Resources Information Centre), EBSCO (full-text articles on a variety of topics from several disciplines), and CBCA (Canadian Business and Current Affairs, which deals with both magazines and newspapers). The Gale Group also provides a wide variety of databases on literature, social sciences, and business. A librarian can help you choose the database best suited to your research. Simply search a specific subject and the database will show how many articles are available under that subject heading. Beware, however: often, far more articles appear than you could possibly use. If you narrow your search terms as much as possible, you'll come up with better results.

Web Pages

Although most people think that the World Wide Web refers to the Internet (and use the terms interchangeably), the Web is actually only *part* of the Internet, the **inter**national **net**work of computers linked to each other to provide and exchange information. Nowadays, the Web is the most used aspect of the Internet, which also facilitates e-mail, listservs, and newsgroups. Web pages are sources of information posted on the World Wide Web that contain images and hypertext (lines of data that allow quick connection to other pages if users click on them). Each Web page (or Web site) has its own address, or URL (uniform resource locator), which allows the user to locate or call up the page onto the computer screen.

Advantages

Information on the Web is updated virtually daily; you can find absolutely up-to-the-minute information there. In addition, the information is quickly accessible from any computer with Internet access. You can conduct research from home at your leisure, and you have access to data from a wide variety of sources at your fingertips. Many reputable and established institutions (for example, universities, colleges, hospitals, or government bodies) maintain Web sites that offer students a wealth of useful and reliable information.

Disadvantages

Because virtually anyone can post anything on the Web and there are no regulations or censorship, you must be extra vigilant in exercising critical thinking when you assess any information you encounter there. Just because someone posts an account of her personal experiences with taking the antidepressant drug Prozac,

---

Information for Bibliographic References

Whenever you access a Web page, take down the following information, as much as is available:

- URL (Web address)
- Title of the page
- Name of any sponsoring institution or organization
- Name of any large project of which the page is part
- Name of author or creator of the page
- Number of pages or paragraphs (if indicated)
- Date of posting (look for the "last updated" information, usually at the bottom of the page)
- Date of access (when you accessed the site)

---

for instance, doing so does not make her an expert on this drug. While you must critically assess every type of source you encounter, it's particularly important to be absolutely scrupulous when carrying out your assessment of Web pages.

In addition, despite its ubiquitous nature and the immense quantity of information it makes available, the Internet is an extremely incomplete and erratic source. You may draw a blank on a particular topic or find only irrelevant information. Because the most reliable and abundant sources of good information are still at the library, you should consider the Internet as a supplemental, never a singular, source of information.

Finally, another disadvantage of the Internet is its ephemeral nature: information changes constantly, and may in fact change from day to day. If you consult a particular Web page on Monday, the page may have moved (changed address) or altered its contents by Wednesday. For this reason, it's always a good idea to print out any information as it's viewed, directly from the Web page itself if your printer will allow it. This way, as well, you also have a hard copy of the date and Web address on the printed page.

How to find Web pages

Any computer with Internet access can be a vehicle for finding Web pages. To find information on your topic, you must conduct a search on the Internet, a process that can sometimes be as frustrating as it is rewarding. The key to good Internet searches is knowing how to define and narrow your search terms. Here are some pointers in this area:

USE A GOOD SEARCH ENGINE. Always use a search engine to conduct your search. A search engine allows you to type in a subject as a single word (keyword) or phrase related to your topic; it will then scan millions of Web pages to seek that word, and will show the relevant hits or URLs (Web addresses) for pages that contain the keyword(s). It's important to find a search engine that provides as many references as possible and reviews as many entries as possible in searching if you want your results to be most useful. You can choose between standard search engines that scan Web pages individually, or metasearchers (search engines that search through a number of other search engines at once to find the maximum number of hits or matches).

These are some of the most popular search engines:

- AltaVista (www.altavista.com)
- Infoseek (www.infoseek.com)
- Lycos (www.lycos.com)
- HotBot (www.hotbot.com)
- Excite (www.excite.com)
- Google (www.google.com)
- GoTo (www.goto.com)

These are some common metasearch engines:

- Metacrawler (www.metacrawler.com)
- Dogpile (www.dogpile.com)
- Ask Jeeves (www.askjeeves.com)
- Ixquick (www.ixquick.com)
- Yahoo (www.yahoo.com)

USE EFFECTIVE SEARCH METHODS. The number of responses you get to any search depends on the keywords you use in the search. The more specific your search terms, the more likely it is that you'll get references that relate closely to your topic. You can also combine terms using Boolean operators, which work with the vast majority of search engines. Boolean operators are words that force your search to include or exclude terms of your choice. Here's how they work:

1. *Type "and" between two keywords.* Placing the Boolean operator "and" between two keywords forces the search engine to include *only* those Web pages that contain *both* the words. This is useful when your search involves only one part or aspect of a larger topic. For instance, if you simply type "education" as your keyword, you will be inundated with thousands of possible hits. However, if your essay concerns only college-level education, the search phrase "education and college" will yield a much more specific list of possible Web pages, since all hits will contain *both* keywords. You can refine the search even further by combining more than two keywords, as in the search phrase "education and college and Alberta." *Note:* Some search engines require you to use the plus symbol (+) instead of the word "and"; type the symbol between the keywords, *without* leaving spaces between them (for example, "education+college+Alberta"). Always check the help file of the particular search engine you use.

2. *Type "or" between two keywords.* If you seek *either* one word *or* the other, use "or" between the two keywords. For instance, you may conduct a search in which you seek "songs or lyrics" related to a particular musician. *Note:* For this type of search, some search engines require you to simply type the keywords, leaving a space after each, without adding the word "or" (for example, "songs lyrics"). Always check the help function of the particular search engine you use.

3. *Type "not" between two keywords.* In searching for a term that is often associated with another term, you may want to clarify which of the two you seek. For instance, a search for information on the ship *Titanic* will also supply a plethora of pages on the 1997 hit movie *Titanic,* unless you key in a search such as "Titanic not movie" or "Titanic not film." *Note:* Some search engines require you to use the minus symbol (–) instead of the word "not"; type the symbol between the keywords, *without* leaving a space between them (for example, "Titanic–movie"). Always check the help file for the particular search engine you use.

4. *Use phrases.* You can refine a search to pick up only a specific phrase or combination of words *in a particular order* by enclosing the phrase or words in quotation marks (" "). For instance, if you simply write "genetic engineering" as your search term (without quotation marks), the search engine will return all hits that contain the word "genetic" (without "engineering"), those that contain the word "engineering" (without "genetic"), and those that contain both words. If you enclose the entire phrase "genetic engineering" in quotation marks, the search engine will call up only those two words together and in that order.

5. *Seek variations on a word or phrase.* You can use an asterisk (*) to conduct a "wild card" or open-ended search. If you key in the first few letters of a word and add an asterisk at the end, the search engine will seek all words that *begin* with those letters, even if the endings are different. For example, the keyword "authorit*" will produce search results on "authority," "authoritative," and "authoritarian." An asterisk can also replace letters in the middle of a word if you wish to seek variations in spelling; if you type "lab*r," for instance, the search engine will seek "labor" as well as "labour." Again, always be certain to consult the help file of the particular search engine you use, in case it doesn't support this function.

6. *Be careful with spelling, capitalization, and punctuation.* Depending on the search engine you use, a search for "Major" may turn up different hits from a search for "major"; and "Jones" may turn up different hits from a search for "jones." Similarly, "houses" may provide a different list of hits from "house." Always check the search engine you use to see if these mechanical details will make a difference to the search results.

7. *Be flexible.* Finally, the best way to find the sources you seek is to be flexible and persistent in your search. If your first set of hits doesn't provide the information you seek, try again using a different combination of keywords or alternative keywords (try synonyms for some words, such as "hot beverage" for "coffee"). Similarly, approaching your topic from a different angle may also help; a search for information on organic products in Canada can be approached through the topics of farming in Canada, agriculture in Canada, organic produce, organic foods, and so on.

Newsgroups and Listservs

A newsgroup is a public site that publishes messages for anyone to see; anyone who calls up the site can read and respond to the posted messages. A listserv gears a message to a large group of recipients, but only those who subscribe to the list. Recipients may respond either to the entire group or to the individual posting a message.

Advantages

Because they are available on-line, both these sources can provide current information. They also tend to attract participants who are already involved in a particular field, as they deal with specific topics. Listservs, however, usually address more specific topics and are more regulated than newsgroups. Because they serve subscribers, listservs can more easily be monitored; they are often screened to prevent hate literature or abusive messages.

Disadvantages

Newsgroups, unlike listservs, have no controls imposed on the content; participants can post anything they like. For both sources, you may need to wade through a lot of irrelevant material in order to find the specific posting that relates to your research.

How to find newsgroups and listservs

Newsgroups and listservs on particular topics will often be listed in the results of an Internet search. Many of the popular search engines (such as Yahoo and AltaVista) regularly include newsgroups and listservs on their pages. In addition, a keyword search for either "newsgroup" or "listserv" will yield hundreds of results, including specialized search engines that list both newsgroups and listservs.

Experts

Experts are those individuals recognized for their knowledge and experience in a particular field. They often deal with specific subjects directly and on a daily basis.

> ## Information for Bibliographic References
>
> Whenever you contact an expert—in person, by telephone, or by e-mail—take down the following information for your Works Cited or References list:
>
> - Name and title of person contacted
> - Date of interview (if done in person or on the telephone)
> - Date of e-mail message (the expert's message to you)
> - Title (subject line) of e-mail message
> - Date you accessed an e-mail message

Advantages

If you can locate an expert on your topic who is willing to talk to you, you will have a wealth of useful information at your fingertips. Access to current information (facts) and detailed, informed answers to pointed questions are both advantages of talking to an expert.

Disadvantages

The major disadvantage with this type of information is the time involved in finding the person and, sometimes, waiting for an answer to your questions. Never rely solely on interviews for your information.

How to find experts

Many government agencies, associations, foundations, corporations, or other commercial ventures have e-mail addresses and are happy to answer queries. In addition, many individuals operate their own Web sites with e-mail addresses, and some professors, writers, doctors, or other experts are also available this way. If you know of an expert in a particular field, try contacting the person first through e-mail and request a short telephone or an in-person interview. Good sources for interviews are professionals of any sort (for example, doctors, lawyers, professors), government employees, administrators, entrepreneurs, scientific researchers, or creative artists. Obviously, you should choose a professional with expertise in the area you are researching.

Other Media Sources

Other media sources for research include television programs, radio programs, videos, DVDs, films, and sound recordings (such as albums, tapes, and CDs). Television programs, radio programs, and films are interesting, entertaining

---

Information for Bibliographic References

Whenever you use sources from the media, take down as much as is available of the following information to use in your Works Cited or References list:

- Names of writer(s), performer(s), director(s), and producer(s)
- Title of program or series (radio and television); of film, video, or DVD; or of album, tape, or CD
- Title of episode (for a TV or radio program) or song (for an album, a tape, or a CD)
- Production company (for example, Sony Records, Universal)
- Date produced (or, for a radio or television program, date aired)
- Local network (for radio and television programs)
- City of broadcast (for radio and television programs)

---

sources, presented in a format that is both easy and enjoyable to access. In addition, television and radio programs often provide information that is updated daily.

Advantages

The media offer rich resources on a plethora of topics. Watching a video or listening to a recording can be a valuable experience, allowing you to amass data not available through the written word.

Disadvantages

As with Web pages, you must be careful about the media sources you use. It's often difficult to find an entire video or radio recording dealing exclusively with the topic you seek, let alone one that is current. In addition, much of popular media is just that—a popularized, often watered-down version of the information. Unless you use work by serious producers and writers (of documentary films, television programs for educational or public-broadcasting stations, or reliable news reports), you must carefully assess just how much the information has been diluted for a popular audience.

How to find other media sources

Like other sources, you can locate filed copies of some television programs, films, recordings, and so on at libraries. These will be filed according to subject, title, and author (films are often filed by the director or producer). Some film companies or television stations also keep files of recorded programs, and sometimes allow the public to screen these under controlled conditions. Your local video store, of course, also stocks films on tape.

Assessing Your Sources

When you purchase goods or services, you almost always consult a variety of sources and consider a variety of factors before you make your choice and spend your hard-earned money. Just as you wouldn't buy the first bicycle you see, rent the first video you set your eyes on, or book the first vacation package you hear about, you should never use the sources you encounter without first considering their overall value. Following is a list of the different questions to review while deciding which sources will make their way into your essays.

Assessing the credibility of the author

- Is the author an expert in the field? Does s/he have any professional credentials? Has the writer dealt with this topic before? Always look for material written by specialists or those with acknowledged expertise in a particular field.

- Is the writer well respected? Even someone who has written a number of publications on a particular topic may nevertheless be discredited by the academic or professional community.

Assessing the credibility of the source

- Look for publications that are supported by respected academic or professional bodies (such as universities, professional organizations, and government bodies). Academic and literary journals usually provide fairly reliable material, as do certain national magazines and newspapers. In general, you will find more in-depth and useful information in scholarly or academic publications than in popular magazines. Consider the source of the information and the date of publication (how current is it?), especially when dealing with technology, science, or other topics in which discoveries and change occur on a regular basis. Additionally, examine how each source makes use of its own sources, and how these are indicated and attributed.

- When dealing with Web sites, look for those that operate under the auspices of a university or other reputable body. The author should be identified, and her or his credentials stated or easily verifiable. In addition, assess the quality of the writing, whether the information is current, and whether the site is frequently updated. Ideally, you will be able to verify information from a Web site in other sources as well. It may be helpful to consider the domain (usually the last part of the URL, after the dot), which helps to identify the source of the site, or what type of site it is. The following are some common domains:
    - .com = commercial site
    - .edu = educational site (U.S.)

- .org = organization site (usually a not-for-profit organization)

- .net = network site (a multipurpose domain; may be commercial)

- .gov = government-run site

- .mil = military site (U.S.)

- .ca = Canadian site (other domains exist for other countries, such as .au for Australia, .uk for United Kingdom)

SUMMARIZING INFORMATION

As you begin the note-taking process for your research paper, you may prefer at times to summarize material rather than paraphrase or quote it directly. A **summary** is especially useful for large chunks of information from sources that cannot be quoted in their entirety. In a summary, you provide a condensed version of a text, including all its main points, in about one-quarter to one-third the number of words used in the original (generally, a single paragraph can be summarized in one sentence).

DEFINITION

Summary: a short version of a piece of writing, in your own words, that includes all the major points of the original

Here are the steps in writing a summary:

1. *Read the original.* Read through the original piece of work as you would any other, using the process for critical reading described in Chapter 1. Ensure that you understand the general meaning.

2. *Underline key points.* To differentiate major from minor ideas, look for the topic sentences of paragraphs (which usually indicate main points). Within a paragraph, minor details usually illustrate points already made or expand on earlier ideas.

3. *Write out all the main points in the same order in which they occur in the original.* Give points equal weight to those in the original (for example, if a topic takes up half of the original, it should take up half of the summary). Avoid using the exact phrasing of the original.

4. *Condense the main points further if possible.* Eliminate as much excess material as possible at this stage.

5. *Write the draft summary, using clear, cohesive language.*

6. *Revise to ensure that your summary makes sense and hasn't left out anything essential.*

7. *Revise again, if necessary. Check the word count.*

TIP

Reducing word counts

To reduce the number of words in your summary, eliminate unnecessary words or repetition, such as the following:

- Supporting examples, illustrations, or details (except those absolutely necessary to understanding the meaning of the work)
- Most quotations (use indirect quotes instead)
- Wordiness
- Figures of speech (use paraphrasing instead)
- Multiple short sentences that repeat information and can be combined into longer sentences

Remember, too, that your summary should merely reduce the length of the original, without changing or adding to the original meaning and intent. In other words, your own analysis and opinions should never be included in a summary.

Text and Sample Summary

Here is an excerpt dealing with indoor air pollution. Read over the text and decide how you'd summarize it before looking at the sample summary, which follows the passage.

When we hear the phrase "indoor air pollution," we typically think of smokestacks and vehicle exhausts pouring grey streams of chemical matter into the air. However, much air pollution is invisible to the eye and exists where we least expect it—in our homes, schools, workplaces, and public buildings.

Sick building syndrome (SBS) is a situation in which occupants of a building experience symptoms that seem to be linked to time spent in a building, but no specific illness or cause can be identified (Lindauer, 1999). Building occupants complain of symptoms such as headaches; eye, nose, and throat irritation; a dry cough; dry or itchy skin; dizziness and nausea; difficulty concentrating; fatigue; and sensitivity to odours. While specific causes of SBS remain unknown, contributing factors may include polluted outdoor air that enters a building through poorly located air intake vents, windows, and other openings. Most indoor air pollution comes from sources inside the building, such as adhesives, upholstery, carpeting, copy machines, manufactured wood products, cleaning agents, and pesticides.

In poor countries, fumes from cooking and heating are major contributors to indoor air pollution. Globally, four million people die each year from acute respiratory problems caused by breathing fumes from cooking and heating (Kemps, 1998).

In developed countries, common household, personal, and commercial products contribute to indoor air pollution. For some individuals, exposure to these products can result in a variety of temporary acute symptoms such as drowsiness, disorientation, headaches, dizziness, nausea, fatigue, shortness of breath, cramps, diarrhea, and irritation of the eyes, nose, throat, and lungs. Long-term exposure can affect the nervous system, reproductive system, liver, kidneys, heart, and blood. Some solvents found in household, commercial, and workplace products cause cancer; others, birth defects ("The Delicate Balance," 1994). Some of the most common indoor pollutants include carpeting (which emits nearly 100 different chemical gases), mattresses (which may emit formaldehyde and aldehydes), drain cleaners, oven cleaners, spot removers, shoe polish, dry-cleaned clothes, paints, varnishes, furniture polish, potpourri, mothballs, fabric softener, and caulking compounds. Air fresheners, deodorizers, and disinfectants emit the pesticide paradichlorobenzene. Potentially harmful organic solvents are present in numerous office supplies, including glue, correction fluid, printing ink, carbonless paper, and felt-tip markers.

Many consumer products contain fragrances. The air in public and commercial buildings often contains deodorizers, disinfectants, and fragrances that are emitted through the building's heating, ventilation, and air conditioning system. Some fragrance fumes produce various combinations of sensory irritation, pulmonary irritation, decreases in expiratory airflow velocity, and possible neurotoxic effects (Fisher, 1998). Fragrance products can cause skin sensitivity, rashes, headaches, sneezing, watery eyes, sinus problems, nausea, wheezing, shortness of breath, inability to concentrate, dizziness, sore throat, cough, hyperactivity, fatigue, and drowsiness (DesJardins, 1997). Increasingly, businesses are voluntarily limiting fragrances in the workplace or banning them altogether to accommodate employees who experience ill effects from them.

Indoor air pollution is particularly problematic for sufferers of a controversial condition known as multiple chemical sensitivity (MCS). People suffering from MCS say that after one or more acute or traumatic exposures to a chemical of group of chemicals, they began to experience adverse effects from low levels of chemical exposure that do not produce symptoms in most people. Even individuals who are not diagnosed as having MCS may experience adverse health effects from indoor air pollution. [540 words] [From Linda A.

Mooney et al., *Understanding Social Problems,* First Canadian Edition, Scarborough, Ontario: Nelson Thomson Learning, 2001: 470–71]

Here is a sample summary of the reading.

> Indoor air pollution exists invisibly in many buildings.
>
> With no clear cause, Sick Building Syndrome (SBS) is linked to time spent in a building and may be linked to polluted outdoor air entering a building, though indoor air pollution is usually caused by inside air. SBS causes many physical symptoms.
>
> In poor countries, heating and cooking fumes create indoor air pollution, causing acute respiratory problems and death.
>
> In developed countries, common household, personal, and workplace products contribute to indoor air pollution and result in temporary acute symptoms for some. Long-term exposure can affect the nervous system, reproductive system, vital organs, or blood. Some solvents cause cancers or birth defects. Airborn products in public and commercial buildings are emitted through heating, ventilation, and air conditioning systems and can produce a variety of severe respiratory or neurological symptoms. As a result, some businesses limit or ban fragrances.
>
> Sufferers of multiple chemical sensitivity (MCS) experience adverse effects from low levels of normally harmless chemical exposure, but even healthy people can suffer from indoor air pollution. [173 words]

CITING AND DOCUMENTING SOURCES

The two most common formats for citing and documenting sources in research essays are the MLA (Modern Language Association) and the APA (American Psychological Association) formats. The MLA is used primarily for arts and humanities (including English) papers, while the APA tends to be used for science-related papers, including social sciences. Both require two parts to the documentation process:

1. *In-text citation (parenthetical reference).* For every quotation or paraphrase in your essay, you must include, in the same passage of the essay in which the material appears, an in-text citation (parenthetical reference). This is a short reference to the source of the information (usually just a name and page number or date) that allows the reader to find a longer, more detailed and complete reference at the end of the paper, in the Works Cited or References list. Each item in an in-text citation should have a corresponding listing in the Works Cited or References list at the end of the paper. (For more information

on when to quote or paraphrase, the differences between the two, and how to fit quotes smoothly into your essay, see Appendix 2.)

2. *Works Cited or References.* This is a complete, detailed list of *every* source used in the essay, listed in alphabetical order by authors' last names, and including all of the relevant information necessary for readers to find the original reference sources themselves. The items in the Works Cited or References list should match those in the in-text citations. There should *never* be a source listed on this page that has not already been cited in your essay.

Citing Sources in the Text

Both MLA and APA formats ask you to include a short reference, in parentheses in the body of your essay, following a quote or paraphrase. The basic MLA and APA formats and several variations for each style are discussed below.

MLA format for in-text citations

Basic in-text citation
Include the author's last name and the page number on which the information or quote appeared, separated by a space but no comma or abbreviation (such as "p."). Because the reference is not part of the quote, it should follow the closing quotation mark, but precede the final period of the sentence.

It is interesting to note that "[c]ultures surely differ in how their members express, talk about, and act on various emotions. But that says nothing about what their people feel" (Pinker 365).

In-text citation when the author's name is mentioned in the text
If you happen to mention the name of your author in the essay as an introduction to the quote or passage, you need not repeat the name again in the parenthetical reference. However, you should always include the page number, at the least, in a parenthetical reference; never include it in your own sentence.

Pinker suggests that "[c]ultures surely differ in how their members express, talk about, and act on various emotions. But that says nothing about what their people feel" (365).

In-text citation when more than one work by the same author is mentioned
If your essay refers to two works by the same author published at different times, the reader will not be able to distinguish from just a name and page number which

of the two, or more, books by that author the quote is from. In this case, add an abbreviated version of the title between the author's last name and page number.

> In her definition of intimacy, the author writes, "intimacy means that we can be who we are in a relationship, and allow the other person to do the same" (Lerner, Intimacy 8). However, she does acknowledge that we sometimes "want to be separate, independent individuals—self contained persons in our own right," in contrast to seeking this intimacy with another (Lerner, Anger 29).

In-text citation for a work by two or three authors
When citing a work by two or three authors, always use the last name of each author each time the work is cited. When citing three authors, add commas after the first two last names.

> One theory suggests that "fluctuations in the economy are always preceded by corresponding fluctuations in collective psychology" (Rogers and Koyama 47).

In-text citation for two authors with the same last name
If by some chance you are quoting from two different authors with the same last name, distinguish them in your in-text citations by adding each author's first initial (or the entire first name if the initial is also shared) before the last name in each case.

> These long-term effects can include "high blood pressure, impaired circulation, vision problems, and extreme thirst" (M. Smith 422).

In-text citation for a work by four or more authors
In each case, use only the first author's last name followed by "et al." ("and others") and the page number.

> It is possible that such a waste-disposal unit could be installed in several apartments within the same building, but "specifications must comply with municipal regulations and be posted in common disposal areas" (Colbourne et al. 189).

In-text citation for an electronic source
Because electronic sources often don't include page numbers, MLA format simply requires you to include as much information as you may have. If the source

includes page numbers, use these; otherwise, indicate the paragraph number or even the screen (if the text runs to more than one screen) to identify the location of the source.

> Discussing Lucy Maud Montgomery's novel, <u>Anne of Green Gables</u>, one writer based in Prince Edward Island wrote that it "has captured the hearts of millions world-wide and in turn has heightened the sense of rural majesty and timelessness so intrinsically linked with life in this tiny province" (Sutton par. 1).

APA *format for in-text citations*

Basic in-text citation

With APA style, there are three elements to the basic citation: the author's last name, the date of the publication, and the page reference (page references are necessary for direct quotes, but not for paraphrased passages). Separate the items with commas, and use "p." (to indicate the page) or "pp." (to indicate the pages) before the page number(s). Include the information in a parenthetical reference at the end of the sentence; put the final period of the sentence after the parenthetical reference. In-text citations are *required* only for quoted material; if you paraphrase or summarize, an in-text citation is encouraged but not mandatory.

> It is interesting to note that "[c]ultures surely differ in how their members express, talk about, and act on various emotions. But that says nothing about what their people feel" (Pinker, 1997, p. 365).

In-text citation when the author's name is mentioned in the text

As with the MLA style, if you mention an author's name in your own sentence, it may be omitted from the in-text citation. The date, however, is always included (in parentheses) beside the author's name.

> Pinker (1997, p. 365) suggests that "[c]ultures surely differ in how their members express, talk about, and act on various emotions. But that says nothing about what their people feel."

In-text citation when more than one work by the same author is mentioned

Because a date is included with each in-text citation, the APA system allows readers to distinguish between two works by the same author using the date. If it turns out that you are using two works by the same author and both were published in the *same* year, add "a" after the date of the first work, "b" after the date of the second, "c" after the date of the third, and so on to distinguish these from each other; retain these distinctions in your References list.

> In her definition of intimacy, the author writes, "intimacy means that we can be who we are in a relationship, and allow the other person to do the same" (Lerner, 1989, p. 8). However, she does acknowledge that we sometimes "want to be separate, independent individuals—self contained persons in our own right," in contrast to seeking this intimacy with another (Lerner, 1985, p. 29).

In-text citation for a work by two authors
When citing a work by two authors, always use the last name of each author every time the work is cited. Use an ampersand (&) rather than the word "and" to connect authors' names in the in-text citation.

> One theory suggests that "fluctuations in the economy are always preceded by corresponding fluctuations in collective psychology" (Rogers & Koyama, 1999, p. 47).

In-text citation for two authors with the same last name
If by some chance you are quoting from two different authors with the same last name, distinguish them in your in-text citations by adding each author's initial before her or his last name in each case.

> These long-term effects can include "high blood pressure, impaired circulation, vision problems, and extreme thirst" (M. Smith, 2001, p. 422).

In-text citation for a work by three to five authors
APA asks you to refer to *all* the authors of a work the first time it is mentioned when there are three to five names. Use an ampersand (&) rather than the word "and" before the last author's name in the in-text citation. If you mention the work again after the first in-text citation, however, you may write only the first author's last name followed by "et al." ("and others") in the in-text citation.

> *First citation:*
> It is possible that such a waste-disposal unit could be installed in several apartments within the same building,

but "specifications must comply with municipal regulations
and be posted in common disposal areas" (Colbourne,
Schacter, Kerr, & Masal, 1999, p. 189).

Second and all later citations:

Once the units have been installed, regulations require
"authorized inspections to take place at intervals of no
less than one year apart" (Colbourne et al., 1999, p. 214).

In-text citation for a work by six or more authors

In this case, use the last name of the first author followed by "et al." in every in-text citation, including the first.

Cellular telephone systems have grown within the North American
marketplace "at a rate that would have been inconceivable even
a decade ago" (Lorimer et al., 2000, p. 33).

In-text citation for an electronic source

Indicate the most recent date available for the electronic source as well as a page or paragraph reference, if provided. If neither page numbers nor paragraphs are indicated, you may omit this information.

Discussing Lucy Maud Montgomery's novel, Anne of Green Gables,
one writer based in Prince Edward Island wrote that it "has
captured the hearts of millions world-wide and in turn has
heightened the sense of rural majesty and timelessness so
intrinsically linked with life in this tiny province" (Sutton,
2001, para. 1).

Placement of in-text citations

For both MLA and APA styles, the placement of the in-text citation depends on the length of the quotation. For short quotes that are included within your sentence or paragraph, simply place the parenthetical reference *after* the quoted or paraphrased material, but before the final punctuation of the sentence (the reference is not part of the quote, but it is part of your sentence). With longer quotes that are indented and separated from your own sentence or paragraph, place the parenthetical reference *after both* the quoted passage *and* the final period; do not add a second period after the in-text citation. (For examples of formats for quotations and paraphrases, see Appendix 2.)

Documenting Sources in a Works Cited or References List
MLA format for Works Cited

The Works Cited list, which appears on a separate page at the end of your essay, provides full references for each of the sources cited in your essay. In MLA style papers, entries usually include the author's name followed by the title of the work, publication information, and the date of publication (for humanities subjects, information is usually relevant for a long period of time, so the date is less important than the author and title of the work). As you look through the following samples, notice the format: MLA requires that each listing begin flush with the left margin and that subsequent lines be indented. In addition, underlining is used to indicate book titles, but parts of books (chapter headings or story titles) are enclosed in quotation marks. For other more specific details, see the models below.

If your particular type of source does not appear in this list, consult the MLA style book or Web site:

Gibaldi, Joseph. <u>MLA Handbook for Writers of Research Papers</u>. New
    York: Modern Language Association, 1999.

www.mla.org

For each item, all the information that should be included is listed, in order. Keep in mind, however, that each of these parts may not always be available (for example, some books don't list an author, some Web sites are not paginated, some magazines don't list volume numbers, and so on). If any specific piece of information is not available, simply omit it and list the rest of the information in the order given.

A book by a single author
Warburton, Peter. <u>Debt and Delusion: Central Bank Follies That</u>
    <u>Threaten Economic Disaster</u>. London: Penguin, 2000.

A book by two or three authors
Moriarty, Sandra E., and Tom Duncan. <u>How to Create and Deliver</u>
    <u>Winning Advertising Presentations</u>. Lincolnwood: NTC Business
    Books, 1989.

A book by four or more authors
Only the first author of four or more must be named, followed by "et al." ("and others").

Lehringer, Albert, et al. <u>The Principles of Biochemistry</u>. 2nd ed. New York: Worth, 1993.

A book with no author indicated

In some cases, as with very old books, government publications, or books issued by large companies, it's possible that no author is mentioned. In this case, treat the title as the first piece of information (and arrange the entry alphabetically according to the first word in the title, other than "a," "an," or "the").

<u>The Gentleman's Guide to Etiquette</u>. London: Penguin, 1921.

A book with corporate, association, or government authorship

If a specific author is mentioned, include the name as in a typical entry. If the author is a particular agency or department of government, cite this by listing the province or country first, followed by the agency or department.

Author different from publisher:

British Columbia Ministry of Health. <u>Handbook for Rural Mental Health Workers</u>. Ottawa: Health and Welfare Canada, 1983.

Author same as publisher:

Health Canada. <u>Heart Disease and Stroke in Canada</u>. Ottawa: Health Canada, 1995.

A translation

Tremblay, Michel. <u>Forever Yours, Marie-Lou</u>. Trans. John Van Burek and Bill Glassco. Vancouver: Talon Books, 1975.

A book with an editor instead of an author

Ondaatje, Michael, ed. <u>Lost Classics</u>. Toronto: Knopf Canada, 2000.

A book with an editor and an author

Moodie, Susanna. <u>Roughing It in the Bush; or, Life in Canada</u>. Ed. Elizabeth Thompson. Ottawa: Tecumseh, 1997.

A second or later edition

Harris, Lesley Ellen. <u>Canadian Copyright Law</u>. 3rd ed. Toronto: McGraw-Hill Ryerson, 2000.

A reprint
If the original work and the reprint were not published by the same publisher, you must indicate both publishers, in order of dates; otherwise, indicate only the first date after the title, followed by the usual publication information for the later work.

Original work and reprint by different publishers:
Faulkner, William. <u>The Wild Palms</u>. New York: Modern

    Library, 1939. New York: Random House, 1984.

Original work and reprint by the same publisher:
Lawrence, D. H. <u>Sons and Lovers</u>. 1913. New York: Viking,

    1958.

An introduction, preface, foreword, or afterword
If the author of the introduction, preface, foreword, or afterword is different from that of the rest of the book, begin your entry with the author of the part; then put the author of the rest of the book after the title of the book.

Part and rest of book by same author:
Wylie, Betty Jane. Preface. <u>Reading between the Lines: The</u>

    <u>Diaries of Women</u>. By Wylie. Toronto: Key Porter, 1995.

    ix-xvii.

Part and rest of book by different authors:
Rapoport, Judith. Foreword. <u>Getting Control: Overcoming</u>

    <u>Our Obsessions and Compulsions</u>. By Lee Baer. New York:

    Penguin, 2000. vi-vii.

Essay or chapter in an anthology
Hodgins, Jack. "The Concert Stages of Europe." <u>Canadian Short</u>

    <u>Fiction</u>. Ed. W. H. New. 2nd ed. Scarborough: Prentice Hall,

    1997. 381-94.

Chapter or essay in a collection of works by one author
Porter, Katherine Anne. "St. Augustine and the Bullfight." <u>The</u>

    <u>Collected Essays and Occasional Writings of Katherine Anne</u>

    <u>Porter</u>. Boston: Houghton Mifflin, 1970. 39-48.

Multivolume book

You must indicate if the volume you are using has a separate title from the whole series. Include the volume title after the author's name, and the series title after the volume number; include the total number of volumes at the end of the entry. If you use more than one volume, indicate this as well, after the title of the series. Finally, if you are citing more than one volume and the volumes were published in different years, include the range of years when you indicate the date.

Citing only one volume:

Clarkson, Stephen, and Christina McCaul. <u>Trudeau and Our</u>

<u>Times</u>. Vol. 1. Toronto: McClelland & Stewart, 1990. 2 vols.

Citing more than one volume:

Clarkson, Stephen, and Christina McCaul. <u>Trudeau and Our</u>

<u>Times</u>. 2 vols. Toronto: McClelland & Stewart, 1990-94.

ARTICLES IN PERIODICALS   In entries for all periodicals (including magazines and newspapers), MLA format uses no "p." or "pp." to indicate page numbers. However, MLA does use abbreviations to indicate months (except for May, June, and July) in entries for daily, weekly, monthly, or quarterly periodicals. Never include issue numbers for popular periodicals (though issue numbers *are* included for academic journals). Also note that discontinuous page numbers are indicated by a plus sign (+).

Article in a monthly periodical or magazine

Clements, Nick. "Peaks of Pleasure." <u>Condé Nast Traveler</u> Feb. 2001: 124+.

Article in a weekly or biweekly periodical or magazine

Young, Stephen. "Sleep, Who Needs It?" <u>New Scientist</u> 29 July 2000: 32-33.

Unsigned article in a weekly or monthly magazine

"A Duquette Retrospective." <u>Architectural Digest</u> Jan. 2001: 32.

Published interview

Entries for interviews begin with the name of the person being interviewed, not the interviewer.

Seth, Vikram. Interview. "It's Fugue I Suffer From: Nancy Wigston

Speaks with Vikram Seth." By Nancy Wigston. <u>Books in Canada</u>

Feb. 2000: 28-29.

Book review

Lyon, Annabel. "Collection of Moody Guys." Rev. of <u>Demonology</u>, by

    Rick Moody. <u>National Post</u> 10 Feb. 2001: B9.

Article in a periodical or journal with continuous pagination
This kind of periodical begins paginating at the beginning of each year, and continues consecutively with each issue; issues later in the year will not begin with page 1, but will continue the pagination from the end of the previous issue.

Roberts, Julian V. "Sexual Assault in Canada: Recent Statistical

    Trends." <u>Queen's Law Journal</u> 21 (1996): 395-421.

Article in a periodical or journal that begins new pagination with each issue
These types of periodicals always begin with page 1 in each issue. Include both the volume number and the issue number (in the example below, 10 is the volume number and 1 is the issue number). Note that the original publication provided the author's initials only.

Caldwell, R. H. "The VE Day Riots in Halifax, 7-8 May 1945."

    <u>Northern Mariner</u> 10.1 (2000): 3-20.

ARTICLES IN NEWSPAPERS   For newspaper entries, identify the section of the paper with a letter or word (for example, "A23" or "Arts/Leisure 18").

Article in a newspaper

Holland, Ward. "Thanks to Quartet's Efforts, Winter Nature Trail

    Ready for Use." <u>Thunder Bay Chronicle-Journal</u> 29 Jan. 2001: A3.

Editorial

"A Fresh Start." Editorial. <u>Halifax Chronicle-Herald</u> 24 Jan. 2001: D1.

Letter to the editor

Michaud-Lalanne, Hortense. Letter. <u>Le Devoir</u> 25 Jan. 2001: A6.

ELECTRONIC SOURCES   Formats for electronic sources (both CD and on-line) have been determined only recently, so they are not as familiar to scholars and academics as those for established print or other media. However, the formats for these sources generally follow the same order of information as all other sources, from author to part of a work to the whole work, and so on. In addition, electronic sources require any other distinguishing features that will help to locate the source, such as the vendor for a CD-ROM (since versions may differ according to vendor), the URL (to locate Web pages), and the date accessed (since some of these sources are updated or change on a regular basis). As always, include as much information as is available. Note that in MLA style, URLs are enclosed in angle brackets (< >).

For all periodical references from on-line sources, include the number of pages or paragraphs, if given, after the title and before the retrieval date (see the entry for on-line magazine article, below).

Use the models below as your guides, and consult the MLA Web page for the most recent entries.

Article from an on-line journal

Grant, Stanley S. "Prenatal Genetic Screening." <u>Online Journal of</u>

<u>Issues in Nursing</u> 5.3 (2000). 5 Feb. 2001 <http://

www.nursingworld.org/ojin/topic13/tpc13_3.htm>

Article from an on-line magazine

Vaz-Oxlade, Gail. "Severance Survival." <u>Chatelaine</u> Oct. 1998. 15

pars. 8 Feb. 2001 <http://www.chatelaine.com/read/money/

sevsurv.html>

An on-line book

MLA requires both the original publication information for an on-line book (that is, the place, publisher, and date when it was published in print form), if available, and the original date of electronic publication, if available, as well as the date of access. You should also include any sponsoring or associated university or organization, if one is mentioned, after the date of electronic publication.

Austen, Jane. <u>Emma</u>. 1815. Aug. 1994. U of Berkeley. 29 Jan. 2001

<http:/sunsite.berkeley.edu/~emorgan/texts/literature/

american/1800-1899/austen-emma-754.txt>

Material from an on-line database

Insert the name of the database after the full record for information retrieved there.

Aly, Shahla. "One Man's Junk Is Also His Gold: Profitable Junk

Removal Service Relies on Dependable Technology." <u>Northern</u>

<u>Ontario Business</u> Sept. 2000: 29. <u>CPI.Q</u> (Gale Group). Toronto

Ref. Lib. 2 Feb. 2001.

Material from a database accessed via the World Wide Web

Cowen, Ron. "Repaired Hubble Finds Giant Black Hole" [abstract].
Science News 4 June 1994: 356-57. Discover Science. GaleNet.
Toronto Public Lib., Toronto. 21 Jan. 2001 <http://
galenet.gale.com/>

Material from a CD-ROM issued periodically (or updated regularly)

Katynski, Liz. "Machine World: When High-End Equipment Breaks Down,
Fix It." Manitoba Business 1 Apr. 1999: 18-21. Canadian Business
and Current Affairs (CBCA). CD-ROM. SilverPlatter. Jan. 1999.

Material from a CD-ROM issued in a single edition (not updated on a regular basis)

"Ablate." The Oxford English Dictionary. 2nd ed. CD-ROM. Oxford:
Oxford UP, 1992.

E-mail message

St. Onge, Ginette. "L'Ancetre Cheeses." E-mail to author. 6 June 2000.

On-line posting (newsgroup or listserv)
Include the name of the forum or listserv ("Soc.college" in the example below), if
available, after the date of the message.

Siegel, Darren. "Serious Admission Questions." Online posting. 30
Jan. 2001. Soc.college. 10 Feb. 2001. <http://x57.deja.com/
threadmsg_cfxp?thitnum=20&AN=722194640.
1&mhitnum=O&CONTEXT=98142943S.1656422470>

Personal or professional Web site
When citing a Web site, identify the page with a title (if one appears) or some
descriptor (such as "home page"). Begin with the name of the author or creator
of the page, if given, followed by the title of the site itself. Also include the latest
revision date or date the site was last updated before the date of access.

King, Stephen. Stephen King Official Web Presence. 2 Feb. 2001.
17 Feb. 2001 <http://www.stephenking.com/>

OTHER MEDIA SOURCES Begin entries for other media sources such as films,
videos, DVDs, radio programs, episodes of television programs, and sound record-

ings with the name of the person(s) most relevant to your own essay. For instance, if your paper focuses on the director of a film or program, you may begin with the director's name; if your essay focuses on the contents of the film or program itself, begin with the title, followed by the names of the significant people involved in creating the work. As always, include as much information as is available.

Film, video, or DVD

Essay that focuses on the director:

```
Fleming, Victor, dir. The Wizard of Oz. Prod. Mervyn
    LeRoy. Perf. Judy Garland, Frank Morgan, Ray Bolger,
    Bert Lahr, Jack Haley. MGM, 1939.
```

Essay that focuses on the content:

```
The Wizard of Oz. Dir. Victor Fleming. Perf. Judy Garland,
    Frank Morgan, Ray Bolger, Bert Lahr, Jack Haley. MGM, 1939.
```

Episode of a television or radio program

For television and radio programs, begin with the name of the episode, if available.

```
"The Drought." Sex and the City. Dir. Matthew Harrison. Writ.
    Michael Patrick King. Prod. Darren Starr. Perf. Sarah Jessica
    Parker. Bravo, Montreal. 10 Feb. 2001.
```

A sound recording (LP, cassette, CD)

Indicate only those recorded formats *other* than CD (such as audiocassette, audiotape [for reel-to-reel], or LP).

Entire work:

```
Jeffers, Susan. Feel the Fear and Do It Anyway. Audio-
    cassette. Simon and Schuster Audio, 1994.
```

One item from a larger work:

```
Beatles. "No Reply." Beatles '65. LP. Capitol Records, 1965.
```

Computer software

If the author is listed, begin with the author's name, followed by the title of the software.

```
Adobe PageMaker. Vers. 6.5. Computer software. Adobe Systems, 1999.
```

Encyclopedia article

Only the title of the article and the edition of the encyclopedia are required to identify this type of source.

```
Hofner, James A. "Himalaya." World Book. 2001 ed.
```

Personal interview

Indicate if the interview is a "personal interview" (in person) or via telephone, after the name of the person being interviewed.

```
Conde, Zalia. Telephone interview. 13 June 2000.
```

Lecture

```
Gossin, Enid. "Fad Diets." Food for Thought [course]. Classroom
    lecture. Seneca College, King City, ON. 14 Oct. 2000.
```

Public presentation

```
Borenstein, Raphaela. "Moving from Private to Public
    Organizations." Presentation. Annual Meeting of Pharmaceutical
    Companies of Canada, Montreal. 21 Oct. 1996.
```

APA format for References

The References list, which appears on a separate page at the end of your essay, provides full references for each of the sources cited in your essay. In APA style papers, entries usually begin with the author's name followed by the date of publication, the title, and publication information. Because information in sciences tends to change on a regular basis and research may quickly become obsolete, the date is important to a reader, and is included up front. Notice that APA, like MLA, begins each entry flush with the left margin. Subsequent lines of the entry are indented. Underlining is used to indicate book titles, but parts of books (such as chapter headings or article titles) are not enclosed in quotation marks. Capitalize only the first letter of the first word of the title and subtitle.

If your particular type of source does not appear in this list, consult the APA style book or Web site:

```
American Psychological Association. Publication manual of the
    American Psychological Association (5th ed.). Washington:
    Author.

www.apa.org
```

For each item, all of the information that should be included is listed, in order. Keep in mind, however, that each of these parts may not always be available (for example, some books don't list an author, some Web sites are not paginated, and some magazines don't list volume numbers). If any specific piece of information is not available, simply omit it and list the rest of the information in the order given.

A book by a single author

Warburton, P. (2000). Debt and delusion: Central bank follies that threaten economic disaster. London: Penguin.

A book by two authors

Moriarty, S. E., & Duncan, T. (1989). How to create and deliver winning advertising presentations. Lincolnwood, IL: NTC Business Books.

A book by three or more authors

In the APA system, *all* authors are listed, regardless of how many there are.

Lehringer, A. L., Nelson, D. D., & Cox, M. M. (1993). The principles of biochemistry (2nd ed.). New York: Worth.

A book with no author indicated

In some cases, as with very old books, government publications, or books issued by large companies, it's possible that no author is mentioned. In this case, treat the title as the first piece of information (and arrange the entry alphabetically according to the first word in the title, other than "a," "an," or "the").

The gentleman's guide to etiquette. (1921). London: Penguin.

A book with corporate, association, or government authorship

If a specific author is mentioned, include the name as in a typical entry. If the author is a particular agency or department of government, cite this by writing the province or country first, followed by the agency or department. If the publisher of the work is the same as the corporation or government agency, indicate this by writing "Author" where the publisher's name usually appears.

Author different from publisher:

British Columbia Ministry of Health. (1983). Handbook for rural mental health workers. Ottawa: Health and Welfare Canada.

Author same as publisher:

```
Health Canada (1995). Heart disease and stroke in Canada.
     Ottawa: Author.
```

A translation

```
Tremblay, M. (1975). Forever yours, Marie-Lou (J. Van Burek & B.
     Glassco, Trans.). Vancouver: Talon Books. (Original work pub-
     lished 1971)
```

A book with an editor instead of an author

```
Ondaatje, M. (Ed.). (2000). Lost classics. Toronto: Knopf Canada.
```

A book with an editor and an author

```
Moodie, S. (1997). Roughing it in the bush; or, life in Canada.
     (E. Thompson, Ed.). Ottawa: Tecumseh Press.
```

A second or later edition

```
Harris, L. E. (2000). Canadian copyright law (3rd ed.). Toronto:
     McGraw-Hill Ryerson.
```

A reprint

```
Faulkner, W. (1984). The wild palms. New York: Random House.
     (Original work published 1939)
```

An introduction, preface, foreword, or afterword
Whether or not the author of the introduction, preface, foreword, or afterword is
different from the author of the rest of the book, begin your entry with the author
of the part. Notice that APA format includes the name of the author of the whole
book before the book's title, whether or not that author wrote the part as well.

Part and rest of book by same author:

```
Wylie, B. J. (1995). Preface. In B. J. Wylie, Reading
     between the lines: The diaries of women (pp. ix-xvii).
     Toronto: Key Porter Books.
```

Part and rest of book by different authors:

Rapoport, J. (2000). Foreword. In L. Baer, <u>Getting con-</u>
<u>trol: Overcoming our obsessions and compulsions</u> (pp. vi-
vii). New York: Penguin.

Essay or chapter in an anthology

Hodgins, J. (1997). The concert stages of Europe. In W. H. New
(Ed.), <u>Canadian short fiction</u> (2nd ed., pp. 381-394).
Scarborough, ON: Prentice Hall.

Chapter or essay in a collection of works by one author

Porter, K. A. (1970). St. Augustine and the bullfight. In <u>The</u>
<u>collected essays and occasional writings of Katherine Anne</u>
<u>Porter</u> (pp. 39-48). Boston: Houghton Mifflin.

Multivolume book

You must indicate if the volume you are using has a separate title from the whole series. Include the volume title after the author's name, and the series title after the volume number. If you use more than one volume, indicate this as well, after the title of the series. Finally, if you are citing more than one volume and the volumes were published in different years, include the range of years when you indicate the date.

Citing only one volume:

Clarkson, S., & McCaul, C. (1990). <u>Trudeau and our times:</u>
<u>Vol. 1.</u> Toronto: McClelland & Stewart.

Citing more than one volume:

Clarkson, S., & McCaul, C. (1990-1994). <u>Trudeau and our</u>
<u>times.</u> (Vols. 1-2). Toronto: McClelland & Stewart.

ARTICLES IN PERIODICALS   In entries for all periodicals (weekly, monthly, or quarterly) except newspapers, APA format uses no "p." or "pp." to indicate page numbers. These abbreviations are used, however, in entries for newspapers. Also note that even discontinuous page numbers are all listed, separated by commas.

Article in a monthly periodical or magazine
APA format includes a volume number with all periodical entries (except those for newspapers), if available (*Condé Nast Traveler*, below, does not use volume numbers). In addition, APA considers the volume number to be part of the title, and underlines it and any punctuation that immediately follows it.

Clements, N. (2001, February). Peaks of pleasure. <u>Condé Nast</u>
　　<u>Traveler,</u> 124-130, 177-178.

Article in a weekly or biweekly periodical or magazine

Young, S. (2000, July 29). Sleep, who needs it? <u>New Scientist,</u>
　　<u>167,</u> 32-33.

Unsigned article in a weekly or monthly magazine

A Duquette retrospective. (2001, January). <u>Architectural Digest,</u>
　　<u>71,</u> 32.

Published interview
In APA style, an interview is treated as a work by the interviewer, and that person's name is listed first.

Wigston, N. (2000, February). It's fugue I suffer from: Nancy
　　Wigston speaks with Vikram Seth. [Interview with Vikram Seth].
　　<u>Books in Canada,</u> 28-29.

Book review

Lyon, A. (2001, February 10). Collection of moody guys. [Review
　　of the book <u>Demonology</u>]. <u>National Post,</u> p. B9.

Article in a periodical or journal with continuous pagination
This kind of periodical begins paginating at the beginning of each year, and continues consecutively with each issue; issues later in the year will not begin with page 1, but will continue the pagination from the end of the previous issue.

Roberts, J. V. (1996). Sexual assault in Canada: Recent statis-
　　tical trends. <u>Queen's Law Journal, 21,</u> 395-421.

Article in a periodical or journal that begins new pagination with each issue
These types of periodicals always begin with page 1 in each issue. Include both the volume number and the issue number (in the example below, 10 is the volume number and 1 is the issue number).

Caldwell, R. H. (2000). The VE Day riots in Halifax, 7-8 May
1945. <u>Northern Mariner, 10</u>(1), 3-20.

ARTICLES IN NEWSPAPERS   For newspaper entries, APA style uses the abbreviations
"p." or "pp." for page number(s) and identifies the section of the paper with a
letter or word (for example, "A23" or "Arts/Leisure 18").

Article in a newspaper

Holland, W. (2001, January 29). Thanks to quartet's efforts, winter
nature trail ready for use. <u>Thunder Bay Chronicle-Journal,</u> p. A3.

Editorial

A fresh start. [Editorial]. (2001, January 24). <u>Halifax
Chronicle-Herald,</u> p. D1.

Letter to the editor

Michaud-Lalanne, H. (2001, January 25). [Letter to the editor].
<u>Le Devoir,</u> p. A6.

ELECTRONIC SOURCES   Formats for electronic sources (both on CD and on-line)
have been determined only recently, so they are not as familiar to scholars and academics as those for established print or other media. However, the formats for
these sources generally follow the same order of information as all other sources,
from author to part of a work to the whole work, and so on. In addition, electronic
sources require any other distinguishing features that will help to locate the source,
such as the vendor for a CD-ROM (since versions may differ according to vendor),
the URL (to locate Web pages), and the date accessed (since some of these sources
are updated or change on a regular basis). As always, include as much information
as is available. Note that in APA style, URLs are not enclosed in angle brackets.

For all periodical references from on-line sources, include the number of pages
or paragraphs, if given, after the title and before the retrieval date (see the entry
for on-line magazine article, below).

Use the models below as your guides, and consult the APA Web page for the
most recent entries.

Article from an on-line journal

Grant, S. S. (2000). Prenatal genetic screening. <u>Online Journal
of Issues in Nursing, 5</u>(3). Retrieved February 5, 2001, from
http://www.nursingworld.org/ojin/ topic13/tpc13_3.htm

Article from an on-line magazine

Vaz-Oxlade, G. (1998, October). Severance survival [Electronic version]. <u>Chatelaine.</u> Retrieved February 8, 2001, from http://www.chatelaine.com/read/money/servsurv.html

An on-line book

Austen, J. <u>Emma.</u> (1994, August). Retrieved January 29, 2001, from http://sunsite.berkeley.edu/~emorgan/texts/literature/american/ 1800-1899/austen-emma-754.txt

Material from an on-line database

Insert the name of the database after the full record for information retrieved there.

Aly, S. (2000). One man's junk is also his gold: Profitable junk removal service relies on dependable technology. <u>Northern Ontario Business, 20,</u> 29. Retrieved February 2, 2001, from CPI.Q online database.

Material from a database accessed via the World Wide Web

Cowen, R. (1994). Repaired Hubble finds giant black hole [abstract]. <u>Science News, 145</u>(23), 356-357. Retrieved January 21, 2001, from GaleNet database (Discover Science) at http:// galenet.gale.com/

Material from a CD-ROM issued periodically (or updated regularly)

Katynski, L. (1999, April 1). Machine world: When high-end equipment breaks down, fix it. <u>Manitoba Business,</u> 356-357. Retrieved from SilverPlatter database (Canadian Business and Current Affairs), CD-ROM, January 1999 release.

Material from a CD-ROM issued in a single edition (not updated on a regular basis)

Ablate. (1992). <u>Oxford English Dictionary.</u> Oxford: Oxford University Press. Retrieved October 23, 2000, from <u>Oxford English Dictionary</u> database, CD-ROM.

ONLINE MESSAGES   Because e-mail messages can be sent by anyone with access to a particular e-mail address (not just the registered user), and because many of these messages are not retrievable by the public at large, APA considers these to be personal correspondence, and entries do not appear in a References list. Instead, include only an in-text citation in which you state the name of the person writing to you, the words "personal communication," and the date, as shown in the two examples that follow.

E-mail message
Do not include an entry in the list of References, but include an in-text citation, as follows.

```
(G. St. Onge, personal communication, June 6, 2000)
```

On-line posting (newsgroup or listserv)
Do not include an entry in the list of References, but include an in-text citation, as follows.

```
(D. Siegel, personal communication, January 30, 2001)
```

Personal or professional Web site
When citing a Web site, APA asks that you identify the page with a title (if one appears) or some descriptor (such as "home page"). Begin with the name of the page's author or creator, if given, followed by the title of the site itself. Also include the date of revision or the date the site was last updated, after the creator's name and before the title of the page.

```
King, S. (2001, February 2). Homepage. Stephen King official Web
     presence. Retrieved February 5, 2001, from http://
     www.stephenking.com/
```

OTHER MEDIA SOURCES   Begin entries for other media sources such as films, videos, DVDs, radio programs, episodes of television programs, and sound recordings with the name of the person(s) most relevant to your own essay. For instance, if your paper focuses on the director of a film or program, you may begin with the director's name; if your essay focuses on the contents of the film or program, begin with the title, followed by the names of the significant people involved in creating the work. As always, include as much information as is available.

Film, video, or DVD
APA style includes the medium (film, video, or DVD) in brackets after the title.

Essay that focuses on the director:

```
Fleming, V. (Director), LeRoy, M. (Producer), & Langley,
     N. (Writer). (1939). The wizard of Oz [Videotape].
     Washington: MGM/UA Home Video, Inc.
```

Essay that focuses on the contents:

```
The wizard of Oz [Videotape]. (1939). Fleming, V.
    (Director), LeRoy, M. (Producer), & Langley, N.
    (Writer). Washington: MGM/UA Home Video, Inc.
```

Episode of a television or radio program

For television and radio programs, APA considers the writer to be the author, and puts that person's name first.

```
King, M. P. (Writer), & Harrison, M. (Director). (2001). The drought.
    In D. Starr (Producer), Sex and the city. Montreal: Bravo.
```

A sound recording (LP, cassette, CD)

APA identifies all formats, as well as spoken-word recordings (as opposed to music recordings).

Entire work:

```
Jeffers, S. (Speaker). (1994). Feel the fear and do it
    anyway [Cassette]. New York: Simon and Schuster Audio.
```

One item from a larger work:

```
Beatles. (1965). No reply. On Beatles '65 [LP]. London:
    Capitol Records.
```

Computer software

```
Adobe PageMaker (Version 6.5) [Computer software]. (1999). San
    Jose, CA: Adobe Systems, Inc.
```

Encyclopedia article

APA requires full publication information, including page references. Include the author's name, if available.

```
Hofner, J. A. (2001). Himalaya. In World Book (Vol. 9, pp. 233-
    234). Chicago: World Book Inc.
```

Personal interview

APA considers personal, unpublished interviews to be one form of private correspondence, along with letters, e-mails, and on-line postings. Therefore, APA doesn't include these sources in a References list. Instead, include an in-text citation in which you write "personal communication" plus the date, as shown below.

```
(Z. Conde, personal communication, June 13, 2000)
```

Lecture

Gossin, E. (2000, October 14). Fad diets. <u>Food for thought</u>
  [course]. Classroom lecture presented at Seneca College, King
  Campus, King City, ON.

Public presentation

Borenstein, R. (1996, October 21). <u>Moving from private to public</u>
  <u>organizations.</u> Presentation at the annual meeting of
  Pharmaceutical Companies of Canada, Montreal, QC.

MLA-Style Essay

Eva Tihanyi

26 May 2002

Female Spirituality: When the Personal Is Religious

Picture this: a young woman in jodhpurs, boots and leather jacket adjusts her silk scarf, stands ready to climb into the open cockpit of her small plane. She seems oblivious to the light wind that further dishevels her already tousled hair, her eyes fixed on the open blue, the sky into which her beloved flying machine will lift her body and with it her indomitable spirit.

The year? 1928. The woman? Amelia Earhart. But it could just as well be now, and it could be any of a thousand women looking upward.

Coincidentally, shortly after I began thinking about writing an article concerning women and spirituality, I came across a copy of *Amelia Earhart and the Search for Modern Feminism*, Susan Ware's absorbing biography. What captured my attention was not what Ware calls the cult of Earhart's disappearance but rather the aviator's extra-ordinary will and pioneering female spirit.

What struck me even more was Ware's description of Earhart's life, how Earhart's "restlessness and constant shifts of direction remind us how few models there were for modern young women desperate to break out of old pat-terns but not quite sure what to replace them with" (35). This was certainly applicable to the subject of the article I was contemplating. Women want to express their spirituality. They are questing for personal meaning, wanting to break free of the status quo.

In other words, we know we want something more than what traditional religion, couched in its centuries of patri-archy, is capable of offering, but we aren't sure what this

Despite what some would like to believe, religion is often more political than it is personal, concerned more with issues of power than of spirit. This is why the god-dess religion of pre-Christian times was discredited and the goddess "re-imaged" into an evil figure. As feminist author Merlin Stone remarks: "We may find ourselves won-dering to what degree the suppression of women's rites has actually been the suppression of women's rights" (228).

Spiritual issues, when filtered through the lens of feminism, take on a decidedly different hue. First of all, most feminists (and I'm not talking here of the "extremists" who give feminism a bad name) tend to see moral issues in a myriad of greys rather than in sim-plistic black and white. To quote Nancy Tuana, author of *Woman and the History of Philosophy*:

> Feminist ethicists are working to reconstruct moral
> theory. Traditional moral theory is criticized for
> positing a conception of people as disinterested,

independent individuals, who are both free and
equals, and of a moral agent as impartial. Many
feminist theorists argue instead for a model of
moral thinking based on relationships, with moral
actions arising out of responsibilities and
affiliations rather than duties or rights." (118)

This, to me, embraces the notion of flexibility, an
ability to comprehend and respond to the greys that lie
between the black and the white--a notion that seems to
escape the bounds of conventional religion and its atten-
dant concerns with right and wrong.

What Tuana describes has very little to do with
"rationality" or "reason" in the traditional sense. It
has everything to do with justice and caring but most of
all with responding to the specific.

Works Cited

Aburdene, Patricia, and John Naisbitt. <u>Megatrends for
Women</u>. New York: Villard Books, 1992.

Hareguy, Darlene. Personal interview. 2 May 1995.

Sewell, Marilyn, ed. <u>Cries of the Spirit: A Celebration
of Women's Spirituality</u>. Boston: Beacon Press, 1991.

Stone, Merlin. <u>When God Was a Woman</u>. New York: Harcourt
Brace Jovanovich, 1976.

Tuana, Nancy. <u>Woman and the History of Philosophy</u>. New
York: Paragon House, 1992.

Ware, Susan. <u>Still Missing: Amelia Earhart and the Search
for Modern Feminism</u>. New York: W.W. Norton & Company,
Inc., 1993.

APA-Style Essay

The Pros and Cons of Certification: A Profession Is Only
as Strong as the Individuals Who Compose It

Nancy Morphet

Georgian College

Although therapeutic recreation has existed as a form
of health care and human service provision for decades,
the field has only recently become more recognized and is
currently acknowledged as the twelfth fastest growing
occupation in the United States (Silvester, 1995). Thus,
as therapeutic recreation continues to evolve in the
United States, so too does the need for the profession to
clearly establish itself as a credible and necessary component of the Canadian health care system. Accordingly,
the efforts of Therapeutic Recreation Ontario (TRO), in
particular, "to build strong support mechanisms for T.R.
practitioners" and "develop standards for the practice of
Therapeutic Recreation in Ontario," have resulted in the
proposal of a certification process, clearly independent
of the process used in the United States (Therapeutic
Recreation Branch, on-line). While there are both positive
and negative implications of a certification process
within the therapeutic recreation profession, the benefits
seem to outweigh the negative consequences. Thus, it is
important to fully understand all aspects of the
certification process, and examine its impact on
professional conduct, education, and other disciplines in
the health care system.

RESPOND IN WRITING

Defined as the "process by which a non-governmental agency or organization grants recognition to persons who have met predetermined qualifications specified by that agency or organization" (National Council for Therapeutic Recreation [NCTR], 1997), certification establishes clear standards for competent practice and professionalism, thereby protecting the interests of consumers, and ensuring credible programs. Indeed, the demand for certification within Canada is evident. Results of a questionnaire completed by 323 individuals employed in parks and recreation (Ontario) indicate that respondents consider it "very" important that certification

> demonstrates the need for specialized skills, provides evidence that a certified person is competent, promotes continued learning, successful performance, guides employers regarding personnel decisions, provides legal backing for personnel decisions, provides protection against liability, and protects jobs for those who are certified. (Nogradi, 1994, p. 29)

Many other reasons supporting the introduction of a therapeutic recreation certification process in Canada have also been cited. For example, by establishing a certification process, the profession is able to monitor its own practice, and has a consistent, uniform system to measure qualifications (NCTR, 1997, p. 1). In addition, certification upholds service quality and accountability, which may result in increased peer recognition, status and validation of the field. Thus, with fierce competition for limited resources, being certified may lend some negotiating power, authority and job security to professionals in the field who may otherwise feel bypassed in the organizational structure (Sylvester, 1998). Of course, with increased status comes increased pay, which in turn ensures that qualified practitioners remain in the field (Hare, 1989). Furthermore, certification provides practitioners with clear expectations, a common body of terminology, and helps "define the future direction of the profession within the social, community, and medical services delivery system" (Latin, on-line, p. 2). Lastly, certification may be advantageous in that through self-regulation and the development a college or certification board, "a unique culture in which formal and informal networking takes place" may develop (Carter, 1998, p. 21).

References

Carter, M. (1998). Increased professionalism: An experience from the United States. Journal of Leisurability, 25 (2), 20-25.

Connolly, P. (1998). NCTRC certification. In F. Brasile & J. Burlingame (3rd ed.), Perspectives in recreational therapy (pp. 401-428). Washington: Idyll Arbor Inc.

Dubois, D. (2000, February 3). Certification. Classroom lecture presented at Georgian College, Barrie, ON.

Hare, L. (1989). The job competencies and educational needs of therapeutic recreationists in Ontario. Journal of Applied Recreation Research, 15 (1), 15-24.

Latin, M. (1998). The importance of certification in therapeutic recreation in Ontario. (n.d.). Retrieved February 8, 2000, from the World Wide Web: http://www.lin.ca/lin/resource/html/essaycon.htm

National Council for Therapeutic Recreation Certification. (1997). 1997 report on the national job analysis project for certified therapeutic recreation specialists. [Brochure].

National Council for Therapeutic Recreation Certification. (n.d.). Homepage. Retrieved from the World Wide Web January 17, 2000: http://www.nctrc. org/ about/vaca.html

Nogradi, G. (1994). The importance and impact of certification for parks and recreation practitioners in Ontario. Journal of Applied Recreation Research, 19 (1), 23-40.

Appendix 1

SUMMARY OF MAJOR DIFFERENCES BETWEEN NONFICTION ESSAYS AND SHORT STORIES (FICTION)

ESSAYS	STORIES
STRUCTURE	
• The main point or idea is called the *thesis*.	• The main point or idea is called the *major theme*.
• Points or ideas must follow a logical organizing principle.	• Points or ideas need not follow an immediately obvious order.
• Specific major points (i.e., an *outline*) can usually be determined by examining the individual essay or article.	• The underlying structure may be difficult to determine.
• Paragraph structure, sentence structure, and language use must be correct.	• Paragraph structure, sentence structure, and language use may be unconventional.
• Text does not usually contain dialogue (except for narrative essays).	• Text usually contains dialogue.
LANGUAGE USE	
• Uses Standard English	• Language may be informal or formal, and may contain unconventional dialects.
• Uses full, correct sentences; uses fragments for effect only	• May contain sentence fragments or irregular grammar
• Vocabulary is appropriate to the audience; language is clear and succinct, and contains no slang or jargon.	• Vocabulary may contain slang, jargon, or obscenity.
• May use figurative language	• Regularly uses figurative language
• The manner in which the author conveys her or his feelings about the subject is called the *tone*.	• The feeling created by the story is called the *mood* or *tone*.

ESSAYS	STORIES
CONTENT	
• Facts are taken from reality and persons mentioned are actual people who exist.	• "Persons" mentioned are referred to as *characters*. Characters are never real people (even if the names of real people are used).
• Ideas are based on facts—events that really happened in the real world.	• Ideas are based on reality, but are not facts (events described never actually took place in the real world).
AUTHOR	
• The author is a real person; s/he uses her or his real name when referring to herself or himself.	• The author (a real person) is distinguished from the *narrator*, the fictional "voice" telling the story. The narrator may or may not be a character in the story.

Appendix 2

USING QUOTATIONS AND PARAPHRASES

This appendix answers some common questions about how and when to use paraphrases and quotations in essays and research papers. (*Note:* In-text citations in this appendix follow MLA format.)

1. What is the difference between a paraphrase and a quotation?

As mentioned in Chapter 1, when you paraphrase, you express the gist of a selection or passage in your own words. A paraphrase may repeat the general contents of a sentence or passage, but it does not use the same language as the original passage. A quotation, on the other hand, is an exact copy of an original piece of writing (including exactly the same punctuation, capital letters—even errors!).

2. When should I paraphrase? When should I quote?

In general, a paraphrase is sufficient, except in the following circumstances:

- When you wish to strengthen your argument by emphasizing a specific detail (such as a statistic) from a quotation or by emphasizing the person you are quoting (such as an expert in a field)

- When the original wording is particularly important, effective, or eloquent (as in the case of fiction, for example) and a paraphrase would not be as forceful

3. Which passages require in-text citations?

Whether you quote *or* paraphrase, you must *always* include an in-text citation. Remember, *any* information that is not either common knowledge or your own, original, data *must* be accompanied by a reference to the original source. Someone else's ideas or information, whether quoted or rewritten by you, must still receive an in-text citation. Otherwise, you may be guilty of plagiarism, one of the worst academic offences.

4. How do I integrate quotations into my essay?

You can integrate quotations into your own sentences and paragraphs in several ways. To blend quotations in smoothly, follow these guidelines:

a. *Make the context of the quotation apparent.*
   Whenever you quote, include enough of the original passage that the reader is not misled. Quotations taken out of context occur all the time in popular media, which is why so many tabloid newspapers and magazines face lawsuits from irate stars! Here's an example of a quotation taken out of context.

Original passage:
[from Marni Jackson, "The Writer as Hero Leaps from the Screen," *Globe and Mail*, 16 Dec. 2000: D22]

Whenever I want to remind myself that writing [. . .] really means muffled sexual intrigue in exotic foreign cities, I watch <u>The Sheltering Sky</u>. This is a rather silly but physically appealing movie about Jane and Paul Bowles [. . .]

Misrepresented quotation:

Marni Jackson believes that <u>The Sheltering Sky</u> is an "appealing movie" (D22).

b. *Introduce or "set up" the quotation for the reader.*
Some kind of introductory phrase or passage should precede the quotations you use. Usually, a mention of the author's name or the title of the selection from which you are quoting is sufficient. Here is an example of a quotation that has *not* been well integrated into the essay:

Many offices have moved to open concept designs. "It's mall thinking brought to the office; devising a tender trap where you can lose track of time working, meeting, eating, and, if necessary, sleeping without ever wondering about the outside world" (Hulsman 53).

To introduce a quotation effectively, try one of the following commonly used strategies:

i. *Run the quotation into your own sentence:*

Many offices have moved to open concept designs, which are intended to create "a tender trap where you can lose track of time working, meeting, eating, and, if necessary, sleeping without ever wondering about the outside world" (Hulsman 53).

ii. *Use a short introductory phrase at the beginning of the quotation:*

Many offices have moved to open concept designs. Hulsman writes, "It's mall thinking brought to the office; devising a tender trap where you can lose track of time working, meeting, eating, and, if necessary, sleeping without ever wondering about the outside world" (53).

Many offices have moved to open concept designs. In "Farewell, Corner Office," Noel Hulsman suggests that these designs are "mall thinking brought to the office; devising a tender trap where you can lose track of time working, meeting, eating, and, if necessary, sleeping without ever wondering about the outside world" (53).

iii. *Use a colon to connect the quotation with the point it illustrates:*

Many offices have moved to open concept designs. These offices introduce an entirely new way of working: "It's mall thinking brought to the office; devising a tender trap where you can lose track of time working, meeting, eating, and, if necessary, sleeping without ever wondering about the outside world" (Hulsman 53).

c. *Introduce quotations separately from each other; do not follow one quotation immediately with another.*
Unless it is unavoidable, have at least a word or two, no matter how small, between two quoted passages.

Weak:
The narrator provides many details about her lover, such as "he takes deeper drags from the cigarette than I do"; "he studies"; "he works as a cashier in the cafeteria" (Potvin 19).

Better:
The narrator provides many details about her lover. She informs us that "he takes deeper drags from the cigarette than I do"; he also "studies" and "works as a cashier in the cafeteria" (Potvin 19).

d. *Make sure that quotations fit grammatically into your sentence.*
You may sometimes need to divide up quoted passages or rearrange your own paragraph so that the quotations contribute to a grammatically correct sentence. When your essay is read aloud, the entire text should remain grammatically correct, including the quoted portions.

Weak:
In Dr. Martin Luther King, Jr.'s speech, "I Have a Dream," he implores us all to change our view about people "will not be judged by the colour of their skin but by the content of their character" (62).

Better:

In his speech, "I Have a Dream," Dr. Martin Luther King, Jr. suggests that all people should be judged "by the content of their character" rather than by "the colour of their skin" (62).

5. What is the correct format to use for quotations?

The format and placement of quotations and in-text citations depends on the length of the quotation (for more about in-text citations, see Chapter 13). Standard formats for short and long quotations are described below.

a. Short quotations

MLA style considers a short quotation to be anything that runs less than five lines on the page; APA considers anything less than 40 words to be a short quotation. Follow these guidelines when using short quotations:
- Incorporate the quotation into your own sentence.
- Use double quotation marks (" "), *not* single quotation marks (' ') or apostrophes, around the quoted material.
- For quotations within the quotation, use single quotation marks.
- Put a comma before the quotation only if a comma would normally appear at this point in the sentence.
- Place the in-text citation after the closing quotation mark but before the final punctuation of the sentence (the citation is not part of the quotation, but it is part of your sentence).

Example:

```
With all of the recent changes in technology, parents are
having a hard time keeping up with their children. In addition,
officials who run our schools "are grappling with the reality
of students often being far smarter on cyber-issues and new
ways of learning than the teachers" (Tapscott 2).
```

b. Long quotations

Anything longer than four lines (MLA) or 40 words (APA) is considered a long quotation. Follow these guidelines when using long quotations:
- Separate the quotation from the rest of the text by indenting one inch or two tabs from each margin.
- *Do not* enclose the quotation in quotation marks.
- For quotation within the long quotation, use double quotation marks.
- In most cases, introduce the quotation with a colon.
- Place the in-text citation after the final punctuation of the final sentence, and on the same line; do not add another period after the in-text citation.

Example:

In his discussion of how new technologies have often created
knowledge gaps between adults and children, Donald Tapscott
describes some of the current differences between them:

> Moms and dads are reeling from the challenges of
> raising confident, plugged-in, and digital-savvy
> children who know more about technology than they
> do. Few parents even know what their children are
> doing in cyberspace. School officials are grappling
> with the reality of students often being far
> smarter on cyber-issues and new ways of learning
> than the teachers. (2)

6. When and how do I make changes to quotations?

Two types of changes—additions or deletions—are sometimes permitted when
you quote. However, these techniques must be used very sparingly, and only if
they do not interfere with the intended meaning and context of the original passage.

a. Additions to quoted material

Any word or words that you add to a quotation must be enclosed in square
brackets: [ ]. You may add material to quotations in three circumstances:
(i) when an addition is needed for clarity, (ii) to render the quotation grammatically correct in your sentence, and (iii) if you wish to acknowledge an
error in the original. Here are some examples of these circumstances:

i. *An addition to clarify an otherwise vague quotation:*

Weak:

The girl tells us, "Her hair was tied up in a kerchief,
wisps of it falling out" (Munro 296).

In this case, "her" refers to the girl's mother, a fact the reader wouldn't
recognize from the quotation. A small addition to the quotation will clarify:

Better:

The girl tells us that "her [mother's] hair was tied up in a
kerchief, wisps of it falling out" (Munro 296).

ii. An addition to correct grammatical inconsistency in your sentence:

Weak:

```
We notice that the girl's fantasies change from "a story
might start off in the old way" to "somebody would be res-
cuing me" (Munro 302).
```

In this case, the quotation does not fit grammatically into the sentence. A small addition can be used to correct this.

Better:

```
We notice that the girl's fantasies change from "a story
[that] might start off in the old way" to ones in which
someone rescued her (Munro 302).
```

Note: If possible, avoid making additions for grammatical purposes; it's better to use only part of a quotation or rephrase your own sentence, whenever possible.

iii. An addition to acknowledge an error in the original:

The original passage, below, contains a spelling error ("quite" has been used instead of "quiet"):

```
Babies often respond well to background voices or sounds of
machinery, and ambient noise rarely disturbs their sleep.
In fact, if it's too quite, a baby may react with alarm.
```

To quote the passage correctly, you must also copy the spelling error. However, to indicate that you recognize this error, add "sic" (Latin for "as it is") in square brackets after the error.

Proper quotation:

```
Smith argues that babies tend to flourish in busy, noisy
environments: "if it's too quite [sic], a baby may react
with alarm," he suggests (41).
```

b. Deletions from quoted material

Deletions are used when you wish to quote only a portion of a sentence or paragraph. To indicate a deletion, use an *ellipsis* (three spaced dots) to replace the deleted word(s). If your deletion bridges two sentences (that is, if you delete the end of a sentence, including the final period), your ellipsis should be four spaced dots. In using an ellipsis, follow these guidelines:

- Be sure that the remaining portion of the quotation fits grammatically into your sentence, even with the deletion.
- Retain enough of the quotation that it still makes sense in your essay. In other words, use an ellipsis *only* to eliminate words you do not need or those that are irrelevant to your argument; never use an ellipsis simply to save space or time.

Original passage:
In the late 80's and early 90's, the atmosphere between the federal government, its negotiators and the Inuit was becoming more positive. It was helped by growing public support for the demands by aboriginal people, and by a series of court challenges across Canada that confirmed aboriginal rights and in some case title to lands they historically used and occupied.

Poor use of ellipsis:
The road to an Inuit homeland was sometimes risky. As Whit writes, "In the late 80's and 90's . . . occupied" (41).

Quotation with two ellipses:
The road to an Inuit homeland was sometimes rocky. As Whit writes, "In the late 80's and 90's, the atmosphere [. . .] was helped by growing public support [. . .] and by a series of court challenges across Canada that confirmed aboriginal rights and in some case title to lands they historically used and occupied" (41).

Glossary

allusion (p. 296): A reference to someone or something from history, literature, the Bible, mythology, popular culture, or any other field that would be recognized by readers. Allusions serve to enhance meaning by connecting something in a text to something in another reference. For example, saying that a couple are "star-crossed lovers" alludes to the original star-crossed lovers in Shakespeare's *Romeo and Juliet* and suggests that the modern couple being mentioned is also doomed.

analogy (p. 247): An extended comparison between two things that is used to help clarify one of them. For instance, you might compare your work at a particular office with being stranded on a desert island: both lack resources, isolate a person, require independent work, and so on.

argument (p. 365): Argument defends or promotes a viewpoint through logical reasoning and clear evidence in order to convince readers that the viewpoint is worth adopting. *See also* **persuasion.**

audience (p. 12): The intended readers for a particular piece of writing.

body: The central section of an essay, after the introduction and before the conclusion. The body contains the main points of the essay and develops these in paragraphs.

brainstorming (p. 133): A collection of techniques used in pre-writing to generate ideas freely about a given topic. Brainstorming includes the cluster technique, freewriting, categories and lists, and the journalist's method.

cause and effect (p. 318): Cause and effect examines what makes things happen and/or what results ensue from particular factors or events.

chronological organization (p. 42): In an outline, a method of organizing points according to when they occur in time. *See also* **outline.**

classification (p. 201): Classification takes a group of things and places them in categories or classes according to a specific principle. Classification may include the process of **division,** taking something large and dividing it into component parts or categories.

classifying principle or **basis of classification** (p. 203): The single concept on which a selection of categories is based; this principle is the means used to develop category headings, and items are organized *according to* the classifying principle. The basis of classification ensures that separate categories are logically connected to each other because each illustrates a different aspect of the same principle.

cliché (p. 78): An overused or outmoded expression, often a comparison, that was at one time fresh and original. Examples are "raining cats and dogs" or "as cold as ice."

coherence: The quality of making ideas cohere or "stick together" in an essay. Coherence is achieved by clear, logical connections between ideas, usually through the use of transitions, repetition, synonyms, and other devices.

communications paradigm or **feedback loop** (p. 2): A model of the communication process that includes the following:

> **sender:** An individual with something to communicate; one who wishes to convey some message.

message: The form in which the communication is sent.

receiver: The person or people at whom the message is targeted.

feedback: The response from the receiver that indicates the message was received and understood.

comparison and contrast (p. 241): Comparison and contrast examines similarities, differences, or both between two related things.

conclusion: The final paragraph of an essay, which summarizes and draws together the main points and may provide final "food for thought."

connotation and denotation (p. 281): Denotation is the literal (dictionary) meaning of a word, while connotation includes implied or associated meanings, not found in the dictionary.

critical reading (p. 7): The process through which one draws inferences and develops logical interpretations of a text by considering the writer, the content (what the writer actually says), and the structure (how the text is put together) in order to understand and respond to that text.

critical thinking (p. 3): The process by which one closely examines and considers a message and, using analysis and logic, formulates an individual assessment of its validity.

deduction (p. 373) or **deductive reasoning:** Reasoning that begins with a general situation or case (a major premise) and then shows how individual cases or specific situations (minor premises) illustrate the first, general, statement. *See also* **induction** or **inductive reasoning.**

definition (p. 280): Definition explains what something **means** or **is** in a particular context. Definitions may be formal or extended. A **formal definition** (or **denotation**) provides a general explanation of what something means in its most basic, common form; an **extended definition** provides a multifaceted, longer explanation of a complex concept or term, often as it applies to a particular situation or context.

description (p. 72): Description re-creates a person, a thing, or a scene in words so that someone else can imagine the subject. Description includes **objective description,** which impartially re-creates a subject in words (to provide information only) and **subjective description,** which re-creates a subject in words to establish an emotional tone or dominant impression.

diction (p. 12): The choice of words and the way in which they are arranged in sentences. Diction includes vocabulary and level of formality, and should take into account the audience of a particular piece.

dominant impression (p. 74): In description essays, a particular mood or emotional tone that permeates the essay and elicits an emotional reaction from the reader.

emphatic organization (p. 43): In an outline, a method of organizing points from the least forceful to the most forceful, leaving the strongest point for last. *See also* **outline.**

example (p. 131): Examples provide concrete illustrations to demonstrate and clarify general ideas or abstract concepts.

exposition: One of the four traditional rhetorical modes, along with description, narration, and argument. Exposition covers modes intending to explain something or inform the reader about something, such as example, process, classification, comparison and contrast, cause and effect, and definition.

facts (p. 5): Irrefutable units of information that can be objectively measured and confirmed.

feedback: *See* **communications paradigm** or **feedback loop.**

figurative language (p. 78): Language that employs comparisons between two things as a means to illuminate the meaning of one. **Similes** use words such as "as," "like," or "similar to" to indicate comparisons, while **metaphors** create direct equivalents between two things.

induction (p. 373) or **inductive reasoning:** Reasoning that begins by examining many different situations or specific cases and then bases a conclusion on the resulting patterns established. *See also* **deduction** or **deductive reasoning.**

inferences (p. 4): Logical conclusions based on, and supported by, facts.

introduction: The opening paragraph(s) in an essay, introducing the topic and thesis to the readers in a way that engages them and prompts them to read on.

irony: In general, a situation in which the reality is recognized as being different from the appearance or expected outcome; a conclusion that is the opposite of what one expected.

jargon: Terminology particular to a specific profession, trade, or group that is not automatically understood by those outside the group.

logical fallacies (p. 374): Errors in reasoning based on faulty logic. (For specific descriptions of logical fallacies, see Chapter 11.)

message: *See* **communications paradigm** or **feedback loop.**

metaphor: *See* **figurative language.**

narration (p. 101): Narration tells a story from beginning to end and includes major events and characters.

opinions (p. 5) or **emotional reactions:** Responses, which may not always be logical, based on strong feelings or personal experiences.

outline (p. 41): A basic plan, or blueprint, of an essay, containing the thesis and main points of support. The three common methods of organization in an essay are spatial, chronological, and emphatic. *See also* **chronological organization, emphatic organization,** and **spatial organization.**

paragraph (p. 6): A single unit of thought in an essay, containing a topic sentence and supporting details.

parallel structure: In an outline, a structure in which each of the supporting points or sentences is presented in the same grammatical format as the others.

paraphrase (p. 11): A repetition, in one's own words, of the ideas contained in a text.

persuasion (p. 365): Persuasion works to convince readers that something is true or to incite readers to action, often through the use of emotional appeals. *See also* **argument.**

point of view (p. 104): The perspective from which a narrative is told. It may be a first-person point of view (the narrator, "I," is part of the action) or a third-person point of view (the narrator is not part of the action).

process (p. 161): Process explains all the steps in how to do something (directions) or examines and explains how something works or functions. A **directive process** provides instructions for how to do something through a series of instructional steps, while an **informative process** explains how something works or happens.

purpose (p. 11): The author's objective, or reason for writing something; what s/he hopes will happen as a result of people reading the selection. An author's purpose may be to entertain, to inform, or to persuade.

reading process (p. 8): A series of steps through the stages of pre-reading, reading, and post-reading, through which a reader can understand and respond effectively to a text.

receiver: *See* **communications paradigm** or **feedback loop.**

rhetorical modes (p. 285): Ways of expressing ideas effectively in prose. The major rhetorical modes include exposition, narration, description, and argument.

sender: *See* **communications paradigm** or **feedback loop.**

simile (p. 78): *See* **figurative language.**

spatial organization (p. 42): In an outline, a method of organizing points according to where they are in space. *See also* **outline.**

style (p. 9): The unique quality given to a piece of writing by an author's choice and arrangement of words and ideas.

subject (p. 31): A very general area of interest, usually expressed in a word or two.

summary (p. 497): A short version of a piece of writing, in your own words, that includes all the major points of the original. A summary is usually between one-quarter and one-third the length of the original.

syntax: The structure or pattern of words in a sentence, clause, or phrase.

theme (p. 13): The major idea or abstract concept being expressed in a literary work. Works of fiction may express several themes in a single text.

thesis (p. 31): The main argument or point of an essay, usually stated in a single sentence. An essay should contain only one thesis.

tone (p. 12): The emotion generated by a piece of work; the impression created of the author's attitude toward her or his subject matter.

topic (p. 31): One specific part or subcategory of a subject, usually expressed in a phrase or clause.

topic sentence (p. 13): The sentence in a paragraph that states its main point (usually the first sentence).

transitional devices (p. 167) or **transitions:** Devices that help to explain logical connections among and between ideas, and to create coherence in essays by providing cues of time or sequence.

unity: The sense that an essay treats only a single main topic, and all parts of the work relate to it.

vantage point (p. 77): The point of view from which the writer describes a scene; all details and movement must follow logically from this point.

voice (p. 47) or **personal style:** The quality in a piece of writing (influenced by diction, sentence variety, and wording in general) that reflects the writer's personality.

writing process (p. 30): A series of steps through the stages of pre-writing, writing, and post-writing used to construct an effective essay.

Copyright Acknowledgments